Understanding the New Statistics

Effect Sizes, Confidence Intervals, and Meta-Analysis

Geoff Cumming

La Trobe University, Melbourne, Australia

Routledge
Taylor & Francis Group
New York   London

Multivariate Applications Series

Sponsored by the Society of Multivariate Experimental Psychology, the goal of this series is to apply complex statistical methods to significant social or behavioral issues, in such a way so as to be accessible to a nontechnical-oriented readership (e.g., non-methodological researchers, teachers, students, government personnel, practitioners, and other professionals). Applications from a variety of disciplines such as psychology, public health, sociology, education, and business are welcome. Books can be single- or multiple-authored or edited volumes that (1) demonstrate the application of a variety of multivariate methods to a single, major area of research; (2) describe a multivariate procedure or framework that could be applied to a number of research areas; or (3) present a variety of perspectives on a topic of interest to applied multivariate researchers.

There are currently 20 books in the series:

- *What If There Were No Significance Tests?* co-edited by Lisa L. Harlow, Stanley A. Mulaik, and James H. Steiger (1997)
- *Structural Equation Modeling with LISREL, PRELIS, and SIMPLIS: Basic Concepts, Applications, and Programming,* written by Barbara M. Byrne (1998)
- *Multivariate Applications in Substance Use Research: New Methods for New Questions,* co-edited by Jennifer S. Rose, Laurie Chassin, Clark C. Presson, and Steven J. Sherman (2000)
- *Item Response Theory for Psychologists,* co-authored by Susan E. Embretson and Steven P. Reise (2000)
- *Structural Equation Modeling with AMOS: Basic Concepts, Applications, and Programming,* written by Barbara M. Byrne (2001)
- *Conducting Meta-Analysis Using SAS,* written by Winfred Arthur, Jr., Winston Bennett, Jr., and Allen I. Huffcutt (2001)
- *Modeling Intraindividual Variability with Repeated Measures Data: Methods and Applications,* co-edited by D. S. Moskowitz and Scott L. Hershberger (2002)
- *Multilevel Modeling: Methodological Advances, Issues, and Applications,* co-edited by Steven P. Reise and Naihua Duan (2003)
- *The Essence of Multivariate Thinking: Basic Themes and Methods,* written by Lisa Harlow (2005)

- *Contemporary Psychometrics: A Festschrift for Roderick P. McDonald*, co-edited by Albert Maydeu-Olivares and John J. McArdle (2005)
- *Structural Equation Modeling with EQS: Basic Concepts, Applications, and Programming, Second Edition*, written by Barbara M. Byrne (2006)
- *A Paul Meehl Reader: Essays on the Practice of Scientific Psychology*, co-edited by Niels G. Waller, Leslie J. Yonce, William M. Grove, David Faust, and Mark F. Lenzenweger (2006)
- *Introduction to Statistical Mediation Analysis*, written by David P. MacKinnon (2008)
- *Applied Data Analytic Techniques for Turning Points Research*, edited by Patricia Cohen (2008)
- *Cognitive Assessment: An Introduction to the Rule Space Method*, written by Kikumi K. Tatsuoka (2009)
- *Structural Equation Modeling with AMOS: Basic Concepts, Applications, and Programming, Second Edition* written by Barbara M. Byrne (2010)
- *Handbook of Ethics in Quantitative Methodology*, co-edited by Abigail T. Panter and Sonya K. Sterba (2011)
- *Longitudinal Data Analysis: A Practical Guide for Researchers in Aging, Health, and Social Sciences*, co-edited by Jason T. Newsom, Richard N. Jones, and Scott M. Hofer (2011)
- *Structural Equation Modeling with MPlus: Basic Concepts, Applications, and Programming* written by Barbara M. Byrne (2012)
- *Understanding The New Statistics: Effect Sizes, Confidence Intervals, and Meta-Analysis*, written by Geoff Cumming (2012)

Anyone wishing to submit a book proposal should send the following: (1) author/title; (2) timeline including completion date; (3) brief overview of the book's focus, including table of contents and, ideally, a sample chapter (or chapters); (4) a brief description of competing publications; and (5) targeted audiences.

For more information, please contact the series editor, Lisa Harlow, at Department of Psychology, University of Rhode Island, 10 Chafee Road, Suite 8, Kingston, RI 02881-0808; phone (401) 874-4242; fax (401) 874-5562; or e-mail LHarlow@uri.edu. Information may also be obtained from members of the editorial/advisory board: Leona Aiken (Arizona State University), Daniel Bauer (University of North Carolina), Jeremy Biesanz (University of British Columbia), Gwyneth Boodoo (Educational Testing Services), Barbara M. Byrne (University of Ottawa), Scott Maxwell (University of Notre Dame), Liora Schmelkin (Hofstra University), and Stephen West (Arizona State University).

Front cover: Detail is from *Treasure* by Claire Layman, and is used with her generous permission.

Routledge
Taylor & Francis Group
711 Third Avenue
New York, NY 10017

Routledge
Taylor & Francis Group
27 Church Road
Hove, East Sussex BN3 2FA

© 2012 by Taylor & Francis Group, LLC
Routledge is an imprint of Taylor & Francis Group, an Informa business

Version Date: 20110518

International Standard Book Number: 978-0-415-87967-5 (Hardback) 978-0-415-87968-2 (Paperback)

Visit the Taylor & Francis Web site at
http://www.taylorandfrancis.com

and the Psychology Press Web site at
http://www.psypress.com

Printed and bound in the United States of America by
Edwards Brothers Mallloy

For Lindy

Contents

Preface

The "new statistics" of this book's title are not themselves new, but adopting them as the main way to analyze data would, for many students and researchers, be new. It would also be an excellent development. Let me explain.

"Children in the new program made significantly greater gains, $p < .05$." In many disciplines, that's the standard way to express a conclusion. It relies on *null hypothesis significance testing* (NHST), which uses $p < .05$ or $p < .01$ to establish a result as statistically significant. However, NHST is a very limited way to analyze and interpret data, because it focuses on the narrow question, "Is there an effect?" Other disciplines, including physics and chemistry, seldom use NHST, and usually report results as *estimates* by saying, for example: "the melting point of the plastic was $85.5 \pm 0.2°C$." That's usually much more informative than a statement that an effect is, or is not, statistically significant. The main message of this book is that we should shift emphasis as much as possible from NHST to *estimation*, based on effect sizes and confidence intervals. We should to some extent join physics, chemistry, and other disciplines that make enormous scientific progress with little use of NHST.

For more than 50 years, scholars have explained the limitations of NHST and the advantages of estimation and other preferred techniques, yet in many disciplines we still feel obliged to use NHST. If we can progressively free ourselves from that obligation, I suspect we'll find that what I'm calling "the new statistics" match the way we naturally think of results and the interpretation of research. I don't underestimate the challenge of overcoming years of relying on $p < .05$, but once we are using the new statistics I suspect we'll find that they "feel right." I'll also discuss easy ways to translate between the new and the old.

Effect sizes and confidence intervals provide more complete information than does NHST. Meta-analysis allows accumulation of evidence over a number of studies. Using these new statistics techniques, students and researchers will be better informed and science will progress faster. "Understanding" in the book's title defines two goals: the "why" and the "what." The first is understanding why the new statistics are better and why it's worth the effort to change, and the second is understanding the techniques themselves and how to use them in practice.

"It's hard to change, do I really have to?" "Why now?" In reply I can say that, first, change is already happening. Many journal editors are requiring effect sizes, more articles that report confidence intervals are being published, and meta-analysis is becoming mainstream. Medicine has routinely used confidence intervals since the 1980s. Second, the *Publication Manual of the American Psychological Association* (APA) now recommends: "Wherever possible, base discussion and interpretation of results on point and interval estimates" (APA, 2010, p. 34). That's an unequivocal statement that researchers should report effect sizes and confidence intervals, then use them as the basis for interpreting results. The *Publication Manual* is used by more than 1,000 journals across numerous disciplines, so its advice matters.

Intended Audience

Understanding The New Statistics is designed for use in any discipline that uses NHST, including psychology, education, economics, management, sociology, criminology and other behavioral and social sciences; medicine, nursing and other health sciences; and biology and other biosciences. It includes examples from many such disciplines.

The book assumes users have had at least some encounter with introductory statistics, and is not intended to provide comprehensive coverage of statistics and research methods. I've designed it for three main types of use. First, any course focused on the new statistics can use this book as the core text. Second, a course in any discipline in which the new statistics are part of the curriculum can use it alone or with another textbook. Third, students, researchers, and practitioners who wish to understand the new statistics can use it by themselves or with peers.

I know the pressures on any statistics curriculum. I've designed this book so teachers can assign selected sections or chapters for self-study by students. Students are increasingly electing to learn when and where they want, either alone or in a small group. They discuss at a shared screen or in cyberspace. This book and the software have been developed to meet those demands. They have benefited from years of use by students in their homes, as well as in the classroom and lecture hall.

You may be puzzled by the NHST ritual in which you (1) assume there's no effect, even though you believe and hope there is an effect, then (2) calculate a strange thing called a *p* value, then (3) apply an arbitrary rule that, you hope, rejects the initial assumption you never believed. Then you (4) conclude that, because you rejected the unbelievable possibility of no effect, there must be an effect after all! You wonder why research is done this way. How wise you are. *Understanding The New Statistics* is for anyone who is thinking about alternatives to statistical significance testing. If you aim to become a researcher, if you are curious about how data are likely to be analyzed in the future, or if you simply wish to understand future reports of research, then this book is intended for you. I hope it serves you well.

Features

This book may be the first statistics textbook that is, as much as possible, *evidence-based. Evidence-based practice* is expected in medicine, psychology, and many other professions. It should also be expected in statistics, so a student or researcher should be able to justify their choice of statistical technique by referring to evidence. That's the evidence-based practice of statistics. Cognitive evidence may, for example, suggest that a particular way to present data is easily understood by readers. Therefore, where possible, I support my recommendations with evidence. *Boxes* summarize research on how people understand—or misunderstand—particular statistical concepts, and particular ways to present results.

Learning and teaching should also be evidence based. This book draws on 40 years of my own teaching and researching, but I have also been guided by evidence from cognitive science about how people learn. That has led me to include *exercises* that refer back to earlier chapters, to help build strong and integrated understanding. *Examples* link new ideas back to familiar ideas. *Excerpts* from published research in a range of disciplines show concepts in action. Many ideas are presented in multiple ways—in the text, in examples and exercises, and by the software—to help build good understanding and cater to a range of learners' preferred learning styles. The book encourages active exploration, but provides *step-by-step guidance* at first. There are many opportunities to use your own data, to gain a more practical appreciation of the techniques discussed. Each chapter starts with pointers to what it contains, and closes with *take-home messages* that provide a summary.

I have written the *Users' Guide to "Understanding The New Statistics"* to describe strategies, shaped by cognitive science, for getting the most out of the book and its software. It includes references to research I have found helpful and that you might also find useful. The *Guide* is available from the book's website: www.thenewstatistics.com. I hope it helps make your time with the book effective and rewarding.

Software

I developed ESCI ("ESS-key," Exploratory Software for Confidence Intervals) to provide vivid images and colorful simulations to help make important ideas clear. It also helps you use the new statistics with your own data. The book includes numerous figures from the software, and ESCI activities are integrated into many chapters. You can use the book without the software, but I invite you to use ESCI alongside the book, to the extent you find it helpful. ESCI runs under Microsoft Excel, on a Windows or Macintosh computer, and is a free download from www. thenewstatistics.com. Appendix A explains how to get started with ESCI, and how to get the most from it. The website also provides further tips on loading and using ESCI, and the latest information about versions of Excel that are supported.

Contents

Chapter 1 introduces the new statistics, then *Chapter 2* discusses the advantages that estimation and effect sizes have over NHST.

Chapter 3 introduces confidence intervals (CIs). Enjoy the *dance of the CIs*, and the first three ways to interpret CIs. I discuss recommendations of the *APA Publication Manual* (APA, 2010). *Chapter 4* describes two further ways to interpret CIs. *Chapter 5* explores replication—what happens when you repeat an experiment—for CIs, and for *p* values. CIs give better information, so they win. The sixth way to interpret CIs is based on replication. *Chapter 6* discusses the two simplest, most familiar experimental designs for comparing two conditions, and how to use CIs for each.

Chapter 7 introduces meta-analysis, with an emphasis on the forest plot, which is a neat picture that summarizes a few experiments or a whole research field. *Chapter 8* describes two basic models for meta-analysis. *Chapter 9* outlines the seven steps in conducting a large scale meta-analysis. It explains moderator analysis and gives further examples of the practical value of meta-analysis.

Chapter 10 is an optional extra chapter on the noncentral *t* distribution, which plays a central role in sampling, statistical power, and CIs for Cohen's *d*. *Chapter 11* discusses Cohen's *d*, which is the basic standardized effect size and a very useful measure. *Chapter 12* considers statistical power. In the new statistics, power is replaced by the much better *precision for planning*, the topic of *Chapter 13*. How large an experiment do you need so your CI won't be too wide? *Chapter 14* discusses further effect sizes, including Pearson's correlation *r*, and proportions. *Chapter 15* considers effect sizes and CIs for more complex designs, starting with *randomized control trials* (RCTs). I close with suggestions to assist practical adoption of the new statistics.

Appendixes A, B, and *C* explain how to download and use ESCI, with numerous hints for getting the most out of the software. Look here to find the page you need to explore a concept, or to carry out calculations on your own data.

Acknowledgments

Numerous colleagues and students have contributed to my learning that has led to this book. I thank them all. Bruce Thompson, Sue Finch, Robert Maillardet, Ben Ong, Ross Day, Mary Omodei, and Jim McLennan are valued colleagues who have supported my work in various ways. The contributions of a number of colleagues and students are at least partially recognized by inclusion of their published research in the book. Members of the Statistical Cognition Laboratory at La Trobe University have helped in many ways, most notably Pav Kalinowski, Jerry Lai, and Debra Hansen. A dedicated group worked through the book and made many excellent suggestions. I thank all members of the group, especially Mary Castellani, Mark Halloran, Kavi Jayasinghe, Mitra Jazayeri, Matthew Page, Leslie Schachte, Anna Snell, Andrew Speirs-Bridge, and Eva van der Brugge. Painstaking work by Elizabeth Silver, Jacenta Abbott, Sarah Rostron, and especially Amy Antcliffe led to many improvements. I am grateful to Lisa L. Harlow, Multivariate Applications Series Editor, for her consistent support, and I also thank reviewers of various draft chapters: Dennis Doverspike, University of Akron; Alan Reifman, Texas Tech University; Joseph S. Rossi, University of Rhode Island; Frank Schmidt, University of Iowa; Meng-Jia Wu, Loyola University Chicago; and two anonymous reviewers.

Collaboration with Fiona Fidler has been very rewarding for me, and the many references in this book to her work provide partial recognition of her crucial contribution. Her book *From Statistical Significance to Effect Estimation: Statistical Reform in Psychology, Medicine and Ecology*, to be published by Routledge, is important and highly engaging. My closest colleague, Neil Thomason, has for nearly two decades provided inspiration, wonderful ideas, and an unswerving commitment to sound argument and clear communication. He has contributed to this book far more than he realizes.

After that long list of wise advisors, I emphasize that remaining errors and weaknesses are all my own work. If you find errors, or have suggestions for improvement, especially for the chapters that present material not yet commonly included in textbooks, please let me know. I'm very grateful to Gideon Polya for the artistry of his drawings and his generosity in creating such a broad range to fit the book. I'm greatly indebted to Debra Riegert, senior editor at Psychology Press/Routledge/Taylor & Francis, Andrea Zekus, and Mimi Williams and her colleagues, for their support and professionalism. I gratefully acknowledge the support of the Australian Research Council. Finally, my warmest appreciation is expressed on an earlier page.

1

Introduction to The New Statistics

This book is about how to picture and think about experimental results. I'll start with a simple pattern of results you may have seen many times, but first I should say what this chapter is about. It introduces

- Null hypothesis significance testing (NHST) and confidence intervals (CIs) as two different ways to present research results
- Meta-analysis as a way to combine results, and thus a third way to present them
- The desirability of shifting emphasis from NHST to CIs and meta-analysis, which are important parts of what I'm calling *the new statistics*
- Three ways of thinking that correspond to the three ways to present results
- Evidence-based practice in statistics, statistical cognition, and some relevant evidence
- ESCI (pronounced "ESS-key," Exploratory Software for Confidence Intervals)

A Familiar Situation: Lucky–Noluck

Consider first a simple pattern of results you may be familiar with.

First Presentation: NHST

Suppose you read the following in the introduction to a journal article:

> Only two studies have evaluated the therapeutic effectiveness of a new treatment for insomnia. Lucky (2008) used two independent groups each of size $N = 22$, and Noluck (2008) used two groups each with $N = 18$. Each study reported the difference between the means for the new treatment and the current treatment.
>
> Lucky (2008) found that the new treatment showed a statistically significant advantage over the current treatment: $M(difference) = 3.61$, $SD(difference) = 6.97$, $t(42) = 2.43$, $p = .02$. The study by Noluck (2008)

found no statistically significant difference between the two treatment means: *M(difference)* = 2.23, *SD(difference)* = 7.59, *t*(34) = 1.25, *p* = .22.

What would you conclude? Are the two studies giving consistent or inconsistent messages? Is the new treatment effective? What conclusions about the two studies would you expect to read in the next couple of sentences of the article?

Here are three possible answers:

1. *Inconsistent* "The Lucky result is clearly statistically significant at the .05 level, whereas the Noluck result is clearly not statistically significant. The two results conflict. We can't say whether the treatment is effective, and we should examine the two studies to try to find out why one found an effect and the other didn't. Further research is required to investigate why the treatment works in some cases, but not others."

2. *Equivocal* "One result is statistically significant, and the other statistically nonsignificant, although the two are in the same direction. We have equivocal findings and can't say whether the treatment is effective. Further research is required."

3. *Consistent* "The two results are in the same direction, and the size of the mean difference is fairly similar in the two studies. The two studies therefore reinforce each other, even though one is statistically significant and the other is not. The two results are consistent and, considered together, provide fairly strong evidence that the treatment is effective."

Choose which of the three answers is closest to your own opinion. You could also consider what conclusion would be most likely if such results were discussed in whatever discipline you are most familiar with. I invite you to note down your answers before reading on. Take some time; maybe have a coffee.

Second Presentation: Confidence Intervals

Now suppose that, instead, the introduction to the article described the two studies as follows:

Only two studies have evaluated the therapeutic effectiveness of a new treatment for insomnia. Lucky (2008) used two independent groups each of size *N* = 22, and Noluck (2008) used two groups each with *N* = 18. Figure 1.1 reports for each study the difference between the means for the new treatment and the current treatment, with the 95% confidence interval on that difference.

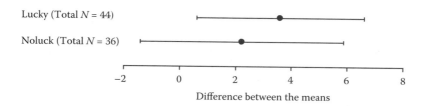

FIGURE 1.1
Difference between the means (mean for new treatment minus mean for current treatment) for treatments for insomnia in the Lucky (2008) and Noluck (2008) studies, with 95% confidence intervals. A positive difference indicates an advantage for the new treatment.

Once again, take a minute to think what you would conclude. Are the two studies giving similar or different messages? Is the new treatment effective? Choose *Inconsistent, Equivocal,* or *Consistent* as coming closest to your opinion. Again, note down your answers.

Third Presentation: Meta-Analysis

Now, finally, suppose the introduction to the article described the two studies, then in Figure 1.2 reported the result of a meta-analysis of the two sets of results. (Chapters 7, 8, and 9 discuss meta-analysis. Think of it as a systematic way to combine the results from two or more related studies.)

> Only two studies have evaluated the therapeutic effectiveness of a new treatment for insomnia. Lucky (2008) used two independent groups each of size $N = 22$, and Noluck (2008) used two groups each with $N = 18$. Each study reported the difference between the means for the new treatment and the current treatment.

Once again, think how you would interpret this result. Is the new treatment effective? How strong is the evidence? Again, note down your answers.

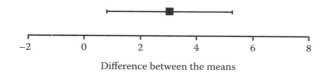

FIGURE 1.2
Difference between the means (mean for new treatment minus mean for current treatment) for treatments for insomnia, with its 95% confidence interval, from a meta-analysis of two studies that compared a new treatment with the current treatment. Total $N = 80$. A positive difference indicates an advantage for the new treatment. The null hypothesis of no difference was rejected, $p = .008$.

Some Terminology

I need to introduce some terminology, which may or may not be familiar
to you. *Statistical inference* is the drawing of conclusions about the world
(more specifically: about some popula-
tion) from our sample data. In the Lucky–
Noluck example we can assume that the
population of interest is the notional set of
all possible differences in scores between the current and new treatments,
for all people affected by insomnia. A researcher should define the population carefully (Which people? What definition of insomnia?), although
often the reader is left to assume. We wish to make a statistical inference
about the population *parameter* of interest, which here is the mean difference in scores.

Statistical inference draws conclusions about
a population, based on sample data.

You are probably familiar with *null hypothesis significance testing* (NHST),
which is the most common way to carry out statistical inference in a range
of disciplines, including many social and
behavioral science disciplines, and some
biosciences. I'll refer to disciplines that
rely at least to a moderate extent on NHST
as *NHST disciplines*. To use NHST you
typically specify a null hypothesis then calculate a *p* value, which you
use to decide whether to reject or not reject the null hypothesis at some
significance level, most commonly .05 or .01. The first presentation of the
Lucky–Noluck results used an NHST format, and the conclusion whether
or not to reject the hypothesis that the population mean difference is zero
hinged on whether or not *p* was less than .05. In other words, a result
was declared statistically significant or not, depending on whether *p* < .05
or not.

Null hypothesis significance testing (NHST)
tests a null hypothesis—usually that there is
no difference—and uses the *p* value to either
reject or not reject that hypothesis.

A second approach to statistical inference is *estimation*, which focuses
on finding the best *point estimate* of the population parameter that's of
greatest interest; it also gives an *interval estimate* of that parameter, to signal how close our point estimate is likely
to be to the population value. The second
presentation of the Lucky–Noluck results
used an estimation format. Figure 1.1
gives point estimates, which are the sam-
ple mean differences marked with the round dots. These are our best
estimates, one from each study, of the true mean advantage of the new
treatment. The 95% CIs are the interval estimates, and the fact that they
are so long signals that our point estimates give only imprecise information about the population values, although any interpretation of CI length
requires understanding of the scale we're using.

Estimation is a second approach to statistical inference. It uses sample data to calculate *point estimates* and *interval estimates* of
population parameters.

The third presentation, in Figure 1.2, combines the Lucky and Noluck results. I calculated it using *meta-analysis*, which is a collection of techniques for the quantitative analysis of the results from two or more studies. At its simplest, it gives a point estimate that is a weighted average of the separate study

> *Meta-analysis* is a set of techniques for the quantitative analysis of results from two or more studies on the same or similar issues.

means. (The weights depend on the sample sizes and variances of the separate studies.) It also gives an overall interval estimate that signals how precise an estimate the weighted average is likely to be.

The Best Interpretation of Lucky–Noluck

All three presentations were based on exactly the same data. Therefore, whatever your interpretations, they should have been the same for all three presentations. Figure 1.1 indicates most clearly that the most justifiable interpretation is *Consistent*—we could even call it the correct answer. The CIs overlap very substantially, and if NHST is used to test whether there is any difference between the two studies, $p = .55$, so the two studies are as similar as could reasonably be expected even if the second was just a repetition of the first. The Lucky and Noluck results are entirely consistent, and therefore reinforce each other. Figure 1.2 shows the extent of reinforcement, where the CI resulting from the meta-analysis is shorter, indicating more precise estimation of the effect of the new treatment. Also the p value of .008 for the combined results would conventionally be taken as fairly strong evidence that the new treatment is more effective.

In later chapters we'll explore the definition and calculation of CIs and discuss several ways to think about them. For the moment it's worth noting two of those ways.

First, a CI indicates a range of values that, given the data, are *plausible* for the population parameter being estimated. Values outside the interval are relatively implausible. Any value in the interval could reasonably be the true value, and so the shorter the interval the better.

Second, CIs can, if you want, be used to carry out NHST. If zero lies within a CI, zero is a plausible value for the true effect, and so the null hypothesis is not rejected. Alternatively, if zero is outside the interval, zero is not so plausible a true value, and the null is rejected. If the intervals in Figure 1.1 are used for NHST, the results match those given in the NHST presentation: The Lucky CI does not include zero, which indicates $p < .05$ and a statistically significant result. The Noluck CI includes zero, which indicates $p > .05$ and statistical nonsignificance. CIs can easily be used to carry out NHST, although doing so ignores much of the valuable information they provide.

The New Statistics Debate

At this point I invite you to reflect on the three presentations of the Lucky–Noluck data. How did you think about each? In each case, what language would you have chosen to describe the results and conclusions, and would that language have varied over the three formats? Did NHST suggest *Inconsistent* or *Equivocal*, but the CI format *Consistent*? Did the different formats suggest that different conclusions are warranted, even though you knew the underlying data were the same, and so conclusions should all be the same? Also, were you interested in knowing how effective the new treatment is, or only whether or not it worked?

In discussions of the three presentations of Lucky–Noluck with groups of researchers, I always ask what they consider the most likely interpretations their disciplinary colleagues would make, or what they would expect to see in the journals with which they are most familiar. The most common opinion, from a number of disciplines, is that NHST is quite likely to suggest *Inconsistent*, and the CI format to suggest *Consistent*. That's only anecdotal evidence—I describe better evidence below—but it supports my contention that Lucky–Noluck illustrates how different ways of presenting results can prompt dramatically different conclusions. NHST is more likely to prompt unjustified conclusions of inconsistency or disagreement, whereas CIs may prompt more justified conclusions of consistency or similarity, at least for the simple pattern of results we've been discussing.

The Lucky–Noluck example is a small illustration of the advantages of estimation over NHST. By *the new statistics* I am referring to a shift from reliance on NHST to the use of estimation wherever possible, and also of meta-analysis whenever it can help. There are further statistical techniques that have great value and can help researchers shift from NHST, but in this book I focus on estimation and meta-analysis. I should quickly say these techniques are hardly new: CIs have been around for almost a century, and meta-analysis for several decades. It's the widespread and routine use of these techniques in disciplines traditionally reliant on NHST that would be new.

The new statistics refer to estimation, meta-analysis, and other techniques that help researchers shift emphasis from NHST. The techniques are not new and are routinely used in some disciplines, but for the NHST disciplines, their use would be new and a beneficial change.

Perhaps you are feeling unsettled by my conclusion that *Consistent* is the best interpretation, and wish to dispute it. You may be thinking there's not enough information to justify "fairly strong evidence" of an effect? Or that, although the results of the two studies are similar, it's an artificial situation, with results falling just either side of the significance boundary, and it's petty of me to criticize NHST for anomalies when results happen to fall close to the decision boundary? In fact, however, CIs provide more and better information than NHST in almost all situations, and not only for Lucky–Noluck.

You might also argue that NHST gives a basis for clear decisions, and often the world needs decisions. After all, the practitioner must decide either to use a therapy with a client, or not; and the regulatory authority must either approve a drug or refuse approval. Yes, we do need to make decisions, but NHST often gives misleading guidance about decisions, as it did for Lucky–Noluck, whereas estimation and meta-analysis present all the available evidence and are thus most informative for making decisions.

Alternatively, you could argue that I'm criticizing not so much NHST as the way some people use it. Appropriate use of NHST with Lucky–Noluck would perhaps involve using NHST to compare the two—and find no statistically significant difference between them. Or perhaps NHST would be applied only to the result of the meta-analysis combining the two. Those are reasonable points to make, but my most fundamental criticism of NHST is not about the way it's used, but that it gives such an incomplete picture, in contrast to the full information provided by estimation. In addition, I'll report evidence that many researchers don't understand NHST correctly and don't use it appropriately. However, even if those problems could be overcome, the more fundamental shortcomings of NHST remain.

You could also protest that we don't know how to interpret the scale of measurement: A difference of 3 may be trivial, and of little practical or scientific value. That's true, and is an important issue we'll discuss in Chapter 2, but it doesn't undermine the conclusion that we have fairly strong evidence of some difference and, most usefully, a numerical estimate of its size—whether we judge that large or small, important or trivial. This book is mainly about the new statistics and how to use them in practice, but the comparison with NHST will come up in several places. In Chapter 15 I'll discuss in more detail a number of queries a skeptic could raise about the new statistics, and give my answers.

In the next chapter I'll discuss further the problems of NHST and describe how statistical reformers have, for more than half a century, been publishing critiques of NHST and advocating a shift to estimation or other techniques. The prospects for achieving real change may now be better than ever before, because the sixth edition of the *Publication Manual of the American Psychological Association* (APA, 2010) strongly recommends CIs, specifies a format for reporting them, and gives many examples. Like earlier editions, it also gives NHST examples, but its detailed guidance for estimation is new. The *Manual* is used by more than 1,000 journals across numerous disciplines—way beyond just psychology—and every year enormous numbers of students learn its rules of style. The new edition states unambiguously: "Wherever possible, base discussion and interpretation of results on point and interval estimates" (p. 34). This is a strong endorsement of the new statistics, which I hope will be influential and lead to improvements in the way research in many disciplines is conducted.

Now I want to discuss three different ways of thinking that are related to my three presentation formats described previously, and which seem to me fundamental to all consideration of statistical reform and the new statistics. Changing our habits of thought may be one of the biggest challenges of moving to the new statistics, but also potentially a valuable outcome of making the change.

Three Ways of Thinking

Dichotomous Thinking

The first presentation format of Lucky–Noluck emphasizes dichotomous decision making: NHST results in a decision that the null hypothesis is rejected, or not rejected. Such dichotomous decision making seems likely to prompt *dichotomous thinking*, which is a tendency to see the world in an either–or way. Experiments are planned, hypotheses formulated, and results analyzed, all within a framework of two completely opposed possibilities: A result is statistically significant or not. The first Lucky–Noluck presentation reports for each study the mean (M) and standard deviation (SD) of the differences, and values of t and p. Our point estimate of the difference between the new treatment and the old is M. Yes, M is reported, but NHST habits may prompt us to skim through the text searching mainly for the p value. Small p usually means success and may elicit joy; large p may elicit disappointment and frustration. Such an either–or outcome goes with dichotomous thinking: We formulate our research in terms of a null hypothesis of zero effect, and finish with a dichotomous decision that we can, or cannot, reject it. *Dichotomy* comes from the Greek "to cut in two," and NHST gives us just two distinct options for decision. It seems plausible that dichotomous thinking and use of NHST are mutually reinforcing. If so, dichotomous thinking may be an obstacle to adoption of the new statistics.

Dichotomous thinking focuses on making a choice between two mutually exclusive alternatives. The dichotomous reject-or-don't-reject decisions of NHST tend to elicit dichotomous thinking.

Why does dichotomous thinking persist? One reason may be an inherent preference for certainty. Evolutionary biologist Richard Dawkins (2004) argues that humans often seek the reassurance of an either–or classification. He calls this "the tyranny of the discontinuous mind" (p. 252). Computer scientist and philosopher Kees van Deemter (2010, p. 6) refers to the "false clarity" of a definite decision or classification that humans clutch at, even when the situation is uncertain. To adopt the new statistics we may need to overcome a built-in preference for certainty, but our reward could be a better appreciation of the uncertainty inherent in our data.

Estimation Thinking

The most salient feature of Figure 1.1 is the CIs. The point estimates are the dots, and the intervals indicate the uncertainty of those point estimates. Figure 1.1 permits dichotomous thinking—if the intervals are used merely for NHST—but there is no reason to limit their use in this way. CIs offer much more, provided we can move beyond dichotomous thinking and adopt *estimation thinking*. Estimation thinking focuses on how big an effect is; knowing this is usually more valuable than knowing whether or not the effect is zero, which is the focus of dichotomous thinking. Estimation thinking prompts us to plan an experiment to address the question, "How much ...?" or "To what extent ...?," rather than only the dichotomous NHST question, "Is there an effect?"

Estimation thinking focuses on "how much," by focusing on point and interval estimates.

Meta-Analytic Thinking

One realization prompted by the use of CIs is that in most single studies the uncertainty is, alas, larger than we'd thought. CIs are in practice usually wider than we'd like, so we usually need to combine evidence from a number of studies. Meta-analysis gives us tools to do that, and so meta-analysis is a vital component in the new statistics. *Meta-analytic thinking* is the consideration of any result in relation to previous results on the same or similar questions, and awareness that combination with future results is likely to be valuable. Meta-analytic thinking is the application of estimation thinking to more than a single study. It prompts us to seek meta-analysis of previous related studies at the planning stage of research, then to report our results in a way that makes it easy to include them in future meta-analyses. Meta-analytic thinking is a type of estimation thinking, because it, too, focuses on estimates and uncertainty. Cumulation of evidence over studies, by meta-analysis, usually gives a more precise estimate, signaled by a shorter CI. That's excellent news, because more precise estimates are best.

Meta-analytic thinking is estimation thinking that considers any result in the context of past and potential future results on the same question. It focuses on the cumulation of evidence over studies.

The Natural Statistics?

I'm arguing that we should move, as much as practical, from NHST to the new statistics, and from dichotomous thinking to estimation and meta-analytic thinking. At one level these are drastic changes, and I don't underestimate the difficulty of breaking the hold of p values and dichotomous thinking. More fundamentally, however, I suspect that the natural way we think about results is (1) to focus on the most direct answer they give to our research question, (2) to consider how precise that answer is, and (3) to think how our answer relates to other results. For an example of the three steps, think of the Lucky and Noluck means and CIs, and the relation between the two results. Based on the three steps, we use our judgment to interpret the Lucky–Noluck results and draw conclusions. But that's simply a description of the new statistics in action! I suspect the new statistics may license us to think about our results in ways we'll recognize as natural, and perhaps the ways we've secretly been thinking about them all along, even as we calculate and publish p values. If my hunch is correct—and it needs to be examined experimentally—then once we've overcome Dawkins' tyranny and van Deemter's false clarity to move beyond dichotomous thinking, we may find that the new statistics feel rather natural. Adopting the new statistics may not feel like shifting to a different world, but as a release from restrictions and arrival at a somewhat familiar place. That place is already inhabited by disciplines that make comparatively little use of NHST, including, for example, physics and chemistry. In addition, NHST and the new statistics are based on the same underlying statistical theory, so in this way as well the new statistics may feel familiar.

Up to this point I've used the Lucky–Noluck example to describe three different ways to present results and, correspondingly, three different ways of thinking. I've also used the example to argue that estimation and meta-analysis can do a better job of statistical inference than NHST, and therefore researchers should, where possible, adopt the new statistics. Most fundamentally, the new statistics are simply more informative, but I would like, in addition, to be able to cite evidence about how researchers understand NHST and estimation. I'll shortly report some cognitive evidence, but first I'll introduce the ideas of evidence-based practice in statistics and statistical cognition.

Evidence-Based Practice in Statistics

Professional practitioners in medicine, health sciences, psychology, and many other fields strive for evidence-based practice. They should be able to justify their treatment recommendation by referring to research showing that the treatment is likely to prove most effective in the circumstances. Clients, legislators, and the community increasingly expect nothing less, and in some cases any other approach may be ethically questionable. I suggest that choice of statistical practices should similarly be evidence based. Relevant evidence is of at least two kinds: statistical and cognitive. The technical discipline of statistics is concerned with studying statistical models and techniques, and with assessing evidence of how suitable they are for a particular situation. Such statistical evidence is undoubtedly important.

The second type of evidence, cognitive evidence, may be just as important if misconception is to be avoided, and readers are to understand results as well as possible.

Statistical Cognition

Statistical cognition is concerned with obtaining cognitive evidence about various statistical techniques and ways to present data. It's certainly important to choose an appropriate statistical model, use the correct formulas, and carry out accurate calculations. It's also important, however, to focus on understanding, and to consider statistics as communication between researchers and readers. How do researchers think about their results; how do they summarize, present, and interpret data; and how do readers understand what they read? These are cognitive questions, and statistical cognition is the research field that studies such questions (Beyth-Marom, Fidler, & Cumming, 2008). As I discuss in Chapter 2, statistical cognition has gathered evidence about severe and widespread misconceptions of NHST, and the poor decision making that accompanies NHST. It is beginning to study the new statistics, and will increasingly be able to advise how new statistical practices should be refined and used. In addition, studies of how best to teach and learn particular statistical concepts should also be helpful in guiding adoption of the new statistics.

> *Statistical cognition* is the empirical study of how people understand, and misunderstand, statistical concepts and presentations.

I want to encourage the evidence-based practice of statistics and so, wherever possible, I'll support recommendations in this book by including boxes with brief accounts of cognitive evidence relevant to the statistical issues being discussed. Often, however, no such evidence is available. Statistical cognition is a small research field, with many vital outstanding questions. Especially in relation to the new statistics there are many interesting cognitive issues that need to be investigated. Occasionally I'll mention some. If you are interested in cognition or learning, and are looking for a research project—or even a research career—you might consider these. Please feel warmly encouraged. This research is important and could be widely influential.

How Do Researchers Think?

Box 1.1 describes my research group's investigation of how leading researchers in three different disciplines interpret results presented in NHST or CI formats, as in the first two Lucky–Noluck presentations. We examined whether NHST might prompt dichotomous thinking, and CIs might prompt estimation thinking.

As often happens in research, we were surprised. As we expected, interpretation of the CI presentation was better on average than interpretation of NHST, but the difference was small. The most striking finding was that those who saw CI results, as in Figure 1.1, tended to split, with some using NHST in their interpretation and others not. Those who used NHST said things like "one's [statistically] significant but the other isn't," and they made such comments even though NHST was not mentioned in the results they saw. Those respondents tended to see the Lucky and Noluck results as different. On the other hand, those who didn't mention NHST said things like "the intervals overlap a lot," and almost all saw the results as similar, a much better interpretation. Yes, the new statistics prompt better interpretation, but you need to think in estimation terms. If you use CIs merely to carry out NHST, you waste much of their potential and may misinterpret experimental results. Estimation thinking beats dichotomous thinking, but merely using CIs doesn't guarantee estimation thinking.

Writing Your Take-Home Messages

At the end of each chapter I suggest take-home messages that express what I think are the chapter's main points. However, it's much better for you to write your own, rather than merely read mine. Therefore, I now invite you to pause, take a coffee break, think (or look) back over the chapter, and write your take-home messages. As possible hints I'll mention that this first chapter used the Lucky–Noluck example to illustrate how different ways of presenting results can prompt different ways of thinking and different interpretations. I argued that estimation can give better interpretation than NHST. However, it's not just the choice of statistical technique that matters, but the underlying thinking adopted by the reader and the researcher. Estimation thinking, which is fundamental to the new statistics, is likely to give better understanding of results than the dichotomous thinking that naturally goes with NHST.

Finally, a word about ESCI. Use of ESCI is integrated into my discussion throughout the book, but in slightly different ways in different chapters. My aim is that you can readily work through the book without using ESCI

BOX 1.1 HOW RESEARCHERS INTERPRET NHST AND CIS

Coulson, Healey, Fidler, and Cumming (2010, tinyurl.com/cisbetter) investigated how researchers think about the Lucky–Noluck results, presented in NHST or CI formats, with the aim of testing the new statistics predictions that CIs elicit better interpretation. We emailed authors of articles published in leading psychology, behavioral neuroscience, or medical journals and presented results in either an NHST or a CI format. We asked researchers, "What do you feel is the main conclusion suggested by these studies?" We then asked them to rate their extent of agreement with statements that the two results are "similar" on a scale from 1 (*strongly disagree*), to 7 (*strongly agree*).

There was little sign of any differences between disciplines, so we combined the three. Overall, there was enormous variability in respondents' interpretations and ratings, with all responses from 1 to 7 being common. Recall that the two studies are actually consistent, and so the best answers are ratings of 6 or 7. The means were 3.75 for NHST and 4.41 for CI. The CI mean was greater by 0.66, 95% CI [0.11, 1.21]. (Square brackets are the CI reporting style recommended in the APA *Publication Manual* and are what I will use throughout this book.) Yes, CIs gave higher ratings, which is good news for the new statistics, even if the difference of 0.66 points on the 1–7 scale is not large. (You noticed that the difference was statistically significant, because the CI did not include zero?) However, there was enormous variability, and mean ratings were close to the middle of the scale, not around 6 or 7. Most respondents performed poorly, even though the pattern of the Lucky–Noluck results was simple and no doubt familiar to many.

We analyzed the open-ended responses to the initial question about the "main conclusion suggested by these studies." We were struck that many respondents who saw the CIs still mentioned NHST. We divided respondents into those who mentioned NHST when interpreting the CIs shown in Figure 1.1 and those who didn't. Figure 1.3 shows for those two groups of respondents the percentages of responses that described the Lucky and Noluck results as similar or consistent, or as different or inconsistent. Those who mentioned NHST were likely (33/55, or .60) to consider the results "different," as dichotomous thinking would suggest. In striking contrast, of those who avoided any reference to NHST almost all (54/57, or .95) gave a better answer by rating the results "similar," as estimation thinking would suggest. In other words, most who mentioned NHST gave an incorrect answer, whereas almost all who did not mention NHST gave a correct answer. The two proportions of respondents who answered correctly by saying "similar" were 22/55, or .40, and

54/57, or .95, for the two groups of respondents, respectively. The difference between those two proportions is .55, [.39, .67]. (In Chapter 14 we'll use ESCI to find such a CI on the difference between two proportions.) In a second study we found evidence supporting this result. Our conclusion was that CIs can indeed give better interpretation, but only if you adopt estimation thinking and regard them as intervals, and avoid merely using them to carry out NHST.

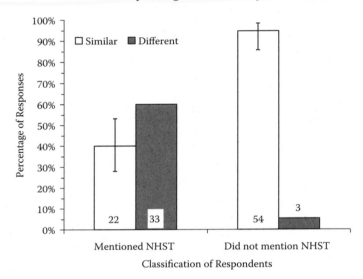

FIGURE 1.3
Percentage of open-ended responses classified as indicating the Lucky and Noluck studies gave "Similar" or "Different" results, for respondents who "Mentioned NHST" or "Did not mention NHST." Error bars are 95% CIs. Numbers of respondents are shown at the bottom. (Adapted with permission from M. Coulson, M. Healey, F. Fidler, & G. Cumming (2010). Confidence intervals permit, but do not guarantee, better inference than statistical significance testing. *Frontiers in Quantitative Psychology and Measurement*, 1:26, 1–9.)

There's a second part to the story. We included medical researchers because medicine has routinely reported CIs since the 1980s, although data interpretation in medical journals is still often based on NHST, even when CIs are reported. Despite their many years of experience with CIs, medical researchers did not perform better than researchers in the other disciplines. It seems that merely using CIs does not guarantee estimation thinking. This conclusion from medicine reinforces our finding that CIs can indeed give better interpretation, but you need to avoid using them just to carry out NHST.

at all, but that using the software adds interest and encourages deeper understanding. Some of the book's main messages are illustrated using simulations in ESCI that I hope make the ideas clear and memorable. In this first chapter I haven't used ESCI yet, but the Exercises will now introduce ESCI, then use it to explore the ideas in the chapter.

Hints for ESCI Exercises

In most chapters the main discussion in the text refers to ESCI, and the exercises at the end of each chapter also use it. At the back of the book there's commentary on most of the exercises. I invite you to take the following approach to using ESCI:

- Focus on understanding. Can you explain the concept to someone else, perhaps using ESCI? Can you draw a picture, make your own example, and recognize the concept when you encounter it elsewhere?
- Look out for images in ESCI that represent a concept. In many cases I hope they are useful for remembering and understanding the concept, and can serve as a signature or logo for it. These may be a picture or a movie—a running simulation. Examples to come include the *mean heap, dance of the CIs*, and diagrams showing *rules of eye*.
- Focus not on the software or the interface, but on the things that really matter—the statistical ideas.
- ESCI is intended first as a playground for understanding statistics, and second as a set of tools for calculating and presenting CIs in simple situations. Watch out for tools you might find useful in the future—perhaps for calculating CIs or for making figures with CIs to present your own data.
- ESCI exercises are at first quite detailed, but I encourage you to explore as widely as you wish, perhaps using your own data and examples. In later chapters they will be much less step-by-step, and I'll mainly give broad suggestions and invite you to use ESCI in whatever ways are most useful for you.

Exercises

1.1 Load and run **ESCI chapters 1–4**. Appendix A can assist.

1.2 Click the bottom tab to go to the page **Two studies**. Compare with Figure 1.4.

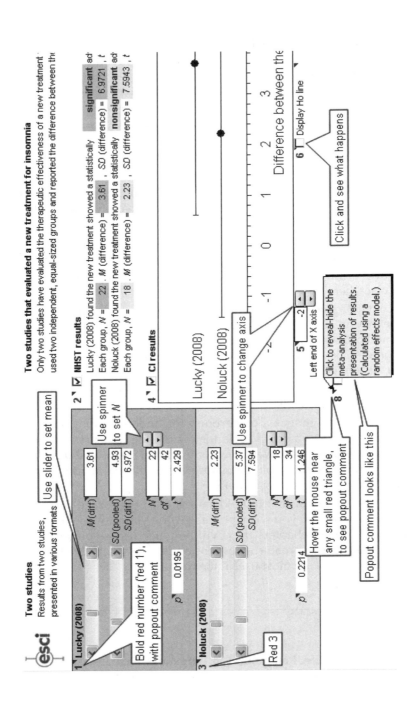

FIGURE 1.4

A partial screen image from the **Two studies** page of **ESCI chapters 1–4**. The Lucky (2008) and Noluck (2008) values have been set to match the first presentation, at the start of this chapter. The callouts point to some features of the display.

1.3 Find red 1 (the bold red 1 near the top left) and read the popout (hover the mouse near the little red triangle). A "slider" looks like a horizontal scroll-bar, and a "spinner" has small up and down arrowheads you can click.

1.4 Use the top slider to set M(diff) = 3.61 for the Lucky study. Use the next slider to set SD(diff) as close as possible to 6.97. (The slider actually sets the pooled SD within groups, and SD(diff) is calculated from that.) Use the spinner to set $N = 22$ for Lucky.

If you ever seem to be in an ESCI mess, look for some helpful popout comments. Appendix A may help. Or experiment with the controls—you won't break any-thing—and see whether you can straighten things out. Or you can close the Excel module (don't Save), then reopen it to start again.

1.5 Note the description of the Lucky results at red 2. This is the NHST version. Check that it matches what you expect.

1.6 At red 3, set the values from the first presentation for Noluck, including $N = 18$. Are the results as you expect?

1.7 Click at red 4 to see the CI results. Do they match Figure 1.1? Reveal the meta-analysis results. Are these also as you expect?

Excel macros are needed to make that work. If you cannot see the figure with CIs, you may not have enabled macros. See Appendix A.

1.8 Hide the CI results (click at red 4) and meta-analysis results. Focus on p for Lucky. How do you think this p would change if

- You increase M(diff); you decrease it?
- You increase SD(diff); you decrease it?
- You increase N; you decrease it?

1.9 Play with the controls at red 1 to see whether your predictions about the p value for Lucky were correct.

There is evidence that making your own predictions like this, then experiment-ing to test them out, can be an effective way to cement understanding. Did you actually make the predictions before you played? It's worth making your best pre-dictions and writing them down, before you start experimenting. That's more effective use of your time.

1.10 Reveal results presented in the CI and meta-analysis formats (click at red 4 and red 8). Play around with the sliders and spin-ners for Lucky and Noluck (at red 1 and red 3), and watch what happens in all three formats. Look for relationships between the formats. Make predictions then test them.

Lots of this book's exercises are like the last one: fairly open ended. They are probably of most use if you adopt strategies such as the following: Take time to explore, collaborate with someone else, set challenges for yourself or others, and write down your conclusions and questions. Where possible, try to find parallels with other statistics books with which you are familiar.

1.11 Focus on the Lucky CI in the CI figure (red 4). Click at red 6 to mark the null hypothesis. Adjust M, SD, and N, and note how p changes and whether the CI covers zero. What is p when the CI includes zero? When it misses zero? When the lower limit (LL) of the CI just touches zero?

1.12 Reveal the meta-analysis results. Play with the spinners at red 5 and red 7—to the right of the display, not shown in Figure 1.4—to see how you can control the horizontal axis in the CI and meta-analysis figures.

1.13 By now you have used every control on this page. Browse around the page and read the popouts, wherever you see little red triangles. Is everything as you expect? Does it make sense?

1.14 Play with the values for Lucky and Noluck, and watch how the meta-analysis result changes. What is the relation between the p value for the meta-analysis result, which is shown just below the meta-analysis figure, and whether the CI crosses zero?

1.15 Watch how the meta-analysis CI relates to the separate CIs for the two studies. Think of the meta-analysis as combining the evidence from the two studies, as expressed by the separate CIs. Usually, the meta-analysis CI will be shorter than each of the separate CIs. Does that make sense?

You can talk about CIs as being long or short, or equivalently as being wide or narrow. Either pair of terms is fine.

1.16 Make the means for Lucky and Noluck very different, so the two CIs don't overlap. Would you regard the two studies as giving *Consistent* or *Inconsistent* results? How long is the meta-analysis CI? Does that make sense?

1.17 Play around further, then write down some conclusions of your own. Do you prefer long or short CIs? Are you comfortable examining a CI figure and deciding whether the result is statistically significant or not?

1.18 Think how you could use this page to invent games to challenge your friends—perhaps show them one format and have them predict what another will look like.

1.19 As you inspect the three formats, do they prompt the three different ways of thinking? To which of the presentations do you find yourself returning? Which seems to give better insight? Can you recognize which type of thinking you are using at any particular moment?

1.20 Revisit your take-home messages. Improve them and extend the list if you can.

That takes time and effort, but the evidence is that generating your own summary is worthwhile and more valuable than merely reading mine.

Sometimes my "take-home messages" include a "take-home picture" or a "take-home movie." These are images, static or moving, that I hope provide vivid mnemonics for a concept and help the concept make intuitive sense. Often, but not always, they come from ESCI. They've become sufficiently embedded in your thinking when you dream about them.

Take-Home Messages

- The way results are presented really matters. Change the format and the researcher may interpret them differently, and a reader may receive a different message.

- Assessing what message a presentation format conveys is a cognitive question that the research field of statistical cognition seeks to answer.

- Evidence-based practice in statistics is desirable, and cognitive evidence can help.

- CIs are more likely to give a better interpretation of results than an NHST format, at least for the frequently occurring pattern of results shown in Figure 1.1.

- *Take-home picture*: The Lucky–Noluck pattern of Figure 1.1. This figure illustrates that a large overlap of CIs can indicate consistency of results, even when one CI includes zero and the other doesn't, so that NHST suggests, misleadingly, that the two studies give inconsistent results.

- NHST may prompt dichotomous thinking, whereas CIs are likely to encourage estimation thinking and meta-analytic thinking.

- The fundamental advantage of estimation, CIs, and meta-analysis is that they provide much fuller information than NHST, which focuses on the very limited question, "Is there an effect?"

- Merely using CIs may not suffice to overcome dichotomous thinking. In addition, CIs should be interpreted as intervals, with no reference to NHST.

- *The new statistics* aim to switch emphasis from NHST to CIs and meta-analysis, and from dichotomous thinking to estimation thinking and meta-analytic thinking.

- NHST disciplines should be able to improve their research by progressively moving to the new statistics.

2

From Null Hypothesis Significance Testing to Effect Sizes

There are two main parts to the statistical reform argument: the negatives and the positives. The negatives are criticisms of NHST, and the positives refer to advantages of estimation and other recommended techniques. Most of this book concerns the positives, but in this chapter I'll first consider the negatives: NHST and how it's taught and used.

This chapter focuses on

- NHST as it's presented in textbooks and used in practice
- Problems with NHST
- The best ways to think about NHST
- An alternative approach to science and the *estimation language* it uses
- The focus of that language, especially effect sizes (ESs) and estimation of ESs
- Shifting from dichotomous language to estimation language
- How NHST disciplines can become more quantitative

NHST as Presented in Textbooks

Suppose we want to know whether the new treatment for insomnia is better than the old. To use NHST we test the null hypothesis that there's no difference between the two treatments in the population. Many textbooks describe NHST as a series of steps, something like this:

1. Choose a null hypothesis, H_0: $\mu = \mu_0$, where μ (Greek mu) is the mean of the population, which for us is the population of difference scores between the new and old treatments for insomnia. It's most common to choose H_0: $\mu = 0$, and that's what we'll do here.

2. Choose a significance level, most often .05, but perhaps .01 if you wish to be especially cautious.

3. Apply the appropriate statistical test, a *t* test, for example, to your sample data. Calculate a *p* value, where *p* is the probability that, if the null hypothesis were true, you would obtain the observed results, or results that are more extreme—meaning more inconsistent with the null hypothesis.

The *p* value is the probability of obtaining our observed results, or results that are more extreme, if the null hypothesis is true.

4. If *p* < .05 (or whatever significance level you chose), reject the null hypothesis and declare the result "statistically significant"; if not, then don't reject the null hypothesis, and label the result "not statistically significant."

Sometimes, in addition to specifying H_0, an alternative hypothesis, H_1, is also specified. For example, if H_0: $\mu = 0$, then perhaps H_1: $\mu \neq 0$, in which case the alternative hypothesis is two-tailed, meaning we're interested in departures from the null that go in either direction—the new treatment being either worse than or better than the old. When a *p* value is calculated we need to include values that are more extreme than our observed result. Lucky (2008) obtained $M = 3.61$, so the set of results that is "more extreme" or "more favoring the alternative than the null hypothesis" includes values greater than 3.61. However, because the alternative hypothesis is two-tailed, the set must also include results less than –3.61. Calculation of *p* includes results farther from zero than our result, in either direction.

A *Type I error* is the decision to reject H_0 when it's true. The probability of rejecting H_0 when it's true is called the *Type I error rate* and is given the symbol α (Greek alpha). This is the prespecified criterion for *p*, which I referred to previously as "significance level."

The *Type I error rate*, labeled α, is the probability of rejecting the null hypothesis when it's true.

A further variation is that the alternative hypothesis may, like the null, be an exact or point hypothesis, H_1: $\mu = \mu_1$. For example, H_1 may be a statement that the new treatment gives, on average, sleep scores 4 units higher on our sleep scale than the old treatment.

Statistical power is the probability of obtaining statistical significance, and thus rejecting the null hypothesis, if the alternative hypothesis is true.

Specifying such a point alternative allows calculation of *statistical power*, which is the probability of rejecting the null hypothesis if H_1 is true. In other words, if there is a true effect, and it has the exact size μ_1 specified by the alternative hypothesis, power is the probability our experiment will find it to be statistically significant. We'll discuss power in Chapter 12. Specifying a point alternative also allows calculation of the *Type II error rate*, labeled β (Greek beta), which is the probability of failing to obtain a statistically significant result, if H_1 is true. Therefore, power = $1 - \beta$.

The *Type II error rate*, labeled β, is the probability of not rejecting the null hypothesis when it is false.

I invite you to examine one or two of the statistics textbooks you are most familiar with, and compare how they present NHST with my description above. Compare the steps in the sequence and the terminology. Note especially what they say about Step 2, the specification in advance of a criterion for statistical significance, perhaps labeled α. Then, for a possibly very interesting comparison, in each book turn to much later chapters where NHST is used in examples. Does the textbook follow its own rules? If its equivalent of Step 2 states that the criterion, or α, must be chosen in advance, in later chapters does it state an α value at the start of each example? Or does it state anywhere that a particular value of α will be used throughout the book? I suspect you might find that, instead, it follows the practice most common in journal articles, which is to calculate and report the p value, then interpret that in relation not to a single prechosen α level, but implicitly in relation to a number of conventional levels, such as .05, .01, and .001. In other words, rather than prespecifying $\alpha = .05$, if you calculate p to be .034, you report the result as statistically significant, $p < .05$, but if you calculate $p = .007$, you claim statistical significance, $p < .01$. If, happily, you obtain $p = .0003$, then you claim statistical significance, $p < .001$. Sometimes use of a set of conventional levels is signaled by asterisks, with more asterisks for smaller p. You could declare the values previously mentioned as statistically significant: .034*, .007**, and .0003***. Sometimes language is used to claim degrees of statistical significance, as when a two- or three-star result is described as "highly statistically significant."

Even if you found the discrepancy I have described between how a textbook introduces NHST and how it uses NHST to analyze data, you may think the difference is no big deal. However, the distinction between (1) setting α in advance and (2) interpreting exact p values, such as .034, on a sliding scale of degrees of statistical significance is vitally important. The two are based on quite different interpretations of the p value. To explain why this matters, I need to describe a little history.

Two Strands in the History of NHST

I'll give here only a very brief sketch of a famous controversy in the early days of NHST. If you are interested in knowing more I recommend Salsburg (2001), which is a book of fascinating stories about famous statisticians and the development of statistics, and which also provides further references. Sir Ronald Fisher made numerous fundamental contributions to statistics, mainly during the first half of the twentieth century. He developed *significance testing*, in which the p value is used as a guide for reaching a judgment about the hypothesis, taking account of all the circumstances. If $p < .01$, he would generally regard the result as clearly significant. He also used .05 as a reference point, although for quite a wide range of p values, perhaps from .01 to .20, he would typically discuss how follow-up experiments could be used to investigate the effect further. Fisher thus regarded p as a measure of strength of evidence against the hypothesis—the smaller the p, the stronger the reason to doubt the hypothesis. He regarded large p values, perhaps $p > .20$, as indicating weak evidence, and he emphasized that such lack of statistical significance should definitely not be taken as meaning the hypothesis is true.

As Salsburg (2001) explains, Jerzy Neyman and Egon Pearson disliked Fisher's approach and developed a more structured form of decision making. They called the hypothesis under test the *null hypothesis* and introduced the *alternative hypothesis*, so their approach became a choice between the two. They required α to be set in advance. The p value was compared with α, and a choice between the null and alternative hypotheses was made according to whether or not $p < \alpha$. Neyman and Pearson also introduced the ideas of *power*, and *Type I* and *Type II errors*.

They considered the Type I error rate, α, as a long-run proportion: If you carry out numerous experiments all with a true null hypothesis, then in the long run, if $\alpha = .05$, you would reject the null hypothesis for just 5% of those experiments. This interpretation of the probability α could only be correct if α were chosen in advance and the data were not permitted to influence the choice of criterion for statistical significance. If $\alpha = .05$ had been chosen, then even $p = .0003$ would lead simply to rejection of the null hypothesis at the $\alpha = .05$ level.

Fisher strongly disagreed with the Neyman–Pearson approach, and both that approach and Fisher's own ideas were extensively criticized. Now, approaching a century later, the criticism continues, but various mixtures of the two approaches are described in numerous textbooks and used by many disciplines as the basis for drawing conclusions from data. Gerd Gigerenzer (1993) described current NHST practices, not as a mixture, but as "an incoherent mishmash" (p. 314) of the ideas of Fisher, and Neyman and Pearson. Raymond Hubbard (2004) referred to an "alphabet soup, blurring the distinctions between p's and α's" (p. 295).

I suspect that many statistics textbooks present NHST using some variation of the steps I set out earlier, which basically take a Neyman–Pearson approach. I also suspect that different disciplines have somewhat different traditions about how NHST is presented. It would be very interesting to know more about how NHST is described in textbooks, and whether that varies over disciplines, but I've been able to find only a few small studies on the topic, and none that make extensive comparisons across disciplines.

It seems the clear structure and decision making of the Neyman–Pearson procedure is appealing. Also, this is the necessary approach if the important topic of statistical power is to be discussed. Therefore, many textbook authors choose it as the framework for presenting NHST. However, researchers seem to have found the requirement to state α in advance too onerous, and unenforceable in practice. It seems irrational to obtain a seemingly clear-cut result with $p = .0003$, but then merely to reject the null hypothesis at the $\alpha = .05$ level. So researchers may teach their students Neyman–Pearson and use that framework to introduce statistical power, but then in practice follow Fisher by reporting exact p values and interpreting these as measures of strength of evidence against the null hypothesis.

If my analysis is even partly accurate, it's not surprising that many students are confused. To some extent students may be expected to learn one rationale and procedure (Neyman–Pearson), but then see a quite different one (Fisher) modeled in the journal articles they read. It would be particularly interesting to investigate whether many textbooks exhibit the discrepancy I described: Do they teach Neyman–Pearson, but then a few chapters later follow Fisher when illustrating how researchers carry out data analysis in practice? It might be tempting to regard a mixture of the two approaches as possibly combining the best of both worlds, but the two frameworks are based on incompatible conceptions of probability. The mixture is indeed incoherent, and so it's not surprising that misconceptions about NHST are so widespread.

I argued in Chapter 1 that NHST can lead to unjustified interpretations of results, whereas estimation provides more complete information. I now turn to a few further problems of NHST and discuss them in terms of how their dangers can be minimized. Box 2.1 reports some relevant evidence from statistical cognition.

BOX 2.1 EVIDENCE OF p VALUE MISCONCEPTIONS

In his important book, *Statistical Inference*, Michael Oakes (1986) gave a scathing critique of NHST and a comparison with other approaches to inference. In his Chapter 3 he reported four statistical cognition experiments that explored the statistical intuitions of psychology researchers and postgraduate students. He found evidence of major misunderstanding of NHST, and also misconceptions about other issues we'll discuss in future chapters, including replication and correlation. In his first study he asked six simple true–false questions about the meaning and interpretation of a p value. Only three of his 70 participants answered all six correctly.

Haller and Krauss (2002, tinyurl.com/nhstohdear) presented Oakes's six questions to psychology students and academic staff in six German universities. As in the Oakes study, a simple experiment was described that gave a p value of .01, then the true–false questions were posed. As an example, consider Question 4:

> "You can deduce the probability of the experimental hypothesis being true."

We know that $p = .01$. If this means a 1% probability that the null hypothesis is true, then there's a 99% probability that the null is false and the experimental hypothesis is true. That's just a statement of the common incorrect belief that p is the probability that the results are due to chance. The correct answer to Question 4 is thus "false," but Oakes reported that 66% of his respondents answered "true."

Haller and Krauss (2002) reported that in their sample 59% of psychology students incorrectly answered "true" to that question, as did 33% of psychology academic staff who did not teach statistics. They also obtained responses from psychology academic staff who taught statistics: 33% of these answered "true" to Question 4, and only 20% answered all six questions correctly. Haller and Krauss described that evidence of NHST misconception among teachers of statistics in psychology departments as "flabbergasting" (p. 7). If a technique is not even understood correctly by its teachers, what hope is there for students and researchers who wish to use it?

Statistical cognition research aims to identify problems, but also to find ways to overcome them. Haller and Krauss (2002) did this by discussing how improved teaching might overcome p value misconceptions. Kalinowski, Fidler, and Cumming (2008) reported a small teaching experiment in which they evaluated two approaches: one proposed by Haller and Krauss, and the other an explanation of the basic logic of NHST. Both approaches were reasonably successful in improving students' understanding of p values. However, it remains an enormous challenge to demonstrate that better teaching could overcome all of the many pervasive misconceptions of NHST and, even if we could achieve that, the fundamental problem would remain that NHST focuses only on the narrow question, "Is there an effect?"

There have been other studies of NHST errors, besides those of Oakes (1986) and Haller and Krauss (2002). My conclusion is that evidence of NHST misconception is now strong. Researchers, students, and even teachers of statistics in psychology all have severe and persisting misunderstandings of p values and what they mean. It's hardly surprising that NHST is so often misused.

Some Selected Problems of NHST

The best summary of NHST problems is Chapter 3 of *Beyond Significance Testing* by Rex Kline (2004). The chapter is available from tinyurl.com/klinechap3 as a free download. Kline described 13 wrong beliefs about *p* values and the way they are used and interpreted. He also explained several major ways that reliance on NHST has damaged research and hampered research progress. His chapter concluded with recommendations about how to avoid or minimize NHST problems, and an outline of his version of the new statistics. I'll now discuss some selected problems of NHST, all of which are additional to the central and fundamental limitation that NHST focuses only on "is there an effect?" By contrast, estimation is much more informative.

What *p* Is, and What It's Not

The *p* value is the probability of getting our observed result, or a more extreme result, if the null hypothesis is true. So *p* is defined in relation to a stated null hypothesis, and requires as the basis for calculation that we assume the null is true. It's a common error to think *p* gives the probability that the null is true: That's the *inverse probability fallacy*. Consider the difference between

The *inverse probability fallacy* is the incorrect belief that the *p* value is the probability that the null hypothesis is true.

1. The probability that you speak English if you are reading this book (close to 1, I would think); and
2. The probability that you will read this book, if you speak English. (Even if one million people read this book—I wish!—that's still a probability close to 0, because so many million people in the world speak English.)

Here's another example of the same distinction. Compare

3. The probability of getting certain results if the null is true (that's *p*); and
4. The probability that the null is true if we've obtained certain results. (We'd like to know that but, alas, *p* can't tell us.)

In both these examples, the two probabilities are fundamentally different. Probability 3 is a conditional probability that's easy to calculate if we assume the null is true. Probability 4 refers to truth in the world, and in a sense must be either 0 (the null is false) or 1 (the null is true), but we don't know which. Anyone can choose his or her own subjective probability that the null is true, but different people will most likely choose different values.

Suppose you run a coin-tossing experiment to investigate whether your friend can use the power of her mind to influence whether a coin comes up heads or tails. You take great care to remove any chance of trickery. (Consult a skilled conjurer to discover how difficult that is.) Your friend concentrates deeply then predicts correctly the outcome of nine of the first 10 tosses. A surprising result! You calculate $p = .011$ as the probability that she would get nine or 10 predictions correct, if the null hypothesis of a fair coin and random guessing were true. (That's Probability 3, the p value.) Are you going to declare statistical significance and buy her the drink she bet you? Or will you conclude that most likely she's just had a lucky day? Sure, .011 is small (and less than .05), but you find her claimed power of the mind *very* hard to accept. You need to choose your own subjective probability that she was lucky, and .011 doesn't give you exact help in making your choice. That's the NHST dilemma, which we usually side-step by using conventions that .05 or .01 are reasonable p value cutoffs for declaring a result as statistically significant. We duck the need for subjective judgment by resorting to a mechanical rule that takes no account of the situation.

Note carefully that .011 was the probability of particular extreme results *if the null hypothesis is true*. Surprising results may reasonably lead you to doubt the null, but p is not the probability that the null is true. Some statistics textbooks say that p measures the probability that "the results are due to chance"—in other words, the probability that the null hypothesis is correct. However, that's merely a restatement of the inverse probability fallacy. It's completely wrong to say the p value is the probability that the results are due to chance. Jacob Cohen (1994), a distinguished statistics reformer, wrote that NHST "does not tell us what we want to know, and we so much want to know what we want to know that, out of desperation, we nevertheless believe that it does!" (p. 997). In other words, we want to know whether the null is true (Probability 4), but p does not measure that—it measures Probability 3. In desperation we believe that p measures Probability 4 and, unfortunately, some textbooks perpetuate the error.

Beware the Ambiguity of "Significance"

If you read in a journal article that "there was a significant reduction in anxiety," does "significant" mean important or large, or just that $p < .05$? The word is ambiguous and can easily mislead. Any good statistics textbook will explain that statistical significance is different from scientific or practical significance. Small p does not guarantee that an effect is "large" or "important." A tiny effect can be highly statistically significant if the experiment is sufficiently large, or a small experiment can find a large effect that's not statistically significant. Distinguish carefully between interpretation of the effect size (ES), and any NHST statement based on *p*. Unfortunately, it's fairly common to find a fallacy I call the *slippery slope of significance*: In the Results section of an article, NHST is reported and an effect is declared to be statistically significant because *p* is small. However, in the Discussion section, and

> I refer to the following fallacy as the *slippery slope of significance*: An effect is found to be statistically significant, is described, ambiguously, as "significant," and then later is discussed as if it had thereby been shown to be "important" or "large."

perhaps the abstract, the effect is described simply as "significant" and is discussed as if it's important, or large. The ambiguous term "significant" silently morphs from one of its meanings to the other. Discussing an ES as large or important requires justification based on informed judgment, whether *p* is large or small.

Kline (2004) recommended that we simply drop the word "significant" and write, "there was a statistical reduction in anxiety," if we're reporting NHST and have rejected the null hypothesis. That's a good idea. An acceptable alternative is to say "statistically significant" if that's the intended meaning, and perhaps "practically significant" or "clinically important" if that's your judgment. I try to avoid using "significant" to mean important, and prefer to find some

> A sidebar like this often gives the definition of a term. If it's a term or expression of my invention I'll usually say so, as I did for the slippery slope of significance, to signal that you probably won't find it in other statistics textbooks.

other word. The vital point is that reading the word "significant" should trigger your ambiguity alarm: Does the author make clear what's intended? Is that justified? Beware the fallacy of the slippery slope of significance.

Beware Accepting the Null

If we conclude that there's a statistically significant advantage of the new treatment for insomnia when there's actually no difference in the population, we're committing a Type I error: We're rejecting the null hypothesis when it's true. NHST limits the risk of Type I errors by requiring small *p* before you reject the null. On the other hand, if we fail to find statistical significance when there is a population difference, we're making a Type II error: We're failing to reject the null hypothesis, even though it's false. Often, however, little attention is paid to Type II errors. Box 2.2 reports evidence of the low power of published research in many areas of psychology. In practice, in many disciplines, statistical power is often low, meaning that the risk of committing a Type II error is often large. In other words, many experiments have a high chance of failing to detect effects when they do exist. We must therefore be careful not to take statistical nonsignificance (the null is not rejected) as evidence of a zero effect (the null is true).

All good statistics textbooks warn of the danger of accepting a null hypothesis, but the trouble is that the acceptance can be hidden. For example,

BOX 2.2 MANY DECADES OF EVIDENCE OF LOW POWER

Cohen (1962) studied 70 articles in the *Journal of Social and Abnormal Psychology*. He chose ES values to label as "small," "medium," and "large," and then estimated the power of the experiments to find effects of various sizes. He found that estimated power varied greatly over studies, but the mean was only .48 (and median .46) to find medium-sized effects. Mean power to find small effects was .18, and only for large effects was mean power as high as .83. In summary, published research in a number of areas of psychology typically had only about a coin-toss chance of finding a medium-sized population effect to be statistically significant ($p < .05$). Cohen described those levels of power as "far too small" (p. 153) and urged researchers to increase their sample sizes and routinely subject their research plans to power analysis. Cohen noted that almost all the published articles reported statistically significant findings and reasoned that, given the low power, many experiments that failed to find statistically significant effects—thus making Type II errors—must have been conducted, but not published. They represent an enormous waste of research effort. Cohen's study was before the arrival of meta-analysis, but we can now recognize that, because the published studies were a biased subset of all studies conducted, meta-analysis of published studies would give biased estimates—most likely overestimates—of population ESs.

Sedlmeier and Gigerenzer (1989) revisited the same journal 24 years later. They found power to be just as low (median .44 to find a medium-sized effect), and even lower if they took account of alpha adjustment procedures used in many articles to account for multiple tests—procedures not in regular use at the time of Cohen's (1962) study. Sedlmeier and Gigerenzer also reviewed studies of power in about 20 other journals from several disciplines. There was variation but, overall, power was similarly disappointingly low. Later studies have suggested little improvement in the following two decades (Maxwell, 2004), despite the efforts of Cohen and others to persuade researchers to consider power seriously.

in the NHST presentation of Lucky–Noluck the *Inconsistent* interpretation amounts to concluding that Lucky found an effect but Noluck did not. The nonrejection of the Noluck null is interpreted as a zero effect. It's absurd to use $M = 2.23$ as evidence that the true value is zero, but hidden under a pile of NHST ritual that's what an *Inconsistent* interpretation does.

If a null hypothesis is not rejected, watch out for another fallacy: the *slippery slope of nonsignificance*. In the Results section, $p >$ .05 prompts a statement that the difference failed to reach statistical significance. That's fine, but in the discussion, or even the abstract, the statistically nonsignificant difference may quietly become no difference. Worse, this may be left implicit, as when the result is contrasted with some other, statistically significant effect. The *Inconsistent* interpretation of Lucky–Noluck includes no explicit statement that Noluck found a difference of zero, but making the contrast and stating the two results are inconsistent implicitly assumes that the statistically nonsignificant effect was zero. Example 2.1 is an example. Beware the fallacy of the slippery slope of nonsignificance.

I refer to the following fallacy as the *slippery slope of nonsignificance*: An effect is found to be statistically nonsignificant then later discussed as if that showed it to be zero.

EXAMPLE 2.1 DOES THIS ANTI-AGING CREAM WORK?

In April 2009 queues formed outside some stores in the Boots chain of pharmacies in the United Kingdom as customers rushed to buy No. 7 Protect & Perfect Intense Beauty Serum. Their eagerness was prompted by media reports claiming that an article in the *British Journal of Dermatology* (Watson et al., 2009) provided scientific proof that the product, marketed as an anti-aging cream, actually worked. The original version of the article had just been published online. It was titled "A cosmetic 'anti-ageing' product improves photoaged skin: A double-blind, randomized controlled trial." It stated, "The test product produced statistically significant improvement in facial wrinkles as compared to baseline assessment ($p = .013$), whereas vehicle-treated skin was not significantly improved ($p = .11$)" (p. 420). The article concluded, "An over-the-counter cosmetic 'anti-ageing' product resulted in significant clinical improvement in facial wrinkles" (p. 420).

The article reported a statistically significant improvement for the active ingredient, but no statistically significant improvement for the control treatment, which was "vehicle," meaning cream lacking the ingredient under test. No direct comparison was reported of results for the treated and control participants, and the conclusion was based on the differing p values. Do you recognize the pattern as classic Lucky–Noluck? The p values (.013 and .11) don't justify the conclusion, and it's a statistical error to claim they do.

Yes, the title of the article sounds convincing, with its statement that the product improves aged skin and that the experiment was a double-blind randomized control trial (RCT). Yes, a double-blind RCT is the gold standard of research designs for this situation. It's not surprising that the media trumpeted the result, but using a good design doesn't guarantee good statistical analysis.

The authors had second thoughts and the official published version, which appeared in the August 2009 printed issue of the journal as well as online, included some amendments. The title became the neutral, "Effects of a cosmetic 'anti-ageing' product on photoaged skin"; it was additionally reported that a comparison of the two conditions gave $p = .10$, and the conclusion claimed only a "[statistically] non-significant trend towards clinical improvement in facial wrinkles." (Watson et al., 2009, p. 419. Note that this is the only version now available. It is the full version originally published online, but with a note explaining the amendments made later by the authors, including changes to the title and the conclusions.) Better science, but perhaps not so likely to trigger media enthusiasm and a rush to buy?

I don't know what prompted the authors' changes, but an article in the journal *Significance* (Bland, 2009) may have contributed. It made the criticism I described previously, as well as other criticisms of the original online version. That original version should not have been published, but we can take this case study as a lesson to never assume that journal referees will find every statistical error. We must always be statistically vigilant and, in particular, watch out for the Lucky–Noluck pattern and the fallacy of the slippery slope of nonsignificance.

If You Use *p*, Report Exact Values

The traditional Neyman–Pearson approach emphasizes making a clear decision to reject the null hypothesis, or not. This requires simply noting whether or not $p < .05$, or, more generally, $p < \alpha$. However, reporting the accurate value of p (e.g., $p = .09$, or $p = .016$) gives extra information and allows any reader either to compare p with a chosen α, or to interpret p as a measure of evidence against the null, as Fisher proposed. The *APA Manual* (2010) states that "when reporting p values, report exact p values (e.g., $p = .031$)" (p. 114), although it permits the use of relative values (e.g., $p < .05$) or asterisks if necessary for clarity in tables. If you use p values, it's best practice and is most informative to report exact values.

> If you report a *p* value, give an *exact* value ($p = .006$), not a *relative* value ($p < .01$).

How to Think About *p* Values

There has been surprisingly little investigation of how researchers think about p values, the interpretations they make, or their emotional reactions to p values that are large or small. These are all great topics for statistical cognition research. One early study was by Rosenthal and Gaito (1963), who asked graduate students and researchers in psychology to rate their degree of confidence in an effect, given a p value. They used p values ranging from .001 to .9, and found that degree of confidence dropped rapidly as p increased. They identified what they called a *cliff effect*, which was a steep drop in the degree of confidence that an effect exists as p increased past .05. Poitevineau and Lecoutre (2001) pointed out that Rosenthal and Gaito's cliff effect was steep but only moderate in size, and not shown by all participants. Their own investigation found that different participants showed different patterns of change in confidence as p increased from very small to large. One extreme pattern is a smooth decrease in confidence as p increases, which fits with Fisher's view of p as a measure of strength of evidence. The cliff pattern is quite different, and is a large and sharp drop in confidence at .05, which fits with a Neyman–Pearson dichotomous decision based on $\alpha = .05$. It seems, from the little evidence available so far, that there are elements of each of these patterns in the ratings given by students and researchers, with most showing the gradual decrease and some showing in addition a small or large drop at .05—in other words an element of the cliff effect. There's considerable variation in patterns shown by different respondents, which is consistent with NHST as it is practiced today being a confused mix of Fisherian and Neyman–Pearson ideas.

> The *cliff effect* is a sharp drop in the degree of confidence that an effect exists for p just below .05 (or another conventional criterion) and just above that criterion.

A good way to think about p is in terms of its definition, as a probability of obtaining particular results assuming that the null is true. Whenever you see a p value, bring to mind "assuming there's actually no difference," or a similar statement of the null hypothesis. However, I suspect researchers may most commonly follow Fisher and think of p as a measure of evidence against the null hypothesis, even though this interpretation of p is only occasionally mentioned in statistics textbooks. Other things being equal, the smaller the p, the more reason we have to doubt the null. In a later chapter I'll demonstrate that p is actually an extremely poor and vague measure of evidence against the null. Even so, thinking of p as strength of evidence may be the least bad approach.

There's also a better way to interpret a p value: Use it, together with knowledge of the null hypothesis and the obtained mean or other ES, to find the CI, as Chapter 4 explains. Then you'll have a much better basis for interpretation.

I now want to turn from NHST to the new statistics—from the negatives to the positives. I'll start with ESs. I'll introduce ESs by considering some aims of science and the language used to express those aims.

The Questions That Science Asks

Think of the questions that science asks. Some typical questions are

Q1 "What is the age of the Earth?"

Q2 "What is the likely sea-level rise by 2100?"

Q3 "What is the effect of exercise on the risk of heart attack?"

Q4 "What is the relationship between pollution level and fish fertility?"

The answer to Q1 may be 4.54 ± 0.05 billion years, where 4.54 is our best point estimate of the true value, and 0.05 indicates the precision of that estimate. It's natural and informative to answer such quantitative questions by giving a best value and an indication of how accurate you believe this is. Similarly, a news website reports, "Support for the prime minister is 62% in a poll with an error margin of 3%," or you look out from the south rim of the Grand Canyon and say to your friend, "I'm guessing it's 10 kilometers to the other rim, give or take 5 k." The answer to Q2 may be 0.37 m, with a range of 0.18 to 0.59 m. The precision, or uncertainty, is indicated by the error margin, the "give or take," or the range of predictions.

The focus of such questions is an *effect*, and the *size* or nature of that effect. We use *effect* to refer to the age of the Earth, support for the prime minister, or distance to the north rim—in fact anything in which we might be interested. Therefore, an *effect size* (ES) is simply the amount of something that might be of interest. Estimating effect sizes is often the primary purpose of empirical science, and so inevitably the primary outcome is one or more ES estimates. "How much" questions, like Q1, Q2, and Q3, naturally lead to "this much" answers, and the main purpose of journal publication is to report those answers.

> An *effect* is anything we might be interested in, and an *effect size* is simply the size of anything that may be of interest.

Many scientists would be astonished to find a chapter in a statistics textbook that explains the importance of reporting ESs. Isn't that obvious? How else could science proceed? NHST disciplines, however, often ask not "how much" questions, but "whether or not" questions, and they publish "statistically significant effect" or "no statistically significant effect" as the dichotomous answer to each.

Chapter 1 described dichotomous thinking, and estimation and meta-analytic thinking. My argument here is that the language used by researchers can indicate which type of thinking predominates. The link may be even stronger: Deliberately choosing estimation language may encourage estimation and meta-analytic thinking, which are the types of thinking favored by the new statistics. Using estimation language to formulate research questions should naturally encourage a focus on ESs and CIs for reporting and interpreting results.

At this point I want to mention the argument of Paul Meehl (1978), the distinguished psychologist and philosopher of science, who published strong criticisms of NHST over several decades. He stated that "reliance on merely refuting the null hypothesis ... is basically unsound, poor scientific strategy, and one of the worst things that ever happened in the history of psychology" (p. 817). Not only was dichotomous decision making impoverished, he argued, but it limited the research aims, and even the theories that researchers formulated. He blamed "the Fisherian tradition [NHST], ... [which] has inhibited our search for stronger tests, so we have thrown in the sponge and abandoned hope of concocting substantive theories that will generate stronger consequences than merely 'the Xs differ from the Ys'" (p. 824). He urged researchers to abandon NHST, and to build theories that were more quantitative, so they could "generate numerical point predictions (the ideal case found in the exact sciences)" (p. 824). Meehl is saying that, for example, focusing on how much better the new Lucky–Noluck treatment for insomnia is than the old should encourage us to consider a quantitative model of how the treatment works. More generally, the new statistics could lead to better theory as well as more informative research, so disciplines could become more quantitative and thus more sophisticated, and better able to explain the world.

The Language Researchers Use

I would like to be able to report evidence that shifting to estimation language encourages the use of ESs and CIs, and leads to better research and more informative results. Lacking such evidence, I would at least like to be able to present evidence about how often researchers use dichotomous or estimation language to present their research aims and report their conclusions. Box 2.3 reports the only study I know of on these issues, and it presents only a partial picture: It didn't examine how research aims are expressed, but found evidence in a leading psychology journal that conclusions are often expressed in dichotomous language.

As an initial tiny investigation of researchers' language I picked up the most recent issue of *Psychological Science*, a leading journal that reports interesting findings across the whole of psychology. I scanned the first 10 articles, looking for brief statements of an article's main aim or question. (I'm not going to give referencing details for that issue, or the words I quote from those articles, because I'm presenting them as typical generic

BOX 2.3 WHAT LANGUAGE DO RESEARCHERS USE?

Hoekstra, Finch, Kiers, and Johnson (2006) examined 266 articles published in *Psychonomic Bulletin & Review*, a leading psychology journal, during 2002 to 2004. They found that 97% of the articles used NHST, and only 6% reported any CIs. They also found that 60% of the articles that used NHST reported a statistically nonsignificant result then made the serious mistake of accepting the null hypothesis and claiming no effect—which sounds like the fallacy of the slippery slope of nonsignificance. In addition, 19% of the articles that used NHST reported a statistically significant effect, then those articles made the mistake of stating, on the basis of statistical significance, that the effect certainly existed, or was important. That sounds like the fallacy of the slippery slope of significance. Hoekstra et al. (2006) interpreted these mistakes as evidence that a majority of researchers did not appreciate the uncertainty in any NHST result, and stated their conclusions using dichotomous language that implied certainty.

fragments of language and don't want to imply criticism of particular authors when I'm quoting only very few of their words.)

I must say I was impressed. Every article investigated interesting issues and reported ingenious experiments that provided relevant evidence and led to valuable conclusions. *Psychological Science* accepts only 10–20% of the manuscripts it receives, and the published articles describe some of the best psychological research from anywhere around the world. However, all 10 articles used NHST to identify effects as statistically significant or not, so dichotomous thinking still thrives. In two of the 10, significance language was avoided, but, even in these two articles, effects were still described as existing or not: p values provided the basis for statements like "proud participants … spent more time manipulating the puzzle … $p = .04$ …," and "no difference was found between reaction times for the proximal and distal postures … $p > .05$…." The reader is left to insert "statistically significant(ly)" at the appropriate point in each sentence. One example diverged from the usual $p < .05$ criterion for regarding an effect as real: "They were also perceived as more dominant by their partners … $p = .07$." A null hypothesis was accepted with the statement, "As Figure 3 shows … the magnitude of this effect was indistinguishable from the magnitude of the adaptation with consistent illumination … $t(13) = 1.82$, n.s." The two points referred to were an easily distinguishable 4 mm apart in Figure 3, which is hardly good evidence for a zero difference, especially given that the unstated p value was .09.

All 10 articles reported means or other ESs, often in figures. Discussion often referred to the ESs. Aims were often expressed in a general way:

"The goal of this study was to explore the mechanism by which gesturing plays a role in learning." Even so, in eight articles it was easy to find a main aim and corresponding conclusion each expressed in a dichotomous way. Here are some examples:

Aim 1: "We predicted that playing a violent video game ... would decrease the likelihood of help."

Conclusion 1: "Participants who played a violent game took significantly longer to help."

Aim 2: "We hypothesized that stressed participants would exhibit increased risky behavior on loss-domain trials but increased conservatism on gain-domain trials."

Conclusion 2a: "Significantly fewer risky decisions (i.e., increased conservatism) were made on gain-domain trials under acute stress."

The usual $p = .05$ cutoff was relaxed in order to make the following conclusion related to the first part of the aim:

Conclusion 2b: "On loss-domain trials, participants showed a trend toward making a higher number of risky decisions under acute stress ... $p < .10$."

Just two studies used estimation language and included no dichotomous statements of aims. One stated, "The current study measured the degree to which the public's interpretation of the forecasts ... matches the authors' intentions." "Measured the degree to which" is the crucial estimation language. Discussion focused on the extent of differences. The aim of the other study was "estimating the financial value of pain." Here "estimating the value of" is the crucial wording. Discussion focused on the price people would pay to avoid pain in various circumstances. Both studies used significance language as well, but were infused with estimation language and estimation thinking, and focused on ES estimates as answers to the research questions asked. Just one of the 10 articles reported CIs, shown in a figure. However, the CIs were not mentioned in the text nor used for interpretation.

I conclude that much excellent current research relies on NHST, dichotomous thinking, and significance language, while also reporting ESs. I can't be sure, but I suspect that at least some of the eight articles that used dichotomous language could have been more informative if estimation ideas had shaped the questions and guided the data analysis and interpretation. The two studies that used estimation language to express their aims, and focused in their discussions on estimated ESs, suggest how future research might be different. Choosing estimation language and CIs, and keeping the focus on ESs, should avoid errors caused by NHST, while also giving answers that are more quantitative. This should contribute to the broader goal of building more quantitative theories, and more quantitative and progressive disciplines.

I suggested previously that scientists in disciplines that don't rely on NHST automatically assume that ESs are the focus of most experiments. I suspect that researchers in NHST disciplines share this intuition about wanting a numerical value from an experiment, and information about how good an answer to our question that value is. The problem is that NHST and dichotomous thinking to some extent suppress those intuitions. If I'm right, moving to estimation thinking and the new statistics will allow such intuitions to flourish, and researchers may thus feel the new statistics are somewhat natural, or even familiar.

Effect Sizes

Jacob Cohen (1990) wrote, "The primary product of a research inquiry is one or more measures of effect size.... Effect-size measures include mean differences (raw or standardized), correlations ... whatever conveys the magnitude of the phenomenon of interest appropriate to the research context" (p. 1310). This accords with my previous definition of an ES as the amount of anything that might be of interest. It can be as familiar as a mean, a difference between means, a percentage, a median, or a correlation. It may be a standardized value, such as Cohen's d (more on this later), or a regression coefficient, path coefficient, odds ratio, or percentage of variance explained (don't worry if some of these aren't familiar). The answer to Q3, about the effect of exercise on risk of heart attack, may be expressed as a percentage change in risk, or a decrease in the number of people in 1,000 who are likely to have a heart attack in one year, or in various other ways, as I will discuss in Chapter 14, but in any case the answer is an ES.

If you measure the attitudes of a group of people before and after you present them with an advertising message, it's natural to think of the change in attitude as an *effect* and the amount of change as the *size* of that effect. However, the term "effect size" is used much more broadly. It can refer to an amount, rather than a change, and there need not be any easily identifiable "cause" for the "effect." The mean systolic blood pressure of a group of children, the number of companies that failed to submit tax returns by the due date, and the ratio of good to bad cholesterol in a diet are all

A p value is *not* an ES. It cannot provide the answer to an estimation question.

TABLE 2.1

Examples of ES Measures

Sample ES	Description	Example
Mean, M	Original units	Mean response time, $M = 462$ ms.
Difference between two means	Original units	The average price of milk increased last year by $0.12/L, from $1.14/L to $1.26/L.
Median, Mdn	Original units	Median response time, $Mdn = 385$ ms.
Percentage	Units-free	35.5% of respondents were in favor. 0.7% of responses were errors.
Frequency	Units-free	39 states ran a deficit.
Correlation, r	Units-free	Income correlated with age ($r = .28$).
Cohen's d	Standardized	The average effect of psychotherapy was $d = 0.68$ (see Chapters 7 and 11).
Regression weight, b	Original units	The slope of the regression line for income against age was $b = \$1,350/year$.
Regression weight, β	Standardized	The β-weight for age in the regression was .23.
Proportion of variance, R^2	Units-free	Three variables of age, education, and family status in the multiple regression together gave $R^2 = .48$.
Risk	Units-free	The risk that a child has a bicycle accident in the next year is 1/45.
Relative risk	Units-free	A boy is 1.4 times as likely as a girl to have a bicycle accident in the next year.
Proportion of variance, ω^2 (Greek omega-squared)	Units-free	In the analysis of variance, the independent variable age accounted for $\omega^2 = 21.5\%$ of total variance.

perfectly good ESs. Yes, many things are ESs, but p values are not. Let me emphasize that last point: A p value is *not* an ES, and it cannot provide the answer to a "how much?" estimation question.

Table 2.1 presents some example ESs. Don't worry if some are unfamiliar. In later chapters we'll discuss some of the ESs in the table further, especially Cohen's d, Pearson's correlation r, and proportions. We'll also encounter further ESs. One of the messages of Table 2.1 is that there are many different ESs that can be described and classified in various ways. Another is that many ESs are probably very familiar to you already. Some authors write about ESs as if they are complex and unfamiliar, and the requirement to report ESs is a new and challenging demand for researchers. Indeed, some ESs may be unfamiliar and a little tricky to understand, but many ESs are highly familiar, and many researchers have always reported and discussed in their articles at least basic ESs, such as means or correlations.

All through the previous paragraph I wrote "ESs," although "ES measures" may have been more precise wording. Many writers use "effect size" to refer sometimes to a single value, and at other times to the measure, such as M or d, as I did previously. Often I'll write "ES measure" for clarity, but you need to be aware that "ES" is used in these two ways.

The *population ES* is simply the true value of an effect in the underlying population. The *sample ES* is calculated from the data and is typically used as our best point estimate of the population ES. It is often referred to as an *ES estimate*. Estimated ESs are usually the main results of research, and should be the main focus of interpretation because they are the best information we have about the population.

> We calculate from our data the *sample ES* and use this as our estimate of the *population ES*, which is typically what we would like to know.

What the *Publication Manual* Says

The *Publication Manual* (APA, 2010) is clear about the necessity of reporting ESs:

> For the reader to appreciate the magnitude or importance of a study's findings, it is almost always necessary to include some measure of effect size…. Effect sizes may be expressed in the original units (e.g., the mean number of questions answered correctly; kg/month for a regression slope) and are often most easily understood when reported in original units. It can often be valuable to report an effect size not only in original units but also in some standardized or units-free unit (e.g., as a Cohen's *d* value) or a standardized regression weight. (p. 34)

Sometimes a result is best reported both in original units, for ease of understanding by readers, and in some standardized measure for ease of inclusion in future meta-analyses. There will be examples in later chapters. Sources of advanced advice about ESs include Kirk (2003) and Grissom and Kim (2005).

Further important advice from the *Publication Manual* is the requirement to "mention all relevant results, including those that run counter to expectation; be sure to include small effect sizes (or statistically nonsignificant findings)" (APA, 2010, p. 32). If, as often in the past, a finding is only reported in detail, with its ES, if it reaches statistical significance, then the published literature contains a biased sample of research findings. Other things being equal, smaller ES estimates are less likely to reach statistical significance and so would be more likely to remain unpublished, and thus be at risk of being omitted from meta-analyses. If that happens, meta-analysis of published research would be likely to give overestimates of population effects. It's an important part of meta-analytic thinking to understand that *any* ES found by any well-conducted experiment needs to be available for later meta-analysis, whether the ES is small or large, statistically nonsignificant or significant.

Cohen's Reference Values

Jacob Cohen, the statistical reformer I've mentioned a couple of times, championed the use of statistical power. He hoped that if researchers routinely calculated and reported power, they would realize that power is often very low and so may be prompted to design larger and better experiments with higher power. Box 2.2 describes his early work, which revealed the very low power of much published research. Cohen's (1988) *Statistical Power Analysis for the Behavioral Sciences* is his classic book on statistical power that remains a basic reference. Power, as I discussed earlier in this chapter, requires specification of an exact population ES. Cohen therefore needed ES measures for many situations, and *d* is his basic standardized ES, and the topic of Chapter 11. Now, *d* is expressed in SD units, and is thus a kind of *z* score. Consider, for example, IQ scores, which are often expressed on a scale that has SD = 15 in a large reference population. A difference of 7.5 IQ points is half of one SD, or equivalently *d* = 0.50. A sample value of *d* can be used to estimate the corresponding population ES of Cohen's δ (Greek delta).

Cohen urged researchers to interpret their ESs by making an informed judgment in the research context. He also suggested values that might be regarded as "small," "medium," and "large." For *d* these were 0.2, 0.5, and 0.8, respectively. Therefore, a difference of 7.5 IQ points could be regarded, according to Cohen's suggestion, as a medium-sized effect. Cohen favored knowledgeable interpretation in the situation, but offered his values as a "conventional frame of reference which is recommended for use only when no better basis … is available" (1988, p. 25). His values were, however, shrewdly chosen, and are reasonable for use in some, but far from all, situations. Cohen also suggested .1, .3, and .5 as small, medium and large values of Pearson's correlation *r*.

Interpreting ESs

A focus on ESs can change the way results are reported and discussed. NHST might prompt a researcher to report "children were significantly less anxious after hearing the music, $t(23) = 2.50$, $p = .02$ (two-tailed)" and conclude that "the music significantly lowered children's anxiety." (When you read those statements, did you automatically insert "statistically" before each "significantly"?) That's dichotomous thinking in action, and it tells us little about the experimental result. The mean anxiety scores may, or may not, be reported, but the focus is on *p* values and statistical significance. It would be much more informative to report that "after hearing the music, the decrease in children's anxiety scores had mean $M = 5.1$ units on the anxiety scale, 95% CI [0.88, 9.32]. A decrease of 5 on the anxiety scale is practically beneficial." The focus is on the size of the difference, and the

CI tells us about the precision of the estimated ES. The "practically beneficial" comment is an interpretive judgment by the researcher, based on knowledge of children, the anxiety scale, and the full context. It should be accompanied by a justification. Another researcher may prefer a different interpretation of the ES, but the CI provides information that assists any reader to assess an author's interpretation. The primary interpretation of research should be such judgments about ESs, rather than ritualistic statements about statistical significance based on p values. (Did you notice that the 95% CI does not include zero? You can thus declare the result statistically significant, $p < .05$, if you wish.)

Look back again at those NHST and CI results. Do you feel uncomfortable? Is the conclusion "the music [statistically] significantly lowered ..." still appealing because it seems so clear-cut, so reassuring? In comparison, the very wide CI may be unsettling, even unbelievable. A large amount of careful work over several months, and all we can say is that improvement in anxiety was, most likely, somewhere between about 1 and 9? Sorry, but [0.88, 9.32] corresponds to $p = .02$. (More on that in Chapter 4.) The CI message is accurate, and the apparent certainty of NHST is misleading. We need to come to terms with the large uncertainty in most experimental results and not blame the CIs. Don't shoot the messenger. Appreciating the extent of uncertainty should lead, as I argued in Chapter 1, to metaanalytic thinking and a search for opportunities to cumulate evidence over experiments.

Alternatively, you may be thinking that a statement of significance is more objective—simply note whether or not $p < .05$—whereas the "practically beneficial" interpretation is mere opinion. Yes, interpretation of ESs, like numerous other aspects of research, requires judgment, but readers can make their own interpretations of the published ES values if they wish. I will discuss interpretation of various types of ESs in later chapters. Most basically, the focus should be on ESs because they are of greatest interest, and estimates of ESs are highly informative. The research investigated the effect of music on anxiety, and what we most want to know—what is most valuable for a music therapist—is how large a reduction in anxiety music may give. That's simply the ES, and the CI indicates how good an estimate it is. ESs and CIs together should usually provide the best basis for understanding results.

Sometimes a researcher is fortunate and can choose ESs likely to be familiar to all readers. Examples include height in meters, outcome in number of deaths, value in dollars, and temperature in degrees Celsius. Almost as fortunate is the opportunity to use ESs that are very familiar in the discipline. Thus particular disciplines routinely use response time in milliseconds, attitudes on a 1-to-7 Likert scale from strongly disagree to strongly agree, ability expressed as an age-equivalent score, or blood pressure in millimeters of mercury. Researchers can report and discuss these types of ESs with little ceremony, confident that their readers will have a basic understanding. Even so, they will probably need to explain what particular values or differences mean in the research context, and give reasons to justify interpretive judgments that an ES is, in the context, "large" or "important."

Table 2.1 includes units-free ESs (e.g., Pearson correlations on a scale from –1 to +1) and standardized ESs (e.g., Cohen's *d*, a number of SDs). In many cases a researcher can assume that these will be familiar to readers, although, again, particular values may need explanation in the context, whether or not the researcher chooses to use Cohen's reference values for small, medium, and large. Other ESs are less well known, for example, ω^2 (Greek omega-squared) as a measure of the proportion of variance attributable to an independent variable in an analysis of variance. They may need further explanation, although often a research field develops traditions of using particular measures, and so even a generally little-known ES may be familiar to researchers in that field. In such cases the field may also develop its own reference standards for what's regarded as large or small, important or trivial. Researchers should be wary, however, of writing for only their close colleagues, and should consider as broad a target audience as possible. Research results need to be widely available and reported so practitioners, for example, can readily understand.

I've mentioned Cohen's reference values for some ESs. Many of the tests used in education, psychology, and other disciplines include reference values that can similarly be used to assist interpretation. The Beck Depression Inventory is an example: For the BDI-II (Beck, Steer, Ball, & Ranieri, 1996), scores of 0–13, 14–19, 20–28, and 29–63 are labeled, respectively, minimal, mild, moderate, and severe levels of depression. As a less formal example, a neuropsychologist colleague of mine describes a rough guideline he uses: A decrease of about 15% in the memory score of a client with some brain injury, between two testing times, is the smallest difference he judges likely to be clinically noteworthy. It would be great if increased attention to ES interpretation encourages researchers to develop further formal or informal conventions for what various sizes of effect mean in various contexts.

My conclusion is that a researcher first needs to judge how much can be assumed and how much needs explanation about an ES measure itself, and then should explain and interpret the particular values being reported. Examples 2.2 illustrate a wide variety of types of ESs and various strategies researchers can use to explain and justify their interpretations.

EXAMPLES 2.2 REPORTING AND INTERPRETING EFFECT SIZES

Volcanic Residues in Lake Sediments

Schiff et al. (2008) reported a study of a core sample taken from a lake bed in Alaska. They found 67 layers of tephra—volcanic ash—that had been deposited by 67 eruptions of a nearby volcano. They were interested in the timing of those eruptions, which they estimated from the depths of tephra layers in the core. They carried out several types of mathematical modeling, with much use of CIs. That was all rather complicated, but the main ESs were simple: The researchers discussed depths, layer thicknesses, and particle sizes, all expressed in centimeters; and times in years. They provided graphics to illustrate how depth in the core (expressed in cm) translated into years into the past, and gave tables reporting the size of the ash particles in the various layers and the thickness of those layers. The layers ranged in thickness from 0.1 cm to 8.0 cm, and depths from 3 cm to 562 cm. Estimated eruption times ranged from the present back to 8,660 years ago. The reporting is so comprehensive, and the ESs measures (cm and year) so familiar, that any reader can understand the main findings. The researchers were fortunate in being able to use such familiar ESs, but they took full advantage by presenting well-designed graphs and a clear discussion of the numerous values they observed.

Portion Sizes and Children's Eating

Fisher and Kral (2008) investigated how portion sizes of presented food influenced how much children chose to eat. They discussed portion size in grams and amount eaten in grams and kilocalories. They used percentages freely. The ESs are sufficiently familiar for readers to easily understand the discussion. They spoke, for example, of their adolescents drinking "75% more juice when using a short …, wide glass than a taller …, narrower glass of the same volume" (p. 43), and stated that "Doubling the … size of … a snack … increased energy intake … by 22% (~180 kcal)" (p. 41). The authors also defined the energy density of food; this measure may be unfamiliar to readers, but the explanation given and its close link to weight in grams and energy in kilocalories mean that readers can understand. A typical conclusion was, "When the ED [energy density] of an entrée was

... reduced by 30%, 2- to 5-year-olds consumed 25% fewer [kilo]calories" (p. 41). Fisher and Kral used ES measures that were either very familiar or based on familiar measures, and therefore they could expect readers to readily understand their results and conclusions.

Dropping Out of Medical School

Dyrbye et al. (2010) surveyed students in a number of medical schools to study burnout and serious thoughts of dropping out. Their major ESs were the survey scores, so they described the questionnaires in the survey and referred to previous research that provided evidence of reliability and validity of the measures. They described in detail their own simple scale of "seriousness of thoughts of dropping out," which ranged from "not seriously" to "extremely seriously." They gave reference values for some measures, for example, by reporting that "mental quality of life" (QOL) scores have a mean of 49.2 and SD of 9.5 for the whole U.S. population. They also reported "pre-established thresholds for health professionals" for several of the measures—for example, any score below 33 on the "low sense of personal accomplishment" scale is regarded as "low" for health professionals. These full descriptions and reference values gave a good basis for their discussion of the scores for their medical students and interpretation of relationships between burnout measures and thoughts of dropping out. Once we know about the QOL measures, for example, we can grasp a summary statement that, other things being equal, a one-point-lower QOL score means a student is on average 5% more likely to have serious thoughts of dropping out during the following year. The main ES measures are unlikely to be familiar to readers, so full descriptions and reference values are needed, but then we can understand.

Improvement in Reading Ability

Edmonds et al. (2009) reported a meta-analysis of intervention studies that sought to improve the reading of teenagers with reading difficulties. They used "effect size, d" (p. 266) as their main measure, explained how it was calculated, then used Cohen's reference values (0.2, 0.5, and 0.8) in their discussion. McGuinness (2004) also used d as the main ES in her large and impressive review of research on reading. (I discuss her work further in Chapter 7.) She didn't mention Cohen's reference values, but made statements such as, "Effect sizes were low for comprehension (.10), marginal for word recognition, spelling, and writing (range .30 to .34), moderate for phoneme awareness (.56), and large for nonword decoding (.71)" (p. 148). She described a value of 0.74 as "solid" (p. 127). Her interpretations were thus largely consistent with Cohen's reference values.

These two examples illustrate how a standardized ES, Cohen's *d*, has become widely used and can serve as a good basis for discussion and interpretation. Researchers can use Cohen's reference values or make their own evaluations of size, but should justify their choice in the particular context.

Risk of Colon Cancer

Moore et al. (2004) studied the relation between obesity and the risk of colon cancer. I'll use their study to discuss two ESs: body mass index (BMI) and risk. BMI is calculated as a person's weight in kilograms divided by the square of his or her height in meters. Some experts criticize BMI because it makes no distinction between fat and muscle, but here I'll follow Moore et al., who used BMI and the World Health Organization definitions of BMI <25 as normal, BMI between 25 and 30 as overweight, and BMI >30 as obese. Such reference values are useful for interpretation, but may change as research advances over the years, and different authorities may recommend different cutoffs. The risk of colon cancer is estimated as the proportion of people in a particular group who developed the cancer during a defined period. Relative risk is the ratio of the risks for two different groups of people. One conclusion was that, for people aged 30 to 54, other things being equal, being obese rather than of normal weight is associated with an increase in risk of colon cancer from 1.2 to 1.8 in 1,000, which is a 50% increase in the risk. That's reasonably understandable, but note that it's important to be told the risks as well as the percentage increase, because a 50% increase in risk may have different implications if it's an increase from a one-in-a-million to a 1.5-in-a-million risk, or an increase from a 10% to a 15% risk. Each of those is a 50% increase in risk. (There's more on this in Chapter 14.) Overall, Moore et al. gave sufficient explanation of BMI and risk, and of what various values mean, for their results and conclusions to be understandable to most readers.

Greasing the Wheels

My final example is a cautionary tale. The title of Kim and Ruge-Murcia's (2009) article asks, "How much inflation is necessary to grease the wheels?" The researchers developed a complex mathematical model of one version of an ideal economy. Many strong assumptions were required. They then applied the model to the U.S. economy and concluded that an inflation rate of 0.35% per year leads to optimum results—if their model is correct and all the assumptions apply. Their ES of 0.35% for the inflation rate is familiar and easily grasped by most readers. We might possibly regard it as a low and desirable rate of inflation. However, figuring out what the whole study means in practice, and the extent to which the model and all the assumptions are realistic, is not nearly so straightforward. The simple and familiar final ES may even be misleading, if it tempts readers to overlook the complex underlying theory and its stringent assumptions. No ES can be better than the data and models on which it's based.

The main new statistics message of this chapter is that the focus of research should almost always be ESs. Adopt estimation thinking, use estimation language to express research goals as "how much" questions about ESs, report ES estimates with their CIs, then interpret those estimates. However, there are also new statistics goals beyond ESs and CIs. For example, the answer to Q4 may be a negative correlation between pollution level and fish fertility. A correlation is a perfectly fine ES, but even better may be a function that expresses the relation between the variables. The journal article may present a figure that plots how fertility changes as a function of pollution; there may even be an equation that describes the relation. Beyond "how much" questions are "what is the relation between" questions, whose answers can be even more informative, and the basis for what Paul Meehl (1978) wanted: theories and disciplines that are more quantitative. I hope the new statistics I discuss in this book encourage researchers to go further and develop and test such quantitative models.

It's time for take-home messages. I invite you to write your own before looking ahead to mine. The preceding paragraph includes some reminders.

Exercises

2.1 Choose a journal of interest to you that reports empirical research. It's best if it has relatively short articles. Find examples of poor NHST, including ambiguous use of the word "significant," and use of relative p (e.g., $p < .01$) rather than exact p (e.g., $p = .006$).

2.2 Find an example of the fallacy of the slippery slope of significance: In the Results section of an article an effect is declared "significant," or even "statistically significant," because p is small. In the discussion, or the abstract, that effect is referred to as certain, or notable, or large, without any attempt to justify such an interpretation of the ES.

2.3 Find examples of acceptance of a null hypothesis. Give yourself extra points for finding an example of the fallacy of the slippery slope of nonsignificance: An innocuous statement of "statistical nonsignificance" in the Results section becomes a statement of no difference in the discussion or the abstract.

2.4 Read as much of Chapter 3 of Kline (2004, tinyurl.com/klinechap3) as you find interesting. Focus on pp. 61–70 and 85–91. Decide what attitudes you'll take to NHST that you read in journal articles.

2.5 Read as much of Haller and Krauss (2002, tinyurl.com/nhstohdear) as you find interesting. Do the findings strike you as astonishing, or depressing? Print out the short questionnaire (in Section 2.2 of Haller and Krauss) including the six Oakes questions. Try them out on your friends—and maybe your teachers?

2.6 Scan a few articles that report experimental results. In each article, first identify a concise statement of the main experimental aim, if possible in relation to a single variable. Can you find a dichotomous statement of that aim? Is there also a "how much" statement of the same aim?

2.7 Match some answers to the corresponding aims. Can you find a dichotomous statement that answers a dichotomous question? Can you find a "this much" answer to a "how much" question? In each case, go further and examine the conclusion or interpretation: Is it expressed in dichotomous or estimation language?

2.8 Find a few dichotomous statements of hypotheses or experimental aims. For each write down your own corresponding "how much" question.

2.9 Here's a challenging one: Find two results in a single article that are compared and that have the pattern of Figure 1.1. As in Lucky–Noluck, one should be statistically significant and the other not. (They need not appear in the article's introduction, but could be results reported for two different groups or conditions. See Example 2.1.) How are they compared? Is it concluded that they are different? Is there discussion about why they might be different? Is a null hypothesis implicitly accepted? If so, what wording is used to hide that? Suggest a better way to report and interpret the two results.

2.10 Look back at Figure 1.1. I criticized the strategy of concluding *Inconsistent* just because one result is statistically significant and the other is not. Could you use NHST to examine whether *Inconsistent* is justified? If so, how?

Exercises 2.9 and 2.10 are based on the previous chapter. There's evidence that it helps learning to include questions about issues discussed earlier, so it's best not to just skip them. Also try to find links with the current chapter.

2.11 Work at becoming a "new statistics aware" reader, always alert to misinterpretations caused by NHST, always asking the corresponding "how much" question.

2.12 Find examples of different types of ES estimates. They may be in the text, in tables, or in figures. Look for a mean, a percentage, a measure of change, and a correlation. For any statistical technique that you know about (analysis of variance, regression, chi-square, path analysis, factor analysis, etc.), look for examples of ES estimates.

2.13 For some of your ES examples, find where the ES is discussed or interpreted. Can you find at least one where the ES is given a substantive interpretation? In other words, find a statement about the meaning or importance of the observed size of the effect.

2.14 For an ES without such an interpretation, try to offer your own substantive interpretation: In your judgment, how important, or meaningful, or practically useful is an effect of the size observed? Justify your answer.

2.15 Revisit your take-home messages. Improve them and extend
the list if you can.

Take-Home Messages

- NHST as practiced in many disciplines is an uneasy mixture of Fisher's idea that p is a measure of strength of evidence and the strict Neyman–Pearson rule to choose α in advance then decide between null and alternative hypotheses according to whether or not $p < \alpha$.

- Beware NHST traps. A p value is a tricky conditional probability, assuming that the null hypothesis is true. It is not the probability that the results are due to chance.

- Whenever you read a p value, automatically think, "assuming the null hypothesis is true."

- If reporting a p value, give an exact value, not merely a statement like $p < .05$.

- Beware the ambiguous word "significant." Use it with great care, or avoid it.

- Statistical significance is different from practical importance—as you probably knew. But keep the distinction carefully in mind anyway. Beware the fallacy of the slippery slope of significance.

- Avoid accepting a null hypothesis, even implicitly. Beware the fallacy of the slippery slope of nonsignificance.
- Regarding p as a very rough index of strength of evidence against the null may be the least bad way to think about p.
- Notice the language used to express research aims and conclusions. Wherever possible, prefer estimation language ("how much …?," "to what extent …?") to dichotomous language ("is there a difference …?").
- An effect size (ES) is simply an amount of something that might be of interest. ES estimates from data are our best guide to population ESs. ESs can be as familiar as a difference between means, a percentage change, or a correlation.
- The focus of research is usually effects. Report ESs and wherever possible the CIs, too.
- Interpret ES estimates, using knowledge of the research area and judgment, and justify the interpretation. Cohen's conventional values may be useful. To what extent is each ES large or small, important or unimportant, useful to practitioners?
- The aim is to use estimation language, and estimation, in order to build more quantitative disciplines that make better research progress.

Polya

3

Confidence Intervals

Soon we'll sound the trumpets for the arrival of CIs, but we need to explore several other ideas first. Watch out for the dance of the means and the mean heap, then the margin of error. After that the trumpets won't be far away. Here's the plan for the chapter:

- The population and a random sample
- Sampling: dance of the means and the mean heap
- Errors of estimation, and the margin of error (MOE)
- Confidence intervals at last
- Reporting CIs
- Interpreting CIs: the first three approaches

There are two parts to this chapter: The first covers the first four bullet points and the second covers the last two. The first part is my version of the story that starts with sampling and finishes with CIs. Numerous textbooks give a version of that story. The main novel aspect of my version is that it focuses on understanding the extent of sampling variability—which, unfortunately, some people often underestimate. I hope ESCI pictures and simulations can help you build accurate intuitions about sampling variability. Because those pictures and simulations are so central, in the first part of the chapter I integrate ESCI activities more closely into the discussion than in any other chapter. However, I include many figures, so I hope the discussion is useful even if you don't work with ESCI as you read.

The second part of the chapter comprises the sections Reporting CIs and Interpreting CIs. These go beyond what many other textbooks say about CIs. I don't need to integrate ESCI so closely into those sections.

Population and Samples

We need to start with a population and samples from that population. Suppose you are investigating the climate change awareness of university students in your country. You decide to use the Hot Earth Awareness Test

(HEAT), which is a well-established survey—actually, I just invented it—
that asks questions about a respondent's knowledge, attitudes, and behavior in relation to climate change. You would like to know the mean HEAT
score for students in your country. You plan to test a sample of students to
estimate that mean.

Now we do some statistical assuming. (Box 3.1 gives extra detail, but it's
an optional extra.) Suppose there's a large population of students in your
country, and their HEAT scores are normally distributed with mean of μ
and SD of σ (Greek sigma). You take a random sample of N students from
that population, obtain their scores, and calculate the mean, M, and standard deviation, s, of your sample. You'll use M as your point estimate of
μ. Later you'll calculate a CI to tell us the precision of your estimate—how
close M is likely to be to the unknown μ.

That statistical model based on a normally distributed population and
random sampling underlies many of the most commonly used statistical
techniques. It's the basis for the conventional CIs we discuss here, as well as

---

BOX 3.1 A STATISTICAL MODEL

A statistics textbook says something like, "Consider random variable
X with distribution $N(\mu, \sigma^2)$. Let M be the mean of a random sample,
size N, of X. Then M has distribution $N(\mu, \sigma^2/N)$." Those three sentences summarize the first half of this chapter, but need some unpack-
ing. A *random variable* is simply a variable that can take some range of
values, with various probabilities. The abbreviation $N(\mu, \sigma^2)$ refers, as
you probably guessed, to a normal distribution with mean μ and variance σ^2, which implies standard deviation σ.

The sentences express a very widely used statistical model, based
on a normally distributed population of X scores, with mean μ and
standard deviation σ. The model considers random samples of X
scores, each sample having size N. The sample mean is another random variable M, and is normally distributed, with the same mean
μ and smaller variance σ^2/N. The SD of M is thus $\sigma/\sqrt{N}$. You may
know that the distribution of M is referred to as the *sampling distribution* of M, the sample mean, and that the SD of this distribution is
called the *standard error* (SE). Therefore, SE $= \sigma/\sqrt{N}$. Sample mean
M is a random variable because every time you take another sample
you'll get a slightly different value for M. Take numerous samples
then the numerous values of M form the sampling distribution of M.
The textbook probably also explains how sample statistics M and s
are used as estimates of population parameters μ and σ.

for conventional NHST. It's far from the only possibility, but it's the model I use throughout this book. It makes important assumptions, notably

- *Normality.* In many cases in practice this strong assumption about the population distribution may be justified, in some cases a transformation of the dependent variable improves its appropriateness, and in some cases it's not justified and some other approach should be taken.
- *Random sampling.* There are two vital aspects: First, every member of the population must have an equal probability of being sampled, and second, all sample values must be chosen independently.

You should always keep these assumptions in mind and judge how closely they are met in a particular situation. In our example, the dependent variable is the HEAT score, which we'll refer to as X. It may be reasonable to assume at least approximate normality of HEAT scores in the population of all university students in your country. Considering random sampling, it's unlikely you can ensure that every student has an equal chance of being included in your sample. Perhaps you can sample randomly from a range of disciplines in a variety of universities? You'll need to judge how well you think your sampling strategy will give a sample representative of the population in ways that are relevant for your HEAT research question.

Independence, the second aspect of random sampling I mentioned, is crucially important. You need to make sure you choose each student in the sample separately, rather than, for example, choosing clusters of students who are mutual friends, or who are in the same class. As so often in statistics, care and judgment are needed. This book is not primarily about research design, so I won't extend this discussion. However, I must emphasize that the new statistics require attention to assumptions just as does NHST.

Note carefully the distinction between population and sample:

- The *population* is a supposedly infinite collection of university students in your country, or rather their HEAT scores. It's common, if slightly confusing, to talk interchangeably of the population comprising the students, or the HEAT scores. Anyway, it's the HEAT scores, our dependent variable X, that we assume to be normally distributed. The *population parameters* are the mean μ and standard deviation σ of the population distribution of X scores. The values of μ and σ are fixed but unknown— because we can't ever know the HEAT scores for every student in your country.

The *population parameters* μ and σ have values that are fixed but unknown.

- By contrast, we know the *N* values of *X* that make up our *sample*, and can calculate the obtained sample mean *M* and standard deviation *s*. The *sample statistics M* and *s* have particular values for a particular sample, but if we repeat the experiment—by taking another, independent sample—we would get different values for *M* and *s*.

> The *sample statistics M* and *s* are calculated from our sample data. They would be different for a different sample. We use them as point estimates of μ and σ.

In other words, we don't know μ and σ, but we want to. We do know *M* and *s* for our sample, but we don't especially care about those particular values, except to the extent they tell us something useful about μ and σ.

I'm about to turn to ESCI but, as I've said, I hope you can follow the discussion whether or not you use the software. I suggest you read the exercises, as well as the main text, but skim over references to the fine details of ESCI if you wish. Many of the exercises ask questions. Whether or not you use ESCI to find answers, you can consult the section near the back of the book that provides suggested answers. In any case, focus on the statistical ideas and the many figures I've included in the book.

Exercises

3.1 Open the **CIjumping** page of **ESCI chapters 1–4**. Consult Appendix A for hints, especially the section Strategy for Getting Started With a New ESCI Page.

3.2 Figure 3.1 shows the population, which for us is an idealized representation of all the HEAT scores of students in your country. It has a normal distribution, and the figure shows it's a symmetric bell-shaped curve. Click near red 2 to display the population curve. Use the sliders to change population μ and σ, then set them back to the values μ = 50 and σ = 20, which we'll assume are the population values for your country. (As you change σ, you can see the vertical scale automatically rescaling, so the curve is always displayed with a convenient vertical height.)

3.3 Click near red 2 to fill under the curve with random little blue circles, or data points, as shown in Figure 3.1. ESCI can't display the infinite number of dots that, notionally, make the population, but you get the idea.

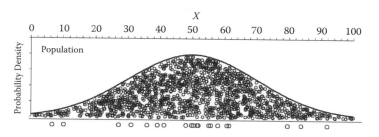

FIGURE 3.1

A part screen image from the **CIjumping** page of **ESCI chapters 1–4**. It shows the normally distributed population, with $\mu = 50$ and $\sigma = 20$, and below, a scatter of points that's a single random sample, $N = 20$, of HEAT scores taken from the population. We use X to refer to the HEAT scores.

3.4 Click the **Clear** button near red 1—nothing happens, but we're getting set. Click near red 4 to **Display data points**. Yes, still nothing, but now a dramatic moment: We're about to take our first random sample.

Text that looks like **Display data points** *refers to text or a label in the ESCI page.*

3.5 Use the spinner near red 3 to select your sample size, perhaps $N = 20$ or whatever you choose. Take a deep breath then click the **Take sample** button. You should see something like Figure 3.1. The scatter of points at the bottom is the 20 data points of our sample. That's our simulated equivalent of finding a random sample of N students and testing them on the HEAT.

3.6 Take more samples. The scatters of data points for successive samples vary greatly. As we'll discuss in later chapters, randomness is intriguing and weird. It's important to develop good intuitions about randomness, although this is a challenge because there's evidence that people often underestimate the extent of random variability.

3.7 Observe your samples of data points carefully. Would you agree that the sampled data points in the long run are about equally often below and above μ? That they tend to cluster fairly close to μ, but values farther from μ are quite common? Just occasionally you get an extreme point? Those features of sampled values follow directly, of course, from the shape of the population and our sampling, which we assume gives every data point in the population an equal chance of being chosen.

Sampling: The Mean Heap and Dance of the Means

The next important idea is the *sampling distribution of the sample mean*. Imagine taking lots of samples from a population—we'll do that with ESCI in a moment. The means of those successive samples vary, but they tend to cluster around the population mean μ. Many such sample means form a distribution, called the sampling distribution of the sample mean. If we could take an infinite number of samples, their means would form a normal distribution, thus demonstrating that the sampling distribution of the sample mean is normal. It's an excellent question why this sampling distribution is normal in shape. The general answer to that question reveals a little magic.

The *sampling distribution of the sample mean* is the distribution created by the means of many samples.

The previous paragraph is an example of explanation that will shortly be followed by ESCI activities. If the text there is unclear, read on, and return after exploring the ideas with ESCI. Or peruse the text, and the ESCI exercises that follow, in parallel.

Some Statistical Magic, the Central Limit Theorem

You might wonder why statisticians choose the normal distribution as a statistical model. The answer is the *central limit theorem*, which is the central result in all theoretical statistics. If you make a variable (let's call it X) by adding up lots of other variables, all independent, then X has, at least approximately, a normal distribution. The amazing thing is that it has a normal distribution pretty much whatever the distributions are of the other variables you add to get X. All those variables can even have distributions of different shapes but, provided they are all independent, their sum X is approximately normally distributed. If more variables are added, X is closer to normal. The normal distribution appears out of thin air, and in this way represents some fundamental aspect of the universe.

Shortly we'll use ESCI to illustrate that the sampling distribution of the sample mean is normally distributed. ESCI currently offers only normal populations, but a future version might offer populations with distributions other than normal—maybe skewed, or with more than one hump, or different in other ways. The amazing thing is that even populations with weird distribution shapes will give a sampling distribution of means that's approximately normal, and closer to normal for samples with larger N. We're talking about two distributions here—the population and the sampling distribution of means. The central limit theorem states that the latter is approximately normal in shape, almost regardless of the shape of the population distribution.

Think of the sample mean as the sum of lots of tiny, independent contributions—the data points in the sample. The central limit theorem states that such sums have approximately a normal distribution. This way of thinking about the theorem gives a link with nature. Suppose you measure some natural quantity in the world, such as the length of adult ants or the time it takes for penguin eggs to hatch. Fairly often, although not always, a large set of such measurements is approximately normally distributed. If ant length or hatching time is determined by the addition of numerous separate influences—perhaps genetic, environmental, nutritional, or random—then the central limit theorem says the result will be approximately normal. No doubt mere addition of independent influences is much too simplistic a biological model, but the idea probably does explain why the normal distribution often appears in nature, at least approximately. The central limit theorem and the normal distribution do seem to express some basic aspects of how the natural world functions.

The Standard Error

The SD of the sampling distribution of the sample mean is called the *standard error* (SE). That may be confusing, so it may be worth making it a chant. Dismay your friends at parties by intoning: *"The standard error is the standard deviation of the sampling distribution of the sample mean."* You can easily explain by pointing to the mean heap— which we'll discover in a moment. We'll use ESCI to picture the SE, and to illustrate the formula:

A chant: "The *standard error* is the standard deviation of the sampling distribution of the sample mean."

$$SE = \sigma/\sqrt{N} \qquad (3.1)$$

which is one of the few formulas you need to explore and remember.

We use ESCI to run simulations, which can be revealing. However, a simulation is not real life. It is vital to keep in mind two major ways that ESCI simulations differ from the usual research situation:

1. A simulation requires that we assume some particular population distribution. You choose a normal distribution, and values of μ and σ, which are shown on the screen. In our role as real-life researchers, however, we never know μ or σ—we are running the experiment to estimate them.

2. We usually take many simulated samples, whereas in real life we almost always can run an experiment only once.

Distinguish carefully between playing around on the computer with simulations of many experiments, and running and analyzing a single experiment in real life.

Exercises

3.8 We'll now work toward generating pictures like those shown in Figure 3.2. Click **Clear** (button near red 1), and click near red 3 to **Display means**. Take a sample. The sample mean is displayed as a green dot just below the scatter of data points.

3.9 Click near red 4 to **Show values**. Values are shown on screen for M and s, the sample statistics for the latest sample you've taken. We can compare these values with the values we've chosen for their population counterparts μ and σ.

"Near red 4" can refer to anywhere in the colored area that has red 4 at its top left corner.

3.10 Click **Take sample** a few times. The means drop down the screen, as in Figure 3.2. Watch the values bounce around, and compare them with the μ value you set. Each click is equivalent to running an experiment, meaning you take a new sample of size N, obtain the HEAT scores for those N students, and then calculate M and s to use as estimates of μ and σ, the unknown parameters we're studying.

3.11 Click **Run-Stop** and watch the sample means dancing down the screen. It's the *dance of the means*, as in Figure 3.2, which illustrates the extent of variation or bouncing around of the mean from sample to sample. (If the dance is a bit slow, try clicking near red 2 to hide the population.) Imagine (or play on your computer) your choice of backing music for the dance.

The *dance of the means* is my name for a sequence of sample means falling down the screen.

3.12 Click **Run-Stop** again to stop the dance, then **Clear**. Now think about two predictions: First, if you change N, what will happen to the dance? For example, will larger N give a more drunken dance—the means tending to vary side-to-side more—or a more sober dance? What about smaller N? Make your predictions—write them down. The two halves of Figure 3.2 illustrate

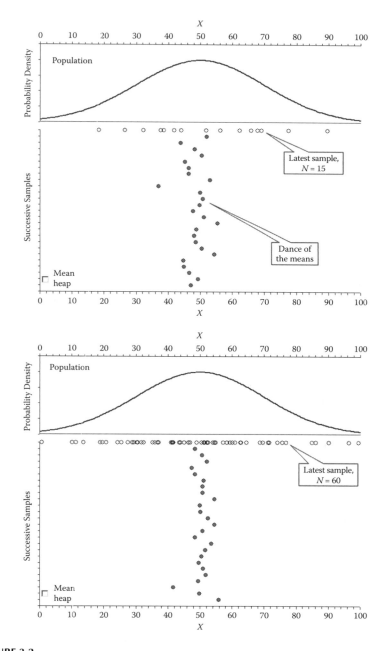

FIGURE 3.2
Dance of the means—the dots dropping down the screen. Upper half: $N = 15$. Lower half: $N = 60$. In each case the population distribution is displayed at the top, and the latest sample appears as the scatter of N data points in a horizontal line just below.

the dance for different values of N. Are your predictions consistent with what that figure shows?

3.13 Second, what would happen if you increase or decrease σ? Any change to the drunkenness of the dance? Which way would it change? Lock in your predictions.

3.14 Experiment to test your predictions. Which change—a different N or a different σ—tends to make more difference?

3.15 Click **Mean heap** near red 5 to see all the means collapse down into a pile of green dots, as Figure 3.3 illustrates. This is the sampling distribution of the mean, and I call it the *mean heap*. Run the simulation to build up a good-sized heap. Do this for various values of N, and keep track of how wide the heap appears: Record for each N your eyeball estimate of the SD of the mean heap. (It may help to recall the rule of thumb that about 95% of the values in a normal distribution lie within 2SD on either side of the mean. If that's unfamiliar, explore Appendix B.) Figure 3.3 shows the mean heap for two values of N. Should we prefer a narrow or a wide mean heap, bearing in mind that we are trying to estimate μ? Translate your conclusion into advice for a researcher who is considering what size sample to take.

> The *mean heap* is my name for the sampling distribution of the sample mean. It's a pile of green dots that represent sample means.

In Figure 3.3, the mean of the latest sample, which has just been added to the mean heap, is highlighted as a large black dot. In ESCI it appears as a dark green dot, the same size as the dots for the other means. Small features sometimes appear to be a little different in the figures than in ESCI, to clarify what the figures show.

3.16 Click **Display sampling distribution curve** near red 6. The normal distribution displayed on the mean heap, as in the lower panel of Figure 3.4, is the *theoretical sampling distribution of the sample mean*. We can compare that with the mean heap, which is the *empirical sampling distribution of the sample mean*—the heap of just the means we've taken so far. The curve is the distribution theoretically predicted from knowing μ, σ, and N. (In ESCI, the curve is scaled vertically so it fits to the mean heap. Take more samples, and both the mean heap and sampling distribution curve grow higher—but not wider; the SD of the sampling distribution remains the same.)

> Take an infinite number of samples and the distribution of their means is the *theoretical sampling distribution of the sample mean*. (The mean heap is my name for the *empirical sampling distribution of the sample mean*.)

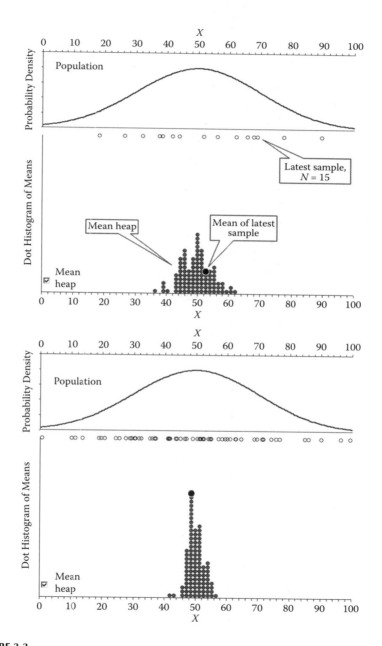

FIGURE 3.3
The mean heap, in each case after taking 100 samples. Upper half: $N = 15$, and the eyeball estimate of the SD of the mean heap may be about 5. Lower half: $N = 60$, and the SD of the mean heap looks to be about 3. The mean of the latest sample is displayed as a highlighted dot when it is added to the heap.

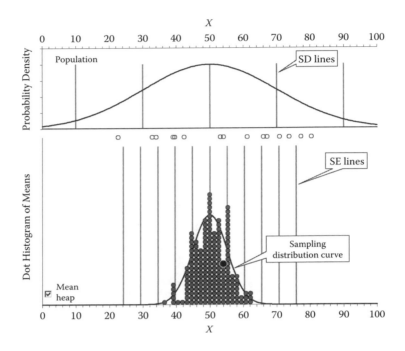

FIGURE 3.4

The upper panel displays the population distribution, with lines marking SD units, showing $\sigma = 20$. Below is the mean heap. The superimposed curve is the sampling distribution of the mean, with lines marking SE units. In this example, $N = 15$, and 200 samples have been taken. The SE $= \sigma/\sqrt{N} = 20/\sqrt{15} = 5.16$.

3.17 The SD of the sampling distribution of the sample mean is given the name *standard error* (SE), so the SE is just a particular SD. Think of the SE as summarizing the breadth or spread of the mean heap—or its curve.

3.18 Click **Display SE lines** near red 6 and see vertical lines marking SE units across the sampling distribution curve. These vertical lines are displayed in the lower panel of Figure 3.4.

3.19 Near red 6 find **Curve SE** and note its value. The popout comment explains that it's the SE of the sampling distribution curve. Does it change if you take further samples? Why?

3.20 Click **Display SD lines** near red 2 (if necessary, click **Display population** first). SD lines for the population curve are displayed, as in the upper panel of Figure 3.4. Compare these with the SE lines for the sampling distribution curve in the lower panel. In each case you can regard the lines as marking $z = 0$ (the mean), and $z = -2, -1$, and $+1, +2$, etc., for the respective normal distributions. (Click **Display means** near red 3 to hide the means, if you want to see the sampling distribution curve more clearly.)

3.21 The sampling distribution is normally distributed—as the curve on the mean heap illustrates—with mean μ and SD of $\sigma/\sqrt{N}$. The vital formula to remember is SE = $\sigma/\sqrt{N}$. Maybe write this formula down, for safekeeping. The mean heap, and its curve, is centered symmetrically under the population, and its SD is smaller than that of the population—by a factor of $\sqrt{N}$.

3.22 If N is made four times bigger, $\sqrt{N}$ becomes twice as large, so the SE should be halved. Compare the lower halves of Figures 3.2 and 3.3, for which $N = 60$, with the upper halves, for which $N = 15$. Does the lower dance seem about half as varied, half as wide as the upper? The lower mean heap about half as wide as the upper? Unfortunately, to halve the amount of variation we need to take a sample four times as big. That's bad news for researchers trying to make precise estimates because, as we'll see, the SE determines precision. A broad mean heap signals a large SE and imprecise estimates.

3.23 This might be a good spot to cross-check with any other statistics textbook you are using. See if you can use ESCI to illustrate the way your other textbook explains sampling and sampling distributions.

3.24 Use the values of σ and N that you set, and which are shown near red 2 and red 3, to calculate SE. Check that the value shown at **Curve SE** is correct.

3.25 Suppose HEAT scores have mean = 50 and SD = 20 in your country. For samples of $N = 30$, what is the SE? (Use the formula to calculate it, then use ESCI to check.) Describe the sampling distribution of the mean.

3.26 That's a typical textbook problem. Invent and solve a few more. Do a few from your other textbook. Maybe invent some, and swap with a fellow learner.

3.27 Recall our chant: "The standard error is the standard deviation of the sampling distribution of the sample mean." If someone asks, "What's a standard error?" you can bring to mind the mean heap as a pile of green dots, then explain about its SD.

3.28 Make up some exercises for discovery learning of the SE = $\sigma/\sqrt{N}$ relation. You could suggest first making predictions, or guesstimates, of the SE of the mean heap (and the sampling distribution curve) for a few widely separated values of N that you nominate. Then, for each of those N values, take at least 50 samples and eyeball the SD of the mean heap—which as you know is the SE. See Figure 3.3 and its caption. Compare those eyeballed estimates with the ESCI values near red 6 for the **Mean heap SE**, which is the SE of the displayed mean heap. What does a graph of those SE values against *N* look like? How accurate were the original predictions? Find someone who doesn't know about SE to try out your exercises.

Errors of Estimation, and the Margin of Error

We take a sample and calculate *M* because we want an estimate of μ. How good an estimate is it? The *estimation error* is $(M - \mu)$, and is different for every sample. The center of the mean heap

Estimation error is $(M - \mu)$, the distance between our point estimate based on the sample and the population parameter we are estimating.

is at μ, and the sample means, shown by the green dots, cluster around μ but generally fall a little to the right or left of μ. The distance away they fall is $(M - \mu)$, the estimation error. We can think of the mean heap, and the sampling distribution of *M*, as the distribution of estimation errors. Most green dots fall fairly close to μ, so have small estimation errors; many fall a moderate distance away; and just a few fall in the tails of the sampling distribution, which signals large estimation errors.

We define the *margin of error* as the largest likely estimation error. The abbreviation is MOE, which you can read out as M-O-E, although I prefer to say it as "MOW-ee." We usually choose "likely" to mean 95%, so there's a 95% chance that the estimation error is less than the MOE, and only a 5% chance that

The margin of error (MOE) is the largest likely estimation error. If "likely" is taken to mean 95%, MOE is approximately 2SE.

we have been unlucky and our sample mean *M* falls in one of the tails of the sampling distribution. You probably know the rule of thumb for any normal distribution: About 95% of the values fall within 2SD on either side of the mean. Therefore, 95% of sample means will fall within about 2SE of the mean of the sampling distribution. (Remember that SE is the SD of that distribution. I sometimes suspect that those terms were selected to be as confusing as possible.) We can therefore state that MOE = 2SE, approximately, and that's the value to remember for eyeballing purposes. More accurately, MOE = 1.96 × SE because 1.96 is the critical value $z_{.95}$ from a normal distribution. (Appendix B does some relevant explaining.)

The 95% of the *M* green dots that fall within MOE (i.e., about 2SE) on either side of μ have estimation error less than MOE, and only the 5% that fall farther than this from μ, within one or the other tail, have estimation error greater than MOE. Warm up the trumpets: The CIs are about to arrive.

Exercises

3.29 With the mean heap, sampling distribution curve, and SE lines displayed, click near red 6 to **Display ±MOE around μ**. Your screen should resemble Figure 3.5. On the bottom axis is a green stripe that indicates a distance of one MOE on either side of μ. At the ends of the stripe, heavier green vertical lines mark a distance of MOE on either side of μ. How many SE units away from μ are the heavier green vertical MOE lines? Is that what you expected?

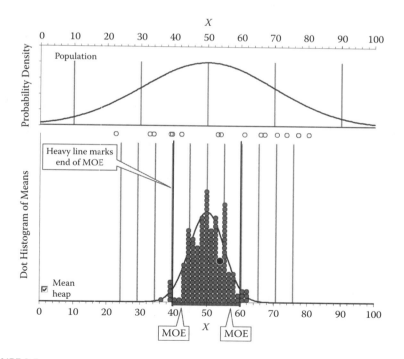

FIGURE 3.5

Same as Figure 3.4, but with MOE marked. The stripe at the bottom, which is green on the screen, extends MOE on either side of the mean μ = 50, where MOE = 1.96 × 5.16 = 10.12. The ends of the stripe are marked with heavier vertical lines. We expect about 95% of means to fall between those lines and, correspondingly, we expect 95% of the area under the sampling distribution curve to fall between those vertical lines.

3.30 What percentage of green dots will fall between those MOE lines? What percentage beyond those lines to the left? Beyond them to the right?

3.31 Click near red 5 to return from the mean heap to the dance of the means, run the simulation, and watch how often a mean falls outside the MOE lines, to the left or right.

3.32 Suppose HEAT scores have $\mu = 50$ and $\sigma = 20$. For $N = 36$, calculate the MOE (i) approximately, and (ii) exactly. Use your answer to (ii) to find an interval that in the long run should include 95% of sample means.

3.33 Set up that situation in ESCI, make sure **Display ±MOE around** μ is clicked on, and note the MOE value shown near red 6. Check that it's the same as you calculated.

3.34 How would you expect MOE to change for different N? For different σ? Test out your predictions. In each case, note about how many green dots fall outside the MOE lines.

3.35 Consider our initial question about the mean HEAT scores in your country. State your aim in an estimation-thinking "how much" way.

CIs at Last: Sound the Trumpets!

We've talked about MOE as describing how sample means clump around μ. Informally, MOE tells us about the "width" of the mean heap, or of the sampling distribution: The green stripe at the bottom of the mean heap, as in Figure 3.5, is 2MOE long and includes 95% of means. In 95% of cases the estimation error is less than MOE, or in other words $|M - \mu| <$ MOE. (The vertical bars mean absolute value, so $|M - \mu|$ equals whichever of $(M - \mu)$ and $(\mu - M)$ is greater than zero.)

Figures 3.1 to 3.5 show simulations, in which we assume μ and σ are known. Now consider Figure 3.6, which shows all we know as typical researchers: our single sample of $N = 15$ data points and their mean. All this ESCI work with simulations is intended to build intuitions about what lies behind such a set of data. Whenever you see a data set, first bring to mind the population and recognize that you don't know its μ or σ. In practice you usually also don't even know whether or not the population is normally distributed, although here we're assuming it is. Next, visualize the dance of the means and the mean heap. We have a single green dot, but it's randomly chosen from the infinite dance. The drunkenness of

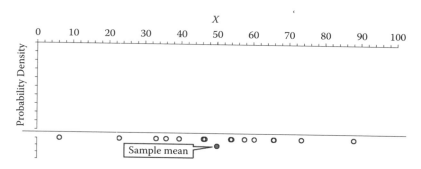

FIGURE 3.6
All a researcher knows: a single sample of $N = 15$ data points and their mean.

the dance—meaning the amount the means bounce around from side to side—or the width of the mean heap, would tell us how far our M might be from the μ we want to estimate. As well as thinking of their own data, researchers should always think about what other values they easily could have obtained, if they'd happened to take a different sample. We could have obtained any of the means in the dance.

We'll use our M to estimate μ, and we want to know how good an estimate it is. Here's a wonderful fact: We can use MOE to provide information about that precision. We rely on this obvious relation: If M is likely to be close to μ—as the last page or two has illustrated—then μ is likely to be close to M. As simple as that. The simulation shows us that, for most samples, M falls pretty close to μ, in fact within MOE of μ. Now we have only a single M and don't know μ. But, unless we've been unlucky, our M has fallen within MOE of μ, and so, if we mark out an interval extending MOE on either side of our M, most likely we've included μ. Indeed, and that interval is the *confidence interval* (CI)!

We define the interval [M – MOE, M + MOE] as the CI. In 95% of cases, that interval will include the unknown population mean μ. That's the inter-val we want, and so we can now celebrate with the trumpets. Recall that MOE = 1.96 × SE = $1.96 \times \sigma/\sqrt{N}$. Therefore,

The confidence interval *on the sample mean M is the interval [M – MOE, M + MOE], which extends MOE on either side of M.*

$$\text{the 95\% CI is } [M - 1.96 \times \sigma/\sqrt{N}, M + 1.96 \times \sigma/\sqrt{N}] \quad (3.2)$$

For eyeballing purposes, use 2 in place of 1.96.

We can label the 95 as the *level of confidence*, C, because it specifies how confident we can be that a CI includes μ. It's also referred to as the *confidence level*. We usually choose $C = 95$, but other values are possible and you can use ESCI to experiment with them.

The level of confidence, *or* confidence level, *is the 95 in "95% CI." It specifies how confident we can be that our CI includes the population parameter μ.*

You might have noticed a problem: MOE is calculated from σ but, you ask, how can we do that when we don't know σ? You're correct, but as a first step we'll assume σ is known and use it to calculate MOE and the CI. As a second and more realistic step, we'll use our sample s as an estimate of σ in our calculation of MOE for the CI. Assuming σ is known, MOE is calculated using $z_{.95} = 1.96$. Dropping that assumption and using s to estimate σ, we need instead to use a critical value of t. As you probably know, using t requires us to choose an appropriate value for the *degrees of freedom (df)*. For our situation, with a single sample, $df = N - 1$, and the critical value we need is $t_{.95}(N - 1)$. Use the **Normal z t** page of **ESCI chapters 1–4** and the notes in Appendix B to find any critical values of z or t that you need. Then,

$$\text{the 95\% CI is } [M - t_{.95}(N - 1) \times s/\sqrt{N}, M + t_{.95}(N - 1) \times s/\sqrt{N}] \quad (3.3)$$

Exercises

3.36 Display the dance of the means, click near red 8 to mark μ with a black vertical line, and click **Display ±MOE around μ**. Compare with Figure 3.7, upper half. Do you have any means beyond MOE? What percentage would you expect in the long run?

3.37 The green stripe at the bottom has length 2MOE. We are going to take a line of that length and place it over each mean to mark an interval extending MOE on either side of the mean. (At this point, make sure that **Assume σ known** near red 7 is clicked on, but **Mean heap** is not clicked.) Near red 7 click **Display CIs**, and there they are. Run the simulation and enjoy the *dance of the CIs*. Music? Compare with Figure 3.7, lower half.

The *dance of the confidence intervals* is the sequence of CIs bouncing around for successive samples, as in Figure 3.7, lower half, and Figure 3.8.

3.38 A CI *includes* μ, or *captures* μ, every time, unless the mean falls outside the MOE lines. Run the simulation and watch. What percentage of CIs will in the long run miss μ? What percentage will miss to the left? To the right?

3.39 All our CIs are the same length because we are using the same MOE value for each. That's calculated from σ, which for the moment we're assuming is known.

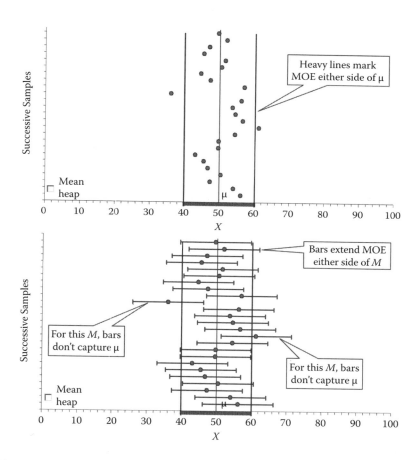

FIGURE 3.7

Dance of the means, $N = 15$ for each sample. A vertical line marks $\mu = 50$. In each half of the figure a stripe at the bottom extends MOE on either side of μ, and the ends of the stripe are marked by vertical lines. Two means happen to fall outside those MOE lines. In the lower half, error bars of length MOE on either side of each mean are displayed: These are the 95% CIs. Only for the two means falling outside the MOE lines does the CI fail to include μ.

3.40 Unclick **Display ±MOE around μ** to hide the MOE lines; then near red 9 click **Show capture of μ**, as in Figure 3.8, upper half. If a CI doesn't capture μ, ESCI displays it in red. Do you have any red CIs? Explain.

3.41 Click off **Assume σ known** near red 7. What happens? Compare with Figure 3.8, lower half. Click on and off a few times and watch carefully. If we drop the assumption that σ is known we are being much more realistic. MOE is now calculated using *s* as our estimate of σ.

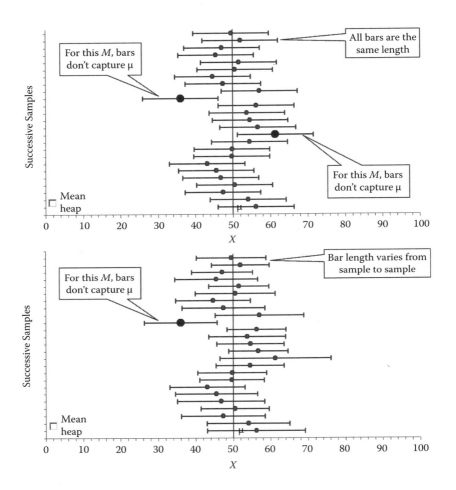

FIGURE 3.8
Dance of the CIs, $N = 15$ for each sample. CIs that miss μ are marked here with a larger black dot for the mean; in ESCI they are red. Upper half: Assuming σ is known. Lower half: That assumption is dropped and each CI is calculated using s for that sample, so the CIs vary in length. Whether a CI captures μ or not may change when the assumption about σ changes, as here for the sample 11th from the bottom.

3.42 Every sample has its own s, and so the CIs vary in length from sample to sample. What would happen for $N = 10$, or even smaller? Would s vary more or less, from sample to sample? Would s typically be a better or worse estimate of σ? Would you expect CI length to vary more, or less, from sample to sample? What about $N = 100$?

3.43 Experiment to test your predictions. Explain.

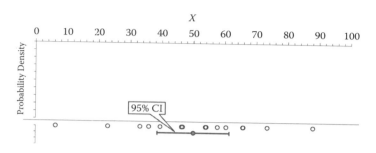

FIGURE 3.9

All that the researcher knows: the data points of a single sample with $N = 15$, as shown in Figure 3.6, but now the 95% CI has been calculated, using s.

3.44 Assuming σ is known, the CI was based on σ and the critical value of z. Without knowing σ, we use instead s and the critical value of t. So the 95% CI is $[M - t_{.95}(N - 1) \times s/\sqrt{N}, M + t_{.95}(N - 1) \times s/\sqrt{N}]$. Suppose you choose $N = 20$, take a sample, and calculate from your data that $M = 44.2$ and $s = 17.5$. Calculate the 95% CI. Use the **Normal z t** page of **ESCI chapters 1–4** to find the critical value of t you need; Appendix B has suggestions to help. While you are using that ESCI page, have a play with the shapes of the t distribution for various values of df, and compare with the normal distribution.

3.45 Calculating that CI is a typical textbook problem. Invent a few more, as varied as you can, and swap with a fellow learner. Work out the answers to each other's problems. (That's a good thing to do with a friend?) Do some similar exercises from another statistics textbook you know.

3.46 Figure 3.9 is the same as Figure 3.6, but now we have calculated the 95% CI using s from our data points. How should we think about that CI?

What does the 95% mean? In general, how should we interpret a CI? We'll discuss that in future chapters, but the figures around here give the basic answer. Our CI is one of an infinite sequence of possible CIs generated from the infinite dance of the means—from the infinite collection of samples, any of which we might have obtained in our experiment. In the long run, 95% of those CIs will capture μ, and 5% will miss. CIs that miss are shown in Figure 3.8 with a larger black dot, and in ESCI are shown in red.

It's a basic CI slogan: "It might be red!" We can be 95% confident that our CI captures μ, but it might be red. In your lifetime of calculating and reading and considering numerous

For any CI bear in mind, "It might be red!" It might be one of the intervals that don't capture μ, although in real life we'll never know.

95% CIs, around 95% will include the population parameters they estimate, and 5% will be red. It's a great convenience that ESCI can display in red the CIs that miss μ. Alas, in real life CIs don't come in color: You can never be sure whether any particular CI should be red or not.

3.47 Return to ESCI **CIjumping** and set up the dance of the CIs, showing capture, as in Figure 3.8. What do you expect if we change C, the level of confidence? Would 99% CIs be narrower or wider than 95% CIs? You are aiming for higher confidence of capturing μ, so would you need a narrower or a wider net? What about 90% or 80% CIs? Lock in your predictions.

3.48 Near red 7 is the spinner to set C. Read the popout. Change C and test your predictions. Does it make sense that CIs some-times change color as you change C? (*Note*: The spinner will give you values up to 99, but you can type in values up to 99.9. Type in a value, then press Enter on your keyboard.)

3.49 Play around with C. Think back to Figure 3.5, the mean heap, and MOEs and the percentage of the mean heap they include. Any surprises as you vary C over a wide range?

3.50 Set C = 95, the value we almost always use. Click **Assume σ known** on, so CIs are all the same length. Make sure capture of μ is indicated by deep green or red. Run the simulation, enjoy the dance of the CIs to your favorite backing music, and watch **Percent capturing** near red 9. What happens near the start of a run? What happens after a minute or two? After 10 minutes? After an hour or more?

3.51 Do it all again without assuming σ known, so the CIs vary in length.

3.52 Do it all a few more times, with various values of N including some very small values, and N = 100, the maximum this simula-tion allows.

3.53 Do it all yet again for various values of C.

Early in a run, after taking a small number of samples, the percentage capturing may differ a bit from C. Do you find it impressive that, after a minute or two, and certainly after 10 minutes or more, the percentage capturing is close or very close to C? Even more impressively, that's true for any N, any C, and whether or not you assume σ is known. Yes, the formulas for CIs predict extremely well how ran-dom sampling behaves. (And the random number generator I am using in ESCI is very good.)

3.54 Study Figure 3.9 again. That's all a researcher knows. That's all that's available for the Results section in a journal article. Whenever you see such a figure, or a Results section, you should bring to mind two underlying things to illuminate how you think about the results. What are they? *Hint*: Look back to Figure 3.6 and the discussion of that.

Reporting CIs

This is a good moment to reflect on the journey so far. I've argued that NHST is deeply flawed, is often misunderstood, and can mislead. If used well, estimation not only avoids the problems of NHST, but prompts researchers to ask "how much?" questions, and these questions are likely to give more informative answers than NHST's dichotomous questions. Estimation is based on point ES estimates, and interval estimates—which are the CIs we've just been discussing. So we've now encountered ESs and CIs, which are the basic building blocks for the new statistics. The main business of the rest of this book is to consider additional ESs, discuss six ways to interpret CIs, and introduce meta-analysis—which itself is based on ESs and CIs.

It's worth celebrating CIs and what they have to offer. (Wine, coffee, or another play with **CIjumping**?) The simple message of this section is that we should always, where possible, report CIs for any ES estimates. Report them in the text, in tables, or in figures, as is most helpful for your readers. I'll now outline what the *Publication Manual* (APA, 2010) says about reporting CIs.

Recommendations of the APA *Publication Manual*

Your discipline may not use the *Publication Manual*, but journals in a very wide range of NHST disciplines refer to it, so its advice is influential. In any case, it says sensible things about CIs. It includes a strong statement about CIs:

> The inclusion of confidence intervals (for estimates of parameters, for functions of parameters such as differences in means, and for effect sizes) can be an extremely effective way of reporting results.... Confidence intervals combine information on location and precision ... they are, in general, the best reporting strategy. The use of confidence intervals is therefore strongly recommended. (APA, 2010, p. 34)

The *Manual* then goes on to make the key recommendation I have already mentioned that researchers should "wherever possible, base discussion and interpretation of results on point and interval estimates" (p. 34).

The *Manual* specifies that a CI reported in text should be shown in the square bracket format I have been using in this book: $z = 0.65$, 95% CI [0.35, 0.95]. Here's another example: $M = 30.5$ cm, 95% CI [18.0, 43.0], which shows that the units of measurement (cm) should not be repeated in the square brackets. You might think the simple matter of how to report a CI in text would have been decided years ago, and some nice, clear format would be everyone's choice. Surprisingly, however, not even medicine has settled on a format that has become widely used, even though it has routinely reported CIs since the 1980s. I hope the *Manual's* […, …] format will quickly become familiar as signaling a CI. The *Manual* uses the same format for other levels of confidence, so you could, for example, report a mean response time as $M = 625$ ms, 99% CI [564, 686]. My recommendation, though, is to use 95% CIs unless there are good reasons for choosing some other level of confidence. It's challenging enough to build up good intuitions about the standard 95% level of confidence without trying to cope with CIs having a variety of levels. There's more about that in Chapter 4.

To report a CI, use this format: "The mean response time was $M = 567$ ms, 95% CI [512, 622]." For subsequent intervals, you can omit the "95% CI" if the meaning is clear.

The *Manual* says the "95% CI" (or other level of confidence) should appear before the square brackets for the first CI reported in any paragraph, but can be omitted for any further CIs reported in the same paragraph. So a later report in the same paragraph might be $z = 1.12$, [0.66, 1.58]. However, I hope the […, …] format will become so familiar for 95% CIs that the "95% CI" need only be stated once at the start of an article.

Chapter 5 in the *Manual* includes many examples of tables, and it's excellent that four of those examples include CIs. The wise advice is, "When a table includes point estimates, for example, means, correlations, or regression slopes, it should also, where possible, include confidence intervals" (APA, 2010, p. 138). To show CIs in a table you can either use the […, …] format, or use separate columns for the values of the interval endpoints: the lower limit (LL) and upper limit (UL) of each interval.

Tables 3.1 and 3.2 illustrate those two formats recommended by the *Manual,* using a small proportion of the data reported by Strandberg-Larsen, Grønbœk, Andersen, Andersen, and Olsen (2009). The tables show point and interval estimates for the relative risk of postneonatal mortality, defined as an infant dying between 28 days and one year after birth, for various levels of drinking by the mother. The risk for mothers reporting no drinking is used as the comparison, so the first row of data shows

TABLE 3.1

An Example Table Reporting the Association of Alcohol
Consumption During Pregnancy With Infant
Postneonatal Mortality

Alcohol Consumption (Average Drinks/Week)	Relative Risk of Postneonatal Mortality (Adjusted)	95% CI
0	1.00	—
0.5–1.5	0.82	[0.48, 1.39]
2–3.5	0.68	[0.27, 1.71]
4 or more	2.91	[1.22, 6.95]

Source: Data from K. Strandberg-Larsen, M. Grønbœk, A.-M. N.
Andersen, P. K. Andersen, & J. Olsen (2009). Alcohol
drinking pattern during pregnancy and risk of infant
mortality. *Epidemiology, 20,* 884–891.

TABLE 3.2

A Second Example Table Reporting the Association of
Alcohol Consumption During Pregnancy With Infant
Postneonatal Mortality

Alcohol Consumption (Average Drinks/Week)	Relative Risk of Postneonatal Mortality (Adjusted)	95% CI	
		LL	UL
0	1.00	—	—
0.5–1.5	0.82	0.48	1.39
2–3.5	0.68	0.27	1.71
4 or more	2.91	1.22	6.95

Source: Data from K. Strandberg-Larsen, M. Grønbœk, A.-M. N.
Andersen, P. K. Andersen, & J. Olsen (2009). Alcohol
drinking pattern during pregnancy and risk of infant
mortality. *Epidemiology, 20,* 884–891.

relative risk of 1.00. The values of relative risk are adjusted to allow for
differences in many other characteristics, including maternal age, socioeconomic status, and smoking status. The tables suggest that levels of
drinking up to an average of 3.5 drinks per week have little impact on
postneonatal mortality, but a mean consumption of four or more drinks
per week increases risk. The point estimate is an increase by a factor of
about 3 but, despite the study analyzing data for about 80,000 births, the
CI is wide—from about a 20% increase in risk to an increase by a factor of
about 7. Having the CIs certainly gives a fuller picture of the results than
either just the point estimates, or those estimates plus the information that
only for the bottom row does the increase reach statistical significance.

Interpreting CIs

In this and the next two chapters I'll describe six ways to think about and interpret CIs. The first is based on the definition of a CI. The following five I'll describe in an order that's convenient for presentation, but it is not an order of priority or preference. It's helpful to have many possibilities in mind for interpreting CIs, and to use whichever one or ones are most illuminating in a particular situation. After I've discussed them all, Table 5.1 provides a summary.

It may seem surprising, but the experts are not fully agreed on how best to interpret CIs. Of the six approaches I'll describe, only the first, which is based on the definition of the level of confidence, is fully endorsed by everyone. The others each attract quibbles or criticism from one or another expert. I'll explain something about some of the issues, but mainly I'll take a pragmatic approach and discuss approaches to interpretation that seem valuable to me. All six interpretations I describe are, in my view, reasonable as well as often useful in practice.

CI Interpretation 1: One From the Dance

As I mentioned, it's always correct to think of the CI calculated from our sample data as one from the potentially infinite sequence of intervals that we'd obtain if the experiment were repeated indefinitely. Each interval is just one randomly chosen from the dance of the CIs. As you inspect your interval, have in your mind's eye the dance of similar intervals. You realize that if your interval is narrow, most likely the dance is quite sober, but the wider your interval, the more varied (and wider) the dance is likely to be. Most likely your interval captures the parameter you wish to estimate, but, by chance, you may have an interval that doesn't include the parameter and that ESCI would show in red. Never forget, "It might be red!" Example 3.1 refers to the first interpretation of a CI.

Interpretation 1 of a CI. Our CI is one from the dance—an infinite sequence of repeats of the experiment. Most likely it captures the parameter we're estimating, but, "It might be red!"

CI Interpretation 2: Interpret Our Interval

It's tempting to say that the probability is .95 that μ lies in our 95% CI. Some scholars permit such statements, while others regard them as wrong, misleading, and wicked. The trouble is that mention of probability suggests μ is a variable, rather than having a fixed value that we don't know. Our interval either does or does not include μ, and so in a sense the probability is either 1 or 0. I believe it's best to avoid the term "probability," to discourage

---

EXAMPLE 3.1 INTERPRETATION 1—
ONE FROM THE DANCE

We should always have in mind that our 95% CI is one from an infinite sequence of repeated experiments. Researchers rarely write about this basic way of interpreting CIs, but I can give one example that comes close. Scott, Lambie, Henwood, and Lamb (2006) reported an analysis of New Zealand crime statistics. Referring to a set of 96 convictions for rape, one question they examined was the relative chance that an intruder rapist (a person who intruded into a residence to commit the crime), compared with a nonintruder rapist, had a previous conviction for trespass. The ES they used was the odds ratio, which is one way of expressing relative chances, or relative risk. Their estimate was 5.91, 95% CI [1.72, 20.35], meaning that the odds for having such a previous conviction were about six times higher for intruder that nonintruder rapists. The authors wrote that the "odds of an intruder rapist [compared with a non-intruder] having a prior trespassing conviction lies 95% of the time, between 1.72 and 20.35" (p. 270).

When they referred to 95% of the time, they no doubt had in mind the definition of a CI as one from an infinite sequence of CIs from repeated experiments. Their wording, however, doesn't make that clear and may, I suspect, be confusing for many readers. If you wish to use Interpretation 1 in writing, it needs to be explained more fully. The key point is that the 95% refers to the whole process of taking a sample and calculating a CI, 95% of which will capture μ. Any particular CI, such as [1.72, 20.35], either does or does not capture μ, and so the 95% doesn't apply directly to that interval, but to the process that generated it. We should always keep in mind the first interpretation of a CI, but it may not provide the best approach for discussing data.

---

any misconception that μ is a variable. However, in my view it's acceptable to say, "We are 95% confident that our interval includes μ," provided that we keep in the back of our minds that we're referring to 95% of the intervals in the dance including μ, and 5% (the red ones) missing μ.

By saying I'm 95% confident that our CI contains μ, I'm saying that the values in the interval are *plausible* as true values for μ, and that values outside the interval are relatively implausible— although not impossible. We can thus consider substantive interpretation of the

Interpretation 2 of a CI. Our CI is a range of values that are *plausible* for the parameter we're estimating. The LL of our interval is a likely lower bound for the parameter, and the UL a likely upper bound.

various values in the interval. We'd probably first interpret the mean, at the center of the interval, which of course is just our point estimate. We could also consider the lower and upper limits of the interval. The LL is a likely lower bound for the true value of μ, although we know that just occasionally the LL won't be low enough (in 2.5% of cases, i.e., the red intervals that happen to land way to the right in the dance of the means). Similarly, the UL is a likely upper bound for μ (except in the 2.5% of cases in which it's not quite high enough—the red intervals that land way to the left). This interpretation of a CI as a range of values that are plausible for μ is probably the most widely used approach, and is often my favorite. For example, in discussing Tables 3.1 and 3.2 previously, I spoke of the 95% CI, which was [1.22, 6.95], as suggesting that the risk for the heaviest drinking group of mothers was raised by at least around 20% (referring to $LL = 1.22$) and perhaps by as much as a factor of about 7 (referring to $UL = 6.95$). Examples 3.2 use the second interpretation of CIs.

EXAMPLES 3.2 INTERPRETATION 2—THE INTERVAL AND ITS LOWER AND UPPER LIMITS

Example 3.1 came from Scott et al. (2006). Those researchers also used my second interpretation explicitly: "Confidence intervals are informative because they provide a range of plausible values" (p. 269).

Vaccination for Rubella

Sfikas, Greenhalgh, and Lewis (2007) reported a study of vaccination policies that could eliminate rubella from England and Wales. An important parameter is R_0, which is the average number of further infections produced by a single case of the disease. Sfikas et al. applied a somewhat complicated epidemiological model to a large database of blood samples to estimate $R_0 = 3.66$, [3.21, 4.36]. For any given value of R_0 they could apply their model and calculate the minimum proportion of children that must be vaccinated for the disease to be eliminated. The higher the value of R_0, the more infectious the disease, and so the nearer the vaccination rate must be to 100%. Assuming a single vaccination at birth, they calculated that the proportion of babies who must be vaccinated is .74, [.67, .76]. They commented that the point estimate is useful, but that the CI provides "a realistic idea of the limits within which the true proportion lies" (p. 6). Exactly. They go on to conclude that, in practice, "it may be more prudent … to implement a campaign for which the

---

target vaccination proportion is closer to the upper 95 percentile limit rather than the point estimate in order to lower the risk of an epidemic" (p. 15). That's an example of interpretation of the CI as a range of plausible values of the parameter of interest, then a focus on one of the CI limits as a likely upper-bound estimate that should be adopted as the target for policy.

Does the Speed of Light Vary?

Abdo et al. (2009) is an article in the journal *Nature* with more than 200 authors from many countries. It reports astronomical data from ground stations and a telescope in orbit around the Earth that provide a test of an important challenge that has been made to Einstein's special theory of relativity. The theory postulates that the speed of light in a vacuum is always exactly the same, whereas the challenge suggests that quantum gravity effects might lead to variation in the speed of light over extremely small distances. Previous research had found evidence of invariance of the speed of light, as Einstein's theory predicts, down to 1.6×10^{-32} cm, which is an exceedingly short distance. Abdo et al. reported data that allowed them to push that boundary down even further. Their 99% CI was [1.6×10^{-35}, 1.3×10^{-33}]. They focused on the UL and claimed invariance of the speed of light has now been established down to 1.3×10^{-33} cm, a distance about one-twelfth the size of the previous boundary. They thus offered further support for Einstein's theory.

I don't claim to understand all aspects of Abdo et al. (2009), and my previous explanation is sketchy. You may be wondering why I chose this example. The researchers estimated the distance at which they had evidence of invariance of the speed of light and, naturally, they calculated a CI on their estimate. I'm interested because they chose to focus on the upper limit of their 99% CI. Their data gave reasonable evidence of invariance at even shorter distances, but they elected to choose the conservative end of their interval and claim they had shown invariance just down to 1.3×10^{-33} cm. Of course, the 99% CI they calculated for their data would be wider than the 95% CI, so the upper limit would be greater for the 99% than the 95% interval. By using the 99% CI, they were thus adding a further degree of conservatism.

Examples 3.2 prompt me to make two further comments. First, what confidence level should we choose? Some statisticians advise choosing a level to suit how concerned we are that our CI includes the parameter we're estimating. If it's a life and death matter, choose a 99% or even 99.9% CI to increase our confidence that our CI includes the true value. If we're not so concerned about the occasional miss, we might choose to report an 80% or 90% interval, these, of course, being considerably shorter than the 99%, let alone the 99.9% CI. That's reasonable advice, but, even so, my recommendation is to use 95% routinely, unless there are strong reasons for choosing some other value. I've seen so much evidence of misinterpretation of CIs—as some of the boxes throughout this book report—that I feel it's best to concentrate on understanding 95% CIs well, without the additional complexity of trying to interpret intervals with various different levels of confidence. However, in the next chapter we'll discuss how to translate easily between a 95% CI and an interval with some other level of confidence, so you should be able interpret a result, whatever level of confidence is reported. The Abdo et al. (2009) situation, in which the researchers chose one limit as the primary finding, is a case where it could be justifiable to use a 99% CI, or an interval with some other level of confidence you judge appropriate for the situation. The Sfikas et al. (2007) example of estimating the percentage of babies that need to be vaccinated is another case where the UL of a CI is used, and it may be prudent public policy to choose 99% or some other high level of confidence, rather than the 95% chosen by the authors. These are also cases in which we could consider a one-sided CI, rather than the usual two-sided CIs I've been discussing. One-sided CIs are not often used, but I discuss them in Chapter 4.

My second comment is that I hope you are getting the feeling that our approaches to the interpretation of a CI, two of which I've discussed so far, are very general. I'm deliberately choosing examples ranging over psychology, criminology, economics, ecology, medicine, astronomy, and other disciplines. Whatever the ES, whatever the situation, you can most likely use any of our six approaches to the interpretation of a CI.

CI Interpretation 3: The MOE Gives the Precision

As we discussed, the MOE is the largest likely error of estimation, and so the MOE is a measure of the *precision* of our experiment. A third approach to CI interpretation is to use the MOE as indicating how close our point estimate is likely to be to μ, or the largest error we're likely to be making. It's easy to get tangled up in language about precision, because our measure of precision is MOE, but *increased* precision means

Interpretation 3 of a CI. The MOE, which is the length of one arm of our CI, indicates the precision and is the maximum likely error of estimation.

EXAMPLES 3.3 INTERPRETATION 3— THE MOE GIVES THE PRECISION

Scott et al. (2006) used this third interpretation of CIs by speaking of precision and width and the desirability of narrow intervals. However, they also commented that a wide CI can be "an indicator of uncertainty as to where the result falls" (p. 269), but that may be misleading. We know exactly where our result falls—for example, our *M*. The uncertainty is about the population parameter, and so it may be clearer to say something like, "uncertainty as to where the true value lies." Perhaps they meant "uncertainty as to where the result falls in relation to the unknown parameter." They also made a reasonable comment about the precision of one of their intervals by describing it as "quite broad because of the small sample size" (p. 270). They thus referred to precision and CI width, but not specifically to MOE. The next example focuses on MOE.

The Ages of Rocks

Broken Hill has long been an important mining city in outback Australia, and so there has been intensive study of the complex geology of surrounding areas. Rutherford, Hand, and Barovich (2007) reported estimates of the ages of a number of rock types, based on a large set of chemical analyses of rock samples. Their purpose was to use the age results to evaluate various models of how tectonic plates had moved and interacted in the area around 1.6 billion years ago. They reported their age estimates of the different rocks as, for example, 1594 ± 17 Ma (million years) and 1585 ± 31 Ma, where the ±17 and ±31 were stated to be 95% CIs, and so 17 and 31 were the MOEs. They reported and attended to MOEs throughout the article, for example, by commenting that "errors on mean ages range between 15 and 40 Ma" (p. 70). The precision of age estimates was important for their main conclusion, which was that an important tectonic event occurred between 1585 and 1610 million years ago, but that a previous suggestion of an earlier tectonic event occurring around 1690 million years ago was mistaken.

---

a *shorter* MOE, and an *increase* in the MOE (taking a smaller sample, for example) means *lower* precision.

The 1594 ± 17 format used by Rutherford et al. (2007) (see Examples 3.3) for reporting error margins is common in some disciplines, but it's essential to be sure what quantity is being reported. Those researchers stated explicitly that they were reporting 95% CIs, but the ± format is probably more often used to report the SE or SD. Further, in some disciplines including physics and chemistry it's common to use ± to report measurement error, but without any statistical definition. A report of, for example, 32.5 ± 0.1 mm suggests that the researcher simply judged that the length scale could be read to an accuracy of about 0.1 mm. No statistical definition was intended.

This is a good point to mention the article by Cumming and Finch (2005, tinyurl.com/inferencebyeye), which introduces and explains CIs, and describes a number of ways to interpret them. Many of the issues discussed in this chapter and in the following three chapters are also discussed in that article.

Exercises

3.55 In your own discipline find, or compose for yourself, some examples of interpretation of CIs. Then for each make a second interpretation, based on some different approach to thinking about CIs.

3.56 Identify in each case which of my first three ways to interpret a CI is being used—or perhaps some other way is being used, or a mixture.

3.57 Think of the dance of the means, the mean heap, and the dance of the CIs. Are you dreaming about them yet? You are sufficiently familiar with them when they come up in your dreams.

3.58 Write down your own take-home messages from this chapter.

Reward yourself with chocolate or another play with ESCI if you actually write down your own before turning over to see mine.

Take-Home Messages

- Our statistical model assumes random sampling from a normally distributed population that has mean μ and standard deviation σ, which are fixed but unknown parameters.

- The simplest experiment is to take a single sample of size N from the population, and use sample mean M and sample standard deviation s as estimates of μ and σ.

- Sampling variability is the variability from sample to sample, and is illustrated by the dance of the means: Larger variability gives a wider, or more drunken, dance.

- *Take-home movie*: The dance of the means, as in Figure 3.2.

- The mean heap is the empirical sampling distribution of the sample means. After a notionally infinite number of samples it becomes the theoretical sampling distribution—illustrated in ESCI by the sampling distribution curve.

- *Take-home picture*: The mean heap, as in Figures 3.3, 3.4, and 3.5.

- The sampling distribution of the sample mean is normally distributed, with mean μ and SD of $\sigma/\sqrt{N}$.

- The SD of the sampling distribution is called the standard error, which gives the chant, "The standard error is the standard deviation of the sampling distribution of the sample mean." Just think of the mean heap: The SE measures its spread. It's worth remembering SE = $\sigma/\sqrt{N}$. That's Equation (3.1).

- The green stripe interval in ESCI extends MOE (the margin of error) either side of μ, and includes 95% of sample means. MOE = 2SE approximately, or more exactly MOE = $1.96 \times$ SE = $1.96 \times \sigma/\sqrt{N}$.

- The MOE is the largest likely error of estimation. For 95% of samples, M lands within MOE of μ, or in other words, $|M-\mu| <$ MOE. For 5% of samples the mean falls outside the MOE lines, in a tail of the mean heap.

- The 95% CI extends MOE on either side of M, so the 95% CI is $[M - MOE, M + MOE]$ or $[M - 1.96 \times \sigma/\sqrt{N}, M + 1.96 \times \sigma/\sqrt{N}]$. That's Equation (3.2). Those CIs are all the same length, based on known σ.

- We usually drop the unrealistic assumption of known σ and use s as an estimate of σ. Then the 95% CI is $[M - t_{.95}(N-1) \times s/\sqrt{N}, M + t_{.95}(N-1) \times s/\sqrt{N}]$, where $t_{.95}(N-1)$ is a critical value of t, with $(N-1)$ degrees of freedom. That's Equation (3.3).

- CIs based on s and t vary in length from sample to sample. Smaller N gives greater variation from sample to sample. For very small samples, CI length gives a poor indication of uncertainty, so we shouldn't trust CI length for such samples.

- *Take-home movie*: The dance of the CIs, as in Figure 3.8.

- The level of confidence, C, is usually set to 95, but can be given other values. Larger C gives wider CIs.

- Researchers should, wherever possible, report CIs for any ES estimates they report, then should interpret the ESs and CIs.

- See a CI reported, and automatically think, "It might be red!" Think of a CI as one from a potentially infinite dance of the CIs, C% of which capture the population parameter being estimated. That's the first approach to interpreting a CI. We can be C% confident our CI includes μ. But it just might be red.

- The second way to interpret a CI is as a range of values that are plausible for μ. The LL is a likely lower bound for μ, and the UL a likely upper bound.

- The third approach to interpreting CIs is to consider MOE as the precision of estimation. MOE is the largest likely error of estimation, meaning that the point estimate is likely to be within MOE of the parameter μ.

4

Confidence Intervals, Error Bars, and p Values

This chapter presents more about CIs, including some beautiful pictures and two further approaches to CI interpretation. The main issues are

- Error bars, and how they can show various types of information in figures
- Cat's-eye pictures that show the beautiful shape of a CI
- The fourth approach to interpreting CIs—in terms of their shape
- The relation between CIs and p values
- The fifth approach to interpreting CIs—with reference to p values
- One-sided CIs, which correspond to one-tailed NHST

The Error Bar, a Picture With a Dozen Meanings

Does Figure 4.1 show the mean number of ice creams consumed by 10-year-olds or the median response time to a red stoplight? What do the error bars represent? These are good questions, and Figure 4.1 fails to provide answers. I'll refer to the simple graphic shown on the column and dot in Figure 4.1 as *error bars*, or sometimes simply *bars*. Error bars define a range of values around a point estimate such as a mean. The trouble is that bars can be used to depict various different types of ranges.

> Error bars, or bars, are a simple graphic that marks an interval around a mean or other point in a figure.

When you see Figure 4.1, what questions spring to mind? Probably the most basic concern is the dependent variable, what it measures, and what its values mean. Ice creams or braking times? Then we need to know what the column and the big dot are reporting—perhaps the sample mean, a median, or a frequency? Labels on the figure or the figure caption needs to give clear answers to these questions.

Seeing the error bars should prompt an additional question, because, although the error bar graphic is familiar, it is, unfortunately, ambiguous.

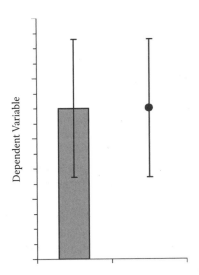

FIGURE 4.1
Two ways to display a mean, or other descriptive statistic, with error bars.

Do the bars show a CI? Or the SE? Or something else? We could refer, only slightly histrionically, to the *tragedy of the error bar*, which is that bars don't automatically state what they are reporting. Seeing error bars needs

The *tragedy of the error bar* is how I refer to the unfortunate fact that error bars don't automatically announce what they represent. We need to be told.

to prompt questions about what they represent. Alas, figures often fail to state what the bars represent, in which case it's impossible to make sense of the figure.

Column or Dot?

Error bars represent some measure of variability or uncertainty, but even the way the point estimate is depicted may influence our perception of variability. Referring to Figure 4.1, consider a further question: Column or dot? Both are common, but which prompts better interpretation? If the vertical axis starts at zero, the height of a column gives a direct representation of effect size that can be useful for appreciating the effect. On the other hand, a column has a sharply defined top end. Yes, we can calculate the sample mean as precisely as we like and picture it with a sharp-topped column. But one main message of this book is that sampling variability is often greater than we suspect. A sharp-topped column may hint that we have precise information about the population. Even if the suggestion is subliminal, that would be misleading. On the other hand, a dot, as in Figure 4.1, reports the sample mean clearly, but may possibly not give such a strong hint about precision. Research is needed to investigate these speculations. In the meantime, I'll generally prefer dots to columns. In either case, however, error bars should be used to provide explicit information about variability or uncertainty.

While we're thinking about columns and dots, I'll mention *Graph Design for the Eye and Mind*, by Stephen Kosslyn (2006). It's a book based on statistical cognition and other research about how people interpret—or misinterpret—graphs. Kosslyn uses the research findings to formulate good advice about how to design figures to report data. He discusses research on the column and dot issue (see pp. 46–53), but doesn't consider what, for me, is the vital question—to what extent does each give an appreciation of the uncertainty in the data? That question awaits investigation. There is much that's useful in Kosslyn's book, although there is nothing on confidence intervals and only a few mentions of error bars.

Confidence Intervals and SE Bars

The most common uncertainty is whether error bars represent a CI, or are SE bars, where *SE bars* are error bars that extend from one SE below to one SE above the mean, or other point estimate. Unfortunately, different research fields have different customs. In medicine, for example, CIs are routinely reported, and so unidentified bars are probably CIs, although they might not be. In some

Standard error bars, or SE bars, extend from one SE below to one SE above the mean. Unfortunately, some researchers and disciplines assume that "error bars" means SE bars.

biological disciplines, however, SE bars are routinely shown in figures, and some researchers regard any mention of "error bars" as automatically implying SE bars. I recommend the safer policy of using the term "error bars" to refer simply to the graphic illustrated in Figure 4.1, without any assumption of a particular meaning.

Should we prefer CIs or SE bars? You won't be surprised to hear that I recommend CIs. To explain why, I need to discuss the role of *N*, the sample size, then introduce the idea of *inferential information*. Figure 4.2 illustrates 95% CIs and SE bars for three samples, of sizes 5, 20, and 80. These are random samples from the same normal population, but I tweaked them a little so they all have the same *M* = 50 and same *s* = 17. That should help comparison of the error bars, which is the aim here. For each sample, the 95% CI is on the left, and the SE bars are on the right. Overall, the two types of bars are very different, with CIs being around twice the length of SE bars, or longer. In addition, both CIs and SE bars show large changes in length with *N*. We'll see that the relation between length and *N* is different in the two cases, and that this difference underlies the advantage of CIs.

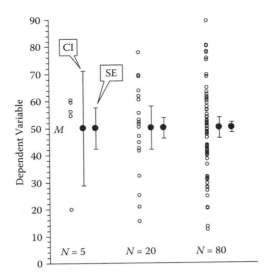

FIGURE 4.2
Three samples, of sizes 5, 20, and 80, displayed as dot plots. All samples have the same mean $M = 50$, and same standard deviation $s = 17$. For each sample, the error bars on the left represent the 95% CI, and on the right are SE bars, which mark ± one SE.

First I'll focus on the CIs, which show an especially marked change in length across the three values of N. Using Equation (3.3) and $N = 5$, MOE for the CI is

$$t_{.95}(N-1) \times s/\sqrt{N} = t_{.95}(4) \times 17/\sqrt{5} = 2.776 \times 7.603 = 21.11.$$

For $N = 5$ the critical value of t is 2.776, and you can use Appendix B and ESCI **Normal z t** to check that the critical value is correct. For $N = 20$, the critical value of t is 2.093 and MOE is 7.96, and for the $N = 80$ sample, the critical value of t is 1.990 and MOE is 3.78.

Now consider the SE bars shown on the right for each sample. Because $SE = s/\sqrt{N}$, these bars also get shorter as N increases. There's a factor of 4 increase in sample size from one sample to the next from left to right across Figure 4.2, which means there should be a factor of $\sqrt{4} = 2$ decrease in SE, from sample to sample. The SE bars in the figure do show that decrease: For the $N = 5$ sample, $SE = 17/\sqrt{5} = 7.60$. For the $N = 20$ sample, $SE = 3.80$ and the bars are half as long. For $N = 80$, $SE = 1.90$ and the bars are again halved in length. Do these values look about right, as you read the SE bars in Figure 4.2?

Compare that pattern for SE bars with changes in the CIs for different values of N. The lengths of the three CIs reflect the three MOEs, which are 21.11, 7.96, and 3.78, from left to right—from the smallest to largest samples. Compare 21.11 and 7.96 to see that the CIs shorten by distinctly more than a factor of 2 from the $N = 5$ to the $N = 20$ samples. From the $N = 20$ to the $N = 80$ samples, the CIs shorten by close to a factor of 2.

Another approach to considering CIs and SE bars is to compare the two sets of bars for each sample. For $N = 5$, the critical value of t is 2.776, considerably larger than 2, and the CI appears considerably longer than double the length of the SE bars. However, for both the $N = 20$ and $N = 80$ samples, the 95% CI appears about double the length of the SE bars, because the critical values of t for those samples are 2.093 and 1.990, respectively—both quite close to 2. Now I need to introduce inferential information and a *rule of eye*.

Inferential Information

CIs give us *inferential information*, which is information that supports an inference about the population. It's calculated from the sample, but informs us about the underlying population. The sample mean, M, gives inferential information when we use it as our

Inferential information is based on the sample data, but tells us about the population.

point estimate of the population mean. A CI provides inferential information because it tells us how precise our point estimate is for μ, the parameter we're estimating.

SE bars usually don't provide accurate inferential information. Often you can interpret SE bars as being, approximately, the 68% CI; there's more about that later in this chapter. Also, as we saw previously, you can double the length of SE bars to get, approximately, the 95% CI. That's a useful *rule of eye*, by which I mean a generally useful guide-

A *rule of eye*: Double the length of SE bars to get, approximately, the 95% CI. This rule is reasonably accurate for means when N is at least 10.

line to remember when interpreting figures (Cumming & Finch, 2005, tinyurl.com/inferencebyeye). Like a rule of thumb, it's not always exact, but it's often helpful. If N is at least 10, the rule is reasonably accurate. For $N = 10$ or less, however, it becomes progressively more in error as N decreases. Figure 4.2 illustrates that, for $N = 5$, the 95% CI is almost three times the length of the SE bars. It would be seriously inaccurate to interpret SE bars when $N = 5$ as a 68% CI, or twice their length as a 95% CI. That's the trouble with SE bars: They don't provide what we want, which is accurate inferential information. CIs by definition provide that information.

Why then are SE bars used so commonly, especially in some disciplines? That's an excellent question. There has been almost no study of how researchers think about or interpret SE bars, but they are probably seen as providing a type of inferential information, perhaps a rough indication of precision. Yes, you can often interpret SE bars inferentially by doubling their length to get, approximately, the 95% CI, but, as we have seen, that strategy fails for small samples. Also, for some measures, including correlations and proportions (see Chapter 14), CIs are not calculated from the SE, so in those cases also SE bars could be misleading. The conclusion must be that CIs should be preferred to SE bars. Medicine agrees and expects researchers to report CIs. In Chapter 6 I'll mention evidence that many researchers don't appreciate the distinction between SE bars and CIs, even though they differ by a factor of about 2! Anyone who doesn't appreciate the difference might prefer SE bars because they are shorter and thus suggest less uncertainty in the data. However that's an illusion, because it's the CI that gives accurate information about uncertainty—because that's what they are designed to do. We should prefer CIs to SE bars. Simple as that.

Descriptive Information

Additional error bar confusion arises when bars are used to convey not inferential, but *descriptive information*. I need to leave error bars for a moment, and say something about descriptive information, which, as you would guess, describes the sample data. It may provide a complete description, like the dot plots in Figure 4.2, which mark *Descriptive information* tells us about the sample data. every data point, or it may be a descriptive statistic that summarizes an important aspect of the sample. In Figure 4.1 the column and dot very likely mark the sample mean, which is the most common descriptive statistic as well as being a point estimate that provides inferential information. Other descriptive statistics are *s*, the median, and the range. You may know about boxplots and frequency histograms, which are descriptive pictures of a sample. All of these give us information about the data points in the sample, their values, and how they are spread.

I've been referring to the set of data as "the sample," and almost always in this book we'll discuss data sets that are random samples from a population, which is our real interest. However, there are other data sets. You might be investigating the world's top 100 performers in your favorite sport. You could plot data showing their performance times or their earnings. Your investigation would be based on a variety of descriptive statistics and pictures, which tell you about those 100 sports people. There's no thought of the data being a random sample from some larger population— it's descriptive information about those 100 people that fascinates you.

There's another reason to be interested in descriptive information. To introduce it, I'll mention Wilkinson and the Taskforce on Statistical Inference (1999, tinyurl.com/tfsi1999), which is the report from a group of statistical experts set up by the APA. I strongly recommend this report, which included much wonderful and down-to-earth advice, including this statement: "As soon as you have collected your data, before you compute *any* statistics, *look at your data"* (p. 597, emphasis in the original). Examining descriptive displays and summary statistics allows you to appreciate the whole data set and identify problems, or intriguing aspects, before you launch into inferential analysis. You may be able to check assumptions. I'll say little more about this vital first step of data analysis, and will usually assume the data we're discussing have undergone this examination.

Error Bars for Descriptive Information

Error bars are sometimes used to report descriptive rather than inferential information, and it's part of the tragedy of the error bar that the same error bar graphic is used for both. Descriptive bars tell us about the spread of data points within the sample. They may indicate the range, from the lowest to highest data points, or interquartile range, but most often indicate the sample standard deviation *s*. Figure 4.3 is the same as Figure 4.2, but with *SD bars* also shown. The SD bars extend a distance *s* below *M* and *s* above *M*, and are the same for all the samples, being ±17 in each case. The data points might appear more widely spread in the N = 80 sample, and the range does increase with N, but that's because larger N makes it more likely that at least a few extreme data points will be sampled. For a given population,

> *SD bars* describe the spread of data points in a sample. For a given population, they don't change systematically as *N* changes.

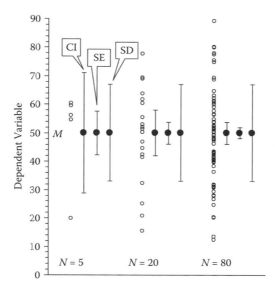

FIGURE 4.3
The same three samples as in Figure 4.2, with an additional set of error bars, on the right for each sample, that show the SD, which is *s* = 17 in every case.

we don't expect any systematic change in s if we take larger or smaller samples. Figure 4.3 illustrates how the CIs and SE bars change dramatically with N, but the SD bars don't.

A small complication is that the sample SD, like the sample mean, provides both descriptive and inferential information and, as Box 4.1 explains, s can be calculated slightly differently for those two purposes. However, I follow common practice by using the same calculation of s, with $(N - 1)$ in the denominator, whatever the purpose. Descriptively, s measures the spread of data points in the sample. Inferentially, whatever the value of N, s is our best estimate of σ, so we expect s to be roughly similar to σ, whatever the sample size. That's why the pattern of SD bars in Figure 4.3 is so different from that for the other bars. Yes, the value of s is likely to bounce around for successive samples, as we saw in Chapter 3, Exercises 3.9 and 3.10, and more so for small N. But s is, on average, close to σ, and that's true for any N. If that's all a bit confusing, focus on Figure 4.3,

---

BOX 4.1 TWO DIFFERENT SDS

Here's an optional extra point about SDs. As you may know, there are two different ways to calculate the SD of a data set. The first uses N in the denominator to give a descriptive statistic, the SD of the data set itself:

$$s_{\text{descriptive}} = \sqrt{\frac{\left(\sum X_i - M\right)^2}{N}} \tag{4.1}$$

You might choose that SD to describe the heights of your 100 top athletes, because you are considering that data set in its own right, and not as a sample from a population. The other formula uses $(N - 1)$ to give an inferential statistic that's the best estimate of σ:

$$s_{\text{inferential}} = \sqrt{\frac{\left(\sum X_i - M\right)^2}{N-1}} \tag{4.2}$$

Only when N is very small is there much difference between the two. I'm going to simplify things by always using the formula with $(N - 1)$ and the symbol s, as I've been using so far. Many textbooks, software packages, and ESCI do likewise. That s is best for estimating σ, which is usually our main concern, but it's also a pretty good descriptive measure of the variation within a data set.

which summarizes the main story: CIs and SE bars vary markedly with *N*, whereas SD bars don't.

To show variability within a sample, SD bars can be useful, but consider using a dot plot—as in Figures 4.2 and 4.3—or a boxplot instead. The main error bar question remains CIs versus SE bars, and on this issue the bottom line is: Report CIs, and if you see SE bars, double them in your mind's eye to get approximate 95% CIs—unless the sample size is less than around 10. The further bottom line is that it's absolutely essential that every figure with error bars states clearly what the bars represent. You'd think that wouldn't need saying, but in a survey of psychology journals (Cumming et al., 2007) we found that 32% of articles that included figures with error bars did not state what the error bars represented. That's terrible because, without that information, the figure is not interpretable. To repeat: It's essential to follow the requirement of the *Manual* (APA, 2010, Chapter 5) that every figure showing error bars must state clearly what the bars represent.

Prefer CIs over SE bars. In any case, a figure showing error bars must state what the bars represent.

Many disciplines have confusions about error bars. Our article in the *Journal of Cell Biology* (Cumming, Fidler, & Vaux, 2007, tinyurl.com/errorbars101) explained SD, SE, and CIs, and offered rules of eye. It's very basic, but was a hit and was downloaded thousands of times. If you are comfortable with the different types of bars illustrated in Figure 4.3 you are ahead of many published researchers out there. Take a pat on the back.

The Shape of a Confidence Interval

I now want to look *inside* a CI and develop a picture to give us a fourth way to interpret CIs. It's a novel picture, but I hope it's helpful for understanding CIs in practical situations. Here's a preview: In Chapter 3 our second interpretation of a CI stated that values inside the CI are plausible as true values for μ, and values outside the interval are relatively implausible, but not impossible. Our fourth interpretation refines that by describing how the plausibility that a value is μ is greatest for values near *M*, in the center of the CI. Plausibility then drops smoothly to either end of the CI, then continues to drop further outside the CI.

The Cat's-Eye Picture

Consider Figure 4.4, which shows the dance of the CIs for samples of size *N* = 15 from a population of Hot Earth Awareness Test (HEAT) scores with

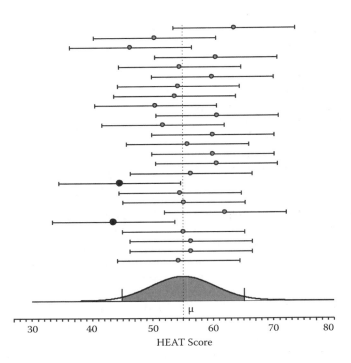

FIGURE 4.4
Dance of the 95% CIs for samples of size $N = 15$ from a normally distributed population of HEAT scores with $\mu = 55$, and $\sigma = 20$ assumed known. If a CI does not capture μ, the sample mean is shown as a large black dot. (In ESCI, those CIs would be red.) The curve at the bottom is the sampling distribution of M. It's a normal distribution and has a mean of 55 and standard deviation of $SE = 20/\sqrt{15} = 5.16$. The shaded area includes 95% of sample means, and therefore extends MOE below and above μ.

mean $\mu = 55$, which is marked by the vertical dotted line. I'll divide my discussion into four steps, but before I start, note that I speak of "where M (or its CI) falls in relation to the unknown μ." In other words, I take a sample and find that its M (or its CI) falls near to, or a little distance from, μ. That wording is a bit awkward, but emphasizes that it's M and the CI that vary, whereas μ is fixed as well as unknown. That's why, as I explained in Chapter 3, I talk about plausibility, not probability. Keep Figure 4.4 in mind, and the dance of the CIs.

1. The curve at the bottom in Figure 4.4 is the sampling distribution of the sample mean, M. The shaded area includes 95% of sample means, so we know from Chapter 3 that it extends MOE on either side of μ. The height of the curve at any HEAT value on the horizontal axis at the bottom indicates the relative likelihood that our M falls at that value. The curve is highest at $\mu = 55$, and so M is

most likely to fall at, or very near, μ. At values a little way from μ, the curve is a little lower and, correspondingly, *M* is a little less likely to fall at those values. The height of the curve decreases smoothly, and at a distance of MOE to the left or right of μ (i.e., at either end of the shaded area) its height is about one-seventh as great as it is at μ. Therefore, *M* is about seven times as likely to land at μ as it is to land at MOE below μ, or at MOE above μ. In brief, the curve tells us how values farther from μ become progressively less likely for our *M*.

2. Now consider estimation error $(M - μ)$, which we encountered in Chapter 3. It's the distance between the *M* of a particular sample and μ. I stated previously that the curve at the bottom in Figure 4.4 is the sampling distribution of *M*, but it's also the sampling distribution of estimation errors, meaning $(M - μ)$ values. Therefore, we can translate all the statements in Step 1 about the relative likelihood of different *M* values into statements about the relative likelihood of different estimation errors. So "*M* is most likely to fall at, or very near, μ" translates to "$(M - μ)$ is most likely to be zero, or very small." The height of the curve tells us how progressively larger values of $(M - μ)$, which occur when *M* falls progressively farther to the right of μ, are progressively less likely. The likelihood that $(M - μ) = $ MOE is only about one-seventh as great as the likelihood that $(M - μ) = 0$, so estimation errors as large as MOE are relatively rare. The curve keeps decreasing beyond the shaded area, so $(M - μ)$ values greater than MOE do occur—and would give red CIs in ESCI—but are progressively even less likely as $(M - μ)$ increases further. [All those statements refer to $(M - μ)$ being positive, meaning *M* falls to the right of μ, but the curve is symmetric, so we can make similar statements about means that fall to the left of μ, for which $(M - μ)$ is negative.] In brief, the curve tells us that estimation errors near zero are most likely, and illustrates how larger estimation errors become progressively less likely.

3. This is the crucial step, probably deserving a drum roll. In practice we don't know μ, and we have only the single value of *M* from our sample. But all the statements in Step 2 about estimation error apply. Therefore, we know that $(M - μ)$ close to zero is most likely, meaning our *M* has most likely fallen close to the unknown μ. Larger estimation errors are progressively less likely, and, correspondingly, it's progressively less likely that our *M* has fallen those larger distances from μ. Now the drum roll: We can take the curve at the bottom of Figure 4.4, which is centered on μ, and center it instead on our *M*—it will indicate the relative likelihood of

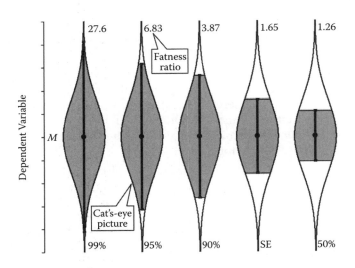

FIGURE 4.5
Cat's-eye pictures of CIs for several levels of confidence, and of SE bars. For each interval the sampling distribution of estimation errors, which is the curve at the bottom in Figure 4.4, plus its mirror image is centered at *M*, the sample mean. In each case the area between the curves that corresponds to the extent of the bars is shaded. The numbers at the top are the fatness ratio, which is the greatest fatness of the shaded area (at *M*) divided by the fatness at either end of the interval.

all possible sizes of estimation error of our *M*. Taking that curve and its mirror image and centering them on *M* is what I did to create Figure 4.5.

4. Figure 4.5 shows several examples of what I call a *cat's-eye picture*, or simply a *cat's eye*. The cat's eye comprises the sampling distribution of estimation errors and its mirror image, centered on *M*, in the middle of the interval. The *fatness* of the picture, meaning the horizontal width between the two curves, indicates the relative likelihood of different estimation errors, within and beyond the CI. Small estimation errors are most likely, as signaled by the fattest part of the picture near *M*. In other words, our *M* has most likely fallen close to μ. Therefore, values close to *M* are the most plausible for μ and are our best bets for μ. The cat's-eye picture then gets progressively less fat for values toward either end of the CI, reflecting the fact that larger estimation errors are progressively less likely, and therefore values

> The *cat's-eye picture* is my name for any of the representations of intervals in Figure 4.5, complete with two sampling distribution curves and a shaded area.

> *Fatness* is my term for the horizontal width of the cat's-eye picture, as in Figure 4.5. Fatness is greatest at *M* and decreases smoothly for values that are progressively farther from *M*. Fatness indicates how the plausibility for μ varies for values within and beyond the CI.

farther from M are progressively less plausible for μ. Values in the unshaded tails beyond the CI are progressively even less fat, and therefore even less plausible for μ, although not impossible. A statistician may prefer to say the fatness of the cat's-eye picture shows how the *relative likelihood* of various values for μ varies within and beyond the CI. Note that fatness, plausibility, and relative likelihood decrease smoothly with distance from M. There's no sudden jump at either limit of the CI. There's little difference in the plausibility of values just inside or just outside a CI.

In brief, the cat's eye summarizes the distribution of plausibility that your estimation error is small, medium, or large. It's highly revealing about what intervals are telling us, so I see it as a beautiful picture.

The shaded area is the region between the two curves that corresponds to a particular CI, as in Figure 4.5. For the 95% CI, the shaded area is about seven times as fat at M as it is at either end of the CI. This reflects the fact that, in the dance of the means, a 95% CI is more likely to land so its M is very close to μ, than it is to land so its upper limit (UL) is very close to μ. In fact, about seven times more likely. And the same for its LL. We could refer to that ratio as the *fatness ratio*. In other words, the fatness ratio is the fatness, or width, of the shaded area at M, divided by the fatness at either the UL or LL of the CI.

The *fatness ratio* is my name for the fatness at M divided by the fatness at either limit of a CI.

Figure 4.5 reports near the top the fatness ratios for the different intervals. It's 6.83 for a 95% CI. In other words, M is about seven times as plausible, or seven times as good a bet for μ, as the UL. And the same for the LL.

In Figure 4.5 each picture is based on the same sample, so each has the same M and s. The two curves of the cat's eye are the same for each and describe how plausibility varies smoothly over the full range of the dependent variable. The five pictures differ only in the percentage of the area between the two curves that's shaded, and that percentage equals the level of confidence. For SE bars, about 68% of the area is shaded, because SE bars mark, approximately, the 68% CI.

In Figures 4.4 and 4.5 the sampling distribution curves are normal distributions because so far I've been assuming σ is known. If we drop that assumption, the sampling distribution curves are t distributions, with $(N - 1)$ degrees of freedom. The cat's eye therefore comprises two t distribution curves rather than two normal curves. However, in most cases the shapes and ratios of fatness reported in Figure 4.5 would change only a little. For most practical purposes Figure 4.5 provides a sufficiently accurate guide, especially considering I'm proposing the cat's-eye picture to assist understanding rather than as a basis for precise calculations. For small N, however, regarding SE bars as a 68% CI can be quite inaccurate.

CI Interpretation 4: The Cat's-Eye Picture

The cat's-eye picture gives us our fourth way to interpret CIs. Our second way, in Chapter 3, referred to interpretation of the interval as giving a range of plausible values for μ. Now we can take that idea further and have in mind the cat's-eye picture that signals how plausibility for μ varies across and beyond the interval. Values close to M are most plausible for μ, and the cat's eye shows how plausibility, or relative likelihood, drops toward LL and UL, then decreases further beyond the interval.

In Chapter 3 we explored how, for a given sample, changing the level of confidence, C, requires intervals of different length. Higher C requires longer intervals: The 99% CI is longer than the 95% CI. There's no change in the sampling distribution of M at the bottom of Figure 4.4, but the shaded area extends farther, to include 99% rather than 95% of the total area under the distribution curve. In Figure 4.5, the

Interpretation 4 of a CI. The cat's-eye picture describes how the plausibility, or relative likelihood, that a value is μ is greatest at M, in the center of the CI, then decreases smoothly to either end of the CI, then drops further beyond the interval.

shaded area for the 99% CI has to extend farther into the skinny tails of the curves to achieve such high confidence, and so there's a large change in fatness across the CI—Figure 4.5 tells us that the fatness ratio is about 28. For the 90% CI, the cat's-eye shading doesn't extend as far. For 50% CIs, only the fat center of the picture is shaded, and so there's little variation in plausibility within the interval, and the fatness ratio is only a little greater than 1. For SE bars there's also only small variation in plausibility within the bars, but quite large tail areas beyond them. Note that the 50% CI is about one-third the length of the 95% CI, so about half the "weight" of a 95% CI is concentrated in the middle third of its length, where fatness varies little.

I'd like to insert an example here, in which a published researcher has referred to the relative plausibility of points within a CI. Alas, I haven't found one, so if you choose to use the cat's-eye picture to help you interpret a CI calculated from your data, you'll be at the forefront of CI interpretation. I'll now make a few suggestions of how we could use the cat's-eye picture to interpret a CI, based on the first sample in Figure 4.4. That's the sample at the bottom, just above the curve, which has $M = 54.3$. The MOE is 10.1 and so the 95% CI is [44.2, 64.4]. Thinking about cat's-eye pictures could lead you to note that

- A value of 54 is about seven times as plausible for μ as a value of 44, or one of 64;
- You can be 95% confident μ lies between about 44 and 64, and 50% confident it lies between about 51 and 57.5—which is about the middle third of the 95% CI (and approximately the 50% CI); and
- Plausibility doesn't change much over the interval from 51 to 57.5, but drops outside that interval.

All those observations are justified and could guide your interpretive comments, but they should not be taken as exact probability statements about our particular interval. As always, bear in mind the dance of the CIs, and remember: Our interval just might be red.

Here's another way to think about the message of Figure 4.5. The distribution of estimation errors, as shown by the curve at the bottom of Figure 4.4, conveys the full information in a sample about μ. Any CI tells us about that full distribution, but to interpret it correctly we need to pay careful attention to the level of confidence, C. It's C that tells us what proportion of the distribution the CI reports, and what percentage of the cat's-eye picture is shaded. I recommend routinely using 95% CIs so we can become skilled at interpreting the 95% cat's eye, and don't need to worry about intervals with the various other shaded shapes shown in Figure 4.5.

I'm not suggesting that journals should publish cat's-eye pictures whenever they show CIs, but I do suggest that imagining a cat's eye can help understanding and interpretation. In Figure 4.6 the error bars on the left are undefined: As in Figure 4.1 we've not been told what they represent, so we can't interpret them and, in particular, can't imagine the cat's eye. If the bars show a 95% CI, the cat's-eye picture in the center is correct, but if they show SE bars, the cat's eye on the right is correct. Those two interpretations of the bars must come from different data sets, with the SE bars signaling much less precise estimation than the 95% CI achieves: For the CI, the plausibility is more heavily concentrated around M. Therefore, for the SE bars, the N of the data set is smaller, and/or s is larger than for the 95% CI. Contrast with Figure 4.5 where all the figures come from the same

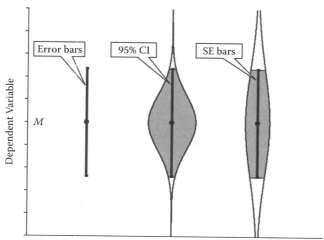

FIGURE 4.6
On the left are undefined error bars. In the center is the cat's-eye picture if the error bars represent a 95% CI. On the right is the cat's-eye picture if they are SE bars.

data. Now check that the fatness ratios of the two shaded areas are as you would expect, and as shown for the 95% CI and SE bars in Figure 4.5. Check that the general shapes of the shaded areas match those shown in Figure 4.5. The two cat's eyes in Figure 4.6 emphasize the dramatic difference between SE bars and 95% CIs, and reinforce my conclusion that it's a tragedy the two are often confused, and that we're often not even told which we are seeing. Can you look at any error bars, as on the left in Figure 4.6, and imagine the appropriate cat's-eye picture superimposed on them?

Finally, I should mention again our first and most basic way to interpret CIs. Whenever considering a single CI calculated from data, bear in mind the infinite dance from which it came. Here you can think of that as an infinite dance of estimation errors, many being small, some medium, and just a few large. The cat's-eye picture summarizes the distribution of plausibility that your estimation error is small, medium, or large. I find the cat's eye highly revealing about what intervals are telling us, so I see it as a beautiful picture—especially the 95% CI cat's eye. I hope you can share this feeling of beauty.

Confidence Intervals and p Values

I hesitate to mention p values, but they give us the fifth way to interpret CIs. It's my least favorite approach, and in Chapter 1 I reported evidence that CI interpretation is better if NHST is avoided. Even so, it's worth discussing the link between CIs and p to give a more complete picture. It's also valuable to be able to read a p value and generate in your mind's eye the corresponding CI. In psychology, almost all statistics textbooks explain p values first, then may or may not cover CIs. In some other disciplines most textbooks explain CIs first, then NHST and p values. Research is needed on the extent to which order might influence the quality of learning and number of misconceptions. I suspect CIs first may be better. Which order did your first statistics textbook use? What's your opinion about order?

In Chapter 1, I introduced the rule that if a 95% CI includes μ_0, we can't reject H_0. Therefore, two-tailed $p > .05$. If the interval does *not* include μ_0, we reject H_0 and note that $p < .05$. This rule makes sense because if μ_0 lies outside the interval it's a relatively implausible value for μ, and therefore it's reasonable to reject it. Conversely, if μ_0 lies in the interval, it's a plausible value for μ, and so we can hardly reject the hypothesis that states it is the value of μ. The boundary case occurs if a 95% CI falls so either of its limits is exactly at μ_0, as in Figure 4.7, in which case $p = .05$.

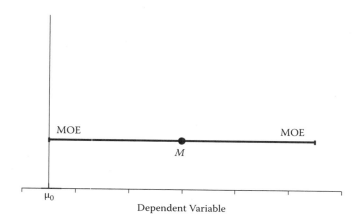

FIGURE 4.7
A CI that falls so one of its limits is at the null hypothesized value, μ_0.

This rule generalizes for other levels of confidence simply by adjusting the p value. For a 99% CI, the p value is .01 if the interval falls so either limit is at μ_0. For a 90% CI, p is .10 if either limit is at μ_0, and so on. For a C% CI with a limit at μ_0, $p = (1 - C/100)$. Figure 4.7 illustrates any of these cases, and Box 4.2, which is an optional extra, explains that formula.

Note my slightly awkward wording, for example, "if the interval falls so either limit is at μ_0," when it might seem clearer to say, "if μ_0 is at one of the limits of the interval." I prefer the first rather than the second wording to emphasize it's the interval that's the variable, not μ_0 or μ, but sometimes · I'll use the second wording. In any case, keep in mind the dance of the CIs.

Box 4.2 explains that, if a C% CI has a limit at μ_0, then two-tailed $p = (1 - C/100)$. The box makes a simple relation look pretty complicated, but does illustrate the fact that NHST and CIs are closely linked. Indeed, they're based on the same underlying statistical model and assumptions. Given this common theoretical base, it may be surprising that they lead to such different thinking and consequences. Anyway, now for a picture that I hope makes the relation between C and p easy to grasp.

The CI Function

Figure 4.8 shows the CI function, another beautiful picture that reveals more about CIs. The easiest way to understand it may be to fire up **ESCI chapters 1–4**, and go to the **CI function** page. Drag the big slider up and down, and see the movable CI, shown in heavy black in Figure 4.8, sweep up and down, changing in length as it goes. The two limits of the interval mark out the big double curves that are the CI function. The left vertical axis

BOX 4.2 THE RELATION BETWEEN C AND p

I stated that if a $C\%$ CI has a limit at μ_0, then two-tailed $p = (1 - C/100)$. Here's an explanation of that relationship. To use NHST for a single group, we calculate the obtained value of t with $(N - 1)$ degrees of freedom by using the formula

$$t_{\text{obt}}(N - 1) = (M - \mu_0)/ (s/\sqrt{N}) \qquad (4.3)$$

which implies that

$$(M - \mu_0) = t_{\text{obt}}(N - 1) \times (s/\sqrt{N}) \qquad (4.4)$$

After calculating $t_{\text{obt}}(N - 1)$ we'd use tables or software (such as ESCI **Normal z t**) to find the corresponding two-tailed p value, which by definition is the probability of obtaining $t > |t_{\text{obt}}(N - 1)|$ if the null hypothesis H_0: $\mu = \mu_0$ is true. To put it another way, $t_{\text{obt}}(N - 1)$ is the critical value of t for that p value, and we write that critical value as $t_{(1 - p)}(N - 1)$. An example is that the critical value of t for a p value of .05 is $t_{.95}(N - 1)$. We can therefore substitute $t_{(1 - p)}(N - 1)$ in place of $t_{\text{obt}}(N - 1)$ in Equation (4.4) to obtain

$$(M - \mu_0) = t_{(1 - p)}(N - 1) \times (s/\sqrt{N}) \qquad (4.5)$$

Now consider CIs and recall from Chapter 3 that Equation (3.3) gave, for a 95% CI

$$\text{MOE} = t_{.95}(N - 1) \times (s/\sqrt{N})$$

so for a $C\%$ interval we would use

$$\text{MOE} = t_{C/100}(N - 1) \times (s/\sqrt{N}) \qquad (4.6)$$

Notice that the MOE of the CI in Figure 4.7 is simply $(M - \mu_0)$, so, for the CI in Figure 4.7, Equation (4.6) gives us

$$(M - \mu_0) = t_{C/100}(N - 1) \times (s/\sqrt{N}) . \qquad (4.7)$$

Compare Equations (4.5) and (4.7) to find that

$$t_{(1 - p)}(N - 1) = t_{C/100}(N - 1). \qquad (4.8)$$

Therefore, $(1 - p) = C/100$ or, equivalently, for the situation of Figure 4.7 we have $p = (1 - C/100)$, which is the relationship we wanted to explain.

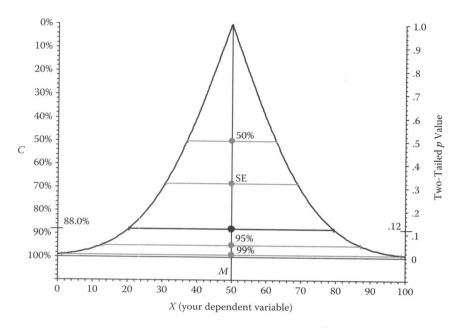

FIGURE 4.8
The CI function, from the **CI function** page of **ESCI chapters 1–4**. It plots the level of confidence C (left axis) and two-tailed *p* value (right axis) against the lower and upper limits of a CI. Fixed intervals are shown in gray, for comparison, and the movable interval, currently set to be an 88% CI, is shown in heavy black.

shows the level of confidence C of the movable CI, and the right vertical axis shows the two-tailed *p* value for that CI when the null hypothesized value lies at either limit of the interval—as illustrated in Figure 4.7. The CI function is sometimes known as the *p* value function. A version was introduced by Poole (1987), and it was discussed by Rothman (2002, Chapter 6).

Can you figure out what's going on here, and why the curves sweep out so sharply at the bottom, at high values of C? Compare with Figure 4.5. For C around 90 or more, the cat's-eye picture in Figure 4.5 is skinny near either of its limits, and so large increases in CI length are needed to yield a modest increase in shaded area and C. Therefore, in Figure 4.8 the CI function sweeps out dramatically near the bottom. It all hinges on the shape of the normal or *t* distribution that defines the cat's eye and, to achieve high levels of confidence, our CI needs to extend into the tails of that distribution.

I'm not going to write out lots of small steps to suggest how you can use the **CI function** page in ESCI, as I did for **CIjumping** in Chapter 3. Explore the CI function as you wish. Here are a few pointers.

- Enter M, SD, and N for your single sample. Adjust these values to control the position and width of the function.
- Observe the relation between CI length, C, and p values. Compare with Figure 4.5.
- Click below red 3 to display a cat's-eye picture on the main CI. Watch how the shading changes as you zoom the CI up and down. The fatness ratio, which is reported below red 3, also changes, but the two mirror-image curves of the cat's eye remain the same. The percentage of the area shaded always matches the level of confidence. Use the spinner below red 3 to change the amount of bulge: This changes the vertical scale of the cat's-eye picture, but doesn't change the fatness ratio or the interpretation.
- Click below red 1 to regard SD as the population value, so the CI is based on z, or to regard SD as the sample value, in which case the CI is based on t. See how the function changes, as well as the shape of the cat's eye. If N is large there's little change, but if N is small there's considerable change—because, as you know, the t distribution differs greatly from the normal distribution at very small df.

Translating Between a 95% CI and p

The next step is to investigate how, in your mind's eye, to skip back and forth between any p value and the corresponding 95% CI. First, notice in Figure 4.5 or Figure 4.8 that a 99% CI is roughly one-third longer than a 95% CI. If μ_0 lies at the end of a 99% CI, p is .01, so if we're looking at a 95% CI, we know that if μ_0 lies about one-third of MOE beyond the end of the interval, p must be .01. Apply that logic for CIs with other levels of confidence, and we can read any p value from where our standard 95% CI lies in relation to a hypothesized value. That turns out to be very useful.

Figure 4.9 shows the left arms of several CIs, with the 95% CI in bold as a reference interval. The dotted vertical lines mark where the CIs with various levels of confidence, C, have their lower limit. These lines are labeled with the corresponding two-tailed p value, meaning p when μ_0 lies at the position of the dotted vertical line. So, for example, the 99% CI has its lower limit at the line labeled with the p value .01. The fractions indicate distances from the left end of the 95% CI, in units of MOE (of that 95% CI), so the 99% CI extends approximately an extra one-third of MOE beyond the end of the 95% CI.

I suggest it's worth remembering those four fractions, as approximate benchmarks for the corresponding four p values. They state that $p = .01$ when μ_0 lies about one-third of MOE beyond the end of a 95% CI, and $p = .001$ when it lies about two-thirds MOE beyond. Inside a 95% CI, about

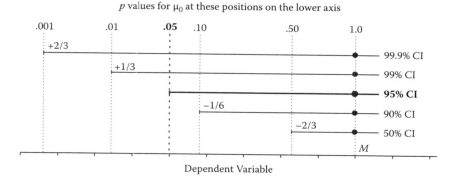

FIGURE 4.9
Left arms of a number of CIs for the same data, as labeled at the right. The null hypothesized value, μ_0, can be given any value on the horizontal axis at the bottom. If μ_0 has the value marked by the heavy dotted vertical line, then $p = .05$, as marked at the top of that line. If μ_0 has the value marked by any of the light dotted vertical lines, then two-tailed p has the value marked at the top of that line. The dotted vertical lines also mark the ends of the CIs corresponding to the various p values. The four fractions are approximate benchmarks worth remembering. They state how much longer or shorter the MOEs are than the MOE for the 95% CI, which is shown in bold and serves as a reference.

one-sixth of MOE back from the end gives $p = .10$, and about two-thirds of MOE back from the end (or one-third MOE out from M) gives $p = .50$. Keep those benchmarks in mind, and interpolate for values between those reference points.

For practice, look back at Figure 1.1 and eyeball the p values from the figure showing the 95% CIs for Lucky and Noluck. For Lucky, zero (the null hypothesized value) lies beyond the interval but not as far away as one-third of MOE. So p will be less than .05 but not as small as .01. If you estimated around .02, you are getting the idea fast. For Noluck, zero is further back from the limit of the CI than one-sixth MOE, so we know p is greater than .10, but zero is well beyond the benchmark for .50. If you estimated around .20, you are, again, doing very well.

Here's a bigger challenge: Run this guesstimating backwards. Read the first presentation of Lucky–Noluck, which reported M and p, and try to generate in your mind's eye the figure showing the two 95% CIs. Note that we're using $\mu_0 = 0$, and for each study you know M and the p value. For Lucky, M is around 3.6 and p is .02, so you know the 95% CI will extend most of the way from 3.6 toward zero, but will stop short by less than one-third of MOE. Therefore, the lower limit of the 95% could be around 0.5 or a little more, which suggests that MOE is around 3. Therefore, the 95% CI is roughly [0.6, 6.6]—which Figure 1.1 shows is a pretty good eyeballing result. For Noluck, consider M of about 2.2 and p of about .20, so we know the interval extends from 2.2 past zero, and by more than one-sixth MOE because p is greater than .10. I guesstimated MOE to be a bit more than 3, which Figure 1.1 shows to be about right, or maybe a bit short. It's close enough for eyeballing purposes.

You can play around with p and the position of μ_0 in relation to a 95% CI by using the **CI and p** page of **ESCI chapters 1–4**. Use the big vertical slider to move the 95% CI up and down, changing its position relative to μ_0, which remains fixed. Click to show or hide an axis showing a wide range of p values, the four benchmarks, and the accurate p value. Use the page for guessing games: For example, hide p values and the benchmarks, position the CI as you wish, and then compete with someone else to estimate p. Click to reveal the p value. Who's more accurate? Another example: Compete with someone else to position the CI to give some stated target p value. You'll both quickly become fast and accurate, and you'll have a useful skill that most researchers lack—or perhaps don't even realize is possible.

In a world full of p values, but lacking CIs, it can often be revealing to generate in your mind's eye what the 95% CIs would look like, given only some p values. Note, for example, what happens for $p = .30$, or some other value that's clearly not statistically significant. The CI is quite long relative to the ES—which is the distance from M to μ_0—so there's considerable uncertainty and, almost certainly, no justification for accepting the null hypothesis. Translating to a CI may be the best way to interpret a p value.

I've mostly been using the normal distribution, to keep things simple. I've therefore usually been assuming σ is known, or that we're using very large samples. I mentioned that if we drop that assumption and use the t distribution with $df = (N - 1)$, the cat's-eye pictures would change shape a bit, and the CI function would be different—most noticeably when N is very small. The **CI and p** page allows you to click to display the 95% CI and p values based on t rather than z: The two are displayed side-by-side, so you can compare, consider the benchmarks, and see how the difference varies as you change N. The figures, from Figure 4.4 onward, and the benchmarks I've suggested describe intervals and p values based on z. For our estimation purposes, they are all accurate enough to be practically useful. Just bear in mind that if N is small, say, less than about 10, our eyeballing may be a little astray.

I discussed cat's-eye pictures, benchmarks for p, and various other things in this chapter in an article in the journal *Teaching Statistics* (Cumming, 2007).

CI Interpretation 5: The Relation Between CIs and *p* Values

The fifth way to interpret a CI is in terms of p values: Note where the 95% CI lies in relation to μ_0, then estimate p. It's my least favorite approach to finding meaning in a CI, but it's still worth being able to do such eyeballing. More useful may be the ability to run this process backwards and generate in your mind's eye the 95% CI, given only μ_0, the sample mean, and *p*. If you can do that, you have additional insight into the great mass of research that's published with *p* values, but not CIs. And you have a valuable skill I suspect is rare.

Interpretation 5 of a CI. Where a 95% CI falls in relation to the null hypothesized value signals the *p* value. Use the benchmarks to eyeball an estimate of *p*.

At this point you may be expecting examples of how CIs can be interpreted with reference to *p* values. I'm not going to include any, however, because I don't want to encourage this approach. You'll recognize such examples easily enough by mention of inclusion or exclusion of a null hypothesized value, or stating of a *p* value. There are also exercises at the end of the chapter.

One-Tailed Tests, One-Sided CIs

So far in this book I've discussed two-tailed NHST and two-sided CIs. You may have wondered whether I've avoided one-tailed tests because they are a strength of NHST that estimation can't match. Not so! *One-sided CIs* are analogous to one-tailed tests but, as usual, the estimation approach is better. Strangely, most NHST textbooks describe one-tailed tests, but even textbooks that include CIs rarely mention one-sided intervals—which can, however, be useful, and are worth knowing about. I'll use an example and Figure 4.10 to explain.

One-sided CIs are analogous to one-tailed tests, but more informative.

Suppose a well-established therapy for a certain type of wrist injury in elite cyclists gives, after 20 sessions, the ability to lift with the injured wrist an average 520 g in a standard exercise device; the SD is 88 g. You are estimating the effectiveness of a new therapy, but are only interested if it's better. You observe a group of $N = 31$ cyclists use the new therapy and calculate $M = 548$ g for their ability to lift in the exercise device.

Let's assume that the mean and SD stated for the standard therapy are population values, perhaps estimated precisely by a meta-analysis. So, for NHST, we'll use H_0: $\mu_0 = 520$ g as the null hypothesis. Then Figure 4.10 panel A shows the sampling distribution of *M*, for $N = 31$ and $\sigma = 88$ g, and the rejection region for a two-tailed statistical significance test with $\alpha = .05$. We'll reject the null hypothesis if *M* falls in a shaded tail area, meaning $M > 551$ or $M < 489$. However, we're only interested in whether the new therapy is *better*, so we could justifiably use a one-tailed test, as illustrated in panel B. That rejects the null hypothesis if $M > 546$—an easier criterion to meet than the 551 of the two-tailed test. The key thing about the one-tailed test is that, yes, it makes statistical significance easier to obtain, but we should only choose it when the situation is genuinely

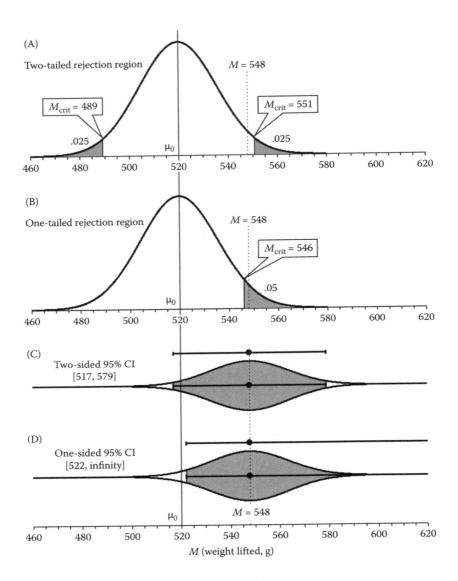

FIGURE 4.10
Panel A shows the sampling distribution of *M*, the mean weight lifted by a group of *N* =
31 cyclists recovering from a wrist injury, and the two-tailed rejection region when α = .05,
and μ_0 = 520 g is the population mean and σ = 88 g is the population SD. Panel B shows the
same for a one-tailed test. Critical values are shown as M_{crit}. Assuming *M* = 548 is observed,
as marked by the dotted vertical line, panel C shows two images of the two-sided 95% CI,
and panel D a one-sided 95% CI.

asymmetric and we only care about one specified direction of effect. Also, we have to commit in advance to using the one-tailed test.

For your $N = 31$ cyclists you calculated $M = 548$ g, as marked by the dotted vertical line in the figure. That would reject the null hypothesis, with $\alpha = .05$, if we had committed to a one-tailed test, but not if we were using the two-tailed test. Panel C shows the 95% CI around $M = 548$. That conventional two-sided interval includes the null value, 520, consistent with the result of the two-tailed test. Panel D shows the 95% one-sided CI around $M = 548$ to be [522, infinity], meaning the interval extends indefinitely to the right. The one-sided CI does not include 520, consistent with the result of the one-tailed test. If we think of whether or not the CIs include the null value, there's a direct correspondence between, respectively, the two- and one-tailed tests, and the two- and one-sided intervals.

Note that the curves of the cat's-eye picture are identical in panels C and D. In Figure 4.5, CIs with various levels of confidence have different percentages of the cat's eye shaded, but the curves are always the same. This is similar in Figure 4.10 for two-sided and one-sided CIs: The difference is in which 95% of the area we choose to shade. For the two-sided CI, 2.5% of the area of the cat's eye lies beyond each end of the CI, whereas for the one-sided CI, all 5% of the area outside the interval lies to the left. The one-sided CI extends indefinitely to the right, because the cat's-eye picture extends indefinitely both ways. In practice there's an upper limit to what any human wrist can lift, but I can't give an exact value for that, so I'll state "infinity" as the upper limit (UL) of the CI.

I should mention that we need to be careful of how a one-sided CI is described. I've seen an interval such as that shown in panel D described as

- A lower end-point CI
- A lower one-sided CI
- An upper one-sided CI
- An upper-tailed one-sided CI

I suggest that "lower end-point CI" is the least ambiguous, and thus what we might prefer. However, always state the numerical limits or refer to a figure to make clear which one-sided interval you mean—is the short arm below or above the mean?

> Refer to a one-sided CI like that in Figure 4.10 as a *lower end-point CI*, but also report values or a figure for clarity.

We can use any of our approaches to interpreting a CI to think about a one-sided CI. Considering the dance of the CIs, in the long run 95% of one-sided CIs will include the population mean, just as we expect for two-sided intervals. In the two-sided case, the red CIs that don't capture the population mean will split between those missing high and those missing low, whereas all 5% of one-sided intervals that miss will miss high (for the lower end-point case, as in panel D). We can say we're 95% confident our one-sided interval includes the true value. We can say the lower limit (LL) of the one-sided CI (522 for our example) is a likely lower bound for the true value, meaning that for 5% of replications the LL will exceed the true value. Compare that with the LL of the two-sided CI (517 for our data), which is also a likely lower bound, but with a different meaning of "likely" because the LL of the two-sided CI will exceed the true value for just 2.5% of replications.

Calculating a One-Sided CI

ESCI doesn't display one-sided CIs, but it's easy to calculate them if you wish. Note again the cat's-eye picture in panel D, in which 5% of the area is below the interval. The 90% two-sided CI has 5% of the area of the cat's eye below and another 5% above, so its LL is the same as the left limit of the one-sided 95% CI illustrated. To find a 95% one-sided interval, use ESCI or any other software to find the 90% two-sided interval, then choose the LL or UL of that CI as your single limit of the one-sided 95% CI that you seek.

The short arm of a one-sided 95% CI is the same as either arm of a two-sided 90% CI.

You may recall $z_{.95} = 1.960$ is the critical value we use to calculate the MOE of a two-sided 95% CI. For a two-sided 90% CI we use $z_{.90} = 1.645$, so that's the value we need to calculate the one-sided 95% CI. Now, 1.645 is 16% less than 1.960, so the lower arm of the one-sided CI in panel D should be 16% (about one-sixth) shorter than either arm of the two-sided CI in panel C. To my eye, that's about what the figure shows. Here's a different example: If $M = 10.0$, 95% CI [6.1, 13.9], then the upper end-point one-sided 95% CI is [–infinity, 13.3].

Two-Sided or One-Sided CIs?

It's useful to know about one-sided CIs because they provide an additional option. A one-sided CI parallels the one-tailed test and gives additional information beyond the test result, but I'd rather think about one- and two-sided CIs without reference to NHST. The key is to bear in mind panels C and D of Figure 4.10. Think of the cat's-eye picture and decide which CI is more appropriate, given your research questions. Arguably you should do that in advance of collecting data, just as you need to commit to a one-tailed test in advance. However, if you refrain from interpreting CIs merely to carry out NHST, and appreciate how one- and two-sided CIs relate, I'm comfortable with your choosing between a one- or two-sided CI as you analyze your data. Is it more informative for your readers who are interested in the new wrist therapy if you report and discuss your findings using the two-sided CI in panel C or the one-sided CI in panel D? Which fits better with your research aims?

Examples 3.2 in Chapter 3 included a CI for the vaccination rate needed to avoid an epidemic, and a CI for the tiny distance down to which a prediction of Einstein's special theory of relativity has been confirmed. In each case the researchers chose to interpret the UL of their two-sided CI, that being in each case a conservative value. Each team of researchers could reasonably have chosen instead to use upper end-point one-sided CIs.

I don't use one-sided CIs often, but it's unfortunate that they are usually ignored even by textbooks that cover CIs. They provide a useful additional option for understanding and communicating research results. Also, I suspect that understanding one-sided CIs, via the cat's-eye picture, probably increases our understanding of estimation in general.

In the next chapter I discuss replication, and what's likely to happen if you repeat your experiment over and over. That discussion follows on from what we've been considering in this section and gives the sixth approach to CI interpretation.

It's time for you to write your take-home messages from this long chapter. Have you been jotting them down as we go? Here are some hints, before I give you my list:

- Many types of error bars. Inferential and descriptive statistical information.
- Beautiful pictures of CIs. The fourth way to interpret CIs.
- The relation between CIs and *p* values. The fifth way to interpret CIs.

Exercises

4.1 You are listening to a research talk about an evaluation of a children's fitness program. The speaker displays Figure 4.11, which depicts the average improvement in performance scores after the program. You raise your hand and ask what the error bars represent. The speaker is flustered and anxiously consults colleagues, but eventually says "a confidence interval." You decide to wait until after the talk to seek confirmation it's a 95% CI. Assuming it is, suggest three interpretations without mentioning NHST or a *p* value. In each case identify which interpretation you're using.

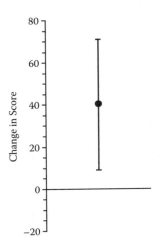

FIGURE 4.11
Mean improvement in children's performance after a fitness program.

4.2 The speaker is unsettled by your question, stops and consults notes, then apologizes and states that the figure shows SE bars. On this assumption suggest three interpretations, without mentioning NHST or a *p* value.

4.3 Now interpret the result using a *p* value, first assuming a 95% CI, then assuming SE bars.

4.4 Suppose the speaker now stated that *N* = 5. Would any of your previous answers change? How?

4.5 Use the **Normal z t** page of **ESCI chapters 1–4** to find the fatness ratio for the cat's-eye picture for a 95% CI when *N* = 30 and when *N* = 5. Compare with the ratio for σ known. *Hint*: You can use **Normal z t** to find the height of the *z* or *t* distribution at any point by clicking near red 5 to turn on **Heights**. Click to display **Two tails** then move the slider to find the height you want. To find, for example, the fatness ratio for a 95% CI, you could divide the height at the center of the distribution by the height at the .05 tail boundary.

4.6 Find an example in your own work or in a journal article, or invent an example, for which using the cat's-eye picture is helpful for interpreting a CI. Explain.

4.7 Use the **CI and p** page to find a benchmark, additional to those shown in Figure 4.9, for *p* = .20. *Hint*: Some eyeballing is required.

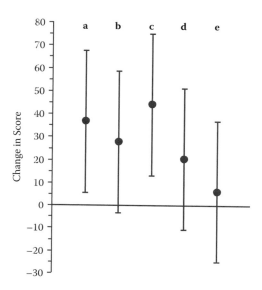

FIGURE 4.12
Some example means with 95% CIs.

4.8 Suppose Figure 4.12 shows means and 95% CIs, and that N is large or σ known. The vertical axis represents change scores and so we choose zero to be the null hypothesized value. Considering each result independently, estimate two-tailed p for each result.

4.9 Sketch a figure showing the mean and 95% CIs for the following results. Consider each independently, and assume in every case that N is large or σ known, and zero is the null hypothesized value:

  (i) $M = 5$ and two-tailed $p = .60$
  (ii) $M = 20$ and two-tailed $p = .15$
  (iii) $M = 15$ and two-tailed $p = .002$

4.10 In Figure 4.12, suppose result **b** is a 90% CI. Estimate p. Suppose result **d** is a 99% CI. Estimate p.

4.11 Find, in your own discipline, a report of a one-sided CI, or (probably easier) a one-tailed test. Is it used appropriately? What would you recommend?

4.12 Before reading on, check your own take-home messages. Revise or expand if you wish.

Take-Home Messages

- In a figure, a dot may be preferable to a column to represent a sample mean or other point estimate, because the sharp top of a column may suggest unwarranted precision.
- It's often valuable to show CIs as error bars in a figure. CIs provide inferential information, meaning information based on the sample that informs us about the population.
- The familiar error bar graphic is, unfortunately, used to show a range of different quantities. It's essential that every figure with error bars states clearly what the bars represent.
- Unfortunately, SE bars are common in some disciplines. SE bars don't give clear descriptive information or accurate inferential information. Always prefer CIs to SE bars.
- Choose 95% CIs unless there are good reasons to use a different level of confidence.
- A rule of eye is that double the length of SE bars gives, approximately, the 95% CI. The rule is reasonably accurate in many cases, but not all. For example, when $N < 10$ the 95% CI is longer than double the SE bars.
- Bars may also be used to represent descriptive information about a sample, for example, the SD or range.

- The sampling distribution of the sample mean is also the sampling distribution of estimation errors. Place that distribution (and its mirror image) on a CI and obtain the beautiful cat's-eye picture of a CI, which shows how plausibility, or relative likelihood, varies across and beyond the interval.

- *Take-home picture*: The cat's-eye picture of a 95% CI, as in Figure 4.5.

- Plausibility of a value for μ is greatest at M in the center of a CI. For a 95% CI it drops to about one-seventh at either limit. For a 50% CI it drops little to either limit but there are large tails beyond the interval. A 99% CI has to extend into the thin tails to achieve such a high level of confidence.

- The cat's-eye picture gives our fourth way to interpret CIs, by indicating how plausibility varies across and beyond the interval.

- The CI function is two smooth curves that plot the level of confidence, C, and two-tailed p value against the lower and upper limits of a CI.

- *Take-home movie*: At the **CI function** page, turn on the cat's eye and sweep the slider up and down to see how CI length and the cat's eye shaded area change with C.

- If a 95% CI lands with one limit at the null hypothesized value μ_0, two-tailed $p = .05$. Use the four benchmarks to estimate p for any position of a 95% CI in relation to μ_0. Approximately: One-third MOE of the 95% CI out from M gives $p = .50$; one-sixth MOE back from a limit of the CI gives $p = .10$; one-third MOE beyond a limit gives $p = .01$; and two-thirds MOE beyond a limit gives $p = .001$.

- Those benchmarks also allow imagining in the mind's eye the 95% CI, given μ_0, M, and p. That's a useful ability in a world that reports p values, but often not CIs.

- Our fifth way to interpret CIs is in terms of p values, although this is nonpreferred and may often not give the best interpretation.

- One-sided CIs correspond to one-tailed NHST, but are more informative. Choose one- or two-sided CIs depending on the research questions and the context.

5

Replication

What's likely to happen if you repeat an experiment? Suppose you obtain Hot Earth Awareness Test (HEAT) scores for a group of students, and calculate $M = 54.3$, [44.2, 64.4] and $p = .072$ to test the null hypothesis H_0: $\mu_0 = 45$. Does the CI give useful information about the likely result of a repeat of the experiment? Does the p value? These are the two main questions I discuss in this chapter. Those results actually refer to Experiment 1, near the bottom of Figures 5.1 and 5.8, so you could, if you like, scan either of those figures for a peek ahead at what repeats of that initial experiment might give.

This chapter is about what happens if you *replicate* an experiment over and over. Replication is fundamental to good scientific practice, so it's reasonable to ask what the statistical analysis of an initial experiment can tell us about what's likely to happen on replication. I'm most interested, of course, in how CIs compare with p values in the information they give about replication. Here's the plan:

- Replication in science.
- CIs and replication. What's the chance that the mean of a replication experiment will fall inside the CI of the initial experiment?
- Dance of the capture percentages.
- The sixth way to interpret a CI—as a prediction interval.
- p values and replication. What information does a p value give about what's likely to happen next time?
- Dance of the p values.
- Intuitions about randomness, and why they matter.

It turns out that CIs give useful information about replication, but p values give only extremely vague information. Considering replication thus gives one further reason to prefer the new statistics.

Replication in Science

Replication is at the heart of science. If you read a study claiming that toast usually lands buttered side down, you'll probably want to find at least one replication before you begin to take the result seriously. That's good scientific practice. A replication experiment inevitably differs a little from the initial experiment—the toast was a little different in shape and dropped in a slightly different way—and so again finding a similar result gives some reassurance that the initial result was not caused by some quirk of the initial experiment.

The most basic reason to want to replicate is to reduce the chance that the initial result was just a fluke—just an unlikely sampling fluctuation, just a CI that misses the parameter and so would appear red in ESCI. Any real-life replication will differ in small ways from the initial experiment, but we can think of an *idealized replication*, in which everything is identical except we take a fresh random sample from the same population. ESCI **CIjumping** does that, so the dance of the means and the dance of the CIs illustrate idealized replication experiments, and idealized replications are what I discuss in this chapter.

An *idealized replication* is identical to the initial experiment, except it uses a different random sample.

Replication is so central to science that it's natural to ask, whenever we read the result of an experiment, "What would happen if we did that again?" Whether the experiment investigated buttered toast or anything else, we can think of it as the first of a string of replications. It would be very helpful if that initial experiment could tell us what those replications are likely to find. In particular, what information does the CI or the *p* value from an initial experiment give us about replication experiments? What do they tell us about what's likely to happen next time?

Confidence Intervals and Replication

Figure 5.1 shows again the results of 25 idealized replications of our experiment in which we obtained HEAT scores from a sample of 15 students in a country where the population of students' HEAT scores has $\mu = 55$ and $\sigma = 20$. For the moment we're assuming σ is known, and so all CIs are the same length. Let's consider our initial experiment, shown as Experiment 1 near the bottom. I'll refer to its CI as the

I refer to the CI given by the initial experiment as the *initial CI*, and the mean of a replication experiment as a *replication mean*.

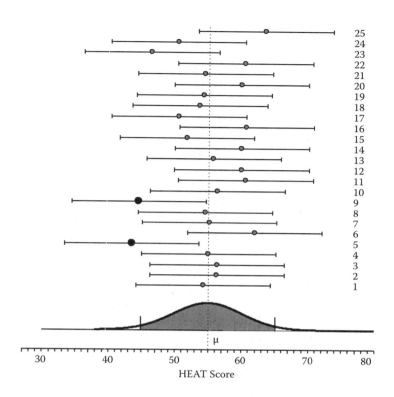

FIGURE 5.1
The 25 simulated results shown in Figure 4.4. The experiments are numbered. Experiment 1, the first experiment, is at the bottom.

initial CI, and the means of replication experiments as *replication means*. What does the initial CI tell us about replication means? What percentage of those means fall within the initial CI? To my eye, in Figure 5.1 the CI of Experiment 1 near the bottom includes all but one of the replication means above it. In considering CIs and replication, that's the question I'll focus on: Given an initial CI, what percentage of replication means are captured by that CI? I'll refer to that percentage as the *capture percentage* (CP) of the initial CI.

You can also think of CP as the percent-   The *capture percentage* (CP) is the percentage chance that, if we carried out one rep-   age of replication means that, in the long
lication experiment, its mean would fall   run, fall within the initial CI.
within the initial CI. Consider the curve at the bottom in Figure 5.1: That's the sampling distribution of the means of all replications, and so the question I'm asking is what proportion of the area under that curve lies within the interval defined by the CI of the first experiment?

Reflect on that for a moment. The sampling distribution curve in Figure 5.1 tells us where replication means will, in the long run, fall. I can focus on any interval I like, for example, from 34 to 54, then the area under the curve corresponding to that interval is the probability a replication mean lands within the interval. The interval 34 to 54 extends for most of the curve left of center, so I'm estimating that the area is a little less than .5, perhaps .45, and so that's my guess of the chance that a replication mean will fall in that interval. That interval is roughly the extent of the CI for Experiment 5, so my estimate of the CP for that experimental result is 45%.

Now consider Experiment 4, which happened to fall so M was almost exactly at μ. The central 95% of the area of the sampling distribution curve is shaded, and its width is 2MOE—the same as the width of each of the CIs displayed. The CI of Experiment 4 happens to line up almost perfectly with the shaded area, and so, if Experiment 4 is our initial experiment, its CP is almost exactly 95%. Returning to Experiment 1, whose CI happened to land a little left of center, what's the area under the curve for that CI? It would be the same length as the shaded area in the figure, but shifted a little to the left. The curve is highest in the center and is symmetric, so any shift from the center reduces the shaded area. The small shift to align the area under the CI for Experiment 1 would decrease the shaded area only a very small amount, and so CP for the first experiment would be a little less than 95% of replication means, perhaps 93% or 94%.

To estimate the area under the curve corresponding to any CI, imagine lines dropping down from each end of the CI to the curve. What's the area between those two imaginary lines? My eyeballing of that area corresponding to the CI for Experiment 6 gives CP of rather more than half the total area under the curve, perhaps 65%. We've already made a rough estimate of 45% for CP for the Experiment 5 interval. That interval misses μ, and so would be shown as red by ESCI. In the long run, 5% of 95% CIs appear red in ESCI, and those 5% of experiments would give CIs with CP less than 50%.

Most generally, the idea is that a CI gives some idea of how wide the dance of the means is. The width of the CI of our initial experiment gives some idea of how widely replication means are likely to dance around. A further important point is that, as we've seen, CP varies, depending on where our initial CI happens to fall. At first sight

Most CIs fall with their M close to μ and have a CP close to 95%. CIs that fall farther from μ have a lower CP. CIs that miss μ have a CP less than 50%.

that might seem surprising. Shouldn't a 95% CI have a .95 chance of including a replication mean? Well, no, as we've seen: If the CI falls so M is close to μ, it would capture close to 95% of replication means, but if the initial CI falls a little way from μ, its CP is less than 95%. If we're unlucky and obtain an extreme initial interval, its CP can even be less than 50%.

A Simulation of CIs and Replication

Now for an investigation of those ideas, using the ESCI page **CIs and replication**. Rather than writing detailed exercises, as in Chapter 3, I'll outline my own exploration and make a few suggestions. I invite you to fire up **ESCI chapters 5–6** and work along with me, but as usual you can follow the bold red numbers on screen, read the popouts, and explore as you wish. Figure 5.2 represents the population by marking μ with a horizontal line and indicating at the left a distance of σ above and σ below μ using vertical shaded bars. I'm using μ = 47 and σ = 50 to give CIs that happen to fit conveniently in the display area. We'll take samples of size N = 15. At the right is the sampling distribution of replication means. The central 95% area under that curve is shaded and marked by horizontal dotted lines.

You can think of Figure 5.2 as similar to **CIjumping**, but tipped on its side because I needed space on the screen for the lower figure as well. Here I'm using a different way of representing the population, by showing μ and σ at the left. Note the SE value of 12.9 reported near red 1. That's σ/√N and is the SD of the sampling distribution curve at the right. Make sure the box near red 2 is checked to indicate we're assuming σ is known.

I clicked the **One initial experiment** button near red 3 to run an experiment. Its 95% CI is shown in Figure 5.3. To estimate its CP of replication means, eyeball the area under the curve that's defined by the range of the CI. To my eye, CP is roughly 90%. If you're working in ESCI you'll have a different CI and different CP. I then unclicked **Shading** near red 2 to

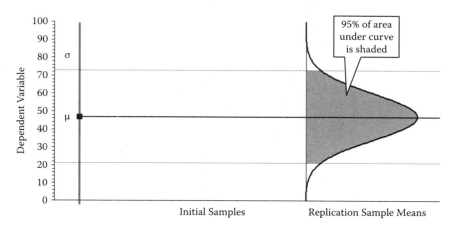

FIGURE 5.2
A figure from the **CIs and replication** page of **ESCI chapters 5–6**, showing the population mean μ and standard deviation σ at left, and the sampling distribution of sample means at right. The central 95% (or C%) of the area under the curve is shaded and marked by horizontal dotted lines.

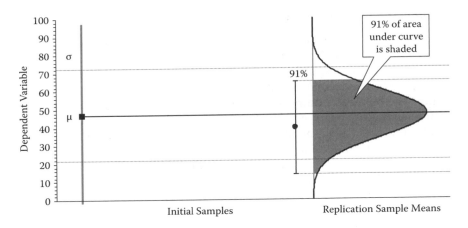

FIGURE 5.3
Click to take one initial sample and display its 95% CI. Its capture percentage (CP) of replication means is marked as 91% and is the shaded area under the sampling distribution curve within the range defined by the CI.

remove shading from the central 95% under the curve, and clicked near red 4 to see CP—which for me is actually 91%—displayed at the top of the CI, and to see the corresponding area under the curve shaded green.

I then clicked to take a further 19 samples, until my display looked like Figure 5.4. You can see my first interval, with CP = 91%, now at the far left. The latest CI is at the right, with CP = 88%—the shaded area under the

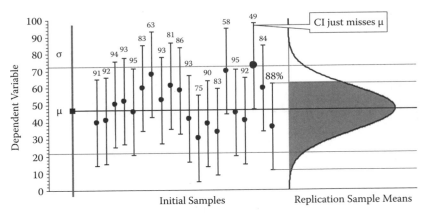

FIGURE 5.4
The first 20 initial samples, each with its 95% CI. The CP for each interval is marked at the top, giving the dance of the CP values. The shaded area indicates the CP for the latest CI, which is 88%. One CI just missed μ and has CP = 49%. Its mean is shown as a large black dot.

curve. I had one red CI, which just missed
µ and had CP 49%. In Figure 5.4 its mean
is shown as a large black dot. We could
refer to the sequence of values as the *dance of the CP values*.

The *dance of the CP values* is my term for the sequence of capture percentages in Figure 5.4.

Let's take stock. Examine Figure 5.4 or your ESCI display. Whatever our initial experiment—represented by its CI—the distribution of replication means will, in the long run, be the sampling distribution curve on the right. Our initial CI will capture some percentage of those replication means—the CP—depending on where it happens to fall in relation to µ. Most CIs fall with their M close to µ, and these have CP close to 95%—the maximum possible. For CIs that happen to fall farther from µ, the area they define under the curve drops and so their CP is lower. CIs that miss µ have CP less than 50%.

Distribution of the Capture Percentages

You may have noticed that in the lower figure ESCI builds a dot histogram of the CP values, as in Figure 5.5. Click **Clear**, take 20 samples, then check that the 20 CP values shown in the upper figure, like Figure 5.4, match the 20 dots in the lower figure. I next clicked the **Run–Stop** button and watched the green shaded area under the curve bounce around, and the dance of the CP values marked on the intervals. When the simulation stopped after 500 samples the lower display looked like Figure 5.5.

Cumming and Maillardet (2006) investigated the distribution of CP values, as shown in Figure 5.5, and found that, in the long run, the mean of the CP distribution for 95% CIs is 83% and the median 90%. The difference between mean and median is, of course, caused by the strong negative skew. The maximum CP is 95% and the most common is 94% to 95%. Most CIs will capture around 85% to 95% of replication means, with some capturing less, and just a few capturing considerably less. On average, a 95% CI captures 83% of replication means. Keep clear the distinction: 95% of such intervals will capture µ—that's the definition of a 95% CI—but on average such an interval captures 83% of replication means.

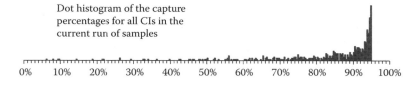

Dot histogram of the capture percentages for all CIs in the current run of samples

0%   10%   20%   30%   40%   50%   60%   70%   80%   90%   100%

FIGURE 5.5
The distribution of CP values of the 95% CIs for 500 samples, with σ assumed known.

Dot histogram of the capture
percentages for all CIs in the
current run of samples

FIGURE 5.6
The distribution of CP values of the 95% CIs for the 500 samples shown in Figure 5.5, with $N = 15$ and σ not assumed known.

The next step is to unclick the box near red 2, so we're no longer assuming σ is known. Now we're using t and s for each sample to calculate the CI for that sample, and so the CIs vary in length. If N is small, they vary greatly in length. Length variation means additional variation in CP values. Most noticeable is that there are now dots indicating CP values greater than 95%, as Figure 5.6 shows for the same 500 samples shown in Figure 5.5. Study the top figure in ESCI to see what's going on: When an interval that happens to be rather long—its s happens to be larger than σ—lands so its M is close to μ, it can span a very large area under the curve, meaning its CP is large and greater than 95%.

Play around with the simulation as you wish. Once you've taken a run of samples, you can click on and off the assumption that σ is known, and also vary the value of C. Watch how the dot histogram changes. If you change N, or the parameters of the population, you need to start sampling again.

Cumming and Maillardet (2006) found, perhaps surprisingly, that the mean and median CP values do not change greatly with sample size. For $N = 10$, mean CP is 86% and median CP is 92%—only a little greater than the 83% and 90% for large N, or σ assumed known. Therefore, for practical purposes, we only need to remember mean 83% and median 90% as a general summary of the information a 95% CI gives about replication. Do researchers know this? Box 5.1 reports our study, which found evidence that researchers generally have quite good understanding of CIs and replication, but tend to underestimate the extent of variability. Many believe, incorrectly, that a 95% CI will in the long run include 95% of replication means, rather than the correct average of 83%.

Consider what the average CP of 83% tells us in practice. As researchers, we have only the one 95% CI calculated from our single data set. We know its CP will most likely be around 90% to 95%, or perhaps more if we used t to calculate the interval, but perhaps its CP is lower, and just possibly it's very much lower. We'll never know the accurate CP of a particular interval, because we don't know μ and can't carry out a very large number of replications. But over a lifetime of working with 95% CIs, average CP will be 83%. We can also say that the probability a single replication will give a mean that lands within our particular CI is .83.

BOX 5.1 RESEARCHERS' UNDERSTANDING OF CIs AND REPLICATION

How well do researchers understand what information CIs give about replication? Cumming, Williams, and Fidler (2004) sent emails to authors of articles in leading journals of medicine, behavioral neuroscience, and psychology, inviting them to visit a website where they saw a mean and 95% CI as in Figure 5.7. They were asked to click to indicate where they thought the means of 10 replications of the original experiment might plausibly fall. As they clicked, horizontal lines appeared to mark where they'd clicked. We then asked for comments about how they did the task, and how they thought about CIs and replication experiments.

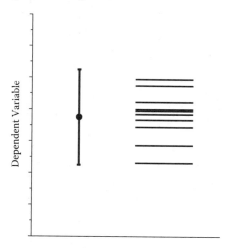

FIGURE 5.7
Respondents saw the mean and 95% CI at left, then clicked in 10 positions where they thought the means of 10 replication experiments might plausibly fall. Lines appeared where they clicked, for example, as at right.

Patterns of responses varied considerably, but Figure 5.7 shows a typical response. Fully 55% of respondents included all 10 means within the CI. In their comments, many stated that they expected that 95% of means would on average fall in the original CI. There were no signs of any differences between disciplines, or between early- and late-career researchers.

We concluded that in some important ways the respondents had good understanding of CIs and replication. They appreciated that the CI gave information relevant for positioning and spreading their 10 responses, and that means are likely to follow, approximately, a normal distribution, as indicated by the bunching of central positions and spreading of upper and lower positions. On the other hand, most believed incorrectly that 95% of replication means will on average fall within the CI. They therefore tended not to spread their responses sufficiently, and to include too many of them within the CI, compared with the accurate average of 83% of replication means falling within a 95% CI. CIs appear much more frequently in medical journals than in journals of behavioral neuroscience or psychology, so it's interesting that the presumed much greater familiarity of medical respondents with CIs was not reflected in any notable differences in their performance.

Overall, we concluded that researchers have quite good understanding of CIs in relation to replication, although here, as in many other cases, they tend to underestimate the extent of sampling variability.

CI Interpretation 6: Prediction Interval for a Replication Mean

Considering replication gives our sixth way to interpret a CI. A 95% CI has a .83 chance of including the mean of a replication experiment. In other words we can regard any 95% CI as an 83% *prediction interval* for a replication mean, meaning it's an interval that has an 83% chance of including the mean of a replication experiment. That 83% chance is an average over the majority of intervals

Interpretation 6 of a CI. A 95% CI has an 83% chance of capturing the mean of a replication experiment, so we can regard it as an 83% prediction interval for a replication mean.

with CP around 90% to 95% or more, and the small proportion of intervals with lower CP. Keep in mind the distributions shown in Figures 5.5 and 5.6, and the chance that we may have been unlucky and obtained a CI with a low CP.

The width of our CI gives a reasonable idea of how much replication means are likely to bounce around, and we can say that there's a .83 chance that a single replication mean will fall within our CI. My conclusion is that a CI gives useful information about what's likely to happen on replication, although as usual we need to bear in mind the possibility that our interval misses μ—and would be red in ESCI—and so gives not such helpful information about replication.

This is the spot for a couple of examples of researchers interpreting a CI as a prediction interval when discussing their results. Alas, I haven't

TABLE 5.1

Six Ways to Interpret a 95% CI for μ

1	One from the *dance*	Our interval is randomly chosen from an infinite sequence, the dance of the CIs. In the long run 95% capture μ, and 5% miss—this is the definition of confidence level. Intervals that miss appear red in ESCI.
2	Interpret our interval: a range of *plausible* values	The interval is a range of plausible values for μ. We're 95% confident that our interval includes μ. Interpret any point in the interval, including the central point *M*, and the lower and upper limits (*LL* and *UL*). Values outside the interval are relatively implausible for μ. The limits are likely lower and upper bounds for μ.
3	MOE gives the *precision*	MOE gives the precision of estimation. It's the likely maximum error of estimation, although larger errors are possible.
4	The *cat's-eye* picture	The cat's-eye picture shows how plausibility, or relative likelihood, varies within and beyond the CI. Plausibility is about 7 times greater at *M* than at a limit.
5	The relation between CIs and *p values*	If the CI falls so either limit is at μ_0, the null hypothesized value, then two-tailed *p* = .05. Use benchmarks to estimate *p* for the CI falling so μ_0 is inside the interval (in which case *p* > .05), or outside it (*p* < .05).
6	*Prediction* interval for a replication mean	On average, a 95% CI is an 83% prediction interval. There's a .83 chance that a 95% CI will capture the mean of a single replication experiment.

found suitable examples, so the exercises at the end of the chapter will have to suffice.

We've now met all six ways I'm suggesting for interpreting a CI. Table 5.1 summarizes the six, for the case of a 95% CI around *M* that estimates μ. All the interpretations can be used for CIs that estimate any other parameter, and for intervals with any level of confidence.

---

p Values and Replication

A CI gives useful information about replication, but does a *p* value? You carry out Experiment 1 in Figure 5.1, calculate *p* = .072, then repeat the experiment. What *p* value is the replication likely to give? Unfortunately, and perhaps surprisingly, the answer is "just about any value," and so the conclusion is that *p* does not give good information about replication. Figure 5.8 shows the same 25 simulated results shown in Figure 5.1, but with the addition of a null hypothesized value μ_0 = 45. Perhaps 10 years ago, when there was less awareness of climate change, a large national

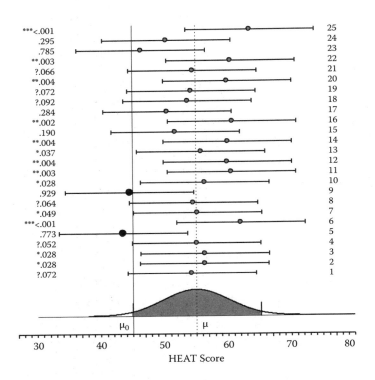

FIGURE 5.8
The 25 simulated results shown in Figure 5.1, but with a null hypothesized value $\mu_0 = 45$ added, and the two-tailed p values shown at left. The p values are labeled with conventional asterisks: *** for $p < .001$; ** for $.001 < p < .01$; * for $.01 < p < .05$; and with "?" for $.05 < p < .10$. The figure illustrates the dance of the means, the dance of the CIs, and the dance of the p values.

survey in our country established that the mean HEAT score for students was 45. Now we take a sample of 15 students—yes, I know, unrealistically small—to estimate how much HEAT scores may have changed over the 10 years. Figure 5.8 shows a few of the infinite sequence of results we might obtain, and gives for each the two-tailed p value for testing that null value of 45.

The sample means in Figure 5.8 bounce around either side of μ, with any of the CIs giving some idea of how wide that dance of the means is. Can

I refer to the bouncing around of p values with replication, as in Figure 5.8, as the dance of the p values.

the dance of the p values add anything to that familiar picture? The p values reflect where the CIs fall in relation to the μ_0 line at 45. We can use the benchmarks from Chapter 4 to confirm that the p values shown are at least roughly correct. If the LL of a CI is close to 45, p is close to .05. For CIs farther to the right, p becomes successively smaller, and for CIs farther to the left, p becomes successively larger. However, it's the distance of M from μ_0 that determines p, and so, for CIs so far to the left that M falls below μ_0, two-tailed p starts decreasing for M farther below μ_0. For this reason, p for Experiment 5 is a little lower than p for Experiment 9.

CIs and p values are based on the same underlying statistical theory, and we discussed in Chapter 4 how it's possible to translate from one to the other. Even so, I suggest that Figure 5.8 shows a dramatic difference in how CIs and p values reflect sampling variability and the information they give about replication. The dance of the means and the dance of the CIs may be wider than we'd like, but at least any single CI gives some idea of the extent that the means bounce around. In stark contrast, however, the dance of the p values ranges from <.001 to .93, which is almost the full range possible for p. Replicate, and we could get just about any p value at all. In other words, any single p value could easily have been very different if we'd just happened to draw some other random sample, and a single p value seems to give very poor information about the whole dance.

Consider our usual research situation in which we have just a single experiment. Would you prefer to know M and the CI, or M and the p value? I suggest that knowing the CI gives some idea of the whole infinite sequence of potential results, whereas knowing p gives hardly any information at all about the potential infinite sequence of p values. To put it differently, the CI is an 83% prediction interval for a replication mean, but a single p value hardly gives a basis for predicting anything at all about replication. Knowing $p = .072$ for Experiment 1 hardly says anything about the full set of p values shown in Figure 5.8.

The Sampling Variability of p

There's a further surprising thing about the variability of p. Consider any introductory statistics textbook you know. Very likely it has a chapter on sampling, with careful explanations of the sampling distribution of the mean, and the SE. If CIs are discussed there may be a figure like Figure 4.4 to illustrate sampling variability for CIs. The experimental design chapter may discuss strategies to reduce sampling variability.

That's all good and proper. The surprising thing is the contrast with p. The sampling variability of p values is large, as Figure 5.8 illustrates, but that basic fact is hardly ever mentioned in statistics textbooks. Far from considering p as subject to large sampling variability, usual NHST practice is to make decisions by comparing the exact calculated p value with an exact criterion such as .05. Alternatively, following Fisher, and as I explain in Chapter 2, a p value accurate to two or three decimal places may be used as an index of strength of evidence against the null hypothesis. In either case, using exact p values suggests that researchers are not aware that p could easily have been very different merely because of sampling variability. Yes, I know that in Chapter 2 I recommended reporting $p = .03$ instead of $p < .05$, because $p = .03$ is more informative about the strength of evidence. It is, but now we know that neither gives us good information about replication or evidence or anything else. In any case, it seems that researchers are very aware of sampling variability in many contexts, but have a blind spot in relation to p. This may be one reason they place too much confidence in NHST.

You may be thinking that I should take my own advice and go back to Chapter 4 and think again about all those calculations and estimates of p values. Indeed! I generally use p values as little as possible and, if I do use them, I regard them as giving only very rough suggestions. I'll certainly never fret about whether p is .04 or .06, and I'll probably hardly notice whether it's .03 or .08. The benchmarks of Chapter 4 are useful to know, but take them and indeed most p values with a very large grain of salt. Similarly, if ever we're examining whether a CI includes a null hypothesized value or not, we shouldn't worry whether it's *just* inside or *just* outside the interval. The smooth shape of the cat's-eye picture tells us that just within or just beyond a CI limit are very similar outcomes.

p Intervals

Suppose you obtain $p = .05$ in an initial experiment. If you repeat the experiment, are you likely to get p within an interval like (.04, .06)? Or (.01, .2)? Or do you need to consider even wider intervals? That's my question here: I discuss p and replication by considering prediction intervals for p. I hope my discussion is understandable, but, if you wish, you can skip to the bulleted conclusions at the end, then go on to the next section, Dance of the p Values.

Let's refer to the p value given by a replication experiment as *replication p*, and let's define a *p interval* as an 80% prediction interval for replica-

I refer to the p value given by a replication experiment as *replication p*, and define a *p interval* as an 80% prediction interval for replication p.

tion p. In Cumming (2008) I discussed p intervals and explained how to calculate them. If $p_{obt} = .05$ is the two-tailed p value we obtain in our initial experiment, then the p interval is (0, .38), which means there's an 80% chance that a replication experiment gives two-tailed p somewhere between 0 and .38, and fully a 20% chance that p is greater than .38. Perhaps surprisingly, based on reasonable assumptions I described in the article, $p_{obt} = .05$ always gives that p interval of (0, .38). Shortly we'll use ESCI **p intervals** to do the calculations.

Why not the 95% prediction interval for replication p? One reason is that 80% intervals are so extremely wide I was worried that if I focused on 95% intervals, which are even wider, people might dismiss my analysis as too extreme. For example, if $p_{obt} = .05$, the 95% prediction interval for two-tailed

p is actually (0, .82), or virtually any value at all. That's consistent with what we saw in Figure 5.8. You might also ask why I don't discuss CIs for p. The answer is that a CI estimates a population parameter, but there's no population parameter corresponding to p, so no CI for p is possible.

My hope is that appreciating how very wide p intervals are should lead researchers to be very cautious in concluding anything from a p value. Perhaps researchers should be required to report the p interval whenever they report a p value, just as they are expected to report a CI with every point estimate. That would be an excellent idea. For example, if a researcher obtained the results in Experiment 1 in Figure 5.8 and wished to report a test of the null hypothesis $\mu_0 = 45$, the report should include a statement like $p = .072$, p interval (0, .44). That's a justifiable way to represent the vagueness of the p value, and requiring the report of such p intervals could be a great way to encourage the adoption of the new statistics.

In Cumming (2008) I explained two ways to calculate p intervals. One is based on the assumption that $M = \mu$, meaning M in the initial experiment estimates the population mean precisely. This is an unrealistic assumption, but it's often made because it simplifies the formulas. The other approach does not require that assumption and is the method used in the **p intervals** page of ESCI, which you can use to calculate the p interval for any p_{obt}.

There are two further slight complications I need to explain. Previously I described p intervals for two-tailed replication p. As an alternative, after calculating two-tailed p_{obt} for the initial experiment it could be reasonable to consider one-tailed p for replication experiments, focusing on results going in the same direction as the initial experiment. If so, you want the p interval for one-tailed replication p. As examples, if two-tailed $p_{obt} = .05$, the p interval for one-tailed replication p is (0, .22), and if $p_{obt} = .072$, the interval is (0, .27).

The second slight complication is quite different, although unfortunately it's easy to confuse with the question of one- or two-tailed replication p. The p intervals I've mentioned so far have been *one-sided*, meaning their left limit is zero, and there's a 20% chance that replication p falls beyond their right limit. For example, I've just stated that when two-tailed $p_{obt} = .05$ the p interval for one-tailed replication p is (0, .22). That's a one-sided p interval because

A *one-sided p* interval has zero as its lower limit, and there's a 20% chance that replication p is greater than the upper limit. A *two-sided p* interval has a 10% chance that replication p falls below its lower limit, and 10% that it falls above its upper limit. (In either case, replication p may be one- or two-tailed: That's a different issue.)

0 is the lower limit. As an alternative, we could consider *two-sided p* intervals, where there's a 10% chance that replication p falls below the left limit of the interval, and a 10% chance that it falls above the right limit. For $p_{obt} = .05$, the two-sided p interval for one-tailed replication p is (.00008, .44). Two-sided p intervals may seem more natural for larger p values. For example, if $p_{obt} = .30$, the interval is (.002, .78). Just to spell

out what that means, if an initial experiment gave two-tailed $p_{obt} = .30$, we know there's an 80% chance that a replication experiment will give one-tailed p falling in that interval, a 10% chance that $p < .002$, and a 10% chance that $p > .78$. As usual, the p interval is extremely wide.

I should also mention that the p interval calculations assume that σ is known and are based on z rather than t, but in Cumming (2008) I reported simulations showing that p intervals based on t are broadly similar. All my general conclusions still hold if σ is not assumed known and calculations are based on t.

You may care to fire up the ESCI **p intervals** page and check the p interval values I've mentioned, and calculate any others you are interested in. Use the slider to set your initial p_{obt}, which is assumed to be two-tailed. You then have a choice of four p intervals. The yellow panel reports p intervals for one-tailed replication p, and the tan panel for two-tailed. Each panel gives both a one-sided and a two-sided p interval. Select with care, and always state clearly which p interval you are reporting.

You might be wondering why I've hardly mentioned N, and why the **p intervals** page doesn't require you to enter a value of N. It may seem surprising, but p intervals depend only on p_{obt} and not on N. Note that p_{obt} is calculated from N and the sample ES. A given p_{obt} may reflect a larger N and smaller sample ES, or smaller N and larger sample ES, but the p interval reflects only the p_{obt}, and not the particular values of N and sample ES that gave it. I explained this further in Cumming (2008).

By now you might be suspicious of my discussion of p values. The intervals might seem so enormously wide, the implications for NHST so drastic, that surely, you think, I have somehow exaggerated things, or hidden something? It's good to be skeptical, and to insist on seeing convincing arguments and clear examples. I believe, however, that the picture I'm painting is fair and accurate. In Cumming (2008) I illustrated in several different ways the large uncertainty in p, and gave several explanations as to why a p value is such a poor basis for inference. I cited references that made the same points. My conclusions were as follows:

- A p value gives only extremely vague information about replication, or what our initial experiment might have obtained instead, simply because of sampling variability.

- A p value is typically a very poor measure of the strength of evidence against a null hypothesis.

- To the extent that it does indicate strength of evidence, a p value typically exaggerates the amount of evidence against the null hypothesis. In most cases, only very small p values ($p < .001$ or, perhaps, $p < .01$) give a reasonable basis for rejecting a null hypothesis. Often in such cases, however, the effect is large and clear, so statistical analysis is scarcely required to reach a conclusion. The effect probably passes the "interocular trauma test," meaning it hits you between the eyes, so very small p hardly tells us anything extra anyway.

- Anything other than a very small p value gives virtually no useful information at all.

Considering CIs and replication, Box 5.1 reported our study that found researchers generally have a reasonable understanding of CIs and replication, although they underestimate to some extent the amount of variation with replication. For p values, however, Box 5.2 reports evidence that researchers underestimate quite considerably the extent of variability of p values with replication. Researchers' judgments about CIs in relation to replication therefore seem to be better than their judgments of p in relation to replication.

In the following final section about p values and replication I'll describe an animation of the dance of the p values and a picture of the distribution of p. It turns out that statistical power is important—as it usually is, if we're using NHST.

Dance of the p Values

The **Dance p** page of ESCI uses a simulation of an experiment comparing two independent groups: an Experimental group (E) and Control group (C). That may strike you as more realistic than the single group experiments I've mainly been using so far. Figure 5.9 illustrates one experiment, after I clicked the button near red 2 to run an experiment, then clicked near red 4 to display the floating difference axis, and again to display a CI on the difference. Let's think of the dependent variable as relaxation scores, where the C population mean is 50 and the E population, with mean 60, refers to people who've had the benefit of your new relaxation therapy. Your therapy thus increases relaxation scores by an average 10 points.

I'm assuming normally distributed populations, each with known standard deviation $\sigma = 20$. Both E and C samples have size $N = 32$. The population ES is the difference between the E and C means, which is 10. This is half of σ, so Cohen's $\delta = 0.50$, as marked in Figure 5.9; that's a medium-sized effect. (There's more about Cohen's d and δ in Chapter 11.) As usual, you can explore the simulation as you wish. Change the E and C means, and σ, and see the population effect size δ change.

I clicked **Display p values** near red 4 and saw $p = .08$ displayed to the left of the CI for the first experiment. I then took a further 24 experiments

---

BOX 5.2 RESEARCHERS' UNDERSTANDING OF p VALUES AND REPLICATION

Lai, Fidler, and Cumming (in press) investigated how researchers think about p values and replication. We conducted three email surveys that asked about p values in three different ways, but I'll describe here just one of the question formats we used. We sent emails to authors of articles published in journals in medicine, psychology, or statistics. Here is a shortened version of what the email presented:

> Suppose you conduct a study to compare a Treatment and a Control group, each $N = 40$. A test of the difference gives $p = .02$ (two-tailed). Suppose you carry out the experiment a further 10 times.

Respondents were then asked to "enter 10 p values that could plausibly be obtained in this series of replications." They typed in 10 p values. Note that the task was parallel with that described in Box 5.1 for our study of CIs and replication.

For each response set of 10 p values we used the spread of the values to calculate an estimate of the respondent's subjective p interval, meaning the interval the respondent thinks has an 80% chance of including p from a replication experiment. We then used a formula from Cumming (2008) to calculate the chance that interval actually has of including replication p.

Many respondents described the task as unfamiliar and difficult. We found great variation over respondents, but 98% of subjective p intervals were too short, meaning respondents almost always underestimated the extent that p varies with replication. On average, estimated intervals were 40% intervals, rather than 80% intervals. Results were similar for respondents from medicine, psychology, and statistics. The other two surveys used different question formats, but gave broadly similar results. We concluded that there's great variability over individuals, but, in general, researchers tend to severely underestimate the extent that p varies over replications of an experiment.

---

and watched the dance of the CIs, until my display appeared as in Figure 5.10. My first experiment, as in Figure 5.9, now appears at the bottom in Figure 5.10. I clicked **Display μ_{diff} line** near red 4 to get the vertical dotted line marking the population ES of 10. As we'd expect, Figure 5.10 shows the CIs bouncing around that line. It also shows the very great

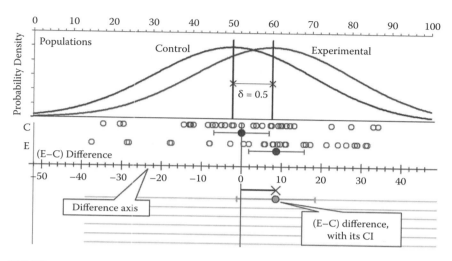

FIGURE 5.9

The **Dance p** page of ESCI, showing one experiment comparing two independent groups, each N = 32. For the Control (C) and Experimental (E) samples, the 32 data points appear as a dot plot, with the sample mean and 95% CI. The lower axis is a difference axis, with zero positioned at the mean of the C sample. The cross and dot beneath it mark the (E – C) mean difference, with the 95% CI on that difference.

variation in p values we first encountered in Figure 5.8. The variation in p is highlighted by asterisks and color patches that shade from bright red for *** to deep blue for $p > .10$. The values are rounded to three decimal places, so a value of .000 means $p < .0005$.

At this point I suggest you watch the video **Dance p**, available from this book's website: www.thenewstatistics.com. It shows the dance of the p values in several different ways. Click **Dance of the p values** near red 4 for one of them. Run a typical experiment and you are visiting the p value casino: Your obtained p is chosen randomly from the infinite sequence of p values, 25 of which appear in Figure 5.10. Obtaining low p is a bit like winning a prize at the casino. Click **Display casino** below the buttons to play.

If you click near red 5, you can turn on sounds to mark different p values. (The sound files must be in the same folder as ESCI; see Appendix A.) A three-star result, meaning $p < .001$, gives a high, bright trumpet, whereas $p > .10$ is marked by a low, sad trombone. Click near red 9 to see little figures that jump for joy at *** but show deep sadness for $p > .10$. The buttons near red 8 let you try them out. I'm speculating that p values can trigger such emotions. It would be intriguing to investigate the extent to which various p values do elicit different emotions. So far as I know, that remains an unexplored question.

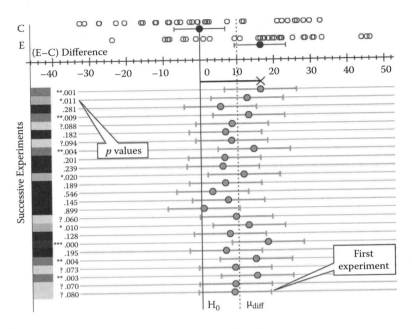

FIGURE 5.10
Twenty-five experiments as they appear in ESCI **Dance p**, with their two-tailed p values shown at left. The first experiment appearing at the bottom is the one shown in Figure 5.9. The p values are marked with asterisks and "?" as in Figure 5.8. They are also marked with color patches that on the screen shade from bright red for *** to deep blue for $p > .10$.

The Distribution of the p Value

Running the simulation builds a frequency histogram of the p values. Click near red 6 to see the histogram. Figure 5.11 shows my histogram after 1,500 experiments. (To speed up the simulation try turning off display of various features, such as p values and the difference axis.) Each small square in a column represents p from one experiment. Above the columns are the percentages of p values that fell in different columns and the percentages expected by theoretical calculation. The horizontal lines, which are red on the screen, mark the column heights expected theoretically, given the number of experiments run so far. Figure 5.11 shows that there's good agreement between theoretical expectations and the results of the 1,500 experiments in my simulation run.

The histogram in Figure 5.11 represents the distribution of the p value for a two-independent-groups experiment, $N = 32$ in each group, with a population ES of $\delta = 0.5$. ESCI reports near red 3 that the power of this experiment is .52 if two-tailed $\alpha = .05$. Power, as we discussed in Chapter 2,

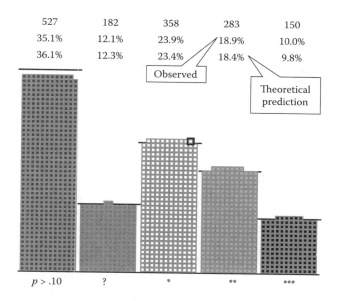

527   182   358   283   150
35.1%   12.1%   23.9%   18.9%   10.0%
36.1%   12.3%   23.4%   18.4%   9.8%

Observed

Theoretical prediction

$p > .10$?   *   **   ***

FIGURE 5.11

The frequency histogram of p values, for 1,500 simulated experiments like those shown in Figure 5.10. The highlighted point at the top of the * column marks p for the most recent experiment. Above each column the top number reports the frequency for that column, then the number below is the percentage of the 1,500 p values that landed in that column. The number below that (red in ESCI) is the percentage expected theoretically in the column. The solid horizontal lines (also red in ESCI) indicate the theoretically expected height of each column.

is the probability that the experiment gives a p value less than .05 for a stated population ES. Power is thus the chance of getting a *, **, or *** result, which is the sum of the probabilities of landing in any of the three rightmost columns in Figure 5.11. Adding the theoretical percentages (red on the screen) for those columns gives 23.4 + 18.4 + 9.8 = 51.6%, or a power of .516. Adding the percentages observed for our run of simulations gives 23.9 + 18.9 + 10.0 = 52.8%, in reasonable agreement with theory.

I chose an example with power around .50 because, as Box 2.2 reported, much research in NHST disciplines has average power of only around .5 to find a medium-sized effect, such as $\delta = 0.5$. My examples are thus typical of much published research.

It turns out that the distribution of p values depends only on power. (I'm still assuming σ is known.) Any experiment, whatever the N and δ, will have the distribution of p shown in Figure 5.11 if the power is .52. The experiment shown in Figures 4.4, 5.1, and 5.8 is a single-group experiment with $N = 15$ and $\delta = 0.5$. This has power .49, so the distribution of *p* is similar, as the similarity of the sets of *p* values in Figures 5.8 and 5.10 reflect.

If you simulate an experiment with higher power, how would you expect the distribution of *p* to differ from that shown in Figure 5.11? Would ** and *** results be more or less frequent? What about an experiment with lower power? Make some guesses and sketch what the histogram might look like in each case.

To check out your predictions, click near red 2 to **Clear** the simulation then adjust the slider near red 7 so the columns have a convenient height. You'll see a pattern like those in Figure 5.12. The columns depict the theoretically calculated distribution of *p* for experiments with power as shown near red 3. You can change the vertical scale at any time with the slider. You can change the power by using any of the controls. Start by using the slider near red 1 to change the E mean. Watch how the E distribution moves and δ changes, and observe the consequent changes in power and the *p* histogram. Then restore the E mean to 60, and adjust *N*. This time δ doesn't change, but power and the distribution of *p* do change.

Here are two questions to explore:

1. How do the *p* distributions compare for various combinations of δ and *N* that give the same power? For example, try δ = 1.0, *N* = 8; then δ = 0.5, *N* = 32; then δ = 0.25, *N* = 128. (As before, adjust the E mean to change δ.) All those pairs of values give power = .52.

2. In general, does power seem more responsive to changes in δ or to changes in *N*?

Figure 5.12 shows the distribution of *p* for four values of power. In every case the distribution is wide—the variation in *p* is large. The top left panel shows the distribution when the null hypothesis is true, so δ = 0 and the alternative hypothesis is the same as the null hypothesis. Therefore power is the same as the Type I error rate, which we set to be α = .05, and so power for the top left panel is .05. When the null hypothesis is true, the distribution in the top left panel applies whatever the value of *N*. The other three panels show the distribution of *p* for larger values of power. The δ values shown give the stated values of power when *N* = 32. The lower left panel describes the distribution of *p* for the experiment illustrated in Figures 5.9, 5.10, and 5.11, with power = .52. I chose also to illustrate power = .8 because, as I'll mention in Chapter 12, power = .8 is often, for planning purposes, regarded as reasonable. Power of .9, as illustrated in the lower right panel, is very high by the standards of most published research in NHST disciplines.

Consider the dilemma if you want to base inference on, for example, p_{obt} = .03. You wish to make a statement about the true value of δ, so you

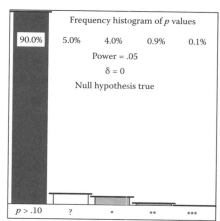

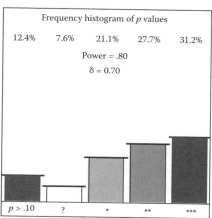

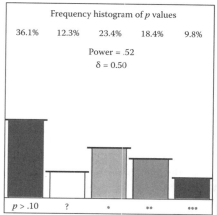

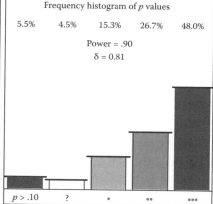

FIGURE 5.12

The distribution of the p value for four values of power. In the top left panel, the null hypothesis is true, so $\delta = 0$. This distribution applies for any value of N. In the other three panels, the value shown for δ gives the stated value of power when $N = 32$. The lower left panel matches Figure 5.11, except with a different vertical scale.

need to consider which distribution of p your value of .03 comes from. Figure 5.12 shows that such a * result has a 4% chance of occurring if $\delta = 0$ (top left panel), and a 23.4% chance if $\delta = .50$ (bottom left panel). Those two likelihoods are different by less than a factor of 6, so $p = .03$ is hardly a good reason for rejecting the null hypothesis in favor of $\delta = .50$. Yes, a *** result is a fairly good reason for rejecting the null hypothesis in favor of $\delta = .50$, but comparing the heights of the ** columns suggests that even a ** result gives only modest grounds for rejecting the null hypothesis in favor of any of the other distributions in Figure 5.12. Such arguments underlie the conclusions I reported earlier that only very small p values may give useful information, and other p values tell us very little. In Cumming (2008) I discussed these issues further.

Note that by comparing heights of the * columns I'm *not* saying that $\delta = .50$ is about six times more probable than $\delta = 0$. To say that would be to commit the inverse probability fallacy we discussed in Chapter 2. All we can say is that the relative column heights give us some idea of how relatively plausible the different values of δ may be, given the results of our single experiment.

The four panels in Figure 5.12 also illustrate one of the main principles of experimental design: It's important to have power as high as possible. High power means a greater chance of the *** (or, perhaps, **) results that give a reasonable basis for rejecting the null hypothesis.

Returning to the two questions I raised earlier, the distribution of p is the same for a particular power, whatever combination of δ and N values give that power. The distribution is thus the same for the three combinations of δ and N I suggested in the first question, and the same as that shown in Figure 5.11 and the lower left panel of Figure 5.12. Note how δ and N influence power: If we halve the population effect size δ, we must multiply N by 4 to achieve the same power. In this way δ generally influences power more than N does. To increase the power of our experiment, looking for a larger population effect may be a better strategy than increasing N. Yes, as a Christmas gift you would like big N, but perhaps you would be even happier to find that the size of the effect you're investigating is large.

There are two main reasons why I'm spending so much time discussing p, even though my overall message is that the new statistics should be preferred to NHST. First, the advantages of CIs in relation to replication may be clearer if they are contrasted with the shortcomings of p in relation to replication. It seems to me that the dance of the p values does that quite emphatically. Second, a CI expresses all the information a data set provides about the population parameter, whereas the previous discussion of the distributions of p in Figure 5.12 suggests that p usually gives a very poor basis for choosing among various hypothesized values of δ. Now I'm going to leave p values and even CIs for a while and talk about the intriguing topic of *randomness*—which has been an underlying theme all through this chapter.

Intuitions About Randomness

So far in this book we've observed many cases of random variability and discussed how large or small it is. Unfortunately, however, researchers and other people tend to hold two misconceptions about variability and randomness that are troublesome for research. In this section I'll describe the misconceptions and encourage you to bear them in mind when analyzing data or reading research results. Here are the two misconceptions:

1. People often underestimate the extent of sampling variability.
2. People often don't understand that randomness is lumpy in the short term and highly predictable in the long term.

As a consequence of these misconceptions, researchers may over-interpret particular aspects of sample data that reflect only random sampling variability. In addition they underestimate the extent to which results are likely to be different if an experiment is repeated, or if results of several similar experiments are compared.

I suggest that we need two strategies to counter these misconceptions, and I hope this book contributes to both. First, demonstrations should help students and researchers understand random variability better and increase awareness of possible misconceptions. Second, we should routinely use CIs to give an accurate picture of uncertainty in data, and thus help any readers of our research reports make better interpretations, less influenced by misconceptions. Those two suggestions seem to me reasonable, but need further empirical investigation. I'll now discuss four examples of randomness to illustrate the issues.

Stars, Glowworms, and Penguins

As a first example, consider Figure 5.13. Look carefully at each of the four squares in turn. For each square, decide whether the points are positioned

1. Randomly, or
2. Randomly but with a bias toward clumping, or
3. Randomly but with a bias toward spacing out of points.

Perhaps ask one or two friends to inspect the four scatters of points and make their judgments also. Write down your answers.

While you're still thinking about Figure 5.13, and before I explain the penguins, I'll describe my second example. Consider Figure 3.1 again. It shows a normal population and a dot plot, or scatter, of 20 data points from that population. You may care to fire up the **CIjumping** page of **ESCI chapters 1–4** and see the live version. Focus first on the dot plot of a sample. As in Figure 3.1, the points are probably scattered haphazardly, with a few little clumps and a gap or two. Take another sample and the new scatter probably shows a different haphazard pattern of clumps,

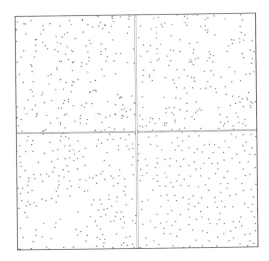

FIGURE 5.13
Four scatters of points, which may represent stars in the sky, glowworms in a cave, or penguin nests on a hillside. For each square, consider whether the points are scattered randomly, or with a bias toward clumping or spacing.

gaps, and single points. Take more samples and watch how successive samples appear different. Try little prediction games—Where will the tightest clump be? Will there be a point or two way out in the tails?—but the samples most likely seem impervious to insight, and your predictions correct only by occasional fluke.

However, if we combine numerous samples together, we'd find close agreement with an exact pattern—the population distribution. Combined over many, many samples, very close to exactly the expected proportions of data points would fall in a narrow interval at μ, and a different proportion in a narrow interval at any other point along the horizontal axis, as signaled by the height of the population normal distribution at that point.

Those observations of samples illustrate the central idea: In the long term, and very long term, randomness is close to perfectly predictable but, in dramatic contrast, in the short term it is haphazard, lumpy, surprising, and not at all predictable. Now, back to my first example and the penguins. Last chance to write down your judgments about Figure 5.13.

In the long term, randomness is highly *predictable*. In the short term, true randomness is often *lumpy*.

In Figure 5.13 the top left square is random, and the other three squares have various degrees of bias toward spacing of points. No square has a bias toward clumping. The short lines in the lower left corner of three of the squares indicate the minimum spacing of points in that square. In other words, draw a circle with that radius around any point in the square, and there will be no other point within that circle. No such limitation applies in the top left square, and so points in that square are positioned randomly.

Did you judge the top left square, or perhaps the top two squares, to have a bias toward clumping? If so, you're in good company: Many people tend to see clumps in truly random patterns or sequences. Ask someone to make random dots on a sheet of paper, and chances are he or she will produce a pattern more like one of the three squares with a bias toward spacing, rather than like the top left square.

Stephen Jay Gould (1991), in one of his fascinating essays about nature, evolution, baseball, and numerous other topics, discussed how glowworms position themselves across the roof of Waitomo Cave in New Zealand. Glowworms are territorial and risk being eaten if they get too close. Gould described the spectacular display of thousands of green dots in the dark, which look totally haphazard unless you look carefully and observe that there are no clumps, but a small minimum spacing between the glowing dots. Gould contrasted this with the pattern of stars in the sky, which in a small area is essentially random and certainly does have apparent clumps. He presented pictures like the top left and bottom left squares in Figure 5.13 to illustrate, respectively, stars in the sky and glowworms in the cave.

I've seen similar patterns in the way penguins space their nests. Chinstrap penguins, for example, usually nest on bleak open hillsides on Antarctic and sub-Antarctic islands. They build nests of small stones, or moss—whatever's available. At first sight the thousands of nests seem randomly positioned, but look closely and you'll realize they're carefully spaced to be beyond pecking distance from any neighbor.

I used the **Random** page of **ESCI chapters 5–6** to make Figure 5.13. That page displays two squares: one with a random scatter of points and the other a scatter of points with a bias toward spacing. Every time you click **Go**, a new random choice is made whether the left or right square will show the random scatter. You choose the number of points, the amount of bias in the spaced square, and whether or not to display the small line in the lower left of whichever is the spaced square. The line indicates the minimum spacing. Test out how well your friends can recognize true randomness. Click to hide the minimum spacing line, click **Go**, wait as the points are generated, guess which scatter is random and which spaced, then display the minimum spacing line to see if you were correct. Note that if you specify too many points, or too large a minimum spacing, the generation of points may be slow or may not run to completion. See the popout comments.

For Figure 5.13 I chose 200 points, and the minimum spacing was 1.5%, 2.5%, and 4% for the top right, bottom left, and bottom right squares, respectively. (The spacing is expressed as a percentage of the length of one side of the squares.)

My third example is another case of clumping in ESCI. Consider Figure 3.1 again. The area under the population distribution curve is filled with a random scatter of points. Does it look random? Do you see clumps and small clear areas? At the **CIjumping** page, click **Fill random** twice to get a new random scatter under the curve. Most likely you'll see different clumps and clearings.

This is a good moment to mention the book *Statistics as Principled Argument*, by Bob Abelson (1995). It contains much that's interesting and wise. Abelson's first law of statistics is "chance is lumpy." However, he makes clear that he's referring to local lumpiness, and that in the long run lumps average out.

Dancing CIs Again

As a fourth and last example of randomness, set up **CIjumping** to show the dance of the CIs as in Figure 3.7, with capture of μ indicated by the color of the CIs. Run the simulation. Do you see sequences or patterns in the way the means dance? Several red intervals may come close together, or there may be none for a while. It can be very tempting to interpret such apparent patterns—that's a great danger when considering real experimental results, just as it is when watching a simulation. Whenever we see patterns in data we need to keep in mind the possibility that they are mere patterns in random sampling variability.

Now **Clear** and start a new dance. Watch near red 9 the percentage of CIs capturing μ. At first this may differ from the C you have set near red 7, and it probably jumps around a lot. After the first couple of hundred samples it settles down and shows only smaller changes. Then, gradually, it makes much smaller changes and gets on average closer to C. If, by chance, there were a clump or two of red intervals near the start, so the percentage capturing was lower than C, the fact that it eventually settles very close to C does *not* mean there's any compensation for the early clumps of red. A random sequence has no such memory. The influence of early clumps is not compensated for, but is gradually diluted as many more samples are taken.

The dance of the CIs illustrates again that randomness close up can be surprisingly suggestive of differences, trends, and patterns. These may tempt interpretation, but that's unjustified. In the very long run, however, percent capturing is very close to C and so, when viewed from a long distance, randomness is very predictable.

You may be thinking that my examples of randomness aren't based on a truly random process like coin tossing or choosing numbers from a well-shaken hat. Instead, I'm using computer simulation, which relies on a *random number generator* to calculate a sequence of numbers that isn't truly random. Yes, ESCI uses a random number generator, but it's a good one, and the numbers it produces are, for all practical purposes, random.

I confess that I've often found ESCI output surprising. The dance of the CIs may start with three red in four samples, or perhaps no red in the first 100 samples. Sometimes I find a programming error, but usually I run the simulation for a long time, apply statistical evaluation to the output, and conclude that the output is just as it should be. I can even examine lumpiness and find that it's lumpy to just the right extent. I'm not immune from the temptation to seek real causes, such as a programming error, for lumps in the randomness!

A Law and a "Law"

Statisticians refer to the long-run predictability of randomness as the *law of large numbers*, which is fundamental in statistical theory. It states that very large random samples resemble the underlying population very closely. It's this law that assures us that, if we keep increasing our sample size N, sample means will tend to be closer and closer to μ. Here the law is operating via the $\sqrt{N}$ in the denominator of the formula for the SE, so for larger N the dance of the means becomes less broad and the mean heap becomes narrower.

> The *law of large numbers* is a law of mathematical statistics. It states that when random samples are sufficiently large they match the population extremely closely.

Box 5.3 reports a classic statistical cognition experiment that found that even researchers tend to underestimate sampling variability and overestimate the chance that a repeat of an experiment will give a similar result. The authors called this misconception of probability the *"law" of small numbers*, which states that many people, including many researchers, believe that small samples behave like very large samples. The law of large numbers is a genuine statistical law, which says that very large samples closely resemble the population. The ironically named law of small numbers, however, labels a human misconception, because small samples actually often differ a great deal from the population, simply because of random sampling variability.

> The *"law" of small numbers* is a widespread human misconception that even small samples match the population closely.

In summary, random variability is often large in the short term, but probability and randomness give good guidance in the long term. If I consider today a few dozen 95% CIs, perhaps none of them is red, but tomorrow I might consider only half a dozen, and two or three will be red. Well,

---

BOX 5.3 THE "LAW" OF SMALL NUMBERS

Tversky and Kahneman (1971) presented the following statement to research psychologists: "Suppose you have run an experiment on 20 subjects, and have obtained a significant result ... $z = 2.23$, $p < .05$, two-tailed. You now ... run an additional group of 10 subjects" (p. 105). The psychologists were then asked to estimate the probability that the results for the second group would be statistically significant, by one-tailed test.

To work out an appropriate answer we could assume that the first experiment estimated the true effect accurately, in which case the second has about a 50–50 chance of obtaining a smaller or larger effect than the first. There are a few complications in the calculations, but a good estimate of the probability that the second study gives $p < .05$, one-tailed is .47.

The median answer given by the psychologists was, however, .85. The participants, including some mathematical psychologists, grossly overestimated the chance that the second experiment would also give a statistically significant result. Tversky and Kahneman (1971) interpreted this result, and those of several related experiments, as indicating that many people severely underestimate the extent of sampling variability. Their research psychologists, including some with a mathematical interest, believed that results even from small experiments are likely to be replicated quite closely. Tversky and Kahneman labeled those misconceptions of randomness and variability "the law of small numbers."

---

they would be red if CIs were colored in real life. On the other hand, I can be sure that close to 5% of the numerous 95% CIs I consider in my lifetime miss the parameter they are estimating. I hope that practice with **CIjumping**, and other ESCI simulations to come, can help us all improve the accuracy of our intuitions about sampling variability. Unfortunately, we're often likely to find that the sampling variability is larger than we'd hoped or expected.

Time for coffee, chocolate, or maybe some well-spiced pea soup. Here are some hints to help you write down your take-home messages from this chapter.

- CIs and replication. What's the chance that a 95% CI will capture a replication mean?

- The sixth way to interpret a CI, as a prediction interval for a replication mean.
- What information does a p value give about what's likely to happen next time?
- Dance of the p values. Distribution of the p value.
- Randomness, lumpiness, glowworms, penguins, and a strange "law."

Exercises

5.1 Consider Figure 5.1. Does the CI of Experiment 1 capture the next replication mean? That's the mean for Experiment 2, so the answer is yes. Does the CI for Experiment 2 capture its next mean? Again, yes. Work your way up the figure, recording (Y for yes, N for no): Y, Y, Y, Y, N, etc. What percentage of the 24 cases give Y? What would you expect the percentage to be in the long run? You could use **CIjumping** to examine a longer sequence. How do these questions relate to the first half of Chapter 5?

5.2 Find some issues raised in the chapter that you think could be interesting to investigate experimentally. Suggest some statistical cognition experiments.

5.3 Figure 5.6 shows that, for $N = 15$, CP values are widely spread around 95% and extend almost up to 100%. What would you expect for larger N, say, $N = 40$ and $N = 200$? Test your predictions.

5.4 I stated that a 95% CI is on average an 83% prediction interval. What about a $C\%$ CI? Cumming et al. (2004) explained how to calculate the prediction percentage for any C and included a graph of the prediction percentage against C. You may wish to read that article. Here's the formula for a 95% CI, expressed in Excel functions, assuming N is very large or σ is known:

Prediction % =
  100 * (2 * (NORMSDIST((NORMSINV(.975)/SQRT(2))) − .5))

You could type that into Excel and verify that it gives 83.422. For any C of your choice, replace the .975 with $(1 − (100 − C)/200)$.

Find the prediction percentage for a 99% CI and a 90% CI. For SE bars, the formula is

$$\text{Prediction \%} = 100 * (2 * (\text{NORMSDIST}(1/\text{SQRT}(2)) - .5))$$

Find that prediction percentage and interpret. Ask your friends to estimate these various prediction percentages. How well do they do?

5.5 I conclude that one reason a CI is valuable is that its width gives useful information about how widely replication means are likely to bounce around. Is this true even for small N? Explain.

5.6 Use the **p intervals** page of **ESCI chapters 5–6** to calculate some p intervals of your choice. Find a couple of examples, in your own work or published in a journal, where a p value is reported. Amend the report by adding the corresponding p interval. Interpret.

5.7 Use the **p intervals** page to calculate p intervals for a set of p values of your choice. Make a table and keep it for reference.

5.8 Suppose you read that $M = 54.3$, [44.2, 64.4], $p = .072$, as at the start of the chapter. Give an interpretation of the CI as a prediction interval, and also give a p interval and interpret. Compare the two prediction interpretations. Repeat for another example.

5.9 Use the **Dance p** page of **ESCI chapters 5–6** to prepare, then deliver, a presentation to your statistics study group or class. You might choose to focus on, for example, the contrast of CIs and p values, or the role of power, or the spread of the distribution of p, or the role of N.

5.10 At the **Random** page of **ESCI chapters 5–6**, set the spinner for some larger number of points; 1,000 is the maximum, but large numbers may be slow to generate. You'll need to set a small minimum spacing, perhaps 1% or less, or the generation may not complete—there may hardly be room for so many points spaced more widely. Experiment with various values of the minimum spacing, and see how well you or your friends can pick which is the random square. How subtle can clumping be and still be discernible?

5.11 Think of the various beliefs about randomness that keep gamblers going back to the roulette wheel, or slot machine, and keep the casinos in business. How might belief in the law of small numbers contribute? What might be the role of apparent clumping in a random sequence?

5.12 Revise your list of take-home messages if you wish.

Polya

Take-Home Messages

- Replication is central to science, and so it's reasonable to ask what information a statistical technique gives about replication.
- To investigate sampling variability we consider idealized replications, such as those illustrated in ESCI simulations.
- The capture percentage (CP) is the percentage of replication means that in the long run fall within the CI of an initial experiment.
- Capture percentages for 95% CIs have mean 83% and median 90%. Most intervals have CP around 90 to 95%, or even more than 95% if based on *t* rather than *z*, and just a few have much lower values of CP. The 5% of intervals that miss the parameter being estimated—and that ESCI shows as red—have CP less than 50%.
- The sixth way to interpret a 95% CI is as an 83% prediction interval for the mean of a replication experiment. There's a .83 chance that our 95% CI will capture the mean of a single replication.
- With replication, *p* values vary enormously. The dance of the *p* values is very wide. In many typical cases, a replication can give almost any *p* value, and obtaining very low *p* is somewhat like winning at a casino.

- *Take-home movie*: Your choice of the dance of the p values, the p value casino, or the sequence of p values to the left in Figure 5.10—on screen, with colored patches. Are you dreaming of dances yet?

- A p interval is the 80% prediction interval for replication p, and p intervals are typically very wide.

- A CI gives useful information about replication, but a p value gives only extremely vague information about replication—about what's likely to happen next time.

- The distribution of the p value is wide and depends on statistical power.

- Only very small values of p (*** results, or just possibly ** results) give reasonably useful information. Other values of p give hardly any information at all and provide a poor basis for inference.

- In the short term, randomness is often surprisingly lumpy, and it can be tempting to interpret such lumpiness as patterns or trends with real causes. Stars or penguins?

- In the very long term, randomness yields very close to the results we expect. That's the law of large numbers in action.

- Uncertainty attributable to random sampling variability is, unfortunately, often underestimated. That's one manifestation of the law of small numbers, which is not a law but a misconception. An important function of CIs is to picture uncertainty accurately and clearly.

6

Two Simple Designs

Many of the simplest experiments compare two conditions, perhaps using the *two-independent-groups* design or the *paired* design. You may be familiar with these designs in the context of the independent-groups *t* test and paired *t* test. This chapter discusses how to use CIs to present and interpret results from these two designs. Here's the agenda:

- The dreadful ambiguity of conventional figures

The two-independent-groups design:

- Displaying the data
- A rule of eye for estimating the *p* value
- Presenting your own data
- Illustrating the great variability with replication

The paired design:

- Displaying the data
- The correlation between measures
- Presenting your own data
- Illustrating why this design can be sensitive

Figures With Error Bars: Even More Ambiguity

Your wine club gives you the onerous task of evaluating a fine red wine from the Napa Valley, California, and another from McLaren Vale, South Australia. To avoid bias, you mask the bottles and label them A and B. It's easy to recruit volunteers, but you need to choose whether to use independent groups of tasters for the two wines, or a single group who taste both, some A then B, and others B then A. After collecting the data, your assistant prepares Figure 6.1. What extra information does a reader need to understand it?

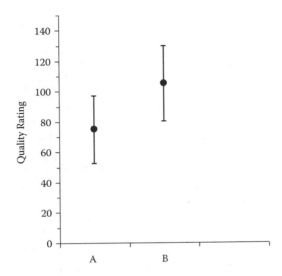

FIGURE 6.1
Mean quality ratings for two wines, A and B, with error bars. What questions need answering before you can interpret the figure?

In Chapter 4 we discussed the tragedy of the error bar—bars are ambiguous and we need to be told what they represent. A further deep ambiguity can lurk in figures, because there's no conventional way to signal whether an independent variable refers to independent groups or is a repeated measure. Without that information we can't use error bars to interpret the figure. If you were considering a *t* test for the data reported in Figure 6.1, you'd immediately ask whether A and B are independent groups, or a repeated measure. We need to ask the same question to be able to interpret the error bars. Every figure with error bars must make clear, with labels or in its caption, the status of each independent variable.

> To interpret a figure with error bars, it's essential to know for each independent variable whether it refers to *independent groups* or is a *repeated measure*.

Pictures of Two Independent Groups

Display the Difference With Its CI

It's best to have the ESs and CIs that relate most directly to the effects we're investigating. You'd think that would hardly need saying, but Figure 6.1 is a common example that may not provide what we want. If our interest

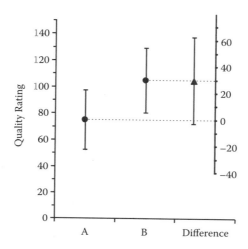

FIGURE 6.2
The two means shown in Figure 6.1. Error bars are 95% CIs. A and B are independent groups, each of size $N = 30$, and the difference between the B and A means is plotted on a floating difference axis, whose zero is aligned with the A mean. The triangle marks the difference on that axis, and the 95% CI on that difference is displayed.

is to score the two wines separately, perhaps to compare with many others, then the figure is fine. However, let's assume that our main interest is to compare the two, in which case we need the point and interval estimates of the *difference* between A and B. Figure 6.2 is a nice solution that still displays M_A and M_B, the two group means, and also $(M_B - M_A)$, the differ-

> Figures are most useful if they present ESs and CIs for effects of primary research interest.

ence between them. (I'm using $(M_B - M_A)$ for the difference, rather than $(M_A - M_B)$, for convenience and to be consistent with ESCI. However it's an arbitrary choice.) The difference is plotted on a difference axis that "floats" so its zero is aligned with the mean of A. The figure displays results for two independent groups of tasters, each of size $N = 30$.

Here's what I did to build such a figure. For the 95% CI on M_A, I used Equation (3.3) to calculate:

$$MOE_A = t_{.95}(N_A - 1) \times s_A / \sqrt{N_A}$$

where the A subscripts refer to the A group. I calculated MOE_B similarly. Then for the 95% CI on the $(M_B - M_A)$ difference we want the MOE for the difference, which is MOE_{diff}. You may recognize the next calculations as very similar to those for an independent groups t test. First, I calculated a pooled estimate of the within-group SD, which we'll assume is the same for the A and B populations:

$$s_P = \sqrt{\frac{(N_A - 1)s_A^2 + (N_B - 1)s_B^2}{N_A + N_B - 2}} \qquad (6.1)$$

Then

$$MOE_{\text{diff}} = t_{.95}(N_A + N_B - 2) \times s_P \sqrt{\frac{1}{N_A} + \frac{1}{N_B}} \qquad (6.2)$$

If sample sizes are large, say, both at least 30, we could use Equation (3.2) and z rather than t. If, as well, the two sample sizes are equal and the two sample SDs are equal, then the formulas become much simpler: $MOE_A = MOE_B$ and MOE_{diff} is just $\sqrt{2}$ times (which is about 1.4 times) larger than either of them. In Figure 6.2, the two groups are each of size 30, and MOE_A and MOE_B are similar, so the conditions stated previously are approximately met, and MOE_{diff} does appear roughly 1.4 times as long as MOE_A and MOE_B.

Does the pattern of error bars in Figure 6.2 look familiar? Compare it with Figure 5.9, which also shows the means of two independent groups, a floating difference axis, and the difference with its CI—which is about 1.4 times as long as the CI on E or C. For successive experiments in a set, Figure 5.10 displays not the separate E and C means and CIs, but the difference with its CI because that's most relevant. Our main interest is the difference between the E and C means, so seeing that difference with its CI is most useful to us.

Once we have that difference and its CI we could choose whichever one or more of the six ways to think of a CI that seem most illuminating in the particular situation. But if we had only Figure 6.1 rather than Figure 6.2 we'd lack the crucial CI on the difference, and thus lack the basis for direct interpretation of what primarily interests us. A new statistics focus on the interpretation of estimates should lead to figures like Figure 6.2 being provided more often.

In Example 6.1, however, what matters for each group and each heading is the match between the data and a theoretical prediction. The difference between group means was not of particular interest, so reporting means and CIs for the separate groups was appropriate. As ever, data presentation and interpretation must be shaped by the research questions.

Independent Means With Their CIs

When we have independent groups, however, the CIs on the separate means can help indirectly. Consider the previous formulas. The CIs on the two means are calculated from s_A and s_B, the two sample SDs. The CI on the difference is based on the pooled SD, which is also calculated from those same s_A and s_B. The CIs on the two means therefore represent the same information about variability as does the CI on the difference. In

> **EXAMPLE 6.1 THE COMPASS USED BY BIRDS**
>
> Zapka et al. (2009) investigated the physiological mechanisms that may underlie birds' ability to use the Earth's magnetic field for navigation. In one of their studies they examined the idea that magnetoreceptors in the upper beak transmit information about compass bearing through the trigeminal nerve from the eye to the brain. They compared orientation performance by European robins with intact trigeminal nerves (control birds), and those whose trigeminal nerves had been severed (treated birds). They reported that control birds oriented at 10°, [350, 30] in the earth's magnetic field, and at 245°, [219, 271] in an artificial magnetic field aligned to 240°. (I'm referring here to compass bearings, magnetic north being 0° and 360°, south 180°, etc.) The treated birds oriented in the same two conditions at 354°, [334, 14], and 264°, [230, 298], respectively. The researchers concluded that both groups could orient reasonably successfully to natural north and to the artificial north induced at 240°, so those robins seem able to navigate without relying on input via their trigeminal nerve. The sample sizes were small (6 and 7) but in all cases the accurate heading (0° or 240°) was well within the 95% CI, and the CIs for the 0° and 240° headings were very well separated. The original article included ingenious circular figures that showed each bird's response as well as the CI, but my purpose here is to illustrate how even CIs reported in text can simply and compactly summarize results and can sometimes give a good basis for interpretation and comparison of groups.

other words, if you knew only the CIs on the means (and the sample sizes), you could figure out the CI on the difference. If the CIs on the means were roughly equal in length, then 1.4 times that length would be a good estimate of the length of the CI on the difference. Therefore, one way to interpret Figure 6.1 is to note the difference between the means, then eyeball an interval about 40% longer than either of the two CIs shown and use that as the CI on the difference.

Overlap of CIs on Independent Means

I'll now describe another approach to thinking about Figure 6.1 that is useful even though it uses p values. In Figure 6.2 you can use the benchmarks of Chapter 4 to eyeball the p value, by noting where the CI on the difference falls in relation to zero on the difference axis. It's $p = .07$; did your eyeball agree? Because the CI on the difference is based on the same variability information as the two CIs on the means, those two CIs can also be used to estimate the p value for the difference. Simply focus on the *overlap* of the two CIs, or the gap between them. Figure 6.2 illustrates the amount of overlap for $p = .07$. Move the B mean a little higher, so the lower limit of the CI on the difference just touches zero, and find that $p = .05$ corresponds to considerable overlap of the CIs on the A and B means. Surprising? Not after a play with ESCI, but first I'll describe an overlap rule of eye.

The Overlap Rule for Two Independent Means

The overlap rule of eye, from Cumming and Finch (2005, tinyurl.com/inferencebyeye), distinguishes three situations:

1. If the 95% CIs on two independent means **just touch** end-to-end, overlap is zero and the p value for testing the null hypothesis of no difference is approximately .01.

2. If there's a **gap** between the two CIs, meaning no overlap, then $p < .01$.

3. **Moderate overlap** (see the following) of the two CIs implies that p is approximately .05. Less overlap means $p < .05$.

Moderate overlap is overlap of about half the average MOE, as in Figure 6.3. MOE, of course, is the length of one arm of a CI, so average MOE is the average of the arm length of the two CIs. Figure 6.3 includes horizontal lines to mark overlap. I express the amount of overlap as a proportion of the average MOE, and refer to it as *proportion overlap*, or just *overlap*. Figure 6.3 shows overlap of a little more than 0.5 and p a little less than .05, illustrating that the rule is often a little conservative—p is often a little less than the rule states. In Cumming (2009) I reported evidence that the rule is reasonably accurate when both sample sizes are at least 10 and the two MOEs do not differ by more than a factor of about 2.

For two independent means, if the two 95% CIs *just touch*, p is approximately .01, and if they *overlap* by about half the average MOE, p is approximately .05.

Rules of eye are approximate and intended for eyeballing, not as a replacement for calculation of exact p values if that's your interest. They give a handy guide for use, for example, when you're listening to a research talk and see a slide showing means with error bars. Check that the means are independent and the error bars are 95% CIs, then use the overlap rule as a rough guide whether some difference of interest would earn * (CIs overlap no more than about half the average MOE) or ** (CIs touch or show a gap). Box 6.1 reports evidence that many researchers in several disciplines have a poor understanding of how the extent of overlap relates to p.

I've strongly recommended 95% CIs over SE bars, but figures with SE bars are still common, especially in some biology disciplines. Unless N is

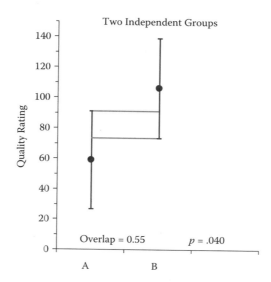

FIGURE 6.3
Two independent means, a little different from those in Figure 6.2, and their 95% CIs. Overlap is the distance between the horizontal lines, expressed as a proportion of the average of the MOEs for the two CIs. The figure illustrates the overlap rule.

small, say, less than 10, SE bars are about half the width of the 95% CI. The overlap rule can therefore be translated to apply to SE bars:

1. If the gap between SE bars on two independent means is about twice the average SE, the p value for testing the null hypothesis of no difference is approximately .01.
2. If the gap is larger, then $p < .01$.
3. If the gap is equal to the average SE, p is approximately .05. Larger gap means $p < .05$.

You can make a picture in your mind's eye to illustrate the third case: Simply halve the lengths of the error bars in Figure 6.3. The rule for SE bars is also reasonably accurate, provided both sample sizes are at least 10 and the SEs of the two groups don't differ by more than a factor of 2. Box 6.1 reports evidence that, alas, many researchers in several disciplines have a poor understanding of the distinction between 95% CIs and SE bars.

ESCI for Two Independent Groups: Compare A B

I suggest now firing up the **Compare A B** page of **ESCI chapters 5–6**. On opening, you'll see a figure like Figure 6.1. Don't for the moment click at

BOX 6.1 RESEARCHERS' UNDERSTANDING
OF ERROR BARS

Belia, Fidler, Williams, and Cumming (2005) reported a study of how researchers understand error bars. We sent emails to authors of articles in leading journals in medicine, behavioral neuroscience, and psychology. The emails included a link to a figure like Figure 6.1 that allowed respondents to click and drag the right-hand mean and its error bars up or down.

There were three conditions, but any respondent saw only one. The CI condition stated that the means were for two independent groups and the bars were 95% CIs. The SE condition was the same, except the bars were SE bars. In the repeated measure condition, the means were for the pretest and posttest for a single group of participants. Respondents were asked to set the right-hand mean so they judged the two means just statistically significantly different at the .05 level. We emphasized that we were asking for eyeballing, not calculations.

We chose the three disciplines because a preliminary study of their journals confirmed that they have very different error bar customs. (That was in 1999–2002. Some practices have changed since then.) In psychology, CIs and error bars were seldom used; in behavioral neuroscience about half the articles included figures with SE bars, but CIs were seldom reported; and in medicine about two thirds of the articles reported CIs as numerical values, but seldom included CIs or SE bars in figures.

Our first finding was that for every discipline and every condition there was a very broad range of responses and, overall, performance was poor: Only 22% of responses were positioned so that p was between .025 and .10. Second, responses were similar for the three disciplines despite the very different experiences the three groups of respondents would have had with CIs and error bars in figures. Third, CI bars were on average set too far apart, corresponding on average to $p = .01$, whereas SE bars were set too close, corresponding on average to $p = .11$. Indeed, the amounts of response overlap or gap were quite similar for CIs and SE bars, suggesting that many researchers did not appreciate the distinction between the two. Fourth, it was popular to set bars just touching end-to-end. For CIs, 34% of responses were just touching, indicating the use of the incorrect overlap rule. For SE bars, 30% of responses were just touching, suggesting the application of the incorrect rule to the wrong type of bars!

Later in this chapter we'll consider the repeated measure design and will find that, for this design, overlap cannot be used to eyeball p for the difference. Therefore, our task is impossible in the paired case. Only 11% of our respondents in this condition recognized the problem.

We had also asked how many years ago a respondent published his or her first journal article. Responses ranged from 0 to 48 years, but there was no sign of any relation with accuracy on the task, so neither long experience nor recent training leads to better understanding of error bars.

We concluded that we'd identified a range of severe misunderstandings that many researchers in each of the three disciplines hold. You might be tempted to respond that CIs and other error bars seem so problematic that even NHST is preferable. You won't be surprised to hear that our response was different: We took the findings as helping to define what's needed if CIs are to be widely and appropriately used. It may be best if new graphical conventions make it immediately obvious what an error bar represents, and whether an independent variable represents independent groups or is a repeated measure. Better guidelines and education are also needed.

red 6 to reveal a second figure, which is for the paired design. The main interest is to investigate the three checkboxes at red 3. Note their popouts. Click the top one to reveal the difference with its 95% CI, displayed on a floating difference axis as in Figure 6.2. Click the next checkbox to mark overlap with horizontal lines and to see values at the bottom for overlap and two-tailed p, as in Figure 6.3. You can now investigate any aspect of the overlap rule of eye for 95% CIs. Here are a few suggestions:

- Adjust the A or B mean so $p = .05$, and note overlap.
- Adjust the A or B mean so overlap = .50, and note the p value.
- Repeat, for $p = .01$, and overlap = 0.
- Try various values of the SDs and Ns to check out the robustness of the rule. Try some very small values of N; change the SDs so the two MOEs differ by a factor of 2 of more. Do you agree that the rule is sufficiently accurate provided both Ns are at least 10, and the two MOEs don't differ by more than a factor of 2?
- With the floating difference axis clicked off, note overlap and imagine what the CI on the difference would look like and where it would fall in relation to zero. Click to display the difference axis to check. Can you find someone willing to make this a competitive challenge?

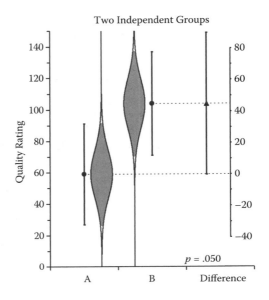

FIGURE 6.4

A figure from ESCI **Compare A B** showing two independent means and their 95% CIs, and the difference with its 95% CI on a floating difference axis. The data are slightly different from those in previous figures. The CI on the difference just touches zero, so two-tailed *p* is .05. Overlap of the CIs on the A and B means is 0.61. The cat's eyes illustrate that overlap is of the "thin ends" of the intervals.

Did you confirm that the rule is usually a bit conservative? If overlap = .50, *p* is often around .036. Have you become slick at eyeballing amount of overlap in terms of proportion of average MOE?

Now click the third checkbox near red 3 to display cat's-eye pictures, and see something like Figure 6.4. Perhaps you were wondering why overlap as large as .5 can give *p* < .05? The cat's eyes indicate that the overlapping is of the "thin ends" of the 95% CIs, and so even a fair amount of overlap is consistent with low *p* and thus some evidence of difference.

Before seeing cat's eyes, the two CIs in Figure 6.1 might suggest that we need zero overlap to have reasonable grounds for concluding that there's a true difference between A and B. In medicine that intuition is stated as a rule in some textbooks, and Schenker and Gentleman (2001) found many examples in medical and health science journals in which authors equated 95% CIs not overlapping with statistical significance at the

Especially in medicine, many people believe, incorrectly, that independent 95% CIs just touching is equivalent to *p* = .05. It's actually approximately equivalent to *p* = .01.

.05 level. The rule that independent 95% CIs just touching is equivalent to *p* = .05 is incorrect, but seems to be widely believed, especially in medicine. Requiring just touching or a gap amounts to using a *p* = .01 criterion, which may be fine, but researchers should be aware of what p criterion they are using. Box 6.1 reports evidence that many researchers in several disciplines believe the incorrect rule.

Example 6.2 describes an experiment that used four independent groups. I prepared Figure 6.5 to show the separate means and CIs, and provide a basis for interpretation. We could also use the overlap rule to eyeball p values from that figure.

EXAMPLE 6.2 RANDOMNESS AND BELIEF IN GOD

Kay, Moscovitch, and Laurin (2010) investigated two factors that might influence people's stated belief that the universe is controlled by God or a similar nonhuman entity. Four small groups of students, 37 in all, served as participants—one group for each combination of the two manipulations. All participants were given an "herbal supplement," which was actually inert. Two groups were led to believe that it may mildly increase anxiety or arousal; two were given no such suggestion. That was the "arousal suggestion" manipulation. All participants then completed a word task. The second manipulation was whether or not the words emphasized chance and randomness. Participants then rated several statements about their belief that God or karma governs the universe. Ratings were on a scale from 1 to 7, where high ratings indicate stronger belief. Kay et al. reported ESs, NHST analyses, and several p values, the smallest being .03. I calculated CIs and prepared Figure 6.5 to display the main result. They suggested that belief in the supernatural may be heightened by thoughts of chance or randomness, unless an alternative explanation is available for the anxiety or arousal that such thoughts are presumed to elicit. For the arousal groups the "herbal supplement" provided such an explanation, so the researchers expected only the randomness-and-no-arousal group to give higher ratings. They interpreted the figure as confirming that expectation: The top left point is higher than the other three points, which are not statistically significantly different.

Their conclusion may be correct, but the pattern of means and CIs in Figure 6.5 suggests the extent of uncertainty. You could consider how much weight to give the p value of .03, and the extent that interval width might influence how you think about the three means that are not statistically significantly different. The experiment used four independent groups, so you can use the overlap rule to compare any two means in Figure 6.5. You could also think of the CIs as prediction intervals and imagine what patterns of the four means might be given by replications of the experiment. In Chapter 15 we'll consider estimation beyond simple comparisons of two means, and also the issue of multiple testing. However, my suggested ways to think about the results raise cautions about the authors' conclusions.

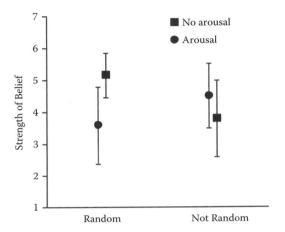

FIGURE 6.5

Mean ratings of strength of belief in the supernatural, with 95% CIs, for the four independent groups used by Kay et al. (2010). Means are slightly offset so all CIs can be easily seen.

I've discussed the rules of eye, despite my recommendation to avoid NHST whenever possible, because they may sometimes prove handy in practice. In addition, eyeballing overlap and p may help bring to mind what the CI on the difference would look like, and how it relates to zero. It's vital to keep in mind, however, the message of Chapter 5: p values give only very vague information. At most we should use p or overlap as a rough guide—along with considering whether the difference is useful or meaningful in the particular context.

ESCI: Data Two

The **Data two** page of **ESCI chapters 5–6** is the first that's designed primarily for you to display your own data. Perhaps you have some suitable data for two independent groups, or you could invent some. Enter that data and see a figure displaying the means and CIs, as in Figure 6.6. As usual, follow red numbers and popout comments to discover what's possible, how to enter data, and how to display various features. For example, you can display the data points as two dot plots and mark overlap of the

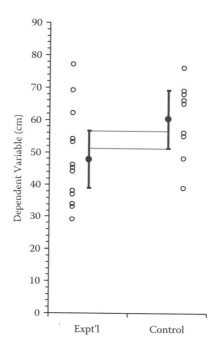

FIGURE 6.6
A figure from ESCI **Data two** showing two independent means and their 95% CIs. The individual data are shown as dot plots, and overlap of the CIs is marked.

CIs, as in Figure 6.6. See Appendix A for further advice. You can click near red 9 to reveal a second figure that also displays the difference between the means, with its CI, on a floating difference axis.

ESCI is not intended to be a fully functioned data analysis tool. One of its limitations is that there's no general import or export capability for data. You need to enter your data either by typing it in, or by using the clipboard to copy and paste it in, one group at a time. Pasting requires the use of **Paste Special/Values**. See the popout at red 1.

Previous ESCI pages have generally used figures with fixed limits for the axes so, for example, you can explore means within only a fixed range, often 0 to 100. Your own data, however, may be large or small, negative or positive, and so **Data two** adjusts the range of the vertical axis to suit the data you enter. The floating difference axis is also changed.

The **Compare A B** page assumes that the SDs of the A and B populations are equal. That's the homogeneity of variance assumption, often made when using an independent groups t test. **Data two** has an option to avoid this assumption by using the Welch–Satterthwaite method, which gives good approximations for p and the CI on the difference without assuming that the A and B SDs are equal. Box 6.2 gives a brief description

BOX 6.2 THE WELCH–SATTERTHWAITE APPROACH

You can skip this explanation if you wish. Just note the final sentence in the box.

For the two-independent-groups design, the conventional approach to calculating t and p for the difference between means, and the CI on that difference, assumes homogeneity of the two population variances. The Welch–Satterthwaite approximation avoids that assumption. For the SE of the difference it uses

$$SE_{WS} = \sqrt{\frac{s_A^2}{N_A} + \frac{s_B^2}{N_B}},$$

where the WS subscript refers to the Welch–Satterthwaite value. This can be contrasted with

$$s_P \sqrt{\frac{1}{N_A} + \frac{1}{N_B}}$$

that appears in Equation (6.2). Recall that s_P is the pooled SD within groups, given by Equation (6.1).

The Welch–Satterthwaite approximation also requires a change to the degrees of freedom. Instead of $df = N_A + N_B - 2$, it uses

$$df_{WS} = \frac{\left(\dfrac{s_A^2}{N_A} + \dfrac{s_B^2}{N_B}\right)^2}{\dfrac{s_A^4}{N_A^2(N_A - 1)} + \dfrac{s_B^4}{N_B^2(N_B - 1)}}$$

That number is often not an integer, and so calculating p, and also MOE for the CI on the difference, requires interpolation between the values given by integer values of df next below and next above df_{WS}. If you select **No** at red 7 in **Data two**, so the approximation is used, you may see a noninteger value of df near red 8.

The conventional approach that assumes homogeneity of variance calculates the pooled within-group SD by weighting s_A^2 and s_B^2 by $(N_A - 1)$ and $(N_B - 1)$, respectively, as in Equation (6.1). If one sample is much larger, it contributes more to the pooled value, and that's appropriate if we're assuming that the two samples are estimating the same population value. By contrast, the Welch–Satterthwaite formula shown above for SE_{WS} weights the contributions of the two samples close to equally. The bottom line is that if the two methods give notably different results, it's probably better to choose Welch–Satterthwaite by clicking **No** at red 7 in **Data two**.

of the method. Click near red 7 in **Data two** to select whether or not you wish to assume homogeneity of variance. Click between **Yes** and **No** to observe how the results change. They usually only differ much when the two samples have considerably different sample sizes and SDs. In such cases it's probably better to click **No** to avoid making the assumption.

I hope **Data two** helps you report CIs and figures with CIs. For either a single group or two independent groups it gives you the numerical values of CIs, for 95% or any other level of confidence, with or without assuming homogeneity of variance. There are a variety of display options. You can also use any Excel editing facilities to change a figure, before copying it to a Word document (see Appendix A for details).

ESCI: Simulate Two

Simulate two lets you simulate independent-groups experiments using population characteristics and sample sizes you specify. The purpose is simple: to get a feel for the amount of variability over replication. Yes, it usually turns out to be surprisingly large. You may feel that earlier chapters made that point, but I feel that it's so important that it's worth exploring replication here, too.

I believe that, whenever you see a mean or any other ES reported with its CI, you should automatically be aware of roughly the range of values that could easily have been obtained instead, simply because of sampling variability. If there are several ESs, you should intuitively appreciate what other patterns of values could easily have been obtained. I don't know of research that has investigated how to develop such intuitions, but I'm hoping that working with simulations will help. **Simulate two** allows you to explore replication for data that's similar to your own, providing that the values are within certain limits.

As usual, you can start by simply exploring. Follow the red numbers, read the popout comments, adjust the controls, and use the buttons to run the simulation. It's too confusing to have all features of the display clicked on at once, so investigate them one or two at a time.

Let's suppose that you entered data into **Data two**, perhaps from your own wine tasting. The sample sizes were 13 and 9, sample means 47.8 and 60.2, and sample SDs 14.6 and 11.7. You found the CIs you wanted, investigated the effect of assuming homogeneity of variance, and made yourself a nice figure for your report. Now you're interested to see what alternative results your experiment might have obtained or, equivalently, what results a replication of your experiment might give. However **Simulate two** needs population parameters, which is difficult because, of course, you don't know them. You can try any parameter values you like, but it's probably most useful to choose values by assuming that your experiment happened to give accurate estimates. Here are some suggestions:

- Click near red 3 in **Simulate two** to enter your two sample sizes, 13 and 9.

- Round off your sample means, and use 48 and 60 as the two population means. Use the spinners near red 7 to enter those values as μ_1 and μ_2. (If the population parameter values are not visible, click to **Show values of population parameters**.)

- **Simulate two** assumes homogeneity of variance, so let's use 13 as the population SD, because 13 is the rounded off average of your sample SDs. Enter 13 for σ near red 7.

- Click **Display difference between means** near red 5. Run the simulation and see how the difference marked in pink varies over replication. We could call it the *dance of the differences*. Its variation is a compounding of the variation in each sample mean, so it's not surprising that the variation of the difference is larger. Correspondingly, we expect the CI on the difference to be about 1.4 times as long as the CI on either mean. The dance you're watching may remind you of Figure 5.10 and the dance of the *p* values.

  > For two independent groups, what I call the *dance of the differences* illustrates how the difference between the means varies over replication even more than either group mean varies.

- Now click **Display difference between means** off, and near red 6 click **Display CIs** and **Display CI overlap** on. Run the simulation and enjoy. (Click to hide extraneous display features as you wish.) Note the large variation in *p*, which is reported below red 9. Yes, this is another version of the dance of the *p* values.

- Take single experiments (button at red 1) and note how the extent of overlap corresponds to the *p* value. Practice translating between the two.

- Click **Display CI overlap** off, run more experiments, and refine your ability to guesstimate *p* by inspecting two CIs and eyeballing overlap or gap. Enjoy.

Whatever parameter values you set, I suspect your main conclusion is that the difference between two independent means varies greatly over replication. Alas, probably surprisingly so.

The Paired Design

Perhaps your volunteers were so keen to taste both wines that you decided to use a *repeated measure* design, in which the N participants in a single group each gave values for both A and B. I'll refer to this simply as the *paired* design, which gives us N pairs of A and B data values. This design may also be appropriate for data from pairs of matched participants. You're probably familiar with the trade-offs that guide the choice between a two-independent-groups and a paired design, but this isn't a book about experimental design so I won't go into detail. I'll just mention that the paired design

> For the *paired design*, as for the paired *t* test, focus on the paired *differences* and the CI for the mean paired difference.

often is more sensitive and gives a more precise estimate of the difference between A and B, although we need to be wary of possible carry-over effects—such as learning or fatigue that means the first measurement from a participant influences the second. You'll arrange, if possible, for some participants to have A first then B, and others the reverse order. We'll see a simulation that highlights why the design is often sensitive. Two key features of the paired design are that measures A and B are correlated, and that we focus on the *differences* from the N pairs.

For a start, go back to **Compare A B**. Click at red 6 to reveal a second figure, which assumes that A and B are measures in a paired design. You'll probably see two figures something like Figure 6.7. If the figure is

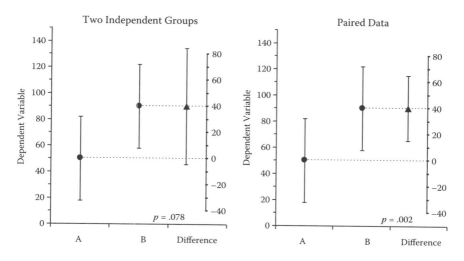

FIGURE 6.7

Two figures from ESCI **Compare A B** showing, at left, two independent means and their 95% CIs, and the difference with its 95% CI plotted on a floating difference axis. Sample size is N = 40 for each group. The figure at right is for the same data values, but in this case A and B refer not to independent groups, but to two measures for a single group of N = 40 participants. Again, means and 95% CIs are shown, including the CI on the mean difference, on a floating difference axis. The correlation between the A and B measures is r = .70. The two-tailed *p* value for testing the difference against zero is shown for each design. The overlap rule may be used in the left panel, but *not* the right.

blank, check that $N_A = N_B$ at red 1 and red 2. The left panel in Figure 6.7 assumes two independent groups, one being $N_A = 40$ values of A, and the other $N_B = 40$ values of B. The focus is on $(M_B - M_A)$, the difference between the two group means. The right panel is based on the same data, but assumes that the data set is $N = 40$ pairs of A and B values. The difference is M_{diff}, the mean of the N paired differences. You can see that the values of $(M_B - M_A)$ and M_{diff} are the same; this is always the case, even though they are described differently. I'm using Figure 6.7 to illustrate the difference between the two designs, but it's highly artificial. In real life, an experiment either has two independent groups or it's a paired design—it can't be both, and so only one of the figures could be correct.

The figure for paired data assumes that the correlation between the two measures is $r = .70$. Because this correlation is substantial, the paired design gives a more precise estimate of the difference between A and B, and a much smaller p value. You can use the slider near red 7 to adjust the assumed correlation of A and B, and watch how the width of the CI on the mean difference changes. Other things being equal, the paired design gives a more precise estimate of M_{diff}, the effect of interest, the higher the correlation between the two measures. If you set a negative correlation, the CI for the difference in the paired design is larger than the corresponding CI for the two-independent-groups design. Such a negative correlation is rare in practice, but does caution that a paired design is not guaranteed to be more sensitive.

For both designs illustrated in Figure 6.7, the CI shown on the floating difference axis is the CI on the difference between A and B, and that's what most interests us. Therefore, in both cases that CI, which is displayed at the right in each panel, is most important for interpretation. However, the vital contrast between the designs is, unfortunately, not made obvious in the display. It's another aspect of the tragedy of the error bar and a big issue for the paired design. Recall that I made a big deal of explaining for two independent groups that the CI on the difference is based on the same information about variability as the CIs on the two group means. Know s_A and s_B and you can calculate the CI on the difference. That's the basis for the overlap rule, which we can apply in the left panel of Figure 6.7. There's a parallel with the t test: You use s_A and s_B to calculate independent groups t.

For the paired design, however, the CI on the difference is based on entirely different information about variability: s_{diff}, the SD of the paired differences. Again there's a parallel with the t test: You need s_{diff} to calculate paired t. Knowing only s_A and s_B is not sufficient to calculate paired t, and it's not sufficient to calculate the CI on the difference in the paired design, which is displayed on the difference axis in the right panel in

For the *paired design*, the CIs on the two measures are virtually *irrelevant* for assessing the difference. No overlap rule is possible.

Figure 6.7. In fact, knowing s_A and s_B, or the CIs on the two separate measures in the paired design, gives virtually *no* information about the CI on the difference. To put it another way, the CI on the difference is sensitive to the correlation between the A and B measures. We found that adjusting r changed the width of the CI on the difference for the paired design—as in the right panel of Figure 6.7—from zero to much wider than either of the A and B CIs. But changing r made no difference to the separate CIs on A and B. Therefore, seeing only the CIs on A and B in the paired design, and not knowing r, leaves us almost totally ignorant about what we really want to know—the precision of our estimate of the difference between A and B.

In summary, Figure 6.7 displays for both designs the CI on the difference, and in both cases that's what we usually need for interpretation. For two independent groups (the left panel) we can consider overlap of the two separate CIs as an alternative to interpreting the CI shown on the difference axis. For the paired design, however, we can't do that, and we must interpret the CI of the mean differences, which is displayed on the difference axis. The contrast arises because the CI on the difference is calculated differently for the two designs.

> Any figure with error bars must make clear the nature of the independent variable(s): independent groups or a repeated measure? Otherwise the figure is not interpretable.

In **Compare A B**, click at red 3 to turn **Display Difference axis** off, then you can inspect the two CIs in the left figure and use the overlap rule to compare the A and B means. You can even generate in your mind's eye the CI on the difference. In stark contrast, in the right figure we don't have sufficient information to do that. We have virtually no idea of the length of the CI on the difference. For the paired design, no overlap rule is possible. Box 6.1 reports evidence that many researchers in several disciplines do not appreciate that overlap of error bars is *irrelevant* in the paired design.

It's a great failing of our graphical conventions that they don't automatically provide the crucial information as to whether an independent variable, such as A versus B, represents independent groups, or a repeated measure as in our paired design example. Example 6.3 is a simple experiment with

---

EXAMPLE 6.3 TELEVISION VIEWING AND OBESITY

Robinson (1999) evaluated an 18-lesson program designed to reduce television viewing by third- and fourth-grade students. He also investigated any associated improvements in eating behavior and body mass index (BMI). He used an intervention group of 92 children and a control group of 100. Before and after the intervention he assessed a number of measures of television viewing habits, exercise, eating habits, and body size and weight. He found that television viewing was reduced by about one-third, and some eating behaviors and BMI were also better in the intervention than the control group.

In Figure 6.8 I've plotted parents' estimates of the number of meals eaten in front of the television. The intervention and control groups are independent, but the baseline and postintervention measures are, of course, on the same children. Therefore, we're justified to use the CIs in the figure to compare the two groups at either time point, but *not* to compare baseline and postintervention means for either group. The CIs on the average change from baseline to postintervention may be much shorter than the CIs shown, but Figure 6.8 doesn't include them. Robinson (1999) reported that the mean difference between the changes on this measure for the two groups was 1.07, [0.18, 1.96]. That's the difference between the groups in the change from baseline to postintervention. The CI is wide, but the result supports his conclusion that there were useful improvements in some eating behaviors.

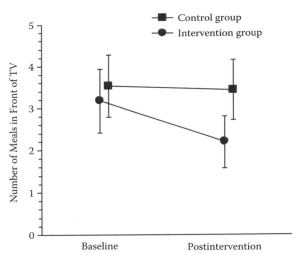

FIGURE 6.8
Means, and 95% CIs, of estimated numbers of meals eaten by children in front of television, for two groups of children at two time points. (Data from "Reducing children's television viewing to prevent obesity. A randomized controlled trial," by T.N. Robinson, 1999, *Journal of the American Medical Association*, 282, 1561–1567.)

one independent-groups and one repeated-measure independent variable. Figure 6.8 reports the means and CIs for one of the measures. In that figure, a line joining the means indicates a repeated measure: That's a useful convention, but not sufficiently well established to solve the problem. When designing a figure, make very clear, using labels or the caption, the nature of the independent variables. When seeing a figure, any reader must automatically ask, what do the error bars show and, for each independent variable, do we have independent groups or a repeated measure? If you can't answer those questions, you can't interpret the figure.

ESCI: Data Paired and Simulate Paired

There are two final ESCI pages to discuss in this chapter, and I can be brief. **Data paired** allows you to present your own data for the paired design. Figure 6.9 is from that page and displays what could be your paired data and, for each pair, a difference score marked by a triangle against the floating difference axis. One data pair and its corresponding difference are highlighted. Compare how the data pairs are represented here with the separate dot plots in the two-independent-groups example in Figure 6.6. The two designs are entirely different, and I hope the different figures make the distinction crystal clear. We need a graphical convention that can make the distinction just as clear when only means and CIs are displayed. In the meantime, the figure caption must describe the design.

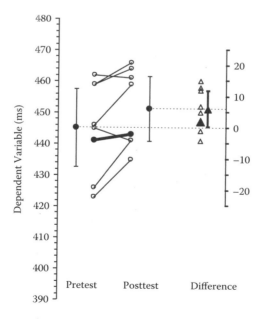

FIGURE 6.9

A figure from ESCI **Data paired** showing means and 95% CIs of pretest and posttest measures, which are response times in milliseconds (ms). The mean paired difference is shown with its 95% CI against a floating difference axis, whose zero is lined up with the pretest mean. The paired data are shown as small circles joined by lines. The differences are shown as triangles on the difference axis. One data pair and its difference are highlighted.

Just to be sure, note the *p* value, shown below red 6. It's .04, which corresponds to the 95% CI on the mean paired difference just missing zero. It's totally irrelevant that the CIs on the pretest and posttest measures show large overlap. **Data paired** doesn't mark that overlap, because for this design it's always irrelevant. The correlation of pretest and posttest is shown below red 7 and is .89 for this data set. The high correlation explains the comparatively short CI on the difference, which indicates that we have a sensitive experiment.

Simulate paired requires population means between 0 and 100, so we can't enter values similar to those of the data set in Figure 6.9. If, however, we subtract 400 from the means and keep the SD the same, we can explore variation over replication for the pattern of data illustrated in Figure 6.9. I used the spinners to enter 45 and 51 as rounded off values for μ_1 and μ_2 below red 8 in **Simulate paired**, and 13 for σ. (Once you change anything the figure goes blank until you click at red 1 to simulate an experiment.) Subtracting 400 to transform from means of 445 and 451 to 45 and 51 changes only the values marked on the vertical axis. The pattern of data and means and all the CIs will be unchanged.

Rather than entering a value for the correlation in the population, we need to enter a value for σ_{diff}, which is the population SD of paired differences. High correlation between the measures suggests that the paired differences don't vary widely, and so their SD, which in the population is σ_{diff}, will be small. I adjusted the value of σ_{diff} until the population correlation, which is shown below red 8, was .89—same as for the data we entered into **Data paired**. Using $\sigma_{diff} = 6$ did the trick. I chose $N = 8$ at red 4 and was set to go.

I clicked to run the simulation. At first I ran single experiments and watched how very widely the value of *p* varied—it's shown below red 10. No surprises there. I also saw that the correlation reported below red 9 varied considerably from experiment to experiment, reflecting the especially large variability of correlation in such small samples.

There's one further observation to describe, and it's an important one— the main reason for building and using **Simulate paired**. I clicked at red 12 to run a sequence. I used the spinner to find a convenient speed— about two experiments per second. Then I focused on how the overall figure, meaning the pretest and posttest means and their CIs, jumped up and down from experiment to experiment. I tried to get a feel for the extent of that jumping, which was often quite large. I then focused on a different thing: the variation from experiment to experiment in the mean difference—the vertical separation between the two dotted lines. If you like, click near red 6 to mark this distance with a pink line. Yes, this vertical distance varied, but

For the *paired design*, the CIs on the two measures are typically wider than the CI on the difference. If so, expect *large* variation over replication in the two means, but *smaller* variation in the mean difference.

usually not nearly as much as the overall variation in the vertical position of the pretest and posttest means. To overstate the observation a bit, the mean paired difference—where the big pink triangle falls on the difference axis—didn't change much, even as the whole configuration including the floating difference axis jumped up and down crazily.

That pattern of variation reflects why the paired design is sensitive. The variability of the paired differences, σ_{diff} in the population, is small compared with the person-to-person variation, σ in the population. The design largely removes interindividual variation and focuses on the differences. It does this most successfully when the correlation is high, which is when σ_{diff} is small compared with σ. Of course, you can use **Simulate paired** to vary any of those parameters and see how things change. Correlations around .8 and .9, as I've been using, are high, but in practice a paired design often gives correlations around those values, so my illustrations are realistic.

Here's one last way to think about the paired design, and a new skill to enjoy. At red 5 click off **Display differences** and **Display data pairs**. Note the long CIs on the pretest and posttest means, and shorter CI on the difference. The CIs tell us we've estimated the pretest and posttest means only with low precision, but the difference much more precisely. Now consider the CIs as 83% prediction intervals for replication means. The two long CIs signal that the pretest and posttest means—in other words, the whole configuration of means and floating axis—will jump up and down considerably with replication. The short CI signals that the difference—in other words, the separation between the two dotted horizontal lines—is likely to vary less over replication. That's exactly what we observed. Once again, CIs tell a beautiful and revealing story, in this case about the patterns of variation that are typical of the experimental design we're using. Relish your ability to hear the story, and see in your mind's eye the patterns of variation over replication, simply by noting the CIs.

It's time for take-home messages. Are you allowed red wine for such special occasions? I'm afraid I've mislaid the key to my labeling of the red wines, so I can't tell you whether it was Napa Valley or McLaren Vale that produced B, the wine my tasters preferred. Anyway, here are some hints to help you write your take-home messages.

- Ambiguity of figures.
- A floating difference axis.
- Overlap rule for the two-independent-groups design.
- Welch–Satterthwaite. **Data two** and **Simulate two**.
- The paired design. Correlation between the two measures.
- **Data paired** and **Simulate paired**.
- Patterns of variability with replication.

Exercises

6.1 In Example 6.3, the mean difference between the changes for the two groups was 1.07, [0.18, 1.96]. Estimate the p value.

6.2 Look back at the cat's-eye pictures in Figure 4.5. When CIs are different lengths because they have different values of C, the curves of the cat's eye are the same, and the only difference is that different proportions of the area between them are shaded. It's the same in **CI function** as you vary C. However, in **Compare A B**, left figure, display cat's eyes then change the SD of one of the groups. The CIs on M_A and M_B are different in length, but the cat's-eye pictures also differ. Why? Why the difference from Figure 4.5?

6.3 In Figure 6.5, estimate the p values for the comparison of arousal with no arousal, for the random and the not random conditions. Do you have any concerns about those estimates?

6.4 Can you use the statistical software package you're most familiar with to generate figures like Figure 6.1, with labels?

6.5 In Figures 6.5 and 6.8 I displaced the means slightly so all the CIs are clearly visible. The *Publication Manual* (APA, 2010, p. 156) suggests this strategy, although its one example uses SE bars, not CIs. Can you find a way to produce such figures?

6.6 In journals or textbooks you read, find a few example figures that permit you to use the overlap rule, for 95% CIs or for SE bars, to estimate p values. Check your estimates.

6.7 In Example 6.1, did you notice that observed bird orientation for the north and 240° magnetic fields was a repeated measure? Each bird was observed in both of those fields, so we have a paired design. Comparing the separate 95% CIs for the two fields ignored the possible correlation between the two measures. What additional information do we need?

6.8 In **Compare A B**, set up $s_A = s_B$ and $N_A = N_B$. Click at red 6 to display the figure for paired data, and near red 3 to turn on the difference axis. Adjust the correlation r near red 7. What value of r gives the shortest possible CI on the mean paired difference, and how long is that CI? Explain. What value of r gives the longest possible CI on the mean paired difference? Explain. How long is that CI compared with the CI on M_A or M_B? When $r = 0$, what happens?

6.9 In journals or textbooks you read, look for example ways to display CIs on separate means and CIs on a difference. Figure 6.7 does this, but there are other ways. Do you have any suggestions?

6.10 Compare Figure 6.5, which shows four independent groups, and Figure 6.8, which shows two groups and one repeated measure—which is indicated by a line joining the relevant means. Can you find example figures that follow this convention for marking a repeated measure? Example figures that don't? Are my captions for those two figures adequate?

6.11 In your other statistics textbook find some interesting exercises for which **Data two** or **Data paired** is helpful. You can enter data into those pages to calculate CIs and get a figure to copy into a report of yours.

6.12 Revisit your list of take-home messages, and revise if you wish.

Take-Home Messages

- Any figure must make clear for each independent variable whether it refers to independent groups or is a repeated measure.
- For interpretation it's best to have an ES estimate and a CI for each effect of primary interest.
- If the $(M_B - M_A)$ difference is of interest, it's best to have the CI for the difference, not just for M_A and M_B separately. A floating difference axis can show that nicely.
- For two independent groups, the overlap rule allows us to use the 95% CIs on the means to assess the difference. If overlap is zero then two-tailed $p = .01$, approximately, and if overlap is .5 of the average MOE then $p = .05$, approximately.
- The overlap rule is sufficiently accurate when both sample sizes are at least about 10 and the two MOEs don't differ by more than a factor of about 2.
- *Take-home picture*: Overlapping 95% CIs for independent groups that illustrate the rule of eye for $p = .05$, including cat's eyes, as in Figure 6.4.
- We prefer 95% CIs to SE bars, but SE bars are usually about half the width of 95% CIs, unless N is small, and so there's an overlap or gap rule for SE bars on two independent means.
- For the two-independent-groups design, the CI on the difference is usually calculated by assuming homogeneity of variance. So are t and p for the independent t test.
- The Welch–Satterthwaite approximation avoids that assumption, and should be preferred when sample sizes and sample SDs differ more than a little.
- **Data two** analyzes your own data for two independent groups, either with or without the assumption of homogeneity of variance, and provides figures to display your data. *Take-home picture*: The CIs and the data displayed as two dot plots, as in Figure 6.6.
- **Simulate two** displays replications of a two-independent-groups experiment. See the dance of the differences, which is wider than the dance of either group mean.
- In the paired design, the focus is on the differences, as for the paired t test. Interpretation must focus on the CI for the mean paired difference, which can be shown against a floating difference axis.

- The correlation of the measures determines how the length of the CI for the difference compares with the lengths of the CIs on the two separate means. The higher the correlation, the shorter the CI for the difference and the more sensitive the design.

- For the paired design, the length of the CI for the difference can be anything from zero to much longer than the CIs on the separate means, which are *irrelevant* for assessing the difference. No overlap rule is possible.

- **Data paired** analyzes your own data for the paired design. *Take-home picture*: The three CIs and the data displayed as pairs of points joined by lines, with the corresponding differences shown against the floating difference axis as in Figure 6.9.

- **Simulate paired** allows the exploration of replication of a paired experiment. Think of the CIs as prediction intervals, and foresee how, typically, the means will jump around a great deal but the mean difference won't change nearly as much.

7

Meta-Analysis 1: Introduction and Forest Plots

Meta-analysis can produce strong evidence where at first sight there seems to be only weak evidence. It can turn long CIs into short ones (well, sort of), find answers in what looks like a mess, and settle heated controversies. Much of what it does can be revealed in a beautiful picture called a *forest plot*. In this chapter I'll discuss forest plots and explain why I think meta-analysis and meta-analytic thinking are so great. Then in Chapter 8 there's more about ESCI and the two most important meta-analysis models. Chapter 9 outlines how to conduct a large meta-analysis and describes even more meta-analysis goodies.

At La Trobe University our large classes of beginning psychology students have for years used ESCI forest plots to discover the basics of meta-analysis. I think meta-analysis is so central to how science should be done that every introductory statistics course should include an encounter with it, and forest plots are the pictures that make that easy.

Here's the menu for this chapter:

- Meta-analysis on a small scale
- The forest plot for Lucky and Noluck, and the basics of forest plots
- What the *Publication Manual* says
- The story of meta-analysis, and meta-analysis making a difference
- Further meta-analysis pages in ESCI

Meta-Analysis on a Small Scale

Combining Two or Three Studies

Figure 7.1 is a combination of the CI and meta-analysis presentations of the Lucky and Noluck results. It's simply a combination of Figures 1.1 and 1.2, and it's our first forest plot. A forest plot is a picture of CIs that present the results from a number of comparable studies, and

A *forest plot* is a CI picture that displays results from a number of studies, and a meta-analysis of those studies.

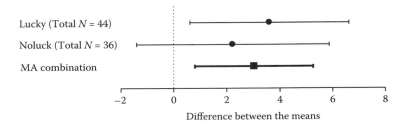

FIGURE 7.1
A forest plot that combines Figures 1.1 and 1.2. It shows the Lucky (2008) and Noluck (2008) results and their meta-analytic (MA) combination.

another CI at the bottom that presents the result of a meta-analysis combining the evidence over all the studies. Lewis and Clarke (2001) said it's called a forest plot because it can look like a forest of lines—there may be dozens of studies each contributing a CI. You could also say it helps us see the forest rather than only the trees.

Before we start playing with ESCI, try the following questions, which ask about your intuitions of small-scale meta-analysis:

7.1 Suppose you have two separate estimates of some ES. The two point estimates are similar, and the two CIs each happen to have MOE = 10 units. (Recall that MOE is the length of one arm of a CI.) Suppose we combine the two results by meta-analysis; what's your guesstimate of MOE for the result?

7.2 Same as 7.1, but now you have three independent estimates, all with MOE = 10.

7.3 Suppose you have two separate results, very similar, and each with $p = .10$. What's your guesstimate of the p value for the combined result?

7.4 Same as 7.3, but now you have three independent results, and each happens to give $p = .10$. (I know that's incredibly unlikely to happen in practice.)

Write down your best guesses in answer to those four questions. In a while I'll introduce an ESCI page that lets you find the answers, but perhaps you can use the **Two studies** page in **ESCI chapters 1–4** to find answers to 7.1 and 7.3?

Time passes … as you and I each fire up ESCI and use the **Two studies** page …

On that page I adjusted things to give Figure 7.2, which helps answer those two questions. I set both Ns large and both *SD*(pooled) values to the maximum, then I adjusted the two *M*(diff) values to be the same and

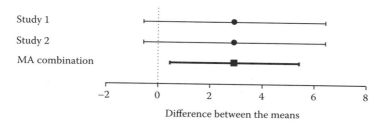

Study 1

Study 2

MA combination

−2   0   2   4   6   8

Difference between the means

FIGURE 7.2

A forest plot to help answer Questions 7.1 and 7.3. It shows the results of two fictitious studies that happened to give the same ES and MOE, and for each of which two-tailed $p = .10$, to test the null hypothesis of zero difference, which is marked by a dotted vertical line. The MOE for the meta-analytic (MA) combination is 29.3% shorter than the MOE of either of the two studies, and its p value is .02.

moved them both until Lucky and Noluck both had $p = .10$, as close as possible. Figure 7.2 is a forest plot that combines the two figures from **Two studies** after I'd made those adjustments. When I was building the **Two studies** page, I deliberately didn't report MOE values, because I hadn't introduced MOE back then in Chapter 1, and I didn't want the page to get too complicated. So we'll have to estimate the MOEs from the figures. Or you can do what I did and scroll right and find the values labeled MOE among the off-screen calculations. They're shaded pink. I noted the MOEs for Studies 1 and 2, and for the meta-analysis. I could have calculated that the meta-analysis MOE was 29.3% shorter, or I could have noted the value conveniently reported by ESCI just below the MOEs. If the MOEs for the two studies were 10 units, as in Questions 7.1 and 7.3, the MOE for the meta-analysis would be about 29% less, or 7.1 units.

The p values of .10 are shown for each study, and for the combined studies $p = .02$ is shown below the meta-analysis figure. You may have obtained slightly different answers, depending on your Ns. When each N is 10 the shrinkage is 34%. For very large N, the meta-analysis MOE is $(1/\sqrt{2})$ times as large as the MOE of either study, assuming those two are the same, meaning it's 29.3% shorter. Remember 30% as an approximate guide to the amount of MOE shrinkage when you combine the results of two similar studies.

The Good News of Meta-Analysis

Did you read Questions 7.1 to 7.4 and think you'd better adjust your first guesses in the pessimistic direction? Just about every time in this book so far the answers to judgment questions I've asked have been discouraging. Almost always, CIs are wider, sampling variability greater, and the result of replication more different than we might have guessed. So perhaps you tweaked your answers to those questions to make the MOEs longer and *p* values larger? I don't blame you—after all, it's one of the main messages of this book that sampling variation is often larger than we'd have guessed.

I'm pleased to say that meta-analysis breaks that mold and often delivers encouragingly good news. Two results combining to give a CI that's about 30% shorter is a very useful increase in precision. Within traditional

Two similar and independent results, when combined, give a CI about 30% shorter (if sample sizes are not too small) than the CI for a single result. They also give a much lower *p* value.

NHST thinking, it may be even more surprising that two results as weak (in traditional NHST terms) as *p* = .10, could combine to give a result as strong (again, in traditional terms) as *p* = .02. The first main conclusion of this chapter is a happy one: Even two or three indications of an effect can, when combined, provide quite strong evidence for the effect. The indications need to broadly agree and must be at least largely independent of each other. If those conditions are met, the combination of evidence is probably encouragingly strong. In many situations, researchers should spend less time worrying about exactly how small a single *p* value is, and more effort looking for any other converging evidence they may be able to find. Even a small amount of separate, converging evidence makes a useful strengthening of a conclusion.

Example 7.1 illustrates how meta-analysis on even a small scale can be very useful. There's further good news: Many disciplines have adopted meta-analysis fairly readily, with little resistance or criticism. It's a component of the new statistics that's rapidly becoming mainstream. That is good news, but the way meta-analysis is usually understood needs to be broadened. So far, appreciation of meta-analysis has usually been restricted to its role in large-scale literature reviews, rather than as a tool for use in various different situations. To put it differently, I suspect that many researchers think of meta-analysis as a set of somewhat difficult and specialized techniques that can be used by statisticians, or researchers with an interest in methodology, to carry out large-scale quantitative reviews of research. In support of this view, any good book on meta-analysis describes a challenging sequence of steps needed to carry out a major meta-analysis. I'll outline that process in Chapter 9, but here I want to highlight meta-analysis at the smaller scale.

Meta-analysis permits us to combine evidence from studies that address similar questions. Combining even two studies can give a useful increase in precision. Researchers can use meta-analysis to combine evidence from related experiments in their research program as

Use meta-analysis whenever it's appropriate, even to combine just two or three results.

we did in Example 7.1, or even from related results within a single experiment. Such small-scale uses of meta-analysis may prove in many situations to be the best way to respond to the disappointingly large uncertainty

EXAMPLE 7.1 ASSESSING THE UNCERTAINTY OF EXPERTS

This is an example of small-scale meta-analysis in action. One of my research interests is the study of decision making by experts. Society often has to rely on expert advice when there's insufficient good evidence to guide decisions, but we'd like to know how uncertain an expert is in a particular case. We'd like from the expert not just a best point estimate, but an interval estimate that has some stated chance of including the true value. (You see why I'm interested in expert decision making—CIs in a different guise!)

The custom is to seek an 80% uncertainty interval around an expert's best point estimate. For example, we might ask our ecological expert to estimate the number of small marine species likely to be lost from a bay at a certain level of water pollution. In addition to a best estimate, perhaps 30, we'd like an 80% uncertainty interval. Just asking the expert to state such an interval— say, (10, 60)—usually gives intervals that are too narrow and that include the true value in only around 50% of situations. In other words, experts often think their estimates are better than they really are. However, research has found that different ways of asking about uncertainty can give more accurate intervals—even just asking separately for the lower and upper limits of the interval helps.

In the article by Speirs-Bridge et al. (2010) we reported one study in which public health experts made forecasts about rates of infectious diseases, and another in which ecological experts gave estimates about the effect of marine pollution. For each study we had data we could use to assess the accuracy of the experts' point estimates, and their 80% uncertainty intervals. One of our aims was to compare two different ways of questioning the experts to establish their 80% uncertainty intervals. The first asked separately for the two limits of the interval, and the second was a slightly more elaborate version in which we didn't specify 80% uncertainty, but asked the participant to nominate the percentage for the interval they gave us. Then we calculated the equivalent 80% interval. In both our studies this second way of questioning gave better uncertainty intervals—meaning intervals that included the true value in closer to 80% of cases. We expressed the difference in accuracy of the intervals given by the two question formats as a Cohen's d value. For our study with public health experts the advantage of the more elaborate format was $d = 0.92$ [−0.12, 1.96], and for the ecological experts it was $d = 0.47$ [−0.21, 1.15]. Both studies thus gave a substantial ES in favor of the second question format, but our precision was low, despite our having assembled as many as 24 public health experts and 34 ecologists to participate in our studies. As so often happens when humans are involved, the variation was large. You may have noticed also that both CIs included zero. We meta-analyzed the two results and obtained $d = 0.60$ [0.04, 1.17] as our overall estimate of how much better our second question format performed. That final CI is still wide, but not as wide as those for the separate studies. We concluded that we had very encouraging evidence from two quite different areas of expertise that the second, slightly more elaborate questioning format is better and definitely worth further investigation. Small-scale meta-analysis, as in Figures 7.1 and 7.2, provided the basis for our conclusion.

revealed by wide CIs. Reporting such a meta-analysis can be as simple as reporting the combined result with its CI, as in Example 7.1, and stating the model of meta-analysis used—Chapter 8 explains about models.

In addition, you may have noticed while working with **Two studies** that you can consider CIs and meta-analysis with little or no reference to p values. Meta-analysis can make NHST largely irrelevant. Perhaps the NHST disciplines will at last shift emphasis from NHST to estimation and other better techniques, not because of the exhortations of statistical reformers, but because wider use of meta-analysis leads to a natural decline in the use of NHST. That would be a great advance.

NHST is almost *irrelevant* to meta-analysis, and so it may be the spread of meta-analysis that helps prompt the retreat of NHST.

I'm arguing that meta-analysis has value much more widely than just as a specialist tool for large literature reviews. This position of mine has two further consequences. First, if meta-analysis will be used as widely as I think it deserves, students should learn the basics of meta-analysis at an early stage. In Cumming (2006b, tinyurl.com/teachma) I argued that software based on forest plots makes it practical to do this, even in the introductory statistics course. I hope ESCI can help.

The second consequence is that meta-analytic thinking is important, right from the start of research planning. If estimation thinking guides our research, we'll probably soon encounter CIs that are wide and data sets that don't seem to permit confident conclusions. We can resolve to design more informative experiments, as we'll discuss in Chapters 12 and 13, but there are usually practical limits. More generally, we should adopt meta-analytic thinking. Think of every result as one line in a forest plot. There may be previous studies and other results from our own research that we can add to the forest plot. We need to bear in mind that future research, by us or others, is likely to contribute further lines. Any study contributes at least one tree, but it's the forest that's important, and the forest plot is a beautiful picture that reminds us of that. Next I'll use ESCI to describe basic features of forest plots.

Forest Plots: The Basics

ESCI Meta-Analysis provides a number of pages for carrying out meta-analysis. The simplest is **Original 7**, which allows you to enter results for up to six experiments, plus one labeled as the "current" study. For each study you enter an identifying name, then the mean, SD, and sample size. The ES of interest is the mean, expressed in the measurement units of the dependent variable. I refer to those units as the *original units*, in contrast to standardized units such as Cohen's *d* that we'll consider in Chapter 11.

Original units are the units in which a dependent variable was originally measured. Examples are centimeters, milliseconds, number of errors, and units on a scale.

I imagined experiments that investigated response times to words. Near red 1 I typed in the units (ms), and then I invented names and data for six past studies and our current study. Figure 7.3 shows what I entered. The ES of each study is represented in the forest plot by a square and the 95% CI by error bars. The dots, with their error bars, report a meta-analysis of the past six studies and—the lower dot—of those six plus our current study. Compare the two dot results, or the two overall means reported near red 3 and red 5 (i.e., 435 and 443 ms), to see what our study has added to the overall picture. Hmm, only a very little?

You may be wondering about the strange stuff near red 16, 18, and 19. We'll get to that in Chapter 8 but, for now, just make sure that **Fixed effect** is clicked at red 16.

Weighting the Studies in a Meta-Analysis

You can see on the screen, or in Figure 7.3, values reported for the means and MOEs, and for the variance of the mean. In Chapter 8 I'll explain formulas for meta-analysis, but here I'll note that meta-analysis calculates a weighted combination of the studies. The usual weighting, which I use in this book and in ESCI, is the inverse of the variance of the ES. We're using here the mean as our ES. Recall that the SD of the mean is $SE = \sigma/\sqrt{N}$. Therefore, variance of the mean is $SE^2 = \sigma^2/N$, which is estimated for each study as s^2/N, where s is the SD of the study.

A meta-analysis usually *weights* the contributing studies by the inverse of the variance of the ES. Large weights go with small SD and large N, and are represented by larger squares in the forest plot.

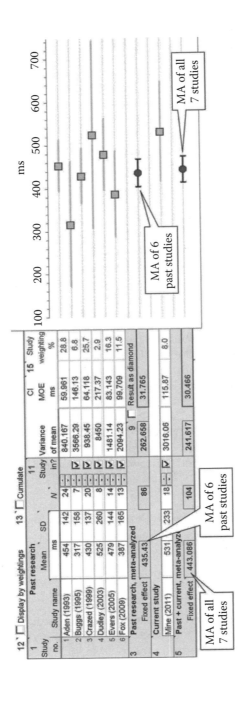

FIGURE 7.3
Data and a forest plot from the **Original 7** page of **ESCI Meta-Analysis**, showing results of six fictitious past studies, then our current study. The values at red 3 and the upper dot in the forest plot report a meta-analysis (MA) of the past six studies. The values at red 5 and the lower dot report a meta-analysis of all seven studies. The forest plot shows 95% CIs.

These estimates of variance are used to calculate the weights, and percentage weights for each study in the overall meta-analysis of seven studies are reported below red 15. A small study with large SD, such as Dudley (2003—one of the fictitious studies appearing in the figures), has large variance of the mean and thus low weight (2.9%) in the meta-analysis. Aden (1993) has relatively small SD and large N, thus smaller variance and higher weight (28.8%). Small weights go with wide CIs, and large weights with short CIs. That's as we'd expect, because both MOE and the weights are calculated from the SE of a study.

One problem with CIs is that wide intervals tend to attract the eye, but give poor information. Short CIs give better information, but appear less prominent. To overcome this problem, we can use the weightings to adjust how the forest plot represents the different studies. Figure 7.4 shows the usual way to do this: The squares representing study means are varied in size, with their areas adjusted to reflect, approximately, the study weights. I clicked at red 12 to get the weighted display. Large and precise studies have large squares marking their mean, and thus attract the eye even though their CIs are short.

Figure 7.4 also illustrates how forest plots often represent the results of meta-analysis with a diamond, rather than a mean marker with error bars. I clicked at red 9 to get diamonds. We can think of the diamond as a stylized version of the cat's eye for a CI.

Meta-Analysis and NHST

I next supposed that someone has published a theory that predicts the mean response time for the word task we're investigating is 300 ms. I clicked at red 6 to add a null hypothesis line to the forest plot, then typed in 300 at red 7 and pressed the Enter key. (The slider doesn't supply values that high.) Figure 7.4 marks that null hypothesized value. You can click at red 8 to show NHST results, or we can just note in the forest plot where the CIs fall in relation to the line at 300. Your skill from Chapter 4 at estimating p values can be useful when inspecting forest plots—if you wish to use NHST. Buggs (1995) and Fox (2009) are not statistically significant ($p > .05$), and are therefore at most risk of not achieving publication. Click to clear their checkboxes below red 11, and thus remove them from the meta-analysis. Note how the meta-analysis results change. Other things being equal, studies giving ES estimates close to a null hypothesized value are more likely to give $p > .05$. If that means they're less likely to be published, then a meta-analysis of published studies will give a biased result—an estimated ES that's likely to be too large.

Clicking to remove those two studies illustrates the *file drawer effect*. If researchers believe $p > .05$ results are unlikely to be published, they're likely to leave the results of such studies in their filing cabinets or on their

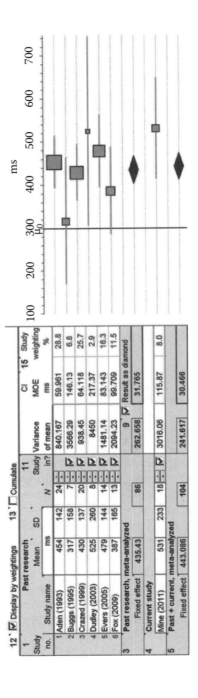

FIGURE 7.4

Same as Figure 7.3, except that a null hypothesis line is marked at 300 ms, the forest plot represents study weights by size of square, and meta-analysis results are shown as diamonds.

hard disks, rather than undertake the large task of writing up and submitting for publication. Or, if the results are submitted to a journal, they are likely to be rejected and

> The *file drawer effect* is the tendency for results that are not statistically significant to remain unpublished. This can seriously bias future meta-analyses.

so end up in the file drawer anyway. The *Publication Manual* (APA, 2010) recognizes the problem by stating, "Mention all relevant results ... be sure to include small effect sizes (or statistically nonsignificant findings) ..." (p. 32). It's essential that results from all well-conducted studies are available for future meta-analysis. Publication decisions based on *p* values are likely to distort the published research literature and bias the results of meta-analyses. That's further bad news about NHST.

Figure 7.3 includes no mention of a null hypothesis or *p* values, yet presents a full picture of multiple studies and their meta-analysis. It thus illustrates that NHST is largely irrelevant to the estimation of ESs, and to the combination of evidence over studies to find more precise estimates. As I mentioned earlier, experience with forest plots and meta-analysis might persuade researchers that NHST is often unnecessary—as well as possibly distorting the published research literature.

Cumulative Meta-Analysis

There's one further trick in the forest plot repertoire. The studies in Figure 7.3 are ordered chronologically. Imagine carrying out a meta-analysis after each successive study became available. That would give a sort of time-lapse movie of how knowledge has advanced, as successive studies provided extra evidence about the ES we're estimating. Click at red 13 to see the cumulative meta-analysis. Rather than illustrating what happens in **Original 7**,

> *Cumulative meta-analysis* refers to a sequence of meta-analyses, each including one additional study.

I'm including an illustration from the next page in **ESCI meta-analysis**. That's **Original 31**, which is exactly like **Original 7** except 30 rather than six past studies can be entered. Figure 7.5 shows the cumulative meta-analysis for the first six studies in the previous figures, plus 10 additional studies. As before, the squares show the weighted results of individual studies. The darker gray dots show the meta-analysis of the first two studies, the first three, and so on. ESCI also reports the mean and MOE for the cumulative results at red 14, to the right of the forest plot.

Examining Figure 7.5 suggests several conclusions:

- Successive cumulative meta-analyses generally home in on a final best estimate of the ES, with the CIs generally becoming shorter.
- As we'd expect, studies with large weights shift the cumulative mean more than studies with small weights. Compare the shifts caused by Golly (2009) and Heavy (2009).

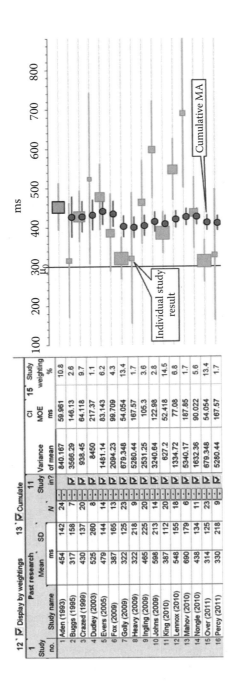

FIGURE 7.5

Part of the screen of **Original 31** showing cumulative meta-analysis (MA) for the first six studies in Figure 7.4, plus a further 10 studies. Results for individual studies are shown by pale gray squares, and successive meta-analytic results are shown by darker gray dots. Error bars are 95% CIs.

- Early studies influence the cumulative result considerably, but studies beyond the first few generally have only a smaller influence. Toward the end of the set, additional studies give diminishing returns, meaning they shift the cumulative mean less.
- I designed Over (2011) and Percy (2011) to have the same weights as Golly and Heavy, and also to be the same distance from the immediately preceding cumulative means. It's clear in the plot that Over and Percy shift the mean much less—only about half as far—as did the two earlier studies. That's a further illustration of the diminishing influence of later studies.

The conclusion is that successive studies added into a meta-analysis give very useful increases in precision, provided the results don't vary too much. (If they differ considerably, the picture is more complicated, as I discuss in Chapter 8.) After a few studies, further increases in precision are smaller, as Figure 7.5 illustrates. The main message, however, is the wonder of meta-analysis: Give it long CIs and it can give back a highly desirable short CI. It's unfortunate that the wonder of meta-analysis has not yet been investigated from a cognitive perspective. Box 7.1 describes one of the very few studies that touch on how people think about meta-analysis. Now, after all this playing with forest plots, I'll report what the *Publication Manual* says about meta-analysis, and then I'll describe some examples of meta-analysis changing the world.

BOX 7.1 THINKING ABOUT META-ANALYSIS

I'd like to know how people think about meta-analysis and interpret forest plots, but the statistical cognition of meta-analysis has hardly been studied. Numerous interesting questions await investigation. I can find only one study to mention here. It's a very early comparison by Cooper and Rosenthal (1980) of traditional reviewing with an early form of meta-analysis based on combining p values. Psychology graduate students and faculty members were randomly assigned to use one or the other reviewing method. All were given a set of seven articles on the same topic and instructed either to read and consider the articles as they usually would if preparing a review, or to apply a set of instructions to calculate a combined p value. They then answered questions about what overall conclusions they felt were justified. The study found that the meta-analysis prompted generally better conclusions—stronger support for the hypothesis of an effect, and a larger estimated ES. Both of those conclusions were justified by the set of results. Cooper and Rosenthal were especially interested to see whether using meta-analysis might prompt their participants to merely apply the procedure and not think critically about the studies. This didn't happen, however, so meta-analysis emerged well from this early evaluation.

What the *Publication Manual* Says

The fifth edition of the *Publication Manual* (APA, 2001) mentioned meta-analysis only a few times, briefly. In striking contrast, meta-analysis appears in the sixth edition of the *Manual* (APA, 2010) in many places. A two-page appendix (pp. 251–252) presents the new Meta-Analysis Reporting Standards (MARS), which are guidelines describing in detail the information that should be included in a report of a large meta-analysis. An example manuscript describes a meta-analysis (pp. 57–59), and two subsections (pp. 36–37, 183) discuss meta-analyses and how they should be reported. There are more than a dozen other mentions of meta-analysis. All that discussion and advice in the sixth edition signals that meta-analysis is now mainstream. That's a great step forward.

As I mentioned earlier, the *Manual* states that all relevant ESs must be reported, even if not statistically significant. That's vital for avoidance of the file drawer effect. The *Manual* emphasizes the point by stating that, "even when a characteristic is not used in analysis of the data, reporting it may … prove useful in meta-analytic studies that incorporate the article's results" (APA, 2010, p. 30). The usual minimum is point and interval estimates of any effect. That information, together with N, should allow its inclusion in a meta-analysis. Reporting as a Cohen's d or a correlation r, as well as in original units, may be even more helpful to a future meta-analyst.

The study of gender differences provides a cautionary tale about incomplete reporting. In the 1970s, reviews of research about the abilities and behaviors of boys and girls usually reported a long list of well-established differences—in verbal ability, mathematical ability, aggressiveness, and so on (Maccoby & Jacklin, 1974). Some differences were large. The published research justified such conclusions, but psychologists interested in gender gradually realized that selective publication was distorting the picture. Some researchers set out to study gender differences, and no doubt some of their studies languished in file drawers, but there was an additional type of incomplete reporting. Numerous researchers primarily studied issues other than gender and, being careful researchers, they explored their data. Often they could compare scores for boys and girls, even though they had no particular interest in gender. They might even prefer to find no difference because then they could simplify things by combining the data for boys and girls. The trouble was that if such a secondary, exploratory analysis gave no statistically significant difference, the researchers were likely to omit any mention of gender from their journal articles, and would certainly not report separate means and SDs for boys and girls. It didn't help that journal space was always at a premium and editors often instructed authors to shorten their manuscripts. Anything of lesser interest had to go, and nonsignificant effects were first overboard. On the other hand, if exploratory subgroup analyses happened to find a statistically significant difference, this result (and, with luck, the means and SDs) would probably be reported, and perhaps given some interpretation in relation to the issues being studied. The published research on gender differences was distorted by studies in the file drawer, but also by selective reporting of subgroup analyses. We might say that the unreported subgroup analyses of gender occupied a secret compartment within the file drawer.

More recent reviews of gender identify fewer and generally smaller differences, and a list of abilities on which there is little if any difference (Hyde, 2007). The study of gender differences is a case study in how estimation and complete data reporting will help reviewers build an accurate picture, whereas old habits of dichotomous thinking, NHST, and selective reporting can easily give a highly distorted picture. Also, pressure of journal space is no longer an excuse for incomplete reporting, because journals now provide online supplementary material to accompany an article.

My conclusion is that the sixth edition of the *Manual* does a good job advising reviewers of research who wish to carry out meta-analysis. That's great but, perhaps even more importantly, it instructs all researchers to bear future meta-analysis in mind as they conduct and report their research. Report complete results, and give sufficient detail—in an online supplement if necessary—to assist the inclusion of your results in a future meta-analysis. That's excellent advice.

Meta-Analysis Making a Difference

I'm emphasizing in this chapter the value of meta-analysis on a small scale. Even so, the main impact so far has been by large-scale meta-analyses used for research synthesis. *Research synthesis* is a term gaining popularity, and meta-analysis is a set of techniques for carrying out research synthesis in a quantitative way. A similar term, widely used in medicine, is *systematic review*. Almost all systematic reviews use meta-analysis for the quantitative combination of evidence. In this section I'll first

Research synthesis and *systematic review* refer to the integration of research evidence, usually by meta-analysis.

sketch briefly the story of meta-analysis, with some examples to illustrate its value, then I'll describe further examples of meta-analysis in medicine, education, and—would you believe—physics.

Gene Glass and the Advent of Meta-Analysis

Early approaches to meta-analysis included combining correlations, or combining p values from different studies. However, the term *meta-analysis* was coined and the basic technique arrived in a big way when Gene Glass gave a famous presidential address to the American Educational Research Association in San Francisco in 1976. Glass was a young educational researcher with statistical interests who had been greatly annoyed by attacks on psychotherapy by H. J. Eysenck. Eysenck had claimed that psychotherapy was ineffective, and there were no evaluative data to prove otherwise. Glass had personally experienced what he felt to be great benefit from psychotherapy, and he believed that he could apply his statistical skills to prove Eysenck wrong. For two years he and Mary Lee Smith labored hard to track down articles, dissertations, and reports that described evaluations of psychotherapy. In those days, before computerized databases and computerized search, Glass and Smith spent many hours in libraries and at the photocopying machine. They located more than one thousand promising documents, only to find on closer inspection that many did not include a control group, or did not provide any measure of therapy outcome.

They judged 375 of the studies adequate for their analysis. Glass then calculated for each an ES for the effect of therapy: "the mean difference on the outcome variable between treated and untreated subjects divided by the within group standard deviation" (Glass, 1976, p. 6). That's Cohen's d, which we'll discuss in Chapter 11. Glass found that many of the reports gave incomplete statistical information, and he had to use his statistical ingenuity to estimate a value for d, given, for example, only means and a p value, or only correlation or regression measures. Overall, the mean advantage of therapy was $d = 0.68$, a substantial and valuable effect. That's equivalent to an average increase of 10 IQ points on an intelligence test with an SD of 15. It's also equivalent to saying that, on average, therapy advances a person at the median (the 50th percentile) of the control distribution to the 75th percentile of that distribution. Glass and Smith also coded their selected studies on a number of important characteristics, including level of training of the therapist and type of psychotherapy. They found that what they classified as client-centered therapies, behavior modification, and rational emotive therapy all produced, on average, very similar improvement. That's an example of meta-analysis going beyond giving just an overall average ES; we'll discuss this further in Chapter 9.

Despite his fears about presenting a novel and possibly strange statistical technique, Glass' presidential address was enthusiastically received. You can read a shortened version in the *Educational Researcher* (Glass, 1976) and a description of the psychotherapy meta-analysis in the *American Psychologist* (Smith & Glass, 1977). Eysenck (1978) responded in a typically outspoken way, in an *American Psychologist* comment titled, "An Exercise in Mega-Silliness." He derided the inclusion of lesser-quality studies as "garbage in—garbage out" (p. 517). Nevertheless, the pioneering work of Glass and Smith has been enormously influential, and their findings have been confirmed by subsequent work by others.

The Glass story is told near the start of Morton Hunt's book, *How Science Takes Stock: The Story of Meta-Analysis* (1997). I highly recommend this book, which reads more like a novel than a textbook. There are tales of the pioneers of meta-analysis, and numerous examples of meta-analysis finding important conclusions in what had seemed like a collection of messy and conflicting results. Hunt reports that Glass was highly critical of NHST, and quotes Glass as saying in an interview, "Statistical significance is the least interesting thing about the results. You should describe the results in terms of measures of magnitude—not just, does a treatment affect people, but how *much* does it affect them? *That's* what we needed to know" (pp. 29–30, emphasis in the original). Exactly.

I'll mention just one of the case studies Hunt describes. A certain program in the United States provided a range of support to low-income pregnant women and mothers with young children. There were strident lobby groups who supported the program, and others who believed it should be abolished. Studies of its effectiveness gave conflicting results. By 1983 it had been running for around a decade, with an ever-growing budget. In advance of Senate hearings on its fate, a meta-analysis was commissioned to synthesize the evaluation studies. This found positive results, especially in terms of increased infant birth-weight, and was probably crucial in the decision to continue the program. This example of meta-analysis reaching a quantitative and well-justified conclusion from a number of studies, many of which were flawed in some way, illustrates how decision making can be evidence based, even in a complex and ideologically charged area of social policy.

There's a lesson also for social and behavioral science research. Possibly the most convincing way to ensure future funding for such research is to show that research, even on messy social questions, can give conclusions that are well supported by evidence and have important practical implications. Few individual studies are able to do that, but meta-analysis often can. The arrival of meta-analysis has probably been crucial for maintaining public support of social and behavioral science research—as well as, of course, deriving from such research conclusions that can improve people's lives.

Hunter and Schmidt

At around the same time, but working independently of Glass, Jack Hunter and Frank Schmidt developed a somewhat different set of techniques for carrying out meta-analysis. They worked mainly in the area of industrial–organizational psychology, and often used correlations as the basis for meta-analysis. They (Hunter & Schmidt, 2004) described a striking example of how meta-analysis has changed conclusions from research, and also business practice. Tests of job aptitude are widely used to select people likely to be most suitable for a particular job. The validity of such tests has been examined in numerous studies, which typically focus on the correlation between test score and some later measure of job performance. Published studies have reported a wide range of correlations, some attaining statistical significance, and some not. One important question was how widely a test could be used. Was a test that seemed valid for a particular job in one company also valid for a similar job in a different company, or for a related but not identical job in the first company? Reviews of the literature generally concluded that validity did not generalize: Tests were usually only valid for the particular job and situation for which they had been designed. That's bad news, of course, because it severely limits the usefulness of tests. It also undermines the general idea of testing. Can we take seriously a test that can't even predict performance in two seemingly similar jobs?

Hunter and Schmidt (2004, Chapter 4) concluded that the widely varying correlations found by individual studies were produced largely by sampling variability and other sources of extraneous variation, such as measurement error. (I'll say more about that in Chapter 9.) The research studies, when synthesized by meta-analysis, actually provided strong evidence that validity generalizes considerably. Within limits, it's justifiable to use a well-developed test of job suitability in a range of different settings. That conclusion has provided important support for job testing and is now widely accepted. Meta-analysis corrected the erroneous conclusions that had originally been drawn from research findings.

In their first chapter, Hunter and Schmidt (2004) gave their own persuasive account of the value of meta-analysis. As an example of a meta-analysis influencing decision making by the U.S. Congress, they described a meta-analysis of studies on the value of producing binary chemical weapons:

> The meta-analysis did not support the production of such weapons. This was not what the Department of Defense (DOD) wanted to hear, and the DOD disputed the methodology and the results. The methodology held up under close scrutiny, however, and in the end Congress eliminated funds for these weapons. (p. 30)

Meta-Analysis in Medicine

Hunt (1997, Chapter 4) described a number of case studies from medicine in which meta-analysis allowed clear conclusions to be drawn from collections of highly variable or even conflicting research studies. Medicine now increasingly uses meta-analysis to synthesize and present the evidence for evidence-based practice, as I'll discuss further in Chapter 9. That's a great development, which is important also for any other discipline wishing to adopt evidence-based practice.

My first medical example includes comparisons with other approaches to reviewing research. Antman, Lau, Kupelnick, Mosteller, and Chalmers (1992) reported a meta-analysis of 17 studies of the effects of oral β-blockers for reducing the risk of mortality in heart-attack survivors. There was clear evidence that the drug therapy is effective. The studies had been published between 1972 and 1988, and the researchers used cumulative meta-analysis to consider how evidence had accumulated during that period. They found that, by around 1982 after the first nine studies had appeared, the issue should have been declared decided. From 1982 the drug should have been used routinely. Unless the later studies asked additional worthwhile questions, it was not justifiable to expend the time and effort running the later studies, and it was not ethical to subject their patients randomized into the control group to the increased risk of the placebo drug—the ineffective sugar pill—instead of the oral β-blocker. Most importantly, a confident recommendation to practitioners could have been made much earlier, with a consequential saving of many lives around the world.

Antman et al. (1992) also examined review articles published during the period covered by the 17 studies. They concluded that many of these did not reflect the then most recent evidence, and did not combine evidence effectively. They often reached poor conclusions and sometimes recommended practices that research had by then shown to be hazardous. Wider use of meta-analysis and better ways to disseminate the results were needed.

My second medical example is heart-rending. Sudden infant death syndrome (SIDS), or crib death, is the death while sleeping of apparently healthy babies. It remained largely inexplicable during most of the twentieth century. When my wife and I were young parents in the late 1970s we carefully followed what seemed to be the best advice for reducing the risk of SIDS: Our three babies slept on their front on a sheepskin. A generation later, Gilbert, Salanti, Harden, and See (2005) reported a meta-analysis of evidence on the effect of sleeping position on risk of SIDS, and also a historical review of the advice given by authors of childcare books, including Doctor Spock, on baby sleeping position. Gilbert et al.'s cumulative meta-analysis found that by 1970 there was reasonably clear evidence that back sleeping was safer than front. The evidence strengthened during subsequent years, although there was little good research until around 1986. However, they also found frequent recommendation of front sleeping, even as late as 1988. They estimated that, if back sleeping had been widely recommended from 1970, as many as 50,000 infant deaths could have been prevented in Europe, the United States, and Australasia. Had meta-analysis been available and used in 1970, much tragedy could have been averted. I'm happy to report that our grandchildren are resolutely put down to sleep on their backs.

The Struggle for Phonics

In a fascinating book titled, *Teaching to Read, Historically Considered*, Mitford Mathews (1966) described how the favored method for teaching reading has changed since the days of Greek slaves teaching rich Romans to read. Numerous methods have come and gone. The pendulum of popularity has swung back and forth between largely phonic (or synthetic) methods and largely whole-word (or analytic) methods. Phonic methods pay careful attention to the ways letters represent sounds, whereas analytic methods emphasize complete words in context. Mathews reviewed the research literature and concluded that synthetic beats analytic, but his voice was only one among many. In many English-speaking countries ideology and fashion, rather than evidence, seemed to guide educational policy on teaching reading, and to shape teachers' beliefs and practices.

Especially during the 1960s and 1970s, large research studies were conducted, and repeated efforts were made to review the evidence. However, conclusions were often equivocal and different experts gave different advice. Entrenched belief, rather than evidence, continued to drive policy and practice. Then the U.S. National Reading Panel (2000) made a concerted effort to bring order to the enormous research literature. To conduct a meta-analysis on the effects of different teaching methods they winnowed 1,072 studies down to only 38 that met their selection criteria—which included requirements as simple as having a control group and providing sufficient statistical information to calculate ESs. The analyses of the Panel were scrutinized and extended, and in some cases corrected, by Diane McGuinness, whose book, *Early Reading Instruction: What Science Really Tells Us About How to Teach Reading* (2004), is impressive and readable. Her discussion in Chapter 5 is based on estimated ESs derived from the meta-analysis of various groups of research studies. She makes a persuasive argument that we now know how to teach reading successfully: It's essential to focus early on phonics, starting with phonemes (sound elements of the language) and how letters most commonly represented them. Mathews was right, in 1966. This is an example of meta-analysis not merely summarizing evidence that gradually accumulates, but determining in decisive fashion a long-standing and heated controversy. There's more, as McGuinness' Chapter 11 describes, but largely thanks to meta-analysis we can now draw clear evidence-based conclusions from an enormous and terribly messy literature. The pendulum should swing no more.

Hard Science and Soft Science

Larry Hedges is a statistician who has made major contributions to the techniques of meta-analysis. In 1987 he published a fascinating article whose title asks the question, "How Hard Is Hard Science, How Soft Is Soft Science?" In the supposedly "soft" social and behavioral sciences we're familiar with disagreement among research findings, but, he asked, what about in physics, the supposedly "hard" discipline, if we go out to the research frontiers? He found that particle physicists who study questions such as, "What is the lifetime of the muon?" and "What is the mass of a charged pion?" often have to contend with differing answers found by different research groups. Hedges found that physicists have developed statistical techniques to combine the results from different laboratories to give a single best estimate, with a CI. Physicists don't use the term "meta-analysis," but Hedges explained that their techniques were very similar to what we know as meta-analysis.

Hedges (1987) went further and applied a measure of heterogeneity to 13 reviews of results from particle physics and 13 meta-analyses in social science. In both cases he included reviews he judged to be representative and of good quality. He found the average amount of heterogeneity to be virtually identical for the physics and social science reviews. In other words, he found the extent of disagreement between studies in a review to be, on average, very similar for physics and the social sciences. Yes, he concluded, physics may in many cases be able to measure to more decimal places, but in terms of the extent of agreement or disagreement among studies at the research frontier, physics may not be any more "hard" a discipline than the social sciences. Meta-analysis seems to be needed in traditionally hard as well as soft sciences, and can also give an additional interesting perspective on how whole disciplines compare. Recently, Petticrew (2001) described how meta-analysis is used in numerous disciplines, ranging from archaeology and astronomy through ecology and law to zoology.

These examples illustrate the great power of meta-analysis to bring order where there's disorder and to settle major disputes. However, I don't want to give the impression that all questions can be answered by applying meta-analysis to existing research, or that meta-analysis is always simple and without challenges. Often an important contribution of a meta-analysis is to highlight deficiencies in existing knowledge and provide guidance for future research. Also, carrying out a large meta-analysis can be a daunting task, and critical analysis and judgment informed by good understanding of the topic area are as important for meta-analysis as for any other way to review research. Even so, meta-analysis does offer magic.

Further Pages in ESCI Meta-Analysis

I've used **Original 7** and **Original 31** for playing with forest plots. **ESCI Meta-Analysis** also provides further pages for your exploration. These are primarily intended to illustrate aspects of meta-analysis and help build intuitions for meta-analytic thinking. They can also, within limits, be used to carry out calculations for the meta-analysis of real data.

First I'll mention a couple of extra things about the two **Original** pages. Excel automatically adjusts the scale of the horizontal axis at the top of the forest plot, depending on the values you type in. That's usually best, but occasionally you might like to stop the axis changing as you experiment, for example, by clicking to include or exclude a study from the meta-analysis. Simply click the checkbox near red 17 to freeze or unfreeze the axis.

One further goodie may lie off the screen, but is signaled at red 20. Scroll right to see a second forest plot, which displays the included studies of the first six or first 30 and only the first summary meta-analysis. It can display by weightings (red 12) but not cumulative meta-analysis (red 13). It's intended for copying to word processing software—I'm trying to encourage everyone to use forest plots whenever they can be useful. This figure, like all others in ESCI, can be edited using any of Excel's facilities. If you wish to include details of the studies as well as the forest plot, you might consider using a selection from a screen capture, as I did to make Figure 7.3 and others like it. Appendix A can assist.

Original two groups carries out meta-analysis of studies that compare two independent groups, for example, an experimental group and a control group. Enter the original units and names for the two groups near red 1, then for each study enter for each group the M, SD, and N. The ES of interest is the difference ($M_2 - M_1$) between the two study means. The variance of this ES is shown and is used to calculate the weights, which are shown below red 6. NHST assumes that the null hypothesis is a difference of zero. Cumulative meta-analysis is not supported.

Standard 7 is a little more complicated because it offers a choice between original units and the simplest type of standardized units. We'll see in Chapter 11 that the standardized ES Cohen's d can be calculated in various ways. The simplest requires that we know a value for σ, the population SD. **Standard 7** requires such a σ and assumes it's the same for all studies entered. That's not quite as unrealistic as it might seem. For example, a number of different IQ tests give scores that have been scaled so that the mean and SD in some large reference population are 100 and 15, respectively. So we might judge it reasonable to use 15 as the σ for a population of children we're studying. Suppose we've found several studies that estimate the mean IQ scores of that population. In **Standard 7**, type in near red 1 the original units ("IQ score"), then 15 as the value of σ, then *M* and *N* for each study. Near red 1, click the radio button—the little clickable circle—next to **Mean** to show the results of the meta-analysis in original units (IQ scores) or the other button, next to *d*, to show them as Cohen's *d* values. Values in original units appear on the screen in blue, and *d* values in purple. The forest plot displays IQ scores or *d* values, as you select. The formula for calculating d_i for a study is

$$d_i = (M_i - \mu_0)/\sigma \qquad (7.1)$$

where M_i is the mean of a study, and μ_0 is the population mean that serves as the reference point from which we wish to measure *d*. ESCI uses the μ_0 value at red 7 as this reference value, and so for *d* to be calculated we need a suitable μ_0 value specified at red 7, and the checkbox at red 6 must be clicked on so the μ_0 reference line is displayed. The popout comments near the *d* radio button and near red 6 explain. As you'd expect by now, **Standard 31** is an expanded version of **Standard 7**. There are also three further pages—**d single group, d two groups**, and **Subgroups**—that I'll discuss in later chapters.

It's time for take-home messages. Playing further with ESCI may help you write yours. Recall that this chapter started with Lucky–Noluck and the combination of two or three studies. ESCI provided forest plots to illustrate some of the basics, including weighting, cumulation, and the file drawer effect. What's the role of NHST? I mentioned the *Publication Manual* then described some case studies. I finished by mentioning further ESCI pages for meta-analysis.

Exercises

7.1 Figure 6.5 reported the results of Kay et al. (2010) about belief in the supernatural. Eyeball a meta-analytic combination of the three lower means and use the overlap rule to compare that with the top left mean. Does that seem justified?

7.2 In your own work, or a journal article, find two or three results that are reasonably independent—perhaps from different studies or different groups—but that relate to the same or similar questions. Does meta-analysis seem justified? Would it be valuable?

7.3 For the results in 7.2, if you have means and SDs on the same measure for each result, use **Original 7** to carry out the meta-analysis.

7.4 In another statistics textbook, try to find examples or exercises that include several results for which meta-analysis seems appropriate, and that can be entered into **Original 7**. Carry out the meta-analysis.

7.5 Figure 7.2 illustrates that the combination of two similar results gives a CI about 30% shorter. Use **Original 7** to explore what happens when you add further studies, all with the same SD and N (make this reasonably large), and means that are the same, or don't differ much. Find the answer to Question 7.2 at the start of this chapter. What happens when you add a fourth, fifth, sixth, and seventh study?

7.6 Use **Original 7** to find the answer to Question 7.4 at the start of this chapter. Give all studies the same mean as well as the same SD and N. Click at red 8 to reveal NHST. Type in various μ_0 values at red 7 until p for each study is close to .10, or whatever you choose.

7.7 Explore what happens to p when you add further identical studies.

7.8 Suppose you have two results that are correlated, for example, two measures of memory performance for a single group of participants. Would it make sense to combine the results by meta-analysis? If you did, what result would you expect? Why?

7.9 Find one or two published meta-analytic reviews in your own discipline. Are forest plots included? What features of meta-analysis discussed in this chapter do the reviews illustrate? Are there conclusions with practical implications?

7.10 Revisit your list of take-home messages. Revise and extend if you wish.

Take-Home Messages

- Meta-analysis is a set of quantitative techniques for combining evidence from a number of related studies.
- A forest plot is a simple and beautiful picture that represents separate results as CIs, and their meta-analytic combination as a further CI.
- Using meta-analysis to combine even only two or three studies can give a very useful increase in precision of estimation—around 30% reduction in CI width when a second study is added, a little more if samples are small.
- Using meta-analysis to combine two or three studies can give a large, even dramatic reduction in the *p* value.
- NHST is largely irrelevant for meta-analysis, and wider use of meta-analysis may help NHST become superseded.
- Studies in a meta-analysis are usually weighted by the inverse of the ES variance. Short CIs mean larger weights, long CIs smaller weights. Forest plots represent study weights by using squares of various sizes, and often show the result of the meta-analysis as a diamond. *Take-home picture*: A forest plot of your choice, perhaps Figure 7.4.
- The file drawer effect is the possibility that results that are not statistically significant are less likely to be published, thus biasing meta-analyses.
- If results are ordered by date, cumulative meta-analysis illustrates how the best combination of evidence has developed over time. The first few studies typically give large increases in precision (narrowing of CIs), and later studies yield progressively smaller changes.
- The sixth edition of the *Publication Manual* (APA, 2010) advises that all ESs of interest must be reported, even if small or not statistically significant—this helps avoid the file drawer effect. The *Manual* also gives detailed guidelines for the reporting of meta-analyses.
- Meta-analysis became widely recognized during the late 1970s and 1980s. It has become increasingly used across a wide range of disciplines, and is essential for research synthesis and for preparing systematic reviews. It assembles the evidence for evidence-based practice.
- There are now numerous examples of research progress as well as practical applications that rely on the results of meta-analysis.
- **ESCI Meta-Analysis** provides pages for data in original units, for a single group and two independent groups; and for data in standardized units (Cohen's *d*), with known σ for a single group.

8

Meta-Analysis 2: Models

This chapter discusses the two most common models for carrying out meta-analysis. There are formulas and calculations, but also pictures and examples, and advice about what to do in practice. Here's the list:

- An overview of the two models, starting with Lucky and Noluck
- The fixed effect model
- The random effects model
- Comparing the two models, and making a choice

If you wish to skip the detail and the formulas, you'll get the main idea if you read just the overview that comes next. You might also find Box 8.1 and Example 8.1 interesting.

Overview of the Two Models for Meta-Analysis

Suppose we've just seen a newly published third study of the treatment for insomnia that Lucky and Noluck evaluated. Figure 8.1 is a forest plot of those two studies from Chapter 1, plus the new study, which I'll call Sleepy1. The means and CIs for the three studies look as though they could easily have come from a dance of the CIs, so I'm happy to regard the three as consistent. We say that the studies are *homogeneous*, because the study-to-study variation in the means can reasonably be accounted for by sampling variation. Meta-analysis of the three studies gives the mean and CI shown at the bottom, labeled MA. That mean is the weighted average of the study means, and its CI is shorter than any of the other CIs, as we'd expect.

Outline of the Fixed Effect Model

So far no surprises, but consider what we're assuming. Without quite saying so, we've been assuming that all the studies in a meta-analysis estimate a single common population ES, which we'll refer to as μ. When studies are as consistent as in Figure 8.1, that seems reasonable. This is

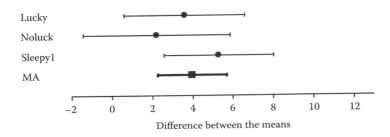

FIGURE 8.1
A forest plot for the Lucky and Noluck studies from Chapter 1, and a third study, Sleepy1, on the same issue. MA is the result of meta-analysis of the three studies. Error bars are 95% CIs.

our first and simplest model of meta-analysis, the *fixed effect* model, which assumes a single fixed μ that is being estimated by each of the studies. This model implies that we're regarding the studies as idealized replications—although possibly with various sample sizes—from a single population with mean μ. The forest plot resembles a dance of the CIs.

Now suppose our recently published third study was not Sleepy1, but Sleepy2, as in Figure 8.2. This time the means and CIs for the three studies hardly seem consistent. Yes, three such CIs could be thrown up by a dance of the CIs, but we're suspicious. The variation over studies seems greater than sampling variation can reasonably explain, and so we say that the studies are *heterogeneous*. The lack of overlap of the CIs suggests that Sleepy2 is estimating a different population ES. If so, our fixed effect model would be wrong, but our second model, the *random effects* model could apply.

If we ignore our suspicions about Sleepy2 and carry out a fixed effect meta-analysis, we get the result labeled "MA fixed effect" in Figure 8.2. The CI is the same width as that in Figure 8.1 but here looks much too short, given the wide variation from study to study in Figure 8.2. The fixed

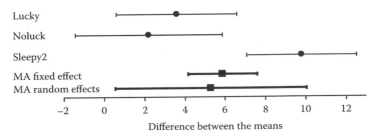

FIGURE 8.2
Same as Figure 8.1 except the third study is Sleepy2, and meta-analytic results are shown for both fixed effect and random effects models.

effect meta-analysis takes no account of heterogeneity, and thus most likely has given us a too-short, overly optimistic CI on the result.

Outline of the Random Effects Model

The random effects model assumes that different studies estimate some-what different values of the population parameter we're investigating. The greater the heterogeneity between studies, the more those different parameter values are likely to vary. If studies are homogeneous, there's no such variation, all studies estimate the same μ, and we have the fixed effect model. The random effects model estimates the overall mean of all the possible parameter values that different studies could estimate. Applying that model gives the result labeled "MA random effects" in Figure 8.2. Its mean is again a weighted average of the study means, although the weighting is slightly different for this model. The random effects model takes account of the heterogeneity by recognizing that there's consider-able uncertainty about where the overall mean of all possible parameter values lies. It acknowledges this uncertainty by producing a very wide CI. Informally, the very wide CI on the random effects mean reflects the large variation of the three study means. To my eye, the wide random-effects CI seems to be a better summary of the three studies in Figure 8.2 than the short fixed-effect CI.

Way back in Exercise 1.16 (you remember it well?), using the **Two studies** page, I suggested that you make the means for Lucky and Noluck very different, so the two CIs don't overlap. The meta-analysis then gives a long CI—longer than either the Lucky or Noluck CIs. In the Commentary on Selected Exercises section at the back of the book, I say, "If, however, the evidence from the two studies conflicts, the meta-analysis CI will be long, reflecting the large amount of overall uncertainty." I didn't say so at the time, but **Two studies** uses a random effects model, and therefore gives a wide CI when studies are inconsistent.

Choosing Between the Models

Until roughly 2005, published meta-analyses most likely used the fixed effect model. It was the first developed and most widely known, and is relatively easy to calculate. However, in many practical situations it's unrealistic, because studies are often heterogeneous, and so we should usually prefer the random effects model, even though it requires stronger assumptions. The random effects model is now becoming the most widely used, and an advantage of using it routinely is that, if applied to homoge-neous studies, it gives the same result as the fixed effect model. So noth-ing's lost by always choosing it. For Figure 8.1, for example, both models give the same result, as displayed in the figure.

The report of any meta-analysis must state clearly what model was used, and every forest plot should likewise state in its caption the model being used. Back in Chapter 1, Figure 1.2 would be the same whichever model was used, but even so the caption should state the model. At the **Two studies** page of **ESCI chapters 1–4**, the popout at red 8 states that a random effects model is used. Throughout Chapter 7 I used the fixed effect model, but didn't always mention that. From now on I, and you, should always state clearly what model we're using.

In Chapter 9 we'll discuss how heterogeneity can lead to valuable insight, if we can find moderating variables that help account for it. However, here the message is that the fixed effect model is simpler, but the random effects model should be our choice. Fortunately, software now makes it easy to see the result of applying either model. Every page in **ESCI Meta-Analysis** allows you to choose between the models with a click of a radio button, so it's easy to compare the two. But make your final click the selection of random effects.

The Fixed Effect Model

Both of our models can combine estimates of any population param-eter, but I'll focus on the simplest case—single means in original units, as **Original 7** and **Original 31** handle. The fixed effect model assumes that there's a single fixed but unknown underlying population mean μ, and that every study estimates this single value. The meta-analysis com-bines data from the studies to give M and

The *fixed effect* model assumes that there is a single underlying population parameter, for example, μ, and all studies are estimat-ing that μ.

its CI as our best point and interval esti-mates of μ. This overall M is calculated as a weighted average of the means of the separate studies, where the weights for different studies reflect the precision of the information about μ each study contributes. As we'd expect, large and precise studies are weighted more heavily than small and imprecise studies.

I'll now use an example in ESCI to show how the fixed effect model gives us point and interval estimates of μ. Suppose we enter data for k studies into **Original 7** or **Original 31**. For each we enter M_i, s_i, and N_i; that is, the sample mean, SD, and size for Study i. Our ES of interest is M_i, which has standard error $= s_i/\sqrt{N_i}$, and so we can label its variance, which is the square of the SE, as $V_i = s_i^2/N_i$. The weight for Study i is the inverse variance, so $W_i = 1/V_i$. The fixed effect model uses these weights to find an overall ES estimate M as a weighted average of the study means:

$$M = \frac{\sum W_i M_i}{\sum W_i} \tag{8.1}$$

(All the summations in this chapter, indicated by Σ, run from $i = 1$ to $i = k$.) The variance of M is estimated as

$$V_M = \frac{1}{\sum W_i} \tag{8.2}$$

and so the SD of M is $\sqrt{V_M}$. We can use this and Equation (3.2) to calculate the $C\%$ CI around M to be

$$\left[M - z_{C/100}\sqrt{V_M}, \quad M + z_{C/100}\sqrt{V_M} \right] \tag{8.3}$$

where, as in Chapter 3, $z_{C/100}$ is the critical value of z for our chosen C. Of course, for $C = 95$, $z_{C/100} = 1.96$.

Incidentally, in these types of discussions "standard error" and "standard deviation" are often used interchangeably. We're talking about effect size measures M_i and M, which are means. Remember that SE is defined as the SD of the sampling distribution of a mean, so it's correct to refer to V_M as the variance of M, and $\sqrt{V_M}$ as either the SE or the SD of M.

We can check any of these formulas against **Original 7**. To keep things very simple, Figure 8.3 shows a meta-analysis of just the first two studies from Figure 7.3. For Aden (1993), the variance is $V_1 = s_1^2/N_1 = 142^2/24 = 840.17$ as shown in the figure. The weights of the two studies are $W_1 = 1/840.17 = 0.00119$ and $W_2 = 1/3566.3 = 0.000280$. The first study weight W_1 as a proportion of the total of the weights is thus

$$\frac{W_1}{W_1 + W_2} = \frac{0.00119}{0.00119 + 0.000280} = .809$$

or 80.9%. Percentages like that appear in the **Study weighting** column near red 15, as in Figure 8.3. The MOE for Aden (1993) is $t_{.95}(24 - 1) \times \sqrt{840.17} = 2.069 \times 28.99 = 59.96$, again, as in the figure. Based on M_1 and this MOE, the 95% CI for the first study is [394.0, 514.0], and this is the interval displayed in the forest plot and reported by ESCI to the right of the forest plot, although not shown in Figure 8.3.

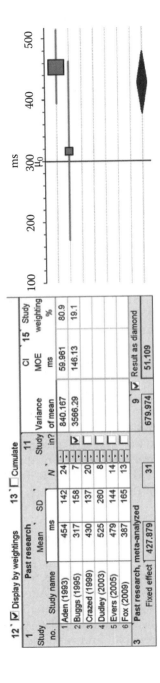

FIGURE 8.3
Data and a forest plot from the **Original 7** page for the first two studies in Figure 7.3. The forest plot shows 95% CIs.

Now for the meta-analysis itself. Using Equation (8.1) our combined point estimate is

$$M = \frac{0.00119 \times 454 + 0.000280 \times 317}{0.00119 + 0.000280} = 427.9$$

as Figure 8.3 reports near red 3. Using Equation (8.2) the variance estimate for M is

$$\frac{1}{W_1 + W_2} = \frac{1}{0.00119 + 0.000280} = 679.97$$

and MOE = $1.96 \times \sqrt{679.97}$ = 51.11. Both values match those in the figure. Using Equation (8.3) the 95% CI around M is therefore [427.9 – 51.11, 427.9 + 51.11], or [376.8, 479.0], as shown by ESCI just to the right of the forest plot.

We can therefore report that the fixed effect meta-analysis of Aden (1993) and Buggs (1995) gives an estimated ES of M = 427.9 ms, [376.8, 479.0]. Now, on to the next model.

The Random Effects Model

The fixed effect model assumes that every study estimates the same μ, but it's almost always more realistic to assume that different studies estimate somewhat different population ESs. Let's say Study i estimates μ_i. The *random effects* model takes this approach, and assumes that there's a population of μ_i values, and that each study estimates a randomly sampled value of μ_i from that population. The model usually goes further and assumes that the μ_i values are normally distributed, let's say with overall mean μ and standard deviation τ. That's lowercase Greek tau, which has the units of M. I'll refer to τ, but also to τ^2, the variance of the distribution of μ_i values, because it appears in various formulas. If $\tau^2 = 0$ (i.e., $\tau = 0$), all the μ_i are the same as μ, and we have the fixed effect model. Sampling variability can reasonably account for variability of the study means, and we say that the studies are *homogeneous*. On the other hand,

> The *random effects* model assumes that there is a distribution of population parameters, and different studies estimate different values from that distribution.

if τ^2 is large, the μ_i being estimated by the different studies are quite different and so the studies are likely to differ a lot, and we can say that the studies are *heterogeneous*.

A set of studies is *homogeneous* if sampling variability can reasonably account for the variation between studies, and *heterogeneous* if variation between studies is larger than this.

As I've mentioned a couple of times, heterogeneity may offer opportunity for insight, if we can find one or more variables that can account for at least some of it. In Chapter 9 we'll discuss such *moderating variables*, or *moderators*, which explain some of the variability of the study means. Meanwhile, the random effects model uses the symbol Q for a measure of the extent of heterogeneity, which influences the calculation of M and, as we saw in Figure 8.2, the width of the CI on M.

A *moderating variable* or *moderator* is a variable that influences the ES being studied in a meta-analysis.

If you know about fixed and random effects in analysis of variance, you might notice a kind of parallel with the two models for meta-analysis we're discussing. If not, don't worry. You might also be thinking that the assumptions of the random effects model are strong and a bit arbitrary: We assume that there's a normal distribution of μ_i values that just happens to account for what could be a wide variety of types of differences from study to study. The random effects model is becoming widely used, but its assumptions are demanding and perhaps often unrealistic. That's a big reason why researchers and statisticians continue to explore new models for meta-analysis, always seeking models that are tractable—meaning formulas can be found and calculations made—and also fit well to sets of real research studies. Keep a lookout for promising new models for meta-analysis.

Heterogeneity and the Random Effects Model

Heterogeneity is central to the random effects model. We'll use Q as our measure of heterogeneity, or variability between study means. It's a standardized measure, the total weighted sum of squares between studies, but saying that may not help much. We calculate it using

$$Q = \sum W_i M_i^2 - \frac{\left(\sum W_i M_i\right)^2}{\sum W_i} \qquad (8.4)$$

If the fixed effect model is accurate, the expected value of Q is just the degrees of freedom, $df = (k - 1)$. (Remember that k is the number of studies in the meta-analysis.) So the next step is to compare Q with df. A Q value close to $(k - 1)$ is consistent with homogeneity and a fixed effect model. A Q value notably greater than $(k - 1)$ indicates that the studies are heterogeneous, the random effects model is needed, and τ^2 is greater than 0. (Remember τ^2 is the variance of the distribution of μ_i.) How great is "notably greater than"? Can we calculate a CI around our Q value? Good questions. Hold those thoughts for a moment.

Next consider T^2, which is an estimate of τ^2 for our studies. The formula is

$$T^2 = \frac{Q - df}{\sum W_i - \dfrac{\sum W_i^2}{\sum W_i}} \tag{8.5}$$

So T^2 is $(Q - df)$, which is the amount by which Q exceeds what we'd expect if $\tau^2 = 0$, divided by a factor that depends only on the weights. This makes sense: Small T^2 means that Q is not notably larger than df, and our estimate of τ^2 is small. Large T^2 means that Q is notably larger than df, there's lots of bouncing around of the M_i, our estimate of τ^2 is large, and we need a random effects model. I'm happy to say that we can calculate a CI around our T value, and this is a CI for τ. The details are too complicated to give here, but are in Chapter 16 of Borenstein, Hedges, Higgins, and Rothstein (2009). We'll just let ESCI do the calculations for us.

Let's see what **Original 7** offers. Figure 8.4 is the same as Figure 8.3, but shows the additional information reported below the meta-analysis results. You've probably noticed the radio buttons near the bottom left in Figure 8.4. These let you select a fixed effect or random effects model for calculation of the meta-analysis result. The popout comment at red 16 explains. (Red 16 is positioned just left of the image shown in Figure 8.4.) The value of Q is reported at red 19. For our two studies, $Q = 4.259$, which is much larger than $df = (k - 1) = 1$. The df is shown just below Q, so it's easy to compare the two values. We seem to have heterogeneity, and therefore suspect that τ^2 may be large. At red 18, ESCI reports T rather than T^2, where T is our estimate of τ. I usually prefer to think about T and τ because they're SDs. ESCI used Equation (8.5) to calculate $T^2 = 7181.3$ then took the square root to find $T = 84.7$ ms, as reported at red 18. ESCI also reports that the 95% CI for τ is [0, 197.6]. With only two studies, it's not surprising that this CI is so enormously wide.

If through sampling variability Q happens to be quite small, $(Q - df)$ can be negative, in which case a negative value is calculated for T^2. However, T^2 is a variance, which cannot be negative, so T^2 is set to zero. Also T, our estimate of τ, is set to zero, so ESCI reports $T = 0$ rather than a negative value. Similarly, if a negative value is calculated for the lower limit of the CI, 0 is reported instead.

There are two further things to mention before we play around by changing some of the data. One more way to think about heterogeneity is to calculate I^2, which is another measure of heterogeneity, by using

$$I^2 = \frac{Q - df}{Q} \times 100\% \tag{8.6}$$

In this equation, $(Q - df)$ is the extra amount of variability between studies beyond what we'd expect under a fixed effect model. Also Q,

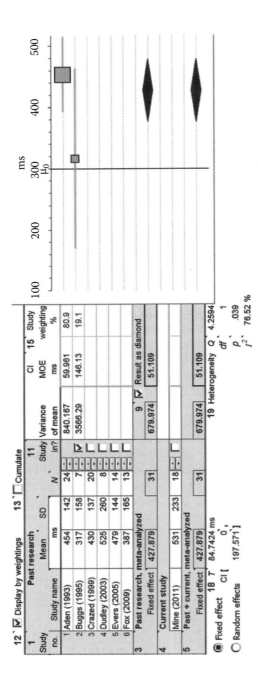

FIGURE 8.4

Same as Figure 8.3, but showing further information at the bottom. Ignore the second copy of the meta-analysis reported at red 5. The label **Fixed effect** near red 3 states the model being used.

the denominator in the equation, is the total variability between studies. So I^2 is the percentage of the total variability that reflects real differences in the μ_i, rather than the bouncing around of sampling variability that **CIjumping** illustrates. Large I^2 signals heterogeneity is large, and close-to-zero I^2 suggests that we have homogeneity. ESCI reports I^2 below Q. In our example, $I^2 = 76.5\%$, again suggesting that we have considerable heterogeneity.

The last thing to mention here is the p value that ESCI reports at red 19. This is a p value calculated from Q for testing the null hypothesis that the studies are homogeneous. In our example, $p = .039$, so we have statistically significant ($p < .05$) heterogeneity, despite having such a small meta-analysis. I'd prefer, of course, to tell you about a CI around Q, but the statisticians advise that this is a situation in which the approximate formulas that the random effects model uses can give us a reasonable value for p, but not such a useful approximation to a CI. Indeed, they advise that the p value for Q probably gives better guidance than the approximation to a CI around T that I described before and that ESCI reports at red 18. Even so, I couldn't resist including that CI in ESCI.

Note that the message from the p value for Q conflicts with the message from the CI for τ. The p value is just less than .05, whereas the 95% CI around T is very wide but includes 0. In other words, Q is large enough to reject the null hypothesis of homogeneity, but the CI around T does not exclude $\tau = 0$ as a plausible value. (Recall that $\tau = 0$ indicates zero heterogeneity, i.e., homogeneity.) Small inconsistencies like this arise because approximations have been used to derive the formulas we need to use. We simply have to live with the occasional disagreements. Rarely, if ever, will they cause real problems. Also, as usual, we shouldn't pay much attention to the precise value of p—or to whether a CI falls so it just includes, or just excludes, a null hypothesized value.

Before switching **Original 7** to the random effects model, it's worth trying different values for M_1 to see what happens to Q and T. I typed in 440, 420, 400, and then 380 for the mean of Aden (1993), but you can try any values you like. (You may want to click at red 17 to freeze the ES axis, so the forest plot doesn't automatically rescale when you change M_1.) I watched as the forest plot changed, Q decreased, its p increased, I^2 decreased, T decreased, and the upper limit of the CI around T also decreased. (Note that in some cases, for example, $M_1 = 400$, ESCI doesn't report a CI for τ because in some circumstances the approximations used to calculate such a CI fail when $df = 1$. Don't worry about this—in virtually every realistic case, ESCI reports a CI at red 18.)

As I made the two study means less different, heterogeneity decreased, as did our estimate of τ, which is the SD of the distribution of μ_i values assumed by the random effects model. I hope that makes sense: As the difference between the two study means decreases, it's less plausible that they're estimating different μ_i, and so not as necessary to prefer a random effects model over the fixed effect model that ESCI is still displaying.

The Random Effects Model in Action

Now for the random effects meta-analysis. As with the fixed effect model, we start with the variance of the ESs for the separate studies, calculate study weights, and then use these to calculate a weighted average that's our overall point estimate of the ES, and a CI. It's all very similar, but the answer may be different because to calculate weights we first calculate a modification of the ES variance for each M_i. The total variability of M_i has two components: The variability of M_i around μ_i, and the variability of μ_i around μ. We estimate the first as V_i and the second as T^2, and therefore our estimate of the variance of M_i is $V_i{}^* = V_i + T^2$, where I'm adding * to symbols to mark the version used with the random effects model.

The weights are once again the inverse variance, so $W_i{}^* = 1/V_i{}^*$. We compute the result of the random effects meta-analysis using a modification of Equation (8.1):

$$M^* = \frac{\sum W_i^* M_i}{\sum W_i^*}$$

(8.7)

The variance of M^* is estimated as

$$V_{M^*} = \frac{1}{\sum W_i^*}$$

(8.8)

which is a modification of Equation (8.2). The SE of M^* is

$$\sqrt{V_{M^*}}$$

and we use this SE to calculate the C% CI around M^* to be

$$\left[M^* - z_{C/100}\sqrt{V_{M^*}}, M^* + z_{C/100}\sqrt{V_{M^*}} \right]$$

(8.9)

which is an adaptation of Equation (8.3).

At **Original 7** we can now click between the two options at red 16 to see the meta-analysis results for either model. Figure 8.5 is the same as Figure 8.4, but shows results for the random effects model. The final CI is dramatically wider, reflecting the large disagreement between the two studies, in other words, large heterogeneity. Click back and forth to see

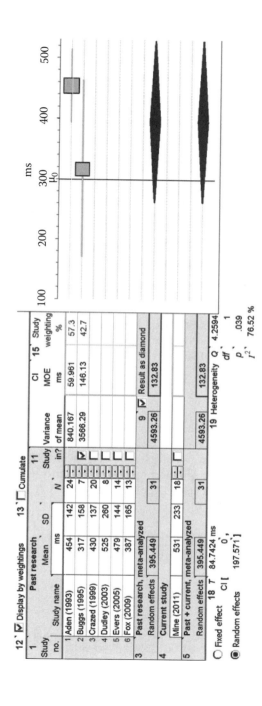

FIGURE 8.5
Same as Figure 8.4, but displaying random effects meta-analysis, as the label near red 3 states. Ignore the second copy of the meta-analysis reported at red 5.

changes in the forest plot, the value of M near red 3, and the CI around M that's shown to the right of the forest plot. If you try this for various values for M_1, the mean for Aden (1993), you'll quickly notice that results from the two models differ only when $T > 0$, because only then is V^* different from V. And T is only greater than zero when $Q > df$. [Recall that Equation (8.5) gives $T^2 = (Q - df)$ divided by a factor depending on the weights.] Therefore, as you try different values of M_1, or make any other changes to the data that you wish, watch for Q to become larger than $df = (k - 1)$ (remember that k is the number of individual studies), so T becomes greater than zero and the results of the two models start to differ. When T is zero, the two models give identical results.

Now, back to the data shown in Figures 8.4 and 8.5. The values of Q, df, p, I^2, T, and the CI on T are all calculated from the study data and are independent of the meta-analysis model chosen, so their values are the same in Figures 8.4 and 8.5.

We can check some calculations, as we did earlier for the fixed effect model. For Aden (1993), the variance needed for the random effects model is $V_1^* = V_1 + T^2 = 840.17 + 7181.3 = 8021.5$. For Buggs (1995), $V_2^* = V_2 + T^2 = 3566.3 + 7181.3 = 10747.6$. Note that the study variance and MOE shown below and left of red 15 are the values for the studies themselves, so, for example, V_1 rather than V_1^* is reported, whichever meta-analysis model is selected. The weights of the two studies for random effects are $W_1^* = 1/8021.5 = 0.000125$ and $W_2^* = 1/10747.6 = 0.0000930$. The proportion weight for the first study is thus

$$\frac{W_1^*}{W_1^* + W_2^*} = \frac{0.000125}{0.000125 + 0.0000930} = .573$$

or 57.3%, as in Figure 8.5. The weights reported at red 15, unlike study variance and MOE, reflect the selected meta-analysis model.

Now for the meta-analysis itself. Using Equation (8.7) our combined point estimate is

$$M^* = \frac{0.000125 \times 454 + 0.0000930 \times 317}{0.000125 + 0.0000930} = 395.4$$

as Figure 8.5 reports near red 3. Using Equation (8.8) the variance estimate for M^* is

$$V_{M^*} = \frac{1}{W_1^* + W_2^*} = \frac{1}{0.000125 + 0.0000930} = 4593.3$$

and MOE = 1.96 × $\sqrt{4593.3}$ = 132.8. Both values match those in the figure. Using Equation (8.9) the 95% CI around M^* is therefore [395.4 – 132.8, 395.4 + 132.8], or [262.6, 528.3], as shown by ESCI just to the right of the forest plot.

Weighting the Studies

A central difference between the two models is the way they weight the studies. The fixed effect model shown in Figure 8.4 weights Buggs (1995) at only 19.1%, because its variance is so high (3566.3), reflecting its small N and slightly larger SD. In contrast, the random effects analysis of Figure 8.5 weights Buggs at 42.7%, because the variances used to calculate the weights are calculated as $V_i^* = V_i + T^2$. When $T^2 > 0$ the variances for the different studies are all larger by this amount, and therefore are overall more similar. As you change M_1 and watch the amount of heterogeneity change, T^2 changes, and also the pattern of weights. Large heterogeneity gives large T^2, which means that the weights are more similar—large and small studies are more similarly weighted. Of course, that's why the sizes of squares in the forest plot often change as you click between the two meta-analysis models.

> The *random effects* model generally weights studies more evenly than does the fixed effect model, because it takes into account the heterogeneity of the set of studies as well as the variance of each study's ES.

   More generally, the different patterns of weights arise because the random effects analysis pays attention to the k different μ_i values. Study i is the only source of information specifically about μ_i, so even if Study i is small it can't be ignored. As I mentioned previously, our estimate of the variance of M_i is $V_i^* = V_i + T^2$. Informally, a study gets one vote that depends on its size (that's V_i, the variance for a particular study mean) and another vote simply for being in the meta-analysis (that's T^2, same for every study). If heterogeneity is large, T^2 is large and so the second vote has increased influence and all the study weights are more similar. Both votes contribute to the study weights, the overall M^* results and, most notably, the width of the CI around that final point estimate.

A Larger Example

I'd like to consider briefly a random effects meta-analysis for more than two studies. Figure 8.6 includes all seven studies and is the same as Figure 7.4, except it shows random effects meta-analysis and includes extra information at the bottom. ESCI reports $Q = 10.51$, somewhat more than $df = 6$, for the overall meta-analysis reported at red 5. In addition, $p = .10$ and $T = 36.9$ ms [0, 75.8]. The I^2 value of 42.9% is an estimate of the percentage of

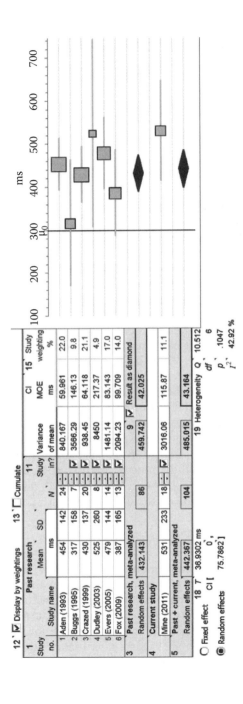

FIGURE 8.6
Same as Figure 7.4, except random effects meta-analysis is shown, as the labels near red 3 and red 5 state, and further information is included at the bottom.

overall variability between studies that reflects true variability in the μ_i that the studies estimate. These values suggest a considerable amount of heterogeneity, although the CI on T includes zero (and $p > .05$) so $\tau = 0$ cannot be ruled out.

Let's think for a moment of all the CIs in Figure 8.6 as prediction intervals and imagine what would happen on replication of all the studies. Imagine an ESCI page **MAjumping** (sorry, it doesn't exist) that allows you to specify μ_i and N_i for each of a number of studies, then produces on each simulation cycle a complete display like Figure 7.4 or Figure 8.6. As we repeated the simulation, all the M_i would bounce around. The M or M^* would also bounce around, although not as much as the M_i. The Q, T, and I^2 would all bounce around considerably, although relatively less if k were larger, meaning that we had more studies in the analysis. I'm suggesting this thought experiment to emphasize that we can't justify any hard and fast conclusion from noting that $Q = 10.51$, or $T = 36.9$ ms [0, 75.8]. The wide CI indicates that a wide range of models is plausible, given our data, all the way from a fixed effect model ($\tau = 0$) to a random effects model with τ around 75 ms. That's a model in which different studies estimate population means (μ_i values) from a distribution with SD as large as 75 ms. There should be no question of trying to decide on a single "correct" or "true" model. That's a form of dichotomous thinking and, as usual, it's better to think in terms of estimation—T as our estimate of τ, and M^* as our estimate of μ, the ES we're studying. As usual, the CIs indicate the precision of our point estimates.

Here's a further observation: Click back and forth at red 16 between the two models and focus on the weights. In agreement with our earlier discussion of weights, the weights for the random effects model vary much less between studies. In the random effects analysis the largest weight is 22.0%—about 4.5 times the smallest weight of 4.9%. In the fixed effect analysis the largest is 28.8%—about 10 times the smallest weight of 2.9%. In the random effects analysis, the largest is not so dominant, and even the smallest makes a contribution. The sizes of squares in the forest plot change accordingly between the two models. If heterogeneity were greater, the weights for the random effects model would vary even less.

Finally, consider how we might think about heterogeneity, especially as part of interpreting meta-analytic results. Box 8.1 describes one of the very few studies on this issue. It highlights how little we know of the cognition of meta-analysis. It identifies heterogeneity and the differing results of different meta-analytic models as a particular interpretive challenge. I suspect that there are useful developments of the forest plot that can represent heterogeneity, and perhaps even the effects of moderating variables, in some ingenious graphical ways that help understanding. You could take that as a challenge.

BOX 8.1 INTERPRETING A META-ANALYSIS

Shrier et al. (2008) studied how eight experts interpreted a series of meta-analyses that combined evidence from randomized control trials (RCTs). The trials assessed the value of giving intravenous magnesium soon after a heart attack—a topic chosen because the evidence is inconsistent. A series of small and medium-sized RCTs had found various results, generally in favor of treatment; then a very large RCT in 1995 found virtually no effect; then further RCTs again found various results. There was therefore considerable heterogeneity in the final set of studies. The researchers prepared five packages of materials, which represented knowledge just after the first RCT was published, after the first three RCTs, then after the first 10, 20, and 23 RCTs. In each case the package included a meta-analysis giving both fixed effect and random effects results, reports of the RCTs themselves, and summaries of review articles on relevant issues that were available at each successive time. The participants were all experts in a relevant medical field and also in meta-analysis. They were given a package, and asked to study it carefully and state their opinion about whether the treatment is effective and whether they would recommend it for clinical use. They were asked to rely only on the materials in the package. After giving their judgments they were given the next package to study. The aim was to obtain judgments based on knowledge available at each of the five successive times. Forest plots provided an essential overview of the information in each package.

Over the first three times the meta-analysis results became more precise. There was little sign of heterogeneity, so the fixed effect and random effects results were very similar. The p value decreased to < .001. Then the results of the very large RCT and some further smaller RCTs arrived, the set of results became heterogeneous, and the two meta-analysis models gave different results. This general pattern persisted to the final time.

The experts differed widely in their judgments and recommendations. Some became more positive toward the treatment over time, others more negative. They also reacted differently to the arrival of the very large study that disagreed with many of the other RCTs. The researchers had clearly given the experts some difficult scientific and clinical judgments to make, exactly as they had intended.

The overall conclusion was simply that even experts who have access to full information can arrive at different judgments.

Interpreting even the best-presented systematic reviews may require careful critical thought and relevant expertise. Carrying out the whole experiment, and finding eight suitable experts willing to spend the many hours needed to participate, was a large task. Even so, with only eight sets of responses, no finer-grain analysis of what caused the differences was possible. At each time point, meta-analysis integrated the mass of evidence, and forest plots revealed patterns and presented overall results, but interpretation was still a challenge. The experiment suggested that interpreting heterogeneity can be a particularly difficult challenge.

It's tempting to ask the extent to which the experts gave "correct" judgments, but of course that's not possible to answer. We can only hope that further research will give more precise estimates, and help explain heterogeneity. Eventually we hope that expert consensus will be possible—this is the closest we can ever come to a correct answer.

Choosing a Model

I've already recommended that we routinely use the random effects model, but here I'll discuss the choice a little further. Some older books advise first examining Q and its p value and then, if $p < .05$ (or whatever other value you choose as a cutoff), conclude that there's statistically significant heterogeneity and thus a random effects model is needed. The trouble with this strategy is that finding $p > .05$ is, as we've seen in Figure 8.6, hardly good grounds for deciding that the studies are homogeneous and a fixed effect model is appropriate. That would amount to accepting the null hypothesis—a bad policy. The good news is that we really don't need to decide: Always use a random effects model. Even if you use that model when heterogeneity is low, you get the same result as the fixed effect model gives. Recall that whenever $Q < df$, we saw $T = 0$ and clicking between the models made no difference. If Q is only a little more than df, the two models give very similar results.

In the past, the complexity of doing the random effects calculations led to the fixed effect model being widely used. Schmidt, Oh, and Hayes (2009) studied meta-analyses published in *Psychological Bulletin*, psychology's leading journal for review articles. They found that the first meta-analysis appeared in 1978, and they examined meta-analyses published up to 2006. They found that fixed effect models predominated, and only around 2003–2004 were there signs of a swing to random effects models. They reanalyzed some of the earlier fixed effect meta-analyses and found considerable heterogeneity. They concluded that many of them produced final interval estimates that were too narrow, because they should have employed random effects models, and these would have given wider CIs. The final CIs for the analyses they reexamined were on average only about half as wide as Schmidt et al. calculated they should be, using random effects models. They cautioned that many published conclusions based on meta-analysis may give overly precise final estimates of effects.

The recommendation of many meta-analysts now is that we should routinely use random effects models. Nothing to lose: Even when they're not necessary, they give useful results, the same as a fixed model would have given—or very similar. Other meta-analysts suggest examining the results of both models to highlight the influence of heterogeneity. I agree that's often worth considering. A forest plot could easily display two CIs at the bottom, one for each model, as in Figure 8.2. Example 8.1 extends the discussion of our research on how researchers think about *p* values that I first described in Box 5.2. The example includes Figure 8.7, which also displays in a forest plot the results given by both meta-analytic models.

More thoughtfully, any choice of model should reflect our conceptualization of the problem and how that matches the assumptions of the model. If you have a set of studies designed to be very similar and all estimating the same ES, it may make sense to choose a fixed effect model. In practice that rarely happens. The random effects approach is our more general tool and should be our routine choice, but it does make strong assumptions, so we should look out for any better options that may emerge.

The *random effects* model should be our routine choice, despite its strong assumptions. If studies are homogeneous it gives results the same as, or similar to, those of the fixed effect model.

If you'd like a more extensive presentation of models for meta-analysis I suggest the excellent book by Michael Borenstein and colleagues (Borenstein et al., 2009). That book's approach and formulas are used in the software, Comprehensive Meta-Analysis (CMA; www.meta-analysis.com), which is becoming widely used. Any page of **ESCI Meta-Analysis** requires the same kind of data for each study—for example, **Original 7** requires *M*, *SD*, and *N* for each. CMA, however, accepts ES information in more than 100 formats, and can combine studies even when their data are entered in a variety of formats. It's flexible and powerful software. You can download a copy and use it freely for a trial period. If you are planning a meta-analysis beyond ESCI's capabilities, you should consider CMA.

It's time for take-home messages. Scan back through this chapter's section headings and figures for some prompts for writing your own take-home messages. Or play a bit more with **Original 7** and let the labels and

EXAMPLE 8.1 THREE SURVEYS OF SUBJECTIVE p INTERVALS

Box 5.2 described our study of how researchers think about p values in relation to replication (Lai et al., in press). It reported that we conducted three email surveys, which asked about p values in slightly different ways. Each survey allowed us to calculate a p interval that a respondent judged would have an 80% chance of including the p value of a replication. Box 5.2 included results only of Survey 1, which found that the respondents' estimated intervals were on average 40.0% intervals, rather than the target 80% intervals. In other words, the average underestimation was $80.0 - 40.0 = 40.0$ percentage points. Yes, the mean just happened to be 40.0, so intervals had, on average, just half the target coverage of replication p. This result of Survey 1 and its 95% CI are shown at the top in Figure 8.7. Surveys 2 and 3 found average underestimation of 29.5 and 30.4 percentage points, respectively, as the figure also shows.

To find an overall best estimate, we applied meta-analysis. Figure 8.7 shows the results for both fixed effect and random effects models. The fixed effect result has a short CI, as we'd expect, but hardly seems to represent the three surveys well because of the considerable difference of the Survey 1 result from the other two results. When I say "considerable difference," I'm noting that the difference is large compared with the CI widths—in fact the Survey 1 CI is not close to overlapping either of the other CIs. It's therefore not surprising to find that heterogeneity was $Q = 20.1$, which is very large considering that there are three studies and so $df = 2$. Also, $I^2 = 90.0\%$. We should therefore prefer the random effects model and it gives, as we'd expect, a much wider CI.

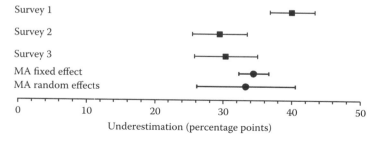

FIGURE 8.7
The average extent of underestimation of subjective 80% p intervals, with 95% CIs, from three email surveys, and the meta-analytic (MA) combination of the three results using a fixed effect model and a random effects model.

> We concluded that the question format of Survey 1 gives somewhat greater underestimation, meaning shorter subjective p intervals. We could only speculate why that is, but our main aim in using three question formats was to avoid a result that may have been dependent mainly on some idiosyncrasy of a single format. Using three formats, with broadly consistent findings, suggests that our overall conclusion is reasonably robust. Yes, the three studies estimated different amounts of underestimation, but they broadly agree that underestimation is severe, around 30 to 40 percentage points—and that's our main conclusion.

popout comments remind you of things. This is also a moment to reflect: If you have followed this long discussion of the two models then you have some important understanding and are ahead of many researchers out there. Take a pat on the back.

Exercises

8.1 Fire up **CIjumping** in **ESCI chapters 1–4**. Enter $\mu = 50$, $\sigma = 20$, $N = 10$, and click near red 4 to **Show values**. Take a single sample, and record its mean M and standard deviation s shown near red 4. Repeat until you have a list of ten M and s values. Type these into **Original 31** as the mean and SD for 10 studies. Enter $N = 10$ for each. Examine the values reported near red 18 and 19. Are these as you expect? Do the two models of meta-analysis give different results? Is this as you expect? Discuss.

8.2 If you have the patience, repeat Exercise 8.1 a couple more times, maybe with different values of N. You could even vary N from sample to sample, but make sure to enter the appropriate N for each study in the meta-analysis. Consider the same questions.

8.3 Revisit Exercise 7.2, which asked you to find results that may be amenable to meta-analysis. If you found some, consider which model you would choose and why.

8.4 In **Original 31**, enter $SD = 10$ and $N = 20$ for every study. (You could type in the values for the first study, then use the **Copy** command and then the **Paste Special/Values** command for the rest.) Type in 1, 2, 3, 4, 5, 6, 7, 8, 9, and 10 as the means of Studies 1–10. Record full information about the meta-analysis for each model. Now enter the same 10 values as the means of Studies 11–20. Again, record full information for each model. Repeat: Enter the same means for Studies 21–30 and record full information. Which quantities remain exactly or approximately the same as you combine 10, then 20, then 30 studies? Which change? Explain.

8.5 Revisit Exercise 7.4, which asked you to find in another statistics textbook several results you could meta-analyze using **Original 7**. Carry out the meta-analysis with both models and compare.

8.6 Invent results for several similar studies in the research area with which you're most familiar. Choose a single group design and data you can enter into **Original 7** or **Original 31**. Within these limitations, make the results as realistic as possible. Carry out the meta-analysis using the two models. Compare and discuss.

8.7 Find several published meta-analyses in journals in your discipline. For each, find any analysis of heterogeneity that's reported. Identify the model(s) used and the justification given for choice of model. Make your own comments.

8.8 Revise your take-home messages if you wish.

Polya

Take-Home Messages

- The fixed effect model for meta-analysis, as used in Chapter 7, assumes that all studies are estimating the same single value of the population parameter, for example, μ. It thus assumes that the studies are homogeneous.

- A fixed effect analysis weights studies by the inverse variance of their means.

- A random effects model assumes a distribution of population parameters, and that different studies estimate different values from that distribution. It may assume that Study i estimates μ_i, where the μ_i have a normal distribution with mean μ and variance τ^2.

- A moderating variable, or moderator, is a variable that accounts for some of the variability of the μ_i.

- If $\tau^2 > 0$, the studies are heterogeneous and a random effects model is needed. Q is a measure of heterogeneity, with expected value $df = (k - 1)$, where k is the number of studies in the meta-analysis.

- T^2 is an estimate of τ^2, and reflects the amount by which Q exceeds df. Large $(Q - df)$ gives large T^2, which indicates large heterogeneity and therefore study means that bounce around distinctly more than **CIjumping** suggests.

- I^2 is the percentage of the total variability of study means that reflects real differences in the μ_i they are estimating, rather than the bouncing around of sampling variability. Homogeneity gives $I^2 = 0$, and large heterogeneity gives large I^2.

- Weights in a random effects meta-analysis reflect both the variance of individual studies and the overall T^2 estimate. They generally differ less over studies than for a fixed effect model.

- The width of the overall CI from a random effects meta-analysis reflects both the combination of evidence over studies (if more studies then narrower CI) and the amount of heterogeneity (if large heterogeneity then wider CI).

- It's usually best, and a safe choice, to use a random effects model, although it makes strong assumptions.

- Careful thought and informed judgment are likely to be needed at many stages in carrying out and interpreting a meta-analysis.

9

Meta-Analysis 3: Larger-Scale Analyses

In Chapter 7 I used forest plots to introduce meta-analysis and described how meta-analysis can summarize messy sets of results and find answers to important questions. In Chapter 8 I described two models and argued that we should almost always choose the random effects model. In this chapter I'll discuss larger meta-analysis projects. The main messages are, first, that doing a large meta-analysis is a big job with many issues to consider and, second, that such an analysis can make an enormous contribution, and even answer research questions beyond the questions addressed by any of the individual studies. That's more meta-analysis magic.

Here's the agenda:

- Seven steps to conducting a full meta-analysis
- Finding moderators that account for ES variation
- Analyzing more than one ES measure
- Correcting for measurement error
- Assessing publication bias
- Meta-analysis becomes mainstream—the Cochrane and Campbell Collaborations

Seven Steps to a Full Meta-Analysis

Anyone who publishes a high-quality large-scale meta-analysis should, in my opinion, receive a gold medal, a large promotion, and a long, fully paid vacation. Such a research synthesis can be an immensely valuable scholarly contribution that brings order to confusion, helps set a future research agenda, and at the same time gives the best evidence-based practical advice. Such a project may take a year or more of work by a team, depending on the range of questions asked and the size and complexity of the relevant research literature. In this chapter I'll outline the steps to undertaking a large-scale meta-analysis and issues to consider. It's a daunting list, but I don't want to be discouraging: Graduate students are increasingly carrying out a small to medium meta-analysis as the first part of their research. Yes, a meta-analysis can take anything from five minutes to more than a year of effort, but somewhere in that vast range may be a project that's right for you. Even if there's already a good meta-analysis on your topic of interest, perhaps you can update and improve it.

I outline below the seven main steps in conducting a large-scale meta-analysis. I've chosen two meta-analytic review articles to illustrate the steps. The first investigates the effectiveness of acupuncture, and I'll mention aspects of that study as I describe the steps. Then I'll outline my second example review, about how we perceive the person we love, also in terms of the seven steps. My steps largely follow a book by Harris Cooper (2010), which I highly recommend. Use it as the text for a reading seminar to help you and some like-minded people develop your understanding of meta-analysis, or as a guide to carrying out your own meta-analysis. At every step there are choices to be made, based on your research goals, knowledge of the research area, and understanding of research methods and meta-analysis. Research synthesis demands creativity and scholarly wisdom; it's no mere mechanical exercise. In the descriptions below of my two examples, note that I'm being very selective and including only small parts of what are two substantial reviews.

A large meta-analysis requires seven steps, as described, for example, by Cooper (2010).

Acupuncture and the Seven Steps

Low back pain is often chronic, but analgesics used for long periods may cease to offer relief and bring damaging side effects. To what extent can acupuncture help? Manheimer, White, Berman, Forys, and Ernst (2005) reported a systematic review, mainly based on meta-analysis, of 33 randomized control trials (RCTs) that compared acupuncture with various comparison treatments. This is an example of a meta-analysis that asks a simple question, especially common in medicine: "What's the effect of this treatment?"

Step 1: Formulate Your Problem

Here you set the scope of your project. You'll probably use an existing theoretical framework to help you decide how to conceptualize the main variables and specify how they are measured. What types of studies will you include? What limits will you set on the questions addressed by studies to be included? What information must those included studies provide?

The question, "What's the effect of acupuncture?" may seem simple, but Manheimer et al. (2005) still needed to decide the scope of their review and operationalize important variables. In recognition of the wide use of acupuncture around the world, they chose to seek studies from many countries, and they elected to include the rather different Chinese, Japanese, and Western styles of acupuncture.

Choices at this first stage may need to be revisited after you work on later steps. For example, research reports you find might require you to refine your variable definitions. Or locating more research than you expected might prompt you to narrow the scope of the whole study, to keep it within your time and resource constraints. The seven steps are not strictly separate and sequential; you may need to move backward and forward as the project proceeds.

Step 2: Search the Literature and Select Studies

You should cast a very wide net to come as close as possible to finding all studies with a chance of providing data you would choose to include. That's the best strategy to minimize the risk of publication bias. Manheimer et al. (2005) searched seven bibliographic databases and contacted experts in six countries, asking for any relevant reports they could provide. They consulted the reference lists of all reviews and reports they retrieved. They made extra efforts to find studies via Japanese sources. They included reports in English, Japanese, Korean, and Chinese, as well as a range of European languages, although resource limitations precluded a search of Chinese databases. They identified 561 potentially relevant reports, then two researchers independently considered these against selection criteria they had established, which required, for example, the random assignment of participants to acupuncture or a control group, and data on outcome measures of pain or functional status. Other criteria reflected definitions adopted for the main variables and decisions about scope. For example, acupuncture was defined as needle insertion, meaning that laser acupuncture was excluded. After applying all selection criteria, 33 studies were included.

Step 3: Code the Studies and Collect Data

Coding the studies and entering the data into your main data file is a large task. Start with a draft coding scheme that specifies all the study characteristics and types of data you wish to record about each study. Among many other things, record information about the participants, the experimental design, the experimental manipulations, and the measures reported. Record statistical information, including sample sizes, ESs, and measures of variance. Box 9.1 has more on this. Test your scheme by coding several studies, then refine it. You may need to train coders and check that they all use the scheme in a similar way. If practical, have every study coded by two coders working independently, or at least have a second coder independently code a proportion of the studies. In either case, use

BOX 9.1 INFORMATION NEEDED
TO CALCULATE EFFECT SIZES

In an ideal world, every report of research would include point and interval ES estimates and descriptions of how these were calculated. Smith and Glass (1977) encountered motley and incomplete statistical information in many of the evaluations of psychotherapy they analyzed, and one of their notable achievements was to find ways to estimate *d* from such fragments. Sadly, more than 30 years later it's still often difficult or impossible to extract sufficient information to calculate ESs and CIs for a meta-analysis.

Meta-analysis requires a point estimate and a relevant variance estimate, so we can calculate the CI that represents the study in the forest plot. Suppose, like Manheimer et al. (2005), we are meta-analyzing differences between group means from RCTs. To calculate the mean difference and its CI we first need either the two group means or the difference. If we are not given the CI on the difference, we need the two group sizes and the SDs or SEs for each group so we can calculate it. If SD and SE information is missing but we are given *t* or the *p* value for a comparison of the groups, we can calculate the CI, although assumptions are required. Things quickly get complicated and statistical advice may be needed. In **ESCI Effect sizes** there are two relevant pages: Both **2 ind means same variance** and **2 ind means general** support the range of options I mentioned earlier in this paragraph. For example, you can enter the means, group sizes, and a *p* value, and ESCI will calculate and display the difference with its CI. The popout comments explain. The Comprehensive Meta-Analysis (CMA) software supports around 20 options for the set of information you enter, to get the difference between two independent means with its CI. Different studies very likely provide different information, so a range of methods is needed to calculate the CIs in the forest plot. A central task of coding is to extract for each study some combination of information sufficient to calculate ESs and CIs.

Embark on a meta-analysis and you are, alas, for some studies likely to have difficulty finding sufficient information. Take that lesson to heart. A key part of meta-analytic thinking is appreciating that our current study will, we hope, be included in future meta-analyses, so we'd better report full and clear statistical information to make that easier.

some measure of agreement between the coders as an indicator of coding reliability. Your final coding scheme should strike a balance between extracting all the information needed for any analyses you contemplate, acceptable coding reliability, and the amount of time and effort needed. Don't code aspects you are unlikely to need; for example, you may not need to record NHST details. It often happens that you simply can't code some characteristic reliably and so you need to find a better way to identify it, or drop it from your plans. My colleagues and I once wanted to record the number of dependent variables used by each of a set of studies, but, surprisingly, often found it impossible to agree on that number. We had to drop that variable from our planned analysis.

Manheimer et al. (2005) reported that for non-English-language reports they relied on one expert, but otherwise two researchers independently extracted all data from the studies. Differences were resolved by discussion, or consultation with a third researcher. They recorded ES data for five types of measures, including pain and return-to-work measures, and for all time points for which data were reported. They decided to define data for times up to 6 weeks following treatment as "short term," and for the meta-analysis they used the data for the time point closest to 3 weeks. Note that such decisions must not be influenced by the results reported in the studies, to avoid biasing the meta-analysis.

Step 4: Choose What to Include, and Design the Analyses

Here you examine your data, consider study quality, and plan your analyses. You may need to drop studies that are deficient in some way. You need to tailor your analyses to the studies and the data you have.

Manheimer et al. (2005) decided that 11 of their 33 studies were so diverse that they could not reasonably be included in a meta-analysis. The other 22 all assessed Chinese acupuncture for chronic low back pain, but compared it with a wide variety of other treatments, sham treatment, or no treatment. These comparison conditions differed so much that the researchers decided to conduct six separate meta-analyses, each combining only two to eight studies, for the six different comparison conditions. It's a little unusual to split a group of studies like that, but it does illustrate that every situation is different, and the meta-analyst needs to make many judgments.

In addition, Manheimer et al. (2005) followed medical custom by giving each included study a score for quality, the score reflecting, for example, how appropriate a procedure for randomization had been used, and the extent to which information was provided about patient dropouts. They could enter the quality score into their analyses to explore whether quality was related to outcomes.

Step 5: Analyze the Data

A meta-analysis may combine data from studies whose results are reported using a variety of ESs. It's a valuable feature of the CMA software that it accepts many different ESs and, in many cases, can convert data entered using one ES measure into a different ES measure. Box 9.2 has more about conversion among different ES measures.

Manheimer et al. (2005) used CMA and random effects models with d as their ES. They concluded that acupuncture is more effective than sham treatment, $d = 0.54$, [0.35, 0.73], but that there's no evidence that it is more effective than other active therapies. Manheimer et al. found no substantial heterogeneity, probably because they conducted several meta-analyses, each combining a small set of similar studies. They included quality scores in their tables and reported no relation between study quality and results. They also looked for any evidence of publication bias in their data sets, but I'll postpone description of that analysis to the section below on publication bias.

BOX 9.2 CONVERSION AMONG DIFFERENT EFFECT SIZE MEASURES

Two ESs often used for meta-analysis are Cohen's d and Pearson's correlation r, and it's possible to convert between the two. To calculate r from a d value, CMA uses

$$r = \frac{d}{\sqrt{d^2 + 4}} \tag{9.1}$$

for the case where $N_1 = N_2$. To do the reverse and calculate d from an r value it uses

$$d = \frac{2r}{\sqrt{1 - r^2}} \tag{9.2}$$

Whenever using any conversion between ES measures we must consider whether the conversion makes conceptual sense, and also check that any necessary assumptions are reasonable. To convert r to d, for example, we need to assume that the data used to calculate r came from a bivariate normal population, and that one of the variables was dichotomized to create the two groups whose mean difference is expressed as d. Borenstein et al. (2009) explain much more about the important topic of conversions among different ES measures.

Step 6: Interpret the Findings

Here, as you'd expect, you discuss your findings in relation to past literature, your theoretical framework, and your initial research questions. Draw out the implications for theory, for future research, and for practice. As you'd also expect, I recommend that interpretation should focus on the overall ES estimates given by your meta-analyses and the CIs on those estimates. In particular, interpret the ESs themselves.

Manheimer et al. (2005) based their discussion on ESs and NHST, but provided a good example of interpreting an ES. They referred to a visual analog scale for severity of pain, which requires that the patient make a mark somewhere on a 10 cm line labeled "no pain" at one end and "worst possible pain" at the other. They reported that an established standard in pain research, widely accepted by researchers and clinicians, is that a difference of 1 cm or more on the scale is regarded as clinically important. In their study, 1 cm corresponds to $d = 0.4$. Therefore, the $d = 0.54$ advantage they found for acupuncture over sham treatment corresponds to 1.4 cm on the scale, which is clearly a clinically important difference.

Step 7: Present the Review

The report of a meta-analytic review usually follows the familiar pattern of introduction, method, results, and discussion. The Meta-Analysis Reporting Standards (MARS) presented in the *Publication Manual* (APA, 2010, pp. 251–252) provide detailed guidance. Expect to see explanations for various choices made at each stage of the review, and critical analysis and discussion of many issues.

Large tables are often used to provide information about all included studies. Manheimer et al. (2005) used one table to describe the 11 included studies not subjected to meta-analysis, but which were mentioned occasionally in the discussion, and another to describe the 22 studies included in the meta-analyses. Forest plots illustrated all the meta-analyses. Further information about the study, and in particular the analyses, was provided as supplementary material available at the journal's website. I'll now turn to my second example meta-analytic review, and again divide my brief description into the seven stages.

Rose-Tinted Glasses, in Seven Steps

Fletcher and Kerr (2010) asked whether love is blind, or maybe insightful? Compared with the acupuncture review, this second example paid much more attention to theory. The researchers studied judgments people make of their partner in a heterosexual romantic relationship. To what extent do we see our loved one through rose-tinted glasses, and to what extent can we judge objectively? They reported two main meta-analyses: one of 98 studies and the other of 48.

Step 1: Formulate Your Problem

Before formulating their meta-analysis questions, Fletcher and Kerr (2010) proposed their own theoretical model of how people think about and make judgments about their partners, and used this new model to underpin their whole project. They defined two separate measures of how people judge, or rate, their partners. Consider ratings of, for example, "warmth" or "attractiveness." Each of the two measures compared the rating of a person made by the person's partner against the rating that person made of him- or herself. I'll refer to *partner ratings* and *self-ratings*, and we can think of these in two equivalent ways. If the partner rating is the rating you make of your partner, then the self-rating is the rating your partner makes of him- or herself. Equivalently, the partner rating could be by your partner of you, in which case the self-rating is your own self-rating. Just keep in mind that partner and self-ratings always refer to the same person.

The first measure was of the extent to which partner ratings are on average higher than the self-ratings. In other words, does your partner generally rate you more highly than you rate yourself? Equivalently, do people generally rate their partners more highly than those partners rate themselves? If so, they are seeing them through rose-tinted glasses, and I'll refer to the difference between the ratings as the rose-tinted glasses (RTG) score, where a larger score means stronger rose tinting.

The second measure is of discrimination, and assesses how well partner ratings and self-ratings correlate in a group. You and your partner may generally agree that you score high on warmth, whereas in another couple both your friend and her partner agree that she is rather low on warmth. (That could be the case whether the average RTG scores are high or low: The two measures I'm describing are largely independent.) If there's such broad agreement within couples, there will be in the group a high correlation between partner and self-ratings. This implies that partner and self-ratings generally agree on who should be rated high and who low. To the extent that the two ratings correlate across the group, people are using the rating scale in a discriminating way and making objective discriminations about their partners. In summary, the RTG score measures average bias within couples, whereas discrimination is a correlation across the whole group that measures the extent that people are accurate in rating their partners high or low.

The general message here is that the researchers presented a substantial theoretical discussion, a new model, and some carefully defined variables as part of this crucial first step. They used that essential preliminary work to specify selection criteria for studies to be included in the meta-analyses.

Important among these were detailed requirements of exactly what judgment procedures had been used and what measures reported, so the researchers could derive estimates of RTG, or discrimination, or both.

Step 2: Search the Literature and Select Studies

Fletcher and Kerr (2010) searched the Web of Science and PsycINFO databases, and used a particularly wide range of search terms because they expected to find relevant studies published in a range of disciplines that were likely to use different terminology. They stated that they were open to studies including homosexual partners, but that all studies they found included only heterosexual relationships.

Step 3: Code the Studies and Collect Data

The researchers encountered a problem with studies that didn't provide full information about whether participating couples were dating, married, or merely sharing a residence; they developed rules to classify such studies. Another problem was that, for married couples, length of relationship was usually reported as length of the marriage. Based on data reported by some studies, they decided that adding 2.5 years to the length data for married couples would improve comparability with data for cohabiting and dating couples. They therefore made that adjustment.

Step 4: Choose What to Include, and Design the Analyses

Fletcher and Kerr (2010) found that they had 38 studies that provided data on both RTG and discrimination, 10 that provided data only on RTG, and 60 only on discrimination. They therefore planned separate meta-analyses on their two basic measures.

Step 5: Analyze the Data

The researchers used CMA and random effects models. They elected to use correlation r as their ES measure, and used CMA to convert ESs reported in other ways into r values. For RTG, d seems to me more understandable, so I used Equation (9.2) to convert the overall average r they reported into d, and found that average RTG was $d = 0.20$, [0.08, 0.30]. I didn't convert the discrimination measure because it is a correlation between partner and self-ratings. Overall, mean discrimination was $r = .47$, [.44, .50].

Fletcher and Kerr (2010) found substantial heterogeneity, meaning variation in mean ESs across studies. I'll postpone description of their moderator analysis until the next section. They also looked for any evidence of publication bias, as I describe in the section below on that topic.

Step 6: Interpret the Findings

Overall RTG of $d = 0.20$ means that, averaging over all the qualities rated by participants, partner ratings averaged $d = 0.20$ higher than self-ratings. That's a rose-tinted glasses effect. The average discrimination measure of $r = .47$ indicates that partner ratings tend to be high or low in broad agreement with high or low self-ratings. Ratings about a partner thus convey a strong element of realism. These two results together indicate that, yes, we do tend to see our romantic partner in a rose-tinted way, but also that we are realistic and discriminate whether a high or low rating is deserved.

The researchers reported CIs, but based their discussion and interpretation on ESs and NHST. They referred to the overall RTG mean, equivalent to $d = 0.20$, as "positive," and the overall discrimination of $r = .47$ as "substantial" and "moderately strong."

Step 7: Present the Review

The first third, approximately, of Fletcher and Kerr's (2010) article was the introduction and discussion of their proposed theoretical model. Much of the final discussion was also based on this model, with considerable attention devoted to theoretical implications of the findings and promising directions for future research. The emphasis on the critical analysis of theory is a strong feature of this review article.

Reflecting on the Seven Steps

I've given just a very brief skip through the seven steps, with selected fragments from my two example reviews. Reading a good meta-analytic review can be fascinating: It gives a bird's-eye view of a whole research literature. It tells a story of how the researchers defined their questions, selected studies that had adequate methodology and reported relevant data, then carried out a meta-analysis and found the best answers to their questions that current knowledge can provide. There's critical comment throughout, and the discussion is related to the wider literature. Please feel encouraged to read some meta-analysis reports, and then do one yourself, even if on a small scale.

Finding Moderators That Account for ES Variation

Fletcher and Kerr (2010) examined whether gender might account for some of the variation in RTG results. They found that 34 of their studies reported separate data for males and females. I converted the r values they reported to d, and obtained average RTG of $d = 0.17$ for women and $d = 0.15$ for men. Clearly any gender difference on RTG was negligible. Recall our definition in Chapter 8 that a moderating variable, or moderator, is a variable that accounts for some ES variation. Fletcher and Kerr found that gender is not a notable moderator of RTG.

Gender is an example of a *dichotomous moderator*—a variable with two possible values. More generally, a *categorical moderator* is a variable with two or more possible discrete values, such as ethnic group or academic grade on a scale from A to F. A *continuous moderator* is simply a variable measured on a continuous scale, such as time spent learning, or age, or cost. *Moderator analysis* seeks to identify moderators and estimate the extent to which they can account for the variability in ES over studies. I will consider two cases: examining a potential dichotomous moderator, and meta-regression, which examines a potential continuous moderator.

> *Moderator analysis* seeks moderator variables that can account for some of the ES variability between studies.

In the early days, meta-analysis was criticized for attempting to combine studies that differed in important ways, but we now understand that differences between studies can be coded as potential moderating variables—for example, gender. If moderators explain some of the variation in outcome of different studies, the meta-analysis may even throw light on questions that haven't been addressed by any of the individual studies in the meta-analysis. That's a wonderful strength of meta-analysis.

Dichotomous Moderators

The **Subgroups** page of **ESCI Meta-analysis** carries out the simplest moderator analysis, which assesses a dichotomous moderator like gender. It's based on **Original 31**, so it needs ESs in original units. You enter the mean, SD, and N for each study. Figure 9.1 is an image from **Subgroups** that shows data I invented for 16 studies that measured response time (RT) in milliseconds (ms) for some task. The wide scatter of the CIs in the forest plot suggests lots of heterogeneity. Recall that I^2 is the estimated percentage of variation over studies that reflects true variation in population ES, rather than sampling variability. The I^2 value reported below red 16 doesn't appear in the figure, but was 87%, confirming that heterogeneity is large. Can we find a moderator to account for some of that?

I imagined that some studies used pictures as stimuli and others used words. In the subgroups column below red 2 I typed "Pics" or "Words" for each study. I left a blank for Study 8, which I imagined didn't use either of those stimuli. Then I clicked at red 5 to see a subgroups analysis, as in Figure 9.2. ESCI displays the groups as red and blue, but here I've made them light and dark gray. The white diamond reports a random effects meta-analysis of all 15 included studies, and the two gray diamonds report

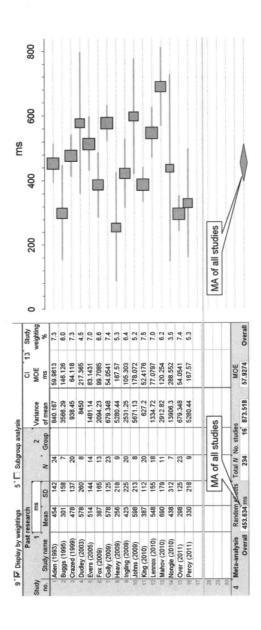

FIGURE 9.1

A part screen image from the **Subgroups** page of ESCI Meta-analysis. Data are shown for 16 studies that measured response time (RT) in milliseconds (ms). The diamond reports a random effects meta-analysis (MA) of all 16 studies. Error bars are 95% CIs. The double line below the studies signals that blank rows have been collapsed to produce this image.

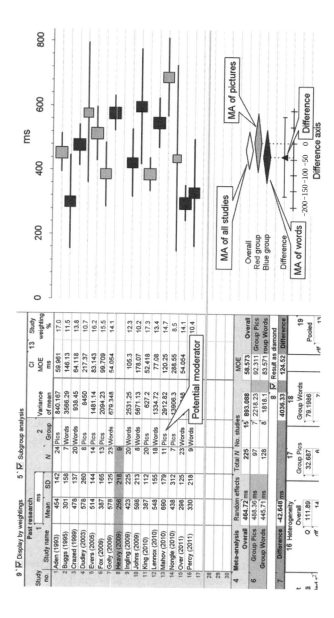

FIGURE 9.2

Same as Figure 9.1, except that the group variable of stimulus type, pictures (Pics) or Words, which is a potential moderator, has been entered in the column below red 2. Study 8 did not use either, so it is grayed out and not included. In the forest plot, means for Pics are light gray and means for Words dark gray. The white diamond reports a random effects meta-analysis (MA) of all 15 included studies. The light and dark gray diamonds show random effects meta-analyses of the separate groups. The difference between the two group means is shown, with its 95% CI, on a difference axis at the bottom.

the results of separate subgroups analyses. Meta-analysis results are also reported in the red 4 and red 6 panels. The red 7 panel reports that the difference between the two group means is –43 ms, meaning responses to Pics (light gray diamond) are on average 43 ms slower than those to Words (dark gray diamond). This difference and its 95% CI are displayed on a difference axis at the bottom. The CI is [–167, 82], which is very wide and indicates that our small set of studies gives a very imprecise estimate of how responses to Pics and Words compare. Also, the CI is wide compared with the 43-ms difference. We conclude that stimulus type is not the moderator we seek.

I next imagined that I could identify gender as another potential moderator, and that most of the studies used either all females or all males as participants. For 14 of the studies I entered a group label, Male or Female, below red 2, as shown in Figure 9.3. This time the group difference reported near red 7 was large, at 153 ms, with CI reported in the same row just to the right of the forest plot as [56, 250]. This difference and its CI are displayed on the difference axis at the bottom of the forest plot. All four CIs displayed at the bottom of the forest plot are wide, as we'd expect given our small number of studies and great variation from study to study. However, the difference between male and female of 153 ms is large, and much larger than the MOE of its CI displayed at the bottom, so we can conclude that gender is one moderator that helps account for the large variation over studies.

Consider the forest plots in Figures 9.2 and 9.3, and in each compare the patterns of light and dark gray squares. Does it seem to your eye that, overall, light and dark differ considerably in the second figure, but hardly at all in the first? Do the diamonds for the two groups, and the difference with its CI marked on a floating difference axis at the bottom, help you appreciate the subgroups analysis? So far as I know, these are novel features of a forest plot for subgroups. They need evaluation, but I look forward to further proposals to make forest plots even more useful by making further features of the meta-analysis easier to grasp.

You may be thinking it's unlikely that almost all studies would use either all females or all males. Yes, indeed. Fletcher and Kerr's (2010) moderator analysis for gender was more complex, because it included studies that presented data only from females, others only from males, and others from both, but the idea is the same as I've illustrated.

Consider a meta-analysis in which every study uses just one level of the moderator, for example, all males or all females. Then our moderator analysis asks a research question—how do males and females compare?—that no

A moderator analysis may be able to address questions that no single study in the meta-analysis has addressed.

single study asked. That's an important way in which meta-analysis can go beyond what any of the contributing studies offer.

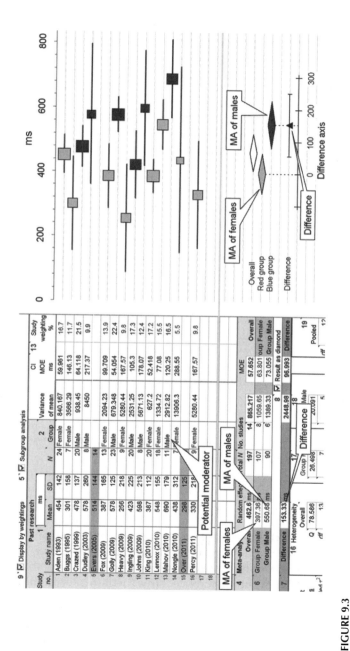

FIGURE 9.3

Same as Figure 9.2 but with gender as the group variable entered in the column below red 2.

Near red 15 you can click to select fixed effect analyses if you wish, but the figures illustrate random effects, our usual choice. For random effects analyses within the groups we need to make one further choice: Will we estimate τ^2 separately for each group, or pool over the groups? If that question seems too daunting, feel free to skip to the next paragraph. Recall that τ^2 is the variation in the true population ES, and we calculate T^2 from our data as an estimate of τ^2. We need T^2 to calculate the random effects weights. We can either calculate a separate T^2 for each group of studies, or we can assume that τ^2 is the same for the populations underlying the two groups and calculate a single T^2 pooled over the groups. With subgroup analysis clicked on at red 5, you can click near red 15 to choose either separate estimates or a pooled estimate of τ^2. If you have many studies in each group, choose separate, but if not, choose pooled unless you have strong reason to think that true ES variation is different for the two groups. For Figures 9.2 and 9.3 I chose pooled. Click back and forth between the two options to see the difference. Often in practice it makes little difference which you choose.

Figure 9.3 may remind you of Figure 6.2, which displays the means of two independent groups and their difference with its CI on a floating difference axis. Yes, there is a parallel. Study means in our subgroups analysis, which are the light and dark gray squares in Figure 9.3, correspond to individual data points in a two-independent-groups design. The main difference is that studies are differentially weighted in the meta-analyses, using weights shown below red 13, whereas all data points are treated equally in calculating the group means in Figure 6.2. There are further small calculation differences between the two situations, but even so it's useful to appreciate the parallel.

There is, however, a crucial contrast between the two situations. If participants are randomly assigned to the two groups, the independent-groups design permits inferences of causality: If a difference emerges, beyond what sampling variability can reasonably explain, then it must have been caused by the different treatments experienced by the two groups. However, in a moderator analysis there is no random assignment of studies to the two levels of the moderator.

A moderator analysis may identify a correlation between a moderator and the main ES, but this does not imply causality.

We may note a large correlation between gender and average RT, but that doesn't justify an inference of causality. The studies using males and those using females may differ in some way other than the gender of their participants, and that other difference may have caused the RT difference. The most the analysis can tell us is that a moderator correlates with an ES difference. Any further interpretation must rely on our judgment in the research situation. The correlation is likely at least to provide a promising suggestion for further research investigation.

Subgroup analysis can be extended to categorical moderators with more than two values. Perhaps the studies in Figure 9.1 used pictures, words, or digits, with each study using just one type of stimulus. We would have three groups, and could carry out meta-analysis of each group and see three group diamonds at the bottom of the forest plot. The parallel is with analysis of variance that compares three independent groups of data points rather than studies. Of course, we could have more than three groups in our meta-analysis and in the analysis of variance. Borenstein et al. (2009) explain further and provide formulas.

Continuous Moderators

Suppose each study in Figure 9.1 reported the average amount of previous experience its participants had at the task, and suppose average experience varied widely over the studies. Amount of experience, a continuous variable, would then be a potential moderator that might account for some of the observed heterogeneity of ESs. Informally, think of calculating the correlation over studies between amount of experience and study means. A substantial correlation would suggest amount of experience is an important moderator. Alternatively, you could calculate the regression of study mean against *Meta-regression* seeks to identify a continuous moderator. amount of experience—informally, think of the straight line of best fit in a plot of study means against experience. Yes, there's a parallel between those simple correlation and regression calculations, and *meta-regression*, which is the analysis we use to investigate a possible continuous moderator. Again, the main difference is that studies are weighted differentially in a meta-regression, as Borenstein et al. (2009, Chapter 20) explain.

I'll illustrate meta-regression with an example from Fletcher and Kerr (2010), who investigated whether RTG score was related to relationship length. Are our glasses more strongly rose-tinted in the first flush of love than after many years together? They found 13 studies that reported RTG and average length of relationship. Figure 9.4 illustrates their meta-regression, carried out in CMA, of RTG against relationship length. The left axis shows RTG as *r* transformed to Fisher's *z*. (There's more on that transformation in Chapter 14.) Equivalent *d* values are shown at right. Length of relationship is shown on a log scale on the horizontal axis, with length in years shown at the top. The negative slope of the meta-regression line indicates much stronger RTG, on average, for shorter relationships: *d* is around 1 for RTG during the first year or two, and declines to around zero after several decades. Over the years, the rose tinting seems to fade.

Note that meta-regression, like other forms of moderator analysis, may address a question that no single study can address. Again, that's a wonderful strength of meta-analysis. However, we are again observing a correlation that doesn't imply causality: Perhaps increasing age is the cause of reduced RTG, and age is confounded with relationship length in our

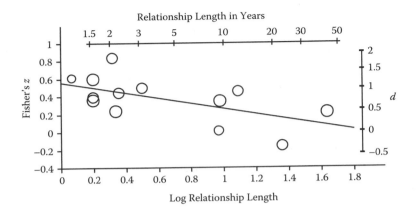

FIGURE 9.4
Meta-regression of rose-tinted glasses (RTG) score against length of relationship. The left axis shows RTG values transformed from *r* to Fisher's *z*, with equivalent *d* values shown at right. The lower axis is log of relationship length in years, and equivalent values in years are shown at the top. Each circle represents a study, with circle area indicating weight in the meta-regression. Plotted from original data kindly provided by Garth Fletcher.

studies. Or perhaps it's a cohort effect, meaning the important factor is year of birth and people contributing data for short relationships, who were mostly born more recently, won't show decreased RTG as they age. Or, again, it may be a selection effect, if couples with high RTG tend to split up and so can't contribute toward the right in Figure 9.4. Any conclusion we draw from the correlation established by meta-regression is a matter for informed judgment in the research context and, as ever, it's important to consider alternatives. We could suggest further research to explore the correlation further, but sometimes that's difficult or impossible.

It's best to identify likely moderators at the planning stage. Draw on your theoretical framework and understanding of the research context. Once you've chosen likely moderators, code the data from your studies that you need for the moderator analyses. In addition, after you've examined all the data, you can carry out further analyses for any other likely looking variables. The risk is that such data snooping may capitalize on chance, so any conclusion about a moderator identified during exploration is especially tentative.

Analyzing More Than One ES Measure

Many research studies include more than one dependent variable, in which case you have a number of options, including

- Choose a single ES for meta-analysis and ignore others.
- Carry out more than one meta-analysis, one for each ES of interest. For example, Fletcher and Kerr (2010) reported separate meta-analyses for RTG and for discrimination.
- Consider in advance how the measures relate conceptually. You may decide that measures of reasoning and of language are both measures of cognitive skill, which is your primary research interest. You could combine the scores into a single measure for meta-analysis, perhaps by averaging, or by converting each to a *d* value then averaging.

I'll describe Peter Wilson's PhD project (Wilson & McKenzie, 1998) on clumsiness in children to illustrate one way to take advantage of having many measures. Wilson located 50 studies that met his inclusion criteria and carried out separate meta-analyses on a large number of different measures of children's abilities. He found an especially large deficit, equivalent to $d = 1.31$, for clumsy children compared with control children on complex visuospatial tasks, which included, for example, visual discrimination of shapes and building with blocks. However, by exploring many measures and focusing on the one that gave the largest overall ES, Wilson risked capitalizing on chance. He knew his conclusion was tentative, and therefore carried out an empirical comparison of groups of clumsy and control children. He used a battery of tests, including 10 visuospatial tasks, and confirmed that clumsy children find such tasks especially difficult. This deficit had not previously been identified as a particular problem for clumsy children. Wilson's project illustrates how meta-analysis can identify a key variable in a messy literature. Meta-analysis plus a follow-up study could shape subsequent theoretical and empirical research on clumsiness.

Correcting for Measurement Error

So far in this book I've focused on sampling variability—the troublesome variation from sample to sample that's pictured in all the dances. It's a common assumption that sampling variability is the only cause of error in our data, and many statistics books don't mention any other source of error. In the real world, however, it's unfortunate that our data also reflect various other types of error, including especially *measurement error*. Measurement error is the difference between the data value we observe and what is, in some sense, the true underlying value. For example, we think of a child as having some true level of verbal ability, say, X_{TRUE}, but when today we gave the child a test of verbal ability we obtained X_{OBSERVED} as the score. Then we can write

$$X_{\text{OBSERVED}} = X_{\text{TRUE}} + e$$

where e is the measurement error—the difference between the true score X_{TRUE} and our observed score X_{OBSERVED}. If we tested the same child tomorrow, we might assume that X_{TRUE} is virtually unchanged, but we are likely to obtain a different X_{OBSERVED} because any number of aspects of the child and the testing situation may be slightly different, which we summarize by saying that the measurement error will be different. One measure of the *reliability* of a test is how well tomorrow's X_{OBSERVED} correlates with today's X_{OBSERVED} across a group of children.

The field of *psychometrics* studies tests and measurement. It develops tests that have, among other desirable properties, high reliability. It has developed sophisticated techniques to quantify and deal with measurement error. An unfortunate separation has developed between the field of statistics, which, as I mentioned, often pays little or no attention to measurement error, and psychometrics, which takes measurement error seriously, but may or may not take full account of sampling variability. It's also unfortunate that a somewhat parallel partial separation has developed within meta-analysis. The most common approach to meta-analysis, which I've been discussing in these three meta-analysis chapters, usually takes little or no account of measurement error, although it could. As I mentioned in Chapter 7, a second major approach to meta-analysis has been developed primarily by Jack Hunter and Frank Schmidt (2004). The subtitle of their book is *Correcting Error and Bias in Research Findings*, which describes their focus on multiple sources of error. They pay careful attention to measurement error and state that all data contain measurement error, to some extent. Usually, however, researchers are most likely to consider measurement error when analyzing data from questionnaires or other tests. Measurement error generally tends to reduce the values of r, d, or other ESs calculated from data. The reduction is small if reliability is high and larger if reliability is medium or low. Hunter and Schmidt provide techniques and software for adjusting the values of ESs, to compensate for the reductions estimated as being caused by measurement error. The techniques require information about the reliability of the ES measures, and they result in an increase in ES values.

In Chapter 7 I mentioned the example from Hunter and Schmidt (2004) of the validity of job aptitude tests. Those researchers applied meta-analysis to a very heterogeneous research literature and found that various identifiable sources of error, an important one of which was measurement error, could largely account for the variation over studies. Their conclusion was that the tests do have a certain breadth of applicability, and this was an important change from what had previously been the accepted view. This example shows that it can be vital to correct for measurement error.

In Chapter 8 I mentioned the study by Schmidt, Oh, and Hayes (2009) of published meta-analyses. Those researchers reported that 63% of the articles they studied took the most common approach to meta-analysis, as I've discussed in these last three chapters, whereas 11% took the Hunter and Schmidt (2004) approach. (The remaining 26% took a variety of other approaches.) Measurement error should more often be considered within statistics and, in particular, as part of meta-analysis. I look forward to developments in guidance and software that will assist researchers to routinely consider measurement error, especially when conducting meta-analysis.

Borenstein et al. (2009) and the CMA software focus on what I've been referring to as the most common approach to meta-analysis. Borenstein et al. included a few pages (pp. 341–352) that outline what they call "psychometric meta-analysis," which is the approach of Hunter and Schmidt (2004), including correction for measurement error. Borenstein et al. also explain how information about test reliability can be used to correct ES values calculated from data. The corrected values can then be entered into CMA, or ESCI, for meta-analysis.

I draw two conclusions from this brief discussion of measurement error. First, we should always be conscious that, in practice, data are likely to reflect measurement error as well as sampling variability. Especially if we suspect that the reliability of our measures is not high, we should consider making some adjustment in our meta-analysis to remove the estimated effect of measurement error. Second, and most important, we should make every effort in designing our research and selecting measures to minimize measurement error. It's far better to reduce it than try to compensate later. Strategies include choosing measures with high reliability, controlling testing conditions closely, and measuring more than once and averaging.

Assessing Publication Bias

We need to cast a wide net when searching for studies for possible inclusion in a meta-analysis, although we can never be sure we've found everything that's relevant. There are, however, ways to estimate whether some types of publication bias have distorted the results of a meta-analysis. I'll describe one common approach: the funnel plot, which is a scatterplot

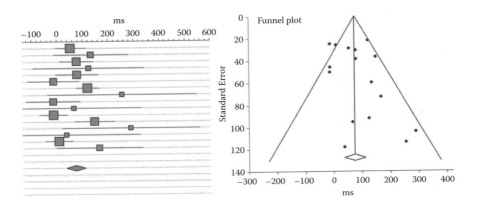

FIGURE 9.5
The left panel is a forest plot of 16 fictitious studies, whose ES is increase in mean RT with fatigue. The right panel is a funnel plot of the same 16 studies. The diamonds report a random effects meta-analysis.

of individual study standard error (SE) against individual study effect size (ES). (With funnel plots, it's even easier than usual to get confused between SEs and ESs.) Figure 9.5 is from the **Subgroups** page of **ESCI Meta-analysis** and shows data for 16 studies that I imagined had reported the mean increase in RT resulting from a given amount of fatigue on a task. The left panel is the forest plot with the result of a random effects meta-analysis, and the right panel is a funnel plot, with a diamond reporting the same result. The vertical axis in the funnel plot represents for each study the standard error of the ES; this is the square root of the variance values shown in the column just to the right of red 2. Note that the SE axis has zero at the top and values increasing downward. That's the custom, although there's no good reason for it. Studies with large N, which I'll call "large" studies, tend to have a small SE and so are plotted as dots near the top, whereas studies with small N, which I'll call "small" studies, tend to have a large SE and appear near the bottom.

The idea is that, at any given value of SE, meaning any given vertical position in the plot, the ESs should be approximately evenly spread to the left and right of the vertical line that marks the overall result of the meta-analysis. Large studies, higher in the plot, should be more tightly bunched near the line because of their smaller SE, and small studies, near the bottom, should spread further from the line because they have a larger SE. The slanting lines, whose funnel shape names the plot, indicate approximately the relative amount of spread we'd expect at different SE values.

We examine the funnel plot, looking for any sign that, for any particular SE, the studies are not spread symmetrically left and right of the vertical line above the diamond, as they should be. Small studies with an ES around zero are likely to be statistically nonsignificant, and thus at risk of not being published and of being missed by the meta-analyst, and therefore not appearing in the funnel plot. If so, lower in the funnel plot there would be dots to the right of the vertical line but fewer dots to the left, around the null hypothesis of zero. Larger studies are at less risk of being missed because they are likely to achieve statistical significance for almost any ES. The funnel plot in Figure 9.5 illustrates a common pattern when there is publication bias: Higher in the plot the larger studies are approximately evenly spread left and right of the line, but smaller studies—lower in the plot—mostly have larger ESs and appear well to the right in the figure. They are not balanced by dots around zero and to the left of the line—perhaps missing studies, not statistically significant, sitting neglected in file drawers or on hard drives.

> A *funnel plot* is a plot of study SE against study ES. Marked lack of symmetry low in the plot suggests that studies are missing because of publication bias.

At the **Subgroups** page, if subgroups analysis is not selected at red 5, then all studies are shown in the funnel plot to the right of the forest plot. You may need to scroll right. The slanting funnel lines may assist in estimating whether dots are missing low in the plot. If you like, you can use the slider below the funnel plot to adjust the slope of the lines so they enclose most of the dots, to help you judge whether small studies with small ESs may be missing. After some practice, you'll be able to look at a forest plot and guess what the funnel plot would look like. In the forest plot, note how the means marked by large squares, which represent large studies, are distributed left and right of the diamond, and then note how the small squares are distributed. To my eye, the asymmetry of small squares revealed by the funnel plot is also pretty clear in the forest plot shown at left in Figure 9.5.

Of course it's rather subjective to examine the funnel plot and judge whether you think there's much sign of publication bias, and the method usually isn't sensitive to small amounts of bias. It also relies on having a spread of study sizes. You can apply a more objective procedure that suggests what studies may be missing by, for example, adding phantom studies marked by dots lower in the funnel plot that are mirror images, around the vertical line, of the studies that do appear. Borenstein et al. (2009) describe that "trim and fill" procedure, as well as a variety of other approaches to estimating possible biases in the set of included studies. The methods typically don't work well with small sets of studies, and all require various assumptions. They can often identify severe cases of bias in study selection, but can never guarantee that our set of studies is free from bias. Using statistical significance to determine whether a study is published is a prime cause of publication bias. This risk of bias provides a further reason for adopting the new statistics.

Other Reasons for Publication Bias

Besides the pernicious influence of NHST there are many other possible causes of bias. Egger et al. (1997), for example, compared RCTs published in leading German-language medical journals with RCTs published by the same authors in English-language journals. They found no difference in the quality of the studies reported in the two types of journals, but results published in English were much more likely to be statistically significant. It seems that researchers direct their lower p value results to English language journals, which are likely to be more influential than journals published in German. Egger et al. concluded that a meta-analysis that ignores non-English-language reports may be biased.

NHST can have a damaging influence even when studies that don't achieve statistical significance *are* published. Boutron, Dutton, Ravaud, and Altman (2010) studied published reports of 72 medical RCTs in which the primary outcome was not statistically significant. They looked for what they called *spin*, meaning that the discussion attempted to divert attention from a nonsignificant main finding, or a definite conclusion was stated that was not justified by the nonsignificant finding or sufficiently by other considerations. They found that 18% of article titles and 68% of abstracts included spin, and 26% of the conclusion sections included what they rated as high-level spin, for example, failing to acknowledge a nonsignificant finding, or recommending the use of a treatment in clinical practice with insufficient justification and despite a nonsignificant finding. The bias here is not nonpublication, but misleading interpretation. Any reader must read with a critical eye, and the meta-analyst must in addition look beyond the words to the data reported.

Perhaps the most sinister and damaging cause of bias is deliberate withholding of negative findings, and here the pharmaceutical industry has a terrible record. A few days before I wrote this section, my local newspaper reported the latest international scandal, as described in the *British Medical Journal* (Eyding et al., 2010). The antidepressant reboxetine has been widely used in Europe, and meta-analysis of published trials indicated its efficacy. However, the German Institute for Quality and Efficiency in Health Care decided to review the drug. They suspected that the manufacturer, Pfizer, was withholding relevant unpublished data. Pfizer at first declined to release further information, but eventually provided data from 10 unpublished studies. Eyding et al. reported a meta-analysis of all published and unpublished trials and concluded that reboxetine is no better than placebo, is less effective than other antidepressants, and has harmful side effects. Their meta-analysis included data from 4,098 patients, but data had been published for only about one-quarter of those. The company had withheld fully three-quarters of the relevant data! In their discussion Eyding et al. referred to eight other cases in which pharmaceutical industry involvement in research has been implicated in selective reporting of more favorable results, or other bias—and that's just for research on antidepressants. It's a life and death issue that all relevant data be publicly available. Researchers should be required to release all data, whatever the outcome. Alas, we have not yet achieved that goal.

Meta-Analysis Becomes Mainstream

Back in Chapter 7 I mentioned that "research synthesis" and "systematic review" are terms used for a review that focuses on integrating research evidence from a number of studies. Such reviews usually employ the quantitative techniques of meta-analysis to carry out the integration. Often such reviews are themselves referred to as "meta-analyses." The three terms are sometimes given different meanings, but often are used more or less interchangeably. I suggest that we shouldn't be too concerned about differences of meaning for the three.

Since 2005 *The Lancet*, a leading medical journal, has included in its instructions to authors the requirement that "the relation between existing and new evidence should be shown by direct reference to an existing systematic review and meta-analysis; if neither exists, authors are encouraged to do their own" (tinyurl.com/lancetma). When introducing that requirement, the editors wrote, "Those who say that systematic reviews and meta-analyses are not 'proper research' are wrong; it is clinical trials done in the absence of such reviews and meta-analyses that are improper, scientifically and ethically" (Young & Horton, 2005, p. 107). Introducing that requirement was a pioneering step, but now journal editors across a number of disciplines are increasingly asking authors of empirical articles to include a reference to an existing meta-analysis, or to do their own. Nothing concentrates the mind of a researcher faster than a rejection letter from a journal, so I'm not surprised that researchers I know are expanding their interest in meta-analysis, and their skills in carrying out meta-analysis in their own research area. Meta-analysis is thus becoming mainstream, and with good reason: Without good understanding of past research, how

> Journals are increasingly requiring empirical articles to refer in their introduction to a relevant meta-analysis.

can we know whether this new study is necessary, or appreciate what contribution it makes? Widespread adoption of meta-analytic thinking by researchers is an excellent development. Better and more easily understood textbooks for meta-analysis are beginning to appear, with, I hope, more to come.

The Cochrane Collaboration

Medicine has led the way in the widespread adoption of meta-analysis. The centerpiece of this development, and the world's primary resource for evidence-based healthcare, is *The Cochrane Library*, an online database of systematic reviews on a vast range of health and medical topics. These are developed and maintained by the Cochrane Collaboration (www.cochrane.org), a network of centers

The *Cochrane Library* is an online database of systematic reviews that support evidence-based healthcare practice.

and researchers that involves, in various ways, more than 28,000 people in over 100 countries, most of them volunteers. The Collaboration, which started in 1993, is named after Archie Cochrane (1909–1988), a British epidemiologist who in the 1970s was an early advocate of evidence-based medicine. He envisaged a library containing the results, data analysis, and conclusions of every controlled clinical trial ever carried out anywhere. The Cochrane Library now contains more than 2,000 reviews, and the Collaboration is aiming for at least 10,000.

I'm lucky that Australia, like an increasing number of countries, has a national subscription, which allows anyone to have free access to the full Cochrane Library. If your country does not have such a subscription you can see the abstract and consumer summary of any review, but will need to find a subscribing library to obtain full access.

The Library includes, of course, numerous reviews that evaluate the efficacy of various drugs for various illnesses, but there are also reviews relating to health policy, cost-benefit questions, psychological treatments, and many other kinds of issues. During some quick browsing of the Library I discovered that

- Meta-analysis of 11 studies suggested that making treatment programs cheaper or free for smokers wishing to quit increases the use of such programs and their success. The differences are small but benefits outweigh costs.
- There is great interest in gluten-free or other exclusion diets for children with autism, and suggestions as to why they may be effective. However, only two small RCTs could be found, with equivocal results. There is currently no good evidence to support the use of such diets. Good research is sorely needed.

- Extracts of St. John's wort are widely used to treat depression, and are often prescribed by physicians in German-speaking countries. The review located 29 studies involving 5,489 patients and concluded that, overall, some extracts are superior to placebo, and are similarly effective as standard antidepressants but with fewer side effects.

Of course, the full reports give more detailed conclusions, sometimes with important qualifications, and more detailed guidance for practice than any brief summary can convey.

The Collaboration website provides open access to extensive resources that may be used by anyone preparing reviews, including Archie and RevMan. Archie is an online file sharing system that helps researchers around the world collaborate on a review, and RevMan is software you install on your own computer and use for many tasks, including carrying out a meta-analysis, and preparing forest and funnel plots. The 22-chapter Cochrane handbook (Higgins & Green, 2008) advises on numerous aspects of preparing a review. You can buy it as a hardcover book, or download the latest version free from the website. There are chapters on all stages of carrying out a review, including my seven steps. Other chapters discuss numerous topics including how to use qualitative evidence, how to use individual patient data, and a range of statistical issues. All these resources help ensure that reviewers follow the best reviewing practices and that reviews are presented in the standard Cochrane format.

Wherever possible, reviews use meta-analysis to integrate evidence from a number of studies, although sometimes there are too few suitable studies for this to be possible. All too often a review tackles an important topic, describes great efforts to locate relevant research, then states that no conclusion can be made because there is little or no relevant evidence. If you are ever seeking ideas for healthcare research, an hour with the Cochrane Library will throw up any number of interesting possibilities.

The Collaboration is keen to communicate with practitioners and the public around the world. Every review has a brief summary in plain language, and many have a podcast. For me, as you'd expect, it's often the forest plots that do the best job of telling the story. Open a review of your choice, read the abstract and plain language summary, then scroll to the end to see the forest plots. There may be a number of these, for different measures or different aspects of the question being addressed. You can see at a glance how much relevant evidence was found, the heterogeneity, and the diamonds that summarize the findings.

The Cochrane Collaboration is a great achievement and provides a wonderful resource, which is essential if evidence-based practice of medicine and health sciences is to flourish. It has been growing at around 20% per year over the last 5 years. It has centers in many countries and large numbers of specialist groups and networks that collaborate in cyberspace. It seeks contributors and users from around the world. There is a Spanish-language version. The Collaboration is meta-analysis in action.

The Campbell Collaboration

What about other disciplines? The *Campbell Collaboration* (www.campbellcollaboration.org) was established in 2000, with aims similar to Cochrane's, for the fields of social welfare, crime and justice, and educa-

> The *Campbell Collaboration* provides systematic reviews, online, in the fields of social welfare, crime and justice, and education.

tion. It, too, is an international network of researchers. It's named after Donald T. Campbell (1916–1996), an American psychologist who argued that public policy should be evidence based, and that policy initiatives should be regarded as experiments and evaluated as such to guide future policy choices.

The Campbell Collaboration has so far released around 60 reviews, all available free online, and many more are in preparation. During some quick browsing I discovered that

- A meta-analysis of 44 studies led to the conclusion that school-based antibullying programs can be effective. Program elements that increase effectiveness have been identified, and also other elements that are counter-productive.
- Parental involvement with children's schooling leads to improved academic performance (average $d = 0.45$, from 18 studies), despite median program length being only 11 weeks.
- Military-style boot camps are often advocated for juvenile offenders, but evidence from 43 studies involving 120,000 participants indicates that they are not effective in reducing future offending.

Once again, the full reports give more detailed conclusions, and guidance for public policy.

Considering psychology, some issues relevant to health and clinical psychology are included in Cochrane. Others, related to education, welfare, or criminal behavior, are included in Campbell. Psychology thus participates in both, but there remain many areas in psychology that don't fit either, at least at present. Psychology needs a broadening of Cochrane or Campbell, or both, or needs to find some other way to support evidence-based practice across the whole discipline and profession.

Meta-Analysis as a Continuing Process

The Cochrane Collaboration has the worthwhile but ambitious aim of updating all its reports every 2 years, Campbell every three. You can imagine what an immense task that is and how many researchers need to be involved, considering the many types of specialist expertise required to update reviews over such a broad range of topics.

At its simplest, updating a meta-analysis may require little more than typing the data for a few new studies into the appropriate page of **ESCI Meta-analysis** and noting the updated overall ES. In reality, however, updating requires each of the seven steps to be revisited, and changes made where necessary. In general we can hope that more precise estimates will result. Conclusions may change little, but the reboxetine example I described earlier is an extreme case in which adding previously withheld data reversed the original conclusions. With more data, additional moderator analyses may become feasible. Improved meta-analytic models may have become available, so better analysis may be possible even without new studies to add. Perhaps the world has changed, so some earlier studies are no longer relevant for the revised form of the main questions we now consider appropriate.

Researchers have so far paid little attention to what's needed to support future updating of meta-analyses, and to develop tools to assist. A good start would be for every systematic review to make full data sets and full details of all analyses available, no doubt online. Journals may need a new category of article that's a brief updating of an earlier review, when full reworking is not required. There are also some subtle questions to consider. For example, a good meta-analysis will, we hope, influence future research, but then the results of that research are hardly independent of the original meta-analysis. Is it justified to combine the new research with the original in an expanded meta-analysis? I expect updating of meta-analyses to receive increasing attention; that would be an excellent development. Regarding any meta-analysis as a work in progress is an important part of meta-analytic thinking.

> Meta-analyses need to be regularly updated to provide the best possible support for evidence-based practice and policy making.

It's time for take-home messages. You might find that browsing through Cochrane or Campbell helps you write yours, although perhaps it's more likely to provide fascinating distraction. Can you recall the seven steps of a major meta-analysis? Moderators, both categorical and continuous? Coping with more than one dependent variable? Measurement error? Publication bias? The Collaborations, and meta-analysis expanding?

Exercises

9.1 Read some recent meta-analytic reviews in your discipline. Identify as many of my seven steps as you can. Is anything important not covered by any of the steps?

9.2 Explore the **Subgroups** page of **ESCI Meta-analysis**. Modify my invented data, or enter your own from a real meta-analysis. Investigate possible dichotomous moderators, including one that accounts for little ES variance, and one that has a strong moderating effect.

9.3 When and why does ESCI gray out a study?

9.4 Note how ESCI displays in the forest plot the result of an analysis for a categorical moderator. Click at red 8 to see an alternative display. Can you find in any published meta-analysis some other display of a subgroups analysis? Can you suggest a better display?

9.5 Click among the three options at red 15. What difference does that make? Explain.

9.6 Find in a published meta-analysis the report of a meta-regression. Is there a figure? Would a figure help? What figure would be best?

9.7 Find some examples in published meta-analyses of different ways to deal with multiple ES measures.

9.8 In **Subgroups**, make sure **Subgroup analysis** is off at red 5, and **Display by weightings** is on at red 9, then explore the funnel plot. Add studies to the analysis, or remove studies, and observe changes in the forest and funnel plots. *Hint*: To remove a study, you can just delete its N.

9.9 In published meta-analyses, note any methods used to examine publication bias. If necessary, look in Borenstein et al. (2009) or elsewhere for an explanation.

9.10 Browse the Cochrane Collaboration website. Is there a Cochrane Center near you that may run local activities? Find some reviews on topics you find interesting, and observe the report structure, especially the forest plots. Suggest improvements to the displays.

9.11 Find some Campbell reports on topics you find interesting. Suggest how the report format could be improved, especially bearing in mind the Cochrane reports.

9.12 Revisit your take-home messages. Improve them and extend the list if you can.

Take-Home Messages

- Meta-analysis may be valuable at any scale, from the quick combination of two or three results to a large-scale team project that reviews a complex research literature.
- The seven steps of a large meta-analysis start with (1) formulation of the problem, then (2) literature search, obtaining of relevant articles and reports, and selection of studies.
- A major step is (3) refining the coding scheme, then coding the studies and extracting information for entry into a data file.
- Then you (4) examine the data, consider study quality, and refine the planned analysis.
- Then comes (5) data analysis, most likely including analysis of moderators.
- Identifying categorical or continuous moderating variables can be a valuable outcome of a meta-analysis. A moderator analysis, for example, meta-regression, may address questions that no individual study in the meta-analysis addressed.
- A moderator analysis may reveal correlation, but doesn't imply causality.

- The final steps are (6) to interpret the findings and (7) to present the review.
- Careful critical thought and expert judgment are needed at every stage of a meta-analysis, for example, to decide how to handle multiple ESs and complex designs.
- A funnel plot is a plot of individual study SEs against study ESs. Asymmetry of the plot for small studies suggests publication bias caused by selective publication of studies that achieve statistical significance.
- Other causes of publication bias may include omission of non-English-language reports and deliberate withholding of studies that find negative results.
- The Cochrane Collaboration is a worldwide network of researchers who prepare systematic reviews on a wide range of healthcare issues. The Cochrane Library provides these reviews online as a resource to support evidence-based practice in healthcare.
- The Campbell Collaboration prepares and publishes systematic reviews to support evidence-based practice and policy making in the social sciences.
- Meta-analyses need to be recent to be most useful, so they should be updated regularly. Researchers need to pay more attention to what's required to support such updating.

10

The Noncentral t Distribution

I find the noncentral t distribution fascinating, but it's an optional extra topic. If you like, read the brief overview, glance at some of the figures, and maybe take a look at the fairy tale. Then you can safely skip to the next chapter. Here's the agenda:

- A brief overview of noncentral t and why we might care.
- Sampling when the null hypothesis is true—first assuming σ is known, and then dropping that assumption.
- Arrival of the s pile, that being the sampling distribution of sample SDs.
- Sampling when the alternative hypothesis is true, first with σ known, then unknown: The beautiful noncentral t distribution emerges.
- Noncentral t: of bumps and tails.
- A fairy tale: the Nulls and Alts in Significance Land.

The Brief Overview

First the one-sentence version: If the null hypothesis is true we need the ordinary familiar t distribution, but if the alternative hypothesis is true—and very often in the world it is—the t statistic turns out to have an interesting humped and skewed distribution called *noncentral t*.

Now for the slightly longer version. Consider taking samples of size N from a normally distributed population—the shape of population that Figure 3.1 illustrates. As usual, the sample mean is M and standard deviation s. You're probably familiar with the test statistic for the one-sample t test:

$$t = \frac{M - \mu_0}{s/\sqrt{N}} \tag{10.1}$$

You probably recall that, if the null hypothesis (H_0: $\mu = \mu_0$) is true, then the statistic calculated using Equation (10.1) has a t distribution with

$df = (N - 1)$. The t distribution, as we saw back in Chapter 3, generally resembles the normal distribution but has fatter tails. We can think of t as measuring how far M is from μ_0 [that's the numerator in Equation (10.1)], in units of $s/\sqrt{N}$ (that's the denominator). Take many samples and we get a pile of t values in the shape of the t distribution. For any sample, we can use tables of the t distribution (or the **Normal z t** page of **ESCI chapters 1–4**) to calculate the p value and carry out NHST.

However, what happens if the null hypothesis is *not* true and some alternative point hypothesis is true? By "point hypothesis" I mean one that states an exact value for μ, for example, H_1: $\mu = \mu_1$. Samples from such a population, with mean μ_1, have M values likely to be close to μ_1 rather than μ_0. As usual we calculate t as the distance from μ_0, as in Equation (10.1). It turns out that the t values for such samples have a *noncentral t* distribution. Noncentral t is asymmetric and requires not only df but an additional parameter, the *noncentrality parameter* Δ (Greek uppercase delta), which depends on the difference between μ_1 and μ_0. The larger that difference, the more the noncentral t distribution is skewed. In contrast, the t distribution that applies when H_0 is true is the distribution we're familiar with—the *central t* distribution, which is symmetric and has $\Delta = 0$ and, therefore, depends on only the single parameter df.

That's the brief story of noncentral t, which arises when an alternative point hypothesis is true. It's important because, in the world, there often is a real effect and so alternative hypotheses often are true. In addition, statistical power is a probability calculated assuming that an alternative point hypothesis is true, so we generally need noncentral t to calculate power. Also, noncentral t is the sampling distribution of Cohen's d and so it's needed to calculate CIs for d, although that's a story for Chapter 11.

If you'd like to skip now to the next chapter, that's fine, but you may care to have a peek at Figure 10.8, which shows the shapes of noncentral t for various combinations of df and Δ. You may also be interested to see the *s pile*, which first appears in Figure 10.3: Just as the mean heap is the sampling distribution of the sample mean, the s pile is the sampling distribution of the sample SD. Finally, you may care to read the section, "A Fairy Tale From Significance Land." If you wish, you could return to this noncentral t chapter after seeing Cohen's d and power in the following two chapters.

Our Sampling Example

I'm now going to use ESCI to illustrate sampling, first with H_0 assumed true, then with H_1 true. In each case we'll first assume that σ is known, which leads to normal distributions, and then that σ is not known, which gives us central and noncentral t distributions. We'll meet the s *pile*, and also the *rubber ruler for t*, which I believe is the key to understanding sampling and t.

Here's our sampling example:

- The dependent variable is X.
- The null hypothesis is H_0: $\mu = \mu_0$, and the alternative hypothesis is H_1: $\mu = \mu_1$.
- The population is normally distributed with mean $\mu_0 = 40$ when the null hypothesis is true, and $\mu_1 = 65$ when the alternative hypothesis is true. Population SD is $\sigma = 15$.
- Sometimes I'll assume σ is known, so z is our test statistic, and sometimes I'll assume σ is not known, so we need to use t.
- I'll take samples of size $N = 6$. Such small samples should give a clearer illustration of the discussion because, when N is small, t distributions are more different in shape from normal distributions.

You may care to make up a cover story in your discipline to give meaning to this example. Perhaps X is the score on a memory test, which is scaled to give $\mu = 40$ and $\sigma = 15$ in some large reference population. We suspect that gifted children have mean $\mu = 65$. We'll take a random sample of $N = 6$ from a famous school, and carry out NHST to investigate the memory ability of children at that school. Or you may prefer to think of X as the number of seeds produced by a flower you are studying, where higher temperature may lead to greater seed production. Or X may be the time in seconds that it takes to process a routine insurance claim: This time might be longer near the end of the working day.

You may find it a bit artificial to dream up such a cover story. Why, you ask, don't we simply take a sample then use the mean and a CI to estimate what's going on? Surely that would be more informative? Yes, indeed. But to explore noncentral t we need to suspend our new statistics instincts and consider NHST for a bit.

Sampling When H_0 Is True: Four Easy Steps

Step 1: Assume That σ Is Known

You may care to join me in firing up the **Sampling** page of **ESCI chapters 10–13**. The next seven figures are from that page. The top panel of Figure 10.1 shows the population when H_0 is true, so its mean is $\mu_0 = 40$

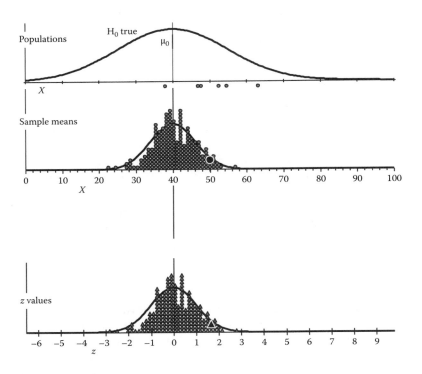

FIGURE 10.1
A figure from the **Sampling** page of **ESCI chapters 10–13** that shows at the top a normally distributed population with $\mu_0 = 40$ and $\sigma = 15$. The second panel shows 201 sample means represented as dots, and in the bottom panel, the z scores for those means represented as small triangles. Sample size is $N = 6$ and the latest sample is shown as the dot plot just under the X axis near the top. The large dot in the second panel at $X = 50.5$ shows the mean M of that latest sample. Each z unit on the bottom axis is $\sigma/\sqrt{N} = 6.12$ of X units, and the vertical lines indicate that zero on the z axis is lined up under $X = 40$. The large triangle in the bottom panel is marked z for the latest sample and is lined up under M of that sample. The curve in the second panel is the theoretically expected sampling distribution of means, which is a normal distribution and identical with the corresponding curve for z values shown in the bottom panel.

and $\sigma = 15$. The second panel shows the mean heap for the 201 samples I've taken so far, each of size $N = 6$, and the curve is the theoretically expected sampling distribution of means—which is normal with mean μ_0 and standard deviation $\sigma/\sqrt{N}$. For any sample mean M, I can calculate the z score:

$$z = \frac{M - \mu_0}{\sigma/\sqrt{N}} \tag{10.2}$$

This measures how far M is from μ_0 in units of $\sigma/\sqrt{N}$, which is the SE, with value $\sigma/\sqrt{N} = 6.12$. I've marked the axis in the bottom panel with those z score units, zero at μ_0.

The dot plot of my latest sample is just below the population curve in Figure 10.1. The large dot in the second panel is the mean of that sample, $M = 50.5$. (This and other values for the latest sample are shown near red 5.) The triangles in the bottom panel are the z scores for my 201 sample means calculated using Equation (10.2), so I'm assuming σ is known. The z axis at the bottom is marked in units of the population SE, which is $\sigma/\sqrt{N}$ and equals 6.12 in terms of X units. Therefore, the heap of triangles in the bottom panel is identical to the heap of dots in the second panel. The large triangle at $z = 1.72$ is for my latest sample and aligns exactly with the large dot in the second panel. The curve in the bottom panel is the theoretically expected distribution of z values, with mean 0 and standard deviation 1, and is identical to the curve in the middle panel.

Step 2: Assume That σ Is Not Known

For my second sampling step I unclicked near red 5 to remove the assumption that σ is known. Figure 10.2 is the result. It's the same as Figure 10.1 except the bottom panel now doesn't show z values, but a heap of t values calculated using Equation (10.1). When we don't know σ we have to use s from the sample instead as our best estimate of σ, just as Equation (10.1) does. The lower axis is the same as before, marked in units of $\sigma/\sqrt{N}$, the population SE. For any sample, t measures how far M is from μ_0, but the "measuring stick" is the *sample* standard error $s/\sqrt{N}$ [the denominator in Equation (10.1)] and this differs from sample to sample.

The dot plot just below the population curve shows the six data points in my latest sample. They happen to be tightly bunched and have $s = 8.45$, rather less than $\sigma = 15$, and so for this sample $t = (50.5-40)/(8.45/\sqrt{6}) = 3.05$, as marked by the large triangle at the bottom in the figure. This is considerably larger than $z = 1.72$ for that sample because t uses $s = 8.45$, which is smaller than the $\sigma = 15$ used to calculate z. If you take more samples, one at a time, with σ still assumed not known, you can compare for each sample the large triangle marking z in the bottom panel and large dot marking M in the second panel. They typically don't line up vertically because s is typically not equal to σ. The key point is that s varies from sample to sample, so our "measuring stick" of $s/\sqrt{N}$ also varies from sample to sample. We'll now investigate this further.

Step 3: The s Pile

The third sampling step, still assuming that H_0 is true and σ is not known, introduces the s pile. That's my name for the sampling distribution of the sample SD, and Figure 10.3 shows a picture. Values of M, the sample mean, bounce around and form the mean heap,

The s pile is my name for the sampling distribution of sample SDs, or s values, as shown in Figure 10.3.

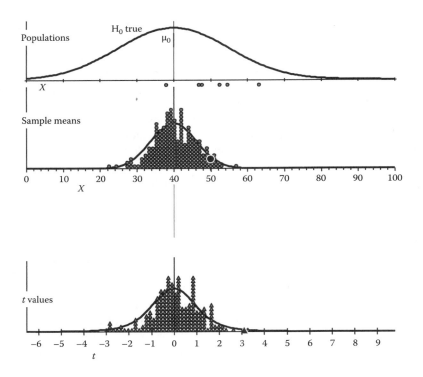

FIGURE 10.2
Same as Figure 10.1 except now we assume that σ is not known. The bottom panel shows
t, calculated using *s* for each sample, rather than *z* as shown in Figure 10.1. The large triangle marks *t* for the latest sample, which is so large because *s* for that sample happens to
be considerably smaller than σ. The curve in the bottom panel is the central *t* distribution
with $df = 5$.

shown in the second panel. In the same way, values of *s*, the sample SD,
bounce around and form the *s* pile, shown in the third panel. Each tiny
square marks *s* for one of my samples, so there are 201 squares in the pile
in Figure 10.3. The large square marks *s* of my latest sample, which is $s = 8.45$ and thus falls to the left of the line marking σ at 15.

The *s* pile is aligned with its zero under *M* of the latest sample. Run
more samples and see the *s* pile shift left and right so it's always aligned
under the latest *M*. That should make it easier to think of *s* as a measure of variation around *M*. The large square in the *s* pile indicates how
the points in the latest sample vary around the large dot in the second
panel. For our latest sample the points happen to be tightly bunched, so
s is small.

There are a few points worth noticing about the *s* pile:

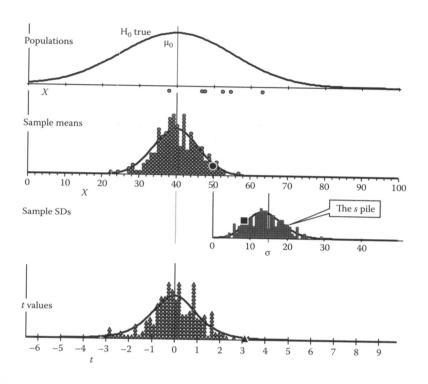

FIGURE 10.3

Same as Figure 10.2 except the s pile is now displayed. This is the sampling distribution of the sample SDs, or s values, from the 201 samples. The s pile is positioned with its zero aligned under the mean of the latest sample. The s value of the latest sample is marked by the large square.

- The s values vary greatly, at least for the small samples ($N = 6$) we're using. There are plenty of values of s less than 10 and greater than 20. Therefore, the "measuring stick" $s/\sqrt{N}$ and the values of t will also vary greatly.

- The distribution of s is positively skewed, with a longer tail of higher values. It's hump-shaped with the maximum lower than σ. The mean of the s values is, in the long run, very close to σ, but more than half the values of s are less than σ.

- If you know about chi-square you may also know that the sample variance s^2 has a chi-square distribution. The sample standard deviation s thus has a chi distribution, with $df = (N - 1)$. That's the curve shown on the s pile in Figure 10.3.

- As N increases, the SD of the s pile decreases—the pile becomes narrower—and the shape of the pile approaches a normal distribution.

You may be wondering why I didn't introduce the s pile much earlier, perhaps back in Chapter 3 along with the dance of the means and the mean heap. Why doesn't **CIjumping** have an s pile? That's a good question, and maybe it should, because back there we discussed how CI width varies from sample to sample when σ is not assumed known, and of course it's variation in s that gives the different widths. I felt, however, that things were already complicated enough for such an early chapter, so I held the s pile until now.

Step 4: The Rubber Ruler for *t*

The fourth step is to introduce the *rubber ruler for t*, which is my name for a measuring stick with zero at μ_0 and sample standard error $s/\sqrt{N}$ as its unit of measurement. Figure 10.4 shows the rubber ruler for *t*, which is marked in units of $s/\sqrt{N} = 8.45/\sqrt{6} = 3.45$, the SE for our latest sample. Now comes the crucial step: Place our sample mean—the large dot—on the rubber ruler, and read off the value of *t*. Figure 10.4 suggests that $t = 3$, approximately. The accurate value reported near red 5 is $t = 3.05$. (The picture is only approximate because M values have been adjusted into bins, so the mean heap looks neat.) Figure 10.4 is a picture of Equation (10.1)

I describe *t* as measured on a *rubber ruler* because *t* expresses the distance of M from μ_0 in units of $s/\sqrt{N}$, which differs from sample to sample.

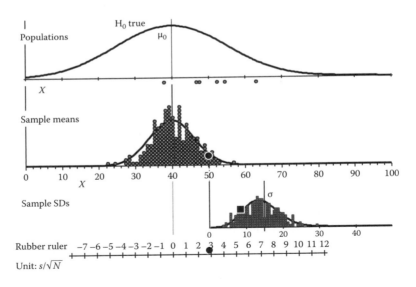

FIGURE 10.4
Same as Figure 10.3 except the rubber ruler for *t* is displayed and the heap of *t* values no longer appears. The rubber ruler has zero at μ_0 and is marked in units of $s/\sqrt{N}$, the SE for the latest sample whose s value is marked by the large square in the s pile. The large dot on the rubber ruler gives the value of *t*.

in action: The numerator in the equation is the distance of the large dot from $\mu_0 = 40$ in the mean heap, and the denominator is the unit of the rubber ruler. Therefore, t is the result we read from the rubber ruler, about 3. Take a few more samples and see why it's a rubber ruler: It stretches in and out from sample to sample because we're assuming that σ is not known, and therefore $s/\sqrt{N}$ varies from sample to sample.

Figure 10.5 puts it all together. I want to make a heap of all the t values given by the rubber ruler for t as it stretches in and out. The t axis allows us to do that because it's marked in units of the *population* SE, which doesn't change from sample to sample. The slanting lines in Figure 10.5 show how the units of the rubber ruler (the sample SE, which changes from sample to sample because we're assuming that σ is not known) map to the t axis. Our t value on the rubber ruler maps to the same numerical value on the t axis, marked by the large triangle. Take more samples and see the lines slant in or out, depending on whether the rubber ruler is stretched out or in, and see the pile of t values build. If s happens to be smaller than σ, the

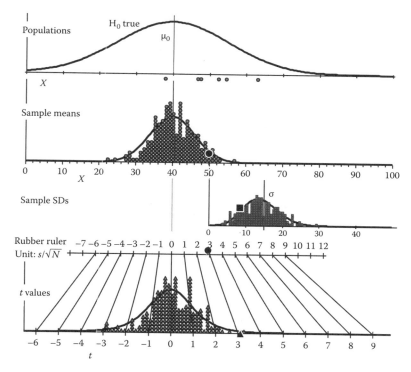

FIGURE 10.5
Same as Figure 10.4 except the heap of t values, as in Figures 10.2 and 10.3, is displayed as well. The slanting lines indicate how units of the rubber ruler for t (the sample SE) map to the units of the t axis (the population SE).

rubber ruler has small units, the lines slant out as in Figure 10.5, and the big triangle showing t is farther from zero than the big dot showing M is from μ_0. If s happens to be larger than σ, the rubber ruler is stretched out, the lines slant in, t is smaller, and the big triangle is closer to zero than M is to μ_0.

The four steps of sampling with H_0 as true resulted in the heap of t values, which in the long run has a t distribution with $df = (N - 1)$. That's the curve displayed in the bottom panel in Figure 10.5 and is the familiar central t distribution. Now we can take the same steps again with just one crucial change: Assume that the alternative hypothesis H_1 is true.

Sampling When H_1 Is True: Noncentral t Arrives

In **Sampling** I clicked near red 1 to display both populations, then near red 2 to assume that H_1 is true. I used $\mu_1 = 65$ for the population, and $\sigma = 15$, same as before. Figure 10.6 shows the result of 196 samples, with **Assume σ known** selected near red 5. The sampling distributions of M and z are normal, just as Figure 10.1 showed for H_0 true—in fact, Figure 10.6 shows those H_0 true heaps as well, in pale gray. No surprises there. I clicked to display as well the s pile and the rubber ruler. I'm now going to jump ahead to the last step of sampling with H_1 true. It's the moment for a drum roll: What do you guess will happen when we unclick near red 5 so σ is assumed *not* known?

Figure 10.7 provides the answer. At bottom left the pale gray curve for samples from the null population changes to the central t distribution, as we'd expect and as Figure 10.2 showed. It's the heap of t values at lower right and its theoretically expected curve that provide the surprise: They're strongly skewed. The curve is actually the noncentral t distribu-

Noncentral t is the sampling distribution of t that emerges when μ_1 is true and σ is assumed not known.

tion. Why is it skewed? Even though my latest sample mean, marked by the large dot, falls very close to μ_1, its t is out to the right. That sample has $M = 64.75$ and $s = 11.19$, so Equation (10.1) gives its t as $(64.75 - 40)/(11.19/\sqrt{6}) = 5.42$. The key is to notice that t is measured from μ_0 even when we're assuming that the alternative hypothesis is true so we're sampling from a population with mean μ_1. It's measured from μ_0 because NHST is based on calculations that assume that the null hypothesis is true: The p value is defined as a certain probability if the null hypothesis is true, and t is calculated using Equation (10.1), which measures how far M is from the null hypothesized value μ_0.

When we assume that the alternative hypothesis is true, the M values cluster around μ_1, but the rubber ruler for t still has its zero at μ_0. Take some more samples and watch how the distance between μ_1 and μ_0 influences t.

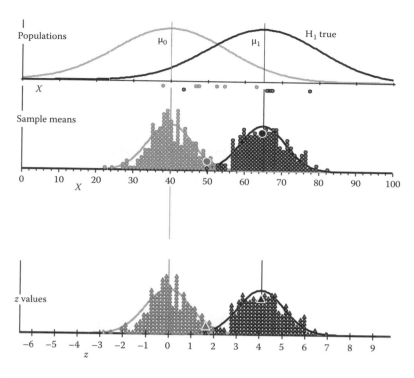

FIGURE 10.6

Same as Figure 10.1, assuming that σ is known, but now the alternative hypothesis is assumed true and 196 samples with size $N = 6$ have been taken from the population with $\mu_1 = 65$, $\sigma = 15$. The population and sampling distributions for the null hypothesis true are still visible, but are shown in pale gray. All sampling distributions are normal.

Samples with $s > \sigma$ give a stretched rubber ruler and values of t bunched mainly to the left of μ_1, whereas samples with $s < \sigma$ give a squashed ruler, as in Figure 10.7, and larger values of t that extend out to the right of μ_1. The occasional quite small values of s usually give very large values of t, so the distribution has a long tail to the right.

You can use the sliders to change μ_0, μ_1, or σ, although the display may take a little time to update. The curve in the lower right of the figure is noncentral t, for $df = 5$ and with a noncentrality parameter Δ that depends on how far μ_1 is from μ_0, and whose value is shown near red 6. The farther μ_1 is from μ_0, the larger is Δ, and the more skewed is the curve. If you change N the display clears and you need to take fresh samples. If Δ is very large the noncentral t curve may not be displayed—see the popout comments near red 6.

Investigations using the **Sampling** page illustrate how the normal, central t, and finally the noncentral t distributions all emerge from simple random sampling—from null or alternative populations, with σ known

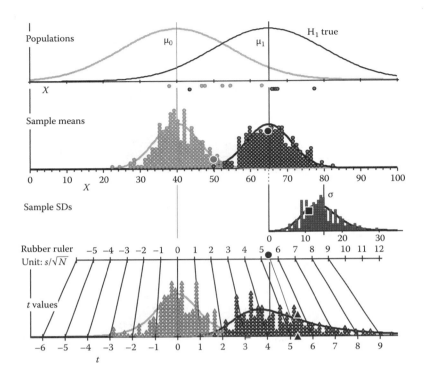

FIGURE 10.7
Same as Figure 10.6 but σ is assumed not known and so the bottom panel shows t not z.
The s pile and rubber ruler for t are also displayed. The bottom right curve is a noncentral
t distribution.

or not known. Why might we care about noncentral t? As researchers we usually don't know σ and very often there's some true effect in the world, so the null is not true. Such cases give noncentral t. That's our main conclusion from this long discussion of the **Sampling** page: When the alternative hypothesis is true and we don't know σ, sampling gives noncentral t. Now let's briefly consider the distribution itself.

The Noncentral t Distribution

The noncentrality parameter Δ is calculated as

$$\Delta = \frac{\mu_1 - \mu_0}{\sigma/\sqrt{N}} \tag{10.3}$$

Comparing Equations (10.3) and (10.2) indicates that Δ is the z score for μ_1, the mean of the population we're sampling *The noncentrality parameter* of noncentral t is Δ. It's the z score of μ_1, and is calculated using Equation (10.3).

from when that noncentral t distribution arises. For our example, $\Delta = (65 - 40)/(15/\sqrt{6}) = 4.08$. Accordingly, in Figure 10.7 the μ_1 line falls at 4.08 on the lower axis.

Figure 10.8 shows the shape of central and noncentral t distributions for a range of values of df and Δ. It shows that the skewness and wide spread of noncentral t are both greater for small df and larger Δ, meaning smaller sample sizes and a larger difference between μ_1 and μ_0. It also illustrates that noncentral t is centered approximately around Δ. If you shift the μ_1

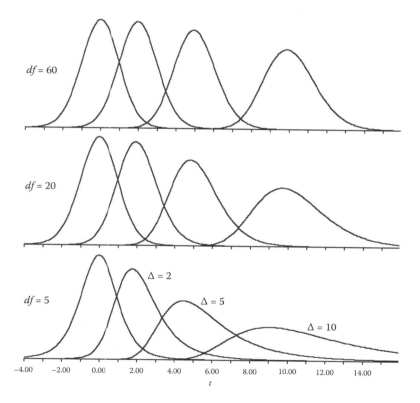

FIGURE 10.8

The central and noncentral t distributions for three values of df. At each df value, the left curve is central t, with $\Delta = 0$, then successive curves have $\Delta = 2, 5$, and 10. (Reproduced from "A primer on the understanding, use and calculation of confidence intervals that are based on central and noncentral distributions," by G. Cumming and S. Finch, 2001, *Educational and Psychological Measurement*, 61, 532–574. Copyright © 2001 Sage Publications, by permission of Sage Publications.)

slider in **Sampling** for our example with $N = 6$, you can see a range of shapes like those in the bottom panel of Figure 10.8.

The **Noncentral t** page of **ESCI chapters 10–13** allows you to investigate central and noncentral t distributions further. As well as adjusting df and Δ, you can show shaded tail areas, which may help appreciation of the asymmetry of noncentral t curves. You can set Δ to be positive or negative, which illustrates that noncentral t for a negative Δ is just the mirror image, reflected around a vertical line through μ_0, of the curve for the corresponding positive Δ. You can also click near red 5 to display a cursor and see the size of tail areas under a noncentral t curve. These are the probabilities of t falling below or above the cursor, which can be set to any chosen value of t.

A Fairy Tale From Significance Land

Once upon a time, many long years ago, there was only one t distribution. It was the familiar symmetric t distribution with a single parameter, df. The Null Hypotheses (the Nulls), who were the high priests in Significance Land, had a monopoly on this t distribution. The Nulls tended to be grumpy because most of them had the very uninteresting value $\mu_0 = 0$, and also because—although they tried to keep this quiet—almost all of them were false! Furthermore, although researchers constantly invoked Nulls, they seemed to be interested merely in rejecting them. Little wonder that morale among Nulls was low, and that they guarded their monopoly on the only t distribution jealously.

One day several smart young Alternative Hypotheses (the Alts) were discussing *their* predicament. There were many more Alts than Nulls, and the Alts tended to be much more interesting and lively than the cantankerous old Nulls. Alts tended to have interesting values (μ_1 values) and were proud of the fact that many Alts were actually true! Surely, researchers should be much more interested in finding true μ_1 values, knowledge that could have practical use in the world, or could perhaps give strong support to a scientist's theory? A few enlightened researchers used estimation and CIs to make their best estimate of true effects, but most researchers still seemed interested only in examining a Null and hoping desperately that they could reject it—as if this told them anything specific about what was actually true!

One especially smart Alt had been watching the Nulls carefully; she wondered whether the Nulls received so much attention because of their t distribution. Researchers seemed to use t values all the time, and students, as part of their induction into the weird statistical significance rituals declared compulsory by the high priests, were given lots of instruction about the t distribution. Perhaps if the Alts could invent some sort of t distribution to suit their wonderful μ_1 values, the monopoly of the Nulls would be broken, and researchers might take Alts more seriously? The Alt think tank thought this an excellent idea. Soon they had developed what they called the *noncentral t* distribution, in contrast to the Nulls' dull old *central t* distribution.

The think tank did a great job. Noncentral *t* is asymmetric and, thus, much more interesting to behold. As well as *df*, it has a *noncentrality parameter* Δ, whose value depends on μ_1 or, more precisely, on the $(\mu_1 - \mu_0)$ difference between μ_1 and the null hypothesized value. Different Alts had different μ_1 values and therefore had differently shaped noncentral *t* distributions. Cool young Alts took to carrying their own distributions with them, clearly visible in the shape of their backpacks. The think tank had designed the new distribution as the sampling distribution of *t* when you sample from a population with mean μ_1. It turns out to have at least two really useful functions. First, unless you know the population standard deviation σ—and you rarely do—then to calculate statistical power it's necessary to find an area under the noncentral *t* distribution. Second, if you use Cohen's *d* you need to use noncentral *t* to calculate a CI for your *d* value.

Alas, even those valuable uses were not sufficient for the new distribution to be a bestseller. Perhaps the Nulls were too entrenched, or perhaps the Alts did not have sufficiently clever media relations? The beautiful, intriguing, and useful noncentral *t* distribution was rarely taught to students, and remained little known among researchers. It's one of the secrets of Significance Land, yet to be fully appreciated.

Noncentral *t* in Action

In the following two chapters we'll need noncentral *t* for the two purposes mentioned above: To calculate power and to find CIs for *d*. Cumming and Finch (2001) discussed noncentral *t* further. I've adapted the fairy tale from Cumming (2006a, tinyurl.com/noncentralt). Kline (2004) and Grissom and Kim (2005) gave further discussions of noncentral *t* and its uses. Now it's time to write your take-home messages.

Exercises

10.1 Try out all the features of the **Sampling** page of **ESCI chapters 10–13**. Click near red 5 to toggle between σ known and not known, and see changes in the bottom panel. What happens for larger sample sizes? For μ_1 closer to or farther from μ_0?

10.2 Explore what the **Noncentral t** page offers. For a fixed non-centrality parameter Δ, what happens as you increase *df* to the maximum of 200? Try various values of Δ.

10.3 At the **Noncentral t** page set Δ = 4.08 and *df* = 5. At red 5 click to display the cursor and move it to *t* = 4.08. What's the probability that noncentral *t* is less than 4.08? What's the value of *t* when the right tail is of size .05?

10.4 Appendix B suggests using **Normal z t** to watch how the central *t* distribution becomes more like the normal distribution as *df* increases. For *df* more than about 30, it's traditionally assumed that the central *t* distribution is sufficiently similar to the normal distribution for researchers to use *z* rather than *t*. Use the **Noncentral t** page to investigate whether the noncentral *t* distribution approaches the normal distribution in shape. How and when?

10.5 To make Figures 10.1 to 10.7 I deliberately stopped the sampling with the most recent sample having small *s* because I wanted to illustrate how large values of *t* are generated; these large values build the impressive right-hand tail of the noncentral *t* distribution. How is the picture different if the most recent sample happens to have *s* > σ? Answer the question for H_0 assumed true, and H_1 assumed true.

10.6 In **Sampling**, investigate how the *s* pile changes for different *N*. Does it approach the normal distribution in shape? How and when?

10.7 Consider the central *t* distribution. What values of *s* tend to give *t* in the tails of that distribution? What does the shape of the *s* pile say about such values of *s*? Why does the central *t* have fatter tails than the normal?

10.8 Find any mention of noncentral *t* in any other statistics textbook you have at hand. Can you discover anything further about the distribution or its uses? Can you use ESCI to help solve any noncentral *t* problems in those textbooks?

10.9 If you use one of the major statistical packages, see whether it has a function to calculate noncentral *t*. If so, use it to find the answers to Exercise 10.3. Compare with the values given by ESCI.

10.10 In **Sampling**, click near red 5 to hide the *s* pile, and also near red 6 to hide the *z*-or-*t* heap in the bottom panel. Click to display the rubber ruler for *t*. Now you can click at red 8 to mark in red the rejection region for conducting NHST with the two-tailed α value you set near red 8. Explore how this rejection region works. Try changing α. Try σ assumed known, then not known. Try sampling when H_0 is true, then when H_1 is true. Explain.

10.11 Revise your take-home messages if you wish.

Take-Home Messages

- The familiar t distribution is central t. When σ is not known, central t is the sampling distribution of the t statistic when sampling from a population with mean μ_0, the null hypothesized value.

- When σ is not known, noncentral t is the sampling distribution of the t statistic when the null hypothesis is *not* true, and we're sampling from a population with mean μ_1.

- Noncentral t requires specification of df and also the noncentrality parameter Δ.

- Central t is symmetric, but noncentral t is asymmetric, with more skew when df is smaller and/or Δ is larger. The long tail is on the side farthest from μ_0.

- The noncentrality parameter Δ can take any positive or negative value and is the z score corresponding to μ_1, so Δ is larger when μ_1 is farther from μ_0.
- *Take-home picture*: The shape of noncentral t in the bottom right of Figure 10.7, or in Figure 10.8.
- Noncentral t approaches the normal distribution in shape as df increases, but only slowly, and more slowly for larger Δ.
- The s pile is the sampling distribution of the sample SD. It has a humped distribution that's positively skewed and approaches the normal distribution in shape as N increases. Values of s less than σ are more common than values greater than σ.
- The rubber ruler for t is marked in units of the sample SE, which is $s/\sqrt{N}$. It illustrates Equation (10.1), which states that t is the distance of M from μ_0, measured in units of $s/\sqrt{N}$, whether the null hypothesis is true and we sample from a population with mean μ_0, or the alternative hypothesis is true and we sample from a population with mean μ_1.
- Noncentral t is needed to calculate power when σ is not known, and CIs for Cohen's d.

Pólya

11

Cohen's d

Cohen's *d* is the widely used standardized ES we've encountered many times already. The idea that *d* is a number of SDs is fairly simple, but in practice there can be tricky choices to make. I suspect that most researchers don't appreciate the wide range of measures that appear in journals with the label "*d*." The first decision is the choice of SD to use for the standardization, and then you need to decide whether to adjust *d* to remove bias. It's essential to think carefully about the choices, then state clearly how you calculate the *d* you report. When you see *d* appearing in an article, it's essential to know how the author calculated that *d*—otherwise, the values are not interpretable. Here are the main topics for this chapter:

- An introduction to *d*
- Pictures of various sizes of *d*
- Options for calculating *d*
- The distribution of *d*: using the rubber ruler for *d*
- CIs on *d*
- Meta-analysis based on *d*

An Introduction to Cohen's d

Cohen's *d* is an ES measure that's simply a number of SDs, but it can be tricky to calculate, tricky to interpret, and tricky to calculate CIs for. So, is it worth the trouble? Yes, for two main reasons. First, it can help readers appreciate the size of an effect. Consider an example: Suppose you find a new numeracy exercise that increases the average score in a class of children by 5 points on an established numeracy test. It's likely that only someone familiar with the particular test could understand what 5 points means. If there's a conversion table provided with the test you could translate 5 points into its equivalent of, for example, 3 months of numeracy age. A much wider group of people would probably understand that. A further option would be to note that the test has been scaled to have SD = 15 in the reference population for the test. If you decide that's a suitable reference for your research, you could express the observed change as $d =$ $5/15 = 0.33$, or one-third of an SD.

The change expressed in SD units can be appreciated most widely, without the need for any familiarity with numeracy tests or numeracy ages, although you should interpret the d of 0.33. There are various approaches you could take. One is to compare it with Cohen's reference values (0.2, 0.5, 0.8 for small, medium, and large, respectively) and pronounce it small to medium. Another is to make your own judgment, taking account of all the circumstances, as to how important and substantial such an effect is. If it was produced by a brief intervention, you might regard it as impressive. Of course, you'll want to see the CI on the point estimate before you get too enthusiastic.

That numeracy example illustrates the first big advantage of Cohen's d: It can help ES communication to a wide range of readers, especially when the original units first used to measure the effect are not widely familiar. The example also raised the question of how to interpret d. In Chapter 2 we discussed a range of ESs, with a focus on choosing a measure and finding a good way to help readers appreciate the size and meaning of effects. Yes, interpretation is a vital issue for any ES measure, but it's especially important for standardized ESs whose SD units may have no immediate natural meaning in a particular context.

The meaning or importance of a change of a particular fraction of an SD may be very different in different circumstances. Suppose a friend excitedly tells you she's improved her marathon time by $d = 0.2$. Personally, I'm impressed by anyone who completes a marathon, whatever the time, but perhaps you're less easily impressed. What do you make of that d? Considering everyone who completes one of the large and famous street marathons, the SD of times may be, say, 40 minutes. If that's the *standardizer*, $d = 0.2$ represents $0.2 \times 40 = 8$ minutes.

The *standardizer* for Cohen's d is the SD that's chosen as the unit of measurement of d. Divide the ES in original units by the standardizer to get d.

Then your friend calls you again, even more excitedly, and says she'd made a mistake and her improvement was really $d = 1.3$! You inquire a bit further and discover that she'd decided to use as the standardizer the SD of times of elite marathoners, which she says is 6 minutes. Her 8-minute improvement suddenly became $d = 8/6 = 1.33$. You express pleasure at her improvement, but also take a moment to explain the importance of choice of standardizer for d, and the need to explain clearly what standardizer is being used whenever d is reported. She calls again a little later and says maybe you're right about the standardizer, but she's been thinking that even a d of 0.1, or even less, may matter. Such a difference may be only a few seconds, but if it's the difference between a top-20 and a top-5 finish, or even the difference between a bronze and a gold medal, then surely even a tiny d may be crucially important? At your next coffee date, you and your friend agree that you're both right: Understanding a value of *d* requires knowledge of both the standardizer and the context, and consideration beyond Cohen's reference values.

It's vital to think of *d* as a ratio: the observed effect divided by some SD. Both numerator and denominator are expressed in original units, and both need interpretive attention. The value of *d* is obviously sensitive to the numerator, but the marathon example shows that it's also very sensitive to the denominator—the SD used as the standardizer. If people don't vary much on some attribute, the SD is small and it may be easy for someone to achieve a large *d* by improving only a little. Conversely, if people vary greatly, SD is large and it may be difficult for a person to achieve even a small *d* improvement. The generality of Cohen's *d* is a great strength, but must also prompt care in interpretation. My first reason for valuing *d* is that it can assist readers' understanding of effects; therefore, it's unfortunate that *d* values are sometimes reported but then not mentioned further. It's important to report *d*, explain the standardizer, and then also discuss what the *d* tells us.

The second reason for valuing *d* is that it permits meta-analysis even when studies have used different original measures. If the studies all estimate the same effect, and if the various measures can all be transformed to *d* using in each case an appropriate SD, then we can meta-analyze the *d* values. In some disciplines, any study on a question is likely to use the same measure. Medicine, for example, often has the luxury of consistency: Numbers of deaths, blood pressure in millimeters of mercury, risk in number of cases in 100,000—these are all natural or at least widely established measures. No transformation to *d* or any other standardized ES is needed if all studies in a meta-analysis use the same original measure. In social and behavioral sciences, however, there is often inconsistency. Reading ability, or anxiety, or socioeconomic status is likely to be measured using different scales by different researchers. Standardization may have challenges, but in such cases it may be the only way to carry out a meta-analysis. Now let's consider pictures that may help the appreciation of various values of *d*.

Pictures of Cohen's *d*

Figure 11.1 is adapted from the **d picture** page of **ESCI chapters 10–13**. It illustrates the separation and overlap of distributions that correspond to $\delta = 0.50$, which is a medium-sized effect if we judge Cohen's reference values to be appropriate in the context. Here, as earlier, I'm using δ for the population ES, and *d* for the sample ES we use to estimate δ. (Sometimes *d*

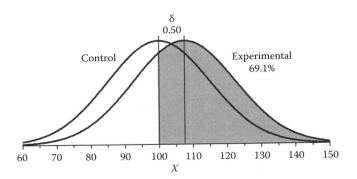

FIGURE 11.1
An image adapted from the **d picture** page of **ESCI chapters 10–13** that shows the extent of overlap corresponding to a population effect of Cohen's $\delta = 0.50$. The shaded area shows that 69.1% of cases from the Experimental distribution fall above the mean of the Control distribution.

is also used as a general label, without specifying whether population or sample is intended.) The **d picture** page uses

$$\delta = (\mu_E - \mu_C)/\sigma_C \tag{11.1}$$

where μ_E and μ_C are the Experimental (E) and Control (C) population means, and σ_C is the control population SD. In the figure, the population SD is the same for E and C, but often a treatment increases the SD of E as well as its mean, in which case we may think of C as the reference distribution and therefore prefer σ_C as the standardizer, as in Equation (11.1).

You may feel that Figure 11.1 shows a clearly visible difference between the two curves, but also very large overlap. Yes, as usual variability is large, perhaps surprisingly large. Even for a difference between means we regard as medium or large there's considerable overlap and thus many individual E cases that fall below many C cases. Another way to think of overlap is to note that, as shown by the shading in Figure 11.1, when $\delta = 0.50$ about 69% of cases in the E distribution will fall above the mean of C, and so the other 31% of E cases will actually fall below the mean of C.

A further way to think of a value of δ is to consider taking a random case from the E distribution and a random case from the C distribution, then finding the probability that the E case is greater than the C case. In other words, what's the chance that a randomly chosen point under the Experimental curve in Figure 11.1 lies to the right of a randomly chosen point under the Control curve? The curves overlap so much that the probability has to be

The *probability of superiority* of E over C is the probability that a randomly chosen value from the E distribution is greater than a randomly chosen value from C.

considerably less than 1. The probability is called the *probability of superiority*, and it's shown in **d picture** below red 3. For δ = 0.50, **d picture** reports it to be .64. So, for a medium-sized effect there's only a 64% chance that a random value from E will be higher than a random value from C.

In **d picture** you can vary the E and C means and SDs, and see how everything changes. You might think in terms of samples rather than populations and click near red 3 to label the difference as *d* rather than δ. You can easily find that the probability of superiority is .58 for *d* = 0.30, a small effect, and .71 for *d* = 0.80. Yes, even for a large effect there's only a 71% chance that a random value from E will be higher than a random value from C.

Figure 11.2 illustrates another way to think about variability and *d*. I opened the **Dance p** page of **ESCI chapters 5–6** and noted that the population means differed by 10 and the population ES was δ = 0.50. I clicked near red 2 to run an experiment and saw the data points for C and E samples. To remove the display of the sample means and their CIs, I scrolled right to see a pink area with a checkbox. I unclicked that box to see the data points uncluttered by means and CIs. I also unclicked near red 1 to hide the populations. I could then watch the patterns of just the E and C data points, their variability, and their overlap, as I clicked to simulate further experiments. I clicked **Display difference axis** near red 4 and stopped sampling when I had an experiment with a difference close to 10, the value in the population. I then unclicked to remove the difference axis. Figure 11.2 shows what I saw. (ESCI doesn't display *d* for the latest experiment, but *d* = 0.51 for the result shown in Figure 11.2, very close to the population value of δ = 0.50). To my eye, the dots in the figure suggest variation and large overlap, rather than E generally exceeding C. I conclude that a mean difference can be substantial and perhaps important even if not immediately visible in the data. Cohen (1988) chose 0.5 as a medium-sized effect because he felt it was "large enough to be visible to the naked eye" (p. 26). Of course, we calculate means and other descriptive statistics to make effects more easily visible. However, we must never become so blinkered by working with means and ESs that we forget the underlying variability. It's essential to plot and examine the data, and appreciate that an effect may be large and important while many individual data points go against the trend.

FIGURE 11.2
Two samples of size *N* = 32 from **Dance p**. There is extensive variation in each sample and extensive overlap, even though *d* = 0.51.

Options for Calculating d

In this section I'll start with the d we've already met that uses a population SD as standardizer, then move on to consider sample SDs as standardizers. In either case, d is a kind of z score. Near the end of Chapter 7 I introduced the **Standard 7** and **Standard 31** pages of **ESCI meta-analysis**. At those pages you enter study means, then ESCI transforms these to d using

$$d_i = (M_i - \mu_0)/\sigma \tag{7.1}$$

where d_i and M_i refer to Study i, and μ_0 and σ are the population mean and SD. We might be entering IQ scores, and be happy to use $\mu_0 = 100$ and $\sigma = 15$ because the IQ test was scaled to have that mean and SD in a reference population. The ESCI pages assume that the μ_0 and σ values you enter are appropriate for all studies. However, if different studies used different IQ measures that are scaled in different ways, we can still use Equation (7.1) to calculate a d_i for each study. We'd simply use the reference population values of μ_0 and σ that are appropriate for each different IQ measure.

The Single-Group Design

If we know an appropriate population σ, that's almost always the best choice of denominator for Cohen's d because it's a precise value. It's much more common, however, to have to use an SD calculated from the sample data as the standardizer. The obvious disadvantage is that such an estimate is imprecise because it includes estimation error. For a single-group design, the general formula for Cohen's d is

$$d = (M - \mu_0)/s \tag{11.2}$$

where s is the sample SD, and μ_0 is a reference value from which we wish to measure d. The value of d is thus simply the distance of sample mean M from reference value μ_0, expressed in units of s. As usual it's a kind of z score.

Table 11.1 shows data I invented for an experiment in which 20 students were randomly assigned to spend the afternoon reading in the library—the Control condition—or reading in the local botanical gardens—the Experimental condition. I'm imagining the weather was fine, and that at the end of the afternoon each student completed a measure of his or her perceived well-being. It's a two-groups experiment, but in this section let's just consider the Control group. Suppose the well-being measure we're using is scaled to have a mean of 40 for young people in our country, so $\mu_0 = 40$. I can then use Equation (11.2) to calculate $d = (42.20 - 40)/10.41 =$

TABLE 11.1

Well-Being Scores for Two Independent Groups

	Control (C)	Experimental (E)
	34	66
	54	38
	33	35
	44	55
	45	48
	53	39
	37	65
	26	32
	38	57
	58	41
Mean	$M_C = 42.20$	$M_E = 47.60$
SD	$s_C = 10.41$	$s_E = 12.46$
Pooled SD		$s_p = 11.48$

0.21 for the Control group. If the test manual reports the SD in an appropriate reference population I would use that σ. However, I'm assuming that no such value is available and I'm forced to use the sample SD of $s_C = 10.41$ as the standardizer, even though, with an N of only 10, my sample SD is an imprecise estimate. Later we'll calculate a CI on d and discover just how imprecise an estimate our d is. The d of 0.21 tells us that the Control mean of 42.2 differs only a little from the reference mean of 40.

You probably know that, for the single-group t test, to test the null hypothesis H_0: $\mu = \mu_0$ you calculate the test statistic

$$t = \frac{M - \mu_0}{s/\sqrt{N}} \qquad (10.1)$$

(That formula appeared back in Chapter 10.) The s used to calculate that t is simply the SD of the group, which was also our choice as the standardizer to calculate d for a single group. Compare Equations (11.2) and (10.1) and note that

$$d = t/\sqrt{N} \qquad (11.3)$$

There's thus a close link: Equation (10.1) states that t measures how far M is from μ_0 in units of $s/\sqrt{N}$, the SE, whereas Equation (11.2) states that d measures how far M is from μ_0 in units of s, the SD. (Recall that SE $= s/\sqrt{N}$.) Therefore, it's not surprising that d will turn out to have the same distribution as t—most commonly a noncentral t distribution.

The Two-Independent-Groups Design

For the two-independent-groups design, the general formula for Cohen's
d is

$$d = (M_2 - M_1)/s \qquad (11.4)$$

where M_1 and M_2 are the two group means. Sometimes $(M_1 - M_2)$ is used
rather than $(M_2 - M_1)$, but it's arbitrary which you choose. Just be consistent, and be sure to state which direction of difference is signaled by a
positive value of *d*. The big question is what to use for *s*: Which SD is best
to choose as the standardizer for *d*? In other words, what units provide
the most appropriate basis for *d*? First, however, note a crucial feature of
Equations (11.2) and (11.4): In both cases the numerator and denominator
both include sampling error. The numerator is a sample mean or difference between sample means and thus is an ES in original measurement
units—perhaps scale units or milliseconds or dollars. The denominator
is in the same original units but is an SD, also estimated from the data.
With estimation error in both numerator and denominator we can expect
values of *d* to bounce around a very great deal with replication.

If we assume homogeneity of variance—in other words, that both
Control and Experimental conditions have the same underlying population variance—then the pooled within-groups SD is a natural choice for
the standardizer. That's calculated using Equation (6.1) and is the same
pooled SD used for the conventional two groups *t* test. Table 11.1 shows
it to be $s_p = 11.48$. Using Equation (11.4) we get $d = (47.60 - 42.20)/11.48 =$
0.47, suggesting that the visit to the gardens prompted a medium-sized
increase in well-being just afterward, although with better knowledge of
the scale and research area we might interpret a *d* of this size differently.

Quite often a treatment increases the SD of scores as well as the mean, so
we might hesitate to make the assumption of homogeneity of variance. We
might prefer to take the Control condition as a baseline for comparison and
use $s_C = 10.41$ as our standardizer, in which case $d = (47.60 - 42.20)/10.41 =$
0.52. Our two *d* values of 0.47 and 0.52 were calculated using the same ES
expressed in original units; they differ only because we made different
choices of standardizer. As I said previously, it's vital to think of *d* as a
ratio whose value depends on both the numerator and the denominator.

The choice between s_p and s_C is a matter for judgment. One consideration is that s_p is based on two groups rather than one and so has larger *df*
and therefore is likely to be a more precise estimate of the population SD
than s_C is. In Table 11.1, s_p is based on $df = (N_C + N_E - 2) = 18$, where N_C and
N_E are the two sample sizes, whereas s_C is based on only $df = (N_C - 1) = 9$.
On the other hand, if samples are very large and there's concern that the
assumption of homogeneity of variance

For two independent groups, the best choice
of standardizer for *d* is usually but not always
s_p, the pooled within-groups SD.

may not be justified, s_C may be a good
choice. The most common choice is s_p, and

that's my recommendation unless there are good reasons for preferring some other option.

As we did for a single group, we can compare d and t. For two independent groups, the conventional t test assumes homogeneity of variance and uses

$$t = \frac{(M_2 - M_1)}{s_P \sqrt{\dfrac{1}{N_1} + \dfrac{1}{N_2}}} \qquad (11.5)$$

Use s_P for s in Equation (11.4) then compare with Equation (11.5) and deduce that

$$d = t \sqrt{\frac{1}{N_1} + \frac{1}{N_2}} \qquad (11.6)$$

Equation (11.5) states that t measures the difference between the two sample means in units of the SE of the difference—that's the denominator. Equation (11.4) states that d measures that same difference in units of the pooled standard deviation s_P. For two groups, as for the single group case, there's a close link between d and t. Equation (11.6) states that link.

To calculate d we should first identify the population SD that makes best conceptual sense as the unit for d, then choose as standardizer the best available estimate of that population SD. So far we've considered a published population σ or some s from our study, but there may be other options. Suppose, for example, we had data for one or more other studies that used the same measure of well-being, also with students. We might judge the control conditions in all those studies to be sufficiently similar that we're prepared to consider them all as estimating the same control population SD we want as our unit for d. We could therefore pool over the several control groups to obtain our best estimate to use as s in Equation (11.2) or (11.4). That strategy could work even if the different experiments investigated different questions and used different treatments—just so long as their control groups were comparable. To pool over two control groups, use Equation (6.1). Having data for even more control groups should give an even more precise estimate to use as the standardizer. Simply extend the formula in Equation (6.1). For three groups, for example, it becomes

$$s_P = \sqrt{\frac{(N_1 - 1)s_1^2 + (N_2 - 1)s_2^2 + (N_3 - 1)s_3^2}{N_1 + N_2 + N_3 - 3}} \qquad (11.7)$$

where the subscripts refer to the three control groups providing data for the pooled estimate. Enter that s_P value into Equation (11.2) or (11.4) to calculate d for our current data. Example 11.1 illustrates d for the two-independent-groups design, and some common shortcomings in how d is reported and used.

EXAMPLE 11.1 USING *d* FOR TWO INDEPENDENT GROUPS

**An Interaction Between Form of a Gene
and Asymmetry of Brain Activity**

Schmidt, Fox, Perez-Edgar, and Hamer (2009) studied how "soothabil-ity" of infants, as rated by their mothers, was predicted by whether the child had the long or short allele form of a particular gene, and whether the child showed greater left or right frontal brain activ-ity. Means for soothability were reported and NHST was the main analysis strategy. On several occasions a *t* value was accompanied by *d*, for example, "$t(34) = 3.51, p = .001, d = 1.20$" (p. 834). The *d* values reported ranged from 0.66 to 1.20. Discussion was in terms of statis-tical significance or nonsignificance, although there was one general statement that was probably a reference to the *d* values: "Although the effect sizes were medium to large, the results need to be repli-cated to ensure their reliability" (p. 836). There was no information about how *d* was calculated. However, when I applied Equation (11.6) to the *t* and *N* values, the *d* values I calculated matched the reported *d* values quite closely. Equation (11.6) assumes that *d* is based on s_p, so I concluded that the researchers most likely used s_p, the pooled within-groups SD, as standardizer for all their *d* values.

   Scanning recent articles in psychology I found that *d* was reported in only a small proportion of articles, although I suspect it would be valuable to know *d* in many more. Of those reporting *d*, most often there was no comment about how *d* was calculated. In addition, there was usually no comment about the *d* values themselves, and discussion and interpretation of the results mainly relied on NHST. Schmidt et al. (2009) largely fit this pattern, although sufficient clues were given for a detective to figure out that s_p was used as standard-izer, and there was one interpretive comment about the sizes of the effects. However, detective work should not be needed—we should be told, and interpretation should make full use of the ES informa-tion reported.

The Paired Design

Table 11.2 presents data I invented for an alternative, possibly less good, design for my study of well-being. A single group of 10 students first com-pleted the well-being measure as a Pretest, spent the afternoon reading in the botanical gardens, then gave well-being scores once again as the Posttest. We therefore have a repeated measure, which gives us paired data. The table reports the (Posttest – Pretest) differences, and the mean and SD of the differences, M_{diff} and s_{diff}. What standardizer should we

TABLE 11.2

Well-Being Scores for a Single Group Tested
Before and After a Treatment

Participant	Pretest	Posttest	Difference
1	43	51	8
2	28	33	5
3	54	58	4
4	36	42	6
5	31	39	8
6	48	45	−3
7	50	54	4
8	69	68	−1
9	29	35	6
10	40	44	4
Mean	$M_{pre} = 42.80$	$M_{post} = 46.90$	$M_{diff} = 4.10$
SD	$s_{pre} = 12.88$	$s_{post} = 10.90$	$s_{diff} = 3.57$
		$s_{av} = 11.93$	

Note: Difference is Posttest minus Pretest.

choose to convert M_{diff}, our ES expressed in original units, into d? The best choice is once again an estimate of the variability of well-being scores in the population, and s_{pre} is an attractive option, leading to

$$d = \frac{M_{diff}}{s_{pre}} = 4.10/12.88 = 0.32 \qquad (11.8)$$

Usually, however, a slightly better estimate is given by an averaging of s_{pre} and s_{post}, using

$$s_{av} = \sqrt{\frac{s_{pre}^2 + s_{post}^2}{2}} \qquad (11.9)$$

which Table 11.2 reports to be 11.93. Therefore, our preferred calculation is

$$d = \frac{M_{diff}}{s_{av}} = 4.10/11.93 = 0.34 \qquad (11.10)$$

and this value is roughly in line with the 0.47 from the two-groups experiment. If the treatment is expected to increase the SD notably, it may be preferable to regard the Pretest condition as a baseline, choose s_{pre} as the standardizer, and use Equation (11.8). However s_{av} is usually the better choice, meaning we'd use Equation (11.10).

Consider again how calculating d relates to t tests. To calculate d in the single and two-groups cases, we used as our standardizer the same SD as the t test. Now, for the paired design, note that the t test uses

$$t = \frac{M_{\text{diff}}}{s_{\text{diff}}/\sqrt{N}} \tag{11.11}$$

Choosing s_{diff}, the SD used in the paired t test, as our standardizer would lead us to calculate

$$d = \frac{M_{\text{diff}}}{s_{\text{diff}}} = 4.10/3.57 = 1.15 \tag{11.12}$$

However, does that seem reasonable? Our ES, expressed in original units, is 4.1 points on our well-being scale, similar to the 5.4 points in the two-groups experiment. In the two-groups case we calculated $d = 0.47$ using our preferred standardizer, s_p. I think it hardly seems reasonable that a slightly smaller ES (4.1 rather than 5.4) gives d more than twice as large (1.15 rather than 0.47) merely because we're using a different experimental design. Equation (11.12) uses the variability over participants in the *difference* between the two treatments as the unit for d. This is estimated by s_{diff}, but seems to me hardly a unit with clear conceptual importance that we'd choose as a measurement unit. A number of statistics texts recognize the option of using s_{diff} as the standardizer, and the CMA software also supports this option. However, I've never found an example in which it seems to me the best choice. If you find an example in which it seems to you the best choice please let me know. Meanwhile, I'll stick with my preference for Equation (11.10).

Using s_{av} for d, rather than s_{diff}, means that our d is comparable with the d calculated for the single group or two-independent-groups designs, because in each case we're using a standardizer that is our best estimate of the SD of well-being scores in the popu-

For the paired design, the best choice of standardizer for d is usually s_{av}, the best estimate of the population SD.

lation. In summary, for the paired design we need s_{diff} for the t test, but s_{av} to calculate d. Using those two different SDs for the two purposes means that for the paired design there's no simple link between d and the t test, as there was for the single group and two-independent-groups designs. So be it.

I have one further comment about the paired design. In Chapter 6 we noted that a high correlation between the two scores generally implies a sensitive design and precise estimation of the mean difference. In Table 11.2 the correlation between Pretest and Posttest is .97 and s_{diff} is less than one-third of s_{av}, so the design is sensitive. The small s_{diff} implies that d standardized against the poor choice of s_{diff} is much larger than d standardized against the good choice of s_{av}. Occasionally you may encounter published values of d that seem too high. It's quite likely, if you dig deep to find out how they were calculated, you'll find that a repeated measure was involved and an s_{diff} used as the standardizer. The more sensitive the experiment, the more such a poor choice of standardizer inflates d.

EXAMPLE 11.2 USING *d* WITH A PAIRED DESIGN

A Multimedia Program to Tackle Eating Disorders

Winzelberg et al. (1998) evaluated a multimedia program designed to reduce the damaging effects of eating disorders in young women. An intervention group who worked through the program, and a control group who didn't, each completed a number of questionnaire measures at baseline and again on completion of the experiment. Analysis used NHST, but the researchers also stated that "effect size was calculated by taking the change score between the first and last measurement for the intervention group and subtracting the change score for the control group.... This difference was ... divided by the pooled standard deviation ... at baseline" (p. 344). In other words, they calculated (posttest – pretest) as a measure of change for the intervention group, and did the same to get the change score for the control group, and then found the difference of the two change scores. That seems to me an appropriate "difference of the differences" way to estimate the effect of the program. They pooled the pretest SD of the two groups to get their standardizer to calculate *d*; again, that seems to me appropriate. ES values ranged from 0.27 to 0.56 for various measures of body image and attitudes toward eating. In discussion, there was one interpretive comment about the "modest" effects of the program. In addition, the ESs for body image (which ranged from 0.48 to 0.56) were compared with values reported in the literature for comparable therapist-provided interventions (which ranged from 0.80 to 1.50) and text-based programs (0.57).

It's interesting that they referred simply to "effect sizes" and did not use *d* (for Cohen's *d*), *g* (for Hedges' *g*), or any other symbol. It's poor practice not to explain, but if you read "effect size" with no explanation it most likely means Cohen's *d*.

Winzelberg et al. (1998) did well by explaining how they calculated their ESs, and by using ES as a metric for making comparisons with published previous evaluations of other approaches to the issue. Consideration is needed as to whether the populations investigated in the previous studies and the Winzelberg study are reasonably comparable, so their standardizers would be comparable, but overall this is an example of standardized ESs being used effectively.

This case illustrates again the general lesson that unless you know how a *d* value was calculated you can't interpret it. Example 11.2 illustrates *d* for the paired design.

I can summarize this discussion by saying that choosing a standardizer requires two steps. First, choose the SD that makes best conceptual sense as a measurement unit. In all cases so far, that's been the population SD for some control or baseline condition. Second, if that population SD is known—as it may be if the test has been scaled to give stated μ and σ in a relevant reference population—then use that σ. If not, use the best estimate available of that σ, noting that different experimental designs may estimate σ in different ways. You should choose your best estimate—for example, s_p or s_{av} or s_{pre}—by using your understanding of the research area and the measures, but *before* examining the data. Otherwise, your choice might be influenced, unconsciously of course, by which gives a preferred value of d.

Finally, be sure to report what standardizer you are using and how it was calculated. Now I have to introduce an additional complication.

An Unbiased Estimate of δ

We've been using d as our estimate for the population effect size δ, but unfortunately d overestimates δ, especially for small samples. Thus d is a *biased* estimate of δ. Fortunately, the bias can be removed by multiplying d by an adjustment factor, to give an unbiased estimate of δ. An *unbiased* estimate has a sampling distribution whose mean equals the population parameter being estimated. In other words, if an estimate is unbiased it will on average neither underestimate nor overestimate the parameter. I'll call the unbiased estimate d_{unb}, which I refer to as

An *unbiased* estimate of a parameter is, on average, equal to the parameter. On average it neither underestimates nor overestimates the parameter.

"dee-un-bee," although you can say it as you wish. The accurate adjustment needed to find d_{unb} was described by Hedges (1981), and that's what ESCI uses. Table 11.3 reports example values of that accurate adjustment factor, and also the percentage bias, meaning the percentage by which d overestimates δ. Hedges also described a very good approximate adjustment, which is

$$d_{unb} = \left(1 - \frac{3}{4\,df - 1}\right) \times d \qquad (11.13)$$

That's what the CMA software uses. The df in the equation is the degrees of freedom of the SD estimate we're using as the standardizer for d. For the single-group and paired-design cases, $df = (N - 1)$, and for the two-independent-groups case using s_p as the standardizer, $df = (N_1 + N_2 - 2)$. The adjustment factor depends only on df. Table 11.3 shows that bias is substantial for small df, meaning small samples. In practice we're almost always using d because we want an estimate of δ. Therefore, we should routinely prefer d_{unb},

I refer to the unbiased estimate of δ as d_{unb}. It's easily calculated from d using Equation (11.13), and probably should be used much more widely.

TABLE 11.3

The Adjustment Factor to Convert d to d_{unb}

Degrees of Freedom df	Adjustment Factor	Percent Bias of d (%)
2	0.564	77.2
5	0.841	18.9
10	0.923	8.4
20	0.962	4.0
30	0.975	2.6
50	0.985	1.5

Note: Multiply d by the adjustment factor to get d_{unb}.

although Table 11.3 suggests that when df is, say, 50 or more, we probably don't need to worry about making the adjustment. Of course, if the software you're using offers d_{unb}, that's almost always the best choice.

Names and Symbols

I now have to mention an unfortunate aspect of current ES practice: The terminology is a mess. The story gets confusing, so, if your eyes start to glaze over, skim ahead a couple of paragraphs and refocus when you get to "My approach in this book …". You'd think something as basic as d_{unb} would have a well-established name and symbol, but it has neither. Further, there are several terms and symbols used for various options for calculating what I'm calling d, and these are used inconsistently. Cohen (1969) originally used d for the population rather than the sample ES. In the early days the two-independent-groups d calculated using s_C as the standardizer in Equation (11.4) was referred to as Glass' d or Glass' Δ (delta), and the two-independent-groups d calculated using s_p as standardizer was referred to as Hedges' g. For example, the important book by Hedges and Olkin (1985, pp. 78–81), which is still often cited, used g in that way, and used d for what they explained as g adjusted to remove bias. So their d is my d_{unb}. By contrast, leading scholars Borenstein et al. (2009, pp. 26–27) *swapped* the usage of d and g, so now their d is the version *with* bias, and Hedges' g refers to my d_{unb}. May be hard to believe, but true. The CMA software also uses g to refer to d_{unb}. In further contrast, Rosnow and Rosenthal (2009) is a recent example of other leading scholars explaining and using Hedges' g with the traditional meaning of d standardized by s_p and *not* adjusted to remove bias. Yes, that's all surprising, confusing, and unfortunate. If you don't really follow, don't worry. The inconsistency of terminology in the literature means it's essential whenever you see a published value of d (or g) to find out how it was calculated. Similarly, it's essential to state clearly how you calculated any d you report.

Another symbol you might encounter for d_{unb} is $\hat{\delta}$, which you can read as "delta hat," where "hat" is used by statisticians to signal "estimate of." In medicine you may encounter SMD, which stands for *standardized mean difference*, another term for Cohen's *d*.

My approach in this book and in ESCI is to use δ for the population ES; *d* for any estimate calculated from data whether it uses σ, s_C, s_p, s_{av}, or some other standardizer; and d_{unb} for

I recommend using δ for the population parameter, *d* for any estimate calculated from data, and d_{unb} for the unbiased estimate of δ. Beware inconsistent use of symbols in the literature.

an unbiased estimate of δ. That's my recommended practice, but it must be supported by explanation of how *d* is calculated. If an article reports *d* and gives no information about how it was calculated, the best guess is usually Equation (11.4): the difference between two-independent-group means, standardized using s_p, with no adjustment to remove bias. But, of course, we shouldn't be left to guess.

Finally, before we turn to ESCI, you might ask why anyone even mentions *d* when d_{unb} is what we really want. That's a fair question. In fact, *d* is much more widely used than d_{unb}, despite virtually all researchers wanting estimates of δ. I suspect it's partly tradition, partly lack of understanding of the bias of *d*, and partly the appeal of *d* as a simple *z* score. Yes, *d* should be reasonably easy to grasp as a number of SDs—as a mean (or mean difference) divided by some SD. That's how I introduced *d* and how ESCI pictures *d*. It's unfortunate that we need to multiply by an adjustment factor to get d_{unb}, which is what we really want. Anyway, d_{unb} should be our routine choice, and should probably be used much more widely than it is. It's fortunate that we now have software that can often do most things for us—except the thinking.

Cohen's *d* in ESCI

In Chapter 6 we discussed two pages from **ESCI chapters 5–6** that support calculations based on your own data for the two-independent-groups and paired designs, and another two that show simulations of those designs. Although I didn't mention it back then, the four pages also support calculation of *d* and d_{unb}. In each case you simply scroll way to the right to reveal a checkbox. Click this, and *d* and d_{unb} are revealed—with a CI for δ, of which more later. Use these pages as you will, but here are a few suggestions to start with:

- In **Data two**, scroll to the right, click at red 11, and see s_p, *d*, and d_{unb} reported at red 12 for the data you enter. ESCI uses the pooled within-groups SD to calculate *d*, so it uses Equation (11.4) with s_p in the denominator. As the popout comments explain, *d* is only shown if **Yes** is selected at red 7 to assume homogeneity of variance. Use this page for d calculations based on your own data for two independent groups.

- **Simulate two** uses the same formula for d as **Data two**. Scroll right, click at red 11, and see d and d_{unb} just to the right of the figure. Note that d is the ES divided by s_p, and both of these values are reported just below red 9. You can therefore click at red 1 to take further experiments and watch how ES and s_p both bounce around, and, consequently, d also bounces around—a lot.

- In **Data paired**, scroll right and click at red 9 to see d and d_{unb} near red 10, calculated using Equation (11.10). The value of s_{av} is shown just above d. Use this page for calculations based on your own paired data.

- **Simulate paired** uses the same formula for d as **Data paired**. Scroll right, click at red 13, and see d, d_{unb}, and s_{av} just to the right of the figure. ES is reported below red 10. You can click at red 1 to take further experiments and watch ES and s_{av} both bounce around, and see how in consequence d also bounces around.

Watching the two **Simulate** pages in action should emphasize that d is a ratio, and both the effect size in the numerator and the standardizer in the denominator are estimates that vary over replication. A d of, for example, 0.5 might come from an ES estimate of 10 divided by a standardizer estimate of 20, or 8 divided by 16, or any of infinitely many other pairs of values. When comparing two d values, we need to be alert to the possibility that the difference is in the standardizer—the unit of measurement of d—and not necessarily in the ES, even if the ES is our primary interest.

Overview of the Calculation and Reporting of d

Here are the summary steps for calculating d:

1. Choose an SD that makes conceptual sense as the unit for measuring d.

2. If you know the population value σ of that SD, use it as standardizer.

3. If as usual you don't know σ, Table 11.4 summarizes the main options for calculating d using an estimate as standardizer.

4. If suitable data from additional experiments are available, consider pooling to get a more precise estimate to use as standardizer.

5. After calculating d using any estimated SD as standardizer, use Equation (11.13) to remove bias and calculate d_{unb}.

TABLE 11.4

Summary of Calculation of d

Design	df	Preferred Standardizer	Equation	Equation Number	Comment
Single group	$(N-1)$	s	$d = (M - \mu_0)/s$	(11.2)	
Two independent groups	$(N_1 + N_2 - 2)$	s_p	$d = (M_2 - M_1)/s_\text{p}$	(11.4)	Consider s_C
Paired design	$(N-1)$	s_av	$d = M_\text{diff}/s_\text{av}$	(11.10)	Consider s_pre

Values of d can be reported in text, tables, or figures. The *Publication Manual* (APA, 2010) gives an example of reporting d and its CI in text along with NHST results: "$t(177) = 3.51$, $p < .001$, $d = 0.65$, 95% CI [0.35, 0.95]" (p. 117). Of course, you don't have to report NHST along with d. The *Manual* also gives on p. 143 an example table that includes a column of d values. Whichever way you choose to report d, don't forget to explain how it was calculated.

In the next two sections I'll discuss the distribution of d, and the calculation of CIs on d. Both are optional extra sections, so feel free to read just the first paragraph of each then skip ahead to meta-analysis based on d if you wish.

The Distribution of d: The Rubber Ruler for d in Action

Consider a single-group design, and suppose we take many samples and calculate d for each. I'm assuming we don't know σ, and use s and Equation (11.2) to calculate d. What is the sampling distribution of those d values? For this simple situation, $d = t/\sqrt{N}$, as Equation (11.3) states, so d and t differ only by the scale factor $\sqrt{N}$, and therefore if we know the sampling distribution of t, we simply divide by the scale factor to get the sampling distribution of d. Chapter 10 explained that the sampling distribution of t is in general the noncentral t distribution. So d is also distributed as noncentral t. In the following I'll use the **d heap** page of **ESCI chapters 10–13** to illustrate the distribution of d. If you are about to skip ahead, that's fine, but note the main message, which is that—as I keep saying—d uses s as its measurement unit, and s varies from sample to sample. Thus d is measured with a "rubber ruler" that stretches and contracts as we take successive samples. You can see the rubber ruler for d in action at the **d heap** page.

You may want to fire up **d heap** and follow as I describe how I made Figures 11.3 and 11.4. I thought of IQ scores, so I set $\mu_0 = 100$ near red 1 as the reference mean and $\sigma = 15$ as the reference population SD, then I set $\mu = 130$, which I'm assuming is the mean IQ of students from our university.

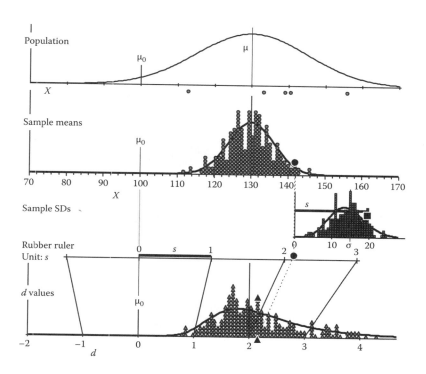

FIGURE 11.3

The **d heap** figure. From the top, it shows the population, the mean heap for samples of size $N = 6$, the s pile for SDs from those samples, the rubber ruler for d marked in units of the latest s, and the pile of d values. The mean of the latest sample is highlighted as the large dot, first in the mean heap, and then dropped down onto the rubber ruler. The SD of the latest sample is displayed as the large square in the s pile, and also as the thick line segment labeled s that appears near the top of the s pile and again as the unit of the rubber ruler. The d for the latest sample is displayed as the large triangle, first in the d pile in the bottom panel, and then dropped down onto the bottom d axis. For the latest sample, the mean of 142.1 is larger than $\mu = 130$, s is larger than σ, and together these give $d = 2.14$.

That's the population shown in the top panel of the two figures. I assume $\sigma = 15$ also for that population. Near red 1, ESCI reports $\delta = 2$, which makes sense because my μ is just $2 \times \sigma$ larger than μ_0. I planned to take samples of size $N = 6$, so I set that value at red 2. I took some samples and watched the mean heap build in the second panel down. (Make sure **Display data points**, **Display heaps**, and **Display distributions** are clicked on near red 4.)

I clicked near red 4 to display the s pile, the next panel down, which is the sampling distribution of sample SDs. Near red 5 I clicked the radio button for s, rather than the button for σ. Note that zero on the horizontal s axis of the s pile is lined up under the mean of the latest

The s pile is what I call the sampling distribution of s. It's a pile of small squares that mark the SDs of samples in the current set.

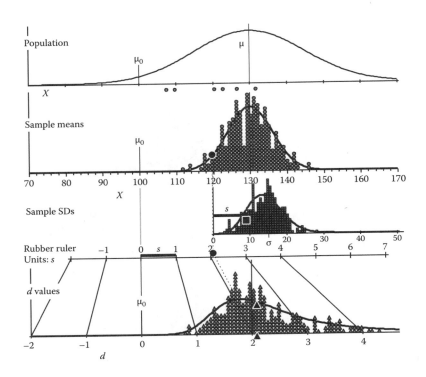

FIGURE 11.4
Same as Figure 11.3, but here the latest sample happens to have a low mean and small s, which together give $d = 2.10$, similar to the value in Figure 11.3.

sample, which is marked by the large dot. This arrangement should help us see the latest value of s, which is marked by the large square, as showing variability about the latest M. Take a few more samples and see the s pile jump around, always lined up underneath the latest M. The numerical values of the latest M and s are reported near red 4.

The data points of the latest sample appear as a dot plot in Figure 11.3 just below the population. Only 5 are visible because one happens to be 171, so it is just off screen to the right. Bearing in mind the off-screen point, their mean looks larger than μ. Accordingly, the large dot in the second panel is to the right of μ, and the value reported near red 4 is $M = 142.1$. The data points appear widely spread and, correspondingly, the SD is $s = 19.6$, rather larger than σ, as marked by the large square and the thick horizontal line segment near the top of the s pile.

Now click **Display rubber ruler** near red 5 to see the rubber ruler, which we'll use to measure d. The ruler has its zero at μ_0, because that's our reference value from which d is measured, and is marked in units of our latest s, as indicated by the thick horizontal line segment labeled "s" on the ruler—same as the line segment in the s pile. The large dot on the rubber ruler for *d* marks the latest *M* and looks to be at about 2.1, so that's our eyeball estimate of *d* for the latest sample. Next click **Display *d* heap** near red 5 to reveal the pile of *d* values at the bottom. The slanting lines show how *s* units on the rubber ruler map to *d* units on the horizontal axis at the bottom. The *d* for the latest sample is shown by the large triangle at $d = 2.14$. That's the value reported near red 5, and we can confirm it by using Equation (11.2) and calculating $d = (142.1 - 100)/19.6 = 2.14$. That completes what's shown in Figure 11.3.

> The *rubber ruler for d* is what I call the axis for measuring *d* that is marked in units of σ, which is constant, or *s*, which changes in size from sample to sample.

As a quick experiment, click near red 5 to choose σ rather than *s* as the unit for *d*. The bottom *d* heap becomes normal and both the rubber ruler and the bottom axis are marked in units of σ, so the slanted lines slant no more: They are vertical, and don't change as we take further samples.

Figure 11.4 illustrates another sample, again using *s* rather than σ, which happens to have a lowish *M* of 119.9 and *s* of 9.48, smaller than σ. These values together give $d = 2.10$. Figures 11.3 and 11.4 illustrate how similar values of *d*, 2.14 and 2.10, can arise from quite different pairs of *M* and *s* values. The rubber ruler is stretched out by the large *s* in Figure 11.3, but squashed by the smallish *s* in Figure 11.4. As I've mentioned a few times, the main message is that *d* is a ratio, and reflects both *M* and the value of *s*—as the rubber ruler illustrates. You can take further samples and watch how a large variation in *s* gives a rubber ruler that stretches and squashes dramatically. The *d* values reflect large variation in both *M* and *s*, so it's not surprising that the distribution of *d* displayed at the bottom is so widely spread.

The distribution of *s* values is shown by the *s* pile. I mentioned in Chapter 10 that the sampling distribution of s^2, the sample variance, is a chi-square distribution. (Don't worry if that's unfamiliar; just skim over these couple of sentences that mention chi-square and chi.) Therefore, the curve shown in the *s* pile, which is the sampling distribution of *s*, the sample SD, is the chi distribution. It's positively skewed with a humped peak a little below σ. Its mean is very close to σ, but values less than σ are more frequent than those greater than σ. Small *s* values tend to give large *d* values, so the predominance of smallish *s* values is one reason the distribution of *d* has a long right tail. The distribution of *d*, based on *s*, is a noncentral *t* distribution with $df = (N - 1) = 5$, and noncentrality parameter Δ given by Equation (10.3):

$$\Delta = \frac{\mu - \mu_0}{\sigma/\sqrt{N}} = \frac{130 - 100}{15/\sqrt{6}} = 4.90 \tag{10.3}$$

When *s* rather than σ is selected near red 5, the value of the noncentrality parameter Δ is reported, also near red 5.

Explore **d heap** as you wish, but here are a few things you could try:

- Use the sliders to change μ_0, μ, or σ, and watch the heaps and curves change, especially the distribution of d. Turn off various aspects of the display if you want to reduce clutter. Note that the noncentral t curve is not displayed if Δ is very large—see a pop-out comment near red 5 for explanation.
- Investigate how various things, especially the shape of the distribution of d and the width of the s pile, change for larger values of N.
- Select σ at red 5, to assume that σ is known and is used to calculate d. The rubber ruler for d stretches no more. Click back and forth between s and σ to appreciate the role of the rubber ruler. Compare what happens when you take further samples, using s and using σ.
- When s rather than σ is being used to calculate d, the value of d_{unb} is shown at red 6. Compare with d for various values of N.

My conclusions from this discussion of the distribution of d are

- Cohen's d based on s has a noncentral t distribution, and there's a strong parallel between the sampling that led to the noncentral t distribution in Chapter 10 and sampling using **d heap** to find the distribution of d.
- The rubber ruler for d emphasizes that d depends on s as well as M. It can thus be a challenge to interpret d values and compare different d values.
- Only with large N is the variability of s markedly reduced, as the s pile shows. If possible, find s with large df to use as a standardizer for d.

Confidence Intervals on d

The brief story is that, because d has a noncentral t distribution, there's no formula that permits the precise calculation of CIs for δ. An *iterative* or successive approximations method is needed. The **CI for d** page of **ESCI chapters 10–13** illustrates how this works. The CI for δ, which I'll also refer to as the CI on d, is usually slightly asymmetric, meaning that its upper and lower arms are different in length. The pages **Data two** and **Data paired** of **ESCI chapters 5–6** allow you to

To calculate a CI on d we need to use an iterative procedure based on noncentral t. The CI is a little asymmetric.

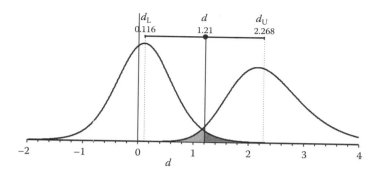

FIGURE 11.5

A figure from the **CI for d** page of **ESCI chapters 10–13**. The 95% CI is shown for $d = 1.21$ for two groups, each of size 8. Homogeneity of variance is assumed. The d_L and d_U values are the lower and upper limits of the CI. Regard these as population values δ_L and δ_U, and then the curves are the sampling distributions of d when δ_L (left curve) or δ_U (right curve) is true. The two small tail areas beyond $d = 1.21$ are shaded.

calculate CIs on d for your own data. If you are not too concerned about how those CIs are calculated, you can simply use the CIs for δ that ESCI reports and skip ahead now to the following section on meta-analysis.

For d based on σ the sampling distribution of d is normal, the complexity of noncentral t is not required, and the conventional formulas of Chapter 3 can be used to calculate CIs. For d based on s, perhaps it's not surprising that having a distribution as strange as noncentral t is likely to make life difficult. Cumming and Finch (2001) explained why CIs on d require a successive approximations strategy, and how to find such CIs. Here I won't attempt a full explanation, but I'll use **CI for d** to illustrate the process. That page finds the CI on d for the two-groups case, assuming homogeneity of variance. I fired up the page then entered values for an example I invented: a d of 1.21 and two sample sizes of 8. Figure 11.5 illustrates at the top the final 95% CI on that d, but the CI you see at first may not be accurate, in which case it is displayed pale gray. We need to adjust things until it becomes the accurate 95% CI on our d, which ESCI signals by displaying the CI in black.

First, what about d_{unb}, which is probably what we really want to know? Use Equation (11.13) and our df of $8 + 8 - 2 = 14$ to calculate the adjustment to be .945. (This is very close to the precise value used by ESCI.) So $d_{unb} = .945 \times d$, and we can easily calculate that our $d_{unb} = .945 \times 1.21 = 1.14$, as ESCI reports near red 1.

An Iterative Procedure for the CI on d

Now comes a tricky bit, but in a moment we'll use ESCI to explore it. Think of the CI on our d shown in Figure 11.5 as a set of plausible values for the population effect size δ. The lower limit of the interval is d_L. Regard this as a population value δ_L, and then the left curve is the sampling distribution of d when δ_L is the true population value. The upper tail of this distribution, beyond our $d = 1.21$, is shaded dark gray and is by definition the one-tailed p value if δ_L is our null hypothesized value. If that's puzzling, think back to the definition of p as the probability of getting our result or a more extreme result if the null hypothesis is true. Here that's the probability of getting d larger than 1.21 if δ_L is the true value, and that's just the area shaded dark gray. For the interval shown around d to be the 95% CI, that dark gray shaded area needs to be .025 so the two-tailed p value is .05. Recall the fifth approach to interpreting a CI, which notes that $p = .05$ when a 95% CI has either of its limits exactly at the null hypothesized value.

That may make better sense if we use ESCI to shift the left curve a bit. You can use the slider near red 6 to do that. Shift it a bit left, and δ is smaller and the upper tail area beyond our d becomes smaller, so p is smaller and the δ value would be rejected at the .05 level. Shift the curve right and δ is larger, the right tail area is larger, p is larger, and this δ would not be rejected. To get an accurate 95% CI we need to shift the left curve so its upper tail area is .025, and shift the right curve so its lower tail area, shaded in light gray, is also .025. The δ_L and δ_U values that give those tail areas are what we need for d_L and d_U, the limits of the CI. The sizes of the two shaded tail areas are shown just below the figure in **CI for d**, and the target sizes are also shown. If you use the sliders carefully until the two shaded tail areas match the .025 target, the interval will turn from gray to black to signal that we have the 95% CI we're seeking. Alternatively, you can click the buttons at red 6 and red 7 and see Excel shift the curves for you. It may take a little time for Excel to do its work. Check that the tail areas are as they should be when Excel finishes and the CI on d turns black.

The tricky thing is that the two curves have the shape of noncentral t distributions, so they change shape as we change δ to slide the curves left or right. It's that change of shape that means we can't make any simple calculation of CIs on d and need to use successive approximations. What are the noncentrality parameters of the two curves? (Skip to the next paragraph if you're not too concerned about that question.) Equation (10.3) gave the formula for the noncentrality parameter Δ for the single sample case. For the two-groups case, the formula is

$$\Delta = \frac{\mu_2 - \mu_1}{\sigma\sqrt{\dfrac{1}{N_1} + \dfrac{1}{N_2}}} \tag{11.14}$$

From Equation (11.1) we have the definition of population effect size δ:

$$\delta = \frac{\mu_2 - \mu_1}{\sigma}. \tag{11.15}$$

Substitute that expression for δ into Equation (11.14) and find a relation similar to that of Equation (11.6):

$$\Delta = \frac{\delta}{\sqrt{\dfrac{1}{N_1} + \dfrac{1}{N_2}}} \tag{11.16}$$

ESCI uses Equation (11.16) to convert between Cohen's δ values and the noncentrality parameter Δ needed to calculate the noncentral *t* curves. The sliders change δ, and thus Δ, and thus the shapes and positions of the curves. ESCI reports the values of Δ_L and Δ_U, which are the noncentrality parameters for the two curves displayed. For the curves in Figure 11.5 they are 0.233 and 4.54, respectively.

Noting the values of d_L and d_U in Figure 11.5, we can report that our *d* = 1.21, [0.116, 2.268]. The two arms of the CI are 1.210 – 0.116 = 1.094 (lower arm) and 2.268 – 1.210 = 1.058 (upper arm), so they differ a little.

A CI on *d* or a CI on d_{unb}?

You may be wondering why I'm describing the CI on *d*, rather than a CI on d_{unb}. If so, that's a good thought. Indeed d_{unb} is our best point estimate of δ, but it turns out that the CI on *d*, as the **CI for d** page calculates, is our best interval estimate for δ. There's no need to adjust the limits of the CI on *d* to remove bias. I explain more about that in Box 11.1.

> The best point estimate for δ is d_{unb}, which is unbiased. The best interval estimate for δ is the CI on *d*.

Use the **CI for d** page of **ESCI chapters 10–13** to explore as you wish. When *d* = 0, the CI is symmetric—after, of course, you have clicked **Find LL** and **Find UL** and you have a black CI on *d*. For larger *d* the two curves generally look increasingly different, although the CI is usually only slightly asymmetric—the two arms differ only a little in length.

Another approach to finding CIs on *d* is to use a formula that allows easy calculation of approximate CIs for *d*, without needing the curve sliding of the accurate noncentral *t* method. Such approximations usually give symmetric intervals. Cumming and Fidler (2009) evaluated one such approximation; we found it to be quite accurate, almost always giving arm lengths within 2–3% of the correct length even for small *N*. However, if ESCI is handy you can have it calculate CIs on *d*, using the noncentral *t* procedure. For the two-independent-groups case use the **CI for d** page of **ESCI chapters 10–13**, or the **Data two** page of **ESCI chapters 5–6**. For paired data use the **Data paired** page of **ESCI chapters 5–6**, which uses the approximate method of Algina and Keselman (2003). I say more about this in Box 11.1. For single-group *d*, calculate CIs by using one of the meta-analysis pages for *d*—to which we now turn.

BOX 11.1 CHOOSING POINT AND
INTERVAL ESTIMATES FOR δ

For both the single-group and two-independent-groups designs, the noncentral t method gives accurate CIs for δ. For the paired design, however, no such accurate method has been found. Algina and Keselman (2003) proposed a method based on noncentral t for finding approximate CIs for this situation, and reported evidence that their method performs well, within limits. The **Data paired** and **Simulate paired** pages of **ESCI chapters 5–6** use their method to calculate CIs on d.

It's legitimate to ask how we can assess the result given by such an approximate method when we can't calculate an exact result to use as a benchmark. After all, if we had an exact method, we'd not be wasting effort on a mere approximation. The solution is to use simulation.

Back in Chapter 3 I discussed the dance of the CIs, and we explored how, if we run that dance in **CIjumping** for a long time, we get very close to 95% of CIs capturing μ—assuming that we've set $C = 95$. Algina and Keselman (2003) ran an extensive series of simulations to evaluate their approximate method. I modified the **Simulate paired** page so I could also carry out such simulations. At each step, ESCI takes a paired sample, uses the Algina and Keselman method to calculate a CI on d, then notes whether that CI captures the population δ specified for that simulation run. ESCI keeps count over many thousands of samples. If close to 95% (assuming I've set $C = 95$) of the intervals capture δ, the method is working well.

For the paired-design case, there are several variables we need to explore: sample size N, population effect size δ, and also the correlation ρ in the population between the two measures. Recall from Chapter 6 that the higher this correlation, the more sensitive the design. Algina and Keselman (2003) reported that for N at least 10, δ between –1.8 and 1.8, and ρ between 0 and .8, their procedure gives 95% CIs that in almost every case capture δ between 95% and 97% of the time. For practical purposes that's a good result, in the absence of any better method.

My investigations confirmed those results and extended them a little. Accordingly, the **Data paired** and **Simulate paired** pages report a 95% CI on d whenever N is at least 6, and δ lies between -2 and 2. (Be sure to scroll right and click to reveal the panels that display Cohen's d and the CI for δ.) Correlation ρ can take any value. Note that the method has been tested only for $C = 95$, so C must be set in ESCI to 95 for CIs to be reported. Popout comments describe those limitations as to when ESCI can calculate a CI on d in the paired case.

In other simulations of mine, ESCI calculates both d and d_{unb} for each of a large number of experiments, and then compares average d and average d_{unb} with δ. For both the single-group and two-independent-groups designs my results confirm that d_{unb} is indeed an unbiased point estimate of δ, whereas d is biased, being on average larger than δ. For the paired design, d_{unb} is a better estimate of δ than is d, although d_{unb} is not entirely unbiased.

I have also investigated by simulation the CI on d, and various other interval estimates for δ including the CI calculated from d_{unb} (for an individual study) that the CMA software uses. I found the CI on d to be clearly the best interval estimate of δ of any I investigated. It's best because it captures δ for very close to $C\%$ of samples. This conclusion applies for both the single-group and the two-independent-groups designs. These simulation results led to my advice that (i) d_{unb} is in general the best point estimate of δ, and (ii) the CI on d is in general the best interval estimate for δ.

Later in this chapter, when discussing meta-analysis of d and d_{unb}, I report that I haven't been able to find any such investigations of which CI on the overall result of the meta-analysis gives the best interval estimate of δ. I therefore follow the practice of Borenstein et al. (2009) and CMA and give a different overall CI, depending on whether d or d_{unb} has been selected as the ES for meta-analysis. I look forward to further research on which of these CIs is better.

It's important to keep these considerations of accuracy in perspective. In practice we should not be too concerned about the precise width of a CI, which is likely to vary—perhaps considerably—on replication. In practice, deficiencies in our experimental procedure, or departures from the assumptions underlying our statistical model, may be more serious problems than whether an approximate method of calculation gives us a 95% or a 96% CI. As ever, careful critical judgment is required, and accuracy of calculation is only one of a number of issues we need to bear in mind.

Meta-Analysis Based on d

The main value of d is to allow meta-analysis of studies that have asked similar questions, but used different measures. As usual with meta-analysis, we need to be satisfied that the studies are sufficiently comparable. Do they estimate a population parameter for which the fixed effect or—more likely—the random effects model is reasonable? If we know a suitable σ that's the same for all studies, life is simple and we can use ESCI pages **Standard 7** or **Standard 31** as discussed in Chapter 7. More often we need to use standardizers calculated from the data to find d for each study, before using meta-analysis to estimate an overall population δ. To assess the comparability of the studies we need to consider both the numerator and denominator of d. In the numerator, are the ESs in original units from the studies sufficiently similar conceptually? In the denominator, are our selected standardizers estimating sufficiently comparable SDs? If both answers are yes we can proceed to the meta-analysis.

A Meta-Analysis of Critical Thinking

I'll use the meta-analysis of critical thinking by Claudia Ortiz (2007) to illustrate what's needed. Her aim was to assess the effectiveness of various critical thinking courses in increasing students' critical thinking skills. She found 52 studies that met her selection criteria. The studies used various measures of critical thinking ability, including the California Critical Thinking Skills Test and the Watson–Glaser Critical Thinking Appraisal. She was satisfied that they all assessed critical thinking, so she answered yes to the numerator question. Considering the denominator, one possibility was to use as standardizer the various SDs published for the various tests, based on the population used in each test's development. However, those populations did not in every case comprise college students, her population of interest, so she decided to use standardizers calculated from the studies themselves. First she calculated a d for each study, using the s_{av} for the particular study, even though some studies reported data for only 10–20 students and so their s_{av} values were imprecise estimates. (She used d rather than d_{unb} throughout her thesis, although, given that some sample sizes were not large, it would have been a desirable refinement to use d_{unb}.) She decided also to pool SDs over the studies that used the same measure to get her best estimate of s_{av} for that measure, using an equation similar to Equation (11.7). For example, she pooled over all the studies using the California Test and used the resulting s_{av} value to calculate d for each of those studies. Similarly, she pooled over the studies that used the Watson-Glaser and used the resulting s_{av} to find d for those studies.

Ortiz (2007) carried out two meta-analyses: one using d based on s_{av} for the individual studies and the other using d based on the pooled s_{av} values. The results were very similar, although the pooled s_{av} strategy not surprisingly gave somewhat shorter overall CIs. Her conclusions, incidentally, were that traditional critical thinking courses in philosophy departments are only moderately effective and produce an average improvement of $d = 0.34$, [0.21, 0.48] in one semester. By contrast, courses based on argument mapping (van Gelder, Bissett, & Cumming, 2004) are much more effective, giving average gains of $d = 0.78$, [0.67, 0.89] in a semester. That's a very impressive increase for any educational intervention, especially one lasting only one semester. Examples 11.3 are further illustrations of meta-analysis based on d.

Meta-Analysis of *d* in ESCI

Once you've decided that meta-analysis based on d is appropriate, and you've calculated d for each study, there are two pages in **ESCI Meta-analysis** that may assist. For a single-group design, fire up the **d single group** page and type in d and N for each study. Similarly, for a two-independent-groups design, **d two groups** requires only d, N_1, and N_2 for each study. It assumes homogeneity of variance and that d from a study is standardized using the s_p of that study. At each of these pages, immediately to the right of the d values you typed in, ESCI reports the corresponding values of d_{unb}. Figure 11.6 shows a part image of the **d single group** page. You need to click one of the radio buttons at red 2 to indicate your choice of d or d_{unb} as the effect size to be meta-analyzed. In Figure 11.6, d_{unb} has been chosen.

After entering d and N data for all studies, click the button at red 4 to trigger the calculation for each individual study of the CI on d. (The CI on d is the best interval estimate of δ, which is why I refer interchangeably to the "CI on d" or the "CI for δ.") This calculation uses the noncentral t procedure I described earlier in the **Confidence Intervals on d** section. If you ever change any of the data, or change C at red 3, you need to click again to trigger recalculation of the CIs for δ. The limits of these CIs are shown below red 15, toward the right in Figure 11.6.

If you simply want to calculate the CI for δ, for your single-group or two-independent-groups d, you can just type the d and sample size(s) into the appropriate page, maybe as Study 1, then click the button at red 4 and see below red 15 the CI you want.

Whether you choose d or d_{unb} as your preferred point estimate of δ, and as the ES for the meta-analysis, the CIs for δ shown below red 15 do not change. As I mentioned earlier, and explain further in Box 11.1, the best interval estimate for δ is the CI on d found by the noncentral t procedure.

EXAMPLES 11.3 META-ANALYSIS BASED ON *d*

Are Positive Self-Statements Valuable?

Wood, Perunovic, and Lee (2009) assessed the value of making positive self-statements ("I'm a lovable person") for people with low or high self-esteem. They reported multiple regression and other analyses, and NHST was prominent. In a small part of the analysis, two of their studies suggested that positive self-statements were detrimental to participants with low self-esteem, with $p = .012$ and $.044$ in the two studies. For participants with high self-esteem, the benefit of such statements "approached but did not reach [statistical] significance in either study" (p. 865) with $p = .10$ and $.06$. The researchers then reported that they used meta-analysis to combine results of the two studies, giving $d = 0.66$, $p = .013$ for the benefit for people with high self-esteem, and $d = -0.72$, $p = .002$ for the detrimental effect of the positive statements for people with low self-esteem. In the discussion was a comment that for people with high self-esteem "the boost was small" (p. 865). There was no comment about why d of 0.66 was considered small.

I'm all in favor of such small-scale meta-analyses, although in this case no information was given about how d was calculated or how the meta-analysis was conducted. We need to know.

Can Shrubs Help Tree Seedlings Grow?

Gómez-Aparicio et al. (2004) reported 146 experiments that over several years studied reforestation of Mediterranean mountains. They explored whether tree seedlings do better if planted in cleared ground or under the canopy of established shrubs. They used random effects meta-analysis to combine their findings and investigate the effects of site, species, and other factors that varied within or across experiments. The authors "chose the standardized difference between means (d index) to estimate the effect of the presence of shrubs on two response variables: seedling survival and seedling growth" (p. 1131). Their description suggests to me that s_p was used as the standardizer, although that was not stated clearly. They found that surrounding shrubs increased seedling survival at 1 year by an overall $d = 0.89$, [0.51, 1.27], an effect they described as "large" and "more than doubled." Surrounding shrubs increased initial seedling growth by an overall $d = 0.27$, [0.15, 0.39], an effect they described as "small" and "consistent." This is a good example of meta-analysis in action within a research program, rather than as a tool for reviewing a whole literature.

> **Evaluating Treatments For Binge Eating Disorder**
>
> Vocks et al. (2010) reported meta-analysis of 38 studies that evaluated psychotherapy, pharmacotherapy (drug), and self-help treatments for binge eating disorder. This is the one example I'll include here of a large-scale meta-analysis. They meta-analyzed several ES measures and used different meta-analysis models for different parts of the overall analysis. They stated that "for between-group effects …, standardized mean differences (… Hedges' d) were calculated" (p. 207). Also, "within-group effects for single treatment groups were computed by dividing the difference of pre- and post-means by the pooled standard deviations at the measurement times" (p. 207). I consulted the references they cited for those ES calculations, which suggested that their Hedges' d is my d_{unb}, the unbiased estimate, but left me suspecting—although I couldn't be sure—that the d they calculated for the within-group effects was not adjusted to remove bias. They meta-analyzed between-group and within-group comparisons separately, and presented tables of overall d values with their CIs, for a number of attitude and behavior measures. Values of d ranged from near zero to 1.5 and more. Their discussion made much of statistical significance or nonsignificance, but also interpreted d values as small, medium, or large using Cohen's reference values. They concluded that, on a range of measures, cognitive behavioral therapy was effective and gave substantial improvement. Pharmacotherapy, mainly using antidepressants, was generally less effective. Self-help gave some large improvements, but any conclusion about self-help is tentative because relatively little evidence was available. Detailed examination of d values on different measures and for different groups of studies led to suggestions of promising lines for future research. Overall, despite uncertainty about how d was calculated, this meta-analysis is a good example of d in action.

So ESCI always reports these CIs on d below red 15, and displays these CIs as the error bars in the forest plot. Try clicking between the two radio buttons at red 2 to change your ES selection between d and d_{unb}. Not only does the highlighting swap between the d and d_{unb} columns, but the green squares in the forest plot that mark the point estimates for the individual studies shift a tiny amount left and right. Those solid green squares display either d or d_{unb}, whichever is selected, and so shift slightly whenever you change that selection. The green error bars that mark the CIs for δ for the individual studies do not change—the green squares simply shift their

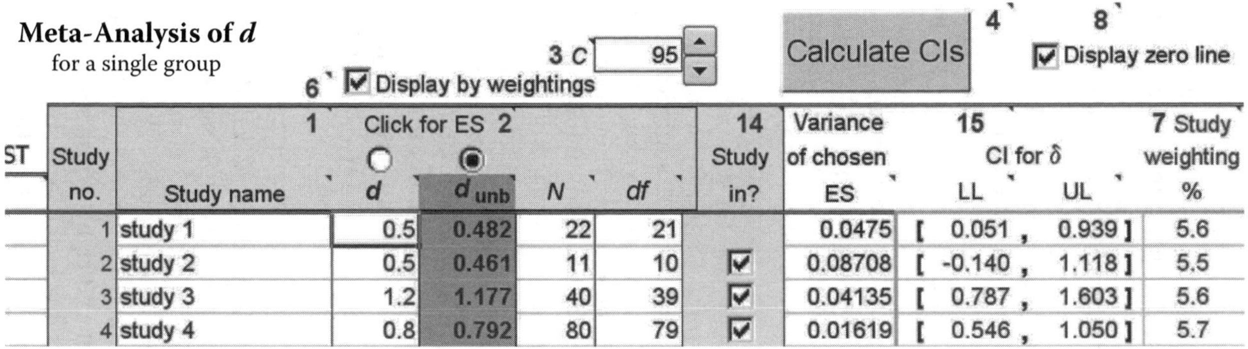

Meta-Analysis of d

for a single group

Calculate CIs

3 C 95

☑ Display by weightings ☑ Display zero line

ST Study no.	Study name	1 Click for ES 2 d	d_{unb}	N	df	14 Study in?	Variance of chosen ES	15 CI for δ LL	UL	7 Study weighting %
1	study 1	0.5	0.482	22	21		0.0475	[0.051 ,	0.939]	5.6
2	study 2	0.5	0.461	11	10	☑	0.08708	[-0.140 ,	1.118]	5.5
3	study 3	1.2	1.177	40	39	☑	0.04135	[0.787 ,	1.603]	5.6
4	study 4	0.8	0.792	80	79	☑	0.01619	[0.546 ,	1.050]	5.7

FIGURE 11.6

A part screen image from the **d single group** page of **ESCI Meta-analysis.** For each study, type your d and N values in the columns below red 2. ESCI calculates and shows the corresponding d_{unb} and df values. Click one of the radio buttons at red 2 to indicate your choice of d or d_{unb} as the ES to be meta-analyzed. In the figure, d_{unb} is selected and this selection is marked by the d_{unb} values appearing in bold and with a gray background (on the screen, a pink background). The variance of the chosen ES (in this case d_{unb}) is shown toward the right, and the next columns to the right show the lower and upper limits (LL and UL) of the CI for δ.

position a little on the fixed green line. Just to the right of the forest plot, below red 16, the lengths of the left and right arms of the CIs are shown.

The weighted average d or d_{unb} value, which is the primary result of the meta-analysis, is reported at red 5 and displayed in red, with its CI, at the bottom of the forest plot. As usual, you can click near red 11 to direct ESCI to use either a fixed effect or a random effects model. The usual results relating to heterogeneity are shown at red 12 and 13.

If you have d values from studies with a two-independent-groups design, simply use the **d two groups** page of **ESCI Meta-analysis**. For each study, type in your d and the two sample sizes, N_1 and N_2, below red 2. The page layout is very similar to that of **d single group**, and all of my discussion applies to either page.

Calculations for Meta-Analysis of *d*

When launching into a meta-analysis with a different ES, the main additional information we need is a formula for the variance of that ES. Given that, we can use the formulas of Chapters 7 and 8 to carry out all the meta-analytic calculations. ESCI uses the formulas given by Borenstein et al. (2009) for the variance of d and d_{unb}. They describe the formulas as very good approximations. CMA also uses these formulas.

You can skip over the formulas and simply let ESCI do the work, but I want to say one thing about them, so I'll include the formulas here. For a single group, the variance of d is

$$V_i = \frac{1}{N_i} + \frac{d_i^2}{2N_i} \tag{11.17}$$

where d_i, N_i, and V_i are the effect size, sample size, and variance of d for Study i. The variance of d_{unb}, which Borenstein et al. (2009) and CMA refer to as Hedges' g, is

$$V_i' = J^2 V_i \tag{11.18}$$

where J is the adjustment factor for converting d to d_{unb}, and V_i' is the variance of d_{unb} for Study i. Note that Equation (11.13) gives an approximate value of J.

For two independent groups, the variance of d is

$$V_i = \frac{N_{1i} + N_{2i}}{N_{1i}N_{2i}} + \frac{d_i^2}{2(N_{1i} + N_{2i})} \tag{11.19}$$

where N_{1i} and N_{2i} are the two sample sizes for Study i. The variance of d_{unb} is again

$$V_i' = J^2 V_i \tag{11.18}$$

although in this case V_i comes from Equation (11.19).

Yes, you can skip over those formulas, but the thing I want to mention is that it's interesting to note that the variance of d is the sum of two components: The first term on the right hand side in Equations (11.17) and (11.19) reflects the variance of the numerator of d, the ES in original units, and the second term reflects the variance of the denominator, the standardizer for d. Yes, uncertainty in both the numerator and denominator of d contribute to the variance of d, and thus to the bouncing around of d with replication.

There's one further thing you may be puzzling about—if not, you can safely skip to the next paragraph. If you click between d and d_{unb}, the variance shown for the individual ES values changes—these values appear in the column headed **Variance of chosen ES**. The values change because ESCI chooses between Equations (11.17) and (11.18), depending on whether d or d_{unb} is to be meta-analyzed. [For the **d two groups** page, ESCI chooses between Equations (11.19) and (11.18).] Those variance values are used to calculate the CI on the overall ES, which is shown just below red 10. Click between d and d_{unb} and watch that CI change a little and, correspondingly, the red error bars on the overall ES, which is displayed at the bottom of the forest plot, also change slightly. Why does the result of the meta-analysis change as you click between d to d_{unb}, but the CIs for the individual studies stay the same? That's an excellent question, and Box 11.1 explains why I've designed ESCI to show such apparently inconsistent behavior. In brief, I don't think we yet have good evidence whether the CI on overall d or the slightly different CI on overall d_{unb} gives the better CI for δ, which is what we want as one important result of our meta-analysis. So I've followed Borenstein et al. (2009) and CMA. Keep an eye out for future developments that may help us decide.

Summary of d and Meta-Analysis

ESCI provides pages that calculate the CI for δ for any d you enter, for either a single-group or two-independent-groups design. As I discussed earlier, I'd prefer d_{unb} as my point estimate for δ, and the CI shown below red 15 as my interval estimate for δ. Considering the meta-analysis, click to choose whether you wish d or d_{unb} to be the ES that is meta-analyzed. I suspect that choosing d_{unb} is likely to give our best overall point estimate of δ—the value is shown near red 5. As I mention in Box 11.1, I'm not sure whether the CI on overall d or the

CI on overall d_{unb} is a better interval estimate of δ. Fortunately, in just about every practical situation there's little problem because these two intervals are very similar. Based on the simulation results I mention in Box 11.1, my guess is that the CI on overall d may turn out to be better, but future research may prove me wrong. Please let me know if you find any research on this issue.

Let me summarize what ESCI provides if you wish to calculate the CI on d for your data, assuming σ is not known:

- For a single sample, use the **d single group** page of **ESCI Meta-analysis**. Type in your d and N, perhaps as Study 1, and click **Calculate CIs**.
- For the two-independent-groups design, you can enter all the data into the **Data two** page of **ESCI chapters 5–6**, or you can enter d, N_1, and N_2 into the **CI for d** page of **ESCI chapters 10–13**, or the **d two groups** page of **ESCI Meta-analysis**.
- For the paired design, you can enter all the data into the **Data paired** page of **ESCI chapters 5–6**.

It's time for take-home messages. We've considered numerous aspects of d, which is the most commonly used standardized ES, and you are justified in feeling pleased if you've followed it all. To prompt some memories and help you write your messages, you may care to revisit some of the many ESCI pages mentioned in this chapter. There are four pages in **ESCI chapters 5–6** that calculate d, d_{unb}, and the CI on d for the two-independent-groups and paired designs. **ESCI chapters 10–13** provides a page that pictures d, another that illustrates how sampling produces the distribution of d, and a third that demonstrates the iterative process of finding the CI on d. **ESCI Meta-analysis** provides two pages for finding CIs and carrying out meta-analysis based on d or d_{unb}.

Exercises

11.1 Use the **d picture** page of **ESCI chapters 10–13** to examine how the C and E distributions appear, for small, medium, and large values of δ. In each case, what proportion of E lies above the mean of C? Explain the meaning of such a proportion in the context of an example of your choice.

11.2 In **d picture**, for a given value of δ, increase the SD of E. What happens to *d*? What happens to the proportion of E that lies above the mean of C? Explain. What standardizer would be best for *d*? Does *d* tell the full story?

11.3 I used IQ scores, scaled so that σ = 15 in a reference population, as my example in which it may be reasonable to assume that a population SD is known and can be used as a standardizer for *d*. It's the example commonly used in textbooks. Can you find another example, perhaps in your discipline?

11.4 Calculate *d* for the Experimental group in Table 11.1. Consider at least two choices of standardizer and justify your preference.

11.5 Equation (11.3) allows you to calculate *d* for the single-group design, given only *t* and the sample size. Equation (11.6) does the same for the two-independent-groups design. Find an example of each design for which *t* and the sample size(s) are reported, but not *d*. You might look in some other statistics textbook or in your favorite journal. Use those simple equations to calculate *d*. Does knowing *d* help you interpret the results?

11.6 Find a small data set for the two-independent-groups design, perhaps in the exercises of another statistics textbook. Calculate *d*. Type the values into the **Data two** page of **ESCI chapters 5–6** and verify your calculation of *d*. Note also d_{unb} and the CI on *d*. Use your selection of those to interpret the results.

11.7 The same as Exercise 11.6, but for a paired design and using the **Data paired** page of **ESCI chapters 5–6**. Calculate the correlation between the two measures, and also calculate *d* using s_{diff} as the standardizer. Discuss.

11.8 Use Equation (11.13) to extend Table 11.3 by adding values of the adjustment factor for additional *df* values. Calculate the adjustment factor given by Equation (11.13) for *df* = 2, 5, and 10, and compare with the accurate values in my table. If you can, set up a spreadsheet and tabulate and graph the adjustment factor for values of *df* from 2 to 50. What do you conclude?

11.9 What terminology does your discipline use for *d*? Can you find any examples in your favorite journals or textbooks of *d* in action? Is the bias of *d* mentioned and, if so, what name and symbol are used for d_{unb}?

11.10 Near the end of the section "The Distribution of *d*: The Rubber Ruler for *d* in Action," revisit the bullet point suggestions for things to try at the **d heap** page of **ESCI chapters 10–13**. Work further on your selection of those.

11.11 I mentioned that the *s* pile is positively skewed, and in the long run a majority of *s* values will fall to the left of σ. I mentioned chi-square, but find out more about the theoretical sampling distribution of s^2, the sample variance. What shape does it have, and what does that say about the *s* pile?

11.12 Use the **CI for d** page of **ESCI chapters 10–13** to verify d_{unb} and the CI on *d* you found for Exercise 11.6. Use **CI for d** to verify d_{unb} and the CI on *d* for a couple of cases of *d*, N_1, and N_2 you type into **d two groups**.

11.13 Use the **d single group** page of **ESCI Meta-analysis** to find the 95% CI for *d*, for the Control group in Table 11.1.

11.14 Find the 95% CI for *d* for the difference between the Control and Experimental groups in Table 11.1, using s_p as the standardizer.

11.15 Find the 95% CI for *d* for the treatment effect in Table 11.2.

11.16 Look for a meta-analysis in your discipline that combines studies that used different measures. How was it done? What common ES measure was used? If *d* was not used, could it have been?

11.17 Suppose you find in the literature just three studies that have investigated whether a new team-building game improves cooperation in the workplace. Each reported a comparison of an experimental group that played the game and an independent control group that spent the time on some irrelevant activity. Unfortunately, each study used a different measure of cooperation. Table 11.5 presents the data. Calculate a suitable *d* for each study and conduct a meta-analysis of the three studies. Explain the main decisions you need to make. Interpret your findings.

TABLE 11.5

Data for Three Studies of Workplace Cooperation

Study	M_C	s_C	N_C	M_E	s_E	N_E
ABC Inc.	11	8	20	16	5	20
PQR Inc.	44	21	8	37	28	9
XYZ Inc.	148	33	15	177	43	11

Note: *M, s, N* are mean, SD, and sample size, respectively; C subscript = control condition, E subscript = experimental condition.

11.18 Revisit your take-home messages. Improve them and extend the list if you can.

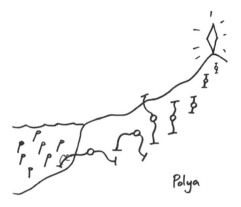

Take-Home Messages

- Cohen's *d* is a standardized ES. It's a mean or difference between means expressed as a number of SDs. It's therefore a kind of *z* score. Choosing an SD to use as the standardizer requires judgment.

- The standardizer must make conceptual sense as a unit to measure ES. If an appropriate population SD is known, it's usually the best choice as standardizer. If not, we want the best available estimate of the most appropriate population SD.

- Expressing a result in terms of *d* can assist interpretation, and also inclusion of the result in future meta-analyses. Don't only report *d*, but discuss what it implies.

- When interpreting any *d* it's essential to know what standardizer was used and how *d* was calculated. When reporting *d* it's essential to state clearly that same information. Beware of terms and symbols that are used inconsistently. For example, Hedges' *g* is currently used with at least two different meanings.

- Think of *d* as a ratio of an ES in original units divided by an SD estimate. Unless the standardizer is a population SD, there's error of estimation in both numerator and denominator, and interpretation must pay attention to both.

- As the **d picture** page of **ESCI chapters 10–13** illustrates, even large d is accompanied by considerable overlap of distributions, and probabilities of superiority that are larger than .5 but not close to 1.0. Even if an effect is large, many individual cases may go against the trend.

- For the two-independent-groups design, if we're willing to assume homogeneity of variance the best choice of standardizer is usually s_p, the pooled within-groups SD. However, if the experimental group is expected to have a considerably larger SD than the control group, we may choose s_C, the control SD, as the standardizer, especially if that group is large.

- If data are available from more than one comparable study, or control group, consider using an SD pooled over studies or groups as the standardizer.

- For the paired design it's almost always best to use s_{av} as the standardizer, calculated using Equation (11.9) from the SD of each of the measures. Using s_{diff}, the SD of the differences, is usually not meaningful and often gives an inflated value of d. Be especially cautious when interpreting d for paired or repeated measure designs: How was d calculated?

- Use Equation (11.13) to adjust d to give d_{unb}, an unbiased estimate of δ. The unbiased estimate d_{unb} should usually be preferred to d, and should probably be used much more widely.

- Four pages in **ESCI chapters 5–6** allow you to calculate d, d_{unb}, and the CI on d for your own data and for simulated experiments.

- When, as usual, σ is not known and s is the standardizer, d has a noncentral t distribution, as illustrated by the **d heap** page of **ESCI chapters 10–13**. The s pile and rubber ruler for d illustrate how the value of d depends on s, which changes from sample to sample. *Take-home movie*: The **d heap** rubber ruler in action.

- Finding accurate CIs on d requires the use of noncentral t and successive approximations, as illustrated by **CI for d**. CIs on d are usually a little asymmetric.

- Meta-analysis based on d can in suitable cases combine results from studies that used a variety of original units measures. There are two pages in **ESCI Meta-analysis** that may assist. To judge whether meta-analysis is appropriate, it's essential to consider the comparability of effects estimated by the different studies, and also the comparability of the standardizers used to calculate d for the different studies.

12

Power

I'm ambivalent about statistical power. On one hand, if we're using NHST, power is a vital part of research planning. Also, funding bodies and ethics review boards often require power calculations. On the other hand, power is defined in terms of NHST, so if we don't use NHST we can ignore power and instead use precision for research planning, as I discuss in Chapter 13. However, I feel it's still necessary to understand power, partly because power calculations are often required, and partly to help understand NHST and its weaknesses. I have therefore included this chapter, although I hope that, sometime in the future, power will need only a small historical mention.

Statistical power has a narrow technical definition, but sometimes "power" is used more broadly to refer to the extent that an experiment provides information to help solve our research problems, and gives us insight about the world. I'll use the term *informativeness* to refer to this more general characteristic of an experiment, and I'll distinguish it from the less important concept of statistical power. Informativeness will remain an important idea, even if we move on from NHST and no longer use statistical power.

In this chapter we'll discuss

- An introduction to power
- A take-home image—the power picture
- Calculating power
- Intuitions about power
- Post hoc power—*illegitimate* power
- What we really want—informativeness
- High power, high informativeness
- Reporting power

Introduction to Power

Back in Chapter 2 I defined statistical power: It's the probability of obtaining statistical significance—and therefore rejecting H_0—if a precisely

Statistical power is the probability of obtaining statistical significance if the alternative hypothesis is true, that is, if there really is a population effect of a stated size.

stated alternative hypothesis is true. It's the chance that we'll be able to reject the null hypothesis if there's a true effect of a particular stated size in the population. Informally, power is the chance that our experiment will identify a particular real effect, if it exists.

Calculating power requires the alternative hypothesis to be a precise statement of an ES, for example, that a new analgesic reduces headache by exactly 1.0 scale units on our 0 to 10 pain scale. It's much more common for researchers to use NHST to test H_0 against a vague alternative, such as $H_1: \delta \neq 0$, and so having to choose a precise value for H_1 is an unfamiliar task. It's also a difficult task because, most likely, the more pain relief the better, and there isn't any exact amount of pain relief in which we're particularly interested. Therefore, the precise H_1 is often an arbitrary choice. In addition, it may or may not be an estimate of the population ES that's true in the world. I'll refer to it as *target* δ to emphasize that

Target δ is a precise value of the population ES that we choose for the H_1. It may or may not be an estimate of the population ES that's true in the world.

it's our choice of a value to use in a power calculation. So target δ is a value that's specified by H_1, and it can be any value we care to choose for our power calculation.

To illustrate some basic features of power I'll discuss the simulation we used in Chapter 5 for the dance of the *p* values. It was a two-independent-groups experiment that evaluated your new relaxation therapy. We assumed that $\delta = 0.5$ for your therapy, and that σ was known. We used groups of size $N = 32$. For power calculations we chose target $\delta = 0.5$, the value assumed true in the simulation. ESCI calculated that, with two-tailed $\alpha = .05$, the power is .52. Back in Chapter 5, Figure 5.11 shows the frequency histogram of the *p* values we obtained in 1,500 simulations of that experiment. Close to 52% of them were less than .05, which illustrates power as the chance that an experiment will reject the null hypothesis when target δ is true in the (simulated) world.

As a further illustration of power, I fired up the **Dance p** page of **ESCI chapters 5–6** and set up the simulation as before, then increased N until ESCI reported near red 3 that power is .80. Using $N = 63$ did the trick. I then ran 1,500 simulations and enjoyed the dance of the CIs and the dance of the *p* values. Figure 12.1, which is analogous to Figure 5.11, shows the frequency histogram of the 1,500 *p* values I obtained. Above each column, the observed and theoretically predicted percentages of *p* values in that column are displayed, where "theoretically predicted" refers to the result of a power calculation using our target $\delta = 0.5$. Adding the observed percentages for the *, **, and *** columns indicates that 80.4% of my *p* values were less than .05, close to the 80.1% total of the three theoretically

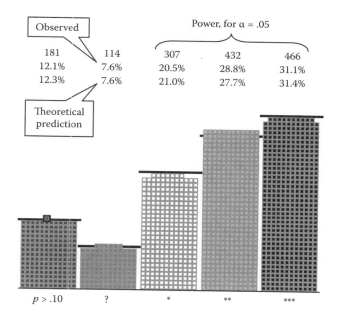

FIGURE 12.1
The frequency histogram of *p* values, for 1,500 simulated experiments that evaluated your new relaxation therapy. The experiments used two independent groups, each with $N = 63$, and $\delta = 0.5$, so, with two-tailed $\alpha = .05$, the power = .80. Back in Chapter 5, Figure 5.11 shows the corresponding histogram when $N = 32$ and power = .52. Above each column the top number reports the frequency for that column, then the numbers below are the observed and theoretically expected percentages of *p* values in that column. The sum of the percentages for the *, **, and *** columns is power.

predicted percentages—which is the power of .80. Here are my comments on this illustration of power:

- We had inside knowledge that the simulation assumed $\delta = 0.5$, and therefore we could select target $\delta = 0.5$ for our power calculation. Because those two values were the same, the percentage (80.4%) of simulated experiments that rejected H_0 matched closely our calculated power of .80. If we simulated many more experiments, the match would be even closer.
- To calculate power we need to know the experimental design, the sample size N, our α, and a target δ. We changed N from 32 to 63 and saw power change. Change any of those features of an experiment and power will change.
- It therefore makes no sense to say "my experiment has power of .85" if you don't tell us all those other things about your experiment.

The most common omission is target δ. Any stated value of power describes a particular experiment, for a stated exact target δ.

> A stated value of statistical power refers to an experiment with a specified design, for stated values of N, α, and target δ. In particular, target δ must be specified.

- The histogram in Figure 12.1 can also tell us power for some other values of two-tailed α. For example, for α = .01 we add percentages for the ** and *** columns and find that 59.9% of my p values were less than .01, close to the 59.1% total of the two theoretically expected percentages. Power was thus .59, which is lower than .80 because we adopted a more stringent α = .01 criterion for statistical significance. Yes, change α, and power will change.
- Power is a single value, say .80, but it's based on a distribution of p values. We found in Chapter 5, and Figure 12.1 further demonstrates, that this distribution of p is very wide. Recall how very wide p intervals usually are: For all but extremely high values of power, any experiment can give a p value from a very wide range.

A more general conclusion from all this discussion of NHST, p values, and power may be that our conclusion in Chapter 5 was correct: It's more informative to use estimation instead, and to have in mind meta-analysis to combine evidence over experiments. I hope this discussion of power may reinforce such new statistics intuitions, which are worth keeping in mind even as I continue to use NHST to discuss power.

It's time for a picture: I believe a picture is needed to make power—like just about any other concept—understandable and memorable. The power picture is my suggestion for a take-home image. I'll use that picture as a context to describe power and how to calculate it.

The Power Picture

Recall the Hot Earth Awareness Test (HEAT)—the fictitious test I introduced in Chapter 3. Suppose we're investigating HEAT scores in our country. The HEAT has population mean $\mu = 50$ and standard deviation $\sigma = 20$ in the reference population used in the development of the test, so we'll use H_0: $\mu = \mu_0 = 50$ as our null hypothesis. We'll take a sample of 10 students—way too small, I know, but small N emphasizes interesting features of the power picture. For such a single-group design, assuming σ is not known, the test statistic is

$$t = \frac{M - \mu_0}{s/\sqrt{N}} \tag{10.1}$$

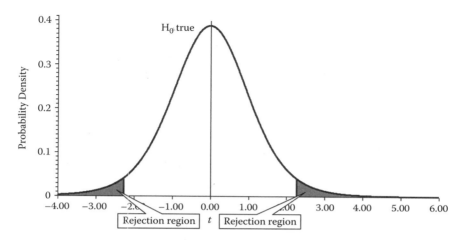

FIGURE 12.2
The distribution of *t* if H$_0$ is true, for a single group with *N* = 10, assuming σ is not known. The rejection region for a two-tailed test with α = .05 is the two shaded tail areas, which extend above *t* = 2.26 and below *t* = −2.26. The curve is the central *t* distribution with *df* = (*N* − 1) = 9.

We encountered that formula in Chapters 10 and 11. We'll choose α = .05 and, as usual, a two-tailed test. We can insert μ$_0$ = 50, *N* = 10, and our sample *M* and *s* into Equation (10.1) to calculate *t*. Figure 12.2 shows the distribution of *t* if the null hypothesis is true. The rejection region for our test is the two tails of that distribution beyond plus and minus the critical value of *t*, which is $t_{.95}(N-1) = t_{.95}(9) = 2.26$. We encountered $t_{.95}(N-1)$ back in Chapter 3, Equation (3.3), when we were calculating 95% CIs. As usual, you can use the **Normal z t** page of **ESCI chapters 1–4** to find that critical value, with help from Appendix B if you wish. Figure 12.2 marks the two tails that make up the rejection region. We reject the null hypothesis if the *t* value we calculate falls in either tail.

A Point Alternative Hypothesis

To calculate power, we need to specify a target δ, which is the exact value stated by the alternative hypothesis. As I mentioned earlier, target δ is a value we choose that may or may not be an estimate of the true population ES. I'll discuss below how we might choose target δ. For our example here, suppose a large national survey reports that the mean HEAT scores for students in Awareland is 68. We hope students in our country are just as aware of climate change issues, so we'll choose H$_1$: μ$_1$ = 68 as our point alternative hypothesis. The corresponding target population ES is then

$$\delta = \frac{\mu_1 - \mu_0}{\sigma} = \frac{68 - 50}{20} = 0.90 \qquad (12.1)$$

In other words, μ_1 is 0.90 of a population SD higher than μ_0. In terms of Cohen's conventions, that's a large effect. To find power we need to know the distribution of the t statistic, as given by Equation (10.1), when the alternative hypothesis is true. Figure 12.3 is an example of what I call the *power picture* and shows that distribution. Power is the area under that H_1 distribution for all values of t in the rejection region, which means power is the large area under that curve corre-

The *power picture* is what I call a figure like Figure 12.3 that displays the distributions of the test statistic, z or t, when H_0 is true, and when H_1 is true.

sponding to the right rejection tail, plus a tiny invisible area under the H_1 curve corresponding to the left rejection tail. We can usually ignore that second, tiny area, although ESCI doesn't. The large area to the right is shaded dark gray, although note that this area includes the right tail rejection area shaded light gray—think of the dark gray continuing behind the light gray.

For our single group example, with $N = 10$, $\alpha = .05$, and target population ES of 0.90, the power is .72. The dark shaded area in Figure 12.3 is 72% of the total area under the H_1 curve. If we run our experiment, and students in our country really do have a mean HEAT score of 68, then

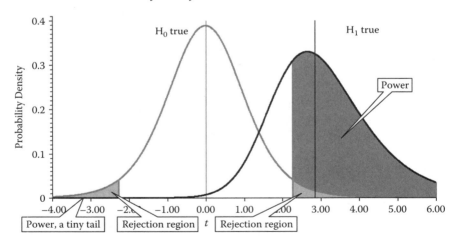

FIGURE 12.3
The example of Figure 12.2, but showing also the distribution of t when H_1 is true. The population ES under H_1 of $\delta = 0.90$ determines the H_1 distribution, which is noncentral t with noncentrality parameter $\Delta = 2.85$ and $df = 9$. The vertical line on the right marks $\Delta = 2.85$. Power = .72, which is the area under the H_1 curve for t in the rejection region. This is the area on the right corresponding to the right rejection area tail, plus a tiny invisible area under the H_1 curve corresponding to the left rejection area tail.

there's a 72% chance that we'll obtain $p < .05$ and can reject the null hypothesis that their population mean is 50. Even with a large population ES we have a $100 - 72 = 28\%$ chance of failure, because our sample size is so small.

You may feel that my example is contrived and unrealistic, and the choice of an exact value for the alternative hypothesis may seem especially artificial. Why not simply use our M and its CI to give an estimated ES for students in our country? The CI would, no doubt, be wide and tell us that we have only an imprecise estimate, but that's the truth. Yes, such doubts about these power discussions are justified, and it's worth keeping in mind the estimation alternative as we continue to discuss NHST.

Sampling Distribution When H_1 Is True

It's easiest to think of power in terms of the power picture and areas under the H_1 curve. How would Figure 12.3 change for a different population ES under H_1, meaning a different value of μ_1 and therefore a different value of target δ? The H_1 curve would shift—to the right for larger δ and to the left for smaller δ. Figure 12.4 is another version of the power picture that illustrates a smaller δ and an H_1 curve shifted left. Less of the curve corresponds to the right rejection tail, so power is smaller. That's what we'd expect: A smaller true effect is less likely to give $p < .05$. In Figure 12.4 I'm using $\mu_1 = 60$, and so $\delta = 0.50$, which gives power of .29.

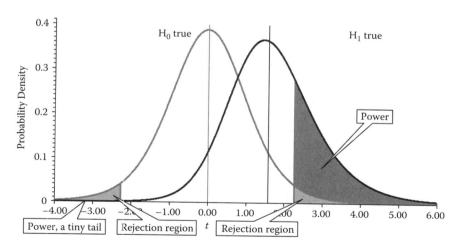

FIGURE 12.4

Same as Figure 12.3, but with population ES of $\delta = 0.50$, so the H_1 curve is shifted left. That curve is a noncentral t distribution with noncentrality parameter $\Delta = 1.58$ and $df = 9$. The vertical line on the right is positioned at $\Delta = 1.58$. Power is now .29.

The H_1 curve is a noncentral t distribution. If that's sufficient (or too much) information about the H_1 distribution, feel free to skip to the next paragraph. To find the noncentrality parameter Δ, recall from Chapter 10 that

When σ is unknown, t is our test statistic. When the alternative hypothesis is true, t has a noncentral t distribution, so power is an area under a noncentral t curve.

$$\Delta = \frac{\mu_1 - \mu_0}{\sigma/\sqrt{N}} \tag{10.3}$$

Substitute from Equation (12.1) to obtain the beautiful relation that

$$\Delta = \delta\sqrt{N} \tag{12.2}$$

The noncentrality parameter Δ simply reflects the target population ES and the sample size. For Figure 12.3, $\delta = 0.90$ and Equation (12.2) gives $\Delta = 0.90 \times \sqrt{10} = 2.85$. This value is marked by the vertical line at approximately the mean of the H_1 curve. Similarly, for Figure 12.4, $\delta = 0.50$ and $\Delta = 0.50 \times \sqrt{10} = 1.58$, and this is the value marked by the vertical line. In any such case, to find power we need to calculate an area under the noncentral t distribution.

This would be a good moment to cross-check with some other statistics textbook you know. If it discusses power, it probably has a figure like Figure 12.3, but note two likely differences. First, it probably assumes that σ is known and therefore shows two normal distributions. That's a perfectly fine way to introduce power, and is the approach I used for the dance of the p values in Chapter 5. It's more realistic, however, to assume that σ is not known, in which case we need the central and noncentral t distributions, as in Figures 12.2 to 12.4.

Second, in Figures 12.3 and 12.4 we're assuming that H_1 is true, so I faded the H_0 curve and the rejection regions to light gray, whereas I highlighted the H_1 curves in black and areas for power in dark gray. Most textbooks simply show two similar curves in their power picture. That may be misleading because it doesn't emphasize that at any moment only one hypothesis can be true. I used the strategy of highlighting and graying out in Chapter 10 when discussing sampling, first assuming H_0 true, then assuming H_1 true. When examining any power picture, it's essential to be clear which hypothesis you are currently assuming true, and it may help if the picture itself makes that obvious.

ESCI's Power Picture

Figures 12.2 to 12.4 come from the **Power picture** page of **ESCI chapters 10–13**. If you fire up that page, you can explore many things about power

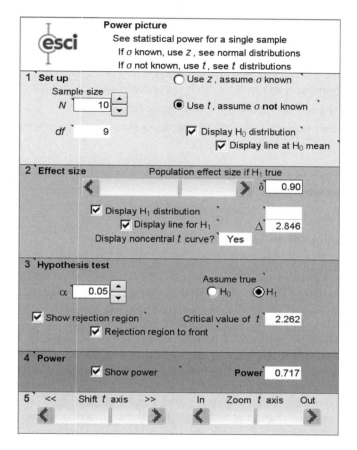

FIGURE 12.5
The control area in the **Power picture** page of **ESCI chapters 10–13**.

for the single-group case. Figure 12.5 shows the control panels; power is reported near red 4. Here are some suggestions:

- Use the spinner near red 1 to select sample size N. Change N freely, because intuitions about sample size are central to understanding power.
- Click the radio buttons near red 3 to specify whether you are assuming that H_0 or H_1 is true. See corresponding aspects of the figure highlighted or faded to gray.
- Click the radio buttons near red 1 to specify whether or not σ is assumed known. Note the change between using z as the test

statistic and seeing two normal curves, and using t and seeing central and noncentral t curves.

- Use the slider near red 2 to change target δ, the population ES if H_1 is true. The H_1 curve shifts left and right: Watch the big changes in its shape and in power, which is reported near red 4.
- Use the spinner near red 3 to change two-tailed α.
- Use this page to calculate power for a single group experiment.

Calculating Power

A Two-Independent-Groups Example

Suppose you plan with a colleague in another country to compare HEAT scores. She can organize a sample of 80 students, and you can find 60. You decide to use $\alpha = .05$, and agree that the difference in mean HEAT scores between countries may only be small, say $\delta = 0.2$, so that's your target δ.

To calculate power for the two-independent-groups case, fire up the **Simulate two** page of **ESCI chapters 5–6**, scroll far right to see checkboxes at red 11 and 12, click them both on, then scroll back left to see a blue panel for power at red 13. Figure 12.6 shows part of the control area for that page, including the panel for power.

Set the two sample sizes at red 3, and use the spinner for C near red 6 to adjust the α value shown at red 13. Adjust the spinners near red 7 for population parameters μ_1, μ_2, and σ until $\delta = 0.2$ is shown in the red 7 area. You can choose any convenient values that give $\delta = 0.2$, which is what's used to calculate power. For example, set $\mu_1 = 50$ and $\sigma = 10$, then adjust μ_2 until you see the δ you want. Click **Another experiment** near red 1 to trigger calculation of d, and power using t. That's how I created the screen shot shown in Figure 12.6. Power is .21 assuming that you'll use t as the test statistic. (Using z it's .22—very similar, as we might expect given the fairly large samples.) Oh dear, such low power! You investigate other options. Increasing both sample sizes to 100 only increases power to .29. However, you find that the seemingly small change of target δ from 0.2 to 0.3 (as before, adjust μ_2 to obtain the δ you want) lifts power to .56. That's better, but hardly good. Hmm, can you just change target δ at whim like that? Later I'll discuss ways to choose and justify target δ, but for the moment we'll assume that it's simply your choice. Using $\delta = 0.4$ gives power .80, and $\delta = 0.5$ gives power .94. Much better. You know that you can also increase power by increasing α, but you agree with your colleague that increasing α is a bad strategy. You recall the conclusion of Chapter 5 that

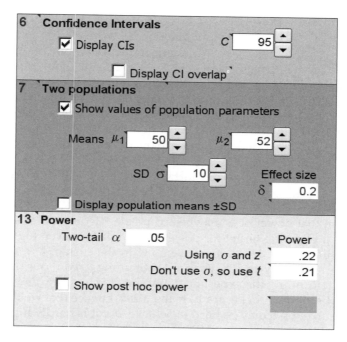

FIGURE 12.6

Part of the control area in the **Simulate two** page of **ESCI chapters 5–6**. Sample sizes are $N_1 = 80$ and $N_2 = 60$.

only very small p values tell us much at all, so you'd strongly prefer to use $\alpha = .01$. You set $C = 99$ at red 6, so $\alpha = .01$, then find that, for $\delta = 0.2$, power is a pathetic .12. For target $\delta = 0.50$, however, power is a more encouraging .82. You agree to hope for the best and go ahead with the experiment using $\alpha = .01$ and two groups of 100.

My imaginary discussion illustrates a common way to use power calculations to guide research planning, by exploring trade-offs between various features that determine power. That's useful because it helps us understand our options, but, on the other hand, it offers scope for fudging: Set δ just a little higher and we'll get a more respectably high value for power. I'll discuss that fudging problem later. First, however, note that the calculations are based on the assumptions we usually make, but which may or may not be reasonable in a particular real-life situation. We're assuming that each sample is a random sample from a normal population, and that the two populations—students' HEAT scores in the two countries—have the same SD. Using those assumptions, we've found that power is often disappointingly low, that larger sample sizes can increase power but only to a moderate extent, and that to use a more reassuring $\alpha = .01$, rather than .05, we pay a considerable price in terms of

In general, power is influenced by sample size, but is influenced more by α and even more by δ, the target population ES.

decreased power. In addition, target δ, the population ES we're aiming to find, has a dramatic influence on power. All of those conclusions are important and quite general facts about experimental design that are highlighted by power calculations. These harsh realities about the difficulty of designing experiments with high power may be a big reason why researchers usually don't calculate or report power. Perhaps they really don't want to know how low it is?

Finally, for this two-independent-groups example, consider the experiment you decided to run: Two groups of 100 seems, by the standards of many research fields, quite comfortable. But even with those groups, it takes a medium-sized effect of δ = 0.5 before power reaches a comfortable .94 using α = .05, or .82 using α = .01. Cohen (1969, 1988) introduced the custom that power of .8 may be acceptable. Medicine also sometimes uses .8 as a planning target for power, although .9 or even higher values are sometimes used. However, if we go with the custom and use power of .8, there's still only an 80% chance of obtaining $p < α$ if our target δ is a true effect. Running the experiment amounts to choosing a p value from the wide distribution in Figure 12.1, and a 20% chance that we'll be disappointed. Power of .8 may be hard to achieve, but it is hardly high enough for comfort. If you run your HEAT study with two samples of 100 and α = .01, then power is .82 and you have an 18% chance of failing to obtain statistical significance even if the true effect is δ = 0.5. Perhaps the slogan for this chapter should be, "No free lunch!"? Meta-analysis of a number of experiments springs to mind: Yes, indeed.

A Paired Design Example

A further and important way to improve things is to use a more sensitive experimental design. Suppose you are interested in possible changes in HEAT scores in your country over the last 2 years. You could compare two independent groups of students at the two times, but, fortunately, 2 years ago a sample of 40 students gave HEAT scores and you are able to test the same students again this year. You decide that the paired design is appropriate, so you investigate the **Simulate paired** page of **ESCI chapters 5–6**. Scroll far right, click at red 13 and 14 then scroll back left to see the blue power panel at red 15. Figure 12.7 shows part of the control area, including the power panel. Set N near red 4, and α by adjusting C near red 7. For the paired design you also need to set a value for the correlation in the population between the two measures. You decide to use .9, because you expect there will be a very high correlation between HEAT scores at the two times. You need to adjust both σ, the SD within each population, and $σ_{diff}$, the SD of the population of

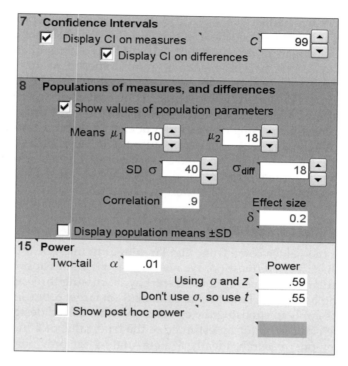

FIGURE 12.7
Part of the control area in the **Simulate paired** page of **ESCI chapters 5–6**. Sample size is
$N = 40$.

paired differences, which together determine the population correlation between the two measures. Recall from Chapter 6 that the higher
this correlation, the more sensitive the design. Here's an easy way to
do it: Set $\mu_1 = 10$ and $\sigma = 40$, then adjust μ_2 until δ is as you want it, for
example, $\delta = 0.2$. Now adjust σ_{diff} until the correlation shown near red
8 is as close as possible to what you want, for example, correlation =
.9. Click **Another experiment** to trigger calculation, and see the power
values near red 15.

You play around with various values and find that, when you set $N =$
40, correlation of .9, and $\alpha = .01$, the power is .55 for $\delta = 0.2$, as Figure 12.7
illustrates. For $\delta = 0.3$ power is a wonderful .93. Even with correlation
of .8, power values are considerably higher than for a comparable two-
independent-groups experiment. Once again you find that N makes a difference, but it's target δ and the correlation between the two measures that
have the really big influences on power.

Yes, the paired design can be powerful and, as we saw in Chapter 6,
it's an attractive design, but, of course, only when it suits the situation.

Might carry-over effects between the two measures be a problem? As ever, careful thinking is needed. In this case, be very clear about the two ways of investigating the question, "Have HEAT scores changed over the last 2 years?" A two-independent-groups experiment that compares beginning students in 2011 with beginning students in 2009 is comparing two cohorts of students. By contrast, a paired design experiment that compares beginning students in 2009 with the same students in 2011 is assessing change in a single cohort of students. At second testing, those students may be different not only because the world is different in 2011 but because they are older and have experienced 2 years at university. Either experiment may give interesting findings, but they are investigating different interpretations of our original question.

Choosing Target δ, Correlation, and α

Where do the values come from that I'm plugging into ESCI to calculate power? That's a good question. We need to choose values appropriate for our particular research situation. I'll start by discussing three approaches to choosing δ and correlation values. I'll focus on target δ, but similar considerations apply to choosing the correlation in the paired design case.

First, we could look for an estimate of the true value of δ in the population. Previous research, ideally a meta-analysis of previous research, might provide a good estimate of δ. More generally, knowledge of the research field may suggest typical values. Perhaps you've already carried out similar experiments and they can suggest values to use in planning the next experiment? Some books suggest running a small pilot study, but usually such a study gives only a poor, imprecise estimate of δ, and we know that small differences in target δ can give large differences in power. The central problem is that, if we had good knowledge of δ, we'd hardly need to run our planned experiment at all.

A second approach is to choose for target δ a value that's of theoretical or practical interest. If the theory you are testing predicts that there's a small to medium-sized effect, you could choose δ = 0.3 as your target ES. Or you might judge a decrease of 3 points on the depression scale you are using to be the minimum improvement that's of clinical interest, or of value to the client, so you choose 3 points as your target ES. You need as well an SD estimate for the depression scale to use as a standardizer. The manual published with the scale, or previous research with the scale, may provide an SD value for an appropriate population. The discussion in Chapter 11 about finding a suitable standardizer may suggest further options. Divide 3 by your chosen SD to get a value of δ to use as the target population ES in your power calculation.

The third and most common approach is to recognize that there usually isn't just a single value of target δ that's of interest. Often it's useful to calculate power for various combinations of values relevant for our intended research. My imagined discussion between you and your colleague as you plan your HEAT experiment is an example, and illustrates how power calculations often alarm researchers about how weak their contemplated experiment is, then guide them to some compromise between what size experiment is achievable and what target δ that experiment can seek with reasonable power.

Now let's consider α. A strategy that's often recommended is to choose an α level that reflects the costs and benefits of making Type I and II errors in a particular situation. For a life-and-death decision about approving a drug for public use we might use α = .001, which Figure 12.1 shows would give, for our earlier example, power of only .32 (the theoretical expectation for the *** column). Low power, yes, but possibly intelligent decision making if we are using NHST. On the other hand, for an exploratory experiment in a little-researched area, we may be looking for hints of anything that could on further investigation prove interesting. We might elect to use α = .10, or some other high value, to reduce the chance of a Type II error. Power would be high, but so would the risk of Type I error. Considering costs and benefits is an appealing strategy for choosing α, but conventions about using α = .05 or .01 are strong, and few researchers would consider α greater than .05.

Does it strike you as disturbingly subjective to have to choose so many values to calculate power? If so, I agree, and I find it even more disturbing that above I could give only vague advice about how to select target values for δ and the population correlation—two features of an experiment that are especially influential on power. Earlier I mentioned the possibility of fudging a power calculation. Yes, the need to specify so many values gives, unfortunately, large scope to choose a set of values that gives a power value to fit your needs, even if it may not represent reality. For target δ there may even be scope to choose both the numerator (3 points on the depression scale, but why not 4?) and the denominator SD we need as a standardizer.

> Exploring how power varies for different values of *N*, α, and target δ (and, for a paired design, correlation) can give insight, but subjectivity of variable choice means power calculations are open to fudging.

A small amount of tweaking of each and we might be able to argue that any of a wide range of δ values is reasonable. I suspect that many power analyses presented to funding bodies and ethics review boards reflect some creative adjustment of various assumptions so the final proposed sample sizes are more or less achievable and target δ values not too unbelievable. You may now be thinking that a quite different approach based on estimation and meta-analysis is especially appealing. Well, I'd never discourage that thought. Next I'll turn to some ESCI pages intended to help build accurate intuitions about power.

Intuitions About Power

There are few formulas in this chapter because I'm more interested in intuitions. Also I can't give you a simple formula for tail areas under the noncentral t distribution, and Figures 12.3 and 12.4 show that we need such tail calculations to find power. We'll let ESCI do the number crunching while we focus on the intuitions. Much of my previous discussion was about how different aspects of an experiment have smaller or larger influences on power. This section continues the theme, but with pictures.

The Two-Independent-Groups Design

Figure 12.8 shows power curves that illustrate how power changes with N for the two-independent-groups design, using t as the test statistic. Sample size N is assumed the same for each group. For groups of different sizes, use **Simulate two**, as discussed in the previous section. The figure uses $\alpha = .05$, and each curve is for a particular value of δ. The curve for $\delta = 0.5$ is highlighted, and three other curves are labeled with their δ values. A

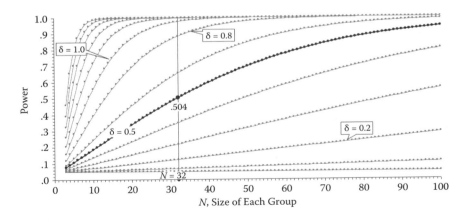

FIGURE 12.8
Power curves for the two-independent-groups design, with $\alpha = .05$, using t as the test statistic. Sample size N, the same for each group, is plotted on the horizontal axis. Each curve is for a particular value of target δ. The curve for $\delta = 0.5$ is highlighted, and three other curves are labeled with their δ values. The N cursor is positioned for power close to .5, for $\delta = 0.5$, and shows $N = 32$ gives that power.

vertical cursor reports power for a chosen N, in this case showing power = .50 when we have two groups of size 32.

Study Figure 12.8 for a moment and consider what messages it's sending. For me, it's saying that target δ is the most important influence on power, and that the power curve is quite different in shape for different values of δ. Even modest experiments, with two groups of 20 or 30, have high power to find large or very large population effects—δ of 0.8 or more. But if we're looking for small effects—δ of 0.2 or 0.3—even groups of 100 have very low power.

Figure 12.9 is similar, but for $\alpha = .01$. It shows in addition a horizontal cursor for power, which is set to power = .8. The vertical N cursor has been placed where the power cursor intersects the $\delta = 0.5$ curve, and shows that, with $\alpha = .01$, two independent groups of size 95 have power of .8 to find a population effect of size $\delta = 0.5$. Compare the two figures. To me they say that, for large and very large δ, power is still in most cases quite high when $\alpha = .01$. However, for small and medium effect sizes, lower α comes at the price of considerably lower power. Not even large N—well, $N = 100$, anyway—can give large power with $\alpha = .01$ unless we're looking for a substantial δ.

Figures 12.8 and 12.9 come from the **Power two** page of **ESCI chapters 10–13**. Figure 12.10 shows that page's control area. At red 1, click to assume that σ is known and z is the test statistic, or σ is not known and therefore t is the test statistic. The spinner at red 1 selects α. Be warned that, when using t, if you change α the whole figure must be recalculated, which requires roughly 3,000 noncentral t calculations. It can take a while, and

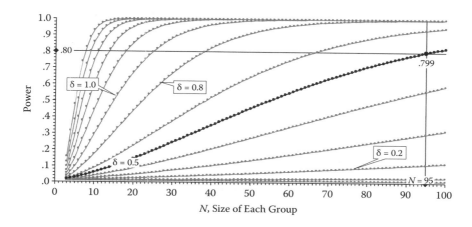

FIGURE 12.9

Same as Figure 12.8 but with $\alpha = .01$. A horizontal power cursor has been added, at power = .8. The N cursor has been moved to where the power cursor cuts the $\delta = 0.5$ power curve, and shows that $N = 95$ for that power and population ES.

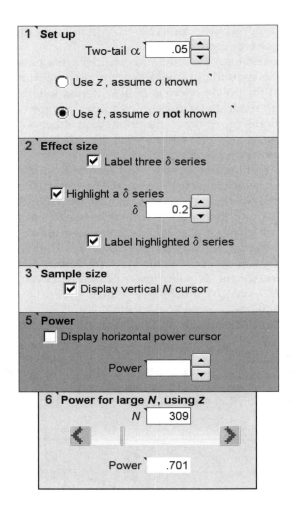

FIGURE 12.10
Control area for the **Power two** page of **ESCI chapters 10–13**. For N greater than 100, use the bottom panel. The values shown tell us that, for $\alpha = .05$ and target $\delta = 0.2$, an N of 309 is needed to achieve power of .7.

nothing seems to be happening. (Here's a hint: If you want to change α by more than a click or two of the spinner, select z, change α, and then switch back to t. It's faster because the calculations for z are much faster than those for t.) The spinner near red 2 selects which curve is highlighted. As usual, explore the checkboxes that control various display features. When the N cursor is displayed, the slider below the figure shifts it left and right. When the power cursor is displayed, the spinner near red 5 shifts it up and down. For values of N larger than 100, which lie beyond

TABLE 12.1

Minimum Sample Size Required to Achieve Various Levels
of Power for the Two-Independent-Groups Design, for Selected
Values of α and δ

Target Power	δ	$\alpha = .05$					$\alpha = .01$				
		0.2	0.3	0.5	0.8	1.0	0.2	0.3	0.5	0.8	1.0
.50		193	87	32	14	9	332	148	55	23	15
.60		245	109	41	17	11	401	178	66	27	18
.70		309	138	51	21	14	481	214	79	32	21
.80		393	175	64	26	17	584	260	96	39	26
.90		526	234	86	34	23	744	331	120	49	32
.95		650	289	104	42	27	891	396	143	58	38

Note: Values are sample size N, where N is the size of each of the two groups. The test statistic is t except that, for $N > 100$, the test statistic is z. For such large sample sizes, using z gives the same or very similar N to that found using t.

the horizontal axis in the figure, use the bottom panel at red 6. This panel calculates power using z, but for such large N the results are very similar to those based on t.

Table 12.1 provides a further approach to building intuitions about power. It shows the smallest N needed to achieve target power shown at the left, for selected values of α and δ. The test statistic is t, except that z is used when $N > 100$.

The Paired Design

For the paired design, use the **Power paired** page of **ESCI chapters 10–13**. Figure 12.11 is from that page and shows the power curves for the paired design, for $\alpha = .01$, using t. The horizontal axis shows N, the number of pairs. The population correlation between the two measures is shown as ρ (Greek rho) and is set to .70. Figure 12.12 shows the control area, including the slider near red 1 that sets ρ. The cursors in Figure 12.11 illustrate that 40 is the smallest N that gives power at least .90. Compare Figures 12.11 and 12.9, and note that $\alpha = .01$ in both. Even with ρ only .70, a correlation likely to be exceeded in many practical cases, the considerably higher values of power in Figure 12.11 illustrate once more the advantages of the paired design—assuming, of course, that it's appropriate for the research situation.

The **Power paired** page provides similar scope for setting values and for exploration of the paired design as **Power two** provides for the two-independent-groups design. The main addition is the slider near red 1 that sets ρ, the population correlation between the two measures. Table 12.2 gives a further perspective on power for the paired design. The left half

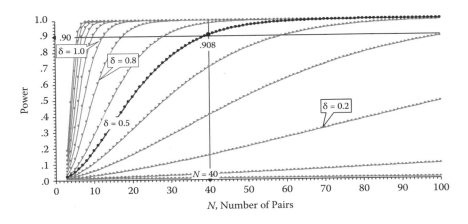

FIGURE 12.11
Power curves for the paired design, with α = .01, test statistic *t*, and population correlation ρ = .70 between the two measures. The horizontal axis shows *N*, the number of data
pairs. The curve for δ = 0.5 is highlighted, and three other curves are labeled. The power
cursor marks .90, and the *N* cursor shows 40 is the smallest *N* giving at least that power.

of the table is for ρ = .50, and the right half is for ρ = .80. Both use α = .01,
so you can compare any *N* in Table 12.2 with those in the right half of
Table 12.1, which also uses α = .01.

Enjoy the generally high power of the paired design, even with modest
values of ρ, for example, in the range .4 to .7. In practice, the paired design
often gives ρ of .8 or even .9 or more, and so even quite small experiments
can have considerable power. Pretest-
posttest experiments with a single group
of participants are a common example of a
paired design. They often have a high correlation between the pretest and posttest
measures, and so are likely to give high power. As usual, we need to be
sure that the paired design is appropriate for our situation, and we don't,
for example, have serious carry-over effects between the two measures.

> A repeated measure design, such as the
> paired design, can give high power, but
> make sure the design is appropriate for the
> particular circumstances.

After all this exploration of how power varies with α, δ, *N*, and other
features of an experiment, I need to mention, or rather warn you about,
post hoc power. Then we can consider ways to increase power.

Post Hoc Power—Illegitimate Power

There's a sinister side to political power, and most people know to
watch out for it. Unfortunately, there's also a sinister side to statistical

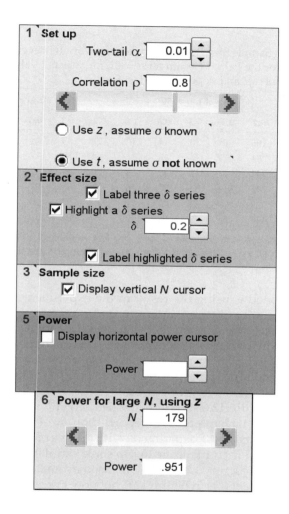

FIGURE 12.12
Control area for the **Power paired** page of **ESCI chapters 10–13**. For N greater than 100, use the bottom panel. The values shown tell us that, for $\alpha = .01$, $\rho = .80$, and target $\delta = 0.2$, an N of 179 is needed to achieve power of .95.

power, and we all need to watch out for that. I'm referring to *post hoc power*, and I'm going to recommend that you never use it and are careful not to be misled by reports of power that are actually values of post hoc power.

Post hoc power is calculated after completing the experiment, using as target δ the effect size d obtained in the experiment. It can easily mislead, so never use it.

The key is δ: What value of target δ is used to calculate power? I've discussed various ways to choose a target value for δ, but the one possibility

TABLE 12.2

Minimum Sample Size Required to Achieve Various Levels of Power for the Paired Design for $\alpha = .01$, for Selected Values of Correlation ρ, and Population Effect Size δ

Target Power	δ	$\alpha = .01, \rho = .50$					$\alpha = .01, \rho = .80$				
		0.2	0.3	0.5	0.8	1.0	0.2	0.3	0.5	0.8	1.0
.50		166	78	30	14	10	70	33	14	8	6
.60		201	93	36	16	12	84	39	17	9	7
.70		241	107	42	19	13	100	47	19	10	8
.80		292	130	51	22	16	117	56	23	11	9
.90		372	166	63	27	19	149	70	28	13	10
.95		446	198	75	32	22	179	83	32	15	11

Note: Values are N, the number of pairs. The test statistic is t except that, for $N > 100$, the test statistic is z. For such large sample sizes, using z gives the same or very similar N to that found using t.

I've not mentioned is using the result of the experiment itself. You may have wondered, why all this concern to find a target value of δ by considering previous research, or choosing an ES likely to be of practical importance? Why not simply carry out the experiment then use d, the ES obtained by the experiment, as target δ for power? Well, yes, we can easily do that, and calculating power using our obtained d for target δ gives us what's called *post hoc* or *observed* power.

For example, Figure 12.6 shows that, when target $\delta = 0.2$, the **Simulate two** page of **ESCI chapters 5–6** reports power of .21 for our two-independent-groups HEAT experiment, with groups of size 80 and 60 and two-tailed $\alpha = .05$. I used that page to run some simulations of the experiment. The first gave $d_{unb} = 0.29$ as the unbiased estimate of δ. Figure 12.13 shows the power panel, as in Figure 12.6, but now I've clicked to show also the value of post hoc power, which is .4. In other words, after running the

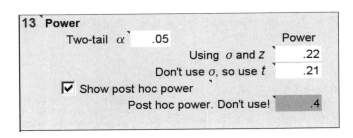

FIGURE 12.13
Part of Figure 12.6, but now post hoc power is displayed. The two-independent-groups HEAT experiment obtained $d_{unb} = .29$, and appears as Replication 1 in Table 12.3.

TABLE 12.3

Results of 10 Replications of the Two-Independent-Groups
HEAT Experiment Shown in Figure 12.6

Replication	Obtained d_{unb}	Two-Tailed p	Post Hoc Power
1	0.29	.09	.40
2	−0.07	.70	.07
3	0.20	.25	.21
4	−0.17	.32	.17
5	0.47	.007	.77
6	0.23	.18	.27
7	0.07	.69	.07
8	−0.02	.90	.05
9	0.11	.52	.10
10	0.56	.001	.90

experiment and observing $d_{unb} = 0.29$, ESCI used that d_{unb} as target δ and calculated power to be .4.

First, there's a small logical problem with post hoc power. Power is the probability that an experiment will reject H_0 if an effect of the stated target size, δ, exists. However, after completing the experiment we've either rejected H_0 or we haven't, and so it doesn't make sense to talk about "the probability that our experiment will reject H_0." OK, we carefully say, "Our experiment, *before we ran it*, had power of .4 to find target δ = 0.29." That's fine. Now let's see what happens if we repeat the experiment a few times.

Table 12.3 shows the results of the first 10 replications of our HEAT experiment, as given by **Simulate two**. The first replication gives post hoc power as shown in Figure 12.13. Based on the values in the table, we can make statements like, "Our experiment, before we ran it, had power of .07 to find target δ = −0.07" (that's based on Replication 2) or, "Our experiment, before we ran it, had power of .90 to find target δ = 0.56" (based on Replication 10).

Those are all perfectly acceptable statements, but do they tell us anything useful? Table 12.3 illustrates the close inverse relation between d_{unb} (or d) and p that we observed in Chapter 5: Small d_{unb} (or d) gives large p, and large d_{unb} (or d) gives low p. It also illustrates the very large variation of p over replication that we saw in the dance of the p values. Examine the d_{unb} and post hoc power columns: Post hoc power has a close and direct relation with d_{unb}. Now examine the p and post hoc power columns: Post hoc power has a strong inverse relation with the p values. Post hoc power, like d_{unb} and p, varies greatly with replication, but the main problem is that it doesn't tell us anything further about our experiment beyond what d_{unb} and p have already told us. It's a mere restatement of our experimental result. The danger is that any statement of a power value is likely to be read as telling us something about the *experiment*, whereas a post hoc power value really only tells us about the result of running the experiment once. A post hoc power value can thus be severely misleading, especially if it's not accompanied by the full statement, as in my examples above, including the target δ value.

Hoenig and Heisey (2001) explained in more detail the reasons for avoiding post hoc power. They described a number of incorrect beliefs held by some researchers about how post hoc power might be able to assist in the interpretation of results found to be not statistically significant. I have never seen a convincing case made for any worthwhile use of post hoc power. I recommend never using it, and I express my disapproval by the gray background shading and the comments at the power panel in **Simulate two** and **Simulate paired**, where you can click if you insist on seeing post hoc power.

I've labeled post hoc power as *illegitimate power* to highlight the contrast with *legitimate power*, which uses a target δ that's chosen for its research interest. It's legitimate power that we've discussed at length in earlier sections of this chapter. Usually we calculate it as part of planning, in advance of running the experiment, but you can calculate legitimate power after collecting the data. The crucial point is that target δ is chosen for its research or practical interest, and is not merely the result of our experiment.

Legitimate power is my name for power calculated for a target δ that's chosen as being of research interest. Contrast it with post hoc power.

So, why am I going on at such length about something we should all avoid? I'm doing so because some widely used computer packages report post hoc power simply labeled as "power" or "observed power." No doubt many users, not understanding how legitimate and post hoc power differ, simply accept what the computer says and report that value as *the* power of their experiment. No doubt it's an awkward extra step for a software package to ask the user for a target value of δ before it calculates power. However, I believe it's reprehensible for software to duck the issue of choosing an appropriate target δ, and simply report post hoc power. At the very least, any post hoc power value should come with a clear label and warning. My recommendation is never to calculate post hoc power and always to watch out for post hoc power being passed off as legitimate power. I strongly recommend the wonderful free software G*Power 3 (tinyurl.com/gpower3). G*Power calculates power for numerous designs and measures beyond the few simple cases I discuss in this chapter and that ESCI supports.

If statistical software reports power without specifying a population ES, it's probably post hoc power. Don't use that value. Be very cautious.

Informativeness

Let's step aside from statistical power for a moment and consider the fundamental aim of experimental research, which is to inform us about the world. We want experiments that answer our research questions, provide useful knowledge, and give us insight into how the world works. We don't have an agreed name for this desirable feature of an experiment, but "strong," "insightful," "good," or "sensitive" come close. However, I think "informative" is best: An experiment is highly *informative* if it gives us useful information and insight about the world. Informativeness is highly desirable and, almost always, the more of it the better.

I refer to the *informativeness* of an experiment as its ability to give information to answer research questions, or to give insight about the world.

I'm introducing informativeness because I want to consider, very generally, how we can improve our experiments. Many books and articles give wonderful advice about ways to improve research. Often they focus on how to increase statistical power, but most of the advice actually applies more broadly and is valuable even if we don't use NHST. I want the benefit of the advice, but without having to use NHST or power. I'll therefore try as much as possible to interpret the advice in terms of increasing informativeness rather than statistical power. If that succeeds, we can follow the advice, but without using NHST.

Many strategies to improve experimental design are likely to increase both informativeness and statistical power. Examples include using larger N, using larger ρ in a paired design, and finding ways to reduce measurement error. On the other hand, increasing α will increase statistical power but is unlikely to change informativeness—the experiment is unlikely to give us greater insight if we use $\alpha = .05$ rather than .01. Informativeness and statistical power are related, but informativeness is the more general concept and reflects better the value of an experiment. Increasing informativeness is more generally beneficial than increasing statistical power. However, I'm not going

Informativeness is related to, but more fundamental than, statistical power, which has meaning only within NHST.

to attempt any quantitative definition of informativeness, which will thus remain a more abstract concept, in contrast to statistical power for which we can calculate a numerical value if we make certain assumptions.

Back in Chapter 2 I introduced Jacob Cohen, the great statistical reformer. Box 2.2 described evidence, first presented by Cohen in 1962, that published research typically has depressingly low power. If researchers realized this, Cohen thought, surely they would stop wasting their time and insist on bigger, better-designed experiments with higher power? His book about power (Cohen, 1969, 1988) was pioneering and remains an important resource, but, alas, Cohen's campaign was not fully successful. Researchers may now be more aware of power, but Maxwell (2004) reported that later surveys have found that the average power of published research is still, in many cases, about as low as Cohen found half a century ago.

Cohen discussed power but his argument can, I believe, be read in terms of informativeness. He wanted researchers to improve their designs and use larger sample sizes—and these are ways to increase informativeness. Maxwell (2004) also couched his advocacy of improved practices in terms of power, but in addition explained the importance of estimation and meta-analysis for achieving scientific progress. Again, I see his main argument as addressing informativeness rather than the narrower concept of statistical power. The *Publication Manual* (APA, 1994) introduced in its fourth edition the advice to "take seriously the statistical power considerations associated with your tests of hypotheses.... Routinely provide evidence that your study has sufficient power to detect effects of substantive interest" (pp. 16–17). Almost identical statements appeared in the fifth and the current sixth editions. That's NHST language, but I'd like to think that the intent is broader: to improve the informativeness of research.

I'm arguing that, if we don't use NHST, and therefore don't use statistical power, the substance of arguments in favor of higher power can usually be recast in terms of increased informativeness. Doing this may actually strengthen those arguments, for example, by removing any hint that merely increasing α, which increases power but not informativeness, might suffice. Increasing informativeness is a fundamental goal of research planning, and thinking in terms of informativeness may allow us to avoid NHST if we wish, but still benefit from so much excellent advice about experimental design.

High Power, High Informativeness

Any discussion of power should consider how power can be increased to improve the experiments being planned. However, I've argued that, more fundamentally, we should be trying to increase informativeness, not merely statistical power. I'll therefore hold until the next chapter my general discussion of how, during research planning, we can improve our intended experiments. There are just two issues I'd like to discuss here in the context of power. They both relate to the question, "Can power be too high?"

In many research situations it's difficult to achieve power that the researchers regard as sufficiently high. A number of studies combined by meta-analysis may be needed before even a moderate amount of evidence can be accumulated. By contrast, consider surveys involving many thousands of people. With such very large samples, CIs are very narrow and even tiny differences are highly statistically significant. It's a waste of time to calculate power or a p value: Power is luxuriously high whatever realistic target δ we choose, and p is minuscule. The focus needs to be on the effects themselves and their interpretation. Some may be highly statistically significant, yet so tiny that they have no importance. It's not a problem that power is too high, but thinking about power or p values may distract us from more important concerns, including the representativeness of our samples and the quality of our survey measures.

Second, note that any experiment has costs, which must be balanced against the value of the knowledge it's likely to provide. Is the size of our proposed experiment justified? Would a smaller, less costly study suffice for our research purposes? These questions are especially pertinent when costs include discomfort and risks to participants. It's highly valuable to know that a small daily dose of aspirin can reduce the risk of heart attack. However, gaining such knowledge usually requires many participants to be randomly assigned to receive the inert placebo pill, and so miss any benefit of aspirin. Clearly, such studies need to be scrutinized by an independent ethical review board before being approved. An analysis based on precision may be better, but an analysis of statistical power is one way to give guidance about the proposed study, so it's large enough to give useful knowledge, but no larger than it needs to be, to minimize participant harm.

Reporting Power

If we decide to calculate power, how should we report it? As I mentioned, the *Publication Manual* advises us to "routinely provide evidence that the study has sufficient power to detect effects of substantive interest" (APA, 2010, p. 30). However, it gives no advice on how to report power, and no power values appear anywhere in its numerous examples.

In medicine, some articles report power, but what about in other disciplines? I took a peek at *Psychological Science*—just one journal in one discipline—but I suspect that what I found is typical for many journals, at least across the social and behavioral sciences. I conducted a full-text search for "power" in the 259 articles published in *Psychological Science* in the last year.

Just 22 articles (8%) mentioned statistical power, of which four reported power values, ranging from .79 to .99. Another 10 made brief comments about experimental design or statistical analysis, mentioning, for example, the combination of groups or the use of meta-analysis as strategies to increase power. All those comments were reasonable, and all can be read as referring to informativeness.

The remaining eight articles all referred to power while discussing effects that were not statistically significant. For example, they suggested that considering power may justify accepting the null hypothesis, or that a result that was found not statistically significant might, with higher power, achieve statistical significance. However, even high power rarely, if ever, provides good grounds for accepting a null hypothesis and concluding that we have a zero effect. The CI always provides much clearer guidance for interpretation, as we've seen in earlier chapters.

The articles did not provide a good example of how to report power—if you must. Suppose you wish to present one of our HEAT experiments to your ethics review board, which requires a power analysis. In the context of your research goals, and bearing in mind available participants and resources, you need to justify your choices of experimental design, α, target δ, ρ (if a paired design), and N. It may be useful to describe how power changes for different values of those variables before you justify the set of values for which you seek approval. Pay particular attention to explaining your choice of target δ. Be as realistic as you can, bearing in mind the risk of fudging. In a journal article a briefer version is needed, but allocate a few words to justifying your choice of target δ.

However, I have yet to find a case in which I think a power analysis is more illuminating than a precision analysis could be. I hope funding bodies and ethics review boards will accept a precision analysis instead and, soon, require one. Considering journal publication, very few researchers have "routinely provide[d] evidence that the study has sufficient power" (APA, 2010, p. 30), as the *Publication Manual* requires. I see no signs that researchers are likely to adopt this advice. It's one of the few guidelines in the *Manual* I don't endorse.

It's almost time to embrace the new statistics and move beyond NHST and statistical power to *precision* as a tool for planning research. That's the topic of the next chapter.

It's time for take-home messages. To help you write yours, you may want to look back over the figures in this chapter. We started with a simulation and a wide spread of p values, then came the power picture for the single-group design, using noncentral t. Two pages in **ESCI chapters 5–6** allow you to calculate power for the two-independent-groups and paired designs. How should we select target δ? Two pages in **ESCI chapters 10–13** present power curves for the two-independent-groups and paired designs. Intuitions about power are important, especially understanding which factors influence power most strongly. Avoid post hoc power! Consider the informativeness of an experiment, not just statistical power. How should we report power, if we choose to?

Exercises

12.1 You are planning a study of attitudes to the length of jail sentences for homicide, using a scale running from –4 to +4, where 0 indicates a judgment that current sentences are about right. Previous research suggests that the population SD for the scale is 1.2. You plan to use a single sample and would like to be able to detect a true effect of 0.5 scale units, using $\alpha = .01$. If you use $N = 100$, what is the power? Explore power for various other choices of effect size, α, and N.

12.2 You wish to use the same scale to compare attitudes in two very different neighborhoods. You would like to be able to detect a difference of 0.3 scale units. Consider power and make recommendations.

12.3 Again using the same scale, you wish to compare attitudes in a single neighborhood, using a single sample of people who respond both before and 3 months after a state election. You would like to be able to detect a change of 0.2 scale units. Previous research using the scale has reported correlations between pretest and posttest attitudes in the range .72 to .89. Consider power and make recommendations.

12.4 If you are using another statistics textbook, find worked examples or exercises about power for which the ESCI pages discussed in this chapter are helpful. Compare the methods used by that other book with ESCI's, and also compare the results.

12.5 A leading researcher in clinical psychology uses the rule of thumb that, roughly speaking, most well-established types of psychotherapy give an improvement of around $\delta = 0.5$ to 0.7, whereas comparisons between any two such therapies are likely to give differences of around $\delta = 0$ to 0.3. Suppose you are planning a two-independent-groups experiment to assess such a therapy, using target $\delta = 0.6$, and a second two-independent-groups experiment to compare two such therapies with target $\delta = 0.2$ for the difference. Compare the two experiments you will need.

12.6 What does the tiny invisible area to the left under the H_1 curve in Figures 12.3 and 12.4 represent? Why is it so small?

12.7 Invent a game to help build your intuitions about power. Challenge a friend to estimate power for an experiment you describe—you'll need to state the design, and also α, δ, and N (and ρ if a paired design). Practice using the **Power two** and **Power paired** pages of **ESCI chapters 10–13** until you can find answers quickly. Develop the game to focus on estimating just one factor, while holding others constant. For example, for a two-independent-groups experiment with $\delta = 0.5$ and $\alpha = .01$, what is the power for $N = 100$? What is N to obtain power = .80? How big a δ can you detect if $N = 100$ and power = .80?

12.8 Use that game, or relevant ESCI pages, or Tables 12.1 and 12.2 to identify some sets of values that seem especially relevant for your discipline. Choose a handful of these to remember, to serve as benchmarks for judgments about published research you read.

12.9 Explore any statistical software you use. Does it give you a value for power? Is this legitimate power, or post hoc power? Is it clearly labeled?

12.10 Even if that software reports post hoc power, perhaps as a default, try to find a way to have it calculate and report legitimate power, after you specify a target population effect size.

12.11 Download G*Power 3 (tinyurl.com/gpower3). Explore as you wish. Use it to check one or two values in Table 12.1 or 12.2.

12.12 Find a journal article in your discipline that mentions statistical power. If possible, find an article that reports a power calculation. Do these articles discuss and use power appropriately? Can you make any recommendations? You could try a full-text search for "power," as I used to investigate power in *Psychological Science*. You should be able to conduct a single search for a whole selected date range of journal issues, before opening only those articles identified as containing the word "power."

12.13 Find a journal article in your discipline that could usefully mention statistical power or report a power calculation, but doesn't. Make your recommendations.

12.14 Larger N gives smaller variation in M over replication—in other words, the dance of the means is narrower for larger N. Similarly, s varies less over replication when N is large. In Chapter 5 we found, perhaps surprisingly, that for a given initial p value, the variation in replication p does not change with N, even for large *N*. Consider the amount of variation in post hoc power over replication. For a given level of legitimate power, would you guess that variability in post hoc power decreases with larger *N*, or remains about the same? Use the **Simulate two** page of **ESCI chapters 5–6** to check out the variation in post hoc power. You could, for example, set up an experiment with $N_1 = N_2 = 8$, then adjust δ until power is about .7. Take 20 experiments and write down the values of post hoc power. Then set up an experiment with $N_1 = N_2 = 64$ and a much smaller δ so power is again about .7. Again record 20 values of post hoc power. Is the amount of variability similar? Try other experiments if you like. What do you conclude about post hoc power?

12.15 Consider every way you can think of to increase statistical power. For each, decide whether you are also increasing the informativeness of the experiment.

12.16 Revisit your take-home messages. Improve them and extend the list if you can.

Take-Home Messages

- I'm ambivalent about statistical power, which is only defined in the context of NHST, so the new statistics do not use it. We should keep in mind our new statistics intuitions even while discussing power within NHST.

- Statistical power is the probability of rejecting H_0 if there is a true population effect of size target δ. The value of power depends on the experimental design, N, α, target δ, and in the paired case ρ, the population correlation between the two measures.

- The informativeness of an experiment is its ability to answer our research questions and give us information about the world. Informativeness is more fundamental than statistical power.

- It's often difficult to achieve high power, and the power of published research is often disappointingly low, despite the efforts of Jacob Cohen and other statistical reformers.

- The power picture shows the distribution of the test statistic when H_0 is true and when H_1 is true. For σ known the test statistic is z and the two distributions are normal. For σ not known the test statistic is t and the distributions are the central and noncentral t distributions. *Take-home picture*: The power picture, for example, Figure 12.3.

- The **Simulate two** page of **ESCI chapters 5–6** allows you to calculate power for the two-independent-groups design, and the **Simulate paired** page for the paired design.

- It's important to build intuitions about power. In general, larger N gives higher power and smaller α lower power, but target δ is even more influential: Small changes in δ can give substantial changes in power. The paired design can give high power, especially if ρ is at least moderately large.

- The power curves of the **Power two** and **Power paired** pages of **ESCI chapters 10–13** illustrate how power varies with N and other aspects of an experiment. These pages also give the values of N shown by Tables 12.1 and 12.2 for selected situations.

- Post hoc or observed power is calculated after data collection, using the Cohen's d obtained in the experiment as target δ. It reflects the result rather than any basic feature of the experiment, and varies greatly with replication. Don't use post hoc power, which can be highly misleading. Watch out for software that reports post hoc power without saying so.

- If you intend to use NHST, a power calculation may be useful, for example, to justify the design and sample sizes of a planned experiment.
- To adopt the new statistics and move beyond NHST, use precision rather than power.

Polya

13

Precision for Planning

Precision is indicated by the width of a CI. Actually it's MOE, the half-width of the CI, or one arm of the CI that's our measure of precision. Higher precision is signaled by a shorter CI, and short CIs are good news. Precision is a highly valuable idea, but not sufficiently recognized or used. It usually contributes to what in Chapter 12 I called the *informativeness* of an experiment.

Most of this book so far has been about using CIs to report and interpret results, and one valuable approach to interpreting a CI focuses on MOE as a measure of precision. This chapter considers a further use of precision—in the planning of experiments. To carry out a precision analysis for planning, we first select a target CI width, and then the analysis tells us what sample size is likely to give CIs no wider than that target. In general, researchers have not yet made precision a central part of their research planning. When they do, they'll no longer need to use statistical power. Precision for planning has the great advantage that it uses, before the experiment, CI concepts and judgments that correspond closely with those we use after the experiment for interpretation. This contrasts strongly with power, which really only applies before the experiment.

Here's the agenda for this chapter:

- Precision as arm length
- Precision for research planning, for three experimental designs
- Precision for planning using ESCI
- Precision with assurance: finding *N* so we can be reasonably assured our CI won't be wider than the target width we've chosen
- Precision for planning using Cohen's *d*
- Ways to increase precision

Precision as Arm Length

Consider any of the HEAT (Hot Earth Awareness Test) experiments we discussed in Chapter 12. To report our main result we'd no doubt use a CI,

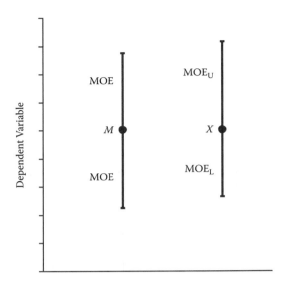

FIGURE 13.1

On the left is a symmetric CI on a sample mean *M*. On the right is an asymmetric CI on some ES measure *X*, the point estimate of the corresponding population ES. The upper and lower arms of the intervals are labeled.

which we'd display as the graphic on the left in Figure 13.1. I've labeled the arms of the CI as MOE because my focus in this chapter is on precision, as pictured by arm length and measured by MOE. Whenever we include a CI in a figure we're using precision to report our results. Precision is also the basis for our third approach to interpreting a CI, as we discussed in Chapter 3—see also Table 5.1. Precision indicates the maximum likely error of estimation, although, of course, larger errors are possible—our CI just may be red, meaning it does not capture μ, or whatever population parameter it's estimating. Vary the level of confidence, *C*, and MOE and thus precision change. Our measure of precision therefore relates to a particular *C*, usually 95.

> I define *precision* as the arm length of a CI, and refer to it as MOE.

Figure 13.1 shows on the left the CI on our sample mean *M*. This CI is symmetric and so the lower and upper arms can both be labeled as MOE. On the right is *X*, the point estimate of a population ES, with a CI that is asymmetric, meaning its two arms differ in length. We've already encountered in Chapter 11 asymmetric CIs on Cohen's *d*. In Chapter 14 we'll find that CIs on correlations and proportions are also generally asymmetric. Figure 13.1 distinguishes the two arms of the asymmetric CI by labeling the upper and lower arms as MOE_U and MOE_L, respectively. For symmetric intervals I'll use MOE for the length of either

> For an asymmetric CI, our measure of precision is MOE_{av}, which is the average of the two arm lengths.

arm. For asymmetric intervals we'll need to label the arms differently, as in Figure 13.1. For asymmetric intervals our measure of precision is simply MOE_{av}, the average length of the two arms, and so

$$MOE_{av} = (MOE_L + MOE_U)/2$$

It may feel strange to say *increased* precision gives *shorter* CI arms, or a *smaller* MOE, but that's what I will do. Watch out for possible ambiguities in what you read or write about precision. Wide CIs mean low precision, and small MOE means high precision. If necessary, add a few words to make what you mean totally clear.

> Take care with language. A shorter CI means lower values of MOE, and greater precision. Larger MOE means worse precision.

Precision for Research Planning

You are investigating the effectiveness of a new reading program and wish to estimate the gain in reading age produced by 12 weeks on the program. How large an experiment do you need? Rather than asking about power to detect a true gain of a stated target size, if it exists, focus on estimation. How wide could a CI be and still give useful information? How short a CI arm length would you like to achieve? What's the maximum error of estimation you can readily accept? You need to answer one of those questions by stating your *target MOE*, which is the precision you want your experiment to achieve, then you (usually meaning ESCI) can calculate what N you need. That's precision for research planning, the topic of this chapter.

> *Target precision*, or *target MOE*, is the precision we want our experiment to achieve.

Within NHST, statistical power contributes to planning, but precision can do a better job in that role. Precision often allows us to avoid NHST both for planning before the experiment, and also for data analysis and interpretation after the experiment. Precision for planning requires no specification of α

> Given a target MOE, precision calculations tell us what N we need. Precision can thus replace power.

and null and alternative hypotheses. Also, it allows us to think in terms of estimation before data collection as well as for reporting our research, and the judgments needed for planning correspond closely with those we use for interpretation of our results. Precision is better than power.

I'll discuss how we can set target MOE, then use this to calculate the N needed so we can expect our experiment to give precision at least that great. We specify a desired arm length, then calculate what minimum N is likely to give us a CI with arms no longer than that. I'll consider three experimental designs: single group, two independent groups, and paired—each for the case where σ is known and we use z as the test statistic, and the more realistic case in which σ is not known and we use t. First I'll use means as our ES, then Cohen's d. There are formulas, but you can let ESCI do the work if you wish.

You may be thinking about the dance of the CIs when t is our test statistic: CI length varies from experiment to experiment. How can we say that N is adequate to give a particular target MOE if arm lengths bounce all over the place? That's an excellent question. Notice that I carefully referred above to N sufficiently large that we can *expect* our experiment to give us sufficiently high precision. The first big step, when we're using t, is to find minimum N that will *on average* give us CI arms no longer than target MOE. In other words, minimum N that's *likely* to give us CI arms no longer than target MOE. Almost 50% of experiments will give MOE greater than our target, the other experiments MOE less than our target. We can't guarantee that our single experiment will have the precision we want, but we can be sure that numerous repeated experiments will on average give at least our desired precision. Later we'll do even better when we consider *assurance*, but, for the moment, we'll consider what minimum N is likely to give arm length no greater than target MOE. Later I'll also explain why, even when we think about variation over experiments, precision is better than power. Now let's turn to the simplest cases of precision analysis.

Finding N for the Single-Group Design

Recall from Chapter 12 that the HEAT has $\mu = 50$ and $\sigma = 20$ in the reference population. Suppose you take a single sample of $N = 10$ students and find $M = 57.0$. Assuming that σ is known, you use Equation (3.2)—remember way back then?—to find the 95% CI by calculating

$$\text{MOE} = 1.96 \times \sigma/\sqrt{N} = 1.96 \times 20/\sqrt{10} = 12.40$$

and so the CI is [44.6, 69.4]. You are a bit disappointed that MOE is so large, although you realize your sample is very small. How large a sample, you wonder, would you need to get smaller MOE, say, 10 instead of 12.4? The 10 is your choice, made by using your judgment, based on your understanding of the HEAT scale and the research context. We'll call 10 your target MOE. You fiddle with the MOE formula a bit and decide that you should express target MOE as a fraction of σ. I'll use f for that fraction, so I can say that your target MOE is $f = 0.5$, because 10 is just half of σ. Our basic formula for target MOE is therefore

We express our chosen target precision as $f \times \sigma$, so f is usually a fraction, for example, $f = 0.5$.

$$\text{Target MOE} = f \times \sigma \qquad (13.1)$$

Think of *f* as a kind of *z* score, a number of SDs. Your fiddling with the MOE formula gave you

$$N = (1.96/f)^2 \qquad (13.2)$$

For *f* = 0.5 you calculate *N* = 15.4. Round that up to 16, obtain the HEAT scores for a sample of *N* = 16 students, and use Equation (3.2) to calculate MOE = 1.96 × $\sigma/\sqrt{N}$ = 1.96 × 20/$\sqrt{16}$ = 9.80. Success! Your MOE is just less than your target of 10—slightly less because we rounded *N* up from 15.4 to 16. You are also pleased to note that we get this MOE every time: We're using *z*, because we're assuming that σ is known, and so MOE doesn't vary from experiment to experiment.

If σ is known, turn around the formula for MOE to calculate N that gives a particular target MOE.

Therefore, if we're using a single sample and test statistic *z*: *To get MOE no more than half of σ we need to use N at least 16.* That's a general statement and a useful one—exactly the information we need to help us plan our study. Choose a different *f* and we'll almost certainly need a different *N*, but Equation (13.2) will give us that *N*. Equation (13.2) states a general relationship, which does not depend on σ: Given only *f*, we can calculate *N*.

Figure 13.2 shows 95% CIs on a sample mean, with arm lengths that are various fractions *f* of σ. The line segment at left marks σ, and the leftmost CI has *f* = 0.5, meaning MOE = 0.5σ, as you used previously. We found that such a CI requires *N* = 16, and this value is reported below the CI as **N using z**. The figure tells us that if we want, for example, *f* = 0.2, we need *N* at least 97. Yes, high precision, meaning small *f*, comes at the price of considerably larger *N*. Equation (13.2) indicates that halving *f* requires *N* four times as large.

Now let's be more realistic and assume that we don't know σ, and so our test statistic is *t*. Box 13.1 explains more about the formulas and tells us that, using *t*,

$$N = [t_{.95}(N - 1)/f]^2 \qquad (13.3)$$

where $t_{.95}(N - 1)$ is the critical value of *t* for a 95% CI. Note carefully that this *N* will give precision of target MOE *on average*, or in the long run, rather than in our single experiment. Figure 13.2 shows near the bottom such values with the label **N using t**. These are the minimum *N* values that give CIs having on average our target MOE. In every case, *N* needs to be a little higher when we use *t* rather than *z*.

Choose *f* = 0.5 and use *t*, and Equation (13.3) tells us that *N* = 18 is required for our average MOE to be no more than 10, our target MOE. That's also the value reported as **N using t** in Figure 13.2 under the leftmost CI. Take a sample of 18 students, test them on the HEAT, and calculate the 95% CI: MOE may be more or less than 10, but repeat the experiment numerous

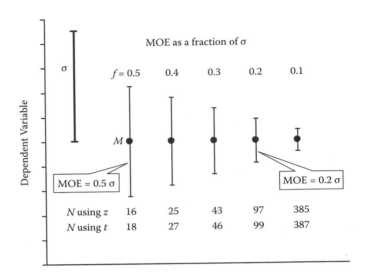

FIGURE 13.2
The line segment at left indicates the population standard deviation, σ. Then 95% CIs on *M* are shown with MOE of various fractions *f* of σ, as shown at the top. Using *z*, **N using z** is the size of a single sample that gives the CI in the figure. Using *t*, **N using t** is the size of a single sample that gives, *on average* over many experiments, the CI in the figure. (In each case a slightly shorter CI may be given, because *N* has been rounded up to an integer.) As Equations (13.2) and (13.3) state, the values of *N* depend only on *f*, not on σ.

times and, in the long run, the average MOE will be 10, or slightly less because *N* has been rounded up to an integer.

Note that the amount of bouncing around of CI arm length would be very different for small and large samples. For the smallest CI shown in Figure 13.2, which requires *N* of 387, there would be hardly any variation of MOE over replication, whereas with *N* of 18 there would be considerable variation. For small samples, the **N using t** in Figure 13.2 will give average MOE no more than our target MOE, but any single experiment could give MOE considerably bigger or smaller than our target.

There's one troubling thing about Equation (13.3). The value of $t_{.95}(N-1)$ we need on the right-hand side of the equation depends on *N*, which is what we are trying to calculate. Change *N*, and $df = (N-1)$ changes and the critical value $t_{.95}(N-1)$ also changes. We need to take an iterative or trial-and-error approach to solving Equation (13.3). We can leave the details to ESCI but, in outline, first use *z* instead of *t* to get an initial estimate of *N*, then check whether, using *t*, this *N* gives a sufficiently short MOE. If not, try $(N+1)$ and again check MOE. Continue until *N* is sufficiently large to give MOE just less than our target MOE.

If σ is not known, *t* is the test statistic. Use Equation (13.3) and an iterative approach to find minimum *N* that gives *on average* a particular target MOE.

BOX 13.1 CALCULATING N GIVEN A TARGET MOE

We specify target MOE as $f \times \sigma$, as in Equation (13.1).

Single-Group Design

Back in Chapter 3 we calculated the 95% CI for a mean, when σ is known and z is the test statistic, as

$$[M - 1.96 \times \sigma/\sqrt{N}, M + 1.96 \times \sigma/\sqrt{N}] \tag{3.2}$$

Therefore, precision is

$$\text{MOE} = 1.96 \times \sigma/\sqrt{N} \tag{13.4}$$

More generally, for a $C\%$ CI using z, precision is

$$\text{MOE} = z_{C/100} \times \sigma/\sqrt{N} \tag{13.5}$$

where $z_{C/100}$ is the critical value of z for the $C\%$ confidence level. The **Normal z t** page of **ESCI chapters 1–4** can provide critical values for z and t (see Appendix B). Substitute MOE $= f \times \sigma$ in Equation (13.5) and find that

$$N = (z_{C/100}/f)^2 \tag{13.6}$$

which for $C = 95$ becomes

$$N = (1.96/f)^2 \tag{13.2}$$

Equation (13.6) is the basic formula for precision for planning with the single-group design, with σ assumed known. It's what the **Precision one** page of **ESCI chapters 10–13** uses to calculate N when using z.

For σ not assumed known and t as the test statistic, back in Chapter 3 we calculated the 95% CI by using Equation (3.3), which gives

$$\text{MOE} = t_{C/100}(N-1) \times s/\sqrt{N}$$

where $t_{C/100}(N-1)$ is the critical value of t for the $C\%$ confidence level. Substitute MOE $= f \times \sigma$ and find that

$$N = [t_{C/100}(N-1)/f]^2 \times (s/\sigma)^2$$

On average, $(s/\sigma)^2 = 1$, so we can calculate

$$N = [t_{C/100}(N-1)/f]^2 \tag{13.7}$$

which for $C = 95$ becomes

$$N = [t_{.95}(N - 1)/f]^2 \qquad (13.3)$$

providing we note carefully that this N gives target MOE *on average*. (Or slightly less because N is rounded up to an integer.) Any single experiment may give precision larger or smaller than target MOE. For very large N, there is little variation in MOE with replication, but small N gives large variation in MOE from experiment to experiment. Think of the s pile in Chapters 10 and 11. Even N up to 50 or more gives noticeable variation in MOE with replication.

Because N appears on the right-hand side in Equations (13.3) and (13.7)—it affects the critical value of t—as well as the left, we need an iterative strategy of successive approximations to solve either of those equations for N. **Precision one** uses Equation (13.7) and an iterative approach to calculate N when using t.

Two-Independent-Groups Design

For the two-independent-groups design, our focus is on the difference between the group means and the CI on that difference. We assume that the two groups are each of size N. Using z, the equation for N that corresponds to Equation (13.6) is

$$N = 2(z_{C/100}/f)^2 \qquad (13.8)$$

which is the smallest N that gives arm length of the CI on the difference between the sample means, calculated using z, no greater than target MOE. The **Precision two** page of **ESCI chapters 10–13** uses Equation (13.8) to calculate N when using z.

Using t, the equation for N that corresponds to Equation (13.7) is

$$N = 2[t_{C/100}(2N - 2)/f]^2 \qquad (13.9)$$

which is the smallest N that gives, *on average*, arm length of the CI on the difference between the sample means, calculated using t, no greater than target MOE. **Precision two** uses Equation (13.9) and an iterative approach to calculate N when using t.

Paired Design

For the paired design, N is the number of data pairs and our focus is on the mean of the differences, and the CI on that mean. Using z, the equation for N that corresponds to Equations (13.6) and (13.8) is

$$N = 2(1 - \rho)(z_{C/100}/f)^2 \qquad (13.10)$$

where ρ is the correlation in the population between the two measures. Equation (13.10) gives the smallest N so arm length of the CI on the mean difference, calculated using z, is no greater than target MOE. The **Precision paired** page of **ESCI chapters 10–13** uses Equation (13.10) to calculate N when using z.

Using t, the equation for N that corresponds to Equations (13.7) and (13.9) is

$$N = 2(1 - \rho)[t_{C/100}(N - 1)/f]^2 \qquad (13.11)$$

which is the smallest N that gives, on average, arm length of the CI on the mean difference no greater than target MOE. **Precision paired** uses Equation (13.11) and an iterative approach to calculate N when using t.

ESCI for Precision for the Single-Group Design

Fire up the **Precision one** page of **ESCI chapters 10–13**. Figure 13.3 shows part of the control area. Figure 13.4 is the main display, whose curve shows how N varies as a function of target precision, using z. If $C = 95$ is set near red 1, the values of N shown on the curve correspond to the **N using z** values shown at the bottom in Figure 13.2. Figure 13.4 shows a vertical cursor positioned at a target MOE of $f = 0.2$ units of σ. This cursor is controlled by the large slider that appears on the screen below the figure. The value of N marked by the cursor is 97, which is the value shown for $f = 0.2$ in Figure 13.2, using z.

The vertical axis in the main figure needs to span a very wide range of N values. Adjust the slider near red 1 that's labeled **Truncate display at**, as shown in Figure 13.3, and the curve disappears for lower values of f. The vertical axis rescales automatically to display a smaller range of N values. Figure 13.5 shows the figure truncated at $f = 0.4$, meaning that 0.4 is the minimum value of f for which the curve is displayed. The curve for N using t is also displayed. Check that the values displayed correspond with those in Figure 13.2 for **N using t**.

Choosing Target Precision

How should we choose our target MOE? For our HEAT experiment we chose 10 score units as our target MOE. That was for the single-group case, but the discussion in this section applies also for other situations,

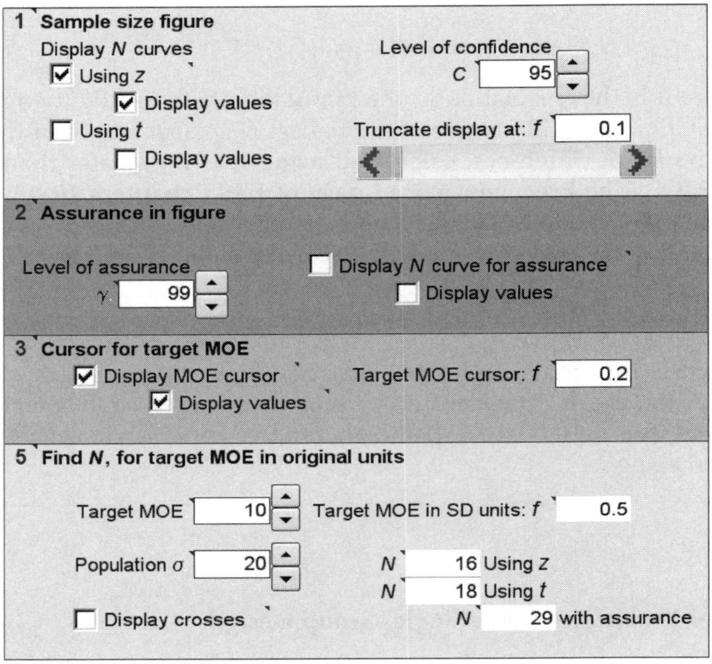

FIGURE 13.3
Part of the control area of the **Precision one** page of **ESCI chapters 10–13**. The checkboxes near red 1 turn on the curves that show how N varies as a function of target MOE. Click at red 3 to turn on a vertical cursor to mark target MOE, which is set by a large slider below the main figure that appears on the screen to the right of the control area.

including the other two designs we're considering in this chapter. We chose 10 by using our judgment in the research situation, based on understanding of the HEAT scale and differences in HEAT scores likely to be of research interest. We expressed that target MOE of 10 original units as $f = 0.5$, meaning 0.5σ. We could do that because we were assuming that we knew $\sigma = 20$. In many situations, however, we don't know σ and use t as the test statistic. Even so, we can still express target MOE as f, in terms of the unknown σ. If we then choose N given by the formulas in Box 13.1 or by one of the ESCI precision pages, we know that, on average, MOE calculated from our data will be no greater than $f \times \sigma$. That will be true, even though we don't know σ and so can't express target MOE $= f \times \sigma$ in original units. After we've run our experiment we shift attention from target MOE and simply report the CI calculated from our data, then use this to guide our interpretation. We could also, if we wish, use s from our experiment to estimate σ. When thinking about the *next* experiment, we would, of course, take into account the extra knowledge we now have—about σ

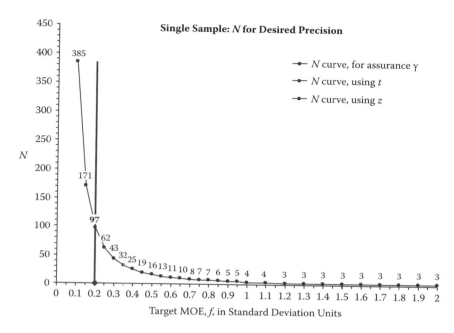

FIGURE 13.4

The main figure of **Precision one**. The curve shows N required to give target MOE for a 95% CI, using z as the test statistic. On the screen this curve is black. In this figure, and the following figures like it, the three legend entries at upper right are distinguished on the screen by color.

as well as the population ES—as we set target MOE to guide our choice of N for that next experiment. Choosing the f for our target MOE is still a matter for judgment, but it's now better-informed judgment.

One way to think about f for planning is in general terms as a fraction of the unknown population SD, much as in Chapter 11 we discussed values of d or δ in numerous contexts as a number of SDs. In either case we might think in terms of Cohen's benchmarks for small, medium, and large ESs, or use our experience in the research context to focus on a relevant fraction of population SD—even if we can't express that σ exactly in original units.

Another approach is to find an estimate for σ, perhaps based on past research—preferably a meta-analysis—and use that as the SD needed to convert our chosen target MOE from original units to f. In Chapter 11 we discussed a range of approaches to finding such a standardizer. ESCI can do the arithmetic: In the panel at red 5, which is shown in Figure 13.3, you can enter your target MOE and a value for known or estimated population SD, both in any original units. The figure illustrates our case where we chose 10 as the target MOE and 20 as the population SD, both in HEAT scale units. ESCI calculates $f = 0.5$ and reports that N is 16 using z, and 18

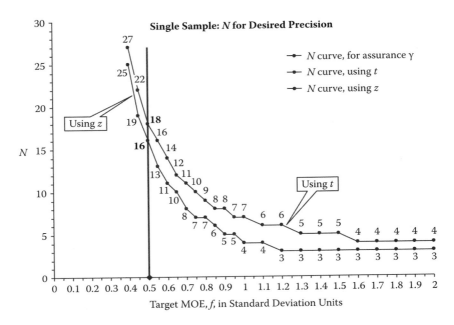

FIGURE 13.5
The main figure of **Precision one**, as in Figure 13.4, except that the curve for *N* using *t* is also displayed, and the curves are truncated at *f* = 0.4. The vertical *N* axis rescales accordingly. On the screen the lower curve, using *z*, is black, and the upper curve, using *t*, is red. The cursor marks *f* = 0.5 and shows *N* = 16 for *z*, and *N* = 18 for *t*.

using *t*, as we found before. Note that this panel is quite separate from the main figure. It's simply a small self-contained calculator that allows you to find *N* for values of target MOE that may not be displayed in the main figure. As usual, see the popout comments for further explanation.

You might be thinking that this is all rather subjective and there could be scope for fudging to get a value of *N* that we find acceptable. That may be true to some extent, depending on how well the research area and the measures we are using are understood. But, after we've run our experiment, the CI calculated from our data gives us precision information directly, and may give useful guidance for planning the next experiment.

The great advantage of precision, compared with power, is that the target MOE we use for planning corresponds closely to MOE of the CI we report after completing the experiment. Both may be in original or standardized units. Both require, for interpretation, our understanding of the measurement scale in the research context. In both cases the examples and discussion of standardizers in Chapter 11 may be relevant. We use our knowledge and judgment to interpret the reported CI, and that's a key part of interpreting our results. As our understanding of the measurement scale and research context develops, our interpretation of the CIs that express our results improves. The same increased understanding can inform our precision analysis for planning.

Choice of target MOE is an important topic for discussion as researchers experiment with using precision for planning. I hope examples are published, and conventions and guidelines developed, but the important point is that improvement in how researchers use precision for planning should naturally accompany—and contribute to—improvement in researchers' interpretations of ESs and CIs based on data.

Finding *N* for the Two-Independent-Groups Design

For the two-independent-groups design I consider only cases in which $N_1 = N_2$, and so we have two groups each of size N. The focus is on the difference between the group means and the CI on that difference. Box 13.1 provides Equations (13.8) and (13.9) for this design, which correspond to Equations (13.6) and (13.7) for the single-group case. Once again, when using t an iterative approach is required, and N is the value that *on average* gives target MOE—or a little less because N is rounded up to an integer.

The ESCI page is **Precision two**, which is very similar in layout to **Precision one**. Figure 13.6 shows its main figure, with truncation at 0.45 and the vertical cursor positioned at $f = 0.5$. Compare with Figure 13.5 and note, for example, the N values marked by the vertical cursor when using z. A single-group experiment needs one group of size $N = 16$ to give a 95% CI on the sample mean with an arm length of 0.5σ. By contrast, a two-independent-groups experiment needs groups each with $N = 31$, a total of 62 participants, to give a 95% CI on the difference of the two means with that same arm length.

Finding *N* for the Paired Design

For the paired design, our focus is on the mean of the differences and the CI on that mean difference. We need to specify a value for ρ, the population correlation between the two measures, and we might look in the literature or rely on our judgment to choose a value for ρ that seems reasonable for the research situation. In Chapter 12 we found that the value of ρ is very influential on power. It's also very influential on precision: Higher ρ means that a much smaller N is needed to achieve our desired precision. Yes, the paired design is sensitive and efficient, for situations in which it is appropriate, and especially so if the two measures are highly correlated.

Box 13.1 provides Equations (13.10) and (13.11) for the paired design. Once again, when using t an iterative approach is required, and N is the value that *on average* gives target MOE—or a little less because N is rounded up to an integer.

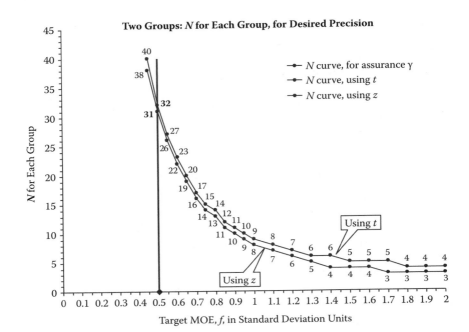

FIGURE 13.6
The main figure of **Precision two**. The lower curve shows N for z, and the upper curve shows N for t, for two independent groups each of size N. The lower axis shows target MOE for a 95% CI on the difference between the two group means.

The ESCI page is **Precision paired**, and Figure 13.7 shows a small part of the control area of that page, including the slider that allows setting of a value for population correlation ρ between the measures. Change ρ and watch the marked changes in the curves of N against f, the target MOE. Figure 13.8 shows the main figure from **Precision paired**, when C = 95 and ρ = .7 have been set near red 1. With these settings, N of 10 for

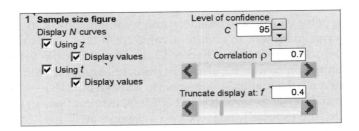

FIGURE 13.7
The top control panel of **Precision paired**. The upper slider allows the setting of a value for ρ, the population correlation between the two measures.

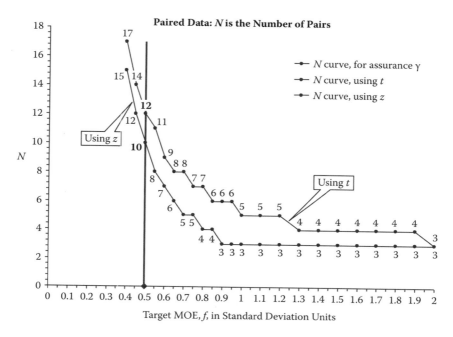

FIGURE 13.8
The main figure from **Precision paired**. The lower curve gives N using z, and the upper gives N using t. The curves relate to 95% CIs and $\rho = .7$.

z and 12 for t are sufficient to achieve the target $f = 0.5$. (For t, have you automatically added the mental comment "on average, in the long run"?) Increase ρ and even smaller N will suffice. Alternatively, aim for greater precision—meaning smaller target MOE—and find that even then N need not be large. Adjust the lower slider at red 1 to shift the truncation of the curves and reveal N for smaller values of f. Note that $N = 3$ is the smallest N that ESCI permits in any precision calculations.

Precision with Assurance

Use t as the test statistic, as we usually must, and so far we can only calculate N that guarantees an arm length that *on average* isn't too large. It's a concern that almost half of the experiments conducted with that N will give MOE greater than our target. The next step is to calculate N so there's a 99% chance that our sample MOE will not exceed the target MOE. The 99% is one possible value of what's called *assurance*, which I'll give the symbol γ (Greek lowercase gamma). Assurance γ is the probability, expressed as a percentage, that our sample MOE is no greater than target MOE. We can choose γ = 99, or γ = 80 (the lowest value ESCI supports), or some other value less than 100. (Some authors use the term "certainty," but "assurance" is becoming the most widely used term and is my preference.) I don't know of any convention to guide our choice of γ, but I'm inclined to choose γ = 99 so that my MOE is rarely larger than target MOE. I try to avoid γ = 95 because that may encourage confusion between γ and C, the level of confidence.

Assurance γ is the percentage of experiments whose MOE is less than target MOE.

You've probably noticed panel 2, which appears on each of the precision pages and in Figure 13.3. Panel 2 provides a spinner to set assurance γ. You can also click to see an additional curve in the figure, which appears above the z and t curves, and gives N for the selected value of γ. Figure 13.9 shows an example from **Precision one**. It's the same as Figure 13.5 except a third curve now gives N with assurance γ = 99. Using t as our test statistic, we noted before (and saw in Figure 13.2) that N = 18 suffices to give, on average, MOE of 0.5σ. Read the value of N where the vertical cursor

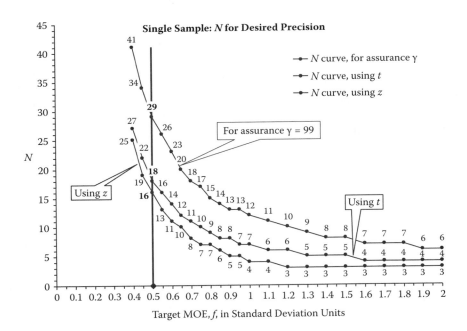

FIGURE 13.9
Same as Figure 13.5, for a single group, but with the curve for N with assurance γ = 99 also displayed. On the screen, the assurance curve is pink.

BOX 13.2 CALCULATING *N* WITH ASSURANCE

When we use t, assurance γ is the percentage of experiments whose MOE is no greater than target MOE. In earlier chapters I mentioned that s^2 has a sampling distribution with the shape of the chi-square distribution. Think also of the s pile, shaped like a chi distribution, which has a single hump and positive skew. When s (or s^2) happens by chance to be large—to be in the upper tail of its sampling distribution—the CI we calculate for that experiment is especially large. We can use knowledge of the sampling distribution of s^2 to calculate how much larger N needs to be so that only a small upper tail of that distribution, with area $(1 - \gamma/100)$, gives a CI that is wider than we want. That's the basis for assurance calculations.

I'm not going to explain those calculations in detail, but the basic formula for the single-group case is

$$N = [t_{C/100}(N - 1)/f]^2 \times [\chi^2_{\gamma/100}/(N - 1)] \qquad (13.12)$$

where $\chi^2_{\gamma/100}$ is the critical value of χ^2 for our selected γ, with $df = (N - 1)$. Note that N appears on the right-hand side of the equation, so, as before with t, we need a step-by-step, successive approximations procedure to find the smallest N that will satisfy our requirement for MOE to be shorter than target MOE on at least γ% of occasions. As usual, ESCI takes care of those details.

intersects the top curve in Figure 13.9, and see that $N = 29$ is needed if we are to be 99% assured that our MOE will be no more than the target $f = 0.5$. We need a considerably larger sample to gain 99% assurance that our MOE won't be longer than we want. Box 13.2 says a little about the calculation of N with assurance.

I suggest that precision calculated with assurance is highly useful, and probably should be our routine practice for finding N during the planning of experiments. We can't be absolutely guaranteed we won't get a CI longer than we want, but select $\gamma = 99$ and we can be pretty sure. Of course, if we use the larger N that's needed to achieve that degree of assurance, our expected MOE will be shorter. Figure 13.9 shows that $N = 27$ gives an expected target MOE of $f = 0.4$, using t. Therefore, if we use $N = 29$, on average our MOE will be a little shorter than $f = 0.4$. Also, on 99% of occasions our MOE will be shorter than target $f = 0.5$, so on only 1% of occasions will it be longer than that target. In summary, on average our MOE will be about 0.4σ and only rarely will it be greater than 0.5σ. That's good information about the precision that our planned experiment will achieve.

Precision Beats Power

Compare precision with power. From Chapter 5 we know that the p value has an extremely wide distribution and so, in advance of our experiment we have very little idea indeed of what p value we'll get, even if target δ used in the power calculation equals δ in the population. All a power analysis can tell us is that, assuming that target δ equals population δ, we have an 80% chance of obtaining $p < .05$—if power is .8 and we're using $\alpha = .05$. In addition, even for very large N, the distribution of p is just as wide, so the uncertainty about our obtained p is just as great, no matter how large N is. In stark contrast, using precision for planning has at least three advantages:

1. It gives us information about arm length, which should be readily interpretable in the research context, and corresponds directly with the CIs we use for interpretation of our results.
2. With an assurance analysis, the information about arm length is fairly detailed, as I described previously: We know both an expected MOE and a likely upper bound.
3. The extent of bouncing around of arm length decreases for larger N, so the uncertainty in a precision analysis, unlike a power analysis, steadily decreases with increasing N.

Yes, precision beats power.

In my assurance example above, N needed to be increased from 18 to 29 when we required 99% assurance that our MOE was no longer than our target $f = 0.5$. That's a 61% increase in N. It's large because, for the particular situation and sample size, CI length bounces around considerably with replication. That observation accords with a general theme of this book that, unfortunately, in many situations the amount of variation over replication is large, even surprisingly large. Think of the dance of the p values. However, with assurance there's good news. For many typical cases that arise in practice, the increase in N required to achieve high assurance is small. For example, use **Precision two** and set a target MOE of $f = 0.3$. For 95% CIs, N needs to be increased from 87 to 108 to achieve assurance of $\gamma = 99$, a more reasonable increase of 24% in sample size. Explore different designs and various targets for MOE and find that the increase in N needed to achieve high assurance can often in practice be modest. Kelley and Rausch (2006, pp. 375–379) discussed this issue in the context of an example in which achieving $\gamma = 99$ required an increase of only 7% in N. Using assurance as well as precision to plan experiments may be one of the rare situations in which sampling variability is often not surprisingly large. Consider also what peace of mind $\gamma = 99$ can give: We're almost guaranteed that our experiment will give a CI no longer than the target used in the assurance analysis.

Precision for Planning Using Cohen's d

This chapter has so far referred to means, but now I'll consider Cohen's d. What N do we need for expected MOE_{av} of the CI on our d to be no more than some target? (Recall from Figure 13.1 that MOE_{av} is the average of the two arms of an asymmetric CI. By "expected MOE_{av}" I'm referring to the long-run average MOE_{av} over many experiments.) That's possible to calculate, but tricky. Recall that to find the CI on an observed d, we need an iterative (i.e., successive approximations) procedure that uses noncentral t. Chapter 11 tells the story, and the **CI for d** page of **ESCI chapters 10–13** can do the work. If we have a two-independent-groups experiment with $N = 20$ for both groups, and observe $d = 0.45$, **CI for d** calculates the 95% CI for δ to be $[-0.18, 1.08]$ and $MOE_{av} = 0.63$. Yes, quite a wide CI, so perhaps we should be using larger N?

You may have noticed that the three precision pages in ESCI have a panel at red 6 for calculations for Cohen's d. This d panel is a self-contained calculator. It uses values of C and γ set in the control panels above it, but has no links with the main figure. Figure 13.10 shows this panel for **Precision one**. The panel for **Precision two** is very similar. Set C near red 1 and γ near red 2, and then use the spinner in the upper right of this panel to set your desired target MOE_{av}. This, like f, is a number of population

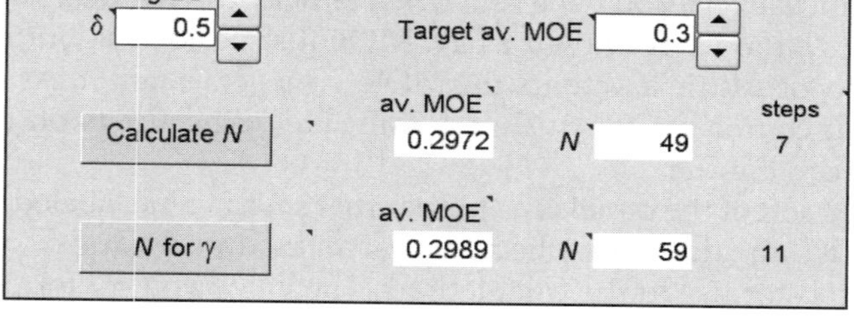

6 Calculate N, for Cohen's d

Planning ES		
δ 0.5	Target av. MOE 0.3	
	av. MOE	steps
Calculate N	0.2972 N 49	7
	av. MOE	
N for γ	0.2989 N 59	11

FIGURE 13.10
The control panel for Cohen's d from **Precision one**. In the panels above this one, as shown in Figure 13.3, $C = 95$ and $\gamma = 99$ have been set. This figure shows results for N after both buttons have been clicked.

**BOX 13.3 PRECISION AND ASSURANCE
CALCULATIONS FOR COHEN'S *d***

My calculations for *d* are partly based on the work of Kelley and Rausch (2006). The idea is that we start with a guess for *N* and use the iterative procedure also used by the **CI for d** page of **ESCI chapters 10–13** to find expected MOE_{av}. If this is larger than the target MOE_{av}, increase *N* and try again. If it's smaller, decrease *N*. Stop when *N* is the smallest that gives expected MOE_{av} that's not greater than the target. That brief version skips over some details, notably how we calculate expected MOE_{av}. But the general picture is that we need two nested iterative or successive approximation procedures, the inner one to find the expected MOE_{av} for a given *N*, and the outer one to try different values of *N* until we home in on the value we want. Finding *N* for a particular assurance complicates the picture further, but the basic idea of nested iterations still applies.

SDs, or, most often, a fraction of the population SD, which is σ. Note that *d* and δ are also expressed as a number of population SDs, so we can think of the target MOE_{av} as a number expressed on the same scale as *d* and δ. Next, click the **Calculate *N*** button to trigger calculation of the smallest *N* that gives on average in the long run MOE_{av} no larger than your target. Box 13.3 describes a little about the calculations, which require a double iteration process that may take some time, perhaps a minute or more. As ESCI labors away, you can watch as successive MOE_{av} and *N* values are shown to the right of the button. At the far right a counter reports the number of main iterative steps taken so far. If ESCI cannot complete the calculation, **No** is shown instead of a value of *N*.

Similarly, you can click the ***N* for γ** button and watch as ESCI finds *N* for the assurance level γ you have set. When either process successfully gives a value of *N*, the value shown as **av. MOE** just beside the button should be equal to, or a little less than, the MOE_{av} you set as target. As usual, see the popout comments for further details, including limits on the values that ESCI can handle.

In the top left of the panel is a spinner that sets a value labeled **Planning ES** and **δ**. It's an added complication that an assumed value of population δ is required for use in the calculations. The value you set for planning δ makes a difference, but not an enormous difference. Figure 13.10 shows that *N* values of 49 (using **Calculate *N***) and 59 (using ***N* for γ**) are needed when δ = 0.5 is the planning value, and other settings (*C*, γ, and target MOE_{av}) are as described above. Change δ to 0.2 and find the *N* values become 44 and 50. Change δ to 0.8 and the *N* values become 57 and 72.

Yes, the planning value you set for δ matters, but the N values I've just described relate to δ values ranging from small (0.2) to large (0.8), which in practice is a very wide range. The differences here in N are nothing like the dramatic differences in power that even a much smaller change in target δ gives. In practice, you usually have a rough idea of the likely δ in your research situation, and can use that as your planning value for δ. To be conservative (and get slightly larger N values), err on the high side when setting your planning δ. Of course, you can try out more than one planning δ.

The **Precision paired** page also includes a panel for Cohen's d. In Chapter 11 I described the approximation I used to calculate CIs on d for the paired design, and the limitations of its applicability. Those limitations apply here also. Our C must be 95 (set that value near red 1) and planning δ can be no larger than 2. The N we calculate for our nominated target MOE_{av} will be an approximation, but it's a reasonably accurate approximation, sufficiently accurate for practical purposes. You'll notice that there's no second button inviting you to click to carry out an assurance calculation. I haven't been able to find any published analysis of such a calculation for the paired design. So far as I'm aware, it remains an interesting problem awaiting a good solution.

The Future of Precision for Planning

I hope precision for planning will become more widely used. I regard precision and assurance calculations for planning as having great value, even though they have to date been seldom used by researchers. They offer quantitative guidance for research planning within the world of estimation, while avoiding the baggage and disadvantages of statistical power. There's a close and natural link from a planning analysis that considers target precision to the reporting of results using CIs—which tell us the precision of our findings. I would like to include published examples of researchers reporting their precision calculations to illustrate the practical usefulness of precision and assurance for planning. Unfortunately, I haven't been able to find suitable examples. It remains a somewhat pioneering exercise to use precision and assurance for planning, put please be encouraged to try. I hope the exercises at the end of this chapter help.

The *Publication Manual* (APA, 2010) acknowledges precision analysis as part of planning. It recognizes that an alternative to power calculations are "calculations based on a chosen target precision (confidence interval width) to determine sample sizes" (p. 31). It also refers to "how sample size was determined ... [based on] precision of parameter estimates" (p. 248). That's important legitimation of the approach.

I used only means and Cohen's *d* in my discussion of precision for planning. However, we could use correlations, proportions, odds ratios—or any other ES measure appropriate for our research—although considerable further statistical development is needed before we will have proven methods for all the ES measures researchers wish to use, and easily accessible software to do the work. Precision hasn't yet received sufficient attention, and assurance has received even less. I'm hoping that wider use of the new statistics will prompt rapid developments. It will be great to have convenient software to easily carry out any precision or assurance analysis we wish, to inform our research planning. Meanwhile, back on planet Earth ...

Actually, there is hope. Researchers are publishing new techniques for precision calculations for various situations, and also investigations of the accuracy and applicability of those techniques. Much of this research is labeled "accuracy in parameter estimation" (AIPE). I mentioned before the work of Kelley and Rausch (2006), which guided my calculations using *d*. More recently, Maxwell, Kelley, and Rausch (2008) reviewed AIPE and compared and contrasted the power and AIPE approaches to planning.

When using precision and assurance for planning, it may be useful to take an exploratory approach and get a feel for how N and f trade off, for various experimental designs in your research situation. In each of the ESCI pages for precision, the main figures show how N varies with target f, for means. The figures make it easy to investigate what happens for various values of f and γ, and to compare different designs. The calculations for Cohen's *d* take longer, and it's not feasible for ESCI to display curves showing how N relates to target MOE_{av}, but it can still be valuable to explore variations. Investigate how N changes as you set different values for MOE_{av}, and different values for planning δ. This may help build intuitions about experiments you could run in your own research context.

Ways to Increase Precision

In Chapter 12, I distinguished statistical power from the informativeness of an experiment. I also need to distinguish informativeness from precision. Informativeness is a very general concept, whereas precision refers specifically to the size of estimation error. The most general way to increase informativeness is to apply ingenuity and creativity—and brainstorming, consultation, deep thought, and the exploration of possibilities—to improve the match between the planned experiment and the research problems it addresses. What experiment will give us the greatest insight into the way the universe works? That's what really matters. More prosaically, increasing the precision of the estimates an experiment gives is likely, in many situations, to improve informativeness. I mentioned in Chapter 2 the call by Paul Meehl (1978) for a shift from NHST and a focus on building a more quantitative discipline of psychology. Increasing precision is likely, in many situations, to contribute to that worthy goal.

When I listen to graduate students presenting their research plans, I'm often impressed with their logic and their care to choose appropriate manipulations and experimental design. However, I'm often dismayed at their optimism that the effects they are so passionate to investigate will actually emerge. In other words, their ingenuity has often identified experiments that potentially are highly informative, but which lack precision, and therefore risk being uninformative. The problem is not confined to students—witness the continuing evidence that much published research typically has low power (Maxwell, 2004).

A vital part of any research planning is repeated brainstorming about how to increase informativeness. Usually, some of that effort should be devoted to improving precision, and it's this aspect I'll focus on here. Gather colleagues or fellow students, and spend time trying to find ways to increase precision. Here are a few suggestions:

- Consider a more sensitive design. Matching? Repeated measures?
- Can you increase ρ in a paired design, perhaps by better matching?
- Increase sample sizes.
- Reduce error of measurement. Consider measuring more than once and averaging.
- Find better measures, likely to have higher reliability and validity.
- Can meta-analysis usefully combine results from several of your studies, or from several outcomes of a large study?

You should be able to extend that list considerably. I'll end by repeating my main point. Calculation of precision and assurance can be a very useful part of research planning, and I hope they become widely used and appreciated. However, they should inform, not replace, careful thought, creativity, ingenuity, and judgment about what experiment is likely to be most informative in your research situation.

It's time again for take-home messages. I started this chapter by defining precision as CI arm length. Precision is better than power. Turn around the formula for a CI and we can calculate N likely to give a particular target precision. Three experimental designs, and three precision pages in ESCI. Assurance as well as precision. Cohen's d. How to increase precision, and what's really important.

Exercises

13.1 Revisit some discussions of CIs, or figures of CIs, in earlier chapters, and recast the discussion, or describe the pictures, in terms of precision.

13.2 Scan any other statistics textbook you are using for any mention of precision. Does it arise as a concept, even by some other name, in connection with calculating or reporting CIs? In connection with interpreting CIs? As part of research planning? In any other way?

13.3 If you, or some friends or colleagues of yours, have knowledge about physics, chemistry, engineering, or some other technical discipline, investigate what's meant in that discipline when you see a measurement reported as, for example, 18.5±0.1. What's meant by the "±0.1" value, and how is it defined and measured? Is there any link to precision as I use the term?

13.4 Could we have a "dance of the precision values"? If so, what use might it have, and how would it relate to the various other dances we've encountered?

13.5 Refer back to Exercise 12.1. In that situation, suppose you would like to achieve precision of MOE = 0.2 scale units, using z. What N would you need? Using t, what N would give you expected precision of that target value? What N would you need to have 90% assurance of obtaining that target precision?

13.6 Refer back to Exercise 12.2. In that situation, what N would you need to achieve precision of MOE = 0.1, using z? Using t, if that's to be the expected precision? With 99% assurance?

13.7 Refer back to Exercise 12.3. Carry out a precision and assurance analysis, and discuss.

13.8 Refer back to Exercise 12.5. Carry out a precision and assurance analysis, and discuss.

13.9 Refer back to Exercise 12.7. Do the comparable things for precision.

13.10 Refer back to Exercise 12.8. Choose a few benchmark cases of N and precision to remember.

13.11 Refer back to Exercise 12.9. Do the comparable things for precision.

13.12 If you are using any other statistics textbook, try to find some worked examples or exercises for which the ESCI precision pages are relevant. Compare the answers given by ESCI and that textbook.

13.13 In your own discipline, try to find in journal articles some use, or even mention, of precision. Compare with the discussion in this chapter.

13.14 Extend the bullet point list of ways to increase precision that I gave near the end of this chapter.

13.15 Revisit your take-home messages. Improve them and extend the list if you can.

Polya

Take-Home Messages

- Precision is measured by the arm length of a CI and is referred to as MOE, the margin of error. For asymmetric CIs we use MOE_{av}, which is the average of the two arm lengths of the CI. MOE varies with C, the level of confidence of the CI.

- Precision is the largest likely error of estimation, as indicated by MOE.

- Watch out for ambiguous language: High or large precision is indicated by short or small MOE, and low or poor precision by a long or wide CI.

- Adopting estimation, and reporting and interpreting CIs means that precision is being reported. Any CI can be interpreted in terms of precision—its arm length—as Interpretation 3 of CIs states. This can often be a valuable approach.

- For planning, precision is better than power and avoids any need to invoke NHST or specify α and null and alternative hypotheses. There is a strong correspondence between the target MOE used in planning and MOE of the CI calculated from data. Similar knowledgeable judgment is needed to set target MOE and, later, to interpret the obtained CI.

- Precision can have a valuable role in research planning. Turn around the formula for a CI, and calculate what N is required to achieve a CI that's not too long.

- If z is the test statistic, we can calculate N to achieve a target MOE. When using t, MOE varies with replication and so we calculate N to achieve a target expected MOE, meaning the average MOE given by an indefinitely large number of replications.

- When using t, we can also calculate N so there's a $\gamma\%$ chance that MOE is no more than a specified target MOE. Then γ is the assurance, and we may choose $\gamma = 99$, for example.

- The pages **Precision one**, **Precision two**, and **Precision paired** of **ESCI chapters 10–13** show, for those three designs, the relation between N and target MOE, which is expressed as f standard deviation units. *Take-home picture*: Three curves of N plotted against target MOE, for z, t, and assurance, as in Figure 13.9.

- Using Cohen's d as the ES, those ESCI pages can carry out precision calculations and assurance calculations for the single-group and two-independent-groups designs. For the paired design, an approximation must be used to calculate CIs on d, and only limited precision calculations can be carried out.

- Precision has so far been little used by researchers for planning, but has great potential. Further developments are needed in techniques, software, and practical guidance for researchers.

- A fundamental aim of research planning is to increase the informativeness of experiments. Increasing their precision can often contribute. Achieving higher precision is often worth great attention and effort.

14

Correlations, Proportions, and Further Effect Size Measures

In earlier chapters, means and Cohen's *d* are almost the only ESs I've discussed. Here I'll go further and consider other measures we can use for the point estimates we want. Correlations and proportions are the main focus, and then I'll briefly mention some other ESs. As usual, I'll emphasize variation with replication, and the value of CIs. Here's the agenda:

- Pictures of correlations
- CIs on Pearson's *r*
- CIs on *r*, and replication
- Comparing two correlations
- The **ESCI Effect sizes** software for effect sizes and CIs
- Proportions and their CIs
- Further effect size measures

Correlation Measured by Pearson's *r*

Suppose you read, for a group of $N = 50$ children, that the correlation between reading scores at age 6 and scores 3 years later was $r = .56$. That's Pearson's *r*, which measures the linear component of the relationship between two variables, tradi-
tionally labeled *X* and *Y*. In our case, *X* and *Y* are the two reading scores. Correlation *r* is a units-free measure, which means simply that it has no units of measurement. It can range between –1 and 1. I'm not going to attempt a full introduction to *r*, with formulas, but will focus on pictures and CIs. As usual, I'm interested in intuitions about the extent of sampling variability, and the insights CIs can give. Correlation *r* is worth our attention because it's so widely used, is interestingly different from means, and is a favored ES for meta-analysis.

> Pearson's *r* is a widely used, units-free measure of *correlation* between *X* and *Y*. It ranges from –1 to 1.

Pictures of Correlations

First some pictures. The scatterplot is a simple graph of Y against X, in our case reading score at age 9 against score at age 6. We have N individuals or items, and each contributes an (X, Y) data pair that appears as one of the N dots in the plot. Figures 14.1 and 14.2 present examples. Scatterplots can be wonderfully revealing pictures of the relations between variables; I recommend using them often. Most textbooks that discuss correlation include scatterplots to illustrate values of r. Unfortunately, these are often stylized diagrams in which dots are carefully arranged into a neat tilted oval shape. Reality is virtually always more messy, more like the haphazard-looking scatters of dots in Figures 14.1 and 14.2.

Inspect the three scatterplots in Figure 14.1 and estimate the correlations they illustrate. How strong is each relation between X and Y? Do the same for the three plots in Figure 14.2. Write down your guesses before reading on.

For a little suspense before giving the answers, I'll describe the ESCI page I used to prepare those figures. It's **See r** in **ESCI chapters 14–15**, and Figure 14.3 shows part of its control area. The idea is that you specify at red 1

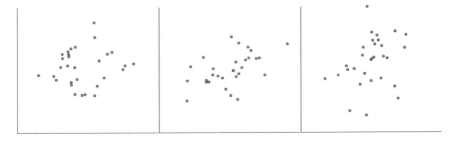

FIGURE 14.1
Three scatterplots, each with N = 30. Each is the plot of Y against X for 30 individuals, represented by 30 dots. What are the r values?

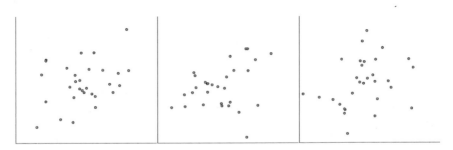

FIGURE 14.2
Another three scatterplots, each with N = 30. What are the r values?

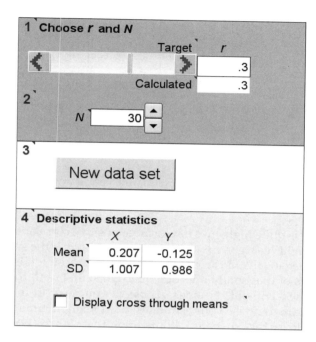

FIGURE 14.3
Part of the control area of the **See r** page in **ESCI chapters 14–15**.

an *r* value that you wish to see illustrated in a scatterplot, and at red 2 a value of *N*. Click the **New data set** button at red 3 and ESCI generates a data set of *N* points for which *r* equals your target *r*, and displays it as a scatterplot.

ESCI generates the data sets from a population having a standard bivariate normal distribution. That's a distribution whose properties include the following: Both *X* and *Y* are normally distributed, the means of *X* and *Y* are zero, and the SDs of *X* and *Y* are 1. We can therefore think of the *X* and *Y* values as being *z* scores. As Figure 14.3 illustrates, ESCI reports at red 4 the mean and SD of *X* and *Y* for the current sample. We expect the means to be around 0 and the SDs around 1, because these are the population values. You may care to fire up **See r** and experiment with various *r* values, then perhaps revise your estimates for the scatterplots in Figures 14.1 and 14.2.

Figure 14.3 shows near red 4 a checkbox labeled **Display cross through means**. Click to see lines that divide the scatterplot into four quadrants. Figure 14.4 shows the three plots of Figure 14.1 with such lines. The lines go through the mean of *X* and mean of *Y* for the current sample. We can use the lines to roughly estimate the number of points in the top right and bottom left quadrants, and note how that compares with the number in the top left and bottom right quadrants. If the first total is much higher than

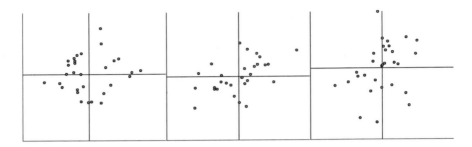

FIGURE 14.4
The same three scatterplots shown in Figure 14.1, with lines drawn through the mean of X and mean of Y to divide the scatterplot into four quadrants.

the second, r is quite high—we have a large positive correlation. If the first total is only a little larger, r is small but still positive. If the second total is higher, r is negative. You can practice estimating those totals of points in the two pairs of diagonally opposite quadrants, first with the cross lines displayed, then without the lines visible so you need to imagine them. Would you care to revise your estimates for r one more time?

Only a little further suspense. I'll mention that Cohen (1988, pp. 79–81) suggested values of .1, .3, and .5 for small, medium, and large values of r, respectively. Note that these differ from the corresponding values of 0.2, 0.5, and 0.8 he suggested for d. In both cases Cohen's reference values are somewhat arbitrary and in many cases won't be suitable; we must not use them as a substitute for knowledgeable judgment in the particular research situation. For r, different authors suggest quite different reference values. Hinkle, Wiersma, and Jurs (2003), for example, labeled r values above .9 as "very high positive," values between .7 and .9 as "high positive," between .5 and .7 as "moderate positive," between .3 and .5 as "low positive," and between -.3 and .3 as "little if any correlation" (p. 109). Take this set of different reference values as a warning that, for r perhaps even more than most ESs, interpretation of values must be made relative to the particular context. You could investigate in **See r** what scatterplots look like, for r = .1, .3, and .5, or any other value of your choice, and perhaps even amend once more your estimated r values for Figures 14.1 and 14.2.

Alright, no further delay. The three scatterplots in Figure 14.1 illustrate, from left to right, r values of .1, .5, and .3. They illustrate correlations that are, by Cohen's convention, respectively small, large, and medium. Figure 14.4 does the same. The middle scatterplot illustrates r = .5, but shows substantial scatter. We'd expect the scatterplot for our reading scores, with r = .56, to look something like that middle plot, although with 50 rather than 30 points. A correlation that is, in Cohen's terms, large still shows a wide range of X values at any given value of Y—or conversely a wide range of Y values at any given value of X. It may be a "large" correlation, but it's not a very close relationship between X and Y.

Figure 14.2 is different: All three scatterplots illustrate $r = .3$. The three are the plots I obtained on three clicks of the **New data set** button in the **See r** page, when I had $r = .3$ and $N = 30$ set at red 1 and 2. To my eye, the amount of variation in overall appearance from plot to plot in Figure 14.2 is considerable. I refer to such plots as *alternative clouds* for r. Simply keep clicking the **New data set** button to see further alternative cloud pictures for a single r. Note carefully that we're not watching the variation in r that's inevitable when we take successive random samples from a population with some fixed correlation ρ (Greek rho). We'll consider that later, but here we are seeing alternative dot pictures that ESCI ensures all have the same r. These vary in appearance, perhaps to a surprising extent.

Alternative clouds for r is my name for different scatterplots that all have the same value of sample r.

I find it a bit difficult to estimate r from realistic scatterplots, such as those in Figures 14.1 and 14.2, although I find the lines added in Figure 14.4 helpful. Sure, it's easy to distinguish $r = .8$ from $r = .2$, and sometimes we are dealing with correlations as large as .8 or more, but estimating values smaller than .5 can be tricky. No wonder many textbooks resort to cartoon scatterplots, in which points are tidily arranged in unrealistic neat clouds.

Here are my conclusions so far:

- At least over the range $r = .1$ to .5, Cohen's small to large correlations, it can be difficult to estimate r from a scatterplot. Adding lines as in Figure 14.4 and considering the relative numbers of dots in the two pairs of diagonally opposite quadrants can help. Usually we need to imagine such lines to help estimate r.
- Even with r as large as .5 there is very considerable scatter, so even a "large" correlation is hardly a very close relationship between X and Y. Of course, that's "large" by Cohen's reference values, but only "low" or "moderate" by those of Hinkle et al. (2003).
- For a given value of r, the scatterplot can look quite different for different samples. Figure 14.2 shows three alternative clouds for $r = .3$.

I invite you to use **See r** for your own explorations. Try large and small N. Try r values over the full range from −1 to 1. Try estimating r with and without the lines turned on.

I have one final thing to say about pictures of correlations. You can make a scatterplot and calculate r whatever the relationship between X and Y. The r of a data set is a measure of the linear component of that relationship, but the plot may suggest that's only part of the story. A departure

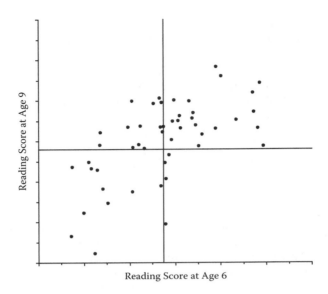

FIGURE 14.5
Invented data for $N = 50$ children showing a correlation of $r = .56$ between reading scores at age 6 and age 9. Note the almost empty lower right quadrant.

from linearity may be readily visible, especially if N is large. You should therefore always examine the scatterplot for any (X, Y) relationship you care about.

I learned that lesson many years ago when some colleagues and I were studying children learning to read. We had reading scores for a large group of children at about age 6, then again at age 9. I remember that the correlation was about .5. I'm glad to say that we printed out the scatterplot of age-9 scores against age-6 scores and made an interesting discovery: Virtually all the points fell in three quadrants, and the lower right quadrant was virtually empty. The data haven't survived, but Figure 14.5 shows the pattern: If a child at age 6 scored below the mean, then at age 9 that child might be below or above the mean—in the lower left or upper left quadrant. However, if a child scored above the mean at age 6, the child was virtually guaranteed of scoring above the mean at age 9, and thus being in the upper right quadrant. That's good news: If a child "gets it" (scores above the mean) by age 6, the child will continue to progress. They can read. If by age 6 they still don't quite get it (they score below the mean), then they may or may not get it by age 9. Few children slip considerably backwards. Our r of about .5 was unsurprising, but didn't tell the whole story. Our

Examine the scatterplot for any (X, Y) relationship you care about.

main conclusion was given not by r but by the pattern revealed by the scatterplot. It's the same old lesson again: Always plot your data in whatever ways are revealing, and think carefully about what the pictures might be telling you. Don't be blinded by calculations of r, CIs, or anything else, but use these along with pictures to seek the messages within your data.

Confidence Intervals on Pearson's r

Consider a CI on, for example, $r = .9$. Because r is bounded at -1 and 1, the CI can't be something like $.9 \pm .2$ because that extends beyond 1. The upper arm, closer to the boundary, needs to be squashed, and so we get an asymmetric CI. We might expect a less extreme value—$r = .6$, for example, would need less squashing and have a less asymmetric CI. It turns out that a good way to do the right amount of squashing and to calculate good approximate CIs for r is to use Fisher's r to z transformation. Yes, that's Sir Ronald Fisher of p value fame. Figure 14.6, from the **r to z** page of **ESCI chapters 14–15**, shows near the left a dot marking $r = .6$, with its 95% CI assuming that $N = 30$. Click the checkbox near red 4 at that page to reveal the large right panel, whose heavy curve is the Fisher r to z transformation, with r plotted vertically and z horizontally. The central part of the curve shows that, for small r, there is close to a linear relation

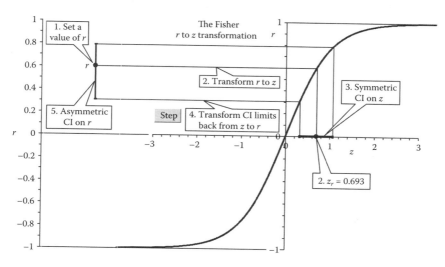

FIGURE 14.6
A figure from the **r to z** page of **ESCI chapters 14–15**. At left is a plot of $r = .6$, with its 95% CI, for $N = 30$. The heavy curve is Fisher's r to z transformation, with r plotted on the vertical axis and z on the horizontal. The horizontal and vertical lines, and the numbered callouts, show how $r = .6$ is transformed to $z_r = 0.693$, a symmetric 95% CI is calculated for z, and then the limits are transformed back to give the asymmetric 95% CI on the original r value. In the **r to z** page, click the **Step** button repeatedly to see the process illustrated step by step.

BOX 14.1 THE FISHER r TO z TRANSFORMATION AND CALCULATING A CI ON r

The Fisher r to z transformation is

$$z_r = 0.5 \times \ln\left(\frac{1+r}{1-r}\right) \tag{14.1}$$

where "ln" is the natural logarithm and I'm using z_r for the result of the transformation to reduce confusion with the critical value of z, which we need in the next equation. For these calculations we need to assume that the population is bivariate normal. Now we use the conventional formula to find a symmetric CI around z_r:

$$\left[z_r - z_{C/100} \times \frac{1}{\sqrt{N-3}} \, , \, z_r + z_{C/100} \times \frac{1}{\sqrt{N-3}} \right] \tag{14.2}$$

As usual, $z_{C/100}$ is the critical value for z, which you can get from the **Normal z t** page of ESCI (see Appendix B). Of course, $z_{.95} = 1.96$. The $(1/\sqrt{N-3})$ term is the SE of z_r. Equation (14.2) gives us z_r values for the two limits of the CI; we transform those two values back to r values using the inverse of the Fisher transformation, which is

$$r = \frac{e^{2z_r} - 1}{e^{2z_r} + 1} \tag{14.3}$$

Let's consider an example. We'll take it step by step, using the numbers in the callouts in Figure 14.6.

1. Set $r = .6$ and $N = 30$.
2. Equation (14.1) gives $z_r = 0.693$ as the transformation of $r = .6$.
3. The SE of that z_r is $(1/\sqrt{30-3}) = 0.192$, and Equation (14.2) gives $0.693 \pm 1.96 \times 0.192$, or [0.316, 1.070] as the symmetric 95% CI that's shown on the horizontal axis in Figure 14.6.
4. Equation (14.3) transforms the LL of the CI on z_r back to $r = .306$, and the UL of the CI on z_r back to $r = .790$. So the 95% CI on $r = .6$ when $N = 30$ is [.306, .790].
5. This asymmetric 95% CI around $r = .6$ appears on the left in Figure 14.6. The two limits of this are also reported near red 3 in the **r to z** page.

between r and z. The ends of the curve show that, as r approaches either of its limits, the curvature increases, with the result that extreme values of r are stretched out when transformed to the z scale. Box 14.1 gives the formulas for using the transformation and calculating a CI on r, but you can leave the donkey work to ESCI if you wish.

We use *Fisher's r to z transformation* to calculate CIs on r. The method is approximate but very good.

Click the **Step** button several times to see a step-by-step demonstration of how the CI on r is calculated. The callouts in Figure 14.6 illustrate the sequence, and their numbers correspond to the following steps:

1. Use the slider near red 1 to set $r = .6$.
2. The $r = .6$ value is carried across to the heavy curve and dropped down to the z axis, at $z_r = 0.693$. That's the transformation in action.
3. A conventional symmetric 95% CI is calculated on the horizontal z axis.
4. The transformation is applied backwards by taking the limits of the CI up to the heavy curve and horizontally back to give the two limits of the 95% CI on r that we seek.
5. See the CI on r.

The curvature of the Fisher transformation means that a symmetric CI on the z axis is transformed back to an asymmetric CI on r. Use the slider near red 1 to change r and watch the CIs. The CI on the z axis is always the same length, and symmetric, but the CI on r changes in length and the degree of asymmetry also changes, being greatest for r near -1 or 1.

Recall from Chapter 4 the cat's-eye picture of a CI in Figure 4.5. Interpretation 4 of a CI uses the cat's eye to indicate the relative likelihood of different values being the true population value. Figure 14.7 is the same as Figure 14.6, but with cat's-eye pictures shown on the CIs. The cat's eye is symmetric for the CI on the horizontal axis, but asymmetric for the CI on r to the left in the figure. At the **r to z** page, simply click near red 2 to display the cat's eye on r, and near red 4 for the cat's eye on z. The cat's eye on the asymmetric CI on r in Figure 14.7 tells us that the best bets for the population correlation ρ (yes, Greek rho, nothing to do with p) are close to r. The longer tail, especially, extends to values that are distinctly less good bets for ρ. You may elect to use the cat's eye to help interpret a CI on r, but you can, of course, use any of our six approaches to CI interpretation that are summarized in Table 5.1—choose any one or more, as seems best in the research context.

Explore the **r to z** page as you wish. Change N as well as r. Do the 95% CIs on r seem to you surprisingly wide? How large an N do you need for r to be what you regard as a reasonably precise estimate of ρ? In other

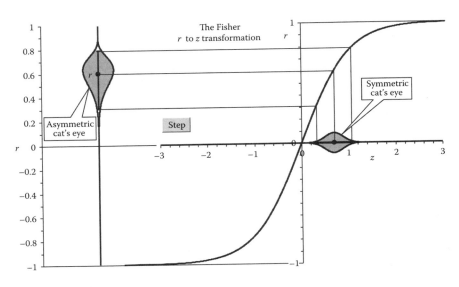

FIGURE 14.7
Same as Figure 14.6, but with cat's-eye pictures. The cat's eye is symmetric for the CI on the z axis, and asymmetric for the CI on r.

words, for the CI to be sufficiently narrow? There's more on such questions in the exercises at the end of this chapter.

Interpretation 5 of a 95% CI states that any value outside the interval can, if considered as a null hypothesis, be rejected at the .05 level. NHST can, however, be more than usually misleading when used with r. The trouble is that many researchers routinely test the null hypothesis of zero correlation in the population, in other words, H_0: $\rho = 0$ (yes, again that's rho), without considering whether that null hypothesis makes sense. Many software packages also routinely report p values, or assign asterisks to r values, assuming a zero null hypothesis. However, when, for example, we consider r as a measure of test–retest reliability, or of validity, and also in many other situations, we're interested in large values and would scarcely consider the possibility that the population value might be zero. Cohen's reference values are completely inappropriate. A reliability estimate as low as r = .6, for example, may be terrible news, and it's irrelevant and misleading even to report that it's highly statistically significantly greater than zero. Far more useful is to report a reliability estimate as r = .6, [.44, .72]—which is the 95% CI if N = 80—and to interpret those values as suggesting very poor, or at best moderate reliability, as we judge appropriate in the situation. Example 14.1 illustrates the problem.

Bruce Thompson (1997), long-time editor of *Educational and Psychological Measurement*, wrote, "I am especially troubled by researchers using statistical tests with a null hypothesis that $\rho = 0$ in validity and reliability

---

EXAMPLE 14.1 LEADERSHIP AND INTELLIGENCE IN GIFTED STUDENTS

One important use of *r* is to assess the reliability and validity of questionnaires and other scales. The best scales, including some IQ tests, can have reliability and validity around .9. Validity can be defined in various ways, an important one being convergent validity, which is the correlation of the measure of interest with another measure already known to be valid. Chan (2007) used a battery of measures to study leadership in gifted Chinese students in Hong Kong. In his discussion he stated, "Leadership giftedness as assessed by the Chinese RRSL [a self-rating scale of leadership] correlated significantly with ... (*r* = .38, *p* < .01, ...) ... the leadership subscale of the SRBCSS [a rating scale used by parents or teachers] ... suggesting that the Chinese RRSL has convergent validity when compared with Chinese SRBCSS leadership scores" (p. 160).

Such a low correlation, around .4, would usually be considered poor evidence for validity. The *N* was 92, so the 95% CI on *r* = .38 is [.19, .54] and so the validity correlation could plausibly have been as low as .2. Perhaps it was the low *p* value that misled Chan (2007) to speak of the result as suggesting convergent validity? Yes, *r* was statistically significantly greater than zero, but was still small. As usual, it would have been much better to report *r* with its CI, and then interpret the point and interval estimates with no reference to the *p* value.

---

studies in which hugely non-zero population effects are expected and demanded" (p. 30). He refused to publish *p* values that tested reliability or validity estimates against zero. Nonsensical null hypotheses seem particularly attracted to *r*, although they can pop up anywhere. Whenever you see a *p* value or statement about statistical significance, automatically think of what null hypothesis is being tested and consider whether it makes sense. Be skeptical of any *p* value, but be especially skeptical of any *p* reported with an *r* value.

CIs on *r*, and Replication

Figure 14.2 illustrates alternative clouds that all have exactly the same *r*. Now for a quite different issue: I want to investigate the sampling variability of *r*, meaning the way *r* varies when we take repeated samples from a population with correlation ρ. I'll use the ESCI page **Sample r** and

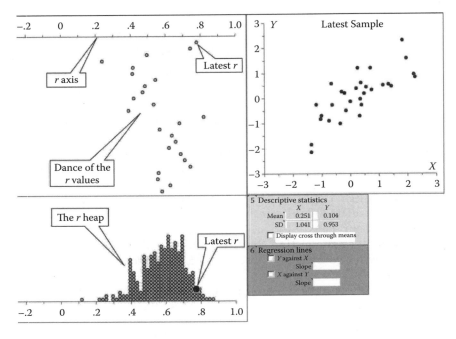

FIGURE 14.8
A part screen image from the **Sample r** page of **ESCI chapters 14–15**. So far, 273 independent random samples of size $N = 30$ have been taken from a standard bivariate normal population whose correlation is $\rho = .6$. The r heap at the bottom shows the 273 r values. The dance of the r values above shows the most recent 25 r values. The latest sample has $r = .78$, which is the top dot in the dance and the large dot in the r heap. This sample is illustrated in the scatterplot at upper right.

The *dance of the* r *values* is my name for the sequence of different r values given by repeated sampling. The r heap is the sampling distribution of r values.

$N = 30$. Figure 14.8 came from that page and shows the *dance of the* r *values*—25 dots dancing on either side of $\rho = .6$. Below is the wide r heap, a pile of dots for all the r values for the 273 samples I've taken so far. The scatterplot at upper right in the figure illustrates the latest sample, for which $r = .78$. The dance is drunken, meaning quite wide, and the r heap has negative skew.

I took a few more samples, then clicked near red 3 to display 95% CIs on the r values in the dance, and at red 4 to mark population ρ with a vertical line at .6 and to mark capture of ρ by the CIs. Figure 14.9 shows the result. The CIs are all asymmetric, as we expect for CIs on r, and they vary greatly in width because r varies so much. In the dance, open circles mark two recent CIs that do not capture ρ and, in the heap, open circles mark values of r in the tails whose CIs did not capture ρ. For the latest sample, $r = .54$,

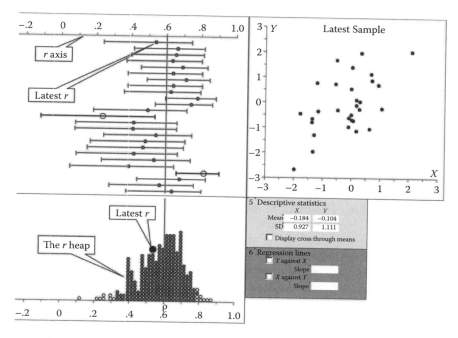

FIGURE 14.9

Same as Figure 14.8, except a further nine samples have been taken. Also, a vertical line marks the population ρ = .6, and 95% CIs are shown on each *r* in the dance. The *r* values whose CIs do not capture ρ are marked by open circles in the dance and in the *r* heap below. The latest sample has *r* = .54, as illustrated by the top dot in the dance and the heavy dot in the heap. This sample is displayed in the scatterplot.

as marked by the top dot in the dance and the large dot in the heap. This sample is displayed in the scatterplot.

   Click to take further samples and watch the great variation in *r*, the CIs, and the scatterplots. I refer to the sequence of scatterplots as the *dance of the r clouds*. Watch the dance of the *r* values, and see the *r* heap build. Explore what happens for different values of *N* and ρ. **Sample r** may remind you of what we found with **CIjumping** in Chapter 3: Sampling variation is often large and the dances wide. Both here with *r* and in Chapter 3 with means, smaller *N* gives larger sampling variability and larger *N* gives dances that are less wide. The main difference here is that the bounds of –1 and 1 on *r* mean that CIs vary in length and are asymmetric, and the *r* heap is skewed.

> The *dance of the* r *clouds* is my name for the sequence of different scatterplots given by repeated sampling.

   In Chapter 3, with means and 95% CIs, after a very long series of samples, very close to 95% of the CIs capture μ. Here, with *r*, our method for calculating CIs on *r* is approximate, so the long-run percentage of CIs capturing ρ may differ a little from 95%, especially for very small *N*. For *N* of 30 or more, long-run capture is almost always between 94% and 95.5%, but for *N* = 10 the long-run capture is around 91%.

The **Sample r** page illustrates the sampling variability of *r*. In Chapter 9 I explained that sample statistics often reflect measurement error as well as sampling variability. It can be especially important to consider measurement error when using *r*, because *r* is so often used with data from questionnaires or other tests that have less than perfect reliability. Any correlation involving scores from such a test is *attenuated*—which simply means reduced—by measurement error. The lower the reliability is, the greater the reduction in our observed *r* value. If we have an estimated reliability for the test, we can calculate an *unattenuated* value for *r*—which is a larger value of *r* obtained after removing the estimated influence of measurement error. Borenstein et al. (2009, pp. 342–344) explain how to carry out such calculations. If you are using tests with less than high reliability, you should consider an adjustment for measurement error. You should also, as I said in Chapter 9, try hard, as part of research planning, to minimize measurement error.

Comparing Two Correlations

Researchers often wish to compare two correlations. The **Two correlations** page of **ESCI chapters 14–15** does this for two independent correlations. Correlations are independent when they come from different groups of participants. Therefore, the correlation of height and weight for a group of boys and the same for a group of girls would be independent. However, if you measure the height–weight correlation in a group of children, then also assess the correlation of those same children's physical activity and eating behaviors, the correlations are not independent. If two correlations are not independent, we can't draw any conclusion from comparing them, and I know of no general way to calculate a CI on the difference. I'll consider only the case of independent correlations.

Suppose you are investigating how medical students learn to interpret X-ray images. The students score the degree of pathology indicated by each image. For a set of 30 images you calculate *r* = .2 between the scores of a beginning student and those of an expert. For another comparable set of 30 images you calculate *r* = .6 between the scores of an advanced student and those of the expert. First, you would interpret the .2 for the beginner and the .6 for the advanced student, each with their CIs, but then you may wish to compare the two. Figure 14.10 shows independent *r* values of .2 and .6, from groups of size 30, with their 95% CIs. The two intervals differ considerably in length and degree of asymmetry, even though *N* = 30 for each. The difference $(r_2 - r_1) = .4$ is plotted as the solid triangle on a floating difference axis, with its 95% CI. It's a bit tricky to calculate the

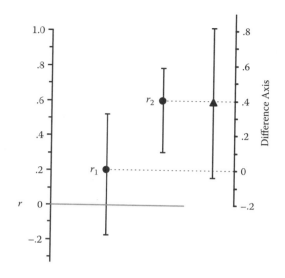

FIGURE 14.10

A figure from **Two correlations**, showing independent correlations of $r_1 = .2$ and $r_2 = .6$, with 95% CIs, when $N = 30$ for each group. The difference $(r_2 - r_1) = .4$ is plotted as the solid triangle on a floating difference axis, with its 95% CI.

CI on the difference between two r values, but ESCI uses a good approximate method described by Zou (2007). The **Two correlations** page reports near red 5 the CI on the difference to be [−.04, .82] and this is the interval shown on the right in the figure. We shouldn't be surprised that this CI is so wide, because it combines uncertainty in each of the two r values as expressed by the individual CIs.

The CI on the difference gives the best basis for comparing two correlations, but consider what that CI tells us. The limits, −.04 and .82, are *differences*, not correlations. The lower limit tells us that the two population correlations may differ by as little as about 0; perhaps both are around .4, halfway between .2 and .6? The upper limit says that the two may plausibly differ by as much as .8; perhaps they are around 0 and .8? Most likely the true difference is somewhere around the center of the CI on the difference, say, between about .2 and .6.

You may have wondered why the second advanced student rated a different set of images. To compare students, surely it's better for each to rate the same set? That's a fair point, but I had to assume different sets for the two correlations to be fully independent, meaning they are calculated for separate sets of people or objects—in this case X-ray images. That makes my example a bit unrealistic, but does emphasize the care needed to ensure that correlations are independent. Example 14.2 is a more realistic case of a comparison of two correlations.

**EXAMPLE 14.2 ASSESSING THE VALIDITY
OF A FOOD QUESTIONNAIRE**

Zou (2007) used the study of Morris, Tangney, Bienias, Evans, and Wilson (2003) to illustrate the calculation of a CI on the difference between two r values. Morris et al. assessed the validity of an eating questionnaire by correlating its scores with the results of a dietary interview. They suspected that males may be less patient in completing the questionnaire, so they compared the validity correlations in their male and female groups. Their 87 males gave a correlation of .36 and their 145 females a correlation of .49. Morris et al. reported that these correlations were not statistically significantly different. I entered $r_1 = .36$ and $N_1 = 87$, and $r_2 = .49$ and $N_2 = 145$ near red 1 in **Two correlations**. The figure showed large overlap of the two CIs, and a wide CI on the difference: That CI was reported near red 5 to be [–.09, .36]. In other words, the validity for females was greater than that for males by .13 [–.09, .36]. Had Morris et al. calculated this CI, they could have stated that the difference between male and female validities is plausibly anywhere in the wide interval [–.09, .36]—a conclusion that's more informative than their statement of no (statistically) significant difference.

The Overlap Rule for Two Independent Correlations

Yes, it's best to examine the CI on the difference, but we may only be given the two r values and their CIs, as in Figure 14.11. Fortunately, the overlap rule we discussed in Chapter 6 for 95% CIs on independent means works also for independent correlations. The rule distinguishes three situations:

A version of the overlap rule can be applied to the 95% CIs on two independent correlations.

1. If the 95% CIs on two independent r values **just touch** end to end, overlap is zero and the p value for testing the null hypothesis of no difference is approximately .01.

2. If there's a **gap** between the two CIs, meaning no overlap, then $p < .01$.

3. **Moderate overlap** (see the following) of the two CIs implies that p is approximately .05. Less overlap means that $p < .05$.

Moderate overlap is overlap of about half the average length of the overlapping arms. In Figure 14.11, the overlapping arms are the upper arm

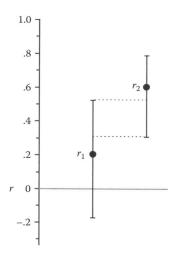

FIGURE 14.11
The same independent correlations shown in Figure 14.10, but here the difference axis is not displayed and the overlap of the two CIs is marked.

of the left CI, and lower arm of the right CI. That figure, from **Two correlations**, shows overlap for our example r values to be a bit larger than moderate. We therefore expect p to be a bit larger than .05, and it is: ESCI reports $p = .072$ near red 4. That p value, a little larger than .05, is also consistent with the CI on the difference extending just past zero on the difference axis, as in Figure 14.10.

In Cumming (2009) I reported evidence that this rule is reasonably accurate when both group sizes are about 30 or more, and the arm ratio (the length of the longer overlapping arm divided by the length of the shorter) is no more than about 2. In other words, the rule requires overlapping arms that don't differ in length by more than a factor of about 2.

ESCI Software for Effect Sizes and CIs

The **ESCI Effect sizes** module provides calculation and graphing of CIs for a range of ESs. At the **Correlations** page you can enter up to 10 r values, each with its N, and see information about the CIs and a figure displaying the correlations with their CIs. Figure 14.12 shows an example. At red 2 I typed in r and N values, then ESCI reported for each 95% CI the limits, arm lengths, and measure of precision MOE_{av}. Figure 14.13 shows the figure. The values I chose illustrate a few interesting points about CIs on r:

2	Input		3	CI limits		4	CI bars		
	r	N		LL	UL		Left	Right	MOE$_{av}$
1	-.9	30		-.952	-.799		.052	.101	.076
2	.9	30		.799	.952		.101	.052	.076
3	.6	30		.306	.79		.294	.19	.242
4	.3	30		-.068	.596		.368	.296	.332
5	0	30		-.36	.36		.36	.36	.36
6	-.9	120		-.929	-.859		.029	.041	.035
7	.9	120		.859	.929		.041	.029	.035
8	.6	120		.471	.704		.129	.104	.116
9	.3	120		.128	.455		.172	.155	.164
10	0	120		-.179	.179		.179	.179	.179

FIGURE 14.12
A part screen image from the **Correlations** page of **ESCI Effect sizes**. Enter r and N values at red 2 and see information about the 95% CIs on those correlations.

- Correlations 1 and 2 (also 6 and 7) show that the CIs on r and $-r$ are mirror images.
- Correlations 2, 3, 4, and 5 (also 7, 8, 9, and 10) show how interval length varies with r, while N remains constant. The CI is much shorter for r close to -1 or 1, meaning a very strong correlation. Also, the extent of asymmetry varies with r: CIs are symmetric when $r = 0$, and have increasing asymmetry as r becomes closer to -1 or 1.
- Comparing CIs for a fixed r, with $N = 30$ and $N = 120$ (e.g., correlations 2 and 7), shows that when N is four times as large, the CI is shorter by a factor of roughly $\sqrt{N} = 2$. This is as we'd expect from Chapter 3, although here the relationship is only approximate.

The **Diff correlations** page of **ESCI Effect sizes** allows you to enter up to 10 pairs of independent correlations, r_1 and r_2, each with its N, and see information about the CIs on the $(r_2 - r_1)$ differences and a figure displaying those differences and CIs. I'll leave you to explore that page and the other pages of **ESCI Effect sizes**, which include pages for single means, paired data, and means for two independent groups. In every case ESCI calculates and reports CIs, and also displays in a figure up to 10 ESs with their CIs.

Now, having spent all of this chapter so far discussing correlations, I'll turn to other effect size measures. First come proportions, then measures of risk.

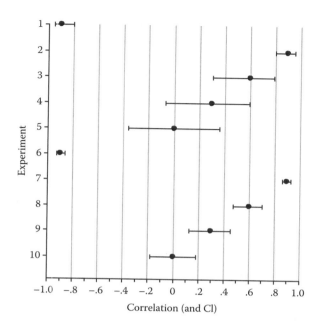

FIGURE 14.13
The figure from the **Correlations** page that displays the correlations and 95% CIs reported in Figure 14.12.

Proportions and Their CIs

If five eggs in a package of a dozen are broken, the proportion broken is simply 5/12 = .42. A proportion is such a fraction, or ratio of two integers, let's say x/N, where N is the total number of things we're considering (12 eggs), and x is the number having some property of interest—five are broken. So x takes some value between 0 and N, and the proportion lies between 0 and 1. The N in the denominator must refer to separate, discrete things—such as eggs.

> A *proportion* is the fraction of a number of discrete things that have a property of interest. It lies between 0 and 1.

   Proportions are another widely used ES that, like correlations, are bounded, but note the difference: Correlations lie between –1 and 1, but proportions between 0 and 1. **ESCI Effect sizes** has two pages for proportions: **Proportions** and **Diff proportions**. At the **Proportions** page you enter up to 10 x and N values, then ESCI calculates proportions as $P = x/N$. Figure 14.14 shows an example. At red 2 I typed in x and N values,

2	Input		3 Proportion	4 CI limits		5 CI bars		
	x	N	P	LL	UL	Left	Right	MOE$_{av}$
1	0	7	0	0	.354	0	.354	.177
2	0	28	0	0	.121	0	.121	.06
3	28	28	1.0	.879	1.0	.121	.0	.06
4	6	7	.857	.487	.974	.37	.117	.244
5	1	7	.143	.026	.513	.117	.37	.244
6	4	28	.143	.057	.315	.086	.172	.129
7	16	112	.143	.09	.22	.053	.077	.065
8	3	7	.429	.158	.75	.27	.321	.296
9	12	28	.429	.265	.609	.163	.181	.172
10	48	112	.429	.341	.521	.088	.093	.09

FIGURE 14.14

An image from the **Proportions** page of **ESCI Effect sizes**. Enter x and N values at red 2 and see the proportions $P = x/N$, and information about the 95% CIs on those proportions.

then ESCI reported the proportions and information about the 95% CIs. Figure 14.15 shows the figure.

You may be familiar with using the normal approximation to the binomial distribution to carry out NHST for proportions and to calculate CIs. That approach is reasonable if N is very large and P is not close to 0 or 1. ESCI, however, uses the method recommended by Newcombe and Altman (2000), which gives good approximate CIs on proportions even when N is small and/or P is close to, or even equal to, 0 or 1. To calculate CIs using either method we need to assume that the N things we're considering are separate or independent.

Are proportions the same as percentages? Well, any proportion can be expressed as a percentage, so I can say 42% of the eggs are broken, but not every percentage is a proportion. I can say it rained 18% of the time yesterday, but that refers to time as a continuous variable. I can't express the 18% as a proportion, with the definition we're using here, because that definition is a ratio with, in the denominator, N discrete things: items, people, events—or eggs. I could measure time to the nearest minute, and say that yesterday it rained for 130/720 of the minutes between 8 a.m. and 8 p.m. Even then, however, I don't have a proportion, as I'm defining it here, because the 720 minutes in the denominator are not separate, independent things.

The example in Figures 14.14 and 14.15 illustrates some interesting points about CIs on proportions:

- Proportions 1, 2, and 3 are examples of CIs when $P = 0$ or 1.
- Proportions 2 and 3 (also 4 and 5) show that CIs on P and $(1 - P)$ are mirror images.

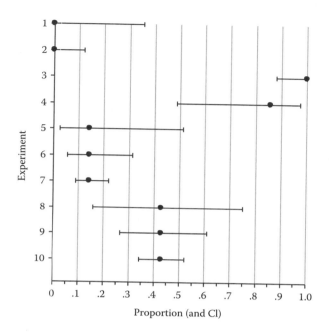

FIGURE 14.15
The figure from the **Proportions** page that displays the proportions and 95% CIs reported in Figure 14.14.

- Proportions 1, 5, and 8 show how interval length varies with *P*, for a fixed *N*. The CI is shorter for *P* close to 0 or 1. Also, the extent of asymmetry varies with *P*: There's greater asymmetry when *P* is closer to 0 or 1.

- Proportions 5, 6, and 7 suggest that, for a fixed *P*, when *N* increases by a factor of 4 the interval becomes shorter by a factor of roughly 2, as we'd expect. However, proportions 1 and 2, and also proportions 8, 9, and 10 show that this relation doesn't hold generally. Yes, larger *N* gives shorter intervals, but the relation doesn't follow a simple rule.

The Overlap Rule for Two Independent Proportions

You are probably seeing many parallels between proportions and correlations. Yes indeed. I'll leave it to you to imagine a sampling page for proportions, like **Sample r** for correlations. Given the parallels, it's not surprising that the overlap rule works for proportions—consider, for example, the CI overlap for proportions 4 and 5 in Figure 14.15. The rule requires the proportions to be independent, meaning

A version of the overlap rule can be applied to the 95% CIs on two independent proportions.

that, for proportions x_1/N_1 and x_2/N_2, the N_1 and N_2 must refer to different sets of things. The rule distinguishes three situations:

1. If the 95% CIs on two independent proportions **just touch** end to end, overlap is zero and the p value for testing the null hypothesis of no difference is approximately .01.
2. If there's a **gap** between the two CIs, meaning no overlap, then $p < .01$.
3. **Moderate overlap** (see the following) of the two CIs implies that p is approximately .05. Less overlap means that $p < .05$. (So $p < .05$ for proportions 4 and 5 in Figure 14.15.)

Moderate overlap is overlap of about half the average length of the overlapping arms. In Cumming (2009) I reported evidence that this rule is reasonably accurate when the arm ratio (the length of the longer overlapping arm divided by the length of the shorter) is no more than about 2. In other words, the rule requires overlapping arms that don't differ in length by more than a factor of about 2. We can, however, use the rule even for very low N, for proportions like 1/2 or 0/3. There's no minimum N for the overlap rule for proportions, whereas for correlations we needed N to be at least around 30.

You could apply the rule to any pair of CIs in Figure 14.15, if the proportions are independent. Proportions 6 and 9, for example, overlap a little less than half the average of the overlapping arms, so I'd estimate a p value of a little less than .05.

The **Diff proportions** page allows you to enter pairs of proportions and see information about the CI on the $(P_2 - P_1) = (x_2/N_2 - x_1/N_1)$ difference. To check the comparison of proportions 6 and 9 I just referred to, type $x_1 = 4$ and $N_1 = 28$ for the first proportion into the first yellow panel near red 3, and $x_2 = 12$ and $N_2 = 28$ into the second yellow panel. ESCI reports the proportions as $P_1 = .143$ and $P_2 = .429$, and the difference as $(P_2 - P_1) = .286$. The 95% CI on the difference is [.048, .486], which easily misses zero, so we know that the p value for the difference is less than .05, as the overlap rule suggested.

Further Effect Size Measures

There are numerous further ESs I could discuss, but I'll mention only a few measures used to express risk, or differences in risk. The main message is that choice of ES can make a crucial difference in how readers understand results. I'll be brief, and won't even discuss CIs. I will, however, mention some good sources of further ES advice.

Suppose the risk that a woman over 40 will die of breast cancer is about 0.4%. This value can be stated in at least three ways, using three different ES measures for risk:

1. The probability of death is about .004.
2. The chance of death is about 0.4%.
3. On average, about four in 1,000 women over 40 will die of breast cancer.

Now suppose that mass screening mammography reduces the risk so that, among women over 40 who participate in the screening, we can say that

- The probability of death is about .003.
- The chance of death is about 0.3%.
- On average, about three in 1,000 participating women will die of breast cancer.

If we focus on the reduction in risk we could say that

- Mass screening reduces the probability of death from .004 to .003.
- Mass screening reduces the chance of death from 0.4% to 0.3%.
- Mass screening reduces the number of deaths from about four to about three in 1,000.
- There is a 25% reduction in risk.
- The *risk ratio* is .75. (The risk ratio is the new risk divided by the old risk.)

All those statements are reasonable, consistent with each other, and typical of statements about risk that appear in mass media and also in medical journals. There is clear evidence, however, that they are not all accurately understood by people in general, or even by many medical practitioners, although some are understood better than others. I'll illustrate with a story told by Gerd Gigerenzer (Gigerenzer, Gaissmaier, Kurz-Milcke, Schwartz, & Woloshin, 2007, pp. 54–55). In Chapter 2 I referred to Gigerenzer as a critic of NHST. He also leads research on the best ways to present information about risk.

Gigerenzer recounts that, in 1995, news media in Britain reported evidence that taking third-generation contraceptive pills increases the risk of a dangerous type of blood clot by 100% over the risk when taking other contraceptive pills. This news led to panic, and many women stopped taking the third-generation pills. As a result, unwanted pregnancies increased and there were an estimated additional 13,000 abortions. The increase in risk of the blood clots was actually from about one in 7,000 to about two in 7,000 women. Yes, that's a 100% increase in risk, but had the result been expressed in terms of one or two in 7,000, perhaps women would have reacted differently. The harm of the extra abortions probably greatly outweighed the harm of what would have been small numbers of extra blood clots expected if women had continued with the third-generation pills. However, a headline announcing a 100% increase in risk no doubt sells more newspapers than fiddly figures about so many in 7,000.

One conclusion from many studies by Gigerenzer and others is that it's usually best to report risk, and changes in risk, in terms of *natural frequencies*. Natural frequencies are simply whole numbers expressing a risk in terms of so many per hundred, or thousand, or other convenient number. Saying that risk increases from one to two in 7,000 gives a clear message that the risk is small, although not to be ignored. It also says doubling the risk gives a risk that's still small. Reporting a comparison of two risks as a percentage difference, or a risk ratio, tends to exaggerate the difference, and also the risk itself, as it did for the report of a 100% increase. There's evidence that people, including health professionals, often severely misunderstand risk reported in that way. In contrast, reporting risks and comparisons of risks in terms of natural frequencies generally gives more accurate understanding.

A risk expressed in *natural frequencies* is stated as so many per hundred, or thousand, or other convenient number.

It's usually best to express risks in terms of natural frequencies.

There's a further twist to this tale. Sedrakyan and Shih (2007) investigated how risks are expressed in medical journals. They studied 119 systematic reviews of evaluations of drug and other therapies that were published in three leading medical journals during 2004–2006. They found that 48% of the reviews did not use natural frequencies to express any of the risks they reported. That's one discouraging result. They also noted that 55% of the reviews reported information on both benefits and harms of the therapies being studied. Of these, about one third presented the probability information relating to benefits and harms using different ESs. In most cases, relative risk was used to express benefits, whereas frequencies were reported for harms. An example of benefit expressed as relative risk is a therapy reported as giving a 150% increase in the chance of a full recovery, or a relative chance of recovery of 2.5 times the chance without the therapy. By contrast, a harmful side effect might be expressed as occurring on average for 12 people in 100. Such reporting may easily give an exaggerated perception of the benefit, but a fairly accurate understanding of the risk of the harm—because that risk was expressed in natural frequencies. Even in the best journals there may be a need for improvement in the choice of ESs. Gigerenzer et al. (2007) explained much more about ways to present risk, with numerous examples.

There is much scope for interesting statistical cognition research on how risk and differences in risk should be presented for best understanding, by professionals and by the public. For example, what graphical representations are best? In the meantime, natural frequencies are usually the best choice. If you see a risk expressed as .004 or .4%, translate it in your head to 4 in 1,000. If you see a risk difference expressed as a percentage or a risk ratio, try to find the two risks being compared and translate them into natural frequencies.

My broader conclusion is that there are often a number of ES measures that a researcher can choose for the analysis and reporting of results. It's vital to choose carefully. If statistical cognition evidence is available to help guide the choice, that's great. If not, we could consider conducting cognitive research on the issue. In any case, we need to think carefully about what ES to choose, appreciating that the effectiveness of our communication with readers can be strongly influenced by the ES measure we use.

Further Information about Effect Sizes

An interesting discussion of the history of ES measures used in psychology and education is given by Huberty (2002). Kirk (1996, 2003) gives classic discussions of ESs. Altman, Machin, Bryant, and Gardner (2000) compiled a book with the beautiful title *Statistics with Confidence* that gives practical guidance on how to use many of the ESs most commonly used in medicine, and how to calculate CIs for these. It has chapters on, among others, means, medians, proportions, correlation and regression, and measures of risk. Grissom and Kim (2005) wrote an important book that gives a detailed discussion of many ESs and their CIs.

It's time for reflection on this chapter, and take-home messages. To help you write yours, recall that I started with correlations and scatterplots. I discussed CIs on *r*, the variation of *r* over replication, and the comparison of two independent correlations. **ESCI Effect sizes** provides pages for a number of ESs, including correlations and proportions, and their differences. Finally, I mentioned ESs for expressing risk and differences in risk.

Exercises

14.1 Use the **See r** page of **ESCI chapters 14–15** to explore the variation in scatterplot appearance for a fixed *r*, as illustrated in Figure 14.2. Try different values of *r* and *N*.

14.2 Use **See r** to practice estimating r from a scatterplot. Challenge a fellow learner. Does it help to display the cross lines through the means? Vary r and N.

14.3 Compare the correlation chapter in another statistics textbook with this chapter. Note any important points made here but not in the other book—or vice versa.

14.4 Use **ESCI Effect sizes** to find answers for correlation exercises in that other textbook.

14.5 Make up some typical textbook exercises about correlation, then use ESCI to solve them. Swap exercises with a fellow learner. Include comparison of independent correlations, and (of course) use of CIs. Make the exercises relevant to a research area about which you know.

14.6 Use the **r to z** page of **ESCI chapters 14–15** to explain to someone who hasn't heard of Fisher's r to z transformation what the transformation does and why we use it.

14.7 Use **r to z** to choose a few benchmarks worth remembering, preferably ones relevant to your discipline. Choose a few pairs of r and N values so that r is just statistically significantly greater than zero, and a few pairs so that the 95% CI is roughly ±.1 or ±.2.

14.8 Use the **Sample r** page of **ESCI chapters 14–15** to investigate how the dance of the r values changes for various ρ and N.

14.9 Explain the difference between alternative clouds for r, and the dance of the r clouds.

14.10 How good are our approximate CIs on r? Use **Sample r** to investigate the percentage capture of 95% CIs, for various ρ and N.

14.11 The r heap in Figure 14.9 shows negative skew. If we transformed all those r values using Fisher's r to z transformation, what's your guess of the shape of the heap?

14.12 Use the **Two correlations** page of **ESCI chapters 14–15** and the overlap rule to estimate p for various comparisons of two r values, then check against p reported near red 4. Challenge someone else.

14.13 **Two correlations** uses Fisher's r to z transformation to calculate an approximate p value for the comparison of two r values. It uses Zou's (2007) method to calculate an approximate CI on the difference. Assess how well these two methods agree. For example, choose $C = 95$ then adjust things so that the CI just touches zero on the floating difference axis. Does the reported p value equal .05?

14.14 Scan your favorite journal for articles that use *r*. Can you find any examples of a CI on *r*? Find some cases where CIs were not used, but you think they should have been.

14.15 Enter *r* and *N* values into the **Diff correlations** page of **ESCI Effect sizes**. Enter the same values into the **Two correlations** page of **ESCI chapters 14–15** and check that the CI on the difference is the same.

14.16 Adapt Exercises 14.3, 14.4, 14.5, 14.12, and 14.14 to apply to proportions rather than correlations. Use the **Proportions** and **Diff proportions** pages of **ESCI Effect sizes**.

14.17 Find the website of Gerd Gigerenzer's Max Planck Institute in Berlin and browse for results about how risk is understood and how it should best be represented. You may find at least one video of an interesting talk given by Gigerenzer.

14.18 Scan your favorite journal for examples of risk being reported. Note the ES used. If necessary, translate into natural frequencies and assess whether that's an improvement.

14.19 Watch out for media reports of recent research findings that include statements about risk, or a change in risk. Ask your friends to interpret. If necessary, translate into natural frequencies and again ask them to interpret. Any better?

14.20 What ESs not mentioned in this book are used in your discipline? Can you calculate CIs for them? Try to find a way to calculate such CIs.

14.21 If you are familiar with some other statistical software, try to find out how to calculate CIs for correlations and proportions, and their differences. Can you display these CIs?

14.22 Revisit your take-home messages. Improve them and extend the list if you can.

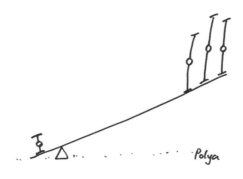

Polya

Take-Home Messages

- Pearson's correlation r is a widely used ES. It's a units-free measure that lies between –1 and 1. It measures the linear component of the relation between two variables, usually labeled X and Y. Correlation r refers to N pairs of values, each being (X, Y).

- A scatterplot is a beautiful picture of the relation between X and Y, in which each data pair is represented by a dot. For a given r value, the appearance of the scatterplot can vary considerably, as Figure 14.2 illustrates.

- Cohen suggested $r = .1, .3$, and $.5$ for small, medium, and large correlations, respectively, but other reference values have also been suggested. Interpretation of any r value is highly dependent on context.

- It can be a little difficult to estimate r by inspection of a scatterplot, although imagining lines that divide the display into quadrants can help. Compare the numbers of points in the diagonally opposite pairs of quadrants to estimate r.

- If repeated samples of N data pairs are taken from a bivariate normal population, we get the dance of the r values, which may appear wide unless N is very large. Those r values form the r heap, which is skewed toward 0, meaning it has a longer tail closer to 0. The scatterplots for successive samples are likely to vary greatly in appearance.

- Assuming that the sample is from a bivariate normal population, we can use Fisher's r to z transformation to calculate an approximate CI on r. For given N, the CI is shorter for r closer to –1 or 1. The CI is typically asymmetric, the longer tail being closer to 0.

- If two correlations come from different groups they are independent, and we can calculate an approximate CI on the difference $(r_2 - r_1)$. Given 95% CIs on r_2 and r_1, the overlap rule gives approximate information about the p value for the difference.

- **ESCI Effect sizes** allows the calculation and display of CIs on correlations, and differences between two independent correlations. It also supports the calculation and display of CIs for a number of other ESs.

- The proportion, $P = x/N$, where x and N are integers and $0 \leq x \leq N$, is another useful ES that is bounded. It lies between 0 and 1. **ESCI Effect sizes** allows the calculation and display of CIs on proportions, and differences between two independent proportions. CIs on proportions are typically asymmetric.

- Many other ESs are used by researchers. An important class of ESs is those expressing risk, or differences in risk. In general, it's better to express risk using natural frequencies, for example, 4 in 1,000, rather than as probabilities (.004 or .4%).

- Two risks can be compared by stating both as probabilities (.004 and .003), by using a risk ratio (.003/.004 = .75), by stating the difference as a percentage (the second is 25% less than the first), or by using natural frequencies (3 rather than 4 in 1,000). In general, risk ratio and percentage difference may be poorly understood and may exaggerate the difference. Natural frequencies usually give better understanding.

- It's vital to consider carefully what ES is best for presentation of a research result, especially considering how clearly and accurately it conveys the message to readers. Statistical cognition evidence, where available, can offer valuable guidance.

15

More Complex Designs and The New Statistics in Practice

Researchers often use more than one measure and more than two conditions. Can the new statistics cope with realistically complex situations, such as factorial designs, multivariate analyses, and model fitting? That's the first question I discuss in this chapter, and my answer is "increasingly, yes, although sometimes it takes extra effort."

My second question concerns the practicalities of adopting the new statistics, given all the pressures of the modern research world. I'll discuss a number of strategies that may help.

As a unifying theme I'll use a general strategy for estimation that won't surprise you at all: Find the ES most appropriate for the research question, place a CI on it, then make a figure and interpret the ES and its CI. That's the first section:

- A four-step general strategy for estimation

The reasons for preferring the new statistics to NHST are just as strong for complex designs as they are for the simple situations we've been discussing. I've chosen a few topics to illustrate how we can gain the advantages of the new statistics more widely. I'll start with

- Analysis of variance (ANOVA) designs, especially randomized control trials (RCTs)

I'll then take a side-step and discuss

- General issues that ANOVA designs raise, including multiple testing and data exploration

Then I'll return to discuss further types of analysis:

- Model fitting
- Multivariate analyses
- Continuous data

Finally, I'll move on to my second question and discuss strategies for putting the new statistics into practice.

A General Strategy for Estimation

Grayson, Pattison, and Robins (1997) noted that "attacks on significance testing ... have largely taken place in the context of simple models with few parameters" (p. 69). Their comment largely applies to this book so far, because I've mainly discussed single samples, single correlations, and the simple two-condition designs of Chapter 6. To what extent is the new statistics beneficial for more complex designs? To address this crucial question, I'll first state explicitly a general strategy for estimation that we've used many times in earlier chapters. Here's a small example to illustrate it: In Chapter 12 we considered an experiment to compare the HEAT (Hot Earth Awareness Test) scores for groups of students from two countries. If we'd run that experiment, we could have entered the data into the **Data two** page of **ESCI chapters 5–6** and clicked near red 9 on that page to reveal a figure like Figure 15.1. This shows the two means with their CIs, and the difference between the means with its CI, displayed on a difference axis. This example

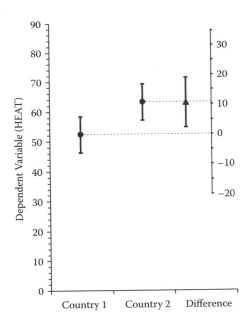

FIGURE 15.1

A figure from the **Data two** page of **ESCI chapters 5–6** showing means and 95% CIs for an imaginary experiment that compared HEAT scores for independent groups of 30 students from two countries. The solid triangle marks the difference between the means, with its 95% CI, on a floating difference axis.

illustrates our general strategy for estimation, which has the following four steps:

1. Choose one or more ESs most relevant to the research question.
2. Place CIs around those ESs.
3. Make a figure.
4. Interpret.

The ES of primary interest in our experiment is the difference between the means; and the CI on that difference, as displayed in Figure 15.1, is what we need to guide our interpretation. You may feel that this example is by now so familiar that it's not necessary here, but I've included it and the figure to emphasize that our four-step strategy often requires more than is traditionally reported: probably just the separate means, perhaps with CIs, but not the difference with its CI—which is what's crucial for interpretation.

I'm going to use the four-step strategy to suggest how estimation can be used in a range of more complex situations, starting with ANOVA designs.

ANOVA Designs: Randomized Control Trials (RCTs)

ANOVA designs are factorial designs with two or more independent variables, each of which may be a between-groups variable or a repeated measure. I'll first discuss ANOVA designs that are RCTs, because the RCT design is very widely used across medicine, psychology, and a range of other disciplines, and is often regarded as the gold standard for providing evidence to support evidence-based practice. In addition, it raises important interpretive issues because it includes both independent groups and the within-groups variable of testing time.

The upper panel of Figure 15.2 shows invented data for an RCT in which participants were randomly assigned to a Treatment group that received therapy for anxiety, or a Control group that didn't. The figure reports means and 95% CIs for anxiety test scores at four time points. At first sight, the results look encouraging for the therapy: The groups were similar at Pretest, the Control group changed little with time, and the Treatment group showed improvement that was maintained after therapy at the two follow-up measuring times.

How can we use CIs to guide interpretation? Recall the discussion in Chapter 6 about using CIs to compare means. Because our two groups are independent, we can use the CIs to compare the Treatment and Control

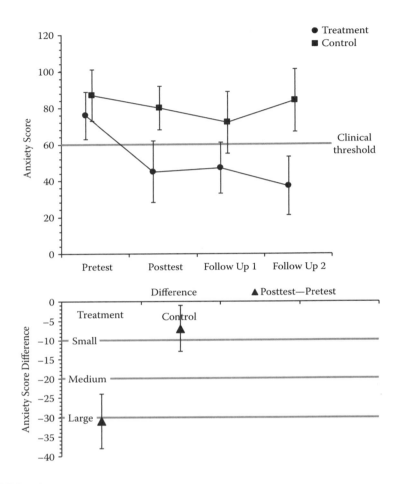

FIGURE 15.2
Data from a fictitious RCT of a therapy for anxiety. The upper panel shows invented means
and 95% CIs for two independent groups, with measures at four time points. The gray line
labeled "clinical threshold" marks a reference value. The lower panel shows for each group
the mean (Posttest–Pretest) difference with its 95% CI, and marks three reference values for
ES changes. Note that the vertical scales differ in the two panels. The figure comes from the
Figure page of **ESCI chapters 14–15**.

means at any time point. Do that first for Pretest and Posttest, and conclude that the pattern of means and CIs for the two groups support our
initial observation that the groups had comparable averages at the start,
and that at Posttest the Treatment group had scores averaging considerably lower than the Control group.

Within a group, however, the situation is different because time point
is a within-group variable, and so the four measures for a group are

correlated. Therefore, we cannot use the displayed CIs to compare, for example, the Pretest and Posttest means for a single group. For the paired design in Chapter 6 I used a floating difference axis to display the mean of the differences with its CI. An RCT is more complex and so it's better to use a separate figure, as in the lower panel of Figure 15.2, which shows the mean (Posttest–Pretest) difference, with its CI, for each group. Those CIs are appropriate for assessing the improvement in any group and for comparing the improvement of different groups. Here, as usual, we're benefiting from the repeated measure design by seeing CIs in the lower panel that are much shorter than those in the upper panel, thus indicating relatively precise estimation of changes over time. (Note that ESCI sets each vertical scale to fit the data being presented, and here the vertical scales in the two panels are different.) The lower panel shows a large and very clear difference in the average size of change in the two groups. We could similarly plot means and CIs for any other within-group comparison of interest, for example, Follow Up 1 versus Posttest.

CIs on means may be used to assess differences for independent groups, but not a repeated measure.

Knowledge of anxiety, the clinical condition under study, and the anxiety scale should guide interpretation of the results. The gray line in the upper panel at 60 marks what I'm assuming is the threshold for anxiety to be considered clinically distressing. We can conclude that both groups initially averaged above that score, and after therapy the Treatment group averaged below the threshold. Further knowledge of the scale may permit statements about the initial and final average severity of anxiety in the groups. The lower panel includes three reference values for changes in anxiety score. Reference values may reflect established conventions within a relevant body of professionals, or the clinical judgment of the researchers. I recommend using reference values, where possible, but authors need to justify and explain them. Reference

Mark reference values for ESs and ES differences in figures, if that helps interpretation.

values can guide interpretive statements. For example, inspecting the lower panel in Figure 15.2 might prompt statements such as "the average decrease in anxiety in the Control group was at most small, and quite likely negligible," and "in the Treatment group, it was between medium-large and very large."

The editors of the *British Medical Journal* describe a similar approach when they ask for interpretation of CIs: "There will always be some uncertainty … Using wording such as 'our results are compatible with a decrease of this much or an increase of this much' … is more accurate and helpful to readers than 'there was no effect …'" (tinyurl.com/bmjcis).

As well as interpreting the figure showing means and CIs, we should examine individual data, perhaps by including dot plots in the figure, as in Figures 6.6 and 6.9. We could also use additional ES measures, for example, a count of the number of participants in each group who meet diagnostic criteria for clinical anxiety or severe clinical anxiety, and then examine how those numbers change with therapy.

A traditional analysis would probably apply an omnibus ANOVA model to the data in the upper panel of Figure 15.2. Interpretation would be in terms of the interaction between group and time, perhaps with post hoc tests to examine components of the interaction, despite such tests probably having low power. The hope would be that the analysis shows comparability of the groups at Pretest and a statistically significantly lower score for the Treatment group at the other time points. However, "the problem is that omnibus tests ... do not usually tell us anything we really want to know" (Rosenthal, Rosnow, & Rubin, 2000, p. x). I expect that our estimation approach based on Figure 15.2 would be more informative.

Box 15.1 describes evidence that published reports of RCTs, at least in psychiatry and psychology, often provide only incomplete information. Fidler, Faulkner, and Cumming (2008) described guidelines for reporting RCTs that we developed partly in response to that evidence. The guidelines start with examination of the main patterns in the data, then preparation of figures to show means and CIs. We explained how to use the statistical software SPSS or Excel to produce relevant figures. We considered moderators and then integration of our results into a meta-analysis. Our aim was to use the new statistics to give researchers and practitioners what they say they want from RCTs, including especially an estimate of the size of the effect, which is highly relevant for evidence-based practice. Rather than repeat what we included in that book chapter, I'll now describe what ESCI offers.

ESCI for the Analysis of ANOVA Designs

Figure 15.2 comes from the **Figure** page of **ESCI chapters 14–15**. Figure 15.3 shows part of the control area of that page and part of the data displayed in Figure 15.2. The page can display up to four data series, each with up to four points. You type in labels for the data series and the points, so Figure 15.3 shows the labels "Treatment" and "Control" for Series 1 and 2, and "Pretest," etc., for Points 1, 2, and 3. Checkboxes at the left indicate that Series 1 and 2, but not 3, are being displayed. Values of the means are entered in the columns labeled **Mean**, and MOEs in the columns labeled **Bars**. For every case in Figure 15.3 the lower cell for **Bars**, labeled "–", is blank, which prompts ESCI to use the same value for both upper and lower arms of the CI. As usual, popout comments give full explanations.

At the top in Figure 15.3 are checkboxes for each point. If exactly two of those four checkboxes are checked, then **Figure** displays the difference between the means for those two points, for each series selected for display.

BOX 15.1 WHAT RESEARCHERS WANT FROM RCTs

For her dissertation in clinical psychology, Cathy Faulkner examined how published RCTs were analyzed (Faulkner, Fidler, & Cumming, 2008). She located 193 reports of RCTs of psychological therapies published in prominent psychiatry and psychology journals during 1999–2003. She found that 99% of her reports used NHST for analysis and interpretation, and only 31% reported any CIs. Worse, only 2% of articles made any use of CIs for interpretation. That's a common finding, even in medicine: Even if CIs are reported, they are very often ignored and not used to inform interpretation, which is largely based on NHST. In a second study, she surveyed the authors of her RCT articles by email, to ask them what information they most wished to know when they read a report of an RCT. They told her they wished to know (a) whether there is an effect, (b) how large the effect is, and (c) to what extent the effect is clinically important. They rated all three as very important. Faulkner made the reasonable assumption that practicing psychologists are likely to have similar preferences. She contrasted these preferences with what the RCT articles provided: They focused on NHST to answer (a) and, in many but not all cases, they included discussion about (c). CIs and discussion to address (b) were largely missing. She concluded that reports of RCTs often don't provide the information that practitioners say they want.

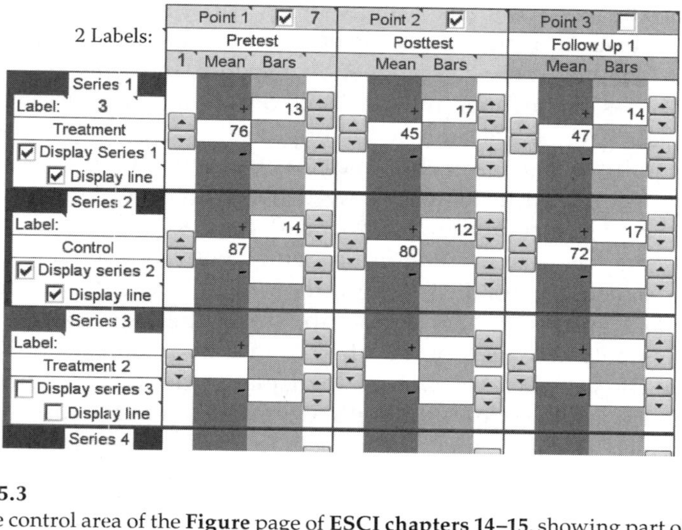

FIGURE 15.3
Part of the control area of the **Figure** page of **ESCI chapters 14–15**, showing part of the data displayed in Figure 15.2. **Figure** displays data for up to four data series, each with up to four points. To enter data, use the spinners or type in values.

In Figure 15.3, only Points 1 and 2 are checked, so the mean (Posttest–Pretest) difference is displayed for the Treatment and Control series, as in the lower panel of Figure 15.2. You need to enter the MOEs for the CIs on the differences. Because the four points within a series are assumed correlated, ESCI can calculate the differences but not the CIs. Enter those MOEs in the **Bars** column below red 8, not shown in Figure 15.3. Also not shown are the areas at red 6 and red 9 where you type in your labels and specify the values to use as reference values, if you wish these to be displayed. Figure 15.2 shows example reference values, marked by gray lines: "Clinical threshold" at 60 in the upper panel and the three values for changes in anxiety score in the lower panel.

Using CIs to compare means and evaluate differences can be a good way to interpret RCTs.

In Figure 15.2 the means for Treatment and Control, for each of the four points, are slightly offset horizontally, so CIs can be easily seen even if they overlap. Use the spinner at red 5 to adjust the amount of horizontal offset. Being able to offset means so all error bars are clearly visible is a crucial feature of any graphical software for the new statistics. Many standard statistical packages cannot yet do this, but let's hope they soon will.

Figure has spinners beside the data cells, as Figure 15.3 shows. These provide values between 0 and 200, and allow you to easily explore changes in the figures by adjusting means and CIs. Alternatively, simply type in your values, whether or not they lie within that range.

The general approach I've described for the analysis of RCTs can be applied to the more complex designs **Figure** can display—up to four data series—and beyond, but always keep in mind the distinction we discussed in Chapter 6 between independent groups and repeated measures. As we discussed above for an RCT, if the different data series come from independent groups, we can use the upper-panel CIs to compare groups at a time point. When, as is often the case, the points within a data series represent a repeated measure, we need the differences and their CIs in the lower panel to compare results at different points. You can also use **Figure** to display data for a design in which both independent variables vary across groups. For this design, the points in each series represent independent groups and we can use the CIs in the upper panel to assess differences between any points, whether in the same or different series. In **Figure** you can click below red 3 to display or not display lines joining the means in a data series. I think it's a good convention to use such lines for a repeated measure, and to omit them for independent groups, but the convention is far from universal, so beware. In any case, you need to make crystal clear in the figure caption the status of each independent variable as varying across participants (i.e., independent groups) or within participants (i.e., a repeated measure).

Interpretive Issues Prompted by ANOVA Designs

I'll now step aside for a moment from discussing more complex designs and consider some interpretive issues raised by the new statistics. This is a convenient moment, because ANOVA designs provide a natural context for discussing these issues. You may already have been thinking about some of the queries or doubts I'll mention. I'll frame them as objections posed by a skeptic, followed by my response.

Covert NHST

Skeptic: *"Your conclusions are, or should be, consistent with what p values indicate, so you're conducting NHST by stealth, and it would be better to have it out in the open."* First, an interpretation of, for example, the Treatment group ES in the lower panel of Figure 15.2 as "around large" is consistent with the NHST conclusion of a statistically significant decrease, but is preferable because it's more informative—the CI gives information about precision. Second, it's true that taking nonoverlap of independent 95% CIs as reasonably clear evidence of a difference is approximately equivalent to using a $p < .01$ criterion. However, considering the CIs as ranges of plausible true values, and bearing in mind the cat's-eye picture, gives a clear interval-based rationale for the conclusion, keeps the focus on ESs, and suggests how large the difference is likely to be. Estimation conclusions, even if consistent with those of NHST, are likely to be more informative.

Decisions

Skeptic: *"You are avoiding clear decisions, which are often needed in practice."* Yes, we often need to make decisions, such as whether or not to use this therapy, or approve that procedure for use in schools. In a famous article titled "Conclusions vs. Decisions," the eminent statistician John Tukey (1960) described such decisions with the words, "let us decide to act for the present as if" (p. 424), meaning that we should take account of the best evidence available now, whether that's weak or strong. Evidence may be provided by a single study, but preferably is combined over studies, most likely by meta-analysis. Tukey distinguished such decisions from scientific conclusions, which should be "withheld until adequate evidence has accumulated" (p. 425). Again that's meta-analysis, but it emphasizes that the conclusion should wait until we feel the evidence is sufficiently strong, or estimates sufficiently precise. Yes, we can distinguish decisions and conclusions, but the commonality is important: Both should be based on the best evidence we have at the moment, and that's given by estimation, not p values.

Subjectivity and Fuzzy Interpretations

Skeptic: *"Interpretations of ESs such as 'medium to large' and 'most likely negligible' are subjective, fuzzy, and hard to summarize."* Yes, interpretation of ESs is based on judgment, but so are numerous other aspects of planning, conducting, and reporting research. Such wording is intended to capture not only the ES but also the uncertainty, as expressed by the CI. Therefore, any less fuzzy wording would be claiming too much precision and would misrepresent the data by downplaying uncertainty. Recall my argument in Chapter 2 that statements of statistical significance can suggest certainty, but that such certainty is illusory, whereas CIs give an accurate picture of the uncertainty in the data.

More than One Degree of Freedom

Skeptic: *"The problem is that you are considering only simplistic comparisons of means, thus missing insight provided by interactions and other effects with more than one degree of freedom."* Yes, omnibus effects that are more complex than a comparison, and which therefore have more than one degree of freedom, can sometimes provide insight, but in many cases they don't match closely the research questions being asked, and may be difficult to interpret. The *Publication Manual* (APA, 2010) states the following: "Multiple degree-of-freedom effect-size indicators are often less useful than effect-size indicators that decompose multiple degree-of-freedom tests into meaningful one degree-of-freedom effects—particularly when the latter are the results that inform the discussion" (p. 34). I agree. I recommend Rosenthal and Rosnow's (1985) book titled *Contrast Analysis: Focused Comparisons in the Analysis of Variance*, which explains how to use contrasts and simple comparisons to analyze ANOVA designs, and why that approach can give better interpretations. The authors explain why planned comparisons, specified in advance, can be especially valuable. Rosenthal et al. (2000) developed the approach further, but I still like the accessibility of the 1985 book.

Other ES Measures

Skeptic: *"You are ignoring other ES measures that, with complex designs, provide valuable information."* Yes, my simple comparisons use means and differences as ESs in original units, or we could use Cohen's d as in Chapter 11. Other ESs are indeed used with ANOVA designs. When Cohen (1988, Chapter 8) discussed such designs, he introduced an effect size measure, f, which is the SD of the standardized group means. The G*Power software uses f, but otherwise it's little known, although it probably deserves to be more widely used, because it's expressed in original units and I suspect may be easier to interpret than the measures I'll mention now. The ES measures most commonly used with ANOVA are estimates of the proportion of total variance that's attributable to an independent variable. Slightly different approaches measure this as η^2 (Greek eta-squared) and ω^2 (Greek omega-squared). Most widely used is η^2, although estimates of ω^2 are less biased. Grissom and Kim (2005, Chapter 6) and Hays (1973, Chapters 10 and 12) explained these ESs and provided formulas for calculating them. Grissom and Kim (pp. 124–127) discussed issues of definition, estimation, and interpretation of such ESs for ANOVA.

It can be a challenge to interpret ES measures that are a proportion of variance, including η^2 and ω^2, and, in the context of multiple regression, R^2. One problem is that they are expressed in squared units, such as ms^2 or cm^2, which may be less intuitive than the original units, milliseconds or centimeters. Another problem is that they are proportions of total variance, and this total may depend on many things, including experimental design, and numbers of levels of the independent variables. It can therefore be hard to appreciate what, for example, $\eta^2 = .04$ or $R^2 = .30$ mean. ESs that are proportions of variance can be useful, but we should recognize their challenges. If appropriate, consider using comparisons of means instead, as Rosenthal and Rosnow (1985) described.

Multiple Comparisons

Skeptic: *"By making many comparisons of pairs of means, you are ignoring the problem of multiple comparisons and an inflated Type I error rate."* If we carry out a number of statistical significance tests, some are likely to give $p < .05$, even if all null hypotheses are true. The more tests, the greater the chance that we'll incorrectly reject a null hypothesis and thus commit a Type I error. This is the well-known problem of multiple testing and α inflation. Students of NHST learn about the Bonferroni correction and post hoc test procedures that protect against the problem, typically by making the tests more conservative, to keep the Type I error rate down but at the cost of increasing the risk of committing a Type II error. The mainstream view is that Type I errors are the major concern, and therefore multiple comparisons are problematic, a simple $p < .05$ criterion applied to each comparison separately is untenable, and the Bonferroni correction or some other protection strategy is needed. On the other hand, a number of scholars, for example, Rothman (1990), have presented cogent arguments that such a protection strategy is overly conservative and risks missing important findings. They are comfortable with using a possibly large number of tests, just so long as any statistically significant result is regarded as an interesting possibility needing further investigation, rather than an established finding.

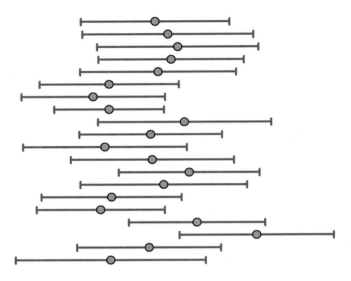

FIGURE 15.4
The dance of the CIs: mean and 95% CI for the first 20 samples, each with $N = 25$, and with σ not known, from the **CIjumping** page of **ESCI chapters 1–4**.

Using estimation does not make the issue of multiple comparisons go away. Figure 15.4 shows the dance of the CIs for the first 20 samples in a set from the **CIjumping** page of **ESCI chapters 1–4**. Focus on one of the largest sample means—which lie farthest to the right in the figure—and one of the smallest, and compare their CIs. Not much overlap, or even a gap! You could use the overlap rule and judge $p < .05$ or even $p < .01$, or you could ignore NHST and think in terms of cat's-eye pictures for both CIs, and conclude that there's quite strong evidence of a difference between the underlying population means. However, those samples all come from the same population, so any conclusion of a difference would be spurious. Looking at the data and comparing extreme results, as we did just then, is a bad strategy, likely to prompt overinterpretation of what's really just sampling variability. That's capitalizing on chance, and likely to give erroneous findings.

In the estimation world there's no well-established CI adjustment comparable to the Bonferroni correction. I think that's a good thing, because I'd prefer to rely on careful judgment than on an arbitrary numerical adjustment. Recall my conclusion in Chapter 5 that, nearly always, a p value conveys very little information. There's little point in calculating a "corrected" criterion for evaluating a p value when on replication p could easily be markedly different.

Considering judgment, one issue is the number of comparisons of potential interest. Another is whether comparisons chosen for interpretation are specified in advance, preferably with some theoretical rationale, or are selected post hoc after inspecting the data. Those two issues combine to give a continuum: With few effects, all specified in advance, we can reach reasonably confident conclusions. At the other extreme, however, we examine many means or comparisons and focus on any effect that seems interesting, thus running the risk of capitalizing on chance and obtaining spurious findings. How conservative should we be? Rothman's (1990) answer was that "scientists should not be so reluctant to explore leads that may turn out to be wrong that they penalize themselves by missing possibly important findings" (p. 43). In other words, we shouldn't be too conservative, and should explore our data for possibly important findings.

Use exploration of data, and judgment, but be wary of the risk of capitalizing on chance.

Exploratory Data Analysis

Skeptic: *"You've mentioned data exploration, but that risks capitalizing on chance and unjustified interpretations."* The previous objection focused on the negative—the problem of multiple comparison and inflated α; this objection concerns the same underlying issue but hints at the positive—the insight that may be given by data exploration. My comments here therefore overlap with my previous comments. I suggest considering two stages of data analysis. After first examining the data, Stage 1 focuses on the small number of effects you've specified in advance as addressing your main research questions. In Figure 15.2 these probably include the two differences in the lower panel and their comparison. You can have reasonable confidence in conclusions about those effects. Then Stage 2 is a full exploration of everything. The trade-off is that Stage 2 risks spurious findings by capitalizing on chance. Keep in mind the dance of the CIs, shown in Figure 15.4, and the risk that you are only focusing on effects that are large because of sampling variability. It's often sobering to examine a figure such as Figure 15.2 and imagine what's likely to happen on a full replication. Every CI is just one from a dance, so, on replication, every mean may be considerably different, and the overall pattern of means may look very different. The CIs give us some idea of how different. Also bear in mind that any of our findings may—and probably should—be included in a meta-analysis, which is usually the best way to come close to knowing truth.

Exploration of data is valuable, but effects that emerge as interesting should be suggested for further investigation rather than stated as firm conclusions.

In 1977 John Tukey published a famous book with a bright orange cover titled *Exploratory Data Analysis* (EDA). Tukey introduced many new representations of data and gave numerous examples of data exploration, usually based on several different pictures of the data. Tukey's EDA was detective work: Investigate the data until its messages become apparent. Tukey was well aware of the multiple comparison issue, but regarded exploration as necessary if experimental results are to yield their greatest possible value. Rothman would agree, and so do I. My Stage 2 therefore includes any replotting of data that might be illuminating. Just make clear that findings from exploration need follow up.

A valuable and insufficiently appreciated strategy is to seek converging evidence. Suppose you notice in Figure 15.2 that the Treatment group's mean scores drop from Follow Up 1 to Follow Up 2, suggesting a delayed positive effect of the therapy. Click to select those two time points to display mean differences in the lower panel. For the Treatment group, the differ-

Converging evidence strengthens a result and reduces the risk that we're capitalizing on chance.

ence is encouraging: 10, [3, 17], but are we overinterpreting randomness? Recall the warning in Chapter 5 about interpreting lumps in randomness. Of course, you can suggest further research, and you can search the literature for evidence you could combine with your result by meta-analysis. But first you can search for supporting hints in your current data. If you have any other measure of anxiety, perhaps ratings by the therapist or reports by a close family member of the participant, you could examine whether those measures show a similar late drop. Perhaps you can go back to your therapists and ask them, even if you didn't think to do so at the time. If you split your Treatment group into participants starting with more or less severe anxiety, does the late drop appear in both subgroups? If further data exploration can find any hints of support that are even partly independent of your original observation, then you have stronger grounds for suspecting that you've found a real effect, definitely worth further study.

Now, after stepping aside to cope with interruptions from the skeptic, I'll return to considering further more complex analyses.

Model Fitting

As theorizing in a discipline becomes more sophisticated, data analysis more often focuses on assessing how well a particular model fits a data set. NHST often does an especially poor job of this, primarily because it doesn't give us a measure of how well a model fits a set of data—p values can't tell us that. Such a measure is an ES measure—it quantifies the goodness of fit, which is our primary interest. We'd like such an ES measure to help us compare how well a particular model fits different data sets, and to compare different models fitted to a single data set. Then we could apply our estimation strategy. I have two examples of using ESs and CIs for model fitting.

Categorical Variables and Frequency Tables

Suppose you are interested in the access that corporations have to finance. You survey 20 large and 20 small corporations in your city, and ask them whether they have been able to obtain sufficient finance in the last 2 years. Table 15.1 presents your results. The table entries are the numbers of large and small corporations that stated that they did or did not have adequate access to finance. The traditional analysis of such a frequency table is to use a χ^2 (chi-square) test to examine the goodness of fit of the observed frequencies to the model stated by the null hypothesis. This model is that there is no association between the two categorical variables: large or small corporation, and satisfactory or unsatisfactory access to finance. The test statistic is $\chi^2 = 4.29$ with $df = 1$, $p = .04$, so the traditional NHST decision would be to reject the null hypothesis of no association, with $\alpha = .05$, and conclude that large corporations have better access to finance.

Using NHST to assess goodness of fit encounters the old problem that a p value is not an ES. Two p values don't give a sound basis for comparing, for example, how well a model fits two data sets. In addition, with a medium or large data set, NHST can often in practice be overly sensitive, in that even a small and perhaps unimportant discrepancy between a model and the data can give a small p value and a misleading conclusion that the model does not fit.

To apply my four-step estimation strategy, we first focus on the proportion of corporations having satisfactory access to finance, and compare that proportion for large and small corporations. The proportions are independent, so you could use the **Diff proportions** page of **ESCI Effect sizes**. Type in the two proportions 17/20 and 11/20, and find that the proportions are .85 and .55, and the difference is .3, [.02, .53]. The 95% CI just misses zero, which is consistent with $p = .04$ for the χ^2 analysis. As usual, the estimation approach is

> If two proportions are independent, a CI on the difference may offer an estimation approach to analyzing a frequency table.

TABLE 15.1

Numbers of Large and Small Corporations Having Satisfactory or Unsatisfactory Access to Finance

	Large Corporations	Small Corporations	Total
Satisfactory access	17	11	28
Unsatisfactory access	3	9	12
Total	20	20	40

more informative because it gives us an estimate of the difference, which is the ES most directly relevant to our research question, and a CI to tell us the precision of that estimate. It's not surprising that this small sample gives such a wide CI.

We can use **Diff proportions** when the two proportions are independent. For larger tables of frequencies, for which χ^2 is also the usual NHST approach, we can also calculate the difference between any two independent proportions that are of research interest, again with a CI. Grissom and Kim (2005, Chapter 8) described further estimation approaches to assessing goodness of fit for larger tables of frequencies.

Pictures of CIs to Assess Goodness of Fit

Wayne Velicer and his colleagues have for more than 20 years been developing the Transtheoretical Model of behavior change, which is widely used, especially to help design and evaluate programs to improve people's health-related behaviors. I won't try to summarize the complex model here, but will just say that 15 variables are used to capture a range of people's thoughts, feelings, motivations, and behaviors. If applied, for example, to smoking, the model postulates relationships between those variables and a person's current smoking status—meaning where that person is along a continuum from regular smoker to successful quitter. The model has been developed to predict the size, as well as the direction, of the relationship between a variable and smoking status.

For one large project, the team chose ω^2 as the main ES, an estimate of the proportion of total variance in smoking status attributable to each of a number of predictor variables. The researchers used the model to derive predictions for each variable on a scale of zero, small, medium, and large effects. Then they used expert judgment and existing data sets to calibrate these labels, and decided to regard ω^2 values of .01, .08, and .18 as small, medium, and large, respectively.

I was invited to join the team for the final stage of assessing the model's predictions against results from a new group of 3,967 smokers. Figure 15.5, from Velicer et al. (2008), shows our strategy and main findings. The gray dots mark the model's predictions, at $\omega^2 = 0$, .01, .08, or .18, for zero, small, medium, and large effects, respectively. The short lines mark estimates from the data, with 95% CIs. The predictions fall within the CIs for 11 of the 15 variables, which we interpreted as strong support for most aspects of the model. Because the discrepancies between predictions and data are quantitative, we could examine each and decide whether to adjust our calibration values of ω^2, modify an aspect of the model, or await further empirical testing. In the article we discussed our test of the Transtheoretical Model more broadly as an illustration of the value of CIs

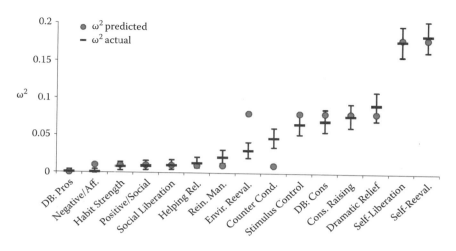

FIGURE 15.5

Comparison of predicted and actual observed ω^2 effect size values for 15 variables listed on the horizontal axis, with 95% CIs shown for the observed estimates. The predictions were derived from the Transtheoretical Model of behavior change, and tested against data from 3,967 smokers. (Reproduced with permission from Velicer, W. F., Cumming, G., Fava, J. L., Rossi, J. S., Prochaska, J. O., & Johnson, J. (2008). Theory testing using quantitative predictions of effect size. *Applied Psychology: An International Review, 57,* 589–608.)

for model fitting, and looked forward to progress that may enable predictions to be fully quantitative, rather than restricted to the four levels of ω^2 that we used.

More generally, proposing models and assessing their fit to data is an enormous, fascinating, and important area of research. As one step in complexity beyond anything I discuss here I recommend Mick McCarthy's (2007) book titled *Bayesian Methods for Ecology.* The ideas and methods he discussed are being applied very widely beyond ecology.

Multivariate Analyses

Multivariate analyses are widely used and likely to become more so. NHST is the usual approach to inference, although ESs and methods for calculating CIs are now available for many types of multivariate analysis. There is also scope for improved textbooks, guidance, and software to encourage greater use of estimation in multivariate analysis.

Different research communities tend to choose different multivariate techniques, and have developed differing customs: Some routinely report

ESs and CIs, although most rarely do. Some use 95% CIs, but others routinely use 90% CIs, so be careful. In some areas discussion continues in the literature about the merits of various ES measures, and further statistical investigation is needed. The good news is that progress continues, and it's increasingly possible to find a suitable ES measure and software to calculate a CI. In the next three short subsections, I'm going to make brief remarks about the use of estimation in the context of just three multivariate techniques.

Multiple Regression

Suppose you are studying the severity of sentences for violent assault. You have a measure of sentence severity, and for a set of offenses you have data about the offender, including age, level of education, and degree of remorse; and about the victim, including gender, age, and severity of injury. You could use multiple regression to investigate the extent to which those variables predict sentence severity. Multiple regression poses many challenges of interpretation, with subtle patterns of suppressor variables—variables that hide the influence of other variables—being just one possible problem. The worst approach, however, is to rely on p values to indicate which variables make large or important contributions. For estimation, the most commonly used ES is R^2, the proportion of variance of the dependent variable that is accounted for by one or more independent variables. The R^2 values, together with CIs on those values, could provide the main guide for interpretation, although, as I've mentioned, R^2 can be challenging to interpret. It's also possible, although less common, to use R values and CIs on those R values for interpretation. Michael Smithson (2001) explained that CIs for R^2 are based on the noncentral F distribution. He discusses CIs for R^2 and other ESs in his little green book, *Confidence Intervals* (Smithson, 2003). He also provides scripts at his website (tinyurl.com/mikecis) to assist the calculation of CIs on R^2 and various other ESs, using SPSS or SAS software.

Multivariate Analysis of Variance (MANOVA)

Again, consider the four-step strategy. Commonly used ESs for MANOVA are η^2 and partial η^2, and both require CIs based on noncentral F. Here, too, the scripts provided by Smithson support use of SPSS or SAS to calculate CIs. Tabachnick and Fidell (2007, Chapters 6 and 7) explain and give examples. The 2007 edition of that text added calculation and discussion of CIs into many of its chapters. It's a good source of estimation advice for many types of multivariate analysis.

Structural Equation Modeling (SEM)

In some disciplines, SEM is a growth industry. SEM investigates network models of interrelated variables, and evaluates the fit of such models to data. Several fit indices can be used as ESs, and the root mean square error of approximation (RMSEA) is perhaps the most often chosen. I'm glad to say RMSEA values are often reported with CIs—usually 90% CIs, and most SEM software reports such CIs, thus providing the basis for our four-step strategy. Tabachnick and Fidell (2007, Chapter 14) and Fabrigar and Wegener (2009) are good sources of advice.

Continuous Data

As a final example area for applying estimation, consider large and complex data sets. These are becoming common and raise interesting issues for analysis. Streams of data that are continuous across space or time, or both, can be valuable, but are especially challenging to analyze. Consider, for example, images produced during brain scans. Statistical techniques are used to identify which brain areas, at which times, show heightened activity when the participant engages in, say, a reasoning task, compared with passively relaxing.

My example is simpler. My colleagues Melanie Murphy, Sheila Crewther, and David Crewther are studying environmental influences on how vision develops. If children or adolescents habitually spend many hours at a computer screen, are they likely to develop shortsightedness? As part of investigating how environmental influences might work they recorded electrical responses in the retina of anesthetized chicks as light is switched on and off. They compared responses for animals previously treated with drug DAAA, which disrupts one aspect of retinal function, or the placebo control drug PBS. They averaged 20 recordings for each chick. Figure 15.6 is their figure showing the recordings averaged for 7 DAAA chicks and 13 PBS chicks. The shaded areas indicate 95% confidence limits.

A smooth curve is plotted, but the voltage was actually recorded every 0.1 ms. At each time point, the 20 voltages for a chick were averaged, then the 7 averages for the DAA chicks were used to calculate the mean and 95% CI plotted at that time point. Similarly, the 13 averages for the PBS chicks were used to calculate the mean and CI for the control condition. Just as in Figure 15.2, the two groups are independent but measurements at successive time points are a repeated measure and are, no doubt, highly

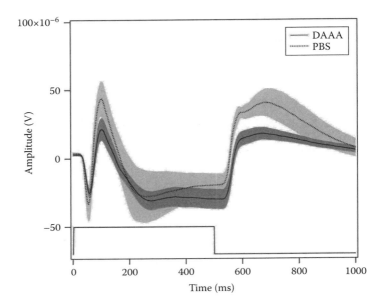

FIGURE 15.6
Recordings in volts (V) from the retina of anesthetized chicks treated with active drug
DAAA ($N = 7$) or placebo drug PBS ($N = 13$). The trace at the bottom signals that light is
turned ON at time 0 and then OFF at time 500 ms. The shaded regions indicate 95% confidence limits. (Unpublished figure courtesy of Melanie Murphy, Sheila Crewther, and David
Crewther.)

correlated from one moment to the next. We can therefore use the shaded
confidence areas to assess the difference between the groups at any time,
but not to assess the change from one time to another within a single
group. Whenever the two stripes don't overlap we have quite strong evidence that the responses in the two drug conditions differ, and at any
time point we can estimate the difference from the figure. This figure is a
lovely example of an ingenious way to display CIs to help readers understand the data and draw justifiable conclusions.

A key point to appreciate is that the CIs are calculated with $N = 7$ for
DAAA, not $N = 7 \times 20 = 140$. It's good to have 20 recordings per chick,
because the average of 20 gives a better estimate of that chick's retinal
function, but those 20 values are correlated because they come from a
single chick. The CI around the DAAA group mean must be calculated
from the $N = 7$ independent values, one from each chick in the DAAA
group. That CI may be wide if there is considerable chick-to-chick variation, but it's the appropriate CI to indicate the precision of our DAAA
average curve, and to guide our comparison of DAAA with PBS. When
sample sizes are small, as they often are in some areas of biology (cell

biology often uses $N = 3$), it is, alas, fairly common to see CIs calculated with N equal to the total number of observations, not the number of animals. That's a bad error, likely to give CIs that are much too short.

I'll now turn from discussing how to use estimation in complex situations to my second question, which concerns the practicality of adopting the new statistics.

The New Statistics in Practice

"I included effect sizes and confidence intervals, but the editor tells me there's no room, and I have to take them out and only report p values. What should I do?" I've been asked that question many times. I hope such questions will quickly fade into history, but we all have to live in the research world as we find it. You may need to write a report or dissertation that pleases the examiners, and we all need to find good journals that will publish our papers. My reply is that the justification for the new statistics is strong, the world should change and is changing, and it's important to keep up our efforts to help it change further.

I don't underestimate the difficulty for many people of switching from reliance on p values. You may agree that the new statistics are desirable, but, if you are in an NHST discipline, you may feel that p-value consciousness is so deeply ingrained that you have to conform. I've taught p values for more than 40 years so I deeply understand those feelings. I've also taught CIs for almost as long, so I know change is possible. I have some suggestions. Our most persuasive reason for using the new statistics may be that it's simply more informative—it gives a more complete picture of what our data are able to reveal.

Core References

Besides this book and ESCI, there are three references I especially recommend as starting points for the new statistics. Keep them handy, and recommend them to others if that might be useful. They are free downloads, and I've given them tiny URLs to make things easier. Kline (2004, Chapter 3, tinyurl.com/klinechap3) gave a pithy overview of why using NHST is almost always a bad idea, and what we should do instead. Wilkinson et al. (1999, tinyurl.com/tfsi1999) is a fine statement of good practice in design and data analysis. Cumming and Finch (2005, tinyurl.com/inferencebyeye) is an introduction to CIs. I could add the easy reading of Hunt's (1997) story of meta-analysis, with many examples.

I also recommend the wonderful book by Fiona Fidler (forthcoming) that tells the story of NHST and statistical reform for medicine, psychology, and several other disciplines.

Pushing the Boundaries

I have a two-part strategy for writing up research. It aims to use the new statistics as fully as possible, and also give statistical reform a nudge ahead. First, I analyze the data as best I can, which usually involves exploration and figures that show the results in various ways. I'll follow the four steps of my general strategy for estimation, and avoid NHST if I can, or use it as little as possible. Making good figures to convey the messages in the data is usually a large part of preparing a research manuscript.

For my second part I'll consider the pragmatics of communicating the research. I may add some short explanations and a reference to justify my analysis strategy. When submitting the manuscript to a journal I might add a sentence to the covering letter stating that I'm following the advice of the *Publication Manual* (APA, 2010) to base interpretation on point and interval estimates. If the editor and referees want changes, I may add some *p* values alongside estimation, but I won't switch from using estimation as the basis for interpretation. The *Publication Manual*'s recommendations are an important imprimatur for the new statistics, and you may choose to refer to them in your courteous letter to the editor explaining why you prefer to make only small changes to your original data analysis.

If you are writing a dissertation, you may decide to include a paragraph or two to outline your analysis strategy, with explanations and a few references, so your examiners can see that your approach is carefully considered and can be justified from the literature.

Many Others Do It

Increasing numbers of researchers are reporting ESs and CIs in their articles, and using meta-analysis. That's good, but in a range of technical disciplines I suspect that many researchers would be bemused by this whole new statistics discussion. Their disciplines, including physics, chemistry, and engineering, have made wonderful progress with hardly a mention of a *p* value. Experimental results are routinely reported as "435 ± 0.5 mm" and there are well-developed practices to cope with the precision of measurements, as quantified by the "± 0.5." When we adopt estimation, we are to some extent merely catching up with those long-established practices. I can also mention that many great advances in the NHST disciplines were accomplished by leading scholars who predated NHST, or elected not to use it. In psychology, prominent examples are Ebbinghaus for memory,

Skinner for behaviorism, and Piaget for child development. In a number of ways, the new statistics are not at all new.

Enjoy the Feeling

I speculated back in Chapter 1 that, once the requirement to focus on p is weakened, we may feel that it's natural to focus on the ES because that's usually the best answer the data can give to our research question. Using CIs rather than p to guide interpretation may also feel natural because CIs are in the same units as the ES and therefore can also be given meaning in the research context. I speculated further that perhaps we'll even recognize ESs and estimation as how we had, informally, been thinking about results, even as we calculated and published p values. So the new statistics might even seem a bit familiar. My speculations need investigation but, if they resonate at all with you, enjoy the feeling.

Evidence-Based Practice of Statistics

We should adopt evidence-based practice in doing statistics, just as in practicing our professional discipline (Fidler & Cumming, 2008). I have tried in this book to refer to cognitive evidence that can inform how we analyze and present results. Yes, there are gaps in the statistical cognition literature, with opportunities for many interesting projects, but we should make the best use of what we have and new evidence as it becomes available. In any debate about what's best, the conclusions should be based on evidence. There's much evidence of the problems of NHST, but we should also be guided by evidence about how people may misunderstand CIs (e.g., Belia et al., 2005), which should prompt us to design figures with CIs carefully, and explain fully our CI-based interpretations.

The point is that, by using the new statistics in appropriate ways, you can be confident that you are doing the right thing and following best practice. You can cite evidence in support.

Scholarly Support

I'd like to close with some quotations. It's easy to find more, for example, at tinyurl.com/nhstquotes. These can add rhetorical weight to our talks or lectures. More importantly, they remind us of the many distinguished scholars who have, over more than half a century, carefully explained the problems of NHST, the reasons why we should instead use estimation or other techniques, and the enhancements to research that improved statistical methods can offer. Curiously, it's difficult to find statements that defend NHST and explain why it should be so widely used. The prospects for statistical reform are now better than ever, and advancing reform is so important that it deserves our persistent efforts.

> The traditional null-hypothesis significance-test method … is here vigorously excoriated for its inappropriateness. (Rozeboom, 1960, p. 428)

> One can hardly avoid polemics when butchering sacred cows. (Rozeboom, 1960, p. 424)

> I'm not making some nit-picking statistician's correction. I am saying that the whole business [NHST] is so radically defective as to be scientifically almost pointless. (Meehl, 1978, p. 823)

> It is remarkable that despite two decades of … attacks, the mystifying doctrine of null hypothesis testing is still today the Bible from which our future research generation is taught. (Gigerenzer & Murray, 1987, p. 27)

> It is time to go beyond this institutionalized illusion [NHST]. We must write new textbooks and change editorial practices. (Gigerenzer, 1993, p. 314)

> Perhaps p values are like mosquitoes. They have an evolutionary niche somewhere and no amount of scratching, swatting, or spraying will dislodge them. (Campbell, 1982, p. 698)

> It is difficult to estimate the handicap that widespread, incorrect, and intractable use of a primary data analytic method [NHST] has on a scientific discipline, but the deleterious effects are doubtless substantial. (Tyron, 1998, p. 796)

> Given the problems of statistical induction, we must finally rely, as have the older sciences, on replication. (Cohen, 1994, p. 1002)

> Many observers have noted the failure of psychology as a cumulative science. Although many reasons can be advanced for this problem, perhaps the most important is the … dichotomous interpretation of significance levels, resulting in over reliance on p values as the main evidence contained in a study. (Rossi, 1997, p. 175)

> It is time for researchers to avail themselves of the full arsenal of quantitative and qualitative statistical tools.… The current practice of focusing exclusively on a dichotomous reject-nonreject decision strategy of null hypothesis testing can actually impede scientific progress.… The focus of research should be on … what data tell us about the magnitude of effects, the practical significance of effects, and the steady accumulation of knowledge. (Kirk, 2003, p. 100)

For one last time, please reach for the coffee or chocolate and write down your take-home messages. I suggest writing a list for this chapter, and another for the whole book. Maybe sleep on those lists before turning ahead and looking at mine. Are you dreaming about the dances yet? For this chapter I'll mention as hints the following: our four-step strategy for estimation; ANOVA designs and RCTs; challenges to the estimation approach, especially multiple testing and data exploration; tables of frequencies; goodness of fit; multivariate analysis; then strategies to support adoption of the new statistics in practice. For the whole book, write as many messages as you like, but I elected to write just six major ones, although each has a few aspects.

Exercises

15.1 Find a simple RCT in your discipline. Type the data into the **Figure** page of **ESCI chapters 14–15**. Explore and discuss.

15.2 For that RCT, find or invent reference labels and values for the ES and ES differences, and display in **Figure**. Discuss.

15.3 If the RCT shown in Figure 15.2 were entered into a meta-analysis, what ES would most likely appear in the forest plot?

15.4 In one or more other statistics textbooks, look for advice about the Bonferroni correction, α inflation, multiple testing, and data exploration. Compare with this chapter. What's your view?

15.5 Find an example of an ANOVA. Consider an alternative analysis based on contrasts or comparisons of pairs of means. Discuss.

15.6 Find an example or two of NHST analysis. Apply the four-step strategy. Discuss.

15.7 Find a simple frequency table example. Use **Diff proportions** to analyze. Discuss.

15.8 Try to find in your discipline the use of a CI picture, perhaps like Figures 15.5 or 15.6, to assess goodness of fit. Or find a case in which such a figure would be useful. Interpret.

15.9 Find in your discipline an example of a multivariate analysis. Was an ES chosen and reported? Was it interpreted? Was a CI reported? Was it interpreted? Discuss.

15.10 Visit the "instructions to authors" websites of your favorite journals. Is there any advice about how to carry out or report statistical inference? Any reference to the APA *Publication Manual*?

15.11 Try to find stories from your teachers, colleagues, or students about attempts they have made to publish articles using the new statistics. What lessons do you draw?

15.12 Revisit your take-home messages for this chapter. Improve the list if you can.

15.13 Do the same for your list for the whole book. Maybe sleep on this list one more time.

Take-Home Messages for Chapter 15

- Our four-step strategy for estimation is as follows: Choose the ESs most relevant for our research questions, calculate CIs on those ESs, make a figure, then interpret.

- For RCTs, the upper panel of Figure 15.2 displays ESs and CIs that support comparisons between the independent groups. Testing time is a repeated measure, so we need differences between selected time points, with CIs, for each group—as in the lower panel. *Take-home pictures*: The figures in those two panels.

- Reference values for ESs may help when interpreting ESs and CIs. Consider displaying them in a figure, as in Figure 15.2.
- To analyze data from complex designs, first examine ESs and CIs for comparisons specified in advance, then explore to identify effects deserving further investigation. Contrast analysis may be superior to omnibus ANOVA.
- Exploration can give valuable insights, but beware the risk of capitalizing on chance. Seek converging evidence if possible.
- Examining the difference between two proportions, with its CI, can be a good way to analyze data in a frequency table, when the two proportions are independent.
- Consider using figures with CIs to assess the fit of a model to data, as in Figure 15.5.
- For multivariate analyses, apply the four-step strategy. Seek the latest advice about what ESs are most appropriate, and what software is available to calculate CIs.
- Figures with CIs can be valuable, even for continuous data.
- Practice evidence-based statistics wherever possible.
- Strategies that may assist in the adoption of the new statistics include citing support from the literature, taking a gradual but firm approach, and drawing on support from others already using the new practices.
- Statistical reform, starting with the new statistics, is sufficiently important to deserve our support.

Take-Home Messages for the Whole Book

- Often, the main aim of research is to estimate one or more ESs. Therefore, formulate research questions in estimation terms. ESs can be as familiar as means or correlations, but choose ES measures most appropriate for the research questions.
- Whenever possible, report a CI with every ES estimate to indicate precision. Interpret both the ES and the CI. We discussed six ways to interpret CIs.

- Results vary with replication, often to a surprising extent. People frequently underestimate sampling variability. The dance of the means and the dance of the CIs can be surprisingly wide. CIs give useful information about the extent of variation over replication.

- NHST has serious flaws and can be damaging to research progress. Its dichotomous decisions can give illusory certainty and hide the true extent of uncertainty that is expressed by CIs. The dance of the p values is very wide indeed.

- Meta-analysis is usually the best way to combine evidence over studies. CIs may be wide, but they give accurate information about uncertainty in data. Meta-analysis is often the best way to reduce uncertainty, increase the precision of ES estimates, and achieve scientific progress. Always consider results in the context of meta-analysis.

- Statistical reform deserves support. Consider undertaking statistical cognition research. Adopt the new statistics as much as possible in your own work, and in any teaching or supervision you do. Encourage your peers also to adopt the new statistics.

Glossary

This is not a complete glossary of statistical terms. It focuses on selected terms that are important in this book, and includes expressions of my invention.

Alternative clouds for *r*: My name for different scatter plots that all have the same value of sample *r*, as illustrated by the **See r** page of **ESCI chapters 14–15**.

Alternative hypothesis (H₁): A statement about a population parameter that is alternative to the null hypothesis in NHST.

Assurance γ: Probability, expressed as a percentage, that our obtained MOE is no larger than target MOE, when using precision for planning. For example, $\gamma = 99$.

Bars: Short for **error bars**.

The Campbell Collaboration: A worldwide collaboration that provides systematic reviews, online, in the fields of social welfare, crime and justice, and education.

Capture percentage (CP): The percentage of replication means that, in the long run, fall within the initial CI.

Cat's-eye picture: My name for the two curves and shaded area between them, as in Figure 4.5, that depicts how plausibility varies across and beyond a CI.

Central limit theorem: A theorem in statistics that states that the sampling distribution of a variable that's the sum of many independent influences almost always has, approximately, a normal distribution.

Cliff effect: A sharp drop in the degree of belief that an effect exists for the *p* value changing from just below .05 (or another significance level) to just above that level.

Clinical significance: Clinical importance.

The Cochrane Collaboration: A worldwide collaboration of healthcare professionals and policy makers that supports evidence-based practice in healthcare.

The Cochrane Library: An online database of systematic reviews that supports evidence-based practice in healthcare.

Cohen's *d*: A standardized ES expressed in units of some appropriate SD. It can often be considered a kind of *z* score.

Confidence interval (CI): An interval estimate calculated from sample data that indicates the precision of a point estimate.

Confidence level (*C*): Same as level of confidence.

Cumulative meta-analysis: Sequence of meta-analyses, each including one additional study.

Dance of the confidence intervals: My name for a sequence of CIs, from successive samples, falling down the screen in ESCI. See Figure 3.8.

Dance of the CP values: My name for the sequence of capture percentages, for successive CIs, as shown in Figure 5.4.

Dance of the differences: My name for the sequence of differences between the two group means, for a succession of replications of a two-independent-groups experiment, as illustrated by the **Simulate two** page of **ESCI chapters 5–6**.

Dance of the means: My name for a sequence of sample means falling down the screen in ESCI. See Figure 3.2.

Dance of the p values: My name for the sequence of bouncing around p values, for successive experiments, as in Figure 5.8.

Dance of the r clouds: My name for the sequence of different scatterplots, given by a succession of samples, as illustrated by the **Sample r** page of **ESCI chapters 14–15**.

Dance of the r values: My name for the sequence of r values given by repeated sampling. See Figure 14.8.

Descriptive information: Information about the data.

d heap: My name for the empirical sampling distribution of d. In ESCI it's a pile of pink triangles that represent d values from many samples. See Figures 11.3 and 11.4.

Dichotomous thinking: Thinking that focuses on a choice between two alternatives, notably the NHST decision to reject or not reject a null hypothesis.

Effect: Anything in which we might be interested.

Effect size (ES): The amount of something that might be of interest. The size of an effect.

Effect size measure: A measure used to express an ES.

Error bars (also bars): A simple graphic that marks an interval around a mean or other point estimate in a figure.

Error of estimation: Same as estimation error.

ES estimate (also sample ES): ES calculated from data and used as an estimate of the population ES.

Estimation: An approach to statistical inference that uses sample data to calculate point and interval estimates of population parameters.

Estimation error (also error of estimation): Difference, for example $(M - \mu)$, between a point estimate calculated from sample data, and the population parameter it estimates.

Estimation language: Language that focuses on ESs, and on "How much?" questions, rather than dichotomous "Is there an effect?" questions.

Estimation thinking: Thinking that focuses on the sizes of effects.

Evidence-based practice: Practice—in medicine, statistics, or another profession—that is based on research evidence.

Fatness: My term for the horizontal width of the cat's-eye picture, as in Figure 4.5. Fatness is greatest at the point estimate, M, and decreases smoothly for values progressively farther from M.

Fatness ratio: My name for the fatness at the point estimate, M, divided by the fatness at either limit of a CI.

File drawer effect: Tendency for results that are not statistically significant to remain unpublished, thus potentially biasing the availability of studies for meta-analysis.

Fisher's r to z transformation: A transformation used to analyze values of r, notably to calculate approximate CIs on r.

Fixed effect model: Simplest model of meta-analysis, which assumes that each included study estimates a single fixed μ.

Floating difference axis: My name for an axis in a figure that has its zero aligned with one sample mean so it can display the difference between two sample means. See Figures 6.2 and 6.7.

Forest plot: CI picture that displays results from a number of studies, and a meta-analysis of those studies. See, for example, Figure 7.4.

Funnel plot: A plot of study standard error (SE) against study ES, used to investigate possible publication bias in a meta-analysis.

Heterogeneity: The studies in a meta-analysis show **heterogeneity** to the extent that ES variation between studies is larger than can reasonably be accounted for by sampling variability.

Heterogeneous: The studies in a meta-analysis are **heterogeneous** if ES variation between studies is larger than can reasonably be accounted for by sampling variability.

Homogeneity of variance: Assumption that population variance is the same for each of the two groups in the two-independent-groups design.

Homogeneous: The studies in a meta-analysis are **homogeneous** if sampling variability can reasonably account for ES variation between studies.

Idealized replication: Repeat of an experiment that is identical to the initial experiment, except it uses a different random sample.

Illegitimate power: My name for **post hoc power**.

Inferential information: Information based on the data, but telling us about the population.

Informativeness: My term for the ability of an experiment to give information to answer research questions, or to give insight about the world.

Initial CI: The CI given by an initial experiment.

Interval estimate: CI. A range of plausible values for a population parameter.

Inverse probability fallacy: Incorrect belief that the p value is the probability the null hypothesis is true.

Law of large numbers: A law of statistics that states that, when random samples are sufficiently large, they match the population closely.

"Law" of small numbers: A widespread human misconception that even small samples match the population closely.

Legitimate power: My name for power calculated for a target δ that's chosen as being of research interest. Contrast with post hoc power.

Level of confidence (*C*, also confidence level): The 95 in "95% CI," where 95% CIs are those that, in the long run, will include the population parameter for 95% of replications.

Limit: Either end of a CI.

Lower limit (LL): Lower end of a CI.

Margin of error (MOE): The length of one arm of a CI.

Mean heap: My name for the empirical sampling distribution of the sample mean. In ESCI it's a pile of green dots that represent sample means. See Figure 3.4.

Measurement error: Difference between an observed data value and what is, in some sense, the true underlying value.

Meta-analysis: A set of techniques for the quantitative analysis of results from two or more studies on the same or similar issues.

Meta-analytic thinking: Estimation thinking that considers any result in the context of past and potential future results on the same issue.

Meta-regression: Moderator analysis that uses regression to seek to identify a continuous moderator.

Moderating variable (also moderator): Variable that influences the ES being studied in a meta-analysis.

Moderator: Same as **moderating variable**.

Moderator analysis: Analysis within meta-analysis that seeks to identify moderator variables that can account for some of the ES variability between studies.

Natural frequencies: A risk expressed in **natural frequencies** is stated as so many per hundred, or thousand, or other convenient number.

Noncentral *t*: Sampling distribution of t that emerges when μ_1 is true and σ is not known. See Chapter 10.

Null hypothesis (H₀): A statement about a population parameter, often $H_0: \mu = 0$, that is tested by NHST.

Null hypothesis significance testing (NHST): An approach to statistical inference that uses a p value to either reject or not reject a null hypothesis.

One-sided CI: CI with one short arm and the other arm extending indefinitely far.

One-sided *p* interval: *p* interval with zero as its lower endpoint.

Original units: Units, such as milliseconds, centimeters, or dollars, in which a data value or ES was first measured.

Paired design: Experimental design comprising one group of *N* participants, each of whom supplies a pair of data values, one on each of two measures, for example, pretest and posttest.

Pearson's correlation, *r*: Measure of the linear component of the relationship between two variables, usually *X* and *Y*.

***p* interval:** An 80% (unless a different percentage is stated) prediction interval for replication *p*.

Point estimate: Single value estimate of a population parameter.

Population: A set of values, usually assumed large or infinite, about which we wish to draw conclusions.

Population ES: ES in the population, usually unknown and to be estimated.

Population parameters: Values, for example, μ and σ, of aspects of a population. They are usually fixed but unknown.

Post hoc power (also illegitimate power): Power calculated after completing the experiment, using as target δ the effect size *d* obtained in the experiment. It can easily mislead, so never use it.

Power: Statistical power.

Power picture: My name for a figure that illustrates power by showing the distributions of the test statistic, usually *z* or *t*, when H_0 is true, and when H_1 is true.

Practical significance: Practical importance.

Precision: Largest likely estimation error, measured by MOE.

Probability of superiority of E over C: Probability that a randomly chosen value from the E distribution is greater than a randomly chosen value from C.

Proportion (*P*): Fraction of a number of discrete things that have a property of interest. It lies between 0 and 1.

***p* value:** Probability of obtaining our observed results, or results that are more extreme, if the null hypothesis is true.

Random effects model: Model for meta-analysis that assumes that different studies estimate somewhat different values of the population parameter being investigated.

Randomized control trial (RCT): Independent-groups experiment in which participants are randomized to receive either the active or the control treatment.

Random sampling: Sampling in which every data value in the population has an equal chance of being sampled, and values are sampled independently.

Reference values: Values used to assist interpretation of an ES. Cohen, for example, suggested reference values for d. Use of any reference values is a matter for judgment.

Relative risk: Risk ratio.

Replication experiment: An idealized replication of an initial experiment.

Replication mean: The mean of a replication experiment.

Replication p: My name for the p value given by a replication experiment.

Research synthesis (also systematic review): Review that integrates research evidence, usually by meta-analysis.

r heap: My name for the empirical sampling distribution of r values. See Figure 14.8.

Risk: Probability, usually of an unwanted event.

Risk ratio (also relative risk): The ratio of two risks or probabilities.

Rubber ruler: My name for a measuring stick that has its zero at μ_0 and, for noncentral t, has sample standard error, $s/\sqrt{N}$, as its unit of measurement; see Figures 10.4 and 10.5. For Cohen's d, it has sample standard deviation, s, as its unit of measurement; see Figures 11.3 and 11.4.

Rule of eye: My name for a useful approximate guideline, especially for interpreting a figure.

Sample: A set of N data values sampled from a population.

Sample ES (also ES estimate): ES calculated from data and usually used as an estimate of the population ES.

Sample statistics: Statistics, for example, M and s, that are calculated from sample data.

Sampling distribution (also theoretical sampling distribution): The distribution of all possible values of a sample statistic.

Sampling variability: Extent to which results vary over replication, or repeated sampling.

Scatterplot: Picture of the relation between X and Y, in which each data pair is represented by a dot.

Significance: Ambiguous term, best avoided.

Significance level: A criterion p value, often .05, .01, or .001, against which an obtained p value is compared.

Slippery slope of nonsignificance: My name for the fallacy that finding a result to be *not* statistically significant is sufficient to justify interpreting it, perhaps in a later section of a report, as zero.

Slippery slope of significance: My name for the fallacy that finding a result to be statistically significant is sufficient to justify interpreting it, perhaps in a later section of a report, as important or large.

s **pile:** My name for the empirical sampling distribution of sample SDs, or *s* values, as shown in Figures 10.3 and 11.3.

Standard error (SE): SD of a sampling distribution.

Standard error bars (also SE bars): Bars that extend from one SE below to one SE above the mean.

Standardized mean difference (SMD): A term used in medicine for Cohen's *d* for a difference.

Standardized units: Units with some generality, such as number of SDs.

Standardizer: The SD chosen as the unit of measurement for Cohen's *d*.

Statistical cognition: The empirical study of how people understand and misunderstand statistical concepts and presentations.

Statistical inference: A method that uses sample data to draw conclusions about a population.

Statistical power (also power): Probability of rejecting the null hypothesis when the alternative hypothesis is true.

Statistical significance: Rejection of the null hypothesis.

Systematic review (also research synthesis): Review that integrates research evidence, usually by meta-analysis.

Target δ: Value of δ, the population ES, used in a power calculation.

Target MOE: Value of target precision specified for calculations of what *N* we need, when using precision for planning.

The new statistics: Statistical techniques, including especially estimation and meta-analysis, that usually provide a better basis for statistical inference than NHST.

Tragedy of the error bar: My name for the unfortunate fact that error bars don't automatically announce what they represent. We need to be told.

Two-independent-groups design: Experimental design comprising two independent groups of participants, of sizes N_1 and N_2, possibly different.

Two-sided *p* interval: *p* interval for which there is an equal chance (e.g., 10% for an 80% *p* interval) that replication *p* falls below the interval and above it.

Type I error: Rejection of the null hypothesis when it's true.

Type I error rate (α): Probability of rejecting the null hypothesis when it's true.

Type II error: Nonrejection of the null hypothesis when it's false.

Type II error rate (β): Probability of not rejecting the null hypothesis when it's false.

Unbiased: An estimate of a parameter is **unbiased** if, on average, it equals the parameter. On average it neither underestimates nor overestimates the parameter.

Units-free: A **units-free** ES is a number, such as a correlation, frequency, or proportion, that has no measurement units.

Upper limit (UL): Upper end of a CI.

Weights: Relative contributions of different studies in a meta-analysis.

Commentary on Selected Exercises

Chapter 1 Exercises Introduction to ESCI, and Comparing Presentation Formats

1.4–1.7   If you enter at red 1 and 3 the values shown in the first Lucky–Noluck presentation, in NHST format, you should see the three versions of the results and close matches with Figures 1.1 and 1.2. Compare with Figure 1.4. Note that the *df* values in the first presentation indicate that Lucky used two groups with $N = 22$, and Noluck two with $N = 18$.

1.8 and 1.9   Increase M(diff), decrease SD(diff), or increase N: In each case see p decrease. Each of those changes, with everything else held constant, suggests stronger evidence of an effect, and the lower p value reflects that.

1.11   When the CI includes zero, $p > .05$; when it misses zero, $p < .05$. When the LL $= 0$, $p = .05$.

1.14   Same answer as for 1.11.

1.15   Meta-analysis combines evidence from the two studies. If the results of the two studies are not too different, the combined evidence will be stronger than the evidence from either study alone, and so the meta-analysis CI will be shorter than each of the separate CIs.

1.16   If the evidence from the two studies conflicts, the meta-analysis CI will be long, reflecting the large amount of overall uncertainty.

1.17   CIs: The shorter the better! Short beats long. Narrow beats wide. A narrow interval means a small amount of uncertainty, and that's a good thing.

Chapter 2 Exercises NHST and Its Flaws, Questions in Science, and ESs

2.1   I kept browsing *Psychological Science*, and I report a few further examples here. Many articles provide examples of poor NHST. Most occurrences of the word "significant" are ambiguous unless accompanied by an explanatory word, such as "statistically" or "practically" or "clinically," or by a p value or other NHST information. Both relative and exact p values are common, and it's easy to find articles that include both.

2.3   Acceptance of a null: "Participants in both conditions felt equally disgusted immediately after watching the film, as indicated by a nonsigificant effect." The slippery slope of nonsignificance: In the Results section: "with no significant differences across groups … $p > .11$ …," but in the Discussion: "All groups were equally accurate in inhibiting the response."

2.6 and 2.7   Most articles include at least one aim or hypothesis expressed in a dichotomous-thinking way. The conclusion of one article was that "viewers needed to see the scene for at least 150 ms during each eye fixation." That's an estimation-thinking answer. However, the introduction did not ask the corresponding estimation question, but stated that "the amount of time viewers need … should … be in the range of 50 to 60 ms. We … tested this hypothesis." That's a dichotomous aim. All analysis was by NHST, and a figure showed ESs, with 95% CIs, but these were not used to interpret the results.

2.8   Dichotomous: "Test of the hypothesis that people perceive fluently processed stimuli as safer than disfluently processed ones." My estimation version: "To what extent do people perceive fluently processed stimuli as safer than disfluently processed ones?" Alternative estimation language: "Estimate the perceived safety of fluently and disfluently processed stimuli, then examine the difference between the two."

2.9   The prediction being tested was that there is a familiar-word preference for CAE [the name of one condition], but no such preference for JM [another condition]. Results: "This prediction was supported by t tests on the familiar-to-unfamiliar ratios …, which were significantly greater than 1.0 … for CAE … $p < .019$, but not for JM … $p > .187$…." A figure showed that the mean ratio was about 1.36 for CAE and 1.19 for JM. Discussion: "Recognition of familiar words is restricted to [CAE, not JM]." In other words, one condition (JM) showed an effect of 1.19, which was not statistically significant ($p > .187$; that probably means $p = .187$), whereas the other condition (CAE) showed an effect of 1.36, with $p < .019$ (which probably means $p = .019$). This is a very similar pattern to Lucky–Noluck, and certainly does not permit the conclusion that the effect is "restricted to" CAE and not JM. We need to see a direct comparison of the two effects using NHST or some other approach, because the interest is to see whether they differ.

2.10 Yes. Apply NHST to the difference between the two results: In the first presentation, examine the difference between the differences. In other words, test the null hypothesis that the difference between the new and the current treatments is the same in the two studies. I reported that $p = .55$ for that comparison, but finding a small p would have given some justification for *Inconsistent*.

2.12 Mean age was 19.6 years. Modal income was $40,000 to $49,999. Percentage: "capturing 52.7% of the variance." Effect size (d) for gender typicality (column heading in a table). Difference from the predicted value was 0.06. Proportion of fear identification was .36. With an ANOVA: $\eta_p^2 = .032$ (that's partial eta-squared). Number of females satisfied with their current roommates was 11 (that's a frequency). In a regression: $b = -27.1$, $\beta = -.22$. Correlation, $r = .47$. Odds ratio was 1.70. Discriminability, $d' = 0.88$. Relative probability $= .64$. Don't worry if some of those are unfamiliar—they are just examples and you no doubt found different examples. The important thing is that they are all quantities that tell us about an effect of interest.

2.13 I found this difficult. One example was an 11% increase in the risk of a cardiovascular event referred to as "notable"; another was correlations of .38 and .44 referred to as "strong." I gave up without finding any example of ES interpretation that seemed to me a full discussion of the implications of the size of the effect.

Chapter 3 Exercises Confidence Intervals

3.2 Experiment with different ways to use the slider—click and drag the thumbnail (the little rectangle you can move), click either side of the thumbnail, click and hold an end arrow, or click repeatedly on an end arrow. Different versions of Excel respond a little differently, so find what works best for you.

3.9 and 3.10 M values will bounce around μ, as the dance of the means illustrates, and s values bounce around σ. We could imagine a dance of the s values—a dance of sample SD values—to illustrate how s varies from sample to sample.

3.12   Larger N means smaller sample-to-sample variation and thus a more sober dance of the means. Smaller N, more drunken—the dance is wider.

3.13   Larger σ gives more variation and thus a wider or more drunken dance; smaller σ gives a narrower or less drunken dance.

3.14   In general, changes to σ influence sample-to-sample variation quite markedly, whereas changes to N may seem to make only moderate changes to that variation. Later we'll see that it's $\sqrt{N}$ that does the work.

3.15   Larger N gives a narrower mean heap, and that's good because the M values are generally close to μ. Achieving large N is often a basic research design goal. I always ask my beginning classes, "What do you want for Christmas?" They know that the response I'm expecting is, "Big N!"

3.19   **Curve SE** is the theoretically expected value calculated for your chosen N and σ, so it remains constant unless you change N or σ. Compare with **Mean heap SE**, which is the SD of the M values obtained in the current set of samples, so it's bound to change as you take further samples. At the start of a new set it can bounce around a lot, then it settles down to be quite close to the theoretically expected value. Run the simulation for an hour or more and it will be very close to **Curve SE**.

3.22   It's bad news for researchers that sample size has its influence via $\sqrt{N}$ because taking a sample four times as large may be four times the expense and effort, but it only divides the SE by two.

3.24   Use the formula $SE = \sigma/\sqrt{N}$ to calculate SE.

3.25   Use the formula $SE = \sigma/\sqrt{N}$ to calculate $SE = 20/\sqrt{30} = 3.65$. Set the values of N and σ in ESCI and **Curve SE** should take this value. The sampling distribution of the mean is normal, with mean 50 and SD of 3.65.

3.28   A graph of estimated SD of the mean heap, or SE recorded from ESCI, when plotted against N should illustrate the $1/\sqrt{N}$ relationship. N needs to increase by a factor of 4 if we want a halving of the SE.

3.29   The heavier green vertical MOE lines appear very close to the SE lines that mark 2SE from the mean. That makes sense because of the rule of thumb that states that 95% of the values in any normal distribution fall within 1.96SD of the mean.

3.30   In the long run, 95% between the lines and 2.5% in either tail.

3.32   For (i) use 2SE to obtain 6.67, and for (ii) use 1.96SE to obtain 6.53. An interval that in the long run will include 95% of sample means is $\mu \pm$ MOE. For (ii) this is the interval [43.47, 56.53].

3.34   Larger N or smaller σ gives smaller MOE. In any case we expect about 5% of green dots to fall outside the MOE lines, about equal numbers in the left and right tails.

3.35   You wish to estimate the mean HEAT score for students in your country, and you also want to know the precision of that estimate.

3.36 and 3.38   Again, 5%, about equally often to the left and the right.

3.40   CIs are red if they don't include μ, meaning M falls farther than MOE away from μ.

3.41   Each sample has its own value of s, and so the calculated CI will differ for each. When you click, some intervals get a bit longer, some a bit shorter. Occasionally, an interval changes color because it changes from including to not including μ, or vice versa.

3.42 and 3.43   When we assume that σ is not known, for small N the variation in s from sample to sample will be greater than for larger N, and so CI length will vary more from sample to sample. With small N, there will be more change when you click **Assume σ known** on and off. Small N will typically give a worse, less precise estimate of σ. (Just as it does for μ. Small N overall tends to be worse.) Try $N = 5$, or even 3 or 2. As usual, large N is best. Very small samples, especially those with $N < 10$, have values of s that bounce around a great deal, so their CI lengths also bounce around a great deal. Such small samples often give a very poor indication of the extent of uncertainty: If N is very small, we can't put great trust in CI length. What do you want for Christmas? Large N!

3.44   For $df = 19$ the critical $t_{.95}$ is 2.093. MOE is 8.19, and the CI is [36.01, 52.39]. The ESCI page **Normal z t**, described in Appendix B, illustrates that the t distribution is very similar in shape to the normal distribution, for large df, i.e., large N. For small and very small N, the t distribution departs from the normal distribution, with the tails getting fatter and the critical value $t_{.95}(df)$ getting progressively greater than 1.96 as N decreases.

3.47   Larger *C*, for example, 99 rather than 95, means that we wish to be more confident of capturing μ, so we'd better throw out a larger net. MOE needs to be larger so that more of the mean heap is within the MOE lines. MOE is calculated using a larger critical value of *z* or *t*, corresponding to .99 rather than .95. Larger *C* gives wider CIs.

3.48 and 3.49   Change *C* and a different percentage of CIs will include μ, so some will need to change color. In every case, (100 − *C*)% of CIs will, in the long run, be red. In this ESCI simulation you can vary *C* up to 99.9 and down to 0.

3.50   The percent capturing typically bounces around a lot near the start of a run, then settles down. It then continues to vary, but slowly gets less variable, and closer and closer to *C*%. After many thousands of samples have been taken, it will be very close to *C*%.

3.51   The varying CI lengths may suggest more variation in the percent capturing, but the pattern is just the same as for σ known and constant CI lengths.

3.52 and 3.53   Again, perhaps surprisingly, the pattern is the same whatever the values of *N* and *C*. Play around with extreme values and see what happens.

3.54   Whenever you see a CI based on data, first remind yourself that our statistical model assumes the existence of an underlying population, although unfortunately you can't simply click to display it. Second, visualize a dance of the CIs, incorporating both a dance of the means and variation in CI widths. The reported CI is just one from that infinite dance, and we can be *C*% confident that CI captures the population parameter. But it might be red!

Chapter 4 Exercises CIs, Error Bars and *p* Values— and Randomness

4.1   Unfortunately, such events happen. If you judge from the figure that the mean and 95% CI are approximately 40, [9, 71], you might say:

- Interpretation 1: "95% of such intervals, from repeats of the experiment, will include μ."
- Interpretation 2: "We're 95% confident that interval includes μ."

- Interpretation 2: "9 to 71 is a range of plausible values for μ."
- Interpretation 2: "9 is a likely lower bound and 71 a likely upper bound for μ."
- Interpretation 3: "31 is the margin of error and the maximum likely error of estimation of μ."
- Interpretation 4: "We're about 50% confident that the interval 30 to 50 contains μ (that's about the middle third of the 95% CI, and thus approximately the 50% CI), and values outside that interval are progressively less plausible for μ."

4.2   Unfortunately, I've seen that happen, too. In your mind's eye, double the length of the interval and interpret as in 4.1.

4.3   For a 95% CI, I used the benchmarks to eyeball p a little more than .01, and for SE bars, $p = .25$. The accurate values are .011 and .20.

4.4   The answers to 4.1 could remain the same, but for 4.2 the SE bars would need to be multiplied by more than 2—in fact by about 2.8—to get the 95% CI. For 4.3 the p values for both the 95% CI and the SE bars are likely to be different. The accurate values are .023 and .27.

4.5   For $df = 29$, then $df = 4$, I clicked for t, **Heights** and **Two tails**, then used the large slider to set $t = 0$. I noted the height at the center of the curve. I moved the large slider until the two tails area was .05 and again noted the height. The ratio of those two heights is what we want. For $df = 29$, the fatness ratio is $.3955/.0524 = 7.55$, and for $df = 4$ it is $.375/.0256 = 14.6$. For μ known the ratio is 6.83, and so the ratio for $N = 30$ is similar, but as usual things are quite different for the very small $N = 4$. Note that I'm not recommending such accurate calculations for routine use, because that may tempt overemphasis of small variations in plausibility.

4.6   The key is to make general statements about plausibility being greatest around M and gradually declining at progressive distances from M, while always keeping in mind that our interval might miss μ and thus be shown in red by ESCI.

4.7   Click near red 2 to display the p value, and perhaps the p scale. Use the big slider to adjust the 95% CI until $p = .20$, then note the relation between the CI limit and $μ_0$. In fact, result **d** in Figure 4.12 illustrates $p = .20$, so the benchmark could be one third of MOE back from the limit.

4.8   Use the benchmarks to estimate values. The accurate p values are as follows, in order from **a** to **e**: .02, .08, .005, .20, and .70.

4.9   Again, use the benchmarks. Figure 4.13 is the accurate picture, in order from the left.

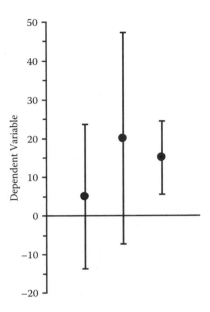

FIGURE 4.13
Means and 95% CIs for the three results in Exercise 4.9.

4.10   Use the benchmarks to eyeball in each case what the 95% CI would be, and then use them again to estimate p. For **b**, $p = .14$, and for **d**, $p = .09$.

4.11   Most likely you can only find a one-tailed test. Try to calculate or estimate the corresponding one-sided CI. Would the one- or two-sided CI be more useful in the situation?

Chapter 5 Exercises Replication and CIs, Replication and p Values

5.1   In Figure 5.1, the CIs for Experiments 4, 5, 9, 16 (just!), 22, and 24 do not capture the following mean. So $18/24 = 75\%$ do. In the long run, expect 83.4% of CIs to include the mean that follows, because this is the average capture percentage for 95% CIs and also the prediction percentage for such CIs. (If you're concerned that successive captures in such a sequence are not independent, consider just every second experiment. Then capture is certainly independent and the long-run answers are the same.) There is more about this approach in Cumming and Fidler (2009).

5.2 I made a few brief mentions of possibilities in the chapter. Consider how people think about p values and how they respond to them, including their emotional reactions.

5.3 Use the **CIs and replication** page of **ESCI chapters 5–6**. Run a simulation of 1,000 or more samples with $N = 40$ and σ assumed not known, and see that the CP values around 95% are less widely spread and do not extend so far toward 100%. Repeat for $N = 200$ and both of those tendencies are stronger.

5.4 A 99% CI is a 93.15% prediction interval, and a 90% CI a 75.52% prediction interval. SE bars give a 52.05% prediction interval, meaning that there's about a coin-toss chance that a replication will give a mean within the initial SE bars and about the same chance that it will fall outside those bars. These answers assume that σ is known or N is large, but the answers are similar for σ unknown and smaller N.

5.5 For small N, and especially for very small N such as N less than around 10, CI width varies greatly from sample to sample, as noted in Chapter 3. Therefore, when N is very small, CI width is much less informative about the amount of bouncing around of replication means.

5.6 If, for example, two-tailed $p = .01$ is reported, you could suggest that it makes sense to consider one-tailed replication p. The p interval is $(0, .083)$, which implies that a replication has an 80% chance of giving one-tailed p in that interval and a 20% chance of giving $p > .083$. That's the one-sided p interval. The two-sided interval is $(.000006, .22)$.

5.7 You might decide to focus on one-tailed replication p, and to include in your table both one-sided and two-sided p intervals. You might choose two-tailed p_{obt} values of .001, .01, .02, .05, .1, .2, .4, and .6. That would be Table 1 in Cumming (2008). For $p_{obt} = .001$, for example, the p intervals are $(0, .018)$ and $(.0000002, .070)$.

5.8 You could speak of the interval [44.2, 64.4] as having a .83 chance of including the mean if the experiment were repeated. For two-tailed $p = .072$, the one-sided p interval for one-tailed replication p is $(0, .27)$, meaning that there's a .80 chance of p falling in that interval if the experiment were repeated. The two intervals have similar prediction percentages, but the CI is probably much more informative and practically useful.

5.9 The **Dance p** video includes brief demonstrations, which you could expand and adapt.

5.10   You may find that, once you know to focus on points that are very close together, you can easily identify the random square, even with a small minimum spacing in the nonrandom square. Try also to look at overall patterns, and get a feel for how random patterns tend to appear.

5.11   The law of small numbers might encourage a gambler to believe that short runs of events should match the long-term probabilities, in which case a black would be more likely after a run of red, for example. That's the gambler's fallacy. In addition, seeing clumping in randomness could emphasize local departures from long-term expectations and thus exacerbate the effect of the gambler's fallacy.

Chapter 6 Exercises Two Designs for Comparing A and B

6.1   Robinson (1999) reported $p = .02$, which seems about right to me.

6.2   In Figure 4.5 and **CI function** the intervals with various values of C all refer to the same data, so the curves of the cat's-eye pictures are the same for every CI. The proportion shaded and the length of the intervals vary only because C varies. In contrast, **Compare A B** displays two CIs with the same value of C—they are both 95% CIs—and they differ in length only when they represent *different* sets of data, for example, when you set s_A and s_B to be different. The cat's-eye picture is fatter for the shorter 95% CI, reflecting the greater concentration of plausibility for that interval, and its greater precision. In other words, any 95% CI spans 95% of the area of its cat's-eye picture, and so if the interval is shorter the cat's-eye shaded area must also be shortened and thus be fatter.

6.3   My approximate calculations give $p = .02$ for random and $p = .30$ for not random. For the random condition, the two MOEs differ by a factor of about 2, and all four group sizes are 9 or 10, so both comparisons are close to the robustness limits of the rule of eye.

6.4   You may need to investigate how to change from the default settings of the software.

6.5   When I wanted an ESCI figure to be able to display means slightly offset, I built the figure as an Excel scatterplot, so I could specify both X and Y for every point. I hope ESCI can do the job for you, for common situations at least.

6.6   Double check that the means are for independent groups.

6.7 We need the difference in bearing between the north and 240° fields for each bird, then the mean of those differences with its CI. The researchers did not report the values, but included a figure from which I estimate 230°, [190, 270] for the control and 265°, [235, 295] for the treatment group. Both CIs include 240°, which was the change in magnetic field orientation, so both groups on average did well. CI widths for the change were not notably shorter than the CIs for orientation in the separate fields, suggesting only a small correlation between the two measures.

6.8 When $r = 1$ the measures are perfectly correlated, all the paired differences are the same, and the CI on the mean difference has zero length. When $r = -1$, the A and B measures are maximally different and so the length of the CI on the difference takes its maximum value, which happens to be twice the length of the CIs on M_A or M_B. When $r = 0$, the CIs on the difference are very similar for the two designs, which makes sense because independence implies zero correlation. If N is very large, the CIs on the difference are virtually identical. Therefore, even a small positive correlation improves the sensitivity of the paired design over that of the two-independent-groups design.

6.9 You could suggest one figure for the separate means and another for the difference with its CI. The world awaits ingenious solutions.

6.10 This convention is worth using and encouraging, but it's easy to find figures with independent means joined by lines, and repeated measures that aren't. So it's still necessary to make clear in the labels or caption the status of each independent variable. My two captions probably do a reasonable job of that. It would be very interesting to know how widely that convention is used in various disciplines, and whether any discipline has developed some other way of indicating reliably the status of independent variables in a figure.

Chapter 7 Exercises Meta-Analysis and Forest Plots

7.1 All the results are from independent groups, so it's justifiable to consider meta-analysis. Kay et al. (2010) predicted that the top left mean would be larger than the other three, and so one of their analyses was a comparison of that mean with the average of the other three, giving $p = .03$. My eyeballing suggestion is an informal way to carry out that comparison.

7.2   If the results are independent, you can make a judgment about the conceptual sense of combining them—are the questions being asked sufficiently similar? If you decide that meta-analysis is appropriate, the result is likely to be valuable.

7.4   You may have found that almost impossible. Textbooks rarely discuss replication or present more than one data set or example for any issue. Meta-analytic thinking has yet to sweep the world, but it should.

7.5   Note that MOEs for the cumulative results are reported in **Original 7** below red 14 to the far right. Add a second study and MOE decreases by 29%. Add a third and the decrease is 18% of the MOE after two. Add fourth, fifth, sixth, and seventh studies and the successive MOE decreases are 14%, 11%, 9%, and 7%, with each percentage referring to the MOE of the just-preceding meta-analysis result. The final result with seven studies has MOE reduced by 62% from the MOE of a single study.

7.6   I set up identical individual experiments each with $p = .10$. Combining two gives $p = .02$, as I reported earlier. Combining three gives $p = .004$, so this is the answer to Question 7.4. Combine more and p is even smaller.

7.7   I tried studies each with $p = .20$. Combine two and $p = .07$, then three gives .026, four .010, five .004, six .002, and seven .001. This demonstration relies on the studies all having identical results—which never happens on planet Earth. Even so, we can expect p values to decrease markedly when studies giving similar results are combined, but the detail of p, and how it changes, depends on where the different CIs lie in relation to μ_0.

7.8   If two results are estimating the same effect, it could make conceptual sense to meta-analyze, but a correlation between the two decreases the total amount of information the two together give us about the effect. Therefore, we'd expect the CI on the meta-analytic combination to be longer than if the two were independent. Independent results give 29% shortening; correlated results give less shortening. The higher the correlation, the less shortening we'd expect of the combined CI compared with the CI of either individual study. Note that this relation is exactly the reverse of our conclusion when we considered in Chapter 6 the paired design and focused on the *difference* between the means of two correlated results, rather than the meta-analytic combination of correlated results. If that's cryptic, don't worry; just note that meta-analysis is usually most appropriate and most effective when applied to independent results.

Chapter 8 Exercises Fixed Effect and Random Effects Models

8.1 and 8.2   I did this for two sets of 10 samples, all with $N = 10$. When I entered the first set into **Original 31** as the results of 10 studies, I obtained $T = 4.36$, $[0, 8.27]$, $Q = 15.5$, $p = .08$, and $I^2 = 42.0\%$. I therefore happened to get a moderate amount of heterogeneity, the two models gave slightly different values for M, and the random effects analysis gave a CI on M that was about 38% longer than the CI from the fixed effect model. My second set gave $T = 0$, $[0, 4.95]$, $Q = 6.34$, $p = .71$, and $I^2 = 0\%$. Therefore, the two models gave the same final CI. The results I obtained for my two sets of studies are both reasonable, and the sort of values we'd expect for a set of studies for which the fixed effect model is true—as it is when we use **CIjumping** with the same μ to generate the result of each study. Yes, it would be quicker and easier if **MAjumping** existed, but I hope you get the idea.

8.3 and 8.5   If you did find results you judged suitable for meta-analysis, first consider the studies and the questions they address. Are they so similar that they're close to being replications of a single study? If so, the fixed effect model may be conceptually appropriate. In practice that's unlikely, and so the random effects model is the better choice. In any case, consider the various statistics that describe the amount of heterogeneity, and compare the results given by the two models.

8.4   The question is, which quantities change substantially with k, the number of studies being combined, and why? There's no variation in $M = 5.5$, for any k and either model. The CI on M gets shorter as k increases, as we'd expect, and in each case is roughly one third longer for the random effects than the fixed effect model. I expected the width of the CI for T to decrease markedly and it did, from $[0, 3.75]$ to $[.72, 2.9]$. (I'll quote values first for $k = 10$ then for $k = 30$.) That signals that we're estimating τ less precisely when we have 10 rather than 30 studies. Similarly, the p value for Q decreased from .06 to .01. The value of Q changed considerably, from 16.5 to 49.5, but that increase mainly reflects the increase in k rather than an increase in heterogeneity. It's the comparison of Q and df that indicates the amount of heterogeneity, whereas T and

I^2 are measures that reflect heterogeneity without strong dependence on k. Whatever the k, the value of T is an estimate of τ, and the value of I^2 is an estimate of the percentage of total variability attributable to true variability in the μ_i. Both changed little with k.

8.6   You could do this first for a set of invented studies that are close to straight replications. You'd expect little or no difference between the results of the two meta-analysis models. Beware, however, the difficulty people usually have in generating numbers with about the same amount of variability we'd expect in random numbers. Recall the glowworms and penguins of Chapter 5. You may find that your Q value is much smaller than your df, suggesting that there's considerably less bouncing around than we'd expect. For a second set, you could deliberately introduce large heterogeneity, perhaps by thinking of some studies being of experts and others of novices, so you'd have several studies with small means and several with rather larger means. A random effects model would certainly be needed. We'd hope later to identify expertise as a moderator.

8.7   It would be interesting to know how meta-analytic practices vary across disciplines, and how they've changed in recent years. That's another barely researched area. My guess is that in most disciplines there are mentions of fixed effect and random effects models, and of heterogeneity and Q. These may, unfortunately, be accompanied by a hypothesis test of whether homogeneity can be rejected. There are also, however, quite different approaches to meta-analysis, for example, some that rely on Bayesian models.

Chapter 9 Exercises Larger-Scale Meta-Analysis

9.1   Not all steps can be identified in every meta-analysis report. Customs vary over disciplines. I think of the steps so broadly that they can include almost anything.

9.2   ESCI displays studies in red and blue in the forest plot, but such representation of a moderator is rare. Does it help build your intuitions about dichotomous moderators?

9.3   To be included in a subgroups analysis, a study must have a group label below red 2. Often in practice a study can't be assigned to either group, so has no group label. When subgroups analysis is on at red 5, ESCI grays out such a study and omits it from the overall analysis displayed as the white diamond. See the popout at red 4. But such a study is included in the overall analysis when subgroups analysis is off at red 5.

9.4 Prefer the diamond, which is a fine picture of a 95% CI. I don't know of other ways to picture the results of a moderator analysis, but I'd like to hear of any you find.

9.5 We are conducting a moderator analysis, so we have considerable heterogeneity, and the fixed effect model is inappropriate. The two random effects options probably give very similar results, with group CIs probably more similar for the pooled option.

9.6 It is probably useful to show weightings by varying dot size, as in Figure 9.4. I would like to hear of any other good ways to picture meta-regression.

9.7 A possibility, besides those mentioned in the text, is to seek one or a small number of variables underlying a battery of scores by using, for example, factor analysis, and then applying meta-analysis to the main factor(s).

9.8 Examine the correlation between how the two plots appear until you can examine a forest plot and see the corresponding funnel plot in your mind's eye.

9.9 A well-known approach is to calculate the *fail-safe N*, which is the number of missing studies that, if added to our meta-analysis, would reduce the overall ES to a size we judge not of practical importance. Assume that the added studies average zero ES. If the fail-safe N is very large, any publication bias is probably not invalidating our result.

9.10 The predictable structure is a great feature of Cochrane reports. For me, the forest plots are great, but it would be good to picture moderator information as well. Any ideas?

9.11 Campbell is at an earlier stage of development; the reports don't even have summary and plain language statements in a standard format. More pictures would often help.

Chapter 10 Exercises Noncentral *t*

10.1 Larger sample size means larger *df* and that noncentral *t* has less skew; μ_1 closer to μ_0 means smaller noncentrality parameter Δ and, again, that noncentral *t* has less skew. Smaller Δ also shifts the curve closer to μ_0.

10.2   Noncentral t becomes closer to symmetric as df increases, but only slowly, and even more slowly for larger Δ.

10.3   For those values of Δ and df, the probability that noncentral t is less than 4.08 is .44, the value ESCI reports as the **Left** noncentral t probability below red 5. Use the slider to move the cursor until the **Right** tail probability is .05, and see that $t = 9.18$. Note that you can use the sliders at red 4 to change the range displayed on the horizontal axis.

10.4   When $df = 30$, noncentral t is still distinctly skewed, unless Δ is very small. Noncentral t approaches the normal distribution as df increases, but only very slowly, and even more slowly for large Δ.

10.5   Assume that σ is not known. Whether H_0 or H_1 is assumed true, if $s > \sigma$, the triangle marking t in the lower panel will be closer to zero than the dot marking M is to μ_0 in the middle panel. Note that I said closer to μ_0, not μ_1.

10.6   The s pile is only markedly skewed for quite small N. As N increases, the s pile approaches the normal distribution in shape. The SD of the s pile decreases as N increases, but even for $N = 30$ and larger, the s pile still has noticeable width, meaning that the sample SD still varies noticeably from sample to sample.

10.7   Assume that H_0 is true so we're sampling from the population with mean μ_0. When $s < \sigma$ the rubber ruler is squashed in, the lines down to the bottom axis slant out, and t values are farther from zero. In other words, samples with $s < \sigma$ tend to give t values in the tails of the central t distribution. The s pile shows that $s < \sigma$ is more common than $s > \sigma$. Therefore, there are many t values in the tails, meaning that the central t has fat tails. Very small N accentuates all those tendencies, so the tails of central t are especially fat for very small df.

10.9   Such a function may give you the probability that noncentral t is less than some chosen t value, for chosen values of df and Δ. As the answer to Exercise 10.3 illustrated, the **Noncentral t** page allows you to calculate such probabilities. Set df and Δ near red 1, click near red 5 to show the probabilities, use the slider to set the desired t, then read the probability below the label **Left**.

10.10 With σ assumed known, consider the green curve in the second panel for H_0 assumed true. The vertical red lines that mark the rejection region are positioned so the tail areas of that curve beyond the red lines are each $\alpha/2$. Change α to check this. You can also note the critical value of z that's shown near red 8. That value marks where the red lines are positioned on the rubber ruler. If a sample gives M that falls in the rejection region—to the left of the left red line, or to the right of the right red line—we reject H_0. That's what we do whether the sample giving M came from the null or from the alternative population. Take further samples and the rejection region doesn't change. Now for the second, more interesting, part of the story: With σ assumed *not* known, the rejection region is defined by a critical value of t on the rubber ruler. The critical value is shown near red 8, and for $\alpha = .05$ and $df = 5$, it is $t = 2.57$. Because we don't know σ, the rejection region is calculated using s from our sample and the rubber ruler reflects that s. Take further samples and see the rejection region change as the rubber ruler stretches and squashes. The red lines are always positioned at plus-and-minus the critical t value on the ruler. Note that the rejection region is centered on μ_0 whether we're sampling from the null or alternative population. Take lots of samples from the null population and expect about α of them to give rejection of the null, which is a Type I error; take lots of samples from the alternative population and the proportion of samples that give rejection of the null is the statistical power.

Chapter 11 Exercises Cohen's *d*

11.1 For $\delta = 0.2$, just 57.9% of E lies above the mean of C. For $\delta = 0.5$ and 0.8, the percentages are, respectively, 69.1% and 78.8%, assuming in each case that the SDs are the same for E and C. My example context is the meta-analysis by Glass (1976) that found $d = 0.68$ for the average improvement after psychotherapy. This implies that 75% of treated people score higher than the mean of untreated, and one-quarter of treated people would score lower than the mean of untreated. If the two SDs are equal, it also implies that the average treated person scores higher than 75% of untreated people. The probability of superiority is .685.

11.2 Using the SD of C as the standardizer, as **d picture** does, if the SD of E increases, d remains unchanged, but a smaller proportion of the area under the E curve lies above the mean of C. When I doubled the SD of E for $d = 0.68$, the percentage of E exceeding the mean of C decreased from 75.2% to 63.3%. The best standardizer for d is a matter for judgment, but where a treatment is expected to change the SD markedly, it may be best to regard C as the reference and use the SD of C as the standardizer. The SD of E needs to be considered before interpreting a d value in terms of percentages. The value of d may not tell the full story.

11.3   There are other test instruments developed in psychology or education that are scaled to have a stated mean and SD in a large and carefully selected reference population. I would like to hear of examples from other disciplines.

11.4   Considering the Experimental group by itself, and therefore using s_E as the standardizer, $d = (47.60 - 40)/12.46 = 0.61$, where $\mu_0 = 40$ is our reference mean for measuring d. Considering both groups, s_p probably gives the best estimate of population SD, so would be a good choice of standardizer for the difference between Experimental and the comparison value of 40. This gives $d = (47.60 - 40)/11.48 = 0.66$. If the treatment is expected to change the SD markedly, we could choose to use Control as a reference, and thus use s_C as the standardizer to obtain $d = (47.60 - 40)/10.41 = 0.73$. Yes, choice of standardizer can make a big difference to d.

11.5   My experience is that t values are very often reported, but d values rarely. I hope d is reported more often in the future, but meanwhile I've frequently found it useful to use these beautifully simple formulas to calculate d, given only t and N (or t and N_1 and N_2). Make sure you identify the experimental design, and then choose the formula appropriate to that design. For paired or any other repeated measure design it's often hard to calculate d, because any t value reported is almost certainly based on an SD (e.g., s_{diff}) that's inappropriate as the standardizer for d, and the SD we need is often not reported. Knowing d can help interpretation, especially if the original measure is not widely used or understood.

11.6   It's straightforward to use **Data two** to find CIs in original units, and to see a nice figure. Click at red 9 for the second figure. Click at red 7 to indicate whether or not you are prepared to assume homogeneity of variance. If you are, then you can scroll right and click at red 11 to reveal d and d_{unb} and the CI on d. I'm often prepared to assume homogeneity of variance, unless there are strong reasons against it. I usually prefer to report and interpret d_{unb} and the CI on d.

11.7   If you know a little about Excel, here's another way to explore the ideas of this exercise. Go to **Simulate paired**, scroll right, and click at red 13 to reveal the panel reporting d. Remove protection—see Appendix A for help. Just to the right of the cell reporting the value of d, type in a simple formula: $= ES/s_{diff}$. To get ES, click on the cell below red 10 that reports the value of ES, and for s_{diff} click on the cell just above that shows the value of s_{diff}. (Be sure to click on the cells reporting the numerical values, not the cells with the labels "ES" and "s_{diff}".) Now when you click at red 1 for another experiment you should see the value of d, calculated using s_{av} as the standardizer, and just beside it should be d calculated using s_{diff}. Compare the two values, and note the correlation reported below red 9. Take further experiments. The higher the correlation in a particular data set, the greater the difference between the two values of d. Use a small N to get large variation in correlation from experiment to experiment. If we regard the d based on s_{av} as what we want, the d based on s_{diff} is usually an overestimate and, when the correlation is high, a very considerable overestimate.

11.8   The adjustment factor is referred to as J, so Equation (11.13) becomes $d_{unb} = J \times d$. Equation (11.13) states a good approximation for J. Figure 11.7 is my plot of the accurate value of J against df. Values of J are stated for df = 2, 3, 4, 5, 10, 20, 30, 40, and 50. Equation (11.13) gives approximate J = .571 for df = 2, and approximate J = .842 for df = 5. Those values are only a little different from the accurate values in Figure 11.7. For values of df more than about 8 the values given by Equation (11.13) are the same as the accurate values, to three decimal places. The figure suggests that it's worth using d_{unb} rather than d. Only when df is large, say 40 or 50 or more, does the adjustment have very little effect.

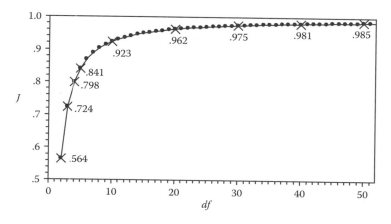

FIGURE 11.7
Accurate values of J plotted against df, where J is the adjustment factor needed to calculate d_{unb}, using the formula $d_{unb} = J \times d$. Values of J are shown for selected df.

11.9   I don't know of other terminology, beyond what I've mentioned in this chapter. Disciplines other than psychology may use other terms or symbols, and I'd like news of any that you know of. I also don't know of any use of d_{unb} in other disciplines, even though I expect it might often be the standardized ES of choice. Please let me know of any examples you find.

11.11 The sampling distribution of s^2 is the chi-square distribution with $df = (N - 1)$, multiplied by a constant, which is $\sigma^2/(N - 1)$. This distribution is positively skewed, has a mean of σ^2, and, for $df > 2$, is a smooth curve with a hump maximum somewhat below the mean of σ^2. The sampling distribution of s is the chi distribution, which is also positively skewed and, for $df > 2$, a smooth curve with a hump maximum a little below the mean, which is very close to σ. Observe the shape of the s pile after taking 300 samples; try this for various values of N. Skew is more pronounced for small N.

11.13 For the Control group in Table 11.1 we found $d = 0.21$, using s_C as the standardizer. Type this d and $N = 10$ into the **d single group** page as the values for Study 1. Click the button at red 4 to calculate CIs, and find that the 95% CI for that d is [–0.42, 0.83]. This CI is wide, as we'd expect with such a small N.

11.14 We found that $d = 0.47$. Enter this and the sample sizes into **d two groups** and find that the 95% CI is [–0.43, 1.35]. The **CI for d** page also gives this result. Again, a wide CI.

11.15 The only way to find these CIs with ESCI is to enter all the data values into **Data paired**, which gives $d = 0.34$, [0.10, 0.58]. The design is sensitive and gives a relatively precise estimate of the effect, as indicated by the relatively narrow CI.

11.16 We'll see in Chapter 14 some further ES measures often used in meta-analyses, sometimes after transformation from various original units measures used in different studies. One is Pearson's correlation r.

11.17 First I decided that the three studies were sufficiently comparable to combine because they all used the same team-building game as the intervention, a two-independent-groups design, and a variety of employees as participants. I decided also that the three different measures of on-the-job cooperation were sufficiently similar. I entered the data into a spreadsheet and used Equation (6.1) to calculate the pooled within-group SD to be $s_p = 6.67$, 24.98, and 37.49 for the three studies, respectively. I then used Equation (11.4) to calculate d, with s_p as the standardizer, and obtained $d = 0.750$, –0.280, and 0.773. I entered those d values and the N_C and

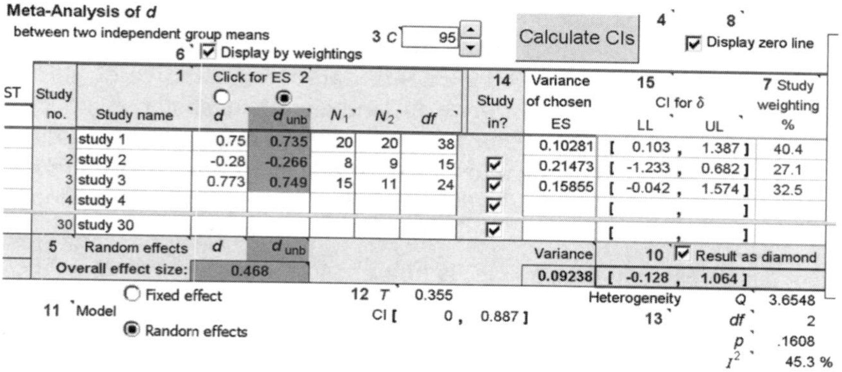

Meta-Analysis of d
between two independent group means

ST Study no.	Study name	d	d_{unb}	N_1	N_2	df	Study in?	Variance of chosen ES	CI for δ LL	UL	Study weighting %
1	study 1	0.75	0.735	20	20	38		0.10281	[0.103 ,	1.387]	40.4
2	study 2	-0.28	-0.266	8	9	15	☑	0.21473	[-1.233 ,	0.682]	27.1
3	study 3	0.773	0.749	15	11	24	☑	0.15855	[-0.042 ,	1.574]	32.5
4	study 4						☑		[,	]	
30	study 30						☑		[,	]	

3 C [95] **Calculate CIs** ☑ Display zero line

6 ☑ Display by weightings

1 Click for ES 2   ○ ◉

14 Variance 15   7 Study weighting

5	Random effects	d	d_{unb}		Variance	10 ☑ Result as diamond
	Overall effect size:	0.468			0.09238	[-0.128 , 1.064]

○ Fixed effect   12 T 0.355   Heterogeneity   Q   3.6548
11 ˙Model   CI [0 , 0.887]   13 ˙ df   2
◉ Random effects   p   .1608
                                                                              I^2 45.3 %

FIGURE 11.8
A part screen image from **d two groups** for the meta-analysis of the data of Exercise 11.17.

N_E values into the **d two groups** page of **ESCI Meta-Analysis**. I clicked to select d_{unb} as the ES to be meta-analyzed, to give an unbiased estimate of the population ES. Figure 11.8 shows part of the screen giving the result of the meta-analysis. The overall ES for a random effects model is $d_{unb} = 0.47$, [−0.13, 1.06]. The CI on the overall d is very similar. I noted that the fixed effect model gave quite similar results, but with a shorter CI; I could see no reason to prefer the fixed effect model. With only three small studies and considerable variation in what the different studies found, it's not surprising that the final CI is so wide and that the statistics Q, I^2, and T suggest that there may be considerable heterogeneity between the studies, although we can't be sure. I conclude that the three studies gave differing outcomes and together can only estimate that the effect of the game may well be positive but could be anywhere between negligible and quite large.

Chapter 12 Exercises Power

12.1   Assume that $\sigma = 1.2$ is known, so target $\delta = 0.5/1.2 = 0.42$. Enter that δ, $N = 100$, and $\alpha = .01$ into the **Power picture** page of **ESCI chapters 10–13**. Click near red 1 to select z as the test statistic, because we are assuming that σ is known. Power is reported as .95. Nice! Change any value to see how power changes. It would be good to retain $\alpha = .01$, but you could set a smaller target δ, although dropping it a little to 0.3 decreases power drastically, to .66.

12.2   Again assume that $\sigma = 1.2$ is known, so target $\delta = 0.3/1.2 = 0.25$. You could use either **Simulate two** or **Power two**. I entered population values at red 7 in **Simulate two** that gave $\delta = 0.25$. Using $N_1 = N_2 = 100$ and $\alpha = .01$, and z as the test statistic, gives power $= .21$. Terrible! Changing α to .05 increases power, but only to .42. We'll either have to live with a larger target δ, or plan to use samples even larger than 100. To calculate power for such larger samples, use the bottom panel in **Power two**, at red 6.

12.3   Again assume that $\sigma = 1.2$ is known, so target $\delta = 0.2/1.2 = 0.17$, which is ambitious. In the **Power paired** page of **ESCI chapters 10–13**, I set $\delta = 0.2$, and $\alpha = .05$. I set $\rho = .72$ to be at the conservative end of the range mentioned, and chose z as the test statistic. I moved the N cursor and read off power. For $N = 100$, power $= .76$, which is barely acceptable. If $\rho = .80$, in the middle of the range, power $= .88$, which is better. We may need to choose a larger target δ, or plan to test more than 100 participants.

12.4   Note carefully whether your other textbook uses normal distributions and z for all power calculations, or uses noncentral t calculations at least for small samples. There may be power curves or tables of values of N that are based on accurate calculations for small samples, even if no mention is made of noncentral t. Note that approximations are often used when power is calculated, so there may be small disagreements between different books, and between other textbooks and the values ESCI calculates. Such small differences rarely matter in practice.

12.5   The **Power two** page of **ESCI chapters 10–13** makes it easy to compare two-independent-groups experiments with targets of $\delta = 0.2$ and $\delta = 0.6$. The comparison emphasizes yet again how sensitive power is to target δ. With target $\delta = 0.2$, even $N = 100$ gives power of only .29, with $\alpha = .05$. With target $\delta = 0.6$, again with $\alpha = .05$, power is .8 for $N = 45$.

12.6   The area under the H_1 curve corresponding to the left rejection tail is so small that it's invisible in those two figures. A value of t that lands in that area is less than -2.26 and gives $p < .05$, so we reject H_0. To calculate power we assume that H_1 is true, and so we're sampling from the H_1 curve. Such a t is a result extremely far into the left tail of the H_1 curve: The result departs sufficiently from H_0 to justify rejection, but it's in the direction opposite to the true population effect. It's therefore extremely unlikely to occur. We're using two-tailed α, and so that tiny left tail under the H_1 curve must be included in the power calculation, but its area is so small that often in practice we can ignore it. You may wish to consider power for one-tailed α and thus a rejection region in just one tail of the H_0 curve, but I don't discuss that in this book, and ESCI doesn't include that case either.

12.7 You could focus on values that are typical for experiments in your discipline. For example, what α is most commonly used? Can you estimate, even roughly, what δ values correspond to the effects typically reported in your discipline? Using t, the answers to the three questions are as follows: power = .82, N = 95, and a little less than $\delta = 0.5$, respectively.

12.8 I remember just two cases, both being two-independent-groups experiments with α = .05. Then I estimate power for any other situation by guessing how different the situation is from those two cases. I remember N = 32 for power = .5 and $\delta = 0.5$. (That's using t. When using z, power = .52 and we have the experiment I used in Chapter 5 to demonstrate the dance of the means. As I reported then, such an experiment has disappointingly lower power, but is typical of those reported in a number of research fields.) I also remember that N = 64 for power = .8 and $\delta = 0.5$.

12.9 If you are not sure whether a value reported for power is post hoc power, try changing the data slightly (make a few of the data values larger or smaller, but don't change N) and running the analysis again. If the value reported for power changes, most likely it's post hoc power.

12.10 It's good practice with any software to learn how to get beyond the defaults. Good defaults can be helpful, but you must not let the defaults make your statistical decisions. Explore any tutorials offered by your software and the help system. These can often be surprisingly useful, perhaps after you have overcome an initial reluctance to try them.

12.11 G*Power 3 comes with extensive help materials. For simple things you can probably just explore. After installing and opening G*Power, in the drop box labeled "Test family" choose "t tests." In the box labeled "Statistical test" choose "Means: difference between two independent means," and in the "Type of power analysis" box read all the options. Note that "post hoc power" is, unfortunately, given a very broad meaning: It refers to the calculation of power, given α, N, and any type of population ES. If you use d resulting from an experiment for that ES you would get what I call post hoc power, but if you use target δ you would get what I call legitimate power, which is no doubt what you want. Explore and enjoy. You should be able to verify that, with ES = 0.5, N = 32 in each group, and two-tailed α = .05, then power = .504, in agreement with ESCI using t as the test statistic. Note that G*Power also displays the power picture, including a noncentral t distribution. Click on the button at the bottom labeled "X-Y plot for a range of values" and explore what curves G*Power can generate.

12.12 and 12.13   Examine any places where NHST is discussed or reported. Look especially at any cases where p values are large and results that are not statistically significant are discussed. If you can, find a report of a power calculation. Is it done well? Does it make clear the target δ used in the calculation?

12.14 I guessed that, because post hoc power is somewhat linked to p values, its amount of variation may remain quite large, even for large N. I described in Box 11.1 how I modified pages in ESCI to run simulations to check various calculations. For this exercise, I modified **Simulate two** to keep track of the post hoc power values calculated for a large number of simulated experiments. ESCI reported the mean and SD of those values. I recorded the SD of post hoc power values for long runs of experiments, for a wide range of N, δ, and α values. I concluded that the amount of variation in post hoc power—the amount of bouncing around with replication—is quite similar for a wide range of experiments, even with large N. It seems to be quite similar at least for N up to 100, and at least for power anywhere in the range .3 to .8. That's one more reason to avoid post hoc power: It doesn't become better behaved even at large sample sizes.

12.15 Improving the experimental design, for example, by using matching or a repeated measure, typically increases both power and informativeness, as does increasing N. Meta-analysis almost certainly increases both power and informativeness. Increasing α increases power but not informativeness. Increasing target δ increases power markedly, but arguably only increases informativeness if you also make the experimental manipulation larger or more effective. Other strategies to refine the experimental procedure or improve measurement can reduce overall error, and thus increase both power and informativeness. I'll discuss those further in the next chapter.

Chapter 13 Exercises Precision for Planning

13.1   Going way back to Chapter 1 and Lucky–Noluck we could discuss Figure 1.1 in terms of the precision of the two studies being quite low in the context of a difference of only about 1.5 between the two means. In other words, the CI arm lengths are large relative to that difference. There are numerous other places where we could reword the discussion or describe a figure with CIs, simply by focusing on arm length. I recommend making a habit, whenever inspecting CIs—whether given as numbers or as error bars in a figure—to note the arm length and think about what its value means as a measure of precision, the maximum likely error of estimation of the effect under investigation.

13.2 I've just scanned the indexes of a dozen statistics textbooks on my shelves without finding a single mention of precision. Some are very well recognized texts. Lockhart (1998), however, is a text that takes CIs seriously and also discusses precision. His definition is the same as mine, and he considers some of the issues raised in this chapter. If you find in your text any presentation or use of precision that you think is interesting, please let me know. I would be especially interested to hear of good alternative ways to explain the analyses of precision and assurance, and to picture the way N varies with f and other characteristics of an experiment.

13.3 My informal discussions suggest that the "±" often refers to a judgment of the finest measurement that can be made by the instrument being used. There's also a well-developed theory of measurement error, used in physics at least, that describes how error compounds when a number of measurements are combined in various ways. I suspect that there's interesting scope to investigate how that theory relates to our uses of CIs and precision.

13.4 Consider the dance of the CIs, as in the lower half of Figure 3.8, which shows CIs based on s whose lengths bounce around because s varies over samples. Focus just on one arm of each CI and we have a dance of the precision values. Use larger N and the s pile is narrower and the precision values don't vary so much over replication. Yes, with larger N they are all generally much shorter, but the proportional variation is also reduced. Use the **CIjumping** page of **ESCI chapters 1–4** to explore these ideas.

13.5 Target MOE is $f = 0.2/1.2 = 0.17$. The figure in the **Precision one** page of **ESCI chapters 10–13** doesn't give N for that f, so type in 0.2 and 1.2 as **Target MOE** and **Population σ**, respectively, near red 5. Set $C = 95$ near red 1 and $γ = 90$ near red 2 then see that $N = 139$ using z, 141 using t (in this case f is our expected MOE), and 161 with 90% assurance.

13.6 Enter 0.1 for target MOE and 1.2 for population σ in the panel near red 5 in **Precision two**. Set $C = 95$ and $γ = 99$, then see that $N = 1107$ using z, 1108 using t (in this case f is our expected MOE), and 1184 with 99% assurance. Yes, they are very large sample sizes, but requiring high assurance makes only a relatively modest increase in N.

13.7 Let's again aim for MOE of $f = 0.1$ scale units. In **Precision paired** let $C = 95$ and $\gamma = 99$, and choose $\rho = .72$, the lower end of the range. Then **Precision paired** tells us that $N = 310$ using z, 313 using t (in this case f is our expected MOE), and 368 with 99% assurance. Using $\rho = .89$, at the high end of the range, the N values are dramatically reduced: 122, 125, and 159, respectively.

13.8 We'll use the Cohen's d panel of **Precision two**. I set $C = 95$ and $\gamma = 99$. Let's choose $\delta = 0.6$ as the planning ES. I tried target $MOE_{av} = 0.2$, but was told "No" by ESCI. I tried 0.25 with the same result. With $MOE_{av} = 0.3$, I found that $N = 90$ would suffice, and $N = 96$ with 99% assurance. The popout comments explain that for the two-independent-groups design, using d, ESCI can only handle values of N up to about 100. (The accuracy of the noncentral t calculations impose this limit.) Considering the second planned experiment, I changed the planning ES to $\delta = 0.2$, and found N values of 86 for **Calculate N** and 89 for **N for γ**—only a little smaller than before, but once again illustrating that achieving very high assurance in some cases does not require a much larger N.

13.9 You could focus on designs and values that are typical for experiments you encounter in your discipline. Can you estimate, even roughly, what values of f are common in your discipline? I confess that I find this quite a challenge, but I feel most comfortable thinking of Cohen's d, even though only a small proportion of reported studies use it. Cohen's d provides a common measurement context within which I can think about results from different fields of research. So I'd focus my game on intuitions about d and N.

13.10 The rough rules of thumb I remember (I'm assuming 95% CIs in all cases):

- z or t doesn't make much difference, provided that N is not too small.
- For the paired design, the value of ρ makes an immense difference, especially when it's greater than around .7.
- You might as well do an assurance analysis, with $\gamma = 99$, but it may also be worth noting what expected MOE the resulting N gives.
- For the two-independent-groups design, $f = 0.28$ needs N around 100, and $f = 0.5$ needs N around 30.

- Think in terms of d whenever appropriate. Using d and a single group, when planning ES = 0.5 and target $MOE_{av} = 0.2$, N is a bit more than 100 (actually 109), and 123 for 99% assurance. Same, but for target $MOE_{av} = 0.3$, N is around 50 (actually 49), and 59 for 99% assurance.

13.11 Please let me know of any good statistical software you find that carries out analyses of precision and assurance, especially if it has good graphics and is very easy to use by researchers in general.

13.12 I suspect that may be hard to do. As I say, if you find any interesting explanations of precision, or good examples of it being used, please let me know.

13.13 Again, please let me know of any interesting examples you find.

13.14 Consult any research design books you have handy. Consider changing the experimental manipulation so that you are likely to be investigating a larger effect—often an especially potent way to improve the chance of success. For example, give 8 weeks of the new reading program, not 4 weeks. Make your experimental procedures more uniform and more carefully controlled, to reduce error variation. Give participants sufficient training so they are all operating at a similar level of understanding of the task—their performance is likely to be more similar. Consider simplifying your experimental design and reducing the number of independent variables or the number of levels of those independent variables so, for a given total amount of experimental effort, the remaining comparisons are likely to give more precise estimates. Use precision for planning when it can assist, but don't let it dominate your thinking.

Chapter 14 Exercises Correlations, Proportions, and Further Effect Size Measures

14.1 Every time you click **New data set** you get a new sample with your chosen r, and the scatterplot varies considerably in appearance. You see alternative clouds for r. Try $N = 10$ and $N = 300$ (the maximum). You may feel that the variation is greater at small and medium N.

14.2 I find that the cross lines are usually helpful for any r or N, and especially for small N, although they are not infallible. For example, they don't help us see that the middle cloud in Figure 14.4

($r = .5$) illustrates a higher correlation than the cloud on the right ($r = .3$), because the upper-left plus lower-right count of dots is actually higher for the middle cloud. When eyeballing a scatterplot, try not to be overly influenced by a couple of extreme points, although when N is small such outlying points have a big influence on the calculated r.

14.3 The other book no doubt has much more about how to calculate r and, most likely, the close relation with regression. It may not have so much about the extent of sampling variability. If it omits CIs, that's unfortunate.

14.4 Just about any statistics software will calculate r for a set of data. (Even ESCI does this: See the **Data paired** page of **ESCI chapters 5–6**. Correlation is reported below red 7.) Any exercise that requires interpretation of a correlation, or comparison of independent correlations, can benefit from the CIs ESCI provides. Any exercise that asks for NHST can probably be answered more informatively with CIs.

14.5 Use CIs and figures whenever they help. Practice thinking in terms of CIs.

14.6 Watch what's revealed as you click the **Step** button several times, and try to build a story.

14.7 If you use correlations as reliability or validity measures, you may regard .9 as large and .7 as low. Or Cohen's benchmarks may seem about right, at least sometimes. You should tailor what you remember to your situation. You can use **r to z** to verify that $r = .1$ needs $N = 385$ for the 95% CI to touch zero. Similarly, $r = .3$ needs $N = 43$ and $r = .5$ needs $N = 16$. As usual, the ES makes an enormous difference in how easy it is to achieve statistical significance. For $r = .5$, $N = 57$ gives a CI whose MOE_{av} is .2, so the CI is roughly $.5 \pm .2$, ignoring asymmetry. For $r = .8$, $N = 17$ gives $MOE_{av} = .2$.

14.8 I expect the width of the dance to halve, approximately, when N is multiplied by 4, keeping ρ the same. For fixed N, the width of the dance increases for ρ closer to zero.

14.9 Alternative clouds for r all have the same value of r, whereas the dance of the r clouds refers to the scatterplots for the sequence of different r values in the dance of the r values.

14.10 **Sample r** reports near red 4 the numbers of captures of ρ by the lower and the upper arms of the CIs; these numbers are usually a little different. Most important, however, is the overall capture percentage of 95% CIs. My tests find that's about 91% when $N = 10$. For N at least 30, and for virtually any value of ρ, it's usually between about 94% and 95%, and almost always between 94% and 95.5%, as I mentioned earlier. The approximation is therefore good, unless *N* is very small.

14.11 It would be approximately normal in shape, and thus close to symmetric.

14.12 The rule is a bit conservative: When overlap is .5, *p* is usually a little less than .05.

14.13 Set *C* as you choose; adjust r_1, r_2, N_1, and N_2 until the *LL* of the CI on the difference is zero; then check how close the *p* value is to $(1 - C/100)$. If $C = 90$, for example, the *p* value should be close to .10. My tests suggest close agreement between the two approximate methods.

14.14 If NHST is used with *r*, try using a CI instead and look for improved interpretation.

14.15 The CIs on the difference should be the same.

14.16 For proportions, ESCI provides only those two pages in **ESCI Effect sizes**. To check the overlap rule, note overlap in **Proportions**, then use the CI on the difference of the same two proportions that's displayed in **Diff proportions** to eyeball the *p* value.

14.18 "Risk" may not appear, but watch for "probability," "chance," "percentages," and "odds."

14.19 Once alerted to the problem, I suspect that you'll often notice media reports of risk, and that they are often not easy to understand accurately.

14.20 Odds ratio (OR) is one other ES often used in medicine and other disciplines.

14.21 You may need to dig deep beyond the default settings, or even learn how to write a script or program. Even then, CIs on differences may be hard to calculate. If you can calculate CIs on differences, try to find what approximate method the software uses. Compare the results with the CIs given by ESCI.

Chapter 15 Exercises More Complex Designs and The New Statistics in Practice

15.1 You may have to choose just one of the several measures reported, and perhaps simplify the design. Estimate realistic CIs if you have to. Is the figure illuminating?

15.2 You may have to invent such values, perhaps using hints in the researchers' discussion of their results. I hope such reference labels and values become much more widely used.

15.3 There are a number of possibilities, depending on the questions being addressed by the meta-analysis. The ES that most directly assesses the effect of the therapy could be the difference between the two differences in the lower panel, which would measure the advantage of treatment over control. A CI would have to be calculated.

15.4 Different research fields and subfields have different customs. If exploration is mentioned, look for advice about the status of the effects it uncovers.

15.5 Some disciplines hardly ever use ANOVA; others use it heavily. Often contrasts are better, as Rosenthal and Rosnow (1985), among others, have argued.

15.6 Finding a suitable ES and calculating the CI may each pose a problem, unfortunately.

15.7 Check that the proportions are independent. Proportions can often do a better job than χ^2.

15.8 Linear regression is another area in which CI pictures can help assess goodness of fit. In any case, consider carefully whether each independent variable varies between or within groups, and make sure to display appropriate CIs to guide interpretation.

15.9 Customs vary, but ESs and CIs are rarely both reported and interpreted. Alas.

15.10 Advice, if any, may only say how to report statistics, but the examples chosen may be revealing. Any mention of the *Publication Manual* may be general, or only for referencing style.

15.11 The most common lesson is that dogged persistence eventually succeeds. Usually.

Appendix A Loading and Using ESCI

ESCI ("ESS-key") is *Exploratory Software for Confidence Intervals*. ESCI runs under Microsoft Excel, and a licensed copy of Excel is required to run ESCI. ESCI for Windows runs under Excel 2010, 2007, or 2003. ESCI for Macintosh runs under Excel 2011.

All ESCI modules that accompany this book are available from www.thenewstatistics.com and may be downloaded freely for noncommercial use. Make sure you save any ESCI module on your own local hard disk before you open and run it. See the document **ESCI Readme** at the website for the latest information about versions of Excel that are supported, and details for using the various different versions. (At the website there is also news about any errors that have been discovered in the book or software.) My custom is that every file name includes the date of last modification, so, for example, **ESCI chapters 1–4 Jul 8 2011** is the version of July 8, 2011. You can thus easily check that you are using the latest version. At the **Intro** page of any module, scroll down to see the license conditions for ESCI.

Note the tabs at the bottom of the Excel display area. These take you to the different pages in an ESCI module.

For Windows: Excel 2010, 2007, and 2003

ESCI runs under any of these versions of Excel. Excel **2010** and **2007** run more slowly than Excel **2003**. In some cases the figure displayed in ESCI responds more immediately to manipulation of the sliders and spinners (see below) in Excel **2003** than in later versions. If you still have Excel **2003**, preserve it carefully.

For Macintosh: Excel 2011

ESCI runs under Excel **2011**, but not under Excel **2008** because that version of Excel cannot run VBA macros (see below), which are used by ESCI for many purposes.

Loading and Running ESCI

ESCI modules are regular Excel workbooks and should open immediately in Excel.

Macros

Many ESCI pages use small programs called "VBA macros" to carry out operations triggered by your clicking a button or carrying out some other action. Therefore, those operations will not work unless macros are enabled. The procedure to enable macros is different for different versions of Excel. See **ESCI Readme** for advice.

Popout Comments

Make sure that **popout comments** are visible when you hover the mouse near any little red triangle. If you can't see them, consult **ESCI Readme** for advice.

Screen Resolution and Display Size

ESCI is designed so the display conveniently fits the screen for **screen resolution** of about 1280 × 800 or 1024 × 768. It may help to use full-screen display: **ESCI Readme** has details of how to do this in the various versions of Excel, and news of any changes relating to screen size or resolution.

You may choose to change your screen resolution: See **ESCI Readme** for details of how to change screen resolution in the various versions of Excel and for various operating systems. However, if you change screen resolution, some aspects of the display may not appear so neat, for example, the neat stacking of means in the mean heap. Alternatively, on any page you can adjust the zoom by changing it from the usual 100%, but, if zoom is changed too far from 100%, labels and values may not fit so well in their cells.

Protection

Pages are protected to reduce the chance of making inadvertent changes, but protection can be removed—no password is needed. See **ESCI Readme** for details on how to remove protection in the various versions of Excel. Take care, and be sure not to save the workbook or, if you wish to save, give it a different name.

On-Screen Controls

In many ESCI pages, *sliders*—which look like small scrollbars—and *spinners*—small controls with up and down arrows—can change what's displayed in the figures. Experiment with different ways to use these controls. Click and hold, or click repeatedly. With a slider you can click and drag the thumbnail (the little rectangle you can move), click either side of the thumbnail, click and hold an end arrow, or click repeatedly on an end arrow. Different versions of Excel respond a little differently, so find what works best for you.

Using Figures Outside Excel

An ESCI figure can be transferred to a Word document. Click on the figure, very close to its edge, to select it: Depending on the version of Excel you may see a highlighted border or little black square handles. Copy, then go to the Word document and paste. **Paste Special/Picture (Enhanced metafile)** works well. (Text like **Paste Special** refers to text or a label or a menu entry on the Excel screen.) Allowing copy and paste of figures requires that figures are not protected. Therefore, they can be accidentally changed. If that happens, try **Undo**. Otherwise, close ESCI—don't Save—then reload ESCI.

An alternative, which I used to make the figures in this book that show part of an ESCI screen, is to use (in Windows) the PRNT SCRN (or PRINT SCREEN) key to transfer an image of the whole screen to the clipboard. Paste this into a Paint program, use the rectangle select tool to select an area of the image, then copy and paste this into your Word document. **Paste Special/Picture (Windows metafile)** works well.

Editing of Figures

Figures can be changed as desired using any Excel editing facilities: Change axis labels, change scaling on an axis, change chart format, etc. It's usually best to edit a figure as you wish, before copying it from ESCI to your Word document.

To deselect a figure, after edit or copy, press the Esc key once or twice. Alternatively, in some versions of Excel, you can simply click elsewhere in the display area.

Number Formats

In most cases ESCI reports numbers to an appropriate number of decimal places. A *p* value, for example, may be reported as .000, meaning it's zero when rounded to three decimal places. That would accord with the APA

Publication Manual (2010), which advises that exact values for p should not be reported if less than .001.

In some cases ESCI uses a general format for numbers to accommodate a very wide range of possible values. In such cases, extremely small or large values may be reported in scientific format: 0.0000045 may appear as 4.5E-06, meaning 4.5×10^{-6}. Similarly, 26,800,000 may appear as 2.7E+07, meaning 2.7×10^{7}.

Sound

The **Dance p** page of **ESCI chapters 5–6** uses five small sound files. These are grouped for download together with **ESCI chapters 5–6**. Make sure those five files are in the same folder with the ESCI module itself, to make them accessible to ESCI. If you don't hear sound when a p value is taken, check that **Sound** is clicked on, near red 5 of the **Dance p** page; that the sound files are in the same folder as ESCI; and, of course, that your speakers are on and volume is sufficient.

ESCI Formulas and Calculations

Most formulas and arrays of data are visible if you scroll right or down, so, if you like, you can see how ESCI does its work. Some formulas need to be placed behind the figures. Similarly, you can examine the VBA code if you wish. In some cases, formulas need to be placed in hidden columns to the left of the display area but you can unhide these columns if you wish. Similarly, on a few pages formulas are placed in hidden rows at the top of the display.

Strategy for Getting Started With a New ESCI Page

- Scan the display, read the labels, and hover the mouse over any little red triangle to see a popout comment.
- A new page may look confusing, but one way to start is to follow the bold red numbers 1, 2, ... , in sequence, reading the popouts as you go. Note that when, in the ESCI exercises, I say something like "click near red 4," I may be referring to clicking anywhere in the colored area that has red 4 in the top left.
- Experiment. See what happens when you click buttons, spinners, radio buttons, checkboxes, or sliders. You won't break anything, usually you can retreat, and if all else fails you can exit

from Excel (don't Save) and start again. Discuss what you see with a peer.

- Discover how ESCI works, yes, but keep your thinking on the statistical ideas—they are the most interesting things, and what really matters.

- As you play around, keep thinking about how you could use ESCI to explain the statistical ideas to someone else. Then have a go at doing that.

- In Chapter 1, just before the start of the first ESCI exercises, see the further hints about using ESCI for statistical learning.

Appendix B ESCI for the Normal and t Distributions, and Values of z and t

The **Normal z t** page of **ESCI chapters 1–4** allows you to investigate the shape of the t distribution for various values of df, and compare it with the normal (z) distribution. You can also display tail areas and read off probabilities for a selected value of z or t. Conversely, you can find the critical value of z or t for a chosen tail area.

You may choose simply to play around to find out what's possible. Appendix A makes some suggestions. In addition, here are some things you could try:

- Near red 1, click t **(and z)**. Near red 4, click **No tails**. Clear all checkboxes, then use the spinner near red 1 to change df and watch as the t distribution changes shape. Only for very small df does it depart far from the normal distribution, shown for comparison in gray.

- However, the tail areas of t and the normal (z) do differ considerably, even for N not very small. For the normal, $z_{.95}$ is the familiar 1.96, where $z_{.95}$ is the two-tailed critical value of z. You can find this value by clicking near red 1 to select z, clicking near red 4 to select **Two tails**, then again to turn on **Areas**, then moving the large slider below the figure until the amount labeled in the figure as **two tails** is .0500, or alternatively the central area is .9500. Click near red 1 to select t, set $df = 29$, again adjust the large slider so that **two tails** is .0500, and then you can see that $t_{.95}(29) = 2.045$ is shown near red 2. This is the two-tailed critical value for t when $N = 30$. You might then find that $t_{.95}(9) = 2.262$. Traditionally, $N = 30$ has often been taken as the smallest sample size at which t and z are practically the same, but the two critical values, 1.96 and 2.045, differ by more than 4%. Therefore, it is not very accurate to use z when $N = 30$ and σ is not known.

- Look below the big slider to see more accurate values than those that are displayed in the figure. If, for example, you want to find $t_{.95}(4)$, you might notice that the slider set on either 2.776 or 2.777 gives the central area marked as .95. Which is correct? Look below the slider and see that 2.7764451 is the accurate critical value for a two-tail probability of .0500000.

Appendix C Guide to the ESCI Modules and Pages

There are two parts to this Appendix. The first lists the ESCI modules, and then for each module the pages are listed with a brief description of what each offers. The second is intended to help you find the most appropriate ESCI page if you wish to analyze your own data.

The ESCI Modules and Their Pages

The ESCI modules are

ESCI chapters 1–4
ESCI chapters 5–6
ESCI Meta-Analysis
ESCI chapters 10–13
ESCI chapters 14–15
ESCI Effect sizes

ESCI chapters 1–4

The pages within this module are as named in bold below. I use the same format for the pages of the other modules, which follow.

Intro—Introductory page. Overview. License information.

Two studies—*Chapter 1*. The Lucky–Noluck example. Explore three presentations (NHST, CI, and meta-analysis) of two studies, one statistically significant and the other not.

CIjumping—*Chapter 3*. See the population, samples, and CIs. Explore sampling, and the mean heap, dance of the means, and dance of the CIs.

Normal z t—*Appendix B* and *Chapter 3*. See the normal and *t* distributions. Find tail areas, heights, and critical values of *z* and *t*.

CI function—*Chapter 4.* See a dynamic graph of level of confidence, C, and the p value, against the two limits of a CI. See cat's-eye pictures.

CI and p—*Chapter 4.* See how two-tailed p varies as a 95% CI falls in different positions relative to a null hypothesized value, μ_0.

ESCI chapters 5–6

Intro—Introductory page. Overview. License information.

CIs and replication—*Chapter 5.* Take an initial sample; see what percentage of replication means it would capture. See the distribution of capture percentages.

p intervals—*Chapter 5.* Calculate 80% p intervals for a chosen value of two-tailed p_{obt}.

Dance p—*Chapter 5.* See how the p value varies with replication. Visit the p value casino. See the distribution of p values. Enjoy the dance of the p values.

Random—*Chapter 5.* Compare a square filled with a random scatter of points, and a square filled with points that are random, but with a minimum spacing between points. Build intuitions about randomness, and the amount of clumping in randomness.

Compare A B—*Chapter 6.* See figures for the two-independent-groups design, and for the repeated measure or paired design. Display the difference between the means, with its 95% CI, on a floating difference axis. For the two-independent-groups design, explore overlap and p values. Explore comparisons between the two designs.

Data two—*Chapter 6.* Display your own data, for the two-independent-groups design. Display means and CIs. Display also the difference between the means and its CI on a floating difference axis. Calculate the CI on the difference either with or without the assumption of homogeneity of variance. Calculate for your own data the means, CIs, and other statistics, including d and d_{unb}, and the CI for δ.

Simulate two—*Chapter 6.* For the two-independent-groups design, see how the figure showing means and CIs varies over replication. See how CI overlap varies over replication. See d and d_{unb}, and the CI for δ. See statistical power.

Data paired—*Chapter 6.* Display your own data, for the paired design. Display the mean difference and its CI on a floating difference axis. Calculate for your own data the means, CIs, and other statistics, including d and d_{unb}, and the CI for δ.

Simulate paired—*Chapter 6.* For the paired design, see how the figure varies over replication. See how the pattern of variation over replication changes as the correlation between the two measures changes. See d and d_{unb}, and the CI for δ. See statistical power.

ESCI Meta-Analysis

Intro—Introductory page. Overview. License information.

Original 7—*Chapter 7*. Meta-analysis of means, in original units for up to seven studies.

Original 31—*Chapter 7*. Meta-analysis of means, in original units for up to 31 studies.

Original two groups—*Chapter 7*. Meta-analysis of the difference between two independent means, in original units, for up to 30 studies.

Standard 7—*Chapter 7*. Meta-analysis of means in original units, or d with σ known, for up to seven studies.

Standard 31—*Chapter 7*. Meta-analysis of means in original units, or d with σ known, for up to 31 studies.

d single group—*Chapter 11*. Meta-analysis of Cohen's d for the single-group design for up to 30 studies.

d two groups—*Chapter 11*. Meta-analysis of Cohen's d for the two-independent-groups design for up to 30 studies.

Subgroups—*Chapter 9*. Meta-analysis of means in original units, for up to 30 studies, plus analysis of two subgroups. See a funnel plot.

ESCI chapters 10–13

Intro—Introductory page. Overview. License information.

Sampling—*Chapter 10*. Take samples from the H_0 or H_1 populations. See the sampling distributions of means, z, and t. See the s pile—the sampling distribution of sample SDs. See normal distributions, central t distributions, and noncentral t distributions.

Noncentral t—*Chapter 10*. Explore noncentral t distributions, and compare with central t. Find areas under the noncentral t curve.

d picture—*Chapter 11*. See how two distributions relate for a chosen value of d or δ.

d heap—*Chapter 11*. Take samples, see the sampling distributions of sample means and SDs. See the s pile, the rubber ruler, and the noncentral t sampling distribution of d.

CI for d—*Chapter 11*. Enter a chosen value of d for the two-independent-groups design; see the iterative process required to use noncentral t to find the CI on d. See also d_{unb}, which is an unbiased estimate of δ.

Power picture—*Chapter 12.* Explore the basic power picture, and calculate power for the single-group design.

Power two—*Chapter 12.* See power curves for the two-independent-groups design, and calculate values of power.

Power paired—*Chapter 12.* See power curves for the paired design, and calculate values of power.

Precision one—*Chapter 13.* See precision curves for the single-group design, and carry out precision and assurance calculations for means and Cohen's d.

Precision two—*Chapter 13.* See precision curves for the two-independent-groups design, and carry out precision and assurance calculations for means and Cohen's d.

Precision paired—*Chapter 13.* See precision curves for the paired design, and carry out precision and assurance calculations for means, and precision calculations for Cohen's d.

ESCI chapters 14–15

Intro—Introductory page. Overview. License information.

See r—*Chapter 14.* Select any target value of Pearson's r and see scatterplots having this degree of correlation.

r to z—*Chapter 14.* See a single r with a CI. Investigate Fisher's r to z transformation, and its use to place a CI on r.

Sample r—*Chapter 14.* Take a sequence of samples, see the dance of the correlations. See r values, with their CIs, and the sampling distribution of r values.

Two correlations—*Chapter 14.* See a figure showing any two r values, with their CIs, and the overlap of these CIs.

Figure—*Chapter 15.* Enter data for up to four data series, each with up to four time points, and see a figure of the means (or other ESs) and CIs. See a second figure showing differences, with CIs.

ESCI Effect sizes

Intro—Introductory page. Overview. License information.

Correlations—*Chapter 14.* Enter values and see a CI figure for Pearson's r correlations.

Diff correlations—*Chapter 14.* Enter values and see a CI figure for the difference between two independent Pearson's r correlations.

Proportions—*Chapter 14*. Enter values and see a CI figure for proportions.

Diff proportions—*Chapter 14*. Enter values and see a CI figure for the difference between two independent proportions.

Means—*Chapter 14*. Enter values and see a CI figure for means, for the single-group design, for any dependent variable with interval scaling.

Paired means—*Chapter 14*. Enter values and see a CI figure for mean differences, for paired data (i.e., a repeated measure).

2 ind means same variance—*Chapter 14*. Enter values and see a CI figure for differences between means, two-independent-groups design, variances assumed equal.

2 ind means general—*Chapter 14*. Enter values and see a CI figure for differences between means, two-independent-groups design, variances not assumed equal.

Known CI limits—*Chapter 14*. Enter values and see a CI figure when the point estimate and lower and upper CI limits are known.

ESCI for Analyzing Your Own Data

To use ESCI to analyze your own data, first choose the subsection in the following that's appropriate for your dependent variable. This may be

- A variable, *X*, in original units,
- Cohen's *d*,
- Pearson's correlation *r*, or
- A proportion.

Then, if necessary, choose the paragraph that's most appropriate. Alternatively, one of the following subsections may be most appropriate:

- Meta-analysis,
- Statistical power, or
- Precision for planning.

These notes describe the ESCI pages that are specifically designed to carry out calculations on your data. Other pages can calculate CIs and provide a figure for a restricted range of values—for example, the **Two**

studies page of **ESCI chapters 1–4**, and the **Compare A B** page of **ESCI chapters 5–6**.

In addition, ESCI includes more specialized calculation pages, including the **Normal z t** page of **ESCI chapters 1–4**, which provides tail areas of the normal and *t* distributions, and critical values of *z* and *t* (see also Appendix B); and the **p intervals** page of **ESCI chapters 5–6**, which calculates *p* intervals. The **Known CI limits** page of **ESCI Effect sizes** provides a figure when you enter any type of point ESs and the limits of the CIs on those ESs.

Original Units Variable, *X*

Single-Group Design, Full Data

At the **Data two** page of **ESCI chapters 5–6**, enter your data as **Group 1** near red 1. At red 3, click **Group 1** and unclick **Group 2**. The page calculates summary statistics and the CI on the mean, and provides a figure.

Single-Group Design, Summary Data

At the **Means** page of **ESCI Effect sizes**, enter *M*, *N*, and either SD or SE, and see the CI and a figure.

Two-Independent-Groups Design, Full Data

At the **Data two** page of **ESCI chapters 5–6**, enter your data near red 1. The page calculates summary statistics, CIs on the means, and the difference and its CI. It also provides two figures.

Two-Independent-Groups Design, Summary Data

The **2 ind means same variance** and **2 ind means general** pages of **ESCI Effect sizes** calculate CIs and provide a figure. The second of those pages uses the Welch–Satterthwaite approximation so the assumption of homogeneity of variance is not required. At either page, enter the means and sample sizes, and some further information: SDs, SEs, a *t* value, or a *p* value.

Paired Design, Full Data

At the **Data paired** page of **ESCI chapters 5–6**, enter your data near red 1. The page calculates summary statistics, CIs on the two measures, the differences, and the mean difference and its CI. It also provides a figure with a floating difference axis.

Paired Design, Summary Data

At the **Paired means** page of **ESCI Effect sizes**, enter either two means or the difference between two means, N, and either the SD or SE of the differences, or a t value, or a p value. See the CI and a figure.

Cohen's *d*

To appreciate what your d implies for overlap of two population normal distributions, see the **d picture** page of **ESCI chapters 10–13**.

Single-Group Design, Summary Data

At the **d single group** page of **ESCI Meta-Analysis**, enter your d and N, and see d_{unb} and the CI for δ. (ESCI does not provide a page for calculating d from full data for the single-group design.)

Two-Independent-Groups Design, Full Data

At the **Data two** page of **ESCI chapters 5–6**, enter your data near red 1. Scroll right, click at red 11, and see near red 12 the value of d_{unb} and the CI for δ.

Two-Independent-Groups Design, Summary Data

Starting with your d, N_1, and N_2, use the **d two groups** page of **ESCI Meta-Analysis**, or the **CI for d** page of **ESCI chapters 10–13**, to calculate d_{unb} and the CI for δ.

Paired Design, Full Data

At the **Data paired** page of **ESCI chapters 5–6**, enter your data near red 1. Scroll right, click at red 9, and see near red 10 the value of d_{unb} and the CI for δ. (ESCI does not provide a page for calculating d from summary data for the paired design.)

Pearson's correlation *r*

To see an example scatterplot for your r, use the **See r** page of **ESCI chapters 14–15**. (ESCI does not provide a page that displays the scatterplot of your paired data set.) ESCI does not have a page primarily intended to calculate r for a paired data set, but you can enter your data into the **Data paired** page of **ESCI chapters 5–6** and see the value of r reported near red 7.

To calculate and display the CI on r, use the **r to z** page of **ESCI chapters 14–15**, or the **Correlations** page of **ESCI Effect sizes**. For the difference between two r values, use the **Two correlations** page of **ESCI chapters 14–15**, or the **Diff correlations** page of **ESCI Effect sizes**.

Proportions

To calculate and display the CI on a proportion, use the **Proportions** page of **ESCI Effect sizes**. For the difference between two proportions, use the **Diff proportions** page of **ESCI Effect sizes**.

Meta-Analysis

Different pages of **ESCI Meta-Analysis** accept summary data for each study expressed in original units, or as Cohen's d. At a particular page, the same information is required for each study. For further details, see the description above of the pages of **ESCI Meta-Analysis**.

Statistical Power

Post hoc power is calculated using the d obtained in an experiment as target δ. I explain in Chapter 12 why that can be misleading and should not be used.

Single-Group Design

To calculate power for your chosen N, α, target δ, and test statistic z or t, use the **Power picture** page of **ESCI chapters 10–13**.

Two-Independent-Groups Design

To calculate power for your chosen N_1, N_2, α, target δ, and test statistic z or t, use the **Simulate two** page of **ESCI chapters 5–6**: Scroll right, click at red 11 and 12, and see power at red 13. For $N_1 = N_2$, you can use the **Power two** page of **ESCI chapters 10–13**, or consult Table 12.1.

Paired Design

To calculate power for your chosen N, α, correlation ρ, target δ, and test statistic z or t, use the **Simulate paired** page of **ESCI chapters 5–6**: Scroll right, click at red 13 and 14, and see power at red 15. You can also use the **Power paired** page of **ESCI chapters 10–13**, or consult Table 12.2.

Precision for Planning

For any design, the ES may be expressed in original units or as Cohen's *d*. Using original units, the test statistic may be either *z* or *t*. **ESCI chapters 10–13** provides three pages for precision for planning: For the single-group design use the **Precision one** page, for the two-independent-groups design use the **Precision two** page, and for the paired design use the **Precision paired** page.

References

Abdo, A. A., Ackermann, M., Ajello, M., Asano, K., Atwood, W. B., Axelsson, M., ... Ziegler, M. (2009). A limit on the variation of the speed of light arising from quantum gravity effects. *Nature, 462,* 331–334.

Abelson, R. P. (1995). *Statistics as principled argument.* Hillsdale, NJ: Erlbaum.

Algina, J., & Keselman, H. J. (2003). Approximate confidence intervals for effect sizes. *Educational and Psychological Measurement, 63,* 537–553.

Altman, D. G., Machin, D., Bryant, T. N., & Gardner, M. J. (Eds.) (2000). *Statistics with confidence: Confidence intervals and statistical guidelines* (2nd ed.). London: British Medical Journal Books.

American Psychological Association. (1994). *Publication manual of the American Psychological Association* (4th ed.). Washington, DC: Author.

American Psychological Association. (2001). *Publication manual of the American Psychological Association* (5th ed.). Washington, DC: Author.

American Psychological Association. (2010). *Publication manual of the American Psychological Association* (6th ed.). Washington, DC: Author.

Antman, E. M., Lau, J., Kupelnick, B., Mosteller, F., & Chalmers, T. C. (1992). A comparison of results of meta-analyses of randomized control trials and recommendations of clinical experts: Treatments for myocardial infarction. *Journal of the American Medical Association, 268,* 240–248.

Beck, A. T., Steer, R. A., Ball, R., & Ranieri, W. F. (1996). Comparison of Beck Depression Inventories -IA and -II in psychiatric outpatients. *Journal of Personality Assessment, 67,* 588–597.

Belia, S., Fidler, F., Williams, J., & Cumming, G. (2005). Researchers misunderstand confidence intervals and standard error bars. *Psychological Methods, 10,* 389–396.

Beyth-Marom, R., Fidler, F., & Cumming, G. (2008). Statistical cognition: Towards evidence-based practice in statistics and statistics education. *Statistics Education Research Journal, 7,* 20–39.

Bland, M. (2009). Keep young and beautiful: Evidence for an "anti-aging" product? *Significance, 6,* 182–183.

Borenstein, M., Hedges, L. V., Higgins, J. P. T., & Rothstein, H. R. (2009). *Introduction to meta-analysis.* Chichester, UK: Wiley.

Boutron, I., Dutton, S., Ravaud, P., & Altman, D. G. (2010). Reporting and interpretation of randomized controlled trials with statistically nonsignificant results for primary outcomes. *Journal of the American Medical Association, 303,* 2058–2064.

Campbell, J. P. (1982). Editorial: Some remarks from the outgoing editor. *Journal of Applied Psychology, 67,* 691–700.

Chan, D. W. (2007). Components of leadership giftedness and multiple intelligences among Chinese gifted students in Hong Kong. *High Ability Studies, 18,* 155–172.

Cohen, J. (1962). The statistical power of abnormal social psychological research: A review. *Journal of Abnormal and Social Psychology, 65,* 145–153.

Cohen, J. (1969). *Statistical power analysis for the behavioral sciences.* New York: Academic Press.

Cohen, J. (1988). *Statistical power analysis for the behavioral sciences* (2nd ed.). Hillsdale, NJ: Erlbaum.

Cohen, J. (1990). Things I have learned (so far). *American Psychologist, 45,* 1304–1312.

Cohen, J. (1994). The earth is round ($p < .05$). *American Psychologist, 49,* 997–1003.

Cooper, H. M. (2010). *Research synthesis and meta-analysis: A step-by-step approach* (4th ed.). Thousand Oaks, CA: Sage.

Cooper, H. M., & Rosenthal, R. (1980). Statistical versus traditional procedures for summarizing research findings. *Psychological Bulletin, 87,* 442–449.

Coulson, M., Healey, M., Fidler, F., & Cumming, G. (2010). Confidence intervals permit, but do not guarantee, better inference than statistical significance testing. *Frontiers in Quantitative Psychology and Measurement, 1:26,* 1–9. Retrieved from www.frontiersin.org/psychology/quantitativepsychology andmeasurement/paper/10.3389/fpsyg.2010.00026/ Also available from tinyurl.com/cisbetter

Cumming, G. (2006a). *How the noncentral t distribution got its hump.* 7th International Conference on Teaching Statistics. Brazil, July. Retrieved from www.stat.auckland.ac.nz/~iase/publications/17/C106.pdf Also available from tinyurl.com/noncentralt

Cumming, G. (2006b). *Meta-analysis: Pictures that explain how experimental findings can be integrated.* 7th International Conference on Teaching Statistics. Brazil, July. Retrieved from www.stat.auckland.ac.nz/~iase/publications/17/C105. pdf Also available from tinyurl.com/teachma

Cumming, G. (2007). Inference by eye: Pictures of confidence intervals and thinking about levels of confidence. *Teaching Statistics, 29,* 89–93.

Cumming, G. (2008). Replication and *p* intervals: *p* values predict the future only vaguely, but confidence intervals do much better. *Perspectives on Psychological Science, 3,* 286–300.

Cumming, G. (2009). Inference by eye: Reading the overlap of independent confidence intervals. *Statistics in Medicine, 28,* 205–220.

Cumming, G., & Fidler, F. (2009). Confidence intervals: Better answers to better questions. *Zeitschrift für Psychologie/Journal of Psychology, 217,* 15–26.

Cumming, G., Fidler, F., Leonard, M., Kalinowski, P., Christiansen, A., Kleinig, A., … Wilson, S. (2007). Statistical reform in psychology: Is anything changing? *Psychological Science, 18,* 230–232.

Cumming, G., Fidler, F., & Vaux, D. L. (2007). Error bars in experimental biology. *Journal of Cell Biology, 177,* 7–11. Retrieved from jcb.rupress.org/content/177/1/7.full.pdf+html Also available from tinyurl.com/errorbars101

Cumming, G., & Finch, S. (2001). A primer on the understanding, use and calculation of confidence intervals that are based on central and noncentral distributions. *Educational and Psychological Measurement, 61,* 532–574.

Cumming, G., & Finch, S. (2005). Inference by eye: Confidence intervals, and how to read pictures of data. *American Psychologist, 60,* 170–180. Retrieved from www.apastyle.org/manual/related/cumming-and-finch.pdf Also available from tinyurl.com/inferencebyeye

Cumming, G., & Maillardet, R. (2006). Confidence intervals and replication: Where will the next mean fall? *Psychological Methods, 11*, 217–227.

Cumming, G., Williams, J., & Fidler, F. (2004). Replication, and researchers' understanding of confidence intervals and standard error bars. *Understanding Statistics, 3*, 299–311.

Dawkins, R. (2004). *The ancestor's tale: A pilgrimage to the dawn of life.* London: Weidenfeld & Nicolson.

Dyrbye, L. N., Thomas, M. R., Power, D. V., Durning, S., Moutier, C, Massie, S., ... Shanafelt, T. D. (2010). Burnout and serious thoughts of dropping out of medical school: A multi-institutional study. *Academic Medicine, 85,* 94–101.

Edmonds, M. S., Vaughn, S., Wexler, J., Reutebuch, C., Cable, A., Tackett, K. K., & Schnakenberg, J. W. (2009). A synthesis of reading interventions and effects on reading comprehension outcomes for older struggling readers. *Review of Educational Research, 79,* 262–300.

Egger, M., Zellweger-Zähner, T., Schneider, M., Junker, C., Lengeler, C., & Antes, G. (1997). Language bias in randomised controlled trials published in English and German. *Lancet, 350,* 326–329.

Eyding, D., Lelgemann, M., Grouven, U., Härter, M., Kromp, M., Kaiser, T., ... Wieseler, B. (2010). Reboxetine for acute treatment of major depression: Systematic review and meta-analysis of published and unpublished placebo and selective serotonin reuptake inhibitor controlled trials. *British Medical Journal, 341*: c4737.

Eysenck, H. J. (1978). An exercise in mega-silliness. *American Psychologist, 33,* 517–519.

Fabrigar, L. R., & Wegener, D. T. (2009). Structural equation modeling. In J. P. Stevens, *Applied multivariate statistics for the social sciences* (5th ed.) (pp. 537–582). New York: Routledge.

Faulkner, C., Fidler, F., & Cumming, G. (2008). The value of RCT evidence depends on the quality of statistical analysis. *Behaviour Research and Therapy, 46,* 270–281.

Fidler, F. (forthcoming). *From statistical significance to effect estimation: Statistical reform in psychology, medicine and ecology.* New York: Routledge.

Fidler, F., & Cumming, G. (2008). The new stats: Attitudes for the twenty-first century. In J. W. Osborne (Ed.). *Best practices in quantitative methods* (pp. 1–12). Thousand Oaks, CA: Sage.

Fidler, F., Faulkner, C, & Cumming, G. (2008). Analyzing and presenting outcomes. In A. M. Nezu & C. M. Nezu (Eds.), *Evidence-based outcome research. A practical guide to conducting randomized control trials for psychosocial interventions* (pp. 315–334). Oxford: Oxford University Press.

Fisher, J. O., & Kral, T. V. E. (2008). Super-size me: Portion size effects on young children's eating. *Physiology & Behavior, 94,* 39–47.

Fletcher, G. J. O., & Kerr, P. S. G. (2010). Through the eyes of love: Reality and illusion in intimate relationships. *Psychological Bulletin, 136,* 627–658.

Gigerenzer, G. (1993). The superego, the ego, and the id in statistical reasoning. In G. Keren & C. Lewis, (Eds.) *A handbook for data analysis in the behavioral sciences: Methodological issues* (pp. 311–339). Hillsdale, NJ: Erlbaum.

Gigerenzer, G., Gaissmaier, W., Kurz-Milcke, E., Schwartz, L. M., & Woloshin, S. (2007). Helping doctors and patients make sense of health statistics. *Psychological Science in the Public Interest, 8,* 53–96.

Gigerenzer, G., & Murray, D. J. (1987). *Cognition as intuitive statistics.* Hillsdale, NJ: Erlbaum.

Gilbert, R., Salanti, G., Harden, M., & See, S. (2005). Infant sleeping position and the sudden infant death syndrome: Systematic review of observational studies and historical review of recommendations from 1940 to 2002. *International Journal of Epidemiology, 34,* 874–887.

Glass, G. V. (1976). Primary, secondary, and meta-analysis of research. *Educational Researcher, 5,* 3–8.

Gómez-Aparicio, L., Zamora, R., Gómez, J. M., Hódar, J. A., Castro, J., & Baraza, E. (2004). Applying plant facilitation to forest restoration: A meta-analysis of the use of shrubs as nurse plants. *Ecological Applications, 14,* 1128–1138.

Gould, S. J. (1991). *Bully for brontosaurus. Reflections on natural history.* New York: Norton. (Chapter 17, pp. 255–268.)

Grayson, D., Pattison, P., & Robins, G. (1997). Evidence, inference, and the "rejection" of the significance test. *Australian Journal of Psychology, 49,* 64–70.

Grissom, R. J., & Kim, J. J. (2005). *Effect sizes for research: A broad practical approach.* Mahwah, NJ: Erlbaum.

Haller, H., & Krauss, S. (2002). Misinterpretations of significance: A problem students share with their teachers? *Methods of Psychological Research Online,* 7(1), 1–17. Retrieved from www.metheval.uni-jena.de/lehre/0405-ws/evaluationuebung/haller.pdf Also available from tinyurl.com/nhstohdear

Hays, W. L. (1973). *Statistics for the social sciences* (2nd ed.). New York: Holt, Rinehart, Winston.

Hedges, L. V. (1981). Distribution theory for Glass's estimator of effect size and related estimators. *Journal of Educational Statistics, 6,* 107–128.

Hedges, L. V. (1987). How hard is hard science, how soft is soft science? The empirical cumulativeness of research. *American Psychologist, 42,* 443–455.

Hedges, L. V., & Olkin, I. (1985). *Statistical methods for meta-analysis.* Orlando, FL: Academic Press.

Higgins, J. P. T., & Green, S. (Eds.) (2008). *Cochrane handbook for systematic reviews of interventions.* Chichester, West Sussex: Wiley.

Hinkle, D. E., Wiersma, W., & Jurs, S. G. (2003). *Applied statistics for the behavioral sciences* (5th ed.). Boston: Houghton Mifflin.

Hoekstra, R., Finch, S., Kiers, H., & Johnson, A. (2006). Probability as certainty: Dichotomous thinking and the misuse of p-values. *Psychonomic Bulletin & Review, 13,* 1033–1037.

Hoenig, J. M., & Heisey, D. M. (2001). The abuse of power: The pervasive fallacy of power calculations for data analysis. *The American Statistician, 55,* 19–24.

Hubbard, R. (2004). Alphabet soup. Blurring the distinction between p's and α's in psychological research. *Theory & Psychology, 14,* 295–327.

Huberty, C. J. (2002). A history of effect size indices. *Educational and Psychological Measurement, 62,* 227–240.

Hunt, M. (1997). *How science takes stock: The story of meta-analysis.* New York: Russell Sage Foundation.

Hunter, J. E., & Schmidt, F. L. (2004). *Methods of meta-analysis: Correcting error and bias in research findings* (2nd ed.). Thousand Oaks, CA: Sage.

Hyde, J. S. (2007). New directions in the study of gender similarities and differences. *Current Directions in Psychological Science, 16,* 259–263.

Kalinowski, P., Fidler, F., & Cumming, G. (2008). Overcoming the inverse probability fallacy. A comparison of two teaching interventions. *Methodology, 4,* 152–158.

Kay, A. C., Moscovitch, D. A., & Laurin, K. (2010). Randomness, attributions of arousal, and belief in God. *Psychological Science, 21,* 216–218.

Kelley, K., & Rausch, J. R. (2006). Sample size planning for the standardized mean difference: Accuracy in parameter estimation via narrow confidence intervals. *Psychological Methods, 11,* 363–385.

Kim, J., & Ruge-Murcia, F. J. (2009). How much inflation is necessary to grease the wheels? *Journal of Monetary Economics, 56,* 365–377.

Kirk, R. E. (1996). Practical significance: A concept whose time has come. *Educational and Psychological Measurement, 56,* 746–759.

Kirk, R. E. (2003). The importance of effect magnitude. In S. F. Davis (Ed.), *Handbook of research methods in experimental psychology* (pp. 83–105). Malden, MA: Blackwell.

Kline, R. B. (2004). *Beyond significance testing: Reforming data analysis methods in behavioral research.* Washington, DC: American Psychological Association. Chapter 3 retrieved from www.apastyle.org/manual/related/kline-2004.pdf Also available from tinyurl.com/klinechap3

Kosslyn, S. M. (2006). *Graph design for the eye and mind.* Oxford: Oxford University Press.

Lai, J., Fidler, F., & Cumming, G. (in press). Subjective *p* intervals: Researchers underestimate the variability of *p* values over replication. *Methodology.*

Lewis, S., & Clarke, M. (2001). Forest plots: Trying to see the wood and the trees. *British Medical Journal, 322,* 1479–1480.

Lockhart, R. S. (1998). *Introduction to statistics and data analysis for the behavioral sciences.* New York: Freeman.

Maccoby, E. E., & Jacklin, C. N. (1974). *The psychology of sex differences.* Stanford, CA: Stanford University Press.

Manheimer, E., White, A., Berman, B., Forys, K., & Ernst, E. (2005). Meta-analysis: Acupuncture for low back pain. *Annals of Internal Medicine, 142,* 651–663.

Mathews, M. M. (1966). *Teaching to read, historically considered.* Chicago: University of Chicago Press.

Maxwell, S. E. (2004). The persistence of underpowered studies in psychological research: Causes, consequences, and remedies. *Psychological Methods, 9,* 147–163.

Maxwell, S. E., Kelley, K., & Rausch, J. R. (2008) Sample size planning for statistical power and accuracy in parameter estimation. *Annual Review of Psychology, 59,* 537–563.

McCarthy, M. A. (2007). *Bayesian methods for ecology.* Cambridge, UK: Cambridge University Press.

McGuinness, D. (2004). *Early reading instruction: What science really tells us about how to teach reading.* Cambridge, MA: MIT Press.

Meehl, P. E. (1978). Theoretical risks and tabular asterisks: Sir Karl, Sir Ronald, and the slow progress of soft psychology. *Journal of Consulting and Clinical Psychology, 46*, 806–834.

Morris, M. C., Tangney, C. C., Bienias, J. L., Evans, D. A., & Wilson, R. S. (2003). Validity and reproducibility of a food frequency questionnaire by cognition in an older biracial sample. *American Journal of Epidemiology, 158*, 1213–1217.

Moore, L. L., Bradlee, M. L., Singer, M. R., Splansky, G. L., Proctor, M. H., Ellison, R. C., & Kreger, B. E. (2004). BMI and waist circumference as predictors of lifetime colon cancer risk in Framingham Study adults. *International Journal of Obesity, 28*, 559–567.

National Reading Panel (2000). *Report.* Washington, DC: National Institute of Child Health and Human Development.

Newcombe, R. G., & Altman, D. G. (2000). Proportions and their differences. In D. G. Altman, D. Machin, T. N. Bryant, & M. J. Gardner (Eds.), *Statistics with confidence: Confidence intervals and statistical guidelines* (2nd ed.) (pp. 45–56). London: British Medical Journal Books.

Oakes, M. W. (1986). *Statistical inference: A commentary for the social and behavioural sciences.* Chichester, UK: Wiley.

Ortiz, C. M. A. (2007). *Does philosophy improve critical thinking skills?* (Unpublished master's thesis). The University of Melbourne, Melbourne, Australia.

Petticrew, M. (2001). Systematic reviews from astronomy to zoology: Myths and misconceptions. *British Medical Journal, 322*, 98–101.

Poitevineau, J., & Lecoutre, B. (2001). Interpretation of significance levels by psychological researchers: The .05 cliff effect may be overstated. *Psychonomic Bulletin & Review, 8*, 847–850.

Poole, C. (1987). Beyond the confidence interval. *American Journal of Public Health, 77*, 195–199.

Robinson, T. N. (1999). Reducing children's television viewing to prevent obesity. A randomized controlled trial. *Journal of the American Medical Association, 282*, 1561–1567.

Rosenthal, R., & Gaito, J. (1963). The interpretation of levels of significance by psychological researchers. *Journal of Psychology, 55*, 33–38.

Rosenthal, R., & Rosnow, R. L. (1985). *Contrast analysis: Focused comparisons in the analysis of variance.* Cambridge, UK: Cambridge University Press.

Rosenthal, R., Rosnow, R. L., & Rubin, D. B. (2000). *Contrasts and effect sizes in behavioral research. A correlational approach.* Cambridge, UK: Cambridge University Press.

Rosnow, R. L., & Rosenthal, R. (2009). Effect sizes: Why, when, and how to use them. *Zeitschrift für Psychologie/Journal of Psychology, 217*, 6–14.

Rossi, J. (1997). A case study in the failure of psychology as a cumulative science: The spontaneous recovery of verbal learning. In L. Harlow, S. Mulaik, & J. Steiger (Eds.), *What if there were no significance tests?* (pp. 175–198). Mahwah, NJ: Erlbaum.

Rothman, K. J. (1990). No adjustments are needed for multiple comparisons. *Epidemiology, 1*, 43–46.

Rothman, K. J. (2002). *Epidemiology, An introduction.* New York: Oxford University Press.

Rozeboom, W. W. (1960). The fallacy of the null hypothesis significance test. *Psychological Bulletin, 57*, 416–428.

Rutherford, L., Hand M., & Barovich, K. (2007). Timing of Proterozoic metamorphism in the southern Curnamona Province: Implications for tectonic models and continental reconstructions. *Australian Journal of Earth Sciences, 54,* 65–81.

Salsburg, D. (2001). *The lady tasting tea: How statistics revolutionized science in the twentieth century.* New York: W. H. Freeman.

Schenker, N., & Gentleman, J. F. (2001). On judging the significance of differences by examining the overlap between confidence intervals. *The American Statistician, 55,* 182–186.

Schiff, C. J., Kaufman, D. S., Wallace, K. L., Werner, A., Ku, T.-L., & Brown, T. A. (2008). Modeled tephra ages from lake sediments, base of Redoubt Volcano, Alaska. *Quaternary Geochronology, 3,* 56–67.

Schmidt, F. L., Oh, I.-S., & Hayes, T. L. (2009). Fixed- versus random-effects models in meta-analysis: Model properties and an empirical comparison of differences in results. *British Journal of Mathematical and Statistical Psychology, 62,* 97–128.

Schmidt, L. A., Fox, N. A., Perez-Edgar, K., & Hamer, D. H. (2009). Linking gene, brain, and behavior: DRD4, frontal asymmetry, and temperament. *Psychological Science, 20,* 831–837.

Scott, D., Lambie, I., Henwood, D., & Lamb, R. (2006). Profiling stranger rapists: Linking offence behaviour to previous criminal histories using a regression model. *Journal of Sexual Aggression, 12,* 265–275.

Sedlmeier, P. & Gigerenzer, G. (1989). Do studies of statistical power have an effect on the power of studies? *Psychological Bulletin, 105,* 309–316.

Sedrakyan, A., & Shih, C. (2007). Improving depiction of benefits and harms: Analyses of studies of well-known therapeutics and review of high-impact medical journals. *Medical Care, 45,* S23–S28.

Sfikas, N., Greenhalgh, D. & Lewis, F. (2007). The basic reproduction number and the vaccination coverage required to eliminate rubella from England and Wales. *Mathematical Population Studies, 14,* 3–29.

Shrier, I., Boivin, J-F., Platt, R. W., Steele, R. J., Brophy, J. M., Carnevale, F., ... Rossignol, M. (2008). The interpretation of systematic reviews with meta-analyses: An objective or subjective process? *BMC Medical Informatics and Decision Making, 8:19,* 1–8.

Smith, M. L., & Glass, G. V. (1977). Meta-analysis of psychotherapy outcome studies. *American Psychologist, 32,* 752–760.

Smithson, M. (2001). Correct confidence intervals for various regression effect sizes and parameters: The importance of noncentral distributions in computing intervals. *Educational and Psychological Measurement, 61,* 605–632.

Smithson, M. (2003). *Confidence intervals.* Thousand Oaks, CA: Sage.

Speirs-Bridge, A., Fidler, F., McBride, M., Flander, L., Cumming, G., & Burgman, M. (2010). Reducing overconfidence in the interval judgments of experts. *Risk Analysis, 30,* 512–523.

Strandberg-Larsen, K., Grønbœk, M., Andersen, A.-M. N., Andersen, P. K., & Olsen, J. (2009). Alcohol drinking pattern during pregnancy and risk of infant mortality. *Epidemiology, 20,* 884–891.

Tabachnick, B. G., & Fidell, L. S. (2007). *Using multivariate statistics* (5th ed.). Boston: Pearson.

Thompson, B. (1997). Editorial policies regarding statistical significance tests: Further comments. *Educational Researcher, 26*(5), 29–32.

Tukey, J. W. (1960). Conclusions vs decisions. *Technometrics, 2*, 423–433.

Tukey, J. W. (1977). *Exploratory data analysis.* Reading, MA: Addison-Wesley.

Tversky, A., & Kahneman, D. (1971). Belief in the law of small numbers. *Psychological Bulletin, 76*, 105–110.

Tyron, W. W. (1998). The inscrutable null hypothesis. *American Psychologist, 53*, 796.

van Deemter, K. (2010). *Not exactly: In praise of vagueness.* Oxford: Oxford University Press.

van Gelder, T., Bissett, M., & Cumming, G. (2004). Cultivating expertise in informal reasoning. *Canadian Journal of Experimental Psychology, 58*, 142–152.

Velicer, W. F., Cumming, G., Fava, J. L., Rossi, J. S., Prochaska, J. O., & Johnson, J. (2008). Theory testing using quantitative predictions of effect size. *Applied Psychology: An International Review, 57*, 589–608.

Vocks, S., Tuschen-Caffier, B., Peitrowsky, R., Rustenbach, S. J., Kersting, A., & Herpertz, S. (2010). Meta-analysis of the effectiveness of psychological and pharmacological treatments for binge eating disorder. *International Journal of Eating Disorders, 43*, 205–217.

Watson, R. E. B., Ogden, S., Cotterell, L. F., Bowden, J. J., Bastrilles, J. Y., Long, S. P., & Griffiths, C. E. M. (2009). A cosmetic 'anti-ageing' product improves photaged skin: A double-blind, randomized controlled trial. *British Journal of Dermatology, 161*, 419–426.

Wilkinson, L., & Task Force on Statistical Inference. (1999). Statistical methods in psychology journals: Guidelines and explanations. *American Psychologist, 54*, 594–604. Retrieved from www.apastyle.org/manual/related/wilkinson-1999.pdf Also available from tinyurl.com/tfsi1999

Wilson, P. H., & McKenzie, B. E. (1998). Information processing deficits associated with developmental coordination disorder: A meta-analysis of research findings. *Journal of Child Psychology and Psychiatry, 39*, 829–840.

Winzelberg, A. J., Barr Taylor, C., Sharpe, T., Eldredge, K. L., Dev, P., & Constantinou, P. S. (1998). Evaluation of a computer-mediated eating disorder intervention program. *International Journal of Eating Disorders, 24*, 339–349.

Wood, J. V., Perunovic, W. Q. E., & Lee, J. W. (2009). Positive self-statements: Power for some, peril for others. *Psychological Science, 20*, 860–866.

Young, C., & Horton, R. (2005). Putting clinical trials into context. *Lancet, 366*, 107–108.

Zapka, M., Heyers, D., Hein, C. M., Engels, S., Schneider, N-L., Hans, J., … Mouritsen, H. (2009). Visual but not trigeminal mediation of magnetic compass information in a migratory bird. *Nature, 461*, 1274–1277.

Zou, G. Y. (2007). Toward using confidence intervals to compare correlations. *Psychological Methods, 12*, 399–413.

Copyright Permissions

Author Index

Names in *italics* are fictitious.

Subject Index

Additional Comments about *Understanding The New Statistics: Effect Sizes, Confidence Intervals, and Meta-Analysis* by Geoff Cumming

"Cumming will be the 'breakthrough' text that finally shows how to analyze and interpret data for many common statistical designs without having to rely on significance testing. ... Its strengths are considerable. It takes a practical, 'hands on' approach ... provides plenty of exercises ... and a very useful computer program to implement the new way of thinking. ... The material ... should be easy even for undergraduates to appreciate. This is an unusual characteristic for a statistics text."

—Joseph Rossi, University of Rhode Island, USA

"Currently, a paradigm shift from the flawed null hypothesis testing model to an effect size and confidence interval approach is taking place. Unfortunately, students taking lower level courses have not been exposed. This book repairs that omission. A very timely and important book!"

—Wayne F. Velicer, University of Rhode Island, USA

"This is as clear a presentation of new approaches for evaluating hypotheses and presenting statistical evidence as one could want. Cumming brings researchers into the new age of statistical discourse."

—Patrick E. Shrout, New York University, USA

"The writing style is breezy and informal. ... It is a unique book ... and it meets an important need. The quality of scholarship is excellent; the author is probably the top world expert on this subject. ... The [accompanying] software ... allows people to 'run their own studies' and see ... just how unstable research findings are across studies when sample size are in the typical small range."

—Frank Schmidt, University of Iowa, USA

"I would recommend the Cumming book to students who want to be on the 'cutting edge' of how to write-up statistics. ... Strengths include the author's passion and long history of research into the most effective methods of teaching statistics. ... The quality of the scholarship is excellent. ... I would definitely purchase the book ... and recommend it to colleagues."

—Alan Reifman, Texas Tech University, USA

"There is a real need for a statistics book that makes the 'new statistics' understandable and can be used as a teaching framework for undergraduates, or graduate students."

—Dennis Doverspike, University of Akron, USA

"[This book will pave] the way for others to demonstrate further the potency of effect sizes and confidence intervals for both univariate and multivariate inferential procedures."

—Lisa Harlow, University of Rhode Island, USA